KU-036-456

PLATE 116 "THE PINEAPPLE", Dunmore Park (302).

STIRLINGSHIRE

AN INVENTORY OF THE ANCIENT MONUMENTS

VOLUME II

THE ROYAL COMMISSION ON THE
ANCIENT AND HISTORICAL MONUMENTS OF SCOTLAND
1963

Published by
HER MAJESTY'S STATIONERY OFFICE
To be purchased from
13A Castle Street, Edinburgh 2
York House, Kingsway, London W.C.2
423 Oxford Street, London W.1
109 St. Mary Street, Cardiff
39 King Street, Manchester 2
50 Fairfax Street, Bristol 1
35 Smallbrook, Ringway, Birmingham 5
80 Chichester Street, Belfast
or through any bookseller

Price £15 net
per set of 2 volumes
ISBN 0 11 491369 2

Printed in Scotland under the Authority of HER MAJESTY'S STATIONERY OFFICE
by T. and A. CONSTABLE LTD., Edinburgh
Wt. 70069 K10

CONTENTS OF VOLUME II

LIST OF FIGURES

LIST OF PLATES

INVENTORY

of the Ancient and Historical Monuments of Stirlingshire (continued)

GARRISON

225. The Garrison, Inversnaid. The remains of the Barrack of Inversnaid stand on a small eminence about 250 yds. NE. of the confluence of the Arklet Water and the Snaid Burn. The Barrack, with those at Kiliwhimen (Fort Augustus), Bernera and Ruthven, was erected in the years following the rebellion of 1715 as part of the Government's plan for controlling the Highlands. The site commands the pass between Loch Lomond and Loch Katrine, and the primary function of the post was to protect the route that ran from Dumbarton via Loch Lomond, Loch Katrine and Loch Tay to join the main Dunkeld-Inverness road at Blair Atholl (cf. No. 523). The Barrack is placed to overlook two fords—those by which, respectively, the Dumbarton road crosses the Arklet Water (cf. No. 521) and the road from Inversnaid Harbour crosses the Snaid Burn (cf. No. 522) before joining the Dumbarton road 80 yds. SW. of the Garrison (Pl. 117).

Sites for all four Barracks were agreed upon in August 1717,[1] the Board of Ordnance being responsible for their erection and maintainance. Early in the following year James Smith was appointed "Surveyor and Chief Director for Carrying on the Barracks" in North Britain, and at the same time Major Thomas Gordon was made Chief Overseer, under Smith, at Inversnaid, with Lieutenants Dumaresque and Bastide as Clerk of Works and Draughtsman respectively.[2] Work began in the spring of 1718 and was continued throughout the summer and autumn, although not without interruption; there is a report of a party of eight masons and quarriers being carried off by armed Highlanders on 8th August.[3] Building contracts were signed on 14th June,[4] the principal contractors being Gilbert Smith, mason, Robert Mowbray, carpenter, and James Syme, slater, all of whom were also engaged upon the Barrack of Kiliwhimen. Work stopped in late autumn but was resumed in the spring of 1719, although in January Smith was replaced by Andrews Jelfe,[5] who is described as "Architect and Clerk of the Works for this office in Great Brittain".[6] By the autumn of 1719 the buildings were approaching completion, Inversnaid being the first of the four Barracks to be finished.

The Barrack is said to have been destroyed during the rebellion of 1745[7] and then rebuilt, but, although plans were made for new buildings at this time,[8] they were not carried out and the structure seen today is that erected in 1718 and 1719. The Garrison was kept in repair until the late 18th century, but a survey of 1823 stated that it was becoming ruinous, the only occupants at that time being two women, one of whom kept "a kind of inn" in one of the barrack blocks.[9] Neither the Engineer Department nor the Barrack Department would admit responsibility for the buildings, and as the site had by that time lost its military significance it was handed back to the Duke of Montrose.

Contemporary plans of the Barrack survive (Pls. 117, 118)[10] and show it as an approximately square enclosure, on the N. and S. sides of which two barrack-blocks faced each other across a courtyard. The W. and E. sides were provided with rampart walks carried on vaulted undercrofts and the entrance was centrally placed in the W. wall. At the NE. and SW. angles of the enclosure towers of two storeys gave flanking fire to the four main walls, the ground floor of the NE. tower being used as a bake-house and brew-house and that of the SW. tower as a guard-room. Loop-holes were also provided in the rear walls of the barrack-blocks and in the vaulted chambers that supported the rampart walks. Provision was made in the plan for towers at the remaining two corners of the enclosure and for the strengthening of the entrance, but there was insufficient money to complete these additional works. The plan as carried out should be compared with those of Kiliwhimen, Ruthven and Bernera,[11] all four Barracks being very much alike; Kiliwhimen and Bernera were slightly larger than Inversnaid, and had more substantial barrack-blocks, but Ruthven provides an almost exact parallel. Credit for these Barracks has been given to J. L. Romer,[12] whose father William Romer had achieved some fame as an expert in the art of fortification; Romer, however,

---

1 P.R.O., *W.O.* 47/30, 228-9.
2 *Ibid.*, 47/31, 57.
3 *Ibid.*, 235.
4 *E.g. Ibid.*, 48/60, list dated June 28, 1720, No. 35.
5 On whom see Colvin, *English Architects*, 318.
6 P.R.O., *W.O.* 47/32, 21.
7 *Stat. Acct.*, ix (1793), 25.
8 B.M. (Map Room), *K. Top. L.* 100.
9 P.R.O., *W.O.* 44/272.
10 National Library of Scotland MS. 1648, Z 3/11, Z 3/16, Z 3/17, Z 3/18. Of these plans, Z 3/17e (Pl. 118) appears to be a preliminary draft, Z 3/17a to incorporate some minor modifications of the original scheme, and Z 3/11a to represent the work actually carried out.
11 National Library of Scotland MS. 1648, Z 3/18.
12 Colvin, *English Architects*, 513, following *D.N.B.*

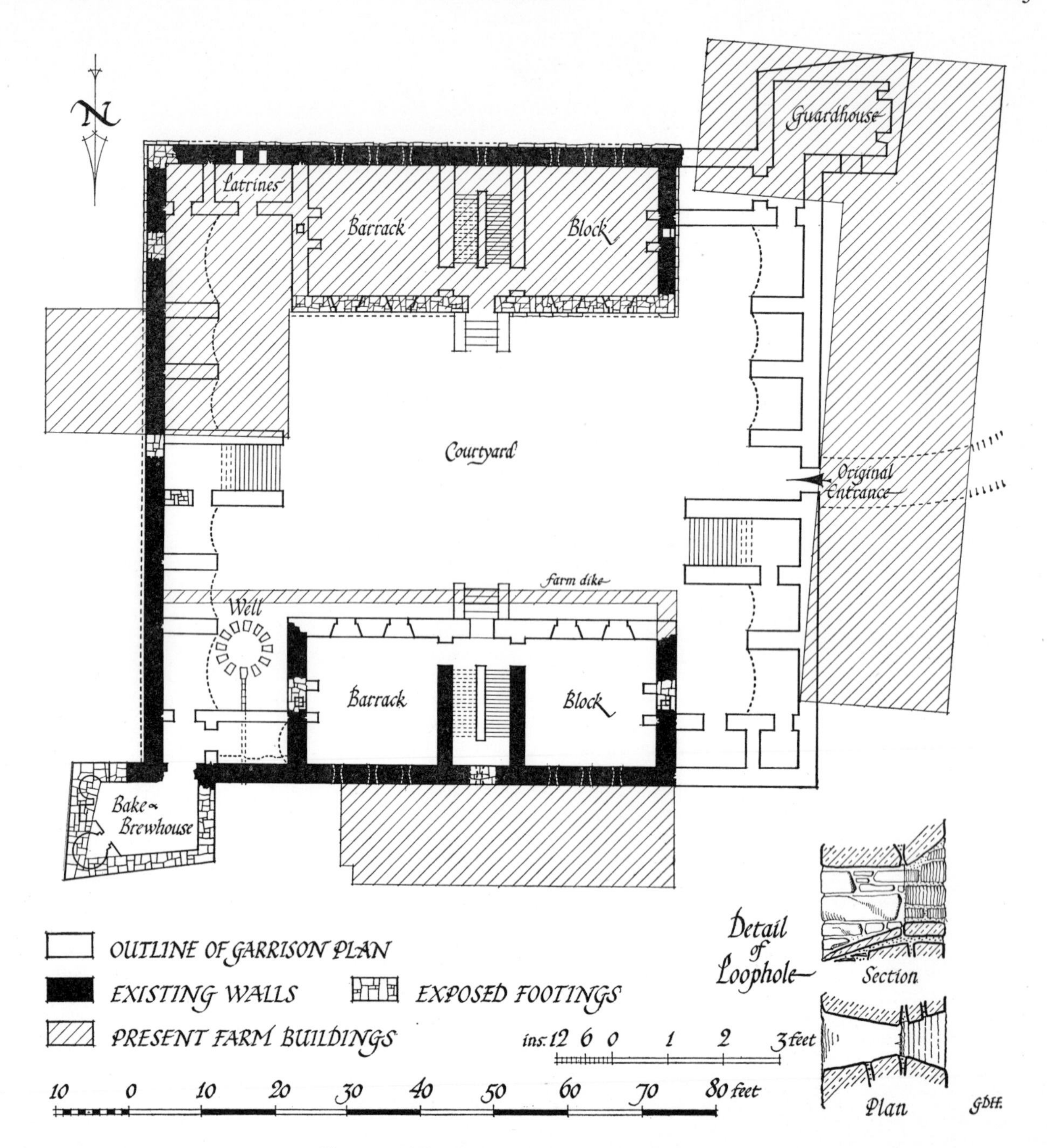

Fig. 112. The Garrison, Inversnaid (No. 225)

replaced Jelfe as Chief Overseer in North Britain only in January 1720,[1] by which date Inversnaid was virtually complete and two years' work had been done on Kiliwhimen. As the erection of the four Barracks had been planned as a single operation as early as 1717, it is clear that Romer did no more than complete a programme which had been laid down by his predecessors, Smith and Jelfe.

The site of the Barrack of Inversnaid is today occupied by farm buildings, many of which, however, incorporate

[1] P.R.O., *W.O.* 47/33, 58.

portions of the original structure (Fig. 112). The masonry is of rubble drawn from a quarry on the N. bank of the Arklet Water, which is marked on a contemporary site-plan (Pl. 117). Nothing remains of the original W. wall of the enclosure or of the SW. tower, the present farmhouse and a byre now occupying these parts of the site. The line of the original approach-road is visible, however, as a slightly hollowed roadway running in an E.-W. direction immediately to the W. of the byre and 53 ft. N. of the SW. angle of the farmhouse. Substantial traces also remain of the two barrack-blocks. Each was of three storeys, and had a central staircase with a barrack-room on either side on each floor; there were windows on the courtyard side only, the outer walls being pierced by loop-holes. Three sides of the N. block remain (Fig. 112, Pl. 119 A) and are incorporated in a sheep-pen: the N. wall rises to a maximum height of 17 ft. 6 in. and contains seven symmetrically placed loop-holes which are splayed both internally and externally and have sloping sills (Pl. 119 B). The doorway now seen in this wall is not an original feature. The gables and stairwell are reduced in height to a few courses and have been adapted for later use, while the S. wall has been replaced by a later wall which runs parallel to the site of the original one but a little to the S. of it. The S. barrack-block has been largely rebuilt and is now used as a barn, but the lower portions of the N. and S. walls and of the W. gable remain to a maximum height of 8 ft. Immediately to the E. of the barrack-block the vents for the private soldiers' latrines can be seen in the S. wall of the enclosure. Of the E. wall of the Barracks, the footings remain along its entire length and the original masonry is preserved to a height of 8 ft. at the S. end. The S. wall of the NE. tower rises to a height of 10 ft., but the N. wall has disappeared completely, and of the W. and E. walls only the foundations are visible. About 15 ft. SW. of the tower is a well, now filled up, but plainly visible on the ground as a circular outline of stones (Pl. 119 C). The well was supplied by an aqueduct fed from a small burn 50 yds. NE. of the Barrack. The aqueduct, which is marked on a contemporary plan,[1] is visible today for about half its length as a channel in the turf about 3 ft. in width and 2 ft. in depth.

NN 348096 28 April 1955
N ii ("Garrison of Inversnaid, Remains of")

HOUSES OF THE 16TH TO 19TH CENTURIES

BURGHS

226. The Burgh of Stirling. The physical development of Stirling has been largely governed by the topography of the site on which it stands (Fig. 113). Here, as at Edinburgh, a "crag-and-tail" formation was adapted for defence by the placing of a castle on the highest point, or "crag", and this left the comparatively gentle downward slope of the "tail" as the site for the development of the burgh. It also led to the alinement of the main street from NW. to SE., but this tendency was modified by the fact that Stirling occupied a key position on the main route from north to south, which crossed the Forth by Stirling Bridge (No. 455), three-quarters of a mile NE. of the town, and then passed through the streets on its way southwards. The earliest surviving town-plan, which was drawn by John Laye in 1725 (Pl. 121),[2] shows clearly how both these factors helped to determine the lay-out of the old town. On the one hand Laye shows a plan laid out predominantly from NW. to SE., and naturally alined upon the Castle (No. 192), to which the burgh owed its origin, while on the other it brings out the importance of the principal deviation from this alinement. This is constituted by St. Mary's Wynd, unnamed by Laye, which descends towards the bridge and gives entry to the town from the north. After climbing to the top of St. Mary's Wynd, through traffic had to descend almost the whole length of the burgh to its SE. extremity before continuing on its way. The other deviation, Friar Street, also unnamed by Laye but shown by him as running N. from the lower end of "Neither Wind", must also be of early origin, as it links the burgh with a harbour on the Forth which was in existence as early as the 12th century.

Of the other streets, the Market Place, now Broad Street, was the most important in the burgh and contained both the Tolbooth (No. 232) and the Mercat Cross (No. 401). Parallel to it and a little to the S. there is a street the upper portion of which Laye designates "Flece Market", the whole now being known as St. John Street. The Market Place and St. John Street, with the streets connecting them, form a rough quadrangle dominated by the Parish Church (No. 131); and from this upper core two parallel streets "Neither Wind", now Baker Street, and Back Row[3], which now forms the lower part of St. John Street, together with Spittal Street, descend to the SE. extremity of the town, and converge at the site of the Meal Market (cf. No. 247) to form what is now King Street. Laye's plan, though of early 18th-century date, clearly preserves an arrangement which goes back to mediaeval times, and probably to the early days of the burgh. The town is shown as still circumscribed by its 16th-century wall, and this indicates that very little expansion took place before the 18th century. The mediaeval boundaries were outgrown, however, in the later part of the 18th and to a much more considerable extent in the 19th century. John Wood's survey,[4] made in 1820, shows that by that date building had begun at the approaches to the town on both the Falkirk and Airth roads, and also in the Allan Park area. To the N. there was already considerable development between St. Mary's Wynd and the Bridge while plans were being made to by-pass the old town

[1] National Library of Scotland MS. 1648, Z 3/11.
[2] *Ibid.*, 1645, Z 2/19.
[3] For the probable origin of this name, see Dickinson, W. C., *Early Records of the Burgh of Aberdeen, 1317, 1398-1407*, S.H.S., xxix, n.5.
[4] *Wood's Town Atlas.*

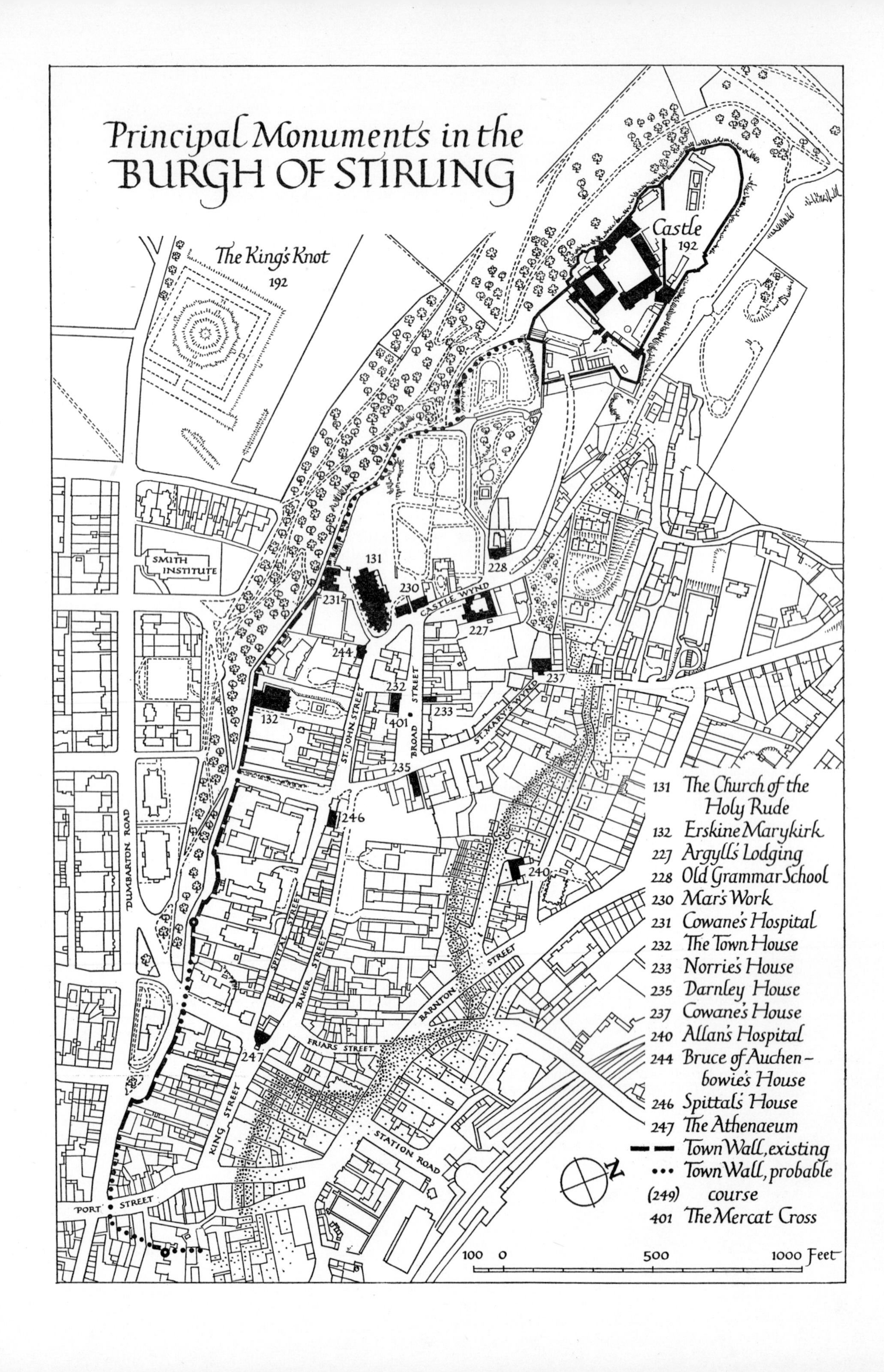
Principal Monuments in the
BURGH OF STIRLING
The King's Knot
192
Castle
192
SMITH INSTITUTE
131
230
228
231
CASTLE WYND
227
244
237
232
BROAD STREET
ST. JOHN STREET
132
401
233
ST. MARY'S WYND
235
246
240
DUMBARTON ROAD
SPITTAL STREET
BAKER STREET
BARNTON STREET
FRIARS STREET
247
KING STREET
STATION ROAD
PORT STREET
131 The Church of the Holy Rude
132 Erskine Marykirk
227 Argyll's Lodging
228 Old Grammar School
230 Mar's Work
231 Cowane's Hospital
232 The Town House
233 Norrie's House
235 Darnley House
237 Cowane's House
240 Allan's Hospital
244 Bruce of Auchenbowie's House
246 Spittal's House
247 The Athenaeum
Town Wall, existing
Town Wall, probable course
(249)
401 The Mercat Cross
N
100 0 500 1000 Feet

with a new through road which would keep to the low ground on the NE. The completion of this scheme, with the building of a new road-bridge in 1831 and the coming of the railway a little later, led to the development of a new town-centre outside the limits of the mediaeval burgh.

No mediaeval buildings survive in the burgh, but several 16th-century town-houses still stand, and others are known from record. These were the homes of nobles and gentry who were attracted to Stirling by the frequent presence of the Court; the most important of them being Mar's Work (No. 230) and the earlier portion of Argyll's Lodging (No. 227). Many others of lesser rank are known to have been erected at about the same period, but have gradually disappeared during the last century and a half (cf. pp. 296 f.); descriptions of individual structures will be found below. It was during the 16th century, too, that the town was enclosed by a stone wall on its S. and E. sides (cf. No. 249).

7993 NS 79 SE Various dates in 1955

227. Argyll's Lodging, Stirling. Argyll's Lodging, the most important surviving town-house of its period in Scotland, stands on the E. side of Castle Wynd, overlooking the only road that links the Castle with the burgh. Although it was thus in close proximity to the houses of the old town, its gardens, which were once extensive, and the fine view that it enjoys over the Forth valley to the Ochils, must have given the Lodging many of the advantages of a country residence.

The building (Pl. 122) is grouped round three sides of an irregular courtyard, the maximum dimensions of which are 55 ft. by 43 ft.; the W. side of the court is occupied by a screen wall, in the centre of which an entrance-gateway gives access from Castle Wynd. Although the plan appears at first sight to be a homogeneous one[1] the building is not all of the same date, and a close examination of the structure reveals a progressive development in which a house of moderate size was extended, by a series of alterations and additions, into the substantial mansion that is visible today. The account that follows is based upon the evidence that was available in 1958, when the partial re-harling of the building made it possible to examine a number of structural features, the existence of which had previously been unsuspected. However, while the broad outline of the architectural development of the building has been established, some problems of interpretation remain, and it is possible that the sequence suggested here may need revision should fresh evidence come to light at some future date.

The original house,[2] which was a simple rectangular block, occupied what is now the NE. angle of the courtyard. It may be ascribed to the 16th century. This building was subsequently reconstructed above the level of the ground floor, and at the same time a short S. wing was added, making the whole structure L-shaped on plan. A little later the house was considerably enlarged by the extension of the main block westwards to what is now the full length of the N. range. These additions presumably took place in the late 16th or early 17th century, but nothing is known of the occupants of the house at this period. In about 1630 the site was acquired by William Alexander, Viscount Stirling and Lord Alexander of Tullibody, who was a prominent figure at the court of Charles I, being celebrated both for his poetical gifts and for his part in the scheme for the colonisation of Nova Scotia.[3] By 1632 Alexander had demolished part of the S. wing of the old house, completed a new E. range and begun a S. range. His second son, Sir Anthony Alexander, joint Master of Works in Scotland, is said to have acted as architect,[4] but there is no contemporary evidence to support this theory and the building accounts cannot be traced. The carved ornamental detail that distinguishes the work of this period is, however, very similar to that at Heriot's Hospital, Edinburgh,[5] and this suggests that one of the master masons employed at the Hospital, perhaps William Ayton, may have had a hand in the work. In June 1633, William Alexander was created Earl of Stirling and Viscount Canada, and at some time between the date of the conferment of these new dignities and his death in 1640 he rebuilt the upper storeys of the W. end of the N. range. After Alexander's death the building passed to his fifth son Charles, but soon came into the hands of the Town Council, which proposed to use it as an almshouse. This scheme was not carried out, however, for in 1666 the site was purchased by Archibald, 9th Earl of Argyll.[6] The date 1674 appears over the doorway of the staircase tower in the SW. angle of the courtyard, and indicates that the S. range was completed and the S. wing added at this time. The wing survived until the middle of the 19th century and is shown in a plan of 1841[7] (Pl. 123); but it has now disappeared except for the lower portion of its W. wall, which fronts Castle Wynd. In 1764 the Lodging was sold by the 4th Duke of Argyll and passed through a number of different hands before being acquired by the Crown about 1800; since that date it has been a military hospital, and it is still in use as such today although now under the guardianship of the Ministry of Works.

THE OLD HOUSE. This name may conveniently be given to the L-shaped block that stood detached in the 16th century in what is now the NE. corner of the court-

---

1 Cf. the account given in *Cast. and Dom. Arch.*, ii, 417 ff. A set of measured drawings of the building was published in Volume I of the *National Art Survey of Scotland* (1921).
2 Reference should be made to the block plans, Fig. 114.
3 Ronald, J., *The Story of the Argyll Lodging*, 74.
4 *Ibid.*, 75.
5 *Inventory of the City of Edinburgh*, No. 56.
6 Ronald, *op. cit.*, 118.
7 P.R.O., *W.O.* 44/554.

Fig. 113. The Burgh of Stirling (No. 226). The numbers refer to the articles in the Inventory, and the stipple represents the approximate NE. limits of the mediaeval burgh

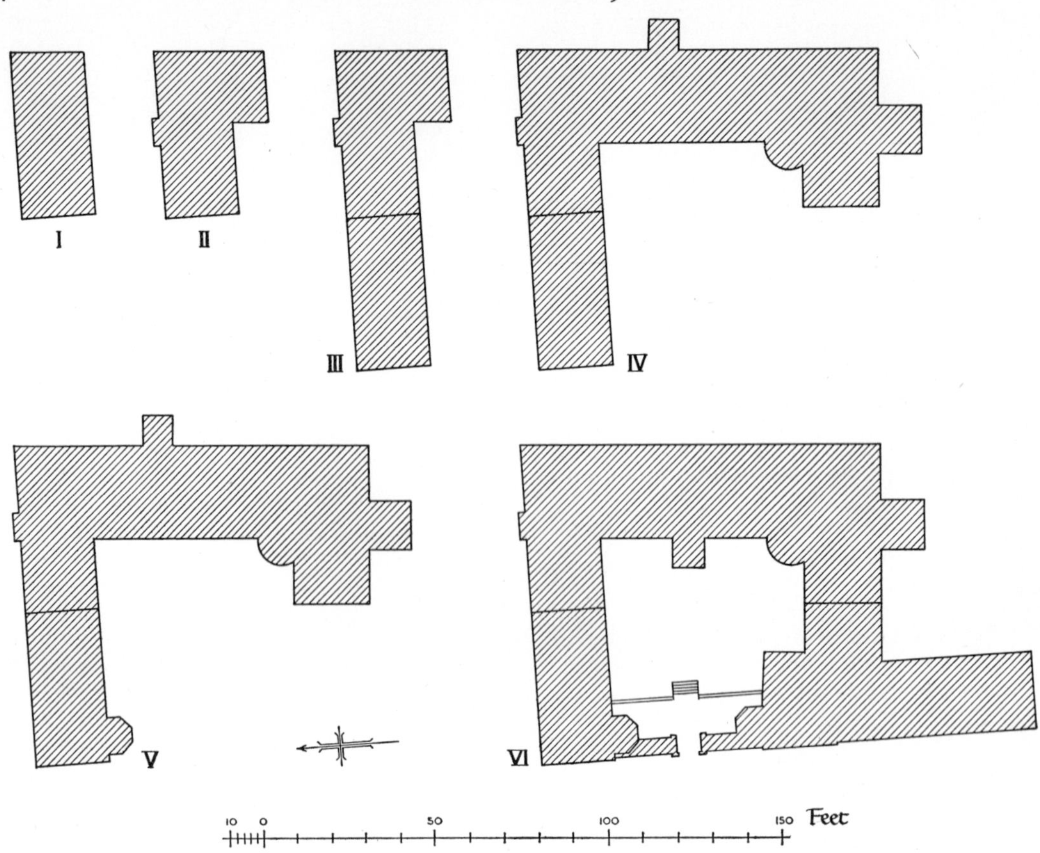

Fig. 114. Argyll's Lodging, Stirling (No. 227); block plans showing phases of construction

yard. It is here treated as a whole, for the purpose of description, but, as already remarked, the greater part of the ground floor is older than the upper floors and the wing.[1] The building comprises a main block alined E. and W., with a wing projecting southwards from its E. end; it rises to a height of four storeys, and in the re-entrant angle of the main block and wing a staircase-tower is corbelled out at first-floor level. Much of the staircase-tower is encased by later masonry, and only the upper part, with its conical roof, is today visible externally. The entrance-doorway, together with a stair leading up to the first floor, was probably contained within the wing, which was partially demolished in 1632 to make way for the present E. range. The windows have either chamfered or rounded arrises, and the walls, which are of harled rubble, finish in an ovolo-moulded eaves-course which returns round the staircase-tower as a mock crenellation; the gables are crow-stepped and have cavetto-moulded skewputs. Some of the windows have been enlarged and others inserted at different periods, and these alterations are noted on the plans (Figs. 115, 116). Within the courtyard a splayed base-course runs the whole length of the N. range. To the W. of the re-entrant angle an original window on the ground floor was extended downwards in the 19th century to form a door. The principal feature of the N. front is an oriel, which is corbelled out at first-floor level and rises to the eaves; it contains a window on both first and second floors. A garden wall of 17th-century date runs N. from the NE. angle of the building. On the E. façade the junction between the surviving fragment of the wing and the building of 1632 is marked by a change in the level of the eaves-course, and to the S. of this point the range clearly assumes a different character.

The ground floor of the main block (Fig. 115) contains two cellars and a kitchen; these are entered from two doors, which once communicated with the wing, and which are now reached from the N. end of the Lower Hall of 1632. The one to the E. leads to the kitchen, which is barrel-vaulted and contains a large fireplace in the E. gable with a semicircular arch. Within the flue, which is now bricked up, there is an oven to the S. and a salt-box to the N. To the E. of the window that lights the apartment from the N. there has evidently been a sink, but only its external outlet is now visible. In the S. wall there is a window, once barred and now blocked up; its existence confirms that the S. wing is later in date than the ground floor of the main block. The door to the

[1] The masonry of the ground floor, and especially the quoins, when exposed in 1958, was observed to differ in character from the masonry and quoins of the upper floors.

W. opens into a corridor from which access is obtained to the two barrel-vaulted cellars on the N. In the S. wall of the corridor and to the E. of the door that opens into the courtyard there are two windows, the easternmost one having been blinded in 1632 by the construction of the E. range. At the end of the corridor a transverse passage leads to an inserted door in the N. wall. At the S. end of the passage there was originally a round-headed entrance-doorway; this was converted into a window in the 17th century, but the window was subsequently blocked. The first floor of the main block (Fig. 115) is now entered from the scale-and-platt stair that rises at the N. end of the Lower Hall of 1632. From the landing of this stair a door to the W. gives access to the turnpike-stair by which the upper floors are reached, while to the N. another door leads to the easternmost of the two apartments that occupy the main block. This has an original garderobe in the NE. angle, but the fireplace is of much later date. There are two doors in the W. wall, but only the one to the S. is original; this leads to what was formerly a single room but is now divided into two. The original room was a spacious one and was lit by windows in the N. and S. walls as well as from the oriel; the latter has a semicircular rear-arch and formerly contained a small window in each return as well as the larger central one. The window in the S. wall has been blocked up and the wall thinned; in the W. wall there is a stone fireplace, now contracted, which has plain jambs and a moulded lintel. When the plaster was temporarily removed from this wall in 1958, it was noticed that in the centre of the wall, and over the present fireplace, there was an old opening, now blocked up; this opening, which is about 7 ft. 10 in. above the present floor-level, is 4 ft. wide and seems originally to have been a fireplace. It has already been mentioned that the ground floor of the old house is of earlier date than the upper floors, and the newly discovered fireplace indicates that, in the W. wall at least, this earlier masonry extends in part as high as first-floor level. The second floor (Fig. 116) originally contained at least two rooms, one occupying the W. portion of the main block and the other the NE. angle and the wing; the wing may, however, have formed a separate apartment, making three rooms in all. These rooms, like those below, have been divided up by partitions, while the E. room, or rooms, has undergone a partial change of floor-level to suit that of the range of 1632. Two doorways originally led to these apartments from the turnpike-stair, but only the one giving access to the W. room remains open. The only features of interest in this room are a garderobe or cupboard in the NW. angle, and a plain fireplace, now contracted, in the W. wall. The E. room is now accessible only from the gallery of the E. range; there is a garderobe in the NE. angle, but it is inaccessible. The third-floor plan (Fig. 116) is like that of the second floor, but is not complicated by the existence of later partitions. In the W. gable of the W. room there is a large fireplace with plain jambs and lintel, but it is now blocked up, as is also the window to the S. of it. Recesses in the wall-head of both the N. and S. walls suggest that the room was formerly lit by dormer windows. The E. room has a garderobe in the NE. angle and a fireplace, now blocked up, in the E. wall. The N. jamb of a window in the W. wall of the old wing also survives close to the re-entrant angle of the staircase-tower and wing, and may be seen from the N. end of the attic of the E. range.

The Addition of 1632. Viscount Stirling's new house was an L-shaped building of three storeys and an attic, the main block of which forms the major part of the present E. range of the Lodging; the wing returns to the W., forming the E. portion of the present S. range, and from it a small outshot of three storeys extends to the S. A circular staircase-tower with a conical roof rises in the re-entrant angle of main block and wing. The masonry is of harled rubble, but quoins and margins are of dressed stone, the former being elaborately carved and the latter chamfered. The walls rise to a moulded eaves-course and the gables are finished with a projecting tabling and moulded skewputs; a stone carved with a crescent, which forms part of the heraldic achievement of the Alexanders, is stepped out about half-way down each of the rakes. Some of the chimney-stacks rise from a scrolled table-course; all are moulded and some have pronounced weathered copings. The splayed base-course on the W. and N. façades is continuous with that of the N. range; it returns round the staircase-tower, which has, in addition, a moulded string-course at first- and second-floor levels. The W. façade (Pl. 124 A) incorporates three rows of symmetrically disposed windows, the uppermost range being dormers, and contains an entrance-porch centrally placed on the ground floor. The porch (Pl. 124 C) is designed to accommodate a door in each of its three external sides, and at the angles fluted pilasters rise from moulded bases to frame the doorways and support a carved entablature. Above the central opening there is a triangular pediment topped by a crescent finial, while in the tympanum a strap-worked cartouche bears the date 1632. The porch is roughly butted against the main structure, and may originally have given access to a doorway in the E. front, where the wall surface shows signs of disturbance. The carriage-drive that led from Broad Street to this doorway can still be traced, and no doubt formed the principal approach to the Lodging until the completion of the courtyard and the construction of the entrance-gateway from Castle Wynd in 1674; and it was probably at this time that the porch was moved to its present position. Above the porch an ornamental frame set within a strap-work border contains the full heraldic achievement of Viscount Stirling (Pl. 124 B). The shield is charged: Quarterly, 1st and 4th, a chevron, in base a crescent, for Alexander; 2nd and 3rd a galley, oars in action, sails furled, flagged, between three cross-crosslets, for Macalastair;[1] over all on an escutcheon the badge of Nova Scotia. Above is a coronet, with helm, wreath and mantling. The crest is a beaver and over it is a label bearing the motto PER MARE PER TERRAS ("By sea and land"). The dexter supporter

[1] But cf. Rogers, C., *Memorials of the Earl of Stirling*, i, 147.

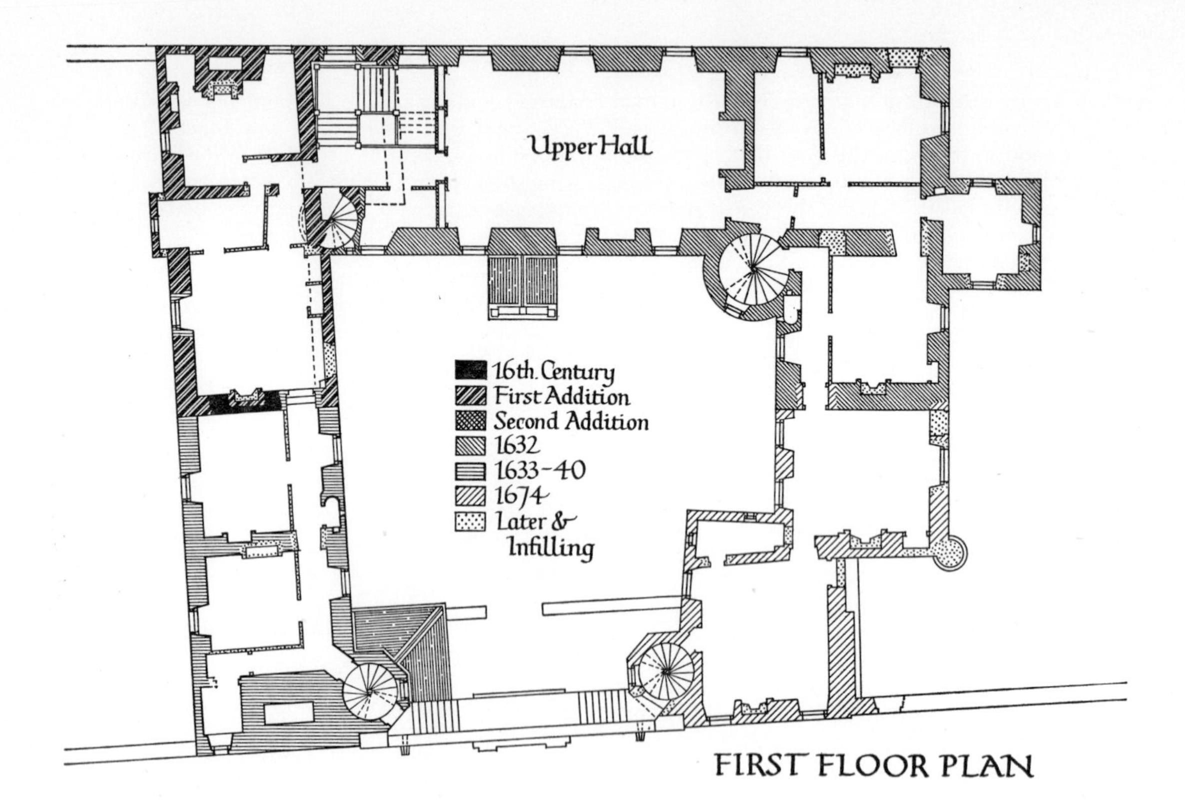

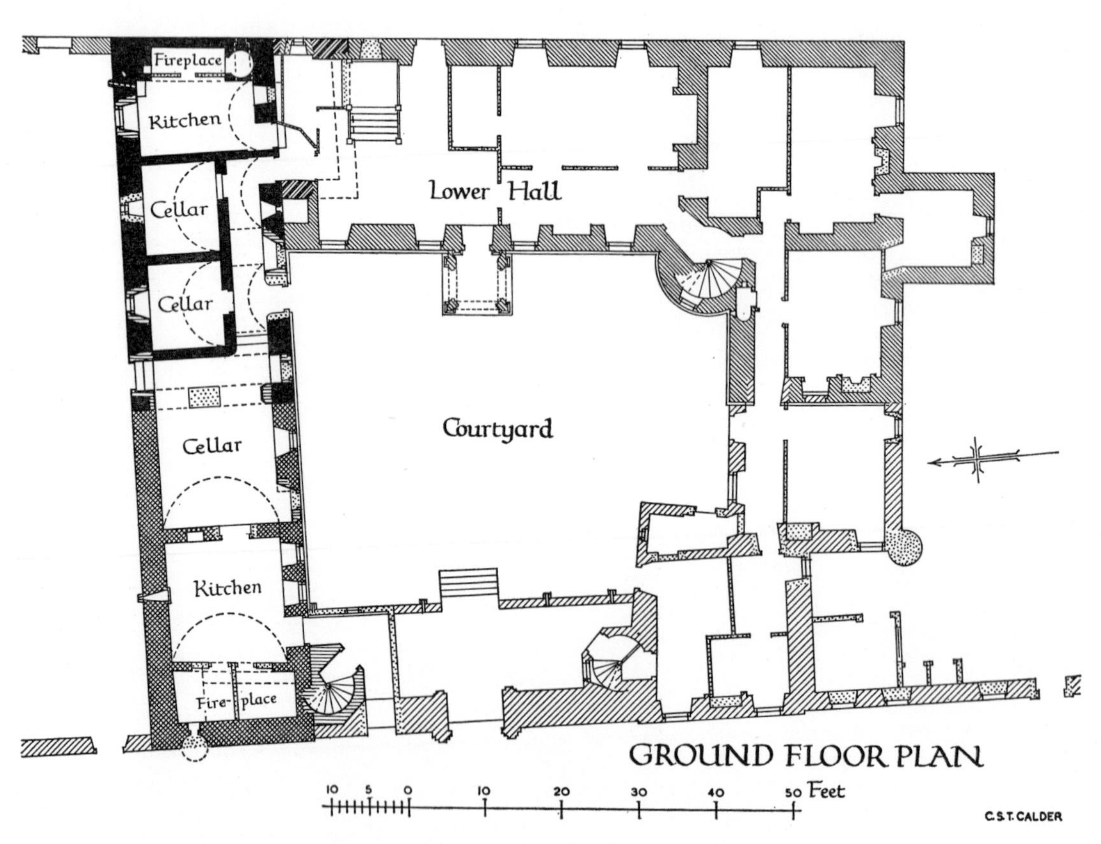

Fig. 115. Argyll's Lodging, Stirling (No. 227); plans of lower floors

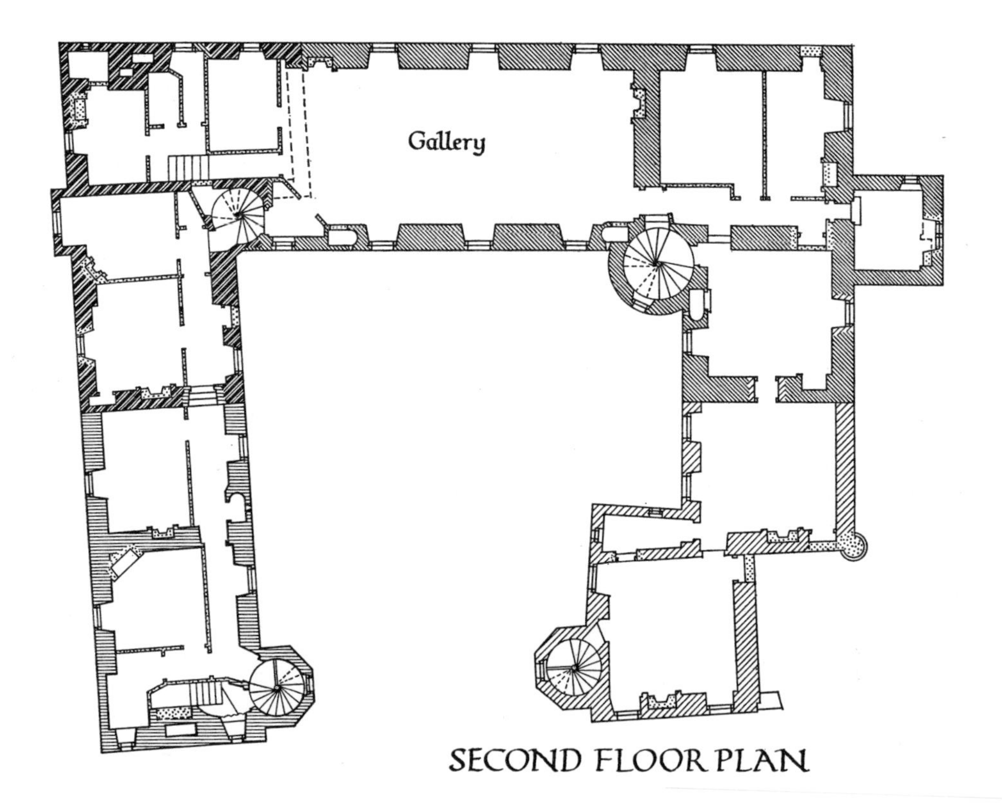

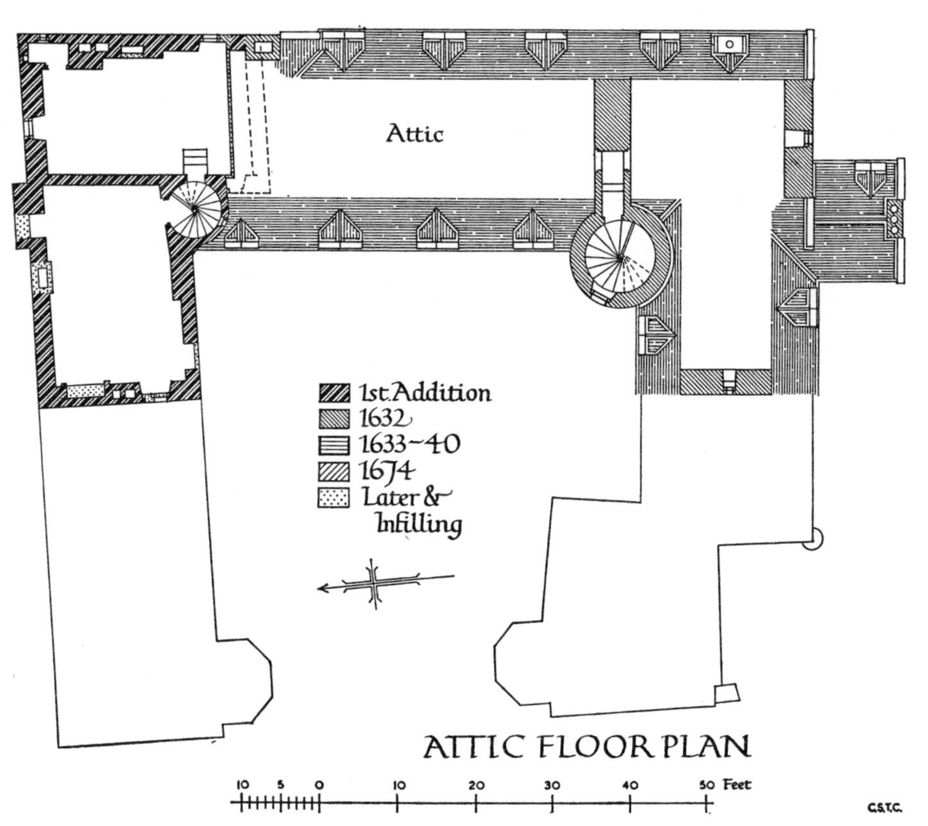

Fig. 116. Argyll's Lodging, Stirling (No. 227); plans of upper floors

is a Red Indian girt about the head and middle with feathers and holding in his right hand a dart; the sinister one is a mermaid, holding in her right hand a mirror. They stand upon a strap-worked cartouche which has the incised inscription AUT SPERO AUT SPERNO ("I either hope for or spurn"). The most varied display of carved detail, however, is to be found in the window pediments, which are carved with strap-work and incorporate the swags, garlands and masks that are characteristic of the period, as well as crescents and coronets of seven points, which refer specifically to Viscount Stirling (Pl. 125 C-E). The three southernmost dormers are further emphasized by flanking pilasters, which are fluted and rise to support the entablature. The pediments of the two windows of the N. façade are similar to those already described, and the windows that light the staircase-tower have strap-worked architraves but no pediments (Pl. 125 B). Within the courtyard the gable wall of the wing is marked by the return of the base-course, above which can be seen a number of decorated quoins which were left in position when the S. range was completed. The E. façade (Pl. 122 B), like the W., contains three rows of symmetrically placed windows with decorated pediments. The ornament here, however, is rather more restrained; the strap-work is confined to the dormer pediments, the southernmost of which contains the date 1632, while one or two new motifs appear on those of the ground and first floors. When the harling was temporarily removed from part of the E. wall in 1958, two blocked-up openings were noticed close to the SE. angle, one at first-floor and the other at second-floor level; both appear to have been doorways, and if so they may at one time have given access to wooden balconies or galleries, which have since disappeared. An entrance-doorway, perhaps once reached from a porch (*supra*), is situated at the N. end of the range, and a little further N., at the junction with the old house, a gablet which carries a chimney-stack raises the roof to the higher level of the earlier building.

The plan of the range of 1632 (Figs. 115, 116) is an interesting one; cellars and kitchens were already available in the N. range, and thus the ground floor as well as the first floor of the new building could be reserved for the principal apartments. The disposition of the rooms on the three main floors is the same; a single large apartment occupies the greater part of the E. range, while there are also two other principal rooms, one in the wing and the other in the SE. angle of the building, the latter opening into a small inner room which is contained within the outshot. The scale-and-platt stair at the N. end of the E. range rises to the first floor and gives access to the older turnpike-stair in the re-entrant angle of the N. and E. ranges, from which the upper floors can be reached. Another turnpike-stair, in the re-entrant angle of the E. range and the S. wing, gives access on each floor to the rooms at this end of the building. The main entrance-doorway from the courtyard leads into the Lower Hall, once a single apartment but now subdivided to provide kitchens and storage-space. In the S. wall there is a large stone fireplace with moulded jambs which support a frieze, cornice and overmantel; at each end of the frieze there is a square raised panel carved with a crescent. The staircase (Pl. 128 B), which occupies the NE. angle of the hall, is of wood and has turned balusters and moulded newel-posts which were originally finished with ball finials, only one of which survives. From the S. end of the hall access is gained to the two other principal apartments on the ground floor, both of which are now subdivided. The one to the E. contains nothing of interest apart from the moulded jambs of an original fireplace, which still flank the modern grate. A door in the SW. angle leads to the inner room, contained in the outshot, in the SW. angle of which there is a fireplace, now blocked up, with plain jambs and a moulded cornice. The room occupying the wing has a similar fireplace in the W. gable wall, but it too is now closed up. To the N. of this fireplace there is a window, which was blinded when the S. range was completed in 1674, and in the N. wall there is a garderobe with a lamp recess. The Upper Hall, which is on the first floor, was probably the most splendid room in the house and fortunately retains enough of its internal decoration to enable the original scheme to be appreciated. It is entered, from the top of the scale-and-platt stair, through a doorway (Pl. 128 A) which has a moulded and lugged architrave and, above, a frieze, cornice and triangular pediment, all in wood. In the E. wall there is a fine stone fireplace (Pl. 126 A-C), the jambs of which are carved in the form of herms; these support a frieze, cornice and overmantel. The frieze is carved in relief with arabesque work and there are traces of painting in gold and white upon the stonework. A series of large shelved cupboards, some with folding doors, forms a partition wall on the N., while there is a smaller shelved recess, now inaccessible, in the W. wall. The walls were originally divided into bays by painted Corinthian pilasters, the pilaster capitals supporting a painted arabesque frieze and a moulded plaster cornice (Pl. 127). The bays between the pilasters may once have contained further painted decoration, though no traces of this now remain, and the N. wall of the room, on which the painting is best preserved, is today sealed off for preservation, as is also the fireplace in the S. wall already described. The room in the SE. angle is now divided by partitions into smaller apartments; its most important feature is the handsome carved-stone fireplace (Pl. 126 D) in the E. wall, which is in the same style as the one in the Upper Hall. The frieze is ornamented with strap-work and contains two oval panels, each painted with a coat of arms, while in the centre there is carved a crescent. The dexter panel is charged: A chevron, in base a crescent, for Alexander, Viscount Stirling, and the sinister one: A pale, for his wife Janet Erskine, whom he married about 1600. Some traces of tinctures show that the panels were coloured. A door in the S. wall gives access to the small room in the outshot. The window in the S. gable of this room seems to be original, but the larger windows in the W. and E. walls have probably been inserted. The room in the wing has also been subdivided; it has a garderobe in the N. wall and a fireplace with plain jambs and moulded cornice in the W. gable. On the second floor a gallery occupies the greater part of the E. range; this has a fireplace in the S. wall and another in the E. wall, but both have been renewed. The small windows that light two garderobes in the thickness of the S. wall are visible from the courtyard, but both garderobes are now inaccessible. The room in the SE. angle has been partitioned off to form two small apartments and a corridor. In the E. wall there is a recess, which seems originally to have been a doorway giving access to an external balcony (cf. p. 282). In the S. wall there is a fireplace, now blocked up, with plain jambs and lintel, to the W. of which a door leads to the small dressing-room in the outshot. There was originally a single window in the gable wall of this room, but this was replaced by the present double window, which has partially destroyed the original fireplace to the W. of it. The room in the wing has a garderobe in the N. wall and a fireplace with moulded lintel and cornice in the W. gable. The turnpike-stair in the re-entrant angle of main block and wing rises to the attic storey, to which it now forms the only approach. There are only two apartments at this level, one occupying the greater part of the main block and the other, which is lit by windows in the gables, the SE. angle and the wing.

Apart from the features noted above, the addition of 1632 is noteworthy for the dressed ashlar margins of the doors and windows, a number of old oak doors with their wrought-iron furnishings, and some ceiling cornices of moulded plaster.

THE W. END OF THE N. RANGE. As it appears today, this part of the building is in large measure the work of the Earl of Stirling, who evidently completed it between the date of the conferment of this title upon him in 1633 and his death in 1640. A building was already standing on the site in 1633, however, for, as mentioned on p. 277, the main block of the old house at the NE. corner of the courtyard had been extended westwards in the late 16th or early 17th century. The alterations of 1633-40 were really no more than an extensive reconstruction of this earlier building, the ground floor of which was retained almost intact, while the upper storeys were renewed.[1]

Although this reconstruction took place only a few years after the completion of the E. range in 1632, the work is of a different character, and lacks the abundance of architectural detail that is such a notable feature of the earlier range. The building comprises three storeys and an attic, and the masonry is of harled rubble with plain dressed quoins and margins; the walls finish in a moulded eaves-course and the gables are crow-stepped. The chimney-stacks have steeply weathered copings like those of the E. range. The arrises of the ground-floor windows are rounded, but those on the upper floors are chamfered. At the W. end of the range there is an octagonal stair-tower, which contains an entrance doorway on the ground floor. Two windows, which light the first floor of the S. façade, have moulded pediments with concave rakes and ball finials. In the tympanum of the westernmost window there is an earl's coronet flanked by the initials E / W S for William, Earl of Stirling; the tympanum of the easternmost window contains a coronet flanked by the initials C / I S for Janet, Countess of Stirling. Above, two dormer windows with plain triangular pediments, one of them surmounted by a crescent, light the second floor. The N. façade is similar to the one overlooking the courtyard, but the first-floor windows have no pediments. The windows on the first and second floors of the W. gable, however, have moulded convex pediments; above there are two small attic-windows, now blocked up.

On the ground floor (Fig. 115) the W. end of the N. range comprises two barrel-vaulted apartments, the one to the W. being a kitchen and the one to the E. a cellar. The kitchen is entered through a round-arrised doorway in the S. wall; there is a stone sink in the N. wall and two windows in the S. wall. In the W. gable there is a large fireplace with a semicircular head, within which may be seen the mouth of an oven, now closed up. The fireplace is now partitioned and used as a fuel store. A door in the E. wall of the kitchen gives access to the cellar, which originally contained a window and an entrance-doorway, both in the S. wall. The doorway was subsequently converted into a window, and this has since been blocked up. Two large meat-hooks hang from the vault. Originally the cellar seems simply to have been butted against the gable wall of the old house, which stands adjacent to it on the E.; but subsequently, perhaps in 1633-40, the gable wall was in large part removed to allow direct internal communication throughout the N. range, and in its place there was substituted a stone arch, which was built flush with the vault of the cellar. At a later date still, presumably after 1841,[2] the arch was itself reinforced by the erection of the rectangular pier of masonry that stands at the E. end of the cellar.

The two main upper floors (Figs. 115, 116) are reached by means of the turnpike-stair in the tower that occupies the NW. angle of the courtyard. Both the first and second floors originally contained two apartments, but these have now been divided up into smaller rooms and are of little interest. The westernmost room on each storey has a closet in the NW. angle and the easternmost a garderobe in the S. wall; some of the fireplaces have been renewed and others inserted, and these details are shown on the plans. At the top of the turnpike-stair, a door to the W. of the one that leads to the second floor gives access to a straight stair, which rises to the attic; but this stair is not original, and the attic, which is now disused, may formerly have been reached from a small turnpike-stair in the SW. angle.

THE ADDITIONS OF 1674. The completion of the S. range, the erection of a S. wing, and the building of the

[1] This fact was made clear when some of the harling was temporarily removed from the S. wall in 1958, as it could then be seen that the masonry of the lower part of the wall was of a different character from that of the two upper storeys. The N. wall may, however, have been more extensively rebuilt than the S. wall, as its masonry, where exposed in 1957, appeared to be homogeneous.

[2] Cf. the plan of this date, Pl. 123.

screen wall that bounds the W. side of the courtyard, may be ascribed to Archibald, 9th Earl of Argyll. Only a fragment now remains of the wing, which was almost entirely destroyed in about 1862,[1] but its lay-out may be seen in the plan of 1841 that is here reproduced as Pl. 123. The work of 1674 is very similar in style to that of 1633-40, with which it was evidently intended to harmonise. Both main block and wing were of three storeys and an attic, and the masonry is of harled rubble with dressed quoins and margins; the windows have chamfered arrises. The walls finish in a moulded eaves-course and the gables are crow-stepped. The W. end of the S. range returns northwards, breaking the regularity of the courtyard, and at the NW. angle of the return an octagonal staircase-tower with a conical roof balances the one at the SW. angle of the N. range; between the two towers the screen wall forms the fourth side of the courtyard and contains an entrance-gateway. There are four doors on the ground floor of the courtyard façade; the one close to the re-entrant angle of the S. range and the return is an insertion, but those in the S. range itself, in the N. wall of the return and in the staircase-tower are original. Over the tower doorway there is a moulded pediment, which contains the date 1674 in raised letters, while above there is carved a vase of flowers. The windows are symmetrically placed, those that light the principal first-floor rooms and the staircase-tower having moulded pediments with concave rakes and ball finials; some of the tympana contain an earl's coronet surmounted by the boar's-head crest of the Argyll family. The second floor is lit by dormer windows, which have plain triangular pediments with ball finials at the apices. The entrance-gateway in the screen wall (Pl. 125 A) has a semicircular head and is framed externally by heavily rusticated pilasters; these support a moulded entablature, the cornice of which returns along the wall-head. Within the courtyard the gateway is flanked by Corinthian pilasters, rising from high pedestal-bases carved with a geometrical pattern in relief. Over the gateway there is an open platt, approached on each side by a flight of stairs within the thickness of the screen walls. The stairs, which have a projecting end-moulding on the treads, were formerly accessible from each of the stair-towers at first-floor level, but the door in the N. tower is now blocked. Within the entrance-gateway there is a terrace from which a central flight of steps descends to the level of the courtyard. Of the S. wing, only part of the W. façade survives and this only to the height of a single storey. The original façade[2] continued the arrangement now found on the gable of the S. range, the three principal floors being lit by symmetrically disposed windows with moulded pediments, some of the tympana of which contained devices in relief, including an earl's coronet and the Argyll crest. Two small windows light the attic in the gable of the S. range, while the upper floor of the wing was probably lit by dormers. On the ground floor there is an inserted bolection-moulded doorway, the architrave of which is carved with a running floral pattern. On the S. side of the main block a circular buttress of 19th-century date marks the original return of the wing. To the E. of this buttress there is an inserted window on both ground and first floors, the former being set within an original doorway and the latter replacing an original window. The dormer pediment of the window situated immediately to the E. of the 1632 gable has the Argyll crest in the tympanum and must have been renewed in 1674. Internally there are two main apartments on the three principal floors, and between them a small closet or dressing-room; the turnpike-stair gives access to the westernmost room on each storey. Doors in the W. wall of the easternmost room and in the S. wall of the westernmost room formerly gave access to the S. wing on each floor, but these have now either been blocked up or made into windows. The ground-floor rooms have been subdivided by later partitions, but apart from one or two minor alterations, which are noted on the plans (Figs. 115, 116), the first- and second-floor rooms retain their original dispositions. The attic is inaccessible. These apartments are of little interest, however, although in the easternmost room on the ground floor the old external base-course of the wing of 1632 is still visible on the E. wall, while in the W. wall there is a fireplace, now blocked, which has a moulded cornice. There is a similar fireplace in the easternmost room on the second floor.

792938 NS 79 SE

Various dates between 1954 and 1958

228. Old Grammar School, Castle Wynd, Stirling. A little to the N. of Argyll's Lodging (No. 227), and on the opposite side of the road, stands the old Grammar School, a very plain structure built to the design of Gideon Gray in 1788.[3] It is rectangular on plan with a staircase-tower to the rear, and rises to a height of three storeys and a garret. The façade has a projecting central feature, lit by two windows on each storey and surmounted by a triangular pediment. There is a moulded eaves-course and the gables have stone copings and moulded skewputs. A later L-shaped building abuts it to the W. The Grammar School was not used for teaching after 1856,[4] and the structure has since been adapted for military use and is featureless inside.

792938 NS 79 SE 21 November 1955

229. Number 30 Lower Castlehill, Stirling. This is a small two-storeyed house of harled rubble with a slated roof and crow-stepped gables. There is a central doorway on the ground floor with a window on either side; three more windows are symmetrically disposed on the first floor. The arrises are wrought with a narrow chamfer and on the lintel of the central first-floor window there is the incised inscription W G 1704 E R. One skewput has

[1] *Stirling Antiquary*, iii, 352.

[2] Illustrated in Ronald, J., *The Story of the Argyll Lodging*, 178.

[3] Hutchison, A. F., *History of the High School of Stirling*, 111.

[4] *Ibid.*, 187.

the initials T C very roughly incised, and the other the initials T R I H in relief. This latter is on a mutual gable and the initials may relate to the building that formerly stood next door.

791940 NS 79 SE 2 June 1955

230. Mar's Work, Stirling. What remains of this large and important mansion[1] stands as a roofless ruin in Mar Place, a few yards N. of the E. end of the Holy Rude Church (No. 131). Only the façade (Pl. 129), which overlooks the top of Broad Street, now survives, and this has been secured against further deterioration by the Ministry of Works, which has strengthened and patched the structure where necessary and has resurfaced what remains of the upper floor in concrete. Though greatly despoiled, and with its former splendour much diminished through the decay of the stonework and, especially, of the elaborately carved details, the façade still presents an impressive appearance. The house as originally laid out must have covered a larger area than now appears at first sight, as traces of two contemporary cellars at the S. end and tusking at the N. end of the existing block imply wings running W., the whole comprising at least three sides of a quadrangular courtyard. The builder was the Earl of Mar[2] who became Regent of Scotland in 1571 and died in Stirling Castle in 1572. Two carved stones (*infra*) show that work was in progress during the years 1570-2. Constructional style and ornamentation alike exemplify Renaissance fashions, and the latter was, no doubt, greatly influenced by James V's Palace in Stirling Castle (pp. 42 f., 196 ff.). The legend that the building was never completed is probably true, as a town plan of 1725 (Pl. 121) shows only the main block and the S. wing, but it seems to have been lived in by one or more of the later earls, no doubt during the 17th century,[3] while repairs were carried out in 1715 to make it fit to accommodate troops.[4] In 1733 the Town took a tack "of the earle of Marr's great lodging, high and laigh, with the closs and well . . . and also of the yaird belonging thereto" for use as a workhouse,[5] and this language implies that a large two-storeyed building was still in existence at that date. A late 18th-century drawing[6] shows the Lodging with its roof still intact, but in 1777 Nimmo describes it as a "ruinous building of good workmanship" and states that stones had recently been taken from it to build a new churchyard at St. Ninians.[7] By 1857, at which time it was acquired by the Town Council,[8] the building was no doubt little more than an empty shell.

On plan (Fig. 117) the existing main block is a parallelogram, alined from N. to S. and measuring approximately 101 ft. 6 in. by 30 ft. 2 in. over all. The walls vary in thickness, the E. and W. side-walls both measuring, in general, 3 ft. 6 in., the longitudinal partitions 2 ft. 3 in. and the transverse ones 10 in. to 12 in. The stonework is faced with ashlar. It is said that some of the building-stone was brought from Cambuskenneth Abbey (No. 130), which passed into the possession of the Earl of Mar before 1562,[9] and this tradition is supported by the presence of a number of ecclesiastical fragments within the existing fabric (*infra*). That these stones were brought from Cambuskenneth Abbey rather than from some other ecclesiastical building in the neighbourhood is, however, no more than a probability; and other possible sources for building materials include the Dominican and Franciscan friaries in Stirling as well as the Hospital of St. James at Stirling Bridge, the stones of which were being used for this purpose in 1567.[10]

The existing frontage, which is described in detail below, rises through two storeys to a denuded wall-head, but the back wall has been trimmed off only a few courses above the level of the first floor and its outer face has been hidden, up to this level, by soil from the Holy Rude graveyard which lies immediately behind. The revetment wall of a garden, and the earth filling behind it, have likewise obscured all details of the N. end at ground-floor level. Internally the ground floor contains nine barrel-vaulted cellars, of which five are to the N. and four to the S. of a central pend which led through the front block into the courtyard. The front entrance to the pend is flanked by semi-octagonal gate-towers, measures 6 ft. 6 in. in width, and has a semicircular arch and checks for the frame of the gate. The inner end of the pend has a segmental arch and shows no checks. The vault of the pend itself is also segmental; its transverse ribs and ridge rib are roll-moulded, heavy and closely set; and in its N. wall there is a segmental-headed recess, no doubt to take a porter's bench. The gate-towers are entered from the E., the interior of the N. one forming a lobby which communicates with the cellar behind while the S. one forms the well, 9 ft. in diameter, of a spiral stair which has now been completely removed. It is possible that a lobby at the stairfoot may originally have given access, through a door, to the cellar behind, but the W. arc of the stair-tower has been renewed as a solid block and no trace of any opening remains except at its N. end, where the renewed masonry seems to abut on an original wall-face. A peep-hole or pistol-hole in the inner face of each tower covers the entrance to the pend, while small loops in the outer faces likewise command the frontage respectively to N. and S. Further defence is provided by three larger gun-loops opening from the adjoining cellars, two on the N. and one on the S. of the entrance. The cellars are both entered and lit from one or other of the side walls, the openings on the W. being spaced at varying intervals and those on the E. conforming to the regular arrangement of the frontage. Internal communication is provided between at least two pairs of cellars, as shown on the plan; three others are certainly

[1] On which see also p. 44.
[2] Sibbald, *History*, 36.
[3] *Ibid.*, 38, 41.
[4] *Stirling Burgh Records*, 1667-1752, 353.
[5] *Ibid.*, 225 f.
[6] National Gallery of Scotland, R.N. 184.
[7] *History*, 311.
[8] *T.S.N.H.A.S.* (1904-5), 27.
[9] *Cambuskenneth*, cv, cix, cxxvi; *P.S.A.S.*, xxxix (1904-5), 155.
[10] Easson, *Religious Houses*, 102, 113 and 158.

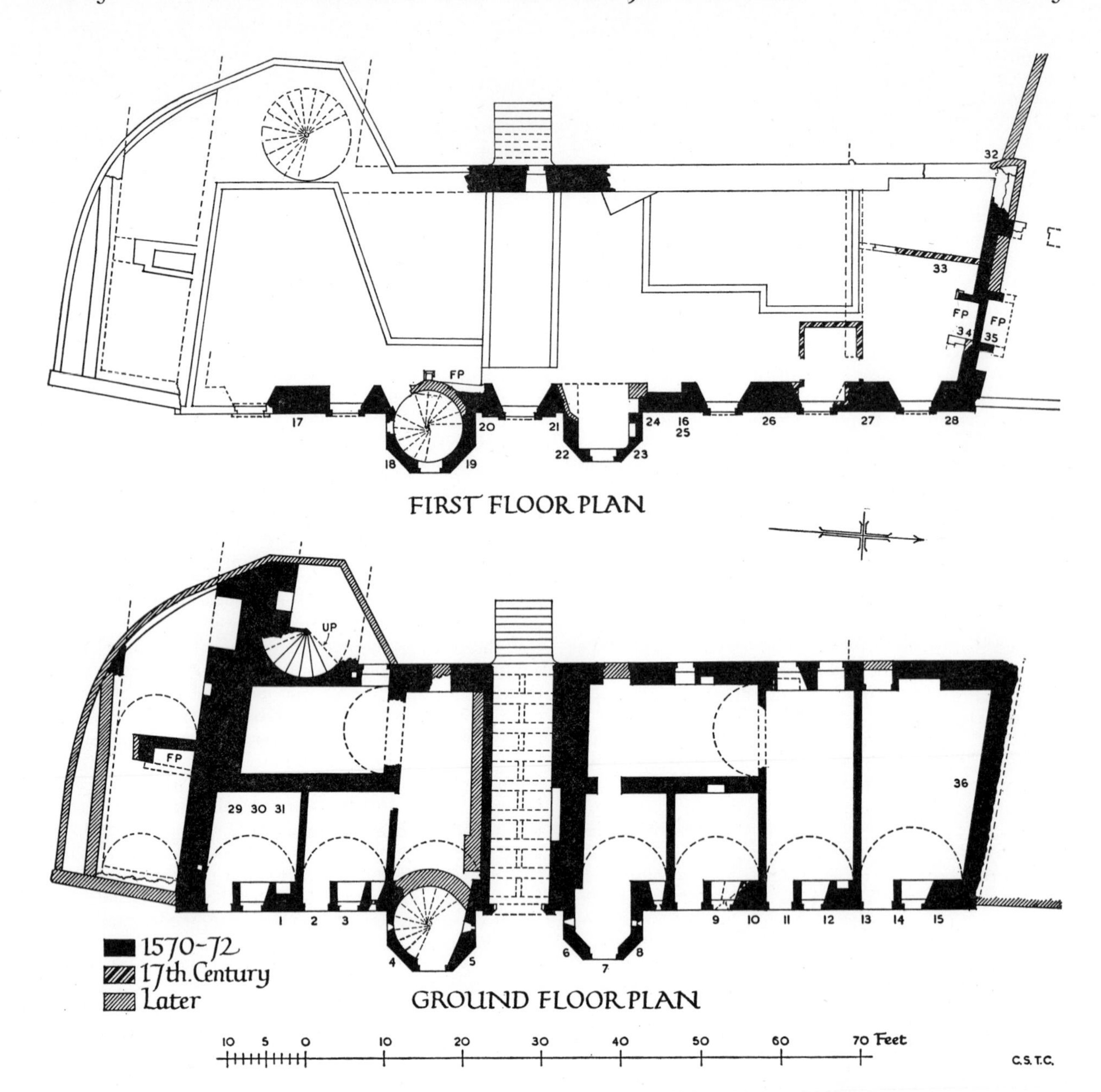

Fig. 117. Mar's Work, Stirling (No. 230)

single chambers. In the internal angle between the main block and the S. wing there remain the lowermost winders of a large newel-stair, 11 ft. 6 in. in diameter; and in what must have been the lobby at its foot there is an aumbry 2 ft. 3 in. wide by 2 ft. 1 in. deep. The two cellars in the S. wing were barrel-vaulted but are now very much ruined; the E. one has a fireplace with a plain lintel and the W. one a small locker and an arched recess, 6 ft. 4 in. wide by 3 ft. 3 in. deep, in its N. wall. Beside the doorway of the southernmost cellar on each side of the main block a vertical drain descends in the thickness of the wall, presumably from a garderobe or laver on the floor above.

The first floor is occupied by a high and spacious hall, with a small room, perhaps a retiring-room rather than a kitchen, to the N. of it. The building as a whole not being strictly rectangular, the front and back dimensions of both these apartments differ; but the mean internal length of the hall is 80 ft. and that of the small room 14 ft. 6 in., the width of both being 23 ft. 5 in. The partition between them, which was of stone, has been demolished and is only represented by the checked rybats and in-go of the E. side of a communicating door situated just N. of the northernmost window of the hall. The small room had a fireplace in its N. wall with jambs projecting 2 ft.; the hall fireplace was somewhat similar, the base of its S. jamb and part of its back, with a relieving arch, surviving in the E. wall behind the stair-tower, though the rest has been destroyed in the repair and refacing of the latter. The projection of these fireplaces, like that of another in the N. gable, to be mentioned shortly, suggests that all of them had canopies. The hall was entered directly from the stair-tower, but the E. jamb of the door has been destroyed in the course of the repairs just mentioned. At ceiling height above this door, and projecting into the stair-well, may be seen the supporting corbel-courses of a small turret which may have led to a parapet or to the roof. Except for a small window above the rear of the pend, the W. and S. walls and the SW. staircase are reduced below the level at which any structural features appear. The N. wall is sufficiently high to show, on its outer side, a broken-down fireplace between an arched recess, now blocked up, and a locker at floor level. Two or three re-used moulded stones can be seen in the jambs of the fireplace; these are corbelled out (*supra*) and originally supported a deep lintel, one broken end of which is still in position. Adjoining the W. side of the recess, and perpendicular to the wall, there is the bottom rybat of a doorway, apparently *in situ*, which marks the position of the lateral wall of a room which once extended N. but is now demolished. All the features just mentioned, as well as the mark of a roof raggle on the N. face of the wall, clearly indicate that some building formerly extended northwards here; but in the present condition of the masonry, and with the walling of the lower storey concealed under the made-up ground (*supra*), it is uncertain whether this was contemporary with or later than the main structure. The NE. corner of the main block shows a finished return with an angle-shaft which suggests that the E. wall of this room was slightly backset from the main façade; but the wall has vanished as a result of the banking-up and revetment of the adjoining garden.

The main façade (Pl. 129), now much weathered and wasted, shows a regular and well-balanced arrangement. It is embellished with nook-shafts at all the angles and corners, as well as with carved ornamentation comprising heraldic and inscribed panels, initial letters, statuettes, masks, and dummy gargoyles fashioned to resemble cannon. Doors and windows have straight lintels and all the openings are moulded. The basement window-sills were once carved but have lost virtually all their ornamentation; those on the first floor appear to have formed part of a continuous string-course, but the mouldings of those N. and S. of the gate-towers have been cut away. All the windows were half-glazed, shuttered and protected by iron grilles, and those surviving in the hall have segmental rear-arches which, like the jambs, are wrought with an edge-roll moulding. Above the string-course the upper-floor windows are advanced from the rest of the façade, and the masonry develops into shallow buttresses which rise to the present wall-head, the outer members of the window mouldings being carried up as edge-rolls.

The archway of the pend projects 7 in. and was originally flanked by a banded nook-shaft, 5 in. in diameter, in each return. The foremost member of the jambs is also a thin shaft with base and capital, otherwise the jamb mouldings run on, unbroken at the springing level, around the arched head, above which there is a hood-moulding carved with a vine-scroll. Over the hood moulding there are the remains of a triangular pediment with rakes which are now broken; the tympanum is plain, but it may originally have contained a decorative or, more probably, an heraldic panel. Above this again the masonry is slightly advanced up to the hall window, the lintel of which, carved with two winged cherubs, forms the bottom of a sculptured framework which contains a large panel exhibiting the Royal Arms of Scotland.[1] The panel (Pl. 131 A) bears in the centre a shield charged: A lion rampant within a tressure flory-counter-flory. The shield is Royally helmed, mantled and has for crest a lion sejant affrontée holding in the dexter paw a sword and in the sinister one a sceptre. The shield is upheld by unicorn supporters, each sustaining a banner; the dexter one bears a Royal saltire and the sinister one a lion rampant. Around the shield is the collar of the Most Ancient and Most Noble Order of the Thistle, from which depends the saltire badge of St. Andrew. On the collar is carved the letter R, and the badge is flanked by the letter I and the figure 6, for Rex Jacobus VI. Below the badge the date 1570 is carved on a label, below which again there is a thistle slip. The motto IN DEFENCE is carved on another label above the coat of arms. The lower half of each side of the frame is sculptured with two upright and opposed dolphins, which rest on a square base carved on each of its three sides with a mask; they bite the rim of an ornate vase which stands between them. The upper half of the frame bears two human figures below a foliaceous capital. The top member of the frame shows, in the middle, a foliaceous ornament flanked on either side by a bird-like monster with a human face.

The gate-towers are symmetrical, and the moulded lintel of each doorway is inscribed with a couplet in raised letters. The N. one reads

> THE MOIR I STAND ON OPPIN HITHT /
> MY FAVLTIS MOIR SVBIECT AR TO SITHT,

and the S. one

> I PRAY AL LVIKARIS ON THIS LVGING /
> VITH GENTIL E TO GIF THAIR IVGING.

---

[1] Such a display of the Royal Achievement was customary where the proprietor was a Crown vassal, in which case he was entitled to place the arms of his feudal superior above his own coat over the principal gate or doorway or over the most important fireplace (Innes of Learney, Sir T., *Scots Heraldry*, 171, 221).

Another couplet appears above the rear arch of the pend; it reads

> ESSPY SPEIK FVRTH AND SPAIR NOTHT /
> CONSIDDIR VEIL I CAIR NOTHT.

Above the entrance to each tower there has been an oillet, constructed partly on the relieving lintel, but the S. one has been blocked up and only the lower half of its margin, represented by a foliaceous swag, now remains. The N. oillet, which is complete, has a moulded margin and, above it, the initial A surmounted by a coronet, evidently for Annabella, daughter of Sir William Murray of Tullibardine, Mar's wife. It may be inferred that the Regent's own initial I, for John, originally stood over the S. oillet, and has vanished in the course of repairs. Above the oillets, in each tower, there is a window with the string-course returning around its head. On the underside of the sill of the N. window, which is now blocked up, there are three cherubs apparently connected by swags issuing from their mouths. On the sill of the S. window there are two mermaids holding up what may be a mirror; their tails are tied with a rope issuing from the mouth of a grotesque head at either end of the sill.

On the lintel of either window there rests an heraldic panel within a carved frame. The N. one (Pl. 130 B) consists of a scroll of oak-leaves and acorns, ending in the mouth of a miniature human figure, with arms bent and upstretched, which is carved as the centre-piece of the top member of the frame. The shield on this panel, which has a wreath and a coronet, is parted per pale charged: Dexter, quarterly, 1st and 4th, a bend between six cross-crosslets fitchée, for Mar; 2nd and 3rd, a pale, for Erskine; sinister, three mullets within a tressure flory-counter-flory, for Murray of Tullibardine. The S. panel (Pl. 130 A) is framed on either side by the upper half of a bearded male figure, set on a vase-shaped pedestal and supporting a moulded upper member. The sloping underside of this is carved with a vase, containing a flower, between the upper halves of two female figures which touch, with one hand, the leaves of the flower in the vase and, with the other, those of a foliaceous capital. The shield, which is supported by two griffons, has coronet, mantling and helm and, for crest, a hand clasping a *sgian dubh*; it is charged: Quarterly, 1st and 4th, a bend between six cross-crosslets fitchée, for Mar; 2nd and 3rd, a pale, for Erskine. The motto is JE PENSE PLVS. The top member of the frame of this panel also acts as the sill of a small window with jambs once moulded or shafted, now much weatherworn; the detail on the lintel of this window is defaced, but a vase still appears carved on the keystone of a rebated relieving-lintel above it.

At intervals along the whole façade, midway between the two ranges of windows, there is a line of carved stones, as under[1]: 1, 4, 8, 9, 10, human and animal masks, of which 1 holds a ring in the mouth and 4 is bearded; 2, 7, 12, 13, initial A with coronet (*supra*); 3, 14, 15, weathered and indistinguishable; 5, crowned R I 6 (*supra*) interwoven with a ribbon; 6, Royal saltire surmounting what may be a thistle slip; 11, an angel holding a scroll inscribed NISI DOMINVS. Above the level of the string-course in the re-entrant angles of the gateway, on the oblique faces of the towers, and between the first-floor windows, there have been decorative shafts evidently intended to carry statuettes, but most of the shafts have now vanished and only one statuette (16) is left. This represents a female corpse wrapped in a shroud and laced (Pl. 131 B). Many of the capitals and base-stops survive, the former being foliaceous and the latter as described serially below. 17. A female figure, now headless, wearing a gown pleated below the waist and open to show the under-skirt. From the waist-belt there hang three elaborate floral pendants. The hands are clasped over the breast. 18. A male figure, now headless, wearing a doublet with puffed shoulders, frilled cuffs and scalloped basque. The hands rest on the waist, which is encircled by a cord. 19. A male figure wearing a close-fitting, high-necked doublet with slight shoulder-puffs, pinked body and sleeves, and a broadly scalloped basque. Two tassels hang from a waist-cord. The right hand supports the left elbow, while the chin rests on the left hand in an attitude of thought. 20. A bearded figure wearing a close-fitting jerkin with a high neck and scalloped basque. The left hand carries a buckler and the right hand holds what may be a cannon-ball. 21. A male figure wearing a helmet with neckguard, a breast-plate with gorget and taces, epaulettes, rerebraces, coudes and vambraces. It holds what seems to be an arquebus, and a powder-horn hangs from the waist. 22. A male figure, now headless, wearing a buttonless doublet with pinked sleeves, pointed neck and scalloped basque, and held in at the waist by a band. The left hand is raised and the right hand rests on the belt. 23. A male figure, now headless, and with its upper portion much damaged. It wears a doublet with a pleated basque, held in at the waist by a knotted cord, and is playing what is probably a lute. 24. A male figure, wearing a tightly fitting cap and a surcoat pleated below the waist and provided with a high collar. The left hand raises the coat, exposing part of the body, while the right grasps what appears to be a leather purse. 25. A female figure facing half-left, the left hand on the hip and the right hand holding a spray of three flowers. It wears a gown, finely pleated at the neck and more broadly below the waist, with zig-zag pinking on sleeves and bodice. A cord about the waist is knotted at the front, with two depending tassels. 26. A female figure, now headless, wearing a gown buttoned above the waist and a surcoat, pleated below the waist and furnished with arm-slits. Before her she holds an open book bearing a much-wasted inscription[2] in incised letters—on the dexter page TR[A]/[T]OVR / [TYM] and on the sinister REVEL/[I]T OVR / CRYM. 27. A male figure, now headless, wearing a buttoned doublet with

[1] The positions of these and the other carved stones may be found by means of the serial numbers, which are shown on the plan (Fig. 117).

[2] The missing letters have been restored from a plaster cast made in 1897 (*T.S.N.H.A.S.*, xxix (1906-7), 92).

pinked sleeves and pleated basque. It is playing what appears to be a kettle-drum hanging at its left side. 28. A male figure, now headless, with the hands resting on the hips. It wears a buttoned doublet with pinked sleeves and a broadly scalloped basque, the top three buttons of the doublet being undone. A broad sash hangs from the waist and bears traces of an illegible inscription.

The following three members of this series are preserved in the S. cellar of the front range. 29. A male figure (Pl. 131 D), now headless, wearing a doublet with pinked sleeves and scalloped basque and having a cord round the waist. The arms are crossed over the breast. 30. A female figure, now headless, wearing a gown with sleeves which are pinked and elaborately ornamented in a spiral design. The hands are clasped across the breast. 31. The figure of a youth wearing a high-necked, buttoned doublet with slight shoulder-puffs and a scalloped basque (Pl. 131 C). It holds across the chest a label bearing the date 1572 in relief.

At the N. end of the main block the following four carved stones, brought from elsewhere, have been built into the masonry at first-floor level during repairs and alterations. 32. A keel-shaped stone. 33. A stone bearing a consecration cross. 34. A stone crudely sculptured with a saltire and chief, the former flanked by the initial I and the figure 4 and having an upturned "foot" at the lower sinister corner.[1] The design is probably a merchant's mark. 35. Part of a hood-moulding and two other moulded stones re-used or inserted in the sides of the fireplace. The stones numbered 32, 33 and 35 have probably come from some church, perhaps Cambuskenneth Abbey (*supra*), as have also part of a moulded base preserved in the N. cellar and several carved fragments built into its walls (36). The built-in fragments differ, however, from those numbered 32 to 35 above in that they are not intrusive but form part of the original structure.

792937 NS 79 SE 27 May 1954

231. Cowane's Hospital, Bowling-green, etc., Stirling. Cowane's Hospital was built as an almshouse in virtue of a legacy of 40,000 merks left by John Cowane, a prosperous Stirling merchant, who died in 1633 (cf. No. 237). The money was to be "bestowed upoun ane hospitall or almoushous to be buildit in sum commodious place within this burgh for sustenying thereintill the nomber of tuelf decayed gildbroder, burgessis and induellars of the said burgh".[2] The building stands between the W. end of the Church of the Holy Rude (No. 131) and the Back Walk (No. 250), on the lip of the Castle Rock and apparently occupying, in part, the line of the Town Wall (No. 249). An older house on the site was demolished to make way for it.[3] Its date, and its purpose as a charitable foundation, are attested by two inscribed panels set over the principal entrance. The uppermost of these reads THIS HOSPITALL / WAS ERECTED AND / LARGLY PROVYDED / BY IOHN COWANE / DEANE OF GILD FOR / THE ENTERTAINEMENT / OF DECAYED GILD / BREITHER, the name IOHN COWANE appearing again below, in larger letters, divided by a merchant's mark resembling an X with a cross-bar, together with the date 16/39. The lower inscription, a Biblical paraphrase, reads I WAS HUNGRIE AND YE GAVE ME MEATE / I WAS THIRSTIE AND YE GAVE ME DRINKE / I WAS A STRANGER AND YE TOOKE ME IN / NAKED AND YE CLOTHED ME / I WAS SICKE AND YE VISITED ME. MAT. 25. 35. The building accounts for the Hospital are preserved[4] and show that construction began in May 1637.[5] The structure was designed by John Mylne, master-mason to the Crown,[6] the work being executed under the direction of James Rynd, a Stirling mason. Freestone for the building was quarried locally as well as at Elphinstone (now Dunmore) and at Plean; stones were also brought from the ruins of Cambuskenneth abbey.[7] The Hospital was approaching completion in 1643, but a number of details, including the fine stone statue of the founder that stands over the entrance doorway, were not finished till about 1648. The statue was to have been carved by William Ayton, a well-known master-mason, but the work seems to have been completed by Mylne himself.[8] The statue is intended to be a portrait, and Mylne worked from a preliminary draft by John Service, a local mason,[9] who was presumably familiar with the features of John Cowane.

The plan of the Hospital (Fig. 118) is one which was uncommon in Scotland at the time, as it is E-shaped, embodying two lateral wings and a central stair-tower projecting from the NE. front (Pl. 132); and in spite of far-reaching alterations and reconstruction in the interior, and the renewal of the roof, the fabric still retains substantially its original appearance and forms a good example of contemporary Scottish work. The main block, which is alined from NW. to SE., measures 74 ft. 2 in. by 27 ft. 5 in.; each wing projects 21 ft. 7 in. and is 21 ft. 9 in. wide; the tower projects 7 ft. 3 in. and is 10 ft. 10 in. wide, but becomes a square of this latter dimension above the main roof-level. The walls vary in thickness, but average about 3 ft. 6 in. except in the tower, where they average about 1 ft. 4 in. The building contains three storeys, the principal one being entered directly on the NE., from the level of a small court made up between the wings, while below this there is a basement which takes advantage of the south-westerly slope of the ground. The first floor is an attic lighted by dormer windows. The tower is carried up to a height of two

[1] This same feature occurs on a stone in the Holy Rude Church (p. 139).
[2] Morris, D. B., *The Stirling Merchant Gild and Life of John Cowane*, 301.
[3] *Castles and Mansions*, 98.
[4] MS. Accounts of Cowane's Hospital, Town Clerk's Office, Stirling.
[5] *Ibid.*, account for period 1635 to October 1637.
[6] *Ibid.*
[7] *Ibid.*, *passim*.
[8] *Ibid.*, accounts for October 1643 to July 1644; 1648 *passim*; July 1649.
[9] *Ibid.*, account for October 1643 to July 1644.

storeys above the rest of the building. The masonry, which has recently been harled, or in parts lime- or cement-washed only, is rubble except in the tower and chimney-stacks, where it is faced in ashlar. The quoins are dressed and backset, as are also the openings of doors and windows which, in addition, have chamfered arrises. The gables are crow-stepped, the skewputs finishing in a cavetto moulding; there is a plain eaves-course, broken here and there by the dormers, and the roof is slated. Along the front there is a plinth, but not elsewhere.

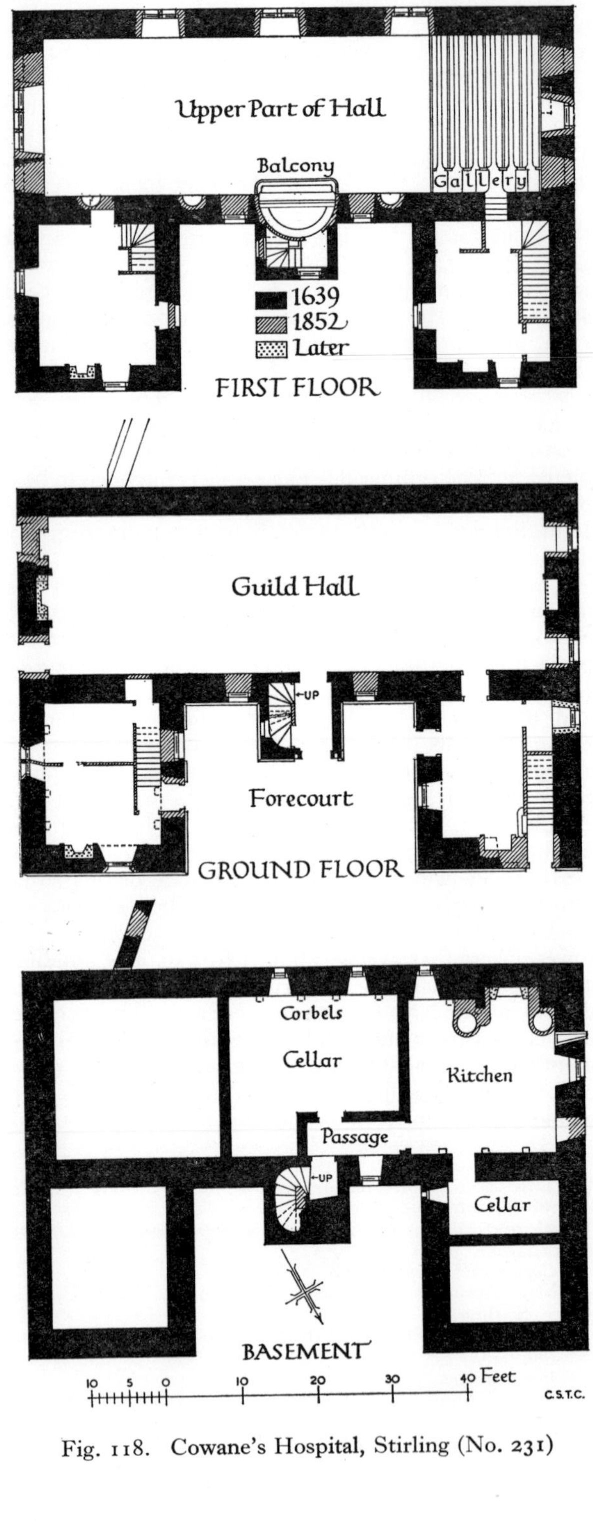

The main entrance and the window above it are not placed centrally in the front of the tower but towards its N. corner. The doorway has a simple, moulded architrave, and in the plinth on either side there is a small recess with a metal bar to serve as a boot-scraper. The upper two storeys of the tower are defined by moulded string-courses and a moulded eaves-course, above which the structure finishes in a leaded ogival roof with a ball-finial and a weather-vane. On the front, between the string-courses, there is a niche containing the statue of the Founder (Pl. 133 A); it is flanked by fluted pilasters rising from a moulded sill and finishing in a moulded and depressed triangular pediment. Below the sill there is a strap-work ornament, and from the semicircular head of the niche there projects a small scallop-canopy. The statue represents the Founder with beard and moustache, and long hair; he wears a ruff and a doublet, buttoned above the waist and skirted below; breeches tied with ribbon below the knees, stockings, and wedge-shaped shoes with buckles. He carries a cloak over his left shoulder and a high-crowned hat in his left hand. The belfry is pierced on its NW., NE. and SE. sides by round-headed, louvred openings treated in much the same manner as the niche, but their flanking pilasters are plain and there is no moulded sill. Some small rectangular openings seen here and there in the masonry of the tower are probably putlog-holes for scaffolding. In the NE. face of the main block there is a pair of original windows, one on the ground floor and the other a dormer, on either side of the tower, but they were blocked up internally during the alterations and are now blind.

The NW. wall of the SE. wing shows an original doorway, now partly blocked up and changed into a window when a stair was inserted (*infra*), and the modern one beside it, converted from a window. On the lintel of the old doorway is inscribed the text AND HE WHICH SOWETH BOVNTIFVLLY SHAL REAPE/BOVNTIFVLLY. 2 CORINTH 9. 6. IOHN COWANE. In the SE. wall there is an original window which differs from all the other survivals in possessing two round-arched lights divided by a mullion. The openings have glazing-grooves and the arrises of the front jambs have been cut back to admit more light. A window in the gable has also been splayed in this manner. All these ground-floor windows have segmental rear-arches. The windows of the upper floor are original and are similarly disposed; those in the side walls are carried up as dormers with gablets which have tabling moulded on the rake and are topped by carved ball-finials. The NW. wing retains its original entrance, in a position corresponding with that of the closed-up entrance in the SE. wing; its lintel is inscribed HE THAT HES MERCIE ON THE POORE LENDETH VNTO / THE LORD AND THAT WHICH HE HATH GIVEN HE / WIL PAY HIM AGAINE. PROV. 19. 17. IOHN COWANE.

Fig. 118. Cowane's Hospital, Stirling (No. 231)

The small window in the NE. wall is a recent insertion. In the centre of the gable of each wing there is an oval panel, within a moulded frame, bearing in relief the date 1639 above the initials I C; the panel on the NW. wing also shows the same merchant's mark as appears on the tower. Other openings in the wings are mentioned below in the description of the interior, as they have greater significance in that context.

The doors and windows of the main block are likewise dealt with below, but the following external details may be noted. The doors in the SE. end, and also the window above them, which latter is wrought with moulded arrises, have backset margins and are finished with a frieze, lightly ornamented with strap-work, a moulded cornice and a strap-work pediment. In the centre of the window-pediment there is a monogram of the Founder's name, and over each doorway the initials J C, for John Cowane, are intertwined. In the NW. gable, below the gallery window, there are three inscribed panels with moulded borders. The lower two show the same wording as those on the tower (*supra*), though the date is 1638, not 1639; the third bears the initials I C in relief with the date 1638 above them and, below, the same merchant's mark as appears on the tower. All the incised inscriptions on the building seem to have been deepened by re-cutting, and much of the strap-work and other ornament has been renewed or added. The dormers on the SW. face have plain gablets with cylindrical finials and cavetto skewputs, but no tabling.

In the original arrangement of the interior, the principal and upper floors of the main block were partitioned off into the several rooms needed for the domestic use of the brethren, and these communicated with a single room on each floor of the wings. An inventory of the plenishing of the Hospital, dated 1st August 1679, shows that there were seven bedrooms which could be occupied by two men each, besides a hall, a dining-room, a business room, servants' and keeper's quarters, a charter house and a victual house[1]; and internal arrangements of this kind can be inferred from structural survivals, such as original doorways, windows and fireplaces which can still be seen (cf. Fig. 118) or are known to be hidden under harling or plaster dressing. Blocked windows, for example, no doubt exist in the SW. wall of the hall, and that there were also fireplaces here is shown by three old chimney-stacks, which are now functionless except for a single vent from the kitchen. In the earlier 18th century, however, probably shortly before 1724, the main block was divided into two halls, an upper and a lower, and from that date "the term 'Gildhall' was regularly applied to the Over Hospital".[2] Thereafter the building was "used for a great variety of purposes, besides being the ordinary meeting place of the Gildry".[3] Later, in 1852, the floor between the upper and lower halls was taken down and the existing single hall, with its high roof, was formed.[4] At the same time communication between the main block and the SW. wing was cut off.

The main entrance, situated in the tower, leads into a lobby which, in turn, gives access to the stair and, at its inner end, to the Guild Hall. The down-going flight is an original wheel-stair of stone, but its width has been reduced by a short length of wall built against the newel, while the opposite face of the stair-well seems to have been cut back, as if to relieve the resulting constriction. The bottom of this stair ends in a small lobby, from which a door opens into a short passage; this gives entry to a large cellar, and also to a kitchen situated in the W. corner of the basement. From the kitchen there is further access to a small cellar underlying part of the NW. wing. The larger cellar is lit by two windows in its SW. wall, and the smaller one and the passage by windows slanting downwards from the forecourt. The kitchen was lighted by three windows, one in the SW. wall and two in the gable, but one of these latter is now below the level of a lane outside and is closed up. Near the W. corner there is an original fireplace with a semicircular head and chamfered arrises, but this has been contracted through the construction, in brick, of a boiler on either side. In the gable wall, beside the fireplace, there is a sink. Corbels in the side walls of both the kitchen and the larger cellar carry the old adze-worked runners and joists of the floor above. As no door- or window-openings appear in the rest of the basement it is to be inferred that the space at the SE. end and in the remainder of the NW. wing was not utilised.

The Guild Hall, which is entered by the lobby in the tower, is the high spacious chamber resulting from the alterations of 1852. It measures 65 ft. 8 in. by 20 ft., the roof is of open timber construction, and there is a gallery at the NW. end and a small balcony in the middle of the NE. side. The walls are plastered above a range of plain Victorian panelling which reaches to the height of the doors, the panels being edged with bolection moulding and the whole finished with a moulded cornice. Both the gallery, which is reached by a stair inserted in the NW. wing, and the balcony, which opens off the head of the stair in the tower, are finished with a wood lining below and plaster above; the ceiling of the balcony is domical. The fronts of the gallery and the balcony are panelled like the body of the hall, the central panel of the former displaying a shield bearing a merchant's mark resembling a 4 reversed. The feet of the principal trusses of the roof, which are arch-braced and alternate with lesser collar-beam trusses, and also the beam-ends of the gallery and balcony, are supported on moulded corbels ornamented with strap-work. At balcony level in the NE. wall three niches have been inserted; these are plain apart from domical scallop heads. A fireplace, which appears to be original but which has been contracted at some time, occupies the space below a large three-light window which has been inserted in the SE. gable; it has fluted jambs, moulded capitals, a segmentally arched lintel moulded on the arris, and a moulded cornice. It is flanked on either side by an inserted doorway with chamfered arrises, the southernmost being closed up

[1] Morris, *op. cit.*, 309 f.
[2] *Ibid.*, 311.
[3] *Ibid.*, 312.
[4] *Ibid.*, 314.

and accommodating a cupboard; they probably replace windows, though the closed one may have been blind from the outset and constructed for the sake of symmetry. In the NW. gable, below the gallery, an original fireplace, now closed up, is centred between two windows the sides of which have been renewed with panelling; another, on the upper level, under an inserted window, is hidden behind the seating of the gallery. The hall is further lighted by three large two-light windows inserted in the SW. side.

The SE. wing is now separated from the main block through the closing-up of the communicating doorways, one on each floor, which have been made into cupboards. Partitions inserted in 1852 subdivide the ground floor into two rooms and a staircase; some of the corbels on which the old upper floor rested still remain in the side walls. The NW. wing now gives admission both to the Hall itself and to the gallery, access to the latter being by means of a stair reached through a doorway inserted in the wing gable. The reconstruction so entailed has led to the blocking of a ground-floor window, and a new fireplace has been substituted for the original one. The fireplace in the upper room is old, as are also those in the other wing though they have been contracted to hold modern grates; the jambs of all are moulded, showing a sunken field.

Inside the tower a dog-legged stair of wooden construction, probably a replacement, rises from the entrance-lobby to the level of the first floor only. Further ascent to the belfry is made by loft ladders through hatches in the floors of the two intervening stages. The lowermost of these is carried on a continuous corbel-course.

BELL. In the belfry there hangs a single bell. It measures $31\frac{7}{8}$ in. in diameter and is inscribed M ADAM DANCKWART ME FVDIT ANNO 1665 / A 1668 / OPPIDVM STERLINI. Between the last two words there is a shield on which the second form of the Burgh arms, a wolf on a crag, are very faintly visible.[1]

OAK CHEST. Within the Guild Hall there is preserved an oak chest (Pl. 133 B), 4 ft. 8 in. long, 1 ft. 9 in. wide and 2 ft. 6 in. high. The lid is bordered, and is also divided into three panels, by raised ornamental strips. The frontal portion of the border has at each end a carved floral device based chiefly on the thistle, and in the centre is inscribed MAN SHAL NOT LIVE BY BREAD ALONE BVT BY EVERIE / WORDE THAT PROCEDETH OVT OF THE MOVTH OF YE LORD. The rest of the border is inlaid with a half-diamond design in woods of contrasting colours. The central panel bears the same inscription, from St. Matthew's Gospel, as appears over the entrance-doorway (*supra*), while the two outer ones contain floral ornament based on the sunflower and the thistle. The front of the chest is bordered and subdivided in the same manner as the lid, but both the upper and the lower portions are inscribed; the upper inscription reads IOHN COWANE'S GVIFTE TO YE CITTIE OF STERLING and the lower one, which divides the date 1636, IT IS MORE BLESSYED TO GIVE THEN TOO RECEIVE. The central panel bears the verses

NO BETTER THOVGHT THEN THINCKE / ON GOD
AND DAYLY HIM TO SERVE /
NO BETTER GVIFT THEN TO YE POORE /
WHYCHE READIE ARE TO STERVE

while the others are carved with thistles within arched inner panels. The ends of the chest each have a single panel within a border inlaid at top and bottom with the half-diamond pattern; in the centre is an elaborate device, based on the thistle, within an intertwined border of diamond shape. The back of the chest is plain. All carving and lettering is in low relief.

BOWLING-GREEN. The E. side of the Hospital is flanked by a flagged terrace, beyond which, at a lower level, lies a bowling-green with a small area of formal garden separating its S. margin from the Town Wall (No. 249), the upper part of which encloses the site on the S. The terrace is 88 ft. 8 in. long by about 18 ft. broad, and projects 28 ft. 9 in. N. of the NE. corner of the Hospital. At its N. end it is approached by a short flight of steps from the roadway, which lies at a lower level; at its S. end a second flight leads up to a similar flagged area at the SE. corner of the Hospital, while in the centre a double flight descends to the bowling-green. The upper terrace projects about 11 ft. S. of the SE. corner of the Hospital, the W. side of the projection being enclosed by a wall which returns from the line of the Town Wall to the Hospital at this point; the return contains a built-up doorway, well below the level of the terrace, which must have led into the garden before the terrace was formed. Both the terraced areas have balustrades, the balusters being square in section and moulded, and of a type which would accord with a date of about 1661 for the formation of the terrace[2]; but plentiful evidence of later reconstruction can be seen—*e.g.* in the broadening of the steps leading down to the bowling-green, in the use of half-round piers, out of keeping with the balustrades, at the top of both flights of steps, and in the fact that most of the balusters have been set upside-down. Morris dates the formation of the bowling-green to 1712, before which date the site may have been in use as a walking-green[3]; a garden is mentioned in 1707.[4] Some carved details from the Holy Rude Church (No. 131), and two Russian guns taken at Sebastopol, are preserved on the lower terrace.

SUNDIAL. Within the garden there stands a shafted sundial bearing a brass dial on which there is an incised "Table of Equations" together with the maker's name and date, "Andr. Dickie Stirling 1727". The shaft appears to be comparatively modern, but stands upon an octagonal base which is evidently older, and which may

[1] For further details about this bell see *P.S.A.S.*, lxxxiv (1949-50), 96 f.
[2] Cf. Morris, *op. cit.*, 305.
[3] *Ibid.*, 305 and 311.
[4] Sibbald, *History*, 34.

have formed part of an earlier sundial, perhaps the one that was purchased for the Hospital from John Buchanan, mason, in 1673.[1]

791936 NS 79 SE
Various dates in 1954 and 1956

232. The Town House, Broad Street, Stirling. The Town House of Stirling stands on the SW. side of Broad Street, at the corner of Jail Wynd. It was built between 1703 and 1705, to the design of Sir William Bruce of Balcaskie, and is one of the first tolbooths in Scotland to be treated in a strictly Classical manner, the steeple alone conceding something to traditional Scottish taste. An earlier tolbooth, which occupied the same site, was found to be in bad condition in March 1698, and the Town Council agreed that it should be rebuilt.[2] In March 1702 Harry Livingstone, a Stirling mason, was sent to Kinross to consult with Sir William Bruce, taking "ane exact account of the breadth and lenth of the ground alongs with him" and having instructions to bring back Bruce's "draught or sceme of the work".[3] Building was begun early in 1703 and both tolbooth and steeple were ready for roofing within a year.[4] The stonework was completed by Livingstone, while John Christie, wright, was responsible for the timber work.[5] The similarity of the Town House to the Mid-Steeple in Dumfries,[6] which was begun in 1705, suggests that Tobias Bauchop, the Alloa mason who designed the latter building, modelled his work on the recently completed tolbooth at Stirling.[7] In 1785 the building was extended eastwards to provide additional accommodation,[8] but the architect, Gideon Gray, who also designed the Old Grammar School (No. 228), followed the original elevational treatment so closely that the junction between the old and the new work is now hardly apparent. A court-house and jail were added to the S. of the Tolbooth, fronting on Jail Wynd and St. John Street, between 1806 and 1811—the court-house itself between 1808 and 1810, the architect being Richard Crichton of Edinburgh.[9]

The Town House as enlarged in 1785 is an oblong building alined nearly E. and W., with a tower in its NW. corner which projects 6 ft. from the N. front (Fig. 119). It contains three storeys, with a garret constructed wholly in the roof, and shows six openings on each floor to the N. and three to the W., all symmetrically arranged (Pl. 134 A). The original portion measures 37 ft. 10 in. in length and, excluding the tower, 29 ft. 3 in. in breadth, but the extension of 1785 increased the total length to 61 ft. 8 in. The wall fronting on Broad Street is faced with ashlar and the one facing Jail Wynd is rendered in cement, the rest of the main building being in rubble. The upper half of the tower, above eaves level, is also ashlar-faced, with a rustic finish at voids and quoins. Elsewhere, both in tower and main block, the quoins are simply backset. The Broad Street façade rests on an ogee-moulded plinth, and finishes in a moulded eaves-course which is carried round the tower as a string-course. The windows on this side are lintelled and have moulded architraves topped with convex friezes and moulded cornices; their sills, which are also moulded, continue on the first and second floors as string-courses. On Jail Wynd the windows have backset margins, some of which have been re-faced in cement, and except in these latter cases all the windows in the N. and W. fronts show traces of bar-holes; but as these occur only in the jambs and in the soffits of the lintels, and were not found in the sills, it is probable that the lower halves of the windows were shuttered and only the upper halves protected by iron grilles. There were two entrances on the ground floor, which corresponded in style with the windows, one being in the N. wall immediately E. of the tower and the other in the W. wall immediately S. of it; the latter has now been converted into a window, the northernmost of the three on that side, and is so shown in Fig. 119. The tower, which is 15 ft. square, contains six storeys and finishes in a moulded cornice. Above this a simple iron railing encloses a parapet-walk, and from this level there rises a wooden belfry with an ornamental ogival roof (Pl. 135 A). The whole is topped by a finial and weather-cock. The tower is lit by windows opening on Broad Street, but the belfry has a louvred opening with a triangular pediment in each of its sides and correspondingly the roof has four lucarnes. Just below the parapet of the tower there are four square clock-faces of wood, each within a moulded stone frame. The 19th-century addition comprises cells, a stair, a court-room which rises through two storeys and, further S., a prison, which is now being converted to domestic use. None of these latter structures is of any particular interest, though mention may be made of the court-house entrance, which is round-headed and has a Gibbs surround, and of the double forestair by which it is approached; this is provided with a stone balustrade, the balusters of which resemble those at Cowane's Hospital (p. 292) and may have been brought thence for use at the court-house.

The constructional history of the main building is not altogether clear. The N. façade of the E. portion appears to have been advanced by a few feet from the front, now removed, of an earlier two-storeyed building, and as a tenement is known to have stood immediately E. of the old tolbooth before its removal,[10] and some items of evidence also go to show that a two-storeyed building was used as part of the accommodation of the Town House in its 1703-85 phase, some portions of the structure, including what may be part of the S. wall of the old tolbooth, have been indicated in Fig. 119 as being

[1] Morris, *op. cit.*, 307.
[2] *Stirling Burgh Records*, 1667-1752, 87 f.
[3] *Ibid.*, 97.
[4] Stirling Council Books (unpublished), 9 Jan. 1703, 25 Dec. 1703, 29 Jan. 1704.
[5] *Ibid.*, 9 Jan. 1703, 8 April 1704.
[6] *Inventory of Dumfriesshire*, No. 127.
[7] Bauchop had previously been associated with Sir William Bruce in an undertaking at Kinross House (*Inventory of Fife, Kinross and Clackmannan*, No. 568).
[8] Stirling Council Books (unpublished), 5 April 1785.
[9] *Ibid.*, 28 Oct. 1806, 8 Oct. 1808.
[10] *Stirling Burgh Records*, 1667-1752, 97, 99.

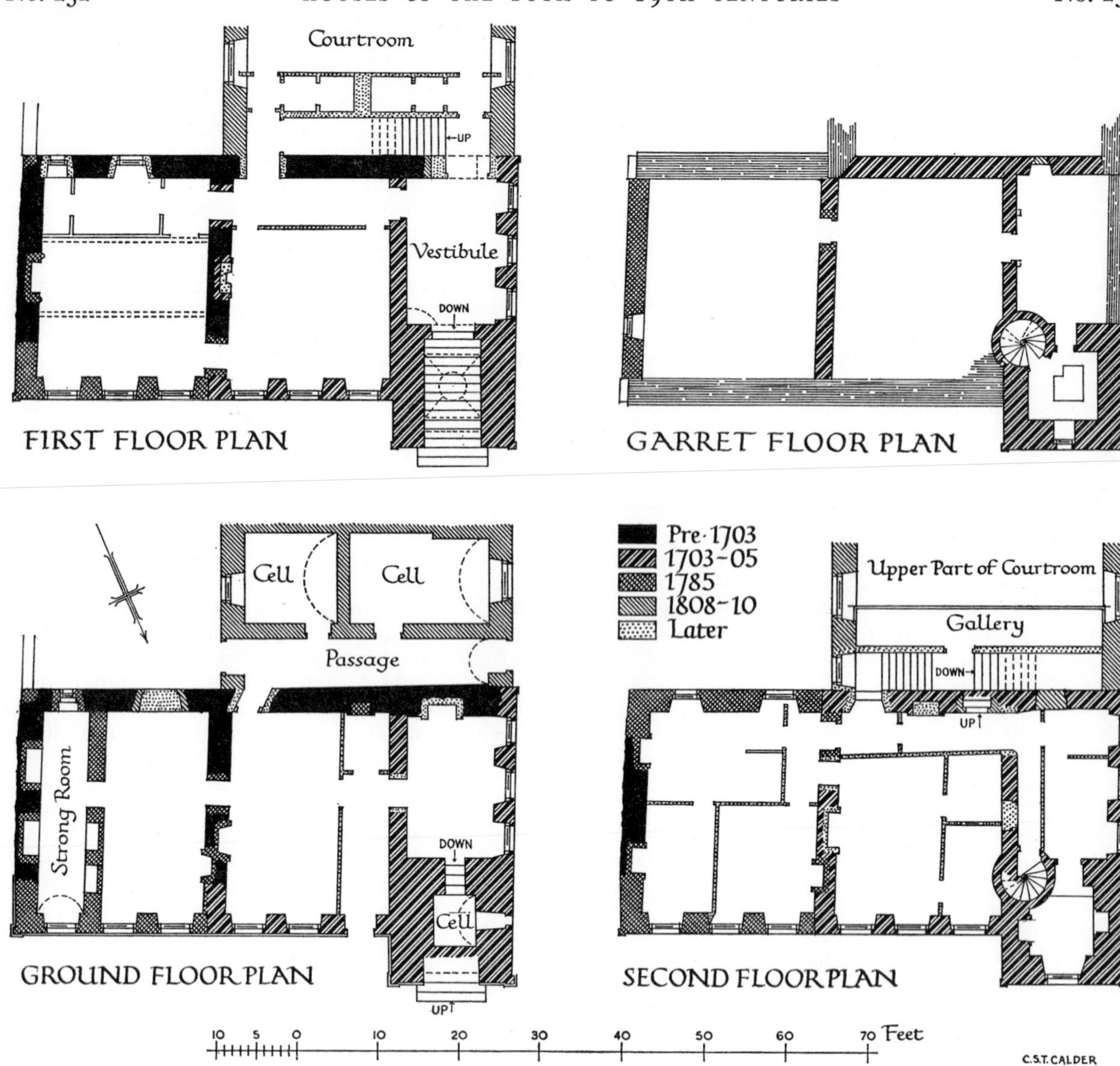

Fig. 119. The Town House, Stirling (No. 232)

older than 1703. This must, however, remain a matter of inference as the greater part of the walling in question —all, in fact, except the outside of the E. gable—is now covered with plaster or woodwork. However this may be, the internal space on each floor is now divided, if more or less recent subsidiary partitions are ignored, by main partitions which rise to the garret, into two large equal apartments with a smaller one behind the tower, the tower itself containing a still smaller room. The E. apartment is subdivided by an additional partition which rises only to the ceiling of the ground floor; this shuts off a long, narrow, vaulted apartment which was evidently used as a strong-room, as each of its side walls contains two presses with iron doors. All the main partitions have been pierced by doors as internal communication became necessary at one time or another, and windows and fireplaces have similarly been inserted or filled up (see Fig. 119). The blocked-up fireplace in the S. wall of the W. room, near its SW. corner, is of interest, seeing that it is asymmetrically placed in the room and may consequently be a feature of the building that existed before 1703. The room behind the tower is reached by a door broken through its W. wall, this having no doubt been done when the external door of this room had been converted into a window (*supra*). Through the N. wall a flight of four steps leads down to a tiny vaulted cell, lit by a small window on the W., no doubt "the holl beneath the steeple" in which a prisoner was confined in 1707.[1]

[1] *Stirling Burgh Records*, 1667-1752, 112.

The position of the "prisons" below the tolbooth, the partition walls of which had to be thickened in 1724,[1] has not been established; they may simply have been small cells occupying part of the room behind the tower.

There is no direct communication between the ground and first floors, as the latter is approached from the street by a wide, straight flight of steps housed in the tower. The outer entrance is a large round-headed arch with a moulded architrave; its keystone is elaborately moulded and is carved with a mask, while the voussoirs flanking it are ornamented with leaves, flowers and fruit. Immediately above there is an empty round-headed niche set within a rectangular frame carved with egg-and-dart ornament. The stairway is plastered and is ceiled with a quadripartite plaster vault having slender wall-ribs and groins springing from foliaceous angle-responds. A bell-hole in the centre of the vault, similarly moulded, is now closed with a painted panel showing the Burgh's later seal,[2] a wolf couchant on a rock, with the motto STIRLINI OPPIDVM. The doorway at the top of the stair has a semicircular head and a continuous roll-and-hollow moulding. The door itself, which is studded with nail heads and is hung on ornamental crook-and-band hinges, appears to be original but may be a replica constructed in the old manner—*i.e.* of two thicknesses of boards, the outer ones vertical and the inner ones horizontal, with their ends dovetailed into the stiles. This doorway opens on to a roomy vestibule from which access is obtained, through a door with a lugged architrave, to the two main rooms on this floor, and also, by another door broken through the S. wall, to the earlier of the 19th-century additions (*supra*). This latter opening was originally arched, with a backset margin, and was presumably broken through when the addition was made, but it has been superseded by a lintelled doorway centred slightly further W., with the result that its W. jamb has been demolished and its E. one partly covered up by the newer masonry. The change was probably made in order to accommodate the foot of a long stair, later inserted in the addition, which rises eastwards to the second floor.

The two main rooms on the first floor are now subdivided by partitions, the W. one to provide a corridor and the E. one a washroom. The W. room is lined with plain wooden panelling and has a dado and a large moulded cornice; the ceiling is plastered. In the centre of the E. side there is a fine stone fireplace (Pl. 135 B) with roll-and-hollow moulding; it is framed by the woodwork, which here consists of a lugged architrave, frieze and moulded mantelshelf above which there is a Classical landscape painted in oil direct on the panelling. The fireplace is flanked by pilasters with panelled pedestals, fluted shafts and pseudo-Ionic capitals. The doorway S. of the fireplace has a lugged architrave and, as its jambs are included in the panelling of the room as a whole, it is to be inferred that this opening dates from 1703-5, a conclusion which would in turn corroborate the idea of a pre-existing tenement to the E. having been utilised as part of the Town House (*supra*). The one to the N. of the fireplace, however, has evidently been broken through, presumably when the building was extended in 1785. The E. room is plastered above a panelled wooden dado, and has an enriched plaster cornice; the ceiling is divided into three equal spaces by two beams resting on scrolled plaster brackets. A fireplace in the centre of the E. side has an inner surround of marble and a moulded wooden mantelpiece delicately carved with swags and wreaths. The doorways are finished with architraves, frieze and cornice, but the architraves are not lugged.

The second floor is now partitioned off into living-rooms, bedrooms and closets, and is reached from the top of the inserted staircase, mentioned above, through a doorway which has been broken out. Formerly, however, there was again no direct communication between this floor and the lower ones and, presumably, before the additions of 1808-10 were carried out, there must have been a forestair or turnpike rising to it from the ground level outside. The position of the head of such a stair is indicated by an original outer doorway, now built up, which is situated in the S. wall of the room to the S. of the tower at this level. Through this room all the rest of the apartments on this floor and on the one above were accessible. The original door to the adjacent room survives, but it has also been built up and its place is taken by another which has been broken through to the S. of it, and which opens into a passage formed by the later partitioning. In this passage there is an original fireplace which has been blocked up. In the tower there is a small room belonging to the original arrangement; this has a fireplace in the E. wall and a giblet-checked locker opposite. The jambs and lintel of this fireplace are wrought with a roll-and-hollow moulding, and a re-used stone of earlier date, with a bead moulding, has been introduced as a relieving lintel above. The wooden door to this room is old, and the window has been renewed in its original style, with glass above and shuttering below. The floor has been raised 1 ft. by the insertion of close-set wooden beams.

The garret, which contains three intercommunicating rooms, is reached by a spiral stair in the SE. angle of the tower; this, however, continues no higher than the garret floor, and the upper parts of the tower are served by wooden loft-stairs. The two larger rooms in the garret have always had a ridged roof, as at present, but two corbels in the E. wall of the room behind the tower suggest that this room was originally covered by a lean-to roof. The old roof-timbering remains, that in the original block having adze-dressed collars and rafters, with heavy sarking-boards, and that in the extension sawn timbers strengthened by a king-post truss. Numerous wooden pegs projecting through the sarking are evidently the remains of an older and heavier roof-covering. A small window pierces the E. gable and another has been blocked up in the S. wall of the room behind the tower; in the E. wall of the central room there is a timber, resembling a lintel, but no trace of any filled-up opening can now be seen below it in the masonry.

---

1 *Ibid.*, 181.

2 Porteous, *The Town Council Seals of Scotland*, 274.

BELLS. The bell that hangs in the fifth storey of the tower is 16 in. in diameter and is inscribed in relief THE COVNSEL BELL OF STERLINE OVDEROGGE FECIT 1656. Below appears the single letter S. In the belfry there hangs another bell, which was recast in 1864, but which bears what is presumably a copy of the original inscription PETRUS HEMONY ME FECIT AMSTELODAMI AD 1669 SIT NOMEN DOMINI BENEDICTUM. The bell of 1669 seems itself to have been a recast of an older bell.[1] At the same level there is a chime of sixteen bells, two of which are inscribed, one bearing the date 1729 with the initials I W and the other the date 1729 alone. An entry in the Burgh Records shows that a set of "musick bells for the towns clock" was bought in London in that year.[2]

793936 NS 79 SE 13 November 1957

233. Norrie's House, 34 Broad Street, Stirling. This house,[3] although partially demolished at the rear and gutted within, is of importance on account of its façade (Pl. 137), which is one of the most pleasing examples of 17th-century architecture remaining in the burgh. It contrasts with the twin-gabled house immediately to the W. both in the quality of its masonry and in its wealth of decorative detail; and it is clear that care has been taken to make a rather narrow street-front as attractive as possible, the rear of the building being treated much more simply.

The façade is four storeys and an attic in height and the masonry is ashlar, some of the stones being of considerable size. The ground floor has lately been used as a shop and is much disfigured, but on each of the three main floors above there is a range of three large windows, closely spaced, above which the façade finishes in a crow-stepped gable which contains a small attic-window and is crowned with a finial carved in the form of a human head. Both quoins and windows have projecting margins; the windows have rounded arrises, and over each there is a moulded cornice and triangular pediment the tympana of which contain texts and initials, the former being incised and the latter in raised letters. Those on the 1st floor, reading from west to east are: ARBOR VITAE SAPIENTIA ("Wisdom is the tree of life") and MURUS AHENEUS: BONA CONSCIENTIA ("A good conscience is a brazen wall"). On the second floor: I N SO[LI] DEO GLORIA ("Glory to God alone") A R. On the third floor: I R 1671 A L. The initials in the second floor pediments presumably represent James Norrie, a prominent Town Clerk of the burgh at the time, and his wife Agnes Robertson, while the date 1671 probably commemorates the erection of the building. The interpretation of the initials in the third-floor pediments is uncertain, but they may represent James Robertson, Norrie's father-in-law, and his wife.[4] At ground-floor level there is a moulded cornice supported at either end by pilasters; these have moulded bases and capitals, are decorated with sunken lozenge-shaped facets, and would pass stylistically as integral members of the earlier work; but as they are not truly bonded into the main wall they may in fact be part of the later shop-frontage.

Norrie's House was reconstructed in 1958-9, after the completion of the foregoing account.

793937 NS 79 SE 1 June 1955

234. Broad Street,[5] Stirling; Lesser Houses and Architectural Details.

NORTH-EAST SIDE. No trace now remains of the fine house that once occupied the corner of St. Mary's Wynd and Broad Street,[6] but some fragments survive from a building which formerly stood a little higher up the street and which is called by Fleming the Elphinstone Lodging.[7] These consist of a dormer pediment now preserved in the Smith Institute (No. 405), a sundial and some carved stones. Three of the carved stones are built into the façade of Numbers 4-6 at first-floor level, two side by side and the third above them. The upper stone is carved in relief with the date 1715 above the initials I B and K M. The dexter stone of the pair below is inscribed LAVS DEO ("Praise to God"), also in relief, and the sinister one, though now blank, is said by Fleming[8] to have borne the inscription HIC PARTA HIC MANEAT ("Here born, here may she remain"). The remaining carved stone and the sundial are built into the front wall of Number 10, the former between the second and third floors and the latter at ground-floor level. The stone is carved with the motto NISI DOMINVS FRVSTRA in raised letters within a sunk panel; the sundial is 1 ft. 10 in. square and has a scalloped edge and Roman numerals. Fleming's sketches and the surviving dormer-pediment suggest an early 17th-century date for this building, although some of the carved details indicate 18th-century alterations.[9]

Numbers 24-26 consist of a rectangular block (Pl. 138 A) four storeys in height, fronting Broad Street, with a wing of two storeys and an attic extending to the rear and entered from a close. The building is no doubt of 17th-century date, but the façade has been altered and refaced at a later period and is now of little interest. About 6 ft. within the pend that gives access to the close is a deep moulded lintel, beneath which there is some disturbance in the wall-face on either side. A similar feature is also found in Norrie's House (No. 233), and suggests that the original central wall of these buildings at ground-floor level was set back some distance from the

---

1 *Stirling Burgh Records*, 1667-1752, 3, 6.

2 *Ibid.*, 205. See also *P.S.A.S.*, lxxxiv (1949-50), 93-5.

3 *Cast. and Dom. Arch.*, v, 15; Fleming, J. S., *The Old Ludgings of Stirling*, 12; *Castles and Mansions*, 427; Small, J. W., *Old Stirling*, pls. 49, 50.

4 *Castles and Mansions*, 429.

5 "Market Place" on Laye's plan. Also known at different times as High Gait and High Street.

6 *Castles and Mansions*, 157 ff.

7 *Ibid.*, 177.

8 *Ibid.*, 178.

9 Illustration in Drysdale, W., *Auld Stirling Biggins*, unnumbered illustration.

street, perhaps within a covered walk. A square staircase-tower rises in the re-entrant angle of main block and wing (Pl. 138 C); it is corbelled out at first-floor level, has a moulded string-course below the topmost window and finishes in a penthouse roof and crow-stepped gables. At ground-floor level there is an entrance-doorway with a bold bolection-moulding and a convex lintel. The wing is entered from a forestair, and the attic is lit by three dormer windows which have moulded segmental pediments (Pl. 138 B). Internally there is little of interest, but a first-floor room in the main block has some wooden panelling and a moulded cornice, while over the fireplace is a painting on plaster of Stirling Castle within a wooden egg-and-dart surround. This room must in its present form be of 18th-century date, but the wing, which Fleming[1] calls Provost Stevenson's Lodging, retains on the attic floor a stone bolection-moulded fireplace dating from the 17th century and on the ground floor a kitchen fireplace, now blocked up, in the gable. Adjacent to Number 24 is Norrie's House (No. 233), to the W. of which stand Numbers 36-38, a 17th-century building of which the rear portion has been demolished although the frontage still remains.[2] This rises to a height of four main storeys and finishes in twin crow-stepped gables (Pl. 137). The ground-floor openings have been altered, but on each of the three upper floors there is a range of four windows symmetrically disposed. The interior has been gutted and possesses no features of interest; the basement is vaulted. A sketch of the rear portion of the building is given by Fleming, who ascribes it to the family of Graham of Panholes.[3]

Numbers 40-52 are tenements of the 18th and 19th centuries, some of three main storeys and some of four, with symmetrically disposed window-openings and, at ground-floor level, pends which give access to the close behind. Internally some of these houses retain ornamental plaster friezes and cornices, while Number 44 has in addition a carved wooden mantelpiece of Adam type in a first-floor room.

SOUTH-WEST SIDE. Apart from the Town House (No. 232), no buildings of interest remain on this side of the street. Set over the passageway of Number 41, however, there is a sunk-moulded panel with a debased ogival head. The panel is carved with two heater-shaped shields, each charged with a mill-rind and a pick. A carving between the shields, shaped like a human head, probably represents a helm affrontée, wreathed and mantled, and at the apex of the panel there appears a slip, probably for crest. This seems to be the stone thought by Fleming[4] to have come from a building known as Lawrie's Turnpike, which formerly stood in Baker Street.

793937 NS 79 SE Various dates in 1954

235. Darnley House, Bow Street, Stirling. This house[5] stands at the N. end of Bow Street, with its façade facing westwards up Broad Street. It is an L-shaped building comprising a main block and a wing which extends to the rear and is entered from a close. The main block is of three main storeys and the wing of four, and in their re-entrant angle there stands a rectangular staircase-tower containing an entrance-doorway and giving access to both main block and wing. The building has been much altered from time to time, has been completely gutted internally and now stands as an empty shell awaiting restoration.[6] The façade is of ashlar, the remainder of the structure being of random rubble. Near the S. gable at ground-floor level an arched pend gives access to the close behind; above there are three windows symmetrically disposed on each of the three upper storeys, those of the attic being dormers. The first-floor windows may have been enlarged. All the windows have chamfered arrises, and over each dormer a moulded cornice incorporating terminal brackets supports a triangular pediment, that to the S. evidently replacing a semicircular one.[7] The distinctive cornice-mouldings suggest a late 16th- or early 17th-century date for the building. The wall originally finished in an ovolo-moulded eaves-course of which only part survives. At fourth-floor level the staircase-tower is corbelled out on a continuous corbel-course; it finishes, like the main block, in crow-stepped gables. The wing is of no special interest, the upper part being of later date than the main block. Internally the only remaining feature of note is the vaulted basement of both main block and wing. A 19th-century panel set into the façade between the first and second floors states that the house was the Nursery of James VI and of his son Prince Henry; but this tradition, like that which associates the building with Lord Darnley, does not seem to be supported by any evidence.[8] More probably the house should be associated with the family of Erskine of Gogar.

793936 NS 79 SE Various dates in 1954

236. Bow Street, Stirling; Lesser Houses. This street has been almost completely cleared of old houses within recent years. The most important of the surviving structures is Darnley House (No. 235), which stands at the N. end of the street. At the foot of the close that is entered from Darnley House stands the shell of Moir of Leckie's Lodging,[9] a building of three main storeys now much ruined but retaining two Venetian windows in its E. wall. Immediately N. of Darnley House there is a four-storeyed rubble building with a vaulted basement, now quite featureless.

794936 NS 79 SE Various dates in 1954

---

1 *Castles and Mansions*, 431.
2 This building was reconstructed in 1958.
3 *Castles and Mansions*, 385. Also *Cast. and Dom. Arch.*, v, 15 f.
4 *Castles and Mansions*, 122, with illustration.
5 Small, J. W., *Old Stirling*, pls. 45 and 46; *Castles and Mansions*, 387.
6 The building was restored in 1957-8.
7 This is shown in the old photograph reproduced as Pl. 139D.
8 *Castles and Mansions*, 387; *T.S.N.H.A.S.* (1910-11), 62.
9 *Castles and Mansions*, 341.

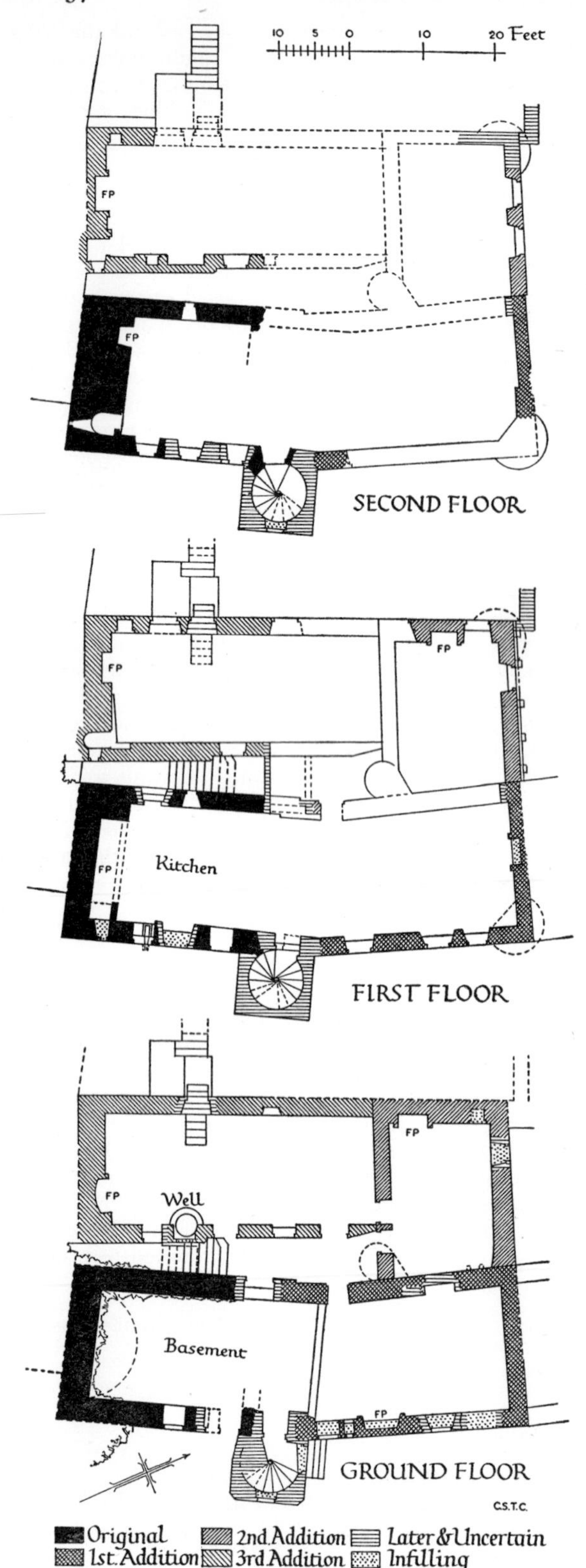

Fig. 120. Cowane's House, Stirling (No. 237)

237. Cowane's House, St. Mary's Wynd, Stirling. This building is traditionally known as Queen Mary's Palace, but there is no evidence to connect it with any member of the Royal house and it seems certain that it was erected during the course of the 16th and 17th centuries as a residence for the Cowane family, whose most conspicuous member was John Cowane, the benefactor of Cowane's Hospital (cf. No. 231). Some portion of the building may be as old as the second half of the 16th century, at which period the Cowanes were already in possession of the property. The structure is not all of the same date, however, and part of it may represent the house that is known to have been built by Andrew Cowane, John Cowane's father, in 1603. Further alterations and additions took place in 1633 and 1697 (*infra*), but by that time the house had passed into the hands of the Schort family, John Schort, who was a nephew of John Cowane, having acquired the property in 1639. The building remained in the possession of the Schort family until 1764, after which it was occupied for brief periods successively as a carpet factory and as a school. By the end of the 19th century the house was in a state of some dilapidation, and it was accordingly unroofed and the upper storey[1] was removed by order of the Town Council.[2] The house stands on the W. side of St. Mary's Wynd, the walls, in places, attaining a height of three storeys; but it is in a highly dilapidated condition, as it has neither roof nor floors and it has also been invaded by herbage and trees from the large garden behind. It represents a complex of structures which has assumed its present form as a result of successive alterations and additions; precise analysis of the remains is consequently difficult, but it seems safe to conclude that the oldest part may date from early in the second half of the 16th century. Two dormer window-pediments from Cowane's House, one of which bears the date 1633 and the other the date 1697, are preserved in the garden of Knockhill House, King's Stables Lane (cf. No. 239). These fragments, which were no doubt removed to their present position when the upper storey of the house was demolished, indicate that additions were made to the building during the course of the 17th century. Minor alterations seem to have been made at still later dates.

The existing remains occupy a space roughly oblong in shape (Fig. 120), 61 ft. 6 in. and 44 ft. in average length and breadth respectively, with a stair-tower 10 ft. 2 in. wide projecting about 9 ft. from the middle of the E. front (Pl. 133 C).[3] On the S. they abut the N. side of a high boundary-wall. Their nucleus is the SE. quarter, where the basement is vaulted and the walls are stouter than elsewhere. This, the original house, presum-

[1] MacGibbon and Ross are in error in stating (*Cast. and Dom. Arch.*, v, 22) that the whole building was removed at this time.

[2] This account follows that of Morris, D. B., *The Stirling Merchant Gild and Life of John Cowane*, 298-9.

[3] For convenience in description the building is regarded as being alined from N. to S., although in fact it lies approximately NNE. and SSW.

ably consisted of a rectangular main block with a stair-turret projecting from it in much the same position as that occupied by the present one. The northern end of this building has been entirely swept away, but the vaulted S. portion survives to a length of some 25 ft. and measures 21 ft. in width over walls 3 ft. 3 in. thick in the basement; the E. wall above is slightly thinner and the W. wall is reduced to 2 ft. 4 in. in thickness. Much of this walling is founded on solid rock which, in places, rises almost to the springing level of the vault. The masonry is rubble with dressed stones at the voids, and the surviving gable is crow-stepped. The walls rise to a height of three storeys, where they finish in an eaves-course moulded with a fillet and quarter-round; above the eaves-course there has been an attic, with dormer windows, now removed. The original openings were wrought with an edge-roll moulding on jambs and lintels; three inserted windows, one on the first floor and two on the second, have backset margins and splayed arrises.

The only access to the whole building is now through a door leading into the basement beside the S. re-entrant angle of the stair-tower. This door has been widened on its S. side, where a new jamb has been inserted; this has led to the destruction of the N. jamb of a small window, the opening of which has been built up. Immediately to the S. again another original door led into the basement, and this, in turn, has been converted into a window. It may be assumed that each of these doors once opened into a separate room, but there is now no trace internally of any partition. On the first and second floors there have also been original doors; the lower one is now partly built up, a window having been formed in its head, and the upper one has been replaced by a small window, its only surviving traces being the sill and a moulded rybat. It is not clear how these doors were reached, but original door-jambs traceable in the well of the existing turret-stair suggest that they were formerly entered across the re-entrant, from the older stairway, by some means not now distinguishable. On the blocking of the first-floor door, another access was broken through near the SW. corner of this room, opening off the head of a straight flight of steps inserted between the W. wall and the latest of the additions, which stands W. of the earliest block; the room is shown to have been a kitchen by a large fireplace with a segmental-arched head which occupies nearly the full width of its S. gable, and has a window, now built up, in its E. end. Also in the E. wall, near the fireplace, there is an original window with a slop-sink in the breast; immediately N. of it is one of the inserted windows, also built up, while there is a small original window in the W. wall. The upper door presumably led into bedroom accommodation on the floor above; the room into which it opens contains, near the SW. corner, a plain fireplace and in the SE. corner a garderobe lit by a small slit-window with a small lamp-recess below it. Of three windows in the E. wall of this room, the S. one is original while the two to the N. are insertions; there is also, in the W. wall, a small window wrought with an edge-roll moulding.

The present rectangular stair-turret with its spiral stair is a reconstruction of uncertain but apparently late date. It was finished with a penthouse roof and a moulded eaves-course. To the height of the first floor the corners are broadly splayed. Its doorway, now built up, is situated in the N. re-entrant angle, and it was formerly lit by two windows with square arrises, now also built up, in its E. wall. The stair communicated with each floor in turn.

The first addition, which averages 21 ft. 6 in. in width, extends 30 ft. 6 in. N. from the turret to the N. gable; it evidently rose to the same height as the part described above, but it was latterly reduced to two storeys and the wall-head was levelled off by a thin, plain and slightly projecting eaves-course. No mutual partition separates the addition from the earlier work, but these are now divided by a low wall evidently inserted after the ruin of the structure. On the ground floor all the openings in the E. wall have been built up—namely, from the turret northwards, a doorway, a small window, a fireplace, and two inserted windows. On the first floor there still remain three windows with edge-roll mouldings like those of the original building but of slighter section; these windows have dressed segmental rear-arches and dressed sconcheons, which latter reach down to the floor level though below the window-sills the embrasures have been built up. In the N. gable there is a plain fireplace. In the W. wall, which stands only to the level of the first floor, there are two doorways, an inserted recess and, beside it on the S., a jamb with edge-roll moulding which suggests the former presence of a locker. At the NE. angle of the extension an angle-turret, which once opened off the second floor, has been almost demolished; all that is left is its continuous corbelling, of four members, which now supports a single course of masonry.

The second addition, which extends W. from the N. end of the first, abutting it in race-bond, altered the plan of the house from an oblong to an L. This addition projects 22 ft. 9 in. and is 18 ft. 8 in. in width; it attained a height of three storeys, but the S. side-wall has been demolished down to first-floor level. In this wall two entrance-doorways set close together imply a subdivision of the ground floor into two rooms, but there is no surviving partition to confirm this. In the W. gable there is a fireplace, and to the N. of this a partly destroyed and built-up locker with giblet checks. In the N. side a small window has been broken out and later filled in, and there are two corbels near the NE. angle the purpose of which is not clear.

The two floors above each contain a single room. The lower one is provided with a fireplace between two windows, the S. one of which is much destroyed, and there is another window in the N. wall; on the upper floor only two windows remain in the N. wall and these have backset sconcheons. A row of five corbels, approximately at the sill level of the first-floor window on the N. side, represents the support for a runner-beam at the head of a penthouse roof which must formerly have covered a single-storeyed outshot. On the NW. corner of the second addition there are remains of an angle-turret corresponding with those on the NE. corner of the first; there are also the lower members of the corbelling of another turret, starting at first-floor level in the re-entrant between the additions. The repetition of the angle-turrets hints that the second addition was erected soon after the first. Two stones pierced by shot-holes, one circular and the other square but set diamondwise, have been reset one on either side of the butt-joint in the masonry of the N. wall just above first-floor level.

The third addition measures 40 ft. 9 in. in length by 18 ft. 8 in. in width and occupies the SW. corner of the site. Its walls originally rose as high as those of the oldest portion and finish similarly in an eaves-course. Between the two structures there is an internal gap tapering in width from fully 6 ft. on the N. to 2 ft. 8 in. on the S., and near the middle of this gap the forestair, already mentioned, ascends to the kitchen door. This stair crosses the bricked-up opening of a well with a segmental-arched head which is inside the third addition. The interior of the third addition now lacks any partitions and the space is entered on the ground floor by either of two doors opening off the N. half of the gap. Between the doors there is a window, and another window S. of the well has been turned into a door; this last leads into a narrow cellar, partly walled by solid rock, below the stair. In the S. gable-end there is a fireplace, and in the W. side-wall a recess with ragged sides may indicate the position of a former window. The features that survive on the first floor include, in the E. wall, a window, and in the W. wall, from S. to N., a giblet-checked locker, two large windows set close together, the N. one of which has been cut down to form a door with steps to the garden, and the S. jamb of a third window; in the S. gable-end there is a fireplace with an edge-roll moulding, and in the SE. corner a garderobe with giblet-checked door-jambs and a window, with rounded arrises, looking into the gap.

On the second floor the disposition of windows, fire-place, garderobe and locker is similar to that below, but in the E. wall there are two additional lockers and a large recess; the recess and the window beside it have backset margins internally. The fireplace consists of a large, plain, joggle-jointed lintel and a moulded cornice supported by fluted pilasters with moulded caps and bases. MacGibbon and Ross[1] illustrate a second and rather similar fireplace, some portions of which appear to be preserved in the garden of Knockhill House and are described under No. 239. The S. gable of this addition is finished with tabling, and the windows of all periods have been half-glazed and barred.

793937 NS 79 SE Various dates in 1956 and 1957

238. St. Mary's Wynd,[2] Stirling; Lesser Houses and Architectural Details. Number 72-76 is a rather plain house of early 18th-century date which, although derelict, preserves an interesting ornamental entrance-doorway (Pl. 140 B) having an architrave decorated with a form of continuous nail-head ornament.[3] There are projecting imposts and a fluted keystone, and above is a moulded cornice and a broken pediment with a wasted floral panel in its centre. This doorway is said to have been brought from a house in Cambusbarron.[4] On the S. gable there is a rounded skewput enriched with cable moulding and with a rosette on its inner face. Adjacent to Number 72, and of similar date, is a house with a moulded skewput similar to the one just described. Number 84 is an old rubble-built house which was extensively restored in 1928, the only remaining features of interest being the relieving arches over the ground-floor windows. On the opposite side of the street is Cowane's House (No. 237), and at the corner of St. Mary's Wynd and Barn Road the Red Lion Hotel. This is a two-storeyed structure of 18th-century date, now somewhat altered and of no great interest. The front corners of the building are rounded on the ground floor and are brought to the square at first-floor level by means of ogival stop-chamfers. Over the door is a panel which bears in relief the initials G T[5] and E G over the date 1733.

794937 NS 79 SE Various dates in 1954

239. King's Stables Lane, Stirling; Indeterminate Remains and Carved Stones. The building traditionally known as the King's Stables[6] stands on the S. side of King's Stables Lane, about 50 yds. above its junction with St. Mary's Wynd. There remains only a stretch of rubble walling about 60 ft. in length and 15 ft. in height. This is plainly the external wall of a substantial building, and a number of doors and windows with chamfered arrises, now blinded, can be traced in the masonry. Any surviving internal features have been rendered inaccessible by the raising of the ground level within, but the doorway with a semicircular head at the NW. end of the wall may originally have given access to a pend. There is insufficient evidence to suggest the character of the building, but it is probably of 17th-century date.

In the garden of Knockhill House, at the lower end of King's Stables Lane, there are some carved stones which originally decorated Cowane's House (No. 237), in St. Mary's Wynd. These consist of: (*a*) Part of a dormer-pediment with a central rectangular panel measuring 1 ft. 7 in. by 2 ft. The panel has a central monogram made up of the letters A, I and C; above appears the date 1633 and below the initials I C and A C, all in raised letters. Both initials and monogram probably relate to John Cowane, founder of the Hospital (No. 231) and his brother Alexander Cowane[7]. (*b*) Part of another dormer-pediment with a fleur-de-lys finial and a central

[1] *Cast. and Dom. Arch.*, v, fig. 1123 on p. 23.
[2] Formerly St. Mary's Vennel.
[3] Measured details in Small, J. W., *Old Stirling*, pls. 37 and 38.
[4] Information from Mr. W. H. Gillespie, A.R.I.B.A., Burgh Architect.
[5] Fleming (*Castles and Mansions*, 458) read these wrongly as J A, and this error vitiates the identification that he suggests.
[6] Fleming, J. S., *Old Nooks of Stirling*, 19 ff.
[7] *Castles and Mansions*, 88, 103.

inscribed panel 1 ft. 4 in. square. At the top of the panel is the date 1697 and in the lower part the initials I S and A S, all in raised letters. Between the initials is what seems to be a tree with a hunting-horn at its base, flanked by charges now somewhat mutilated, which are shown by Fleming[1] as: Dexter, a bow at full bend, stringed and arrowed; sinister, a hunting-knife. This assemblage, which is carved in relief, is evidently intended to be heraldic; the initials are no doubt those of members of the Schort family, which occupied Cowane's House after 1639[2] (cf. No. 237), but no evidence can be found to show that any member of this family held any post in a Royal forest or park, as the charges on the panel would suggest. (*c*) An octagonal stone basin measuring 1 ft. 2 in. by 1 ft. 4 in. over all. The basin is circular within and contains a shallow drain opening through one side, the outer face of which is carved with a human head. Another face is rough, showing that the stone was at one time built into a wall. (*d*) Two moulded fireplace-jambs and part of a lintel of 17th-century type, similar in style to the complete example that still remains in Cowane's House and is described under No. 237.

793938 NS 79 SE 21 November 1955

240. Allan's Hospital, Irvine Place, Stirling. This building seems to have comprised a main block, of which only the ruined N. wall remains, and a wing, extending from its W. end, which is now no more than the shell of a two-storeyed house. The walls have been built of rubble, and the existing N. gable of the wing is crow-stepped and has cavetto-moulded skewputs. The voids have dressed margins with rounded arrises and the windows have been barred with stanchions. In the re-entrant angle there is a separate doorway to each floor, which indicates that the upper rooms were reached by an outside stairway. There is a fireplace with plain jambs and lintel in the gable at first-floor level. The Hospital was founded in 1725,[3] and the character of the fabric of this building would accord well enough with a date early in the 18th century.

794938 NS 79 SE 30 September 1954

241. Doorway, 42 Upper Bridge Street, Stirling. This doorway (Pl. 140 C) is in a house of late 18th- or early 19th-century date which contains no other features of interest. Only the Gibbs surround is original, the pediment having been renewed.

793940 NS 79 SE 1 June 1955

242. 101 Lower Bridge Street, Stirling. This is a small, two-storeyed house, oblong on plan and with a circular stair-tower projecting at the back. The frontage shows, on the ground floor, three windows somewhat irregularly disposed, with the doorway between the two easternmost, and on the upper floor three windows symmetrically arranged. Above is a cavetto eaves-course; the skewputs are moulded. The lower windows retain their original dimensions, but the upper ones have been considerably altered. The doorway has chamfered arrises and, though its head has been raised, the original lintel is still in use; this bears the incised date and initials 17 I S M M 44. Parts of the stone stair and its newel are still intact.

796945 NS 79 SE 10 June 1955

243. Baker Street, Stirling; Lesser Houses and Carved Stones. Like Bow Street (No. 236), Baker Street[4] has lost many of its older buildings within recent years, and extensive rebuilding is now going on; consequently very little remains to be recorded.

North-east Side. The building at the end of the close entered from Number 14 has a chamfered doorway, now blocked, and some round-arrised windows; it may date from the 17th century. Preserved in the wall of an outbuilding on the N. side of the court of Sauchie House there is a panel carved in relief and measuring about 2 ft. by 1 ft. 6 in. The sculpture is in the form of a cartouche supported on each side by a cherub; above the cartouche are two cherubs' heads, while other carvings, now defaced, occupy corresponding positions below. The cartouche bears a much-weathered monogram, of the reversing type, which seems to consist of the initials I and G. The panel is probably of early 18th-century date; it is illustrated by Fleming,[5] who supposes it to have come from the Old Alms House, or Trades Meeting House, which formerly stood in this vicinity.

South-west Side. An heraldic panel is set into the façade of Numbers 27-29 between the first- and second-storey levels. It measures approximately 1 ft. 3 in. by 1 ft. 2 in., and bears, in relief, a shield with helm, mantling and supporters framed within a sunk ogival moulding. The shield is charged: A chevron between three boars' heads erased, each holding a shuttle in its mouth. The supporters are male figures, the dexter one being nude except for a waist-cloth while the sinister one is clad in a coat, breeches, stockings, shoes and bonnet, and carries a shuttle in his left hand. The helm, with barred visor, is shown in profile, as for a peer; it is mantled and wreathed, and has for crest a hand gripping what appears to be a shuttle, accompanied by some unrecognisable device. Beneath the shield there is a label with the motto CONCORDIA. The arms suggest an Elphinstone who possessed a baronial estate and was connected with weaving,[6] but it has been supposed that

[1] *Ibid.*, 88.
[2] Morris, D. B., *The Stirling Merchant Gild and Life of John Cowane*, 299.
[3] *History* (ed. 1817), i, 347.
[4] Known at different times as Middle Raw and Baxter Wynd.
[5] *Castles and Mansions*, 117.
[6] Information from the Lord Lyon.

they belonged to the Incorporation of Weavers, and came from the Weavers' House which formerly stood on this site.[1] The rear portion of Numbers 41-43 has traces of openings with chamfered arrises, now mostly blinded; these suggest that part of the building may be as old as the 17th century. A carved panel with the initials I D and E M below the date 1715, all in relief, is built into the façade of Number 51 at first-floor level.

794935 NS 79 SE Various dates in 1954

244. Bruce of Auchenbowie's House, St. John Street, Stirling. This house (Pl. 139 A) is the last on the SW. side of St. John Street, next to the bowling-green. It measures 45 ft. 8 in. by 21 ft., a wheel-stair projecting 4 ft. 10 in. into the street, and stands to a height of three storeys and an attic. Above the ground floor, which consists of two barrel-vaulted cellars separated by a through passage, the fabric has undergone extensive restoration and has been so much altered that much of the original arrangement has become obscured. On the first and second floors later partitions re-divide the interior, and fireplaces have been renewed, while it would also appear that the projecting stair-tower was an addition. The masonry is of random rubble, with dressed margins and rounded arrises on original rybats where these can be seen; some of the later windows have chamfered arrises and backset margins. The cellars are entered separately from the street and a recess in the front wall of the W. one has probably been the original door, now blocked up. The doorway to the through passage is wrought with a bead-moulding and that to the stair with an ogee moulding. Each cellar is provided with a window to the front and a small locker in the gable-end. Both windows are original, but the W. one is built up and the E. one, in which the W. front has been renewed, has been stanchioned. All the windows above these have been enlarged or restored, and all except the central one on the first floor and the W. one on the second floor show old rybats in one or other of the jambs. The roof has been re-slated, with a modern dormer constructed over the E. attic-room, which was formerly lit by a window, now built up, in the gable; the stair-tower now has a roof of penthouse type, though in the early 19th century it appears to have had a conical one.[2] In the back wall all the windows are insertions of various later periods, the three in the W. half of the building being of comparatively recent date. At the E. end of the wall, on both the first and the second floors, a pair of adjacent door-like openings have been built up and presses have been constructed on their inner sides. Their position suggests that they once provided communication with a wing or stair which is now demolished, and that a wing of this kind once existed at the other end of the house seems certain from evidence which will be discussed shortly. While the E. gable is contemporary with the house, the W. one appears to have belonged to an earlier dwelling, the rest of which has been removed. This W. gable is now finished in a plain cope with a moulded-roll skewput (Pl. 139 C), but the E. one shows four large crow-steps with weathered coping-stones[3] (Pl. 139 B). The quoins of the NE. corner occur only on the third storey; below that height the wall is tusked and at the first-floor level there remains the W. jamb of a window, all indicating that originally there was a two-storeyed E. extension. The vanished S. extension from the W. end of the back wall must have contained at least two storeys, as the lower one was vaulted. Its length is indeterminate, but its width was about 21 ft. Very little of the structure remains, but its N. gable, 1 ft. 7 in. thick, butted against the side wall of the main block where it still remains as a facing, now cemented over. The high W. side of this addition, which was probably an earlier boundary-wall, has been patched up and again acts as a garden-wall between the house and the bowling-green. In it, at first-floor level, there are traces of an opening which may have been either a door or a window; and at the same height further S. there has been inserted a locker, now blocked up, with a flat ogival head and moulded margins.

The original house may be assigned to the 16th century. It is traditionally associated with the family of Bruce of Auchenbowie.[4]

792936 NS 79 SE 17 June 1954

245. St. John Street,[5] Stirling; Lesser Buildings and Architectural Details.

SOUTH-WEST SIDE. The two most important monuments on this side of the street are the Erskine Marykirk (No. 132) and Bruce of Auchenbowie's House (No. 244). About half-way between them is Number 33, a rubble-built house of three storeys which probably dates from the 18th century. The windows are symmetrically disposed on all three floors, and there is a central doorway consisting of a Tuscan porch evidently taken straight out of a pattern-book. The window margins and quoins project slightly, suggesting that the wall surfaces were originally harled.

NORTH-EAST SIDE. Number 36 is a small rubble-built house which was completely restored in 1929. No doubt the shell of the original building remains, but the only surviving features of interest are the relieving arches over windows on the ground and first floors. A moulded dormer-pediment is preserved on the NW. façade of Number 38; it is triangular in shape and has a fleur-de-lys finial and plain dressed margins but no rake mouldings (Pl. 138 D). The tympanum is carved in relief with the inscription: 1612 / BENEDICAM / DOMINUM OM/NI TEMPORE ("I will bless the Lord at all times"). The

[1] *T.S.N.H.A.S.* (1926-7), 32.
[2] *Castles and Mansions*, 214.
[3] This feature is not very common, and where it has been observed it appears to date from the 16th century.
[4] *Castles and Mansions*, 213 ff. Cf. also No. 296.
[5] This street formed the upper part of the old Back Raw. Cf. No. 226.

pediment seems to be one of those illustrated by Fleming,[1] and most probably came from the old house that stood next to the Town House (No. 232) in Broad Street.

792936 NS 79 SE Various dates in 1954

246. Spittal's House, 82 Spittal Street, Stirling. Robert Spittal appears to have acquired a house in this vicinity from Sir James Shaw of Sauchie in 1521,[2] and the inscribed panel (*infra*) that is set between two of the first-floor windows of the existing house suggests, in virtue of the date 1530 that it bears, that this was actually the hospital that he founded. No feature, however, assignable to so early a date can now be distinguished in the structure, which seems to date from the 17th century; while the lettering of the inscription, which is ligatured, and the enrichment of its frame suggest a late 17th- or early 18th-century date. The hospital itself probably stood on another site, although the Spittal Street property no doubt belonged to it. The provenance of the panel is uncertain.[3]

In its present form the house appears, on the side towards Spittal Street, as a two-storeyed block with a partly sunk cellarage, entry being gained at street level; its other side contains three storeys and an attic owing to the steep descent of the ground in the direction of Baker Street. Vaulting survives in a part only of the basement, but apart from this and a 17th-century fireplace, with a roll-and-hollow moulding, in the gable of the SE. room immediately above the cellar, no noteworthy features are to be seen.[4] The interior seems to have been gutted and turned into tenements, probably towards the end of the 19th century; the front has likewise been refaced and the projecting turnpike-staircase removed, while the back, which is partly demolished, has been extensively altered by the blocking of the original voids and the insertion of windows, no doubt in Victorian times.

The memorial panel[5] bears the following incised inscription: THIS HOVS IS FO/VNDIT FOR SVP/PORT OF THE PVI/R BE ROBERT SPIT/TAL TAILLYO/VR TO KING / IAMES THE 4 IN / ANNO 1530 / RS. A pair of scissors, symbolising Spittal's trade, is carved in relief in the centre of the lower part of the panel, the blades intersecting the lowermost five lines of the inscription.

Another example of Robert Spittal's munificence was the erection of the bridge at Bannockburn (No. 457), which still retains an inscription showing his name.

794935 NS 79 SE 1 October 1954

247. The Athenaeum, King Street, Stirling. This building stands in a commanding position at the top of King Street, separating the lower ends of St. John and Baker Streets where they fork. It replaced the old Meal Mercate, pulled down in 1814, and was completed in 1816, after which it became known as the Athenaeum.[6] An extract from the Stirling Guildry Records outlines the proposal for the erection of "a genteel building of three stories in the place where the said Mercate stands, containing two elegant shops with suitable apartments above for an assembly room, library, and reading-room, with a steeple in the centre". Another extract, of the following year, mentions a Mr. Johnstone as being the person with whom the Town Council entered into contract, "for the public building and steeple at the Meal Mercate".[7] Its dominating feature is the tall, square tower (Pl. 134 B), axially disposed and projecting from curved façades which flank it on either side. The tower is divided by moulded cornices into five stages, which are intaken and diminish in height progressively as they rise. The uppermost stage is surmounted by a circular drum incorporating Tuscan pilasters and entablature, and rising to an octagonal spire topped by a finial. The external angles of the tower are splayed, and at its foot there is a later porch surmounted by a statue of William Wallace. The whole building is faced with ashlar, rusticated on the bottom storey, and the rear ends of its curved lateral façades are slightly advanced and straight. Each storey is lit by a range of four windows on either side of the tower; those on the ground floor have semi-circular heads while those on the first and second floors are square-headed with moulded architraves. In addition the first-floor windows have moulded cornices. The walls finish with a moulded eaves-cornice. The only internal feature of interest is the spiral stone stair of the tower, with its open well and wrought-iron balustrading.

795934 NS 79 SE June 1955

248. Spittal Street,[8] Stirling; Lesser Buildings and Architectural Details.

SOUTH-WEST SIDE. Opposite the junction of Spittal Street and Bank Street stands the Old Infirmary, which was built as a bank in 1827.[9] It is a Classical building with a Doric portico, the flanking wings having been added in the late 19th century. The Old South United Free Church stands within the boundaries of the High School, and since 1902 has been utilised as teaching premises. The building, which was erected about the year 1802,[10] is a rectangular block of two storeys; the

1 *Castles and Mansions*, 445.
2 *Ibid.*, 199 f.
3 *T.S.N.H.A.S.* (1897-8), 72 ff. Cf. also *Castles and Mansions*, 200.
4 Reconstruction work carried out in 1959 disclosed a kitchen fireplace at street level in the NW. gable. It has roll-moulded jambs and a semicircular head.
5 For illustration, see *Castles and Mansions*, 114. This indicates the ligatures, which have been expanded in the version given here.
6 *T.S.N.H.A.S.* (1893-4), 45.
7 *Extracts from the Records of the Merchant Guild of Stirling*, 1592-1846, 190, 192.
8 Spittal Street and St. John Street (No. 245) originally formed a single street known as Back Raw.
9 Drysdale, W., *Old Faces, Old Places and Old Stories of Stirling*, 1st series, 255.
10 Drysdale, W., *Auld Biggins of Stirling*, 63.

façade, which looks W., is of ashlar and contains a range of three large round-headed windows on each floor, the upper ones originally lighting a gallery. The High School itself is a 19th-century building, but a fine Renaissance gateway has been utilised in the construction of an entrance at the E. end of the Spittal Street façade. This gateway[1] (Pl. 140 A) measures 7 ft. 6 in. in width and has a semicircular head, its boldly carved ornament incorporating various geometrical devices in the Jacobean manner; it is of late 16th- or early 17th-century date, and no doubt served as the entrance to one of the more substantial dwellings in the burgh. It may be compared with the example at Argyll's Lodging (No. 227). Its original situation is unknown, but at one time it formed part of a building known as the Reservoir, which stood near the corner of Academy Road and Spittal Street.[2]

NORTH-EAST SIDE. At the intersection of Spittal Street and Bank Street there stands the Athenaeum, which is described under No. 247. The building numbered 52 Spittal Street and 5 Bank Street is a much-altered house which may be as old as the 17th century; it retains its moulded skewputs and has a bolection-moulded fireplace on the first floor. Opposite the High School is Spittal's House (No. 246), and adjacent to this is the building known as Glengarry Lodge (Pl. 136), now earmarked for restoration.[3] The front, towards Spittal Street, varies in height from two storeys and an attic to three storeys and an attic in conformity with the eastward declivity of the site, while at the back there is still another storey as the ground falls in that direction also. The attic dormers have lean-to roofs and the gables are crow-stepped. At street level the W. half of the building has been converted into a shop, and the upper floor, reached by a semicircular projecting wheel-stair, is said to have been used for some time as an Episcopal church. The original staircase-windows have been replaced by others having equilateral-arched heads. All the above alterations were presumably carried out in the 19th century. The main entrance is in the W. re-entrant of the staircase; it is wrought with a bead moulding, which also occurs on built-up doors on each floor-level of the back wall, and the type suggests a date in the late 16th or early 17th century. The building is sometimes called the Darrow Lodging, the site having been occupied by a family of that name in the early 16th century.[4]

794935 NS 79 SE Various dates in 1954

249. The Town Wall, Stirling. The site on which the mediaeval burgh grew up was naturally strong and well suited to the purposes of defence (cf. p. 275). The Castle (No. 192) occupied the NW. portion of the rocky outcrop on which the Old Town lay and afforded protection on that side, while to the SW. and S. very steep rock-strewn slopes discouraged all access. Only at the SE. end of the burgh was there no natural obstacle, for, although the ground falls away less steeply to NE. and N. than it does to SW. and S., the River Forth was an effective barrier on this side provided always that the bridge could be held. These natural defences may have been considered sufficient in themselves in early mediaeval times, but it is more probable that Stirling, like other burghs, possessed artificial ones of at least a rudimentary type from an early date. These may have consisted of no more than a palisade,[5] or a ditch and bank bounding the rear portions of the outer burgess-tenements, but nevertheless effectively enclosing the burgh and allowing a measure of control over those who sought to enter or leave. No material evidence of such structures now survives, although a reference to "the port of the burgh" in 1477[6] strengthens the case for their existence.

Both documentary and architectural evidence suggests that the portions of the Town Wall visible today were erected in the 16th century. In 1547, in response to the threat of English invasion, a Council Minute of 26th October assigns a sum of money "to be expendit upone the strengthing and bigging of the wallis of the toun, at this present peralus tyme of neid, for resisting of oure auld innimeis of Ingland".[7] Contributions were also made by the Queen Dowager and certain lords, barons and gentlemen,[8] the work no doubt being carried on under the direction of John Coutis, master-mason to the burgh.[9] Civil disturbances led to further work upon the walls in 1574,[10] and payments for the upkeep of the defences can be traced in the burgh records throughout the 17th century, special precautions being taken at times of crisis as in 1650, and also in 1715 and 1745.

Laye's plan (Pl. 121), drawn in 1725, gives a good idea of the course of the wall as it existed in his day. Beginning at the SE. angle of the Castle, the wall skirts what is now the Valley Cemetery and then follows the S. edge of the natural rock-outcrop until it reaches the "Barras-Yett", which occupied what is now the junction of Dumbarton Road, Port Street and Upper Craigs. From there the wall runs NE. to the Port Street Bastion, beyond which it seems to continue for a short distance in a northerly direction towards Orchard Place, where it dies out altogether. At this point, however, a vulnerable sector of the defences seems to have had the additional protection of a wet ditch which stretched from the wall to the Forth[11]; and the Burgh Mill Dam, shown on Laye's plan, is said to be a vestige of this structure.[12] Laye does not show a North Wall, and it may be assumed that the rear enclosure-walls of the outer tenements were considered

[1] A measured drawing, with details, is to be found in Small, G. W., *Old Stirling*, pl. 36.
[2] *T.S.N.H.A.S.* (1893-4), 110.
[3] This building has been restored since the date of visit.
[4] *Castles and Mansions*, 200.
[5] Cf. Inverness, with its palisade-mound and ditch, and the towns "with good ditches and palisades" mentioned as captured in 1333, in the 14th-century *Chronique* of Jean le Bel (ed. *Société de l'histoire de France*) i, 110.
[6] *Stirling Burgh Records*, 1519-1666, 262.
[7] *Ibid.*, 50.
[8] *Ibid.*, 61.
[9] *Ibid.*, 35, 65.
[10] *Ibid.*, 1667-1752, 376.
[11] Sibbald, *History*, 32; Ronald, J., *Landmarks of Old Stirling*, 223 ff.
[12] Ronald, *op. cit.*, 224.

to give sufficient protection to this part of the town. In 1746 the Town Council, in replying to the charge that they had allowed the rebel army to enter the town too easily, said: "Every one knows that the north part of the town of Sterling is open and without walls, having only some low fences encompassing gardens and parks."[1] The Council were perhaps overstating their case, for portions of the back walls of tenements in Baker Street and St. Mary's Wynd are still visible and are of a substantial nature; but nevertheless it is clear that the Town Wall proper protected the burgh only to the S. and SE. To the N., defence was concentrated instead upon the Bridge, which had its own gates (cf. No. 455), although Laye's plan also shows the St. Mary's Wynd Port which formed a secondary barrier to traffic from the north.

EXISTING REMAINS (Fig. 113). Although Laye's plan indicates that the wall began at the SE. angle of the Castle, no portion is now visible to NW. of Cowane's Hospital (No. 231). Indeed it is possible that the Town Wall proper did not actually connect with the Castle, but either began only in the neighbourhood of Holy Rude Church (No. 131), or else returned towards Argyll's Lodging (No. 227) along the line of the garden indicated by Laye as lying behind Mar's Work (No. 230). A view of the town painted by Vorsterman in 1673 or 1674[2] supports this theory, which, however, cannot easily be reconciled with Laye's plan. Between Cowane's Hospital and the Military Prison the footings of the original wall may perhaps survive, but the upper portion has been rebuilt. The stretch now forming the rear wall of the Prison seems to have been completely rebuilt, but SE. of this point there is a well-preserved section which runs as far as Academy Road. The wall rises to a maximum height of 23 ft. and its thickness at the base, where measured, was 5 ft. The lower portion has a noticeable batter and the uppermost few feet, with the crenelles, are of comparatively recent date. Crudely formed gun-loops can be seen at intervals at a height of from 10 ft. to 15 ft. above the level of the Back Walk (No. 250). The wall is broken at Academy Road and, although the rear wall of the High School no doubt follows the old alinement, little of the original structure survives. South-east of the High School the wall curves inwards, and at least its lower portion is original. Fifty feet SE. of the beginning of the curve a semicircular relieving-arch can be traced in the masonry, but its purpose is obscure. The wall returns sharply at the E. end of the curve and there is a west-looking gun-loop in the return. From this point the wall runs straight to a bastion, beyond which it continues to the Council Offices in Corn Exchange Road, the latter portion being founded on a high base of natural rock.

The bastion (Pl. 141 A), to which access is now obtained from the playground of Allan's Primary School in Spittal Street, is circular on plan and the portion projecting S. of the Wall contains three gun-loops. The interior, the diameter of which is 13 ft. 5 in., is entered from the NE. through a roll-moulded doorway. The structure has plainly been altered, as the floor is now more than 2 ft. above the sill-level of the gun-loops, the interior is lined with brick, and there is a domed roof of rubble with a circular opening in the crown of the vault. This suggests that the bastion has been converted for use as a dovecot at some stage in its history, and it is uncertain how much of the structure that projects N. of the Wall is original.

The Wall is broken by Corn Exchange Road, but reappears E. of the Public Library and continues to a point opposite the junction of Allan Park and Dumbarton Road, where there is a return in which three gun-loops can be seen (Pl. 141 C). From this point the Wall continues to the yard of Messrs. J. & J. Duff, plumbers, where it again originally returned before continuing eastwards to the Barras-Yett; but only a small portion of the return, with an eastward-looking gun-loop, survives. The maximum height of this sector of the Wall is 16 ft. 6 in. externally, and the thickness at the point measured was 6 ft. 3 in. Of the Barras-Yett (or Gate) there are no visible remains as the structure was demolished in 1770[3]; the site, however, has been marked in outline on the roadway at the junction of Dumbarton Road, Port Street and Upper Craigs. A secondary barrier, the New Port,[4] which was situated about half-way up King Street, has also been removed, but it is similarly outlined on the roadway. Of the section of Wall that ran from the Barras-Yett to the Port Street bastion only the last 30 ft. or so survives, incorporated in a building within the yard of the Kinross Company Carriage Works, from which access to the bastion[5] is now obtained.

The Port Street bastion (Pl. 141 B) is a rubble-built structure of one storey, roughly circular on plan externally but rectangular within. The upper storey is of much later date. Near the SE. re-entrant angle of Town Wall and bastion, the latter contains a splayed gun-loop of dressed stone 2 ft. 5 in. in width and 1 ft. high externally. The circular outline of the external wall of the bastion ends on the N. in a rocky outcrop which may have carried the Wall in a northerly direction, as indicated by Laye. The W. wall of the bastion has been disturbed and partly rebuilt; the E. wall is 4 ft. 3 in. thick, and the structure is roofed with a barrel-vault of rubble. In the centre of the floor a hatch measuring 2 ft. by 1 ft. 6 in. gives access to a small and more or less rectangular chamber below ground level. This measures approximately 12 ft. by 7 ft. and is ceiled with a barrel-vault, the crown of which is only 4 ft. 10 in. above the floor. The provision of what appears to be a crudely formed garderobe, with a drain, in the N. wall suggests that the chamber was used as a prison.

No traces of the Wall could be found N. of the Port Street bastion, and the point at which it ended remains

---

[1] *Stirling Burgh Records*, 1667-1752, 279.

[2] Preserved in the Smith Institute, Stirling, and reproduced here as Pl. 120.

[3] Ronald, *op. cit.*, 214.

[4] *Ibid.*

[5] There is no evidence to suggest that part of an "ancient gateway" survives at this point. The vaulted pend which Fleming describes and figures (*Castles and Mansions*, 456) is no more than the undercroft of a house built against the inner face of the Wall in the 17th or 18th century.

uncertain; nor are there any remains of the wet ditch already described, of the St. Mary's Wynd Port, or of the other gates identified by Ronald.[1]

In general, it may be said that the Town Wall is roughly constructed in random rubble, the masonry consisting of large whinstone boulders with an abundance of small pinnings between them. The builders founded it wherever possible on outcrops of natural rock. With the exception of the gun-loop in the Port Street bastion, the loops are rectangular and are crudely constructed in the same material as the rest; the external measurements average 2 ft. in width and 1 ft. in height, the sides splaying out from a width of 8 in. in a measured example. The height at which some of the loops are placed suggests that some sort of timber walk must have been necessary in places, and the reference to "the futegang at the south wall"[2] is probably to a structure of this type. Comparative levels are difficult to judge, however, for the gardens of many of the abutting tenements have undoubtedly raised the ground within, while the construction of the Back Walk (No. 250) may have lowered it without. The many blocked-up doorways now seen in the Wall formed no part of the original structure.

791936 to 797932 NS 79 SE 21 June 1955

250. The Back Walk, Stirling, and Carved Stones. This "ornamental walk" runs along the SW. and W. faces of the Castle Rock from the Dumbarton Road, opposite the end of Allan Park, to Gowan Hill, passing below Cowane's Hospital (No. 231), the Holy Rude cemetery (No. 131) and the Castle (No. 192). It was begun in 1723 by Mr. W. Edmonston of Cambuswallace and finished by the Town in 1791[3]; further work was done on it between 1833 and 1923,[4] and it has evidently been interrupted by the formation of Corn Exchange Road.

Set in the wall of the High School, facing on to the Back Walk at the corner of Academy Road, there is a panel inscribed: ERECTED IN HONOUR OF ROBERT SPETTAL / TAYLOR TO KING IAMES THE FOURTH / DONOR OF THE HOSPITALL IN THIS BURGH / FOR RELIEF OF DECAYED TRADESMEN / THE LIBERAL MAN DEVISETH LEBERALL / THINGS. A pair of shears is represented at the end of the inscription and the date 1530 appears in the top right-hand corner of the panel; this date is, however, certainly not of the 16th century and is probably later than the inscription, which itself suggests a date in the late 17th or early 18th century (cf. No. 246). The word FOURTH appears to be a correction. Another panel, of recent date, which is set in the wall of the High School facing the Back Walk at the corner of Academy Road, records the former position of the Greyfriars Convent (No. 173). It also states that the Hall of the seven Incorporated Trades of Stirling stood on the same site from 1751 to 1907.

At the foot of the path that descends to the Back Walk past the NW. side of Cowane's Hospital (No. 231) there is an alcove containing a stone seat. Let into the back of the alcove there is a re-used stone inscribed VISITA/TION in letters which suggest a 17th-century date. A little further W. there is another seat behind which there is a stone bearing the inscription: TO ACCOMMODATE / THE AGED AND INFIRM / WHO HAD LONG RESORTED / TO THIS SPOT / ON ACCOUNT OF ITS WARMTH / AND SHELTER / FROM EVERY WIND / THIS SEAT WAS ERECTED / 1817.

795932 to 789942 NS 79 SE 8 September 1954

251. The Burgh of Airth. THE OLD TOWN OF AIRTH. Writing in 1723, Johnstoun of Kirkland, after describing Airth village and its harbour, says, "Upon the top of the brae stands the manse with several other houses, which is called the old town of Airth: South southeast from the manse about two large pair of butts stands the house and Kirk of Airth."[5] This settlement is clearly shown on an estate plan of 1764, in the possession of Mr. A. F. C. Forrester of Airth, where it is designated "High Airth"; the plan indicates that from a point on the north drive of Airth Castle (No. 199), some 400 yds. N. of the Castle, the main street of the village ran northwards for about 250 yds. on an alinement which is still preserved by the corresponding portion of the drive. At the N. end of the village a second and shorter street ran westwards, and just outside the limits of the village this latter street gave access to a drive leading up to the manse, which occupied a position approximating to that of Airth Mains Farm.

It seems certain that this was the site of the mediaeval burgh of Airth, which was founded in the reign of William the Lion and refounded as a burgh of barony, with a free port, in 1597.[6] Johnstoun's account implies that the move downhill to the site of the present burgh took place only at the beginning of the 18th century, when Airth began to develop rapidly as a seaport, for he speaks of the tolbooth, the fleshmarket and a number of houses as being under construction in 1723.[7] The Mercat Cross (No. 412), the earliest of the existing structures, bears the date 1697. With the development of Lower Airth the old town on the Hill of Airth soon declined in importance, and although still occupied, as has been said, in 1764, it seems thereafter to have been abandoned, the site being enclosed within the policies of Airth Castle. The replacement, in 1820, of the old Parish Church (No. 137) by the North Church (No. 136) in Lower Airth finally severed the links between the old and new settlements.

There are now virtually no traces of the old burgh, the sites of most of the houses shown on the estate plan of 1764 being today covered by the trees and shrubs that border the north drive of the Castle at this point.

---

[1] *Op. cit.*, 218 ff.
[2] *Stirling Burgh Records*, 1667-1752, 305. This was of timber.
[3] *Stat. Acct.*, viii (1793), 275.
[4] As recorded on a panel behind the stone seat at the foot of the access from Cowane's Hospital.
[5] *Geogr. Collections*, i, 327.
[6] *R.M.S.*, vi (1593-1608), No. 634, and *supra*. p. 17.
[7] *Geogr. Collections, loc. cit.*

LOWER AIRTH. The Airth of the early 18th century evidently had as its core the present High Street, with the Mercat Cross (No. 412) at its wider, or NW., end, while a street leading to the harbour, the modern Shore Road, branched off from its northern corner. The road leading uphill from the opposite corner, in the direction of the church and castle, is also probably an original feature of the village. So far the plan recalls a type of lay-out frequently found in burghs. Main Street, however, has no function in the burghal lay-out, as it avoids the market-place and cuts across the route to the harbour; it is really a section of the highway from Stirling to Falkirk, and was no doubt driven through the eastern fringe of the burgh at the time of the highway's construction. It has now eclipsed the High Street, and has become the main artery of the village.

Little now remains of the buildings of the early 18th century, but the few surviving examples are fortunately representative of the period. These consist mainly of a superior type of dwelling such as might have belonged to the wealthier members of the community. Neat and simple in appearance, the houses gain distinction from their pleasing proportions and fine moulded doorways. The steep-pitched roofs of red pantiles are in sympathy, and formerly the walls were no doubt attractively harled or whitewashed. In situation they have no special prominence, standing for the most part as components of a continuous frontage along with less important dwellings. Ranged as they were on either side of cobbled streets, or grouped around the Mercat Cross, these houses must once have given Airth much the same picturesque qualities as are possessed by Culross,[1] on the opposite side of the Forth. In style and date, however, the houses resemble those at Kincardine, where further characteristics of the local vernacular style are evident, notably the incorporation of nautical motifs in the details.

As is natural in the case of buildings so nearly contemporaneous, these houses show a basic uniformity of design. Each comprises a rectangular plan of two main storeys and an attic. The plan is normally symmetrical, the doorway being central with rooms disposed equally on either side. The location of the stair is not always clear, but it was no doubt generally central, and consequently axial with the entrance-doorway. It follows that the external fenestration was symmetrical too, with the entrance the central feature of the principal frontage. The entrance is treated boldly with a bolection-moulded surround and cornice or pediment, usually incorporating a pulvinated frieze and surmounted by a stone panel. Common external features are the steep pantiled roofs, crow-stepped gables, moulded eaves-courses and back-set margins to windows and angle quoins. The masonry is yellow sandstone rubble. Fig. 121 shows a selection of house-types, including some examples which have vanished.[2] The drawings of the existing houses show them in their original condition in so far as this can be inferred, later alterations being ignored. Descriptions follow of the surviving buildings and are confined to individual characteristics. The houses are numbered as in Fig. 121.

HOUSES IN THE HIGH STREET. The house immediately NW. of the Mercat Cross (Fig. 121, 8) is perhaps the best surviving example of the period, in that it possesses all the basic ingredients of the style. Its main frontage is unaltered and has a central entrance-doorway enriched with a bolection-moulded surround, pulvinated frieze and moulded cornice. Over it is set an oval panel, surrounded by a raised ribbon with knot ends to right and left, which bears in relief the initials and date S P / J H / 1722, all in a cursive hand (Pl. 144 C). At ground level there is a window at either side of the entrance and on the first floor five others, symmetrically disposed, the central one being now a dummy. The ogee-moulded eaves-course returns slightly at the corners, and each gable has a small attic-window. At the rear, in the centre of the NW. wall, a small window lights a landing at first-floor level; beneath it is a doorway, but this probably supplants a former window matching the one above and lighting the space beneath the stair. The plan, which measures 34 ft. 6 in. by 19 ft. 6 in. over all, for the most part retains its original form. A central doorway opens on to the foot of a scale stair which rises on the same axis and divides the ground floor into two single rooms. The one on the right has a large cupboard backing on to the stair-foot and the one on the left has a smaller cupboard in the SE. wall. The stair, except for the first tread which is of stone, is constructed in timber, as is also the original partition on its NE. side. It rises to a landing, and this gives entry right and left to two rooms corresponding with those below. From the landing a small newel-stair rises to two attics.

On the NE. side of the High Street, facing the building just described, there is a row of three houses which deserve mention (Pl. 143). The northernmost one embodies an early building, but it was much restored in 1893. A mutual gable, which is crow-stepped and has a cavetto-moulded skewput, joins this to a smaller dwelling. The latter has been altered, but the modest scale of the windows and their chamfered margins suggest an early 18th-century date. It once possessed a forestair, but today the front elevation comprises an upper range of five windows, symmetrically disposed, and on the ground floor three windows which were evidently arranged to fit in with the forestair. The present doorway is secondary, but there are traces of the original one to the left. The extreme right-hand window also was formerly a door. Adjoining this building is the Elphinstone Inn, which is of considerably later date; its cavetto-moulded eaves-course and the cable-moulded skewput are nevertheless pleasing features.

Just S. of this row of houses is the former site of a building which was demolished a few years ago. It is illustrated in Fig. 121, 4.

HOUSES IN SHORE ROAD. The first house to be described (Fig. 121, 5) is one of a row which stretches along the E.

[1] Cf. *Inventory of Fife*, Nos. 152-8.

[2] The Commissioners are indebted to the Scottish National Buildings Record for information on these vanished structures.

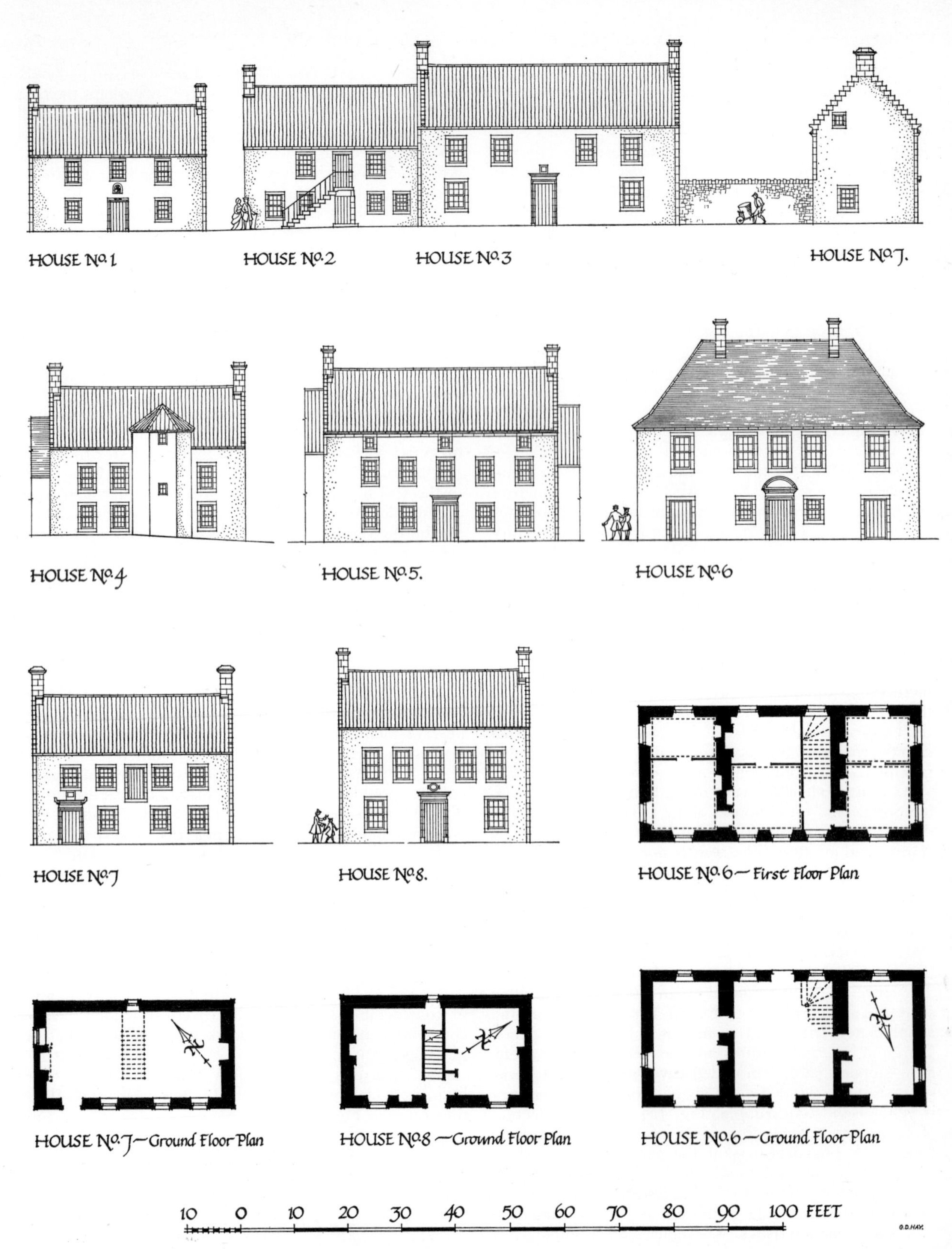

Fig. 121. Burgh of Airth (No. 251); plans and elevations of 18th-century houses

side of Shore Road at its upper end. The special feature of its front elevation is the inclusion of small voids at the wall-head for the purpose of lighting the attic storey. These are now blocked up, but three were originally placed immediately beneath the moulded eaves-course and spaced over alternate voids in the range below. The lintels are integral with a continuous eaves-band, the latter being a horizontal extension of the backset angle-margins. A row of five evenly disposed windows formerly lighted the first floor, but the central one has been cut down to form a doorway for the forestair; the latter is secondary and conceals the original entrance-doorway on the ground floor. This doorway is central and was formerly enriched with a bolection-moulded surround, the left jamb surviving intact with its plinth course. The windows have backset and chamfered margins. On the NW. corner the quoin margin is cut short at the eaves-course of the adjoining building in a way which suggests that the latter is more or less contemporary. The plan, which measures 42 ft. 6 in. by 20 ft. 6 in., doubtless conformed with the standard pattern, but its original arrangement was lost when the house was turned into tenements.

Midway between this row of houses and the corner of Shore Road a small dwelling stands on the E. side. It has been much altered, but the front elevation retains a doorway having bolection-moulded jambs with stopped ends. At the rear there are two small windows having chamfered margins, and these still retain crooks for hanging external shutters.

This part of Shore Road is also interesting for its original cobbled surface and water runnel along the W. side, the latter being well preserved.

The house standing at the corner of Shore Road and the lane leading to South Greens (Fig. 121, 7) is a building of considerable interest. Its main frontage (Pl. 144 A), which faces SW. on to the lane, is of an asymmetrical design very much in keeping with its corner site. This results from the entrance being placed at one end of the façade, namely the one nearest to Shore Road. The doorway is well preserved and has the usual bolection-moulded surround with plinth. Surmounting it is a pulvinated frieze and moulded cornice, the latter displaying two curious lugs at the extremities. On first observation these appear to form the seating of a pediment, now vanished, but a close inspection disproves this and reveals that they were designed specifically as terminal features for the cornice. A mark on the wall-face shows that a stone panel was once set between them. Above the doorway and axial with it occurs the first of the five openings lighting the upper storey. The outer pairs are grouped to conform with the doorway and windows below, and the fenestration is in fact fairly regular apart from the middle window of the upper range. This last, in its present form, looks incongruous, but it was originally a doorway and as such it would have been more in keeping. That it was a door is shown by the fact that the old jambs are still visible beneath the window-sill, while internally it is the only opening that continues down to floor level. The function of this door is not clear, as it might have served either as a hoisting door for stores or as an entrance at the head of a forestair; the former, however, seems more probable on the whole. The rear elevation is plain apart from two small windows vertically disposed in the centre, the lower one now cut down as a door. Each gable contains a small attic-window, that facing on to Shore Road having also a window lighting the ground floor, which matches those on the front elevation. All the windows are finished with backset margins and narrow chamfers.

The building is roofed with pantiles and has an ogee-moulded eaves-course; backset quoins occur on all four corners, that on the N. angle being stopped about 8 ft. from the ground, where a boundary wall formerly linked it with the "Herring House". Extending from the SE. gable is a single-storey building of later date. By reason of its position at a corner, the gables, which have moulded skewputs, became prominent features, their crow-stepped profile being enhanced by tall gable-chimneys, capped with heavy moulded copes which are weathered in the form of a pronounced ogival curve. The house, which measures 37 ft. by 19 ft. 6 in. over all, is now gutted internally, but there is one surviving feature which seems to prove that it was always a single dwelling—namely the two small windows in the rear wall which were evidently designed to light a central scale-stair. On this assumption, the plan does not appear to have been influenced by the location of the entrance near one end, as access to the stair would have been obtainable through the NW. apartment. In the NW. wall of this room there is an original fireplace with lintel and moulded corbels.

The so-called "Herring House" (Fig. 121, 3) is the first of a row which formerly stretched north-eastwards beyond the house at the corner of Shore Road, as last described. The most interesting surviving features are the moulded entrance-doorway (Pl. 144 B), over which is set a square panel bearing in relief the date and initials 1711 W C, and the base-course of the ogee-moulded skewputs, which on the front elevation bear in relief a shield charged with a saltire. The fenestration of the main frontage has been considerably modified, but the central entrance suggests that it was symmetrical and that its original composition probably bore a close resemblance to that of the house at the Mercat Cross (Fig. 121, 8). The angle quoins have backset margins, those at the rear being abbreviated about 8 ft. from the ground to receive a boundary wall. In the SW. gable there is a small attic-window. The crowsteps of the NE. gable are set back from the wall-face, indicating that initially a mutual gable was contemplated serving buildings of equal height. This project appears to have been abandoned, the present adjunct (Fig. 121, 2), which has a forestair, being an example of the smaller type of dwelling to be found in Airth. The house measures 47 ft. by 19 ft. 5 in. over all. Internally it has been much altered, only the fireplace openings in the gables being original. On the assumption that the original staircase was central, all traces of it, together with any openings lighting it, must have been removed when the wide multiple chimney was installed in the SE. wall.

A few feet NE. of the "Herring House" there formerly stood a small house (Fig. 121, 1) possessing a moulded panel which bore the initials and date I M 1733, together with a crown. On the entrance lintel there appeared the initials W M.

The house that is called "The Smithy" (Fig. 121, 6) stands in a central position on the SW. side of Main Street facing the junction of Shore Road. It was evidently of some importance and differs in several respects from the standard pattern. It is larger than the others on plan, measuring 52 ft. by 24 ft. over all, and the ground floor is divided into three, a square central compartment being flanked by cellarage on either side. The former apparently served purely as an entrance hall, as it contains no traces of a fireplace, and both front and rear entrances open directly into it. Originally it no doubt housed the staircase, presumably placed alongside the NW. partition, with the ascent commencing in the W. corner. At one time the room communicated with the cellars, but now only the door in the SE. wall survives. Each cellar contains a fireplace, that in the NW. one having moulded corbels, now partially masked by a later partition. The first floor also has three main divisions, corresponding with those below, but these in turn are subdivided longitudinally by cross-partitions, each having an inner chamber, and the central pair incorporating a passage on their NW. side which presumably received the stair. The rooms are unusually small, but the arrangement seems to be contemporary by reason of the disposition of the fireplaces and the existence of a moulded ceiling-cornice in all but one of the rooms. There are six fireplaces, all of which appear to be original. Four of them are treated uniformly with bolection mouldings. The variants are the one in the back room of the NW. pair, which has a plainer moulding with plinth course, and the one in the rear central room which is larger and has a corbelled lintel. Entry to the central section was by a door at the NE. end of the staircase partition, but this is now sealed off.

Externally the building, which is detached, is distinguished by a hipped roof with bell-cast eaves and has a continuous moulded eaves-course of ogival section. The incorporation of the cellar doors on the main frontage is well managed and in no way belittles its appearance; this is now marred, however, by an abbreviation in height resulting from a rise in the pavement level. The central doorway is surmounted by a heavy segmental pediment (Pl. 144 D) containing a plain tympanum of convex section; the moulded jambs terminate in a plinth course, now almost concealed beneath the pavement. The three windows grouped above the doorway have been altered, the central one and the one to the right being blocked and the latter also having been cut down. Further alteration is evident on the rear elevation, where a forestair has been provided; this was presumably done when the building was converted into flats. Formerly the rear elevation comprised a row of four evenly spaced windows to each storey, the two inner ones on the ground floor forming a group with a central doorway to correspond with that of the main frontage. In the end walls there were formerly two windows at first-floor level, and on the ground floor a small window lighting each cellar. A door-opening in the NW. wall is later. All the windows and the service doors have chamfered margins, but neither these nor the angle quoins are backset.

This structure shows a marked degree of individuality, in both plan and appearance, and seems likely to have been built for some public purpose. It may possibly have been the fleshmarket, noted above as having been under construction in 1723.

899875 (centre) NS 88 NE Various dates in 1955

252. The Burgh of Falkirk. With the exception of those monuments which have been individually described,[1] Falkirk now retains little of architectural interest. It does not appear to contain a single house which, in so far as external features are concerned, can be dated to before the last quarter of the 18th century, though it is possible that older foundations may exist in places underneath the modern buildings. A few facts about the old burgh may, however, be quoted from the rather scanty records.[2] Thus, in 1827 it was still remembered that several old houses, which had had their gable ends turned towards the street, had formerly stood in the High Street, and that one of them had borne a 16th-century date.[3] The burgh's boundary-dyke and ports are also mentioned, in a court minute[4] which runs: "It is statute and ordanit that ilk quarter of the toune of falkirk come forthe dey aboute for buildeing of ane dyk about the said burgh for keipeing forthe of streingeris sua that nane mey enter bot at the ports thairof Viz. the eist and west portis kirkwynd pantaskenes wynde and kow wynde." One of the ports was still partly standing in Kier's time, and another, demolished within the preceding forty years, is known to have borne the date 1585[5]; the latter was probably the one on Kirk Wynd, and it may have stood somewhere near the present Manse Place as Kier states that it was opposite the "Ludging Yard", presumably the Callendar town-house, and this is known to have extended along the E. side of Kirk Wynd in about this position. The East and West Ports were presumably on the High Street, and the only clue to their position is provided by Kier's statement that in his day the town had not expanded much further than the limits indicated by the ports; on this showing a plan prepared in 1802[6] might be taken as evidence that they were placed respectively near Callendar Riggs and the SW. corner of the church-

[1] The Parish Church (No. 140), the Tattie Kirk (No. 141), the Town Steeple (No. 253), the Cross Well (No. 540) and some carved stones (Nos. 426 to 428).

[2] The Commissioners are indebted to Miss D. M. Hunter, Curator of Falkirk Museum, for the information and references incorporated in this article.

[3] Kier's "History of Falkirk" in the *Falkirk Monthly Magazine* of April 1827.

[4] MS. Court Book of Falkirk, preserved in H.M. General Register House, under date 18 May 1647.

[5] Kier, *loc. cit.*

[6] Home, J., *The History of the Rebellion in the Year 1745*, facing p. 169.

yard. Cow Wynd still exists under the same name, which evidently indicates the route by which the burgesses' cattle were led out to pasture on the South Muir.[1] Bantaskine's Wynd is pretty certainly represented by the present Robert's Wynd.[2]

The burgh boundary is not laid down in any surviving charter, but a plan prepared for the Royal Comission on the Royal Burghs of Scotland (1833) shows what was then regarded, perhaps simply on the strength of accepted tradition, as that of the burgh of 1646 (cf. p. 17). The line of this cuts the E. approach to the town near the NW. corner of Callendar Park and the W. one at the West Burn, while its N. and S. arcs lie respectively just N. of Grahamston Station and approximately along the line of Cochrane Avenue. The plan of 1802 (*supra*) shows, in the NE. sector, a curved line evidently representing the boundary wall of garden-enclosures behind houses in the High Street; and though the small scale and general inaccuracy of the plan, which only figures as part of a larger one illustrating the battle of 1746, makes the exact position of this wall somewhat uncertain, it seems safe to infer that it followed the crest of the bluff, now steepened by scarping, that overlooks Callendar Riggs from the W., turned on to a line corresponding in a general way with that of Bank Street, and ended on Kirk Wynd opposite the NE. corner of the churchyard. This wall may or may not have originated in the dyke-building operations ordered in 1647 (*supra*).

The Ordnance Survey Name Book records that the site of the Market Cross is marked in the paving of the street. What is presumably the mark in question can be seen 12 ft. W. of the Cross Well (No. 540).

888799 (centre) NS 87 NE, NS 88 SE
27 November 1958

253. The Town Steeple, Falkirk. The Town Steeple was designed by David Hamilton, and was erected in 1813-4 by Henry Taylor, a local builder, at a cost of £1460. The upper portion was damaged by lightning in 1927 but has been rebuilt.[3] It stands on the foundation of an earlier steeple, dating from 1697.[4]

The Steeple is square on plan, measuring 20 ft. 2 in. externally on each side by 140 ft. in height, and stands free of other buildings except on its E. side. It is built of grey freestone ashlar, channel-jointed in the lowermost of the four stages into which the tower, as distinct from the tapering spire, is divided, and its general appearance will be seen in Pl. 145. The stages are separated by cornices, and each stage is intaken to a greater or less extent from the one below. The lowermost stage is divided unequally into two by a string-course, which is carried through as a transom at the springing-level of the heads of the two large round-headed voids seen at ground level in the centres of the S. and W. sides respectively—the former containing the principal entrance, with a moulded architrave, and the latter a window. Above each of these there is a square-headed blind window with backset margins. The N. side, which has been refaced below the string-course, contains two small round-headed doorways, the W. one blind, and three flat windows with iron bars, centrally placed one above the other, lighting the three rooms within (*infra*). The second stage has inset Doric columns at the angles and, in each side, a large round-headed window. Except on the E. side each of these has a balustrade across its base. All four faces are pedimented. The third stage shows four clock-dials framed by shallow moulded pilasters; as the angles between adjacent pairs of pilasters have been cut back the plan at this stage is an unequal-sided octagon. The fourth stage, which forms the bell-chamber, is a regular octagon with columns at the angles supporting an elaborate double cornice; between the columns are louvred openings, and these are repeated in the plain basal section of the spire, which is octagonal and vertical-sided and is divided from the tapering upper portion by a cornice and a double intake. The spire maintains the octagonal section of the fourth stage, and finishes in a hemispherical capstone surmounted by a ball and weather-cock.

The ground-floor apartment, entered by the main door on the S. side, was presumably intended to serve as a town office, but has now been turned into a shop. The door in the N. side of the tower opens directly on to the foot of a small stone newel-stair in the NE. corner, which gives access to three superimposed rooms, each the full size of the tower; the two upper ones are prison cells, having strongly grated windows and heavy doors with strong external bolts, but the lowermost has a fireplace, a lighter door and less solid gratings, and was no doubt the jailer's quarters. Above the cells the higher stages of the steeple are reached by ladder.

BELL. The bell that hung in the old steeple was disused in 1897, and is now preserved in the Burgh Museum.[5] It is of an unusual shape, being only 17 in. high from the lip to the base of the canons while the diameter is 26 in. It is inscribed IAMES EARLE OF LINLITHGOW AND CALLANDER IOHN MEIKLE FECIT EDINBURGI / 1697 FOR FALKIRK, the lettering being similar to that of the Gargunnock bell (cf. No. 344).

888799 NS 87 NE 22 March 1956

254. The Burgh of Kilsyth. Most of the houses in Kilsyth appear to date from the earlier part of the 19th century, the SW. portion of the town, in particular, having been built about 1820.[6] A number, however, show small windows, with backset dressings, such as suggest a date of up to a century earlier. Of the buildings that possess most character, there may first be mentioned

[1] Love, *Antiquarian Notes and Queries*, iv, section ii, 1.
[2] *Ibid.*, i, 44, and an unpublished note by the same author which, however, quotes no authority.
[3] Johnston, *The Falkirk Steeple*, Falkirk Rotary Club, unpaged.
[4] *N.S.A.*, viii (Stirlingshire), 21.
[5] *P.S.A.S.*, lxxxiv (1949-50), 77.
[6] Ordnance Survey Name Book, Kilsyth parish, 59.

three at the upper end of the High Street. The first, Number 11, is rather tall and narrow and contains three storeys (Pl. 146 A); it is constructed of large squared rubble brought to courses and has backset margins to its voids, V-jointed quoins and a moulded eaves-course. Below the central window on the second floor there is a panel with a cabled border showing the Cordiners' crown and rounding-knife dividing the initials and date 176[?3] / W H. The second house adjoins the first on the N., where the ground is slightly lower; it is of the same general type but has two storeys only, the lower of which has been converted into shops. The gables have plain tabling and the N. one has a rolled skewput. A panel on the front is inscribed 1765 / I M. The third house stands opposite, at the corner of the High Street and the small garden flanking Westport Street (Pl. 146 B). This house is L-shaped on plan, having its main block fronting E. on the High Street and a wing projecting to the back flush with the N. gable. The masonry is squared rubble with dressed quoins and margins, not backset; the gables have plain tabling with rolled skewputs to the front and moulded ones behind. A gablet which rises from the centre of the E. face also has rolled skewputs. The house contains three storeys and an attic. On the ground floor a central opening leads into a pend, at the inner end of which a newel stair leads to the upper storeys. N. of the pend the façade shows a door and two windows, and S. of it another door and one window, the doors having apparently been introduced and the windows enlarged to serve two small shops. The windows on the first and second floors are arranged symmetrically over the lower ones and the pend, and in the gablet there is a single window. A stone dated 1768 is set at the base of the chimney that rises from the gablet. At least one more house of the same date and type is known to have stood on the site of the Gospel Hall, immediately N. of the building first mentioned above. Some carved stones derived from it are noted under No. 434.

Other houses which deserve notice are (i) Number 8 Main Street, a small two-storeyed building with rolled skewputs: (ii) Number 14 Market Street, a two-storeyed building with a steeply-pitched and thatched roof, now covered with corrugated iron sheeting, and a crow-stepped E. gable which bears the date 1735 on an ogival skewput: (iii) A group of three two-storeyed buildings with central gablets, which forms the corner of Newtown and Drumtocher Streets; each building contains several dwellings. Typical of a great many of the smaller houses in the town are those at the S. end of Newtown Street; these recall the colliery "rows", being one-storeyed, though with a habitable attic, and having a single room opening to right and left of a very small lobby inside a central entrance. They are extremely plain, with dressed margins to voids, moulded and corbelled eaves-courses and slated roofs. The smallest houses have ground-floor accommodation on one side only of the entrance.

In 1859 Kilsyth was described as "chiefly occupied by handloom weavers".[1]

7177 NS 77 NW 5 May 1954

TOWNS AND VILLAGES, WITH INDUSTRIAL BUILDINGS

255. Old Houses, Henderson Street, Bridge of Allan. There is little to record in Bridge of Allan, but the easternmost three of a row of four small houses at the W. end of Henderson Street provide a fair sample of work dateable to the turn of the 18th and 19th centuries. Each has two storeys and an attic; a central front door with a flat hood above it; two windows on the ground floor and three above, with attic dormers to the back; harled walls and slated roofs. The dressings are exposed, and the down pipes from the rones are enclosed in chases. Thistle Bank, the westernmost of the three, has a small lobby inside the front door with a front and a back room to the right and the same to the left; from the lobby a stone stair, with iron balusters and a mahogany rail, rises in half a counter-clockwise turn to a small landing from which access is had to five rooms, two to the front and three to the back. The attics, which are not used but which possess fireplaces, are only accessible by a ladder.

789975 NS 79 NE 16 August 1952

256. East Lodge, Bridge of Allan. This house, until recently called Blawlowan, stands on the old road (No. 509) running eastwards from the Allan Water bridge, about 100 yds. NW. of the point where this is crossed by the Sheriffmuir Road (No. 508). It is said to be the last representative of the village of Pathfoot, which was destroyed by Sir Robert Abercromby when he built the wall round the Airthrey Castle policies soon after 1798. The NW. portion consists of a small Georgian dwelling-house, of little interest as it differs in no material way from large numbers of others in the county; but the SE. portion, which is dated by its door-lintel to 1731, is worth noting as it has evidently been part of a long and relatively low house of which the NW. end has been replaced by the later addition. With a central door and four windows on the ground floor, and five windows, correspondingly placed, on the first floor, it must have been a more ambitious structure than the cottage of the time—perhaps an inn, as local tradition states. The reconstruction, however, has now left only the door and two windows on the ground floor and three windows on the first floor, all the openings being chamfered. The interior has been completely modernised. The lintel-inscription reads 17 J B J K 31, with what seems to be a merchant's mark between the two pairs of initials. The first pair no doubt refers to the family of Bryce, in whose possession the house is said to have been for more than 200 years.

804969 NS 89 NW 25 October 1952

257. Blairlogie Village. This very small village has for its main axis the old road mentioned under No. 509, but

[1] Ordnance Survey Name Book, Kilsyth parish, 59.

although some of its cottages possess a certain air of antiquity, and one, at least, showed mud mortar under its harling, none of them seems likely to date from before the latter part of the 18th century. Several carved stones are to be seen, some certainly reset in other than their original positions. The oldest, in the post-office, shows a mason's square, compasses and mallet with the initials S T H B and the date 1728; another bears the initials I A I T, a merchant's mark and the date 1765, and another A W M G and the date 1758. Two undated tabular sundials bear, respectively, a crowned thistle and the initials W F. The Secession church, of 1761-2, is described under No. 129.

828969 NS 89 NW 23 October 1952

258. Cambusbarron Village. The oldest houses now surviving in Cambusbarron are cottages of the later 18th or early 19th century, all more or less renovated. They are in general of harled-rubble construction, with backset dressings; a typical one in Murray Place has a doorway lintel inscribed 17 W D M W 62. A rather similar lintel inscribed J C J S 1769, has been reset in the E. gable of Polmaise Cottages, SE. of the village on the road to St. Ninians. Two cottages in North End, measuring respectively 35 ft. by 19 ft. and 20 ft. 9 in. by 20 ft. 3 in., may be of rather earlier origin though subsequently altered, as some of their windows are unusually small and show narrow chamfers at the arrises, as does also the door of the smaller one. These cottages are said locally to have been weavers' houses; they are now empty and appear to be condemned. Another relic of a textile industry, probably the manufacture of carpets and tartans, which was carried on actively at Cambusbarron in the early 19th century,[1] is to be seen in the old church, a semi-ruinous building on the E. side of The Braes now used for storage by a motor engineer. The main portion of this building is a two-storeyed block measuring 36 ft. 10 in. by 19 ft. 9 in. externally; in its construction, which is of harled rubble with dressed quoins and margins, it resembles the generality of the cottages mentioned above. The street frontage shows four windows equally spaced on either floor, and the built-up hoisting-door in the S. gable together with the fireplaces and chimneys go to confirm the local report that the building was originally a weaving-shed. It has been converted into a church by the addition of an aisle with a three-sided end to the centre of the E. wall; this is 20 ft. wide where it joins the main building and 14 ft. deep, and its quoins are roughly squared and harled over, not carefully dressed and left exposed. Doors at ground-floor level are in the SE. face of the end of the aisle and in the E. wall of the main building, S. of the aisle; the latter opens below an outside stair leading to a door at gallery level in the S. wall of the aisle. Galleries occupy the whole of the aisle and either end of the main building. A bell has been fixed in an iron mounting on top of the chimney on the N. gable

On the W. side of North End, at its S. extremity, there stands a gate-pillar of freestone masonry with a rounded arris, evidently one of a pair. It bears a much-wasted human torso, the companion to which, in even worse condition, is preserved in the garden at Alma House. The pillars, which Fleming implies were at the entrance to a mansion-house,[2] may date from the 17th century.

7792 NS 79 SE 20 May 1955

259. Torbrex Village. Torbrex is a small village standing midway between St. Ninians and Cambusbarron, its houses flanking a narrow and rather twisty central street. The following buildings may be mentioned.

(i) OLD TORBREX HOUSE. This house, which is still inhabited, stands on the NW. side of the street at about the middle of the village. It contains two storeys and is oblong on plan, measuring 44 ft. from SW. to NE. by 19 ft. 9 in. transversely. The walls and openings are faced in cement, and the dressed quoins, which occur only on the SE. front, are backset. The roof, now slated, was originally thatched, and there is no eaves-course. The gables are crow-stepped and the skewputs are finished in heavy roll-and-hollow mouldings. A dated panel (*infra*) indicates that the house was built in 1721 and, although the interior was extensively reconstructed in 1895,[3] it seems probable that the original arrangements were largely preserved. The front door, which is covered by a late porch, is placed in the middle of the SE. front, and is flanked on either side by a window. Three windows on the upper floor are correspondingly spaced. The first-floor window in the middle of the NW. side is original, but the back door and the ground-floor windows on this side appear to be insertions. There is a large room at each end of the house on both floors, and between them a staircase with closet behind it. The stair and the fireplaces, which are all placed in the gables, are known to have been renewed in 1895, and a lean-to building at the NE. end was probably added at the same time. The panel alluded to above is set in the SE. front. It is 1 ft. 11 in. square over a wide, moulded margin, and is crudely carved with a lion rampant, for Buchanan, flanked at the top by the initials J B and M W and at the bottom by the date 1721 and the initials E C, all in relief. The initials have been attributed to John Buchanan, to his wife Ellen Campbell, and to his mother, who may have been one of the Wordies of Torbrex.[4]

(ii) BURNSIDE. This building, which stood at the junction of Torbrex Road with the village street, was largely demolished about the year 1920.[5] Little apart from the foundations now survives, but the house is included here as representing a type of structure once common in the county (cf. p. 49) although no complete

[1] *N.S.A.*, viii (Stirlingshire), 332.
[2] *Castles and Mansions*, 418.
[3] Information from the proprietors.
[4] *Castles and Mansions*, 419; *T.S.N.H.A.S.* (1937-8), 95.
[5] The Commission's officers are indebted to Mr. Gordon of Old Torbrex House, who was present at the demolition of the building, for a description of its construction.

examples appear to survive today. It measures 71 ft. 9 in. by 18 ft. over walls which are about 2 ft. in thickness and are built in rubble with clay mortar. Much of the W. gable remains, and the footings of the S. wall still rise to their full height of 2 ft. although they now form the lower portion of a later roadside dyke. Above these footings the original walling was of turf; the roof was thatched and was supported by perhaps four pairs of crucks the feet of which were recessed into the footings at a height of about 1 ft. 6 in. above the ground. At the time of its demolition the building comprised three separate dwellings.

(iii) WEAVERS' COTTAGES. These cottages (Pl. 148 B), which are good examples of the very numerous weavers' cottages of the 18th century, lie on the NW. side of the village street and about half-way between Torbrex Road and Torbrex Farm Road. They are single-storeyed and the walls are of harled rubble; the slate roofs replaced the original thatch about the year 1912. Although originally comprising two separate dwellings, the building has been altered to form a single house and few features of interest remain. The entrance doorway to the NE. cottage, however, although now blocked up, retains its lintel on which are incised the initials A R and A S dividing the date 1756.

788919 NS 79 SE 31 August 1955

260. St. Ninians Village. Apart from the old parish church (No. 134) and the fragments of an earlier church (No. 133), the village contains few buildings of any architectural interest. Parliament Close, which stands at the corner of Kirk Wynd and Main Street, and the old manse in Kirk Wynd, may date in part from the 17th century and have been treated separately (cf. Nos. 261 and 262). Main Street contained a considerable number of 18th-century houses within recent years, but they were all demolished about 1958. The most interesting of them was "Rollo of Powhousis Lodging", which stood on the W. side of Main Street about 100 yds. N. of its junction with Glasgow Road and Bannockburn Road. This building was L-shaped, the main block measuring 20 ft. by 48 ft. and the wing 20 ft. by 30 ft.; it was rubble-built and probably contained two storeys and an attic, but at the date of visit only the ground floor remained intact, with the E. façade rising to first-floor level. The ground floor, which was vaulted, was then inaccessible, but the principal rooms had evidently been on the first floor, which was reached from Main Street by a forestair; part of a bolection-moulded entrance-doorway remained in the centre of the E. façade at this level. The house is said to have belonged to the family of Rollo of Powhouse and was probably built in 1705.[1]

The other houses in Main Street seem for the most part to have been even simpler in appearance. The majority were plain rectangular blocks of two storeys or two storeys and an attic, the principal façade containing two main ranges of symmetrically disposed windows. The masonry was of harled rubble, relieved only by plain dressed quoins and margins and an occasional moulded eaves-course. The gables were either crow-stepped or tabled, the latter finishing in rolled skewputs, while the roofs were originally of pantile.

A pleasing feature of many of the older houses was the carved panel that was frequently set over the entrance-doorway and contained the date of erection, together with the initials and trade insignia of the builder. No good examples remain *in situ*, but the two early 18th-century panels now incorporated in the façade of Randolph Buildings, Randolph Crescent, will serve to illustrate the type (Pl. 213). The first contains the date 1723, below which are the initials A P and N P and the Hammermen's insignia. The second panel, which is set a few yards to the N. of the first and at a higher level, contains the date 1724 and the initials W A and I S. The devices carved below include a shovel and what appear to be two sheaves of barley, probably representing the emblems of a maltster[2]; but the various drinking-vessels, including a leather bottle and a quaich, which also appear on the panel, suggest that the builder was as much an innkeeper as a brewer. Both panels are carved in relief and are set within a moulded border.

7991 NS 79 SE Various dates to 1958

261. Old Manse, St. Ninians. This building, which served as a manse until the erection of a new structure in 1809,[3] stands on the S. side of Kirk Wynd close to the W. entrance of St. Ninians churchyard. The original house is a rectangular block of two storeys and an attic, and measures 61 ft. 9 in. by 19 ft. 11 in. over walls which average 2 ft. in thickness. The two single-storey outshots, one to the E. and one in the centre of the N. front, have no doubt been added at a later date. The masonry is of harled rubble with dressed-stone margins, and the gables are crow-stepped and have ogival-moulded skewputs. The walls of the N. outshot finish in a cavetto-moulded eaves-course above which there is a penthouse roof with coped gables. There is a doorway in the S. front at ground-floor level, a little to the E. of the centre, and above it the date 1677 has been roughly incised in cement. The inscription, however, at least in its present form, is clearly of no great antiquity. There are three large windows to the W. of the doorway and a range of five on the first floor, all symmetrically disposed, while there are also two smaller windows to the E. of the doorway at ground-floor level; all have chamfered arrises. The lintel of the window over the doorway incorporates the incised initials M A G dividing the date 173[?1]. The initials no doubt represent Mr. Archibald Gibson, who was minister of the parish from 1728 to 1732,[4] and in the absence of any evidence to support the earlier date carved over the doorway it may be assumed that the existing

[1] *Castles and Mansions*, 287; *T.S.N.H.A.S.* (1930-1), 150.
[2] For an illustration of similar emblems, see *P.S.A.S.*, xxxvi (1901-2), 403, fig. 121.
[3] *N.S.A.*, viii (Stirlingshire), 336.
[4] *Fasti*, iv, 314.

house was built in 1731 rather than in 1677. On the N. front there is an original window at first-floor level to the W. of the outshot, and a later one, which has sharp arrises, below. The outshot itself contains an entrance-doorway.

Access was not obtainable to the whole of the interior at the date of visit and the internal arrangements of the house are therefore somewhat uncertain. It seems likely, however, that the building originally comprised two separate dwellings, the ground-floor one being approached by the doorway in the S. front and the first-floor one by a forestair which occupied the position now taken up by the N. outshot. From what was seen of the interior it would appear that few original features survive; the E. room on the ground floor was a kitchen and retains a fireplace with a corbelled lintel. The first floor, which still forms a separate dwelling, is now reached by a wooden stair contained within the N. outshot.

795916 NS 79 SE 26 April 1956

262. Parliament Close, St. Ninians. This close occupies the corner of Main Street and Kirk Wynd and contains what is almost the only surviving group of 17th- and 18th-century houses in the villages. A round-arched gateway in Kirk Wynd gives access to a small but picturesque courtyard, around which there are disposed buildings of several different periods. On the W. side of the close is a house, the façade of which fronts Main Street. It is two storeys and an attic in height and is built of harled rubble, the voids having dressed margins. The slated roof is said to replace original thatch, but the crow-stepped gables and cavetto-moulded skewputs remain. The NW. angle of the building is splayed at ground-floor level, where it forms the junction of Main Street and Kirk Wynd, but it is stopped out to the square above. Within the courtyard a forestair rises to a first-floor doorway, over which there is a panel containing the date 1603 and the initials T W and M A; above is the motto QUI PETITUR VI[N]CIT ("He prevails who is assailed"), all in raised letters. The initials are supposed to be those of Thomas Wordie and his wife.[1] The house may originally have formed two separate dwellings, one entered from the courtyard and the other from Main Street; the interior, however, was gutted by fire early in the 20th century and is now of no interest.

The house occupying the E. side of the court is generally similar in style to that already described. It has a central doorway at ground-floor level, the lintel of which bears the incised initials W W and E D dividing the date 1674. The initials are said to refer to William Wordie and Ellen Doig[2] (cf. No. 294). The interior has been gutted, but there have probably been two main rooms on each of the principal floors; a kitchen fireplace remains in the S. apartment on the ground floor. On the S. side of the court there are offices of 19th-century date, while to the N. there is part of a row of somewhat older cottages which are entered from Kirk Wynd.

795916 NS 79 SE 10 August 1955

263. Chartershall Village. The hamlet of Chartershall was once a settlement of nail-makers, and some traces of this vanished industry deserve to be mentioned. Many of the nailers' houses have fallen into ruin, and those which survive have been reconstructed as ordinary cottages; but the westernmost house in the row S. of the bridge (No. 456) exemplifies the typical plan of two living-rooms, one on each side of the entrance, and a workshop or smithy at the end. The workshop was entered through one of the living-rooms, and also had an external door; traces of this door, now blocked up, can be seen in Pl. 148 A to the left of the third window from the right. The entrance-door of this house has a lintel inscribed W P 1782; in the garden there is a cubical sundial, dug up on the spot, of a type common in the 17th and early 18th centuries.

The larger house by the N. end of the bridge no doubt dates from the turn of the 18th and 19th centuries, but now retains no distinctive features other than its decorated roll skewputs. A ruinous building beside it contains a lintel dated 1770, with the initials R L and E O; this is probably in secondary use.

792902 NS 79 SE 18 May 1955

264. Bannockburn Town. Bannockburn, which evidently existed as a village (*vicus, viculus*) in the later Middle Ages,[3] developed at the end of the 18th century into a small industrial town[4] and subsequently became an important textile centre, particularly for carpets and tartans.[5] This development seems to have been largely due to the enterprise of the Wilson family firm, which organised a regular industrial community in the place with mills, warehouses and ancillary buildings as well as dwellings for workers; siting the mills, dye-houses, etc., mainly on the banks of the Bannock Burn, where adequate water was available for the various industrial processes. The Wilsons evidently had a mill in operation by about 1770, and were erecting workmen's houses some ten years later[6]; the older buildings in the town date from the time of these developments, and some representative structures have accordingly been selected for description. Nothing survives from earlier periods except the bridge, and this is described separately under No. 457.

Of the two mills that survive, the Skeoch Mill, situated on the left bank of the Burn immediately above the bridge, is still operated by Messrs. John Crawford and Co. (Bannockburn) Ltd., the successors of Messrs. William Wilson Ltd. It is now a complex structure of several periods, approximately L-shaped on plan and

1 *Castles and Mansions*, 291.
2 *Ibid.*
3 Boece, H., *Scotorum Historiae, etc.* (1575), 400.
4 "Of late cotton-cloth, and for a long time, all the tartan used by the army, has been manufactured at this village" (*Stat. Acct.*, xviii (1796), 394).
5 *N.S.A.*, viii (Stirlingshire), 332.
6 MS. records of Messrs. William Wilson Ltd., preserved in the National Library of Scotland (uncatalogued).

containing three main storeys and an attic (Pl. 156 A, C). The N. range appears to be the oldest part, and this incorporates the remains of a smaller building which may possibly represent the mill that was in use about 1770. If so, this must have been a small building rather similar to one at Cambusbarron (cf. No. 258). The space between the N. and W. ranges has now been filled with single-storey buildings which include a range of dye-houses; the original dye-houses, however, are thought to have stood on the ground lying W. of the mill. Midway along the N. wall of the N. range an inscribed stone (Pl. 156 B) has been set at third-storey level; the upper part of this bears J C G J W / A J 176[?7] in a pleasing cursive script, and the lower part, which has been cut back to provide a fresh surface, the initials W W, evidently for William Wilson, and the date 1822. The significance of the earlier inscription is unknown, but the later one probably records the date at which the L-shaped structure was built, in whole or in part. The Royal George Mill, the other survivor, stands close to the left bank of the Burn, immediately W. of the main highway through the town (A 9). Its name suggests that it was built at the time of George IV's visit to Scotland in 1822. It is a simple rectangular building, tall and narrow, standing to a height of four storeys and an attic and having at its W. end a lower extension which is probably of much the same date. Viewed from the W. (Pl. 157) it is an impressive structure, but its E. end, to the level of the fourth storey, is now concealed by the highway embankment and the portion left exposed has been remodelled. Like the Skeoch Mill, it is of solid and orthodox stone construction, with gable ends and a pitched roof; the floors are of timber and allow a minimum of headroom. In these respects, and in the plain, forthright treatment of their exteriors in general, both mills are no doubt typical of the handloom-weaving factories that were being built in Bannockburn at this time.

Of the earliest of the Wilsons' housing something is known from record. Two contracts were entered into in 1780[1] with "James Malies wright and mason in St. Ninians" one of which refers to the "new howse" and provides that the materials of the old building are to be used for it and for a proposed dye-house. Drawings for the two houses specified show them to have been terraced, each house being divided into two parts by a central cross-partition and containing four single-room dwellings on each of two main floors. Each part had its own provision for access and internal circulation in the shape of a central entrance opening on a transverse passage with a stair at the rear, the intention having evidently been to provide independent access to each room, which thus became a self-contained unit with its own box-bed, closet and fireplace. Although these houses have now disappeared, others remain which incorporate similar features, notably those in the row situated just N. of the Skeoch Mill; while a cottage at the E. end of Station Road (Numbers 54 and 56) may also be cited for comparison. This is a single-storeyed building of harled rubble, with coped gables and simply moulded skewputs (Pl. 147 D). The slated roof has probably replaced original thatch or pantiles. The building is divided into two main apartments, each of which has an entrance from outside—a feature which may suggest that the original occupant was a craftsman, who used the E. division as a workshop while the larger apartment to the W. served as a dwelling. The lintel of each doorway bears the incised date 1796; the original windows have sharp arrises and provision for external shutters.

Examples of more substantial dwellings of the later 18th century are to be seen in Numbers 26 and 28 Newmarket (Pl. 147 C). These are both simple rectangular blocks of two storeys and an attic, and are built in harled rubble. The original pantiled roofs remain and the gables have a plain coping, the skewputs of the NW. house being simply moulded and those of the SE. one rolled. The front doors are centrally placed in the principal frontage at ground-floor level, and the windows are disposed symmetrically on either side and on the first floor. The lintel of the entrance-doorway of the NW. house bears the incised date 1777, while the other house has a sunk panel over the doorway which contains the incised date 1774 above the initials I H and M I. Internally this house has a central staircase, on either side of which there is a single large room on both the ground and first floors; the NW. apartment on the ground floor has been a kitchen and retains a fireplace with a corbelled lintel. The NW. house probably has a similar plan.

The only other house that calls for mention is Number 17 the Brae (Pl. 147 A, B), an attractive, late 18th-century dwelling on a considerably bigger scale than the two houses in Newmarket already described. The building is a rectangular block of two storeys and an attic, with a partial basement at the NW. end, and measures 41 ft. 3 in. by 28 ft. 5 in. over all. The masonry is harled rubble with dressed, offset quoins and margins, and the walls finish in a plain eaves-band above which there is an ogival-moulded eaves-course. The gable copings are stepped, and finish in rolled skewputs which are wrought with a cable moulding. The entrance-doorway is centrally placed in the SW. façade at ground-floor level; it has a lugged and moulded architrave, a pulvinated frieze and a moulded cornice. A single window is set on either side of the doorway and three more are symmetrically disposed on the first floor; all have sharp arrises. The other elevations are of no particular interest and the conversion of the house into flats has considerably modified the internal arrangements. The original plan probably provided for four main rooms on both ground and first floors and for a central staircase.

The church had been "recently erected" in 1841 to serve a newly formed *quoad sacra* parish.[2] It stands at the junction of Main Street and New Road and is a simple rectangular "preaching kirk"; but the plan has been somewhat modified to conform with the Gothic exterior.

8090, 8190 NS 89 SW Various dates to March 1960

[1] MS. records of Messrs. William Wilson Ltd., preserved in the National Library of Scotland (uncatalogued).

[2] *N.S.A.*, viii (Stirlingshire), 334.

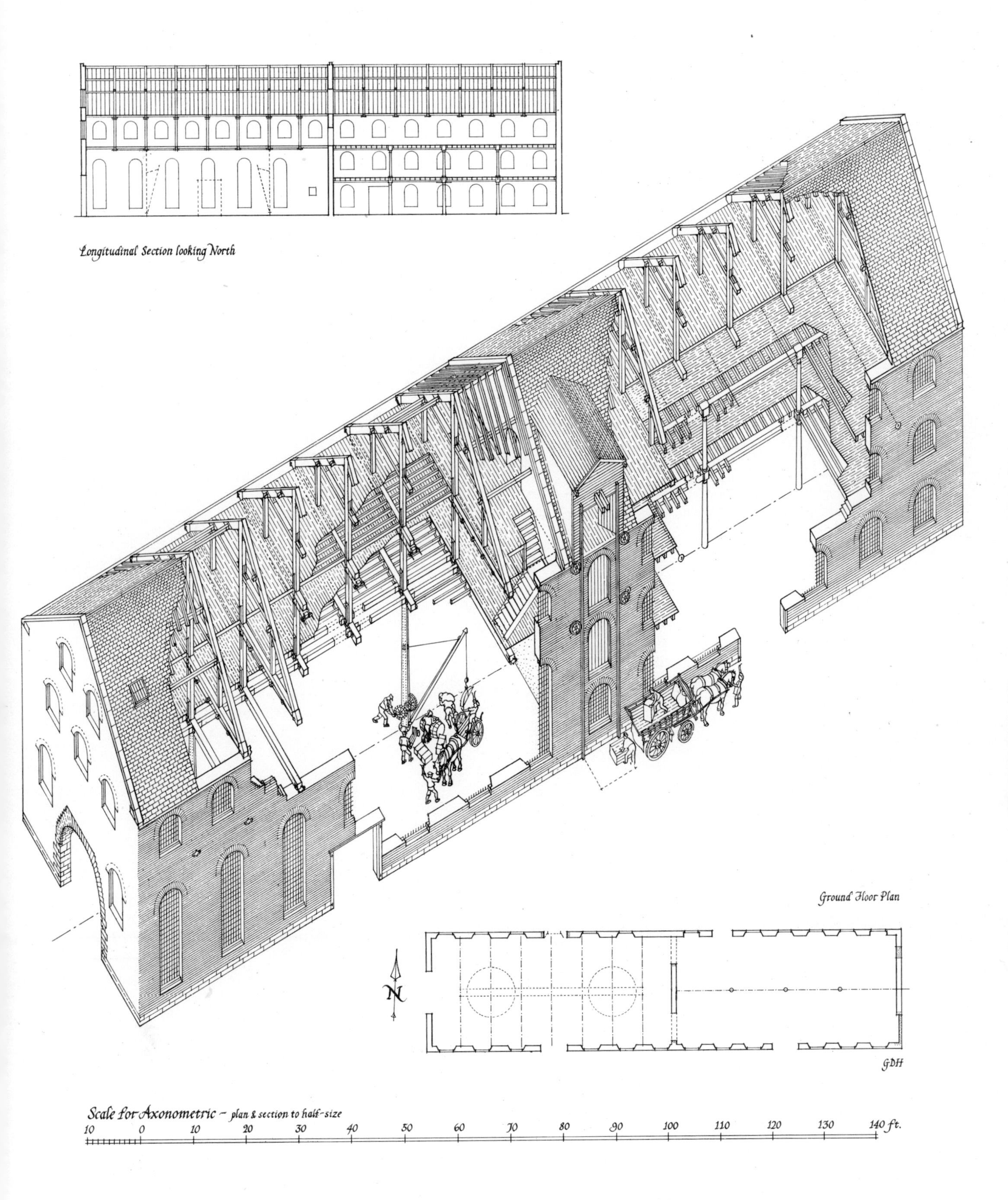

Fig. 122. Engineering shop, Carron Ironworks (No. 265)

265. Engineering Shop, Carron Ironworks. Carron Company was incorporated in 1759 and began to operate in 1760, but no structures of this earliest period have survived within the Works. The engineering shop, however, forms part of a complex of buildings which evidently dates from the beginning of the 19th century, as it first appears in a Works Plan of 1825; and though the rest of the complex has been considerably altered, to adapt it to changing industrial needs, the engineering shop itself has suffered little change beyond the loss of its E. end and the modification of some openings. To judge from a Works Plan dated 1873, it then formed the S. side of a narrow courtyard which was enclosed to the N. by a range of smaller buildings, comprising a brass furnace, a smith's shop and a storehouse; in the centre of the courtyard was an engine house containing machinery actuated by water led into the yard from the E. by a culvert.

The engineering shop (Fig. 122) is a tall, multistoried structure measuring 181 ft. 4 in. by 43 ft. 6 in., and at first was virtually free-standing. It is mainly of interest for its construction, which embodies external load-bearing walls wrapped round an internal framework of timber and primitive iron-construction. It is sturdily built, the walls, which are probably of local brick, being 2 ft. thick and the floors being constructed on the double-floor principle comprising bridging joists and main beams. Cast-iron, the staple site material, has been utilised for making structural connections and internal supports—to the extent that orthodox timber construction has in many cases been dispensed with for a system of butt-joints and cast-iron strengtheners. At about the middle a cross-partition, also 2 ft. in thickness, rises to the full height of the building and divides it into two sections. Both are covered by a massive open-timber roof (Pl. 152) of king-post construction, which incorporates a loft-floor resting on the main ties. Below this level the two sections are treated differently; the W. one having a single upper floor, beneath which is a large machine hall, while the E. one has, in addition, an intermediate floor or mezzanine.

The machine hall, which is adequately lit by tall windows ranged in its side walls, is designed on an impressive scale. Its spacious dimensions, together with the great semicircular entrance at its W. end, are evidence of the size of the machines that it was presumably intended to contain. Its chief asset in this respect, however, is its possession of a clear floor-space, which has been managed in a remarkable way by suspending the floor above from the roof, thus entirely freeing the machine hall of intermediate supports. This has been done by extending the king-posts downwards in the form of pendant-posts, which have their lower ends attached to the main beams of the upper floor by means of cast-iron stirrups. The latter, which are looped round the beam-section, are carried some distance up the sides of the pendant-posts and have their ends gripped together by folding wedges, also of cast-iron. Similarly, the heads of the pendant-posts hang from the roof by means of cast-iron straps, bolted to the former and wedged on to the lower ends of the king-posts.

The upper floor itself, in addition to the main cross-beams, has at its centre a double row of longitudinal beams. The latter, which are set within the depth of the main beams and appear to serve as stiffeners, rest in iron shoes, formed out of heavy castings measuring 4 ft. 6 in. in length by 12 in. in depth (Pl. 154 A). Each pair of castings is bolted together on either side of the main beam, and incorporates slots for retaining the stirrup of the pendant-post, so that a rigid connection results between the various structural members. The last casting but one from each end also incorporates a socket-hole which held the vertical shafts for two derricks which formerly stood in the machine hall. The main beams also support the bridging-joists, which are notched on to stout moulded runners, bolted together at regular intervals along the sides of the main beams. Like the longitudinal beams, the bridging-joists are set within the depth of the main beam, so that the floor, despite its clear span of 39 ft. 6 in., and its heavy boarding 2¼ in. thick, has an overall structural depth of only 12½ in. Another function of the main beams is to tie the side walls together, the ends of the beams being bolted to tie-irons fastened on the external wall-face.

In the eastern section, the upper floor and mezzanine rest on a central row of cast-iron columns, and it is the upper floor that has the uninterrupted floor-area, owing to the roof trusses spanning it. The columns serve as point-supports for the main floor-beams, which run longitudinally; the beams measure 12 in. by 18 in. deep in section and have the inner ends of the bridging-joists notched on to them in the manner already described. The columns (Pl. 154 B-D), which are 12 in. in diameter at the base and Doric in style, are each surmounted by a square iron-casting, about 18 in. square and 20 in. deep, into which are joined the ends of the main beams. The castings have moulded angles, and the eastern and western ones beneath the mezzanine each incorporate a pair of shoes to receive the bridging-joists which here coincide with the beam centres; the central casting on this floor is strengthened by projecting bearing-plates to which the ends of the main beams are bolted. At the level of the upper floor the side walls are again tied together, in this case by iron tie-rods which run beneath the floor.

The roof trusses are of heavy construction, the king-posts, principals and main ties being approximately 11½ in. square over the machine hall and 11½ in. by 6 in. over the remainder; as already indicated, most of the joints are strengthened—if not wholly formed—with cast-iron angle-brackets bolted to the frame. Similarly, the purlins are set between the principals in cast-iron shoes. In order to carry the extra load imposed upon them, the trusses over the western section have their main ties strengthened by pairs of iron tension-rods, 1½ in. in diameter, slung underneath in the form of an inverted bow (Pl. 153 A). Each pair of tension-rods lends support to the underside of the tie-beam by means of cast-iron cradles, fixed at intervals along its length, the rods being slotted through eyes in the cradles and also in the straps attached to the pendant- and king-posts. The ends of the rods are anchored to the feet of the truss, which, although not visible, seem to be contained in iron shoes.

Internally, the plan provides for intercommunication between the two sections at all levels by means of doorways in the cross-partition. There is likewise direct external access to the upper floors from a tier of loading-doors, which is surmounted by a hoist-house at the top. Communication between floors may have been provided either by an outside stair or by loft-ladders, as at present. On the ground floor, in addition to the large opening in the W. gable, there were originally external doorways at the centre of each compartment in the S. wall, and one towards the western end of the eastern compartment in the N. wall. These doorways, which still survive in the eastern compartment, further exemplify the extent to which cast-iron was exploited, their external jambs and heads being constructed of this material. The former consist of 7 in. by 8 in. angles, cast complete with crook hinges, and the latter are cast-iron plates 2 in. thick which extend the full thickness of the wall and project externally as hood-moulds. Similarly, all the windows are built with cast-iron glazing-bars set in timber sub-frames.

The external appearance of the building, which is frank and utilitarian in character, derives mainly from the practical and structural considerations already described. Its flat façades of brick (Pl. 153 B), built in English garden-bond above a stone plinth, 2 ft. 6 in. high, have a regular fenestration, and the W. gable is symmetrical. The S. elevation, however, is interrupted at the centre by the tier of hoisting-doors (*supra*), and both N. and S. elevations have their fenestration varied by the high windows of the machine hall and the square door-openings; the last bay on the N. side of the machine hall does, in fact, omit the window altogether—presumably because of the engine house that formerly stood outside the building at this point. The round brick-arched windows, with their small panes of glass, are pleasing features, as is also the regular pattern of moulded tie-irons that extends across the façade at upper-floor level. Perhaps the most striking feature, however, before it was blocked, was the wide semicircular opening in the W. gable, checked and hinged to receive double doors, and strongly built with rybats and stepped voussoirs of dressed stone.

880824 NS 88 SE 23 March 1960

266. Old Houses, Grangemouth Basin. The Forth and Clyde Canal (No. 552) was begun in 1768 and was opened for traffic in 1790. Grangemouth was founded at its eastern terminal in 1777, and the block of streets lying SE. of the basin exemplifies contemporary town-planning. Apart, however, from its gridiron lay-out and its historical connection with the Canal, this block possesses little interest, as the houses belong to a type which was in common construction at the time and can be matched in great numbers both in this county and elsewhere. They are, moreover, mean examples of their type, and many or most of them have been altered—for example, by the insertion of modern shop-fronts. The original aspect of the block as a whole has been further disguised by a number of incongruous new buildings. What may once have been a house of some pretensions is the one at the corner of South Basin and South Bridge Streets; Numbers 4 and 7 South Basin Street have their front doors flanked by pillars.

Some of the buildings on the NW. side of the basin seem to have formed part of the same original plan, but they are even less noteworthy than the rest.

9282 NS 98 SW 9 December 1952

267. Laurieston Village. The site of Laurieston was feued out in 1756 by Francis, 6th Lord Napier,[1] and the old part of the village is interesting both as an early example of a planned urban settlement[2] and also on account of the early industrial housing that still survives there. The core of the village is Mary's Square, which is pierced from E. to W. by Mary's Street, originally Middle Raw,[3] now forming part of the Edinburgh-Falkirk highway (A 9), and from N. to S. by Boyd Street. Parallel to Mary's Street on the S. is James's Street (South Back Raw), while on the N. Grahamsdyke Street (North Back Raw) follows the converging line of the Antonine Wall[4] and coalesces with Mary's Street at the W. end of the village. Examples of houses which are presumably original and seem to have been comparatively little altered, externally at least, can be seen to good advantage in James's Street; they are one-storeyed buildings with a central door and two windows, or a door and a single window, fronting on the street, each unit being divided internally into a front and a back room. The windows have crooks for external shutters and many of the roofs are tiled. Many of these houses were formerly inhabited by nail-makers.[5] Similar to these are four cottages at the extreme W. end of Mary's Street; but the two-storeyed house with a forestair standing opposite, and the one with roll skewputs at the W. end of Grahamsdyke Street, may probably be rather later than the one-storeyed "raws". The only other building worthy of mention is the church, built in 1788,[6] apparently as a meeting-house for the Macmillanites[7]; this is a plain structure of freestone rubble with backset dressings, its N. end, on James's Street, having an advanced and pedimented central portion topped by a bell-cote and flanked by tall, round-headed windows. The entrance, situated in this advanced portion, is square-headed, and above it there is a blank panel for an inscription. There

---

[1] *N.S.A.*, viii (Stirlingshire), 24.
[2] Cf. Newcastleton, feued in 1793 (*Inventory of Roxburghshire*, No. 71).
[3] This and the other original street-names are given by the *Falkirk Sentinel*, 11th June 1954.
[4] *R.W.S.*, 120.
[5] *Falkirk Sentinel, loc. cit.*
[6] *N.S.A., loc. cit.*
[7] *Stat. Acct.*, xix (1797), 75.

are three square-headed windows in each side-wall. The roof is gabled on the N. and hipped on the other three sides.

9079, 9179 NS 97 NW 29 June 1955

268. Polmont Village. Though the portion of the village that is traversed by the Edinburgh-Falkirk highway is known as the "Newtown of Polmont", and is therefore presumably of later date than that lying at and near the road-junction N. of the old church, the houses in both are of very similar style and probably date in the main from or after the turn of the 18th and 19th centuries. The schoolhouse, for example, which is described separately under No. 269, is dated 1789. What seem to be the oldest houses in the "Newtown" are single-storeyed cottages of about 30 ft. frontage, in many cases joined up in "raws"; they are built of large rubble, generally without backset dressings, and have a central door flanked on either side by a single window. There has been much alteration everywhere.

Little Kerse Cottage, which stands at the NE. extremity of the village on the road to Bo'ness, deserves individual mention for the sake of its external shutters (Pl. 149 c). Crooks for such shutters are a very common feature of small houses and cottages built in the later 18th and earlier 19th centuries, but only here and at Buckieburn Church (No. 152) have the shutters themselves actually been found *in situ*. In other respects the cottage does not differ from the normal type. It has a central door opening on a small lobby, from which access is obtained to a single room on the right and two intercommunicating rooms, front and back, on the left. Beyond these two rooms there is a small outshot, with both internal and external access.

9378, 9379 NS 97 NW 9 May 1958

269. Schoolhouse, Polmont. This schoolhouse, which stands beside the school building nearly opposite the new parish church, deserves mention as an example of a late 18th-century dwelling which is not only precisely dated (1789) but is also virtually intact. The alterations consist of an addition on its E. side, the opening of two doorways to give access to this, and the renewal of the roof and of the fireplaces. When the addition is discounted there remains the structure shown in Fig. 123, an oblong block measuring 36 ft. 3 in. from N. to S. by 20 ft. transversely over walls 2 ft. 3 in. thick, with a wing 11 ft. 8 in. wide projecting 7 ft. 11 in. from its W. face. The walls are faced with well-built squared rubble and the gables finish in tabling; the wing has a hipped roof and its walls are slightly thinner than those of the main block. The appearance of the whole is plain (Pl. 149 F). The entrance, which is centred in the front of the wing, bears the date 1789 on its lintel, and leads, through a vestibule, into an inner lobby off which a room opens to right and left. From the back of the lobby, where a doorway now opens into the addition, access is also obtained to an original stone stair with iron balusters and a mahogany handrail. The first floor contains two rooms

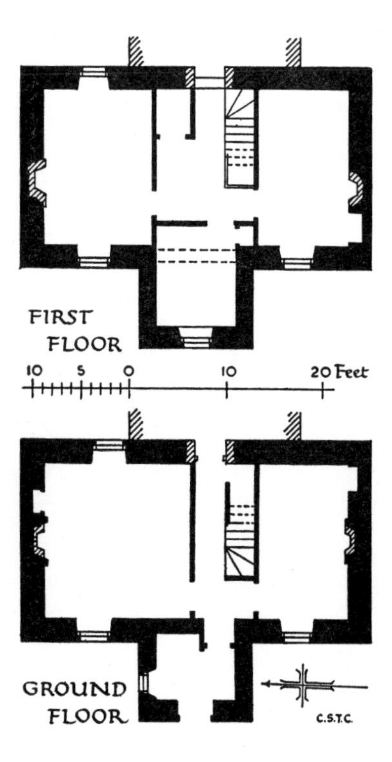

Fig. 123. Schoolhouse, Polmont (No. 269)

corresponding in position with those on the ground floor, together with a smaller room in the wing; this small room, being larger than the vestibule below, encroaches upon the main block and has, in its ceiling, an arched support in line with the W. wall of the latter. All the partitions are original, and in the ground-floor rooms the original mantelpieces and stone fireplace-jambs have been retained.

937792 NS 97 NW ("Sch.") 10 March 1953

270. The Manse, Polmont. The manse, known today as the North Manse, stands some 180 yds. SW. of the parish church. It was built about 1735, *i.e.* a few years after the old parish church (No. 142),[1] but it has been added to on N., W. and E., with the result that only on the S. side can an idea of its original appearance be obtained (Pl. 150 B). As first constructed, it was evidently a plain oblong building of two main storeys and an attic, measuring about 48 ft. by 25 ft. 6 in. over walls 2 ft. 8 in. thick, and having a central doorway and two windows on the ground floor with three windows

[1] *Stat. Acct.*, iii (1792), 346.

symmetrically disposed above. The attics are lit by dormers facing N. and skylights, the E. attic having a small window in the gable as well. The walls are harled, quoins and margins being backset, and the entrance has a fine rusticated architrave. Internal features to be noted are the roomy inner hall, which rises through all three floors as a stair-well now lighted from above; the stone stair, with ornamental iron balusters and mahogany rail; and part of the built-up arch, segmental and originally 5 ft. wide, of the kitchen fireplace in the E. gable on the ground floor.

936791 NS 97 NW ("Kinneil House")
13 January 1953

271. Slamannan Village. Slamannan contains very little of architectural interest, as most of the houses are small, featureless buildings of one or two storeys dating, at earliest, from the beginning of the 19th century. Two, which show rather more character, are worthy of record. (i) Numbers 7, 8, 9 and 10 High Street. These four one-storeyed dwellings have been designed as a block, the outermost two (Numbers 7 and 10) being smaller and lower than the central pair, to which they form wings, having hipped roofs which rise to abut on the gables of Numbers 8 and 9. They are built of squared rubble brought to courses, with V-jointed dressings at voids and quoins. The gables have plain tabling and cavetto-moulded skewputs. The chimneys are ornate. (ii) An unnumbered house in Main Street, formerly the school-house. This has now been subdivided into two flats, and has an outside stair of brick, but it was originally a single dwelling with an inside stair. It measures 34 ft. 7 in. by 18 ft. 9 in. externally; on the ground floor there is a central door with a window, now enlarged, on either side of it, and on the first floor three windows, symmetrically arranged. The door has a lintel bearing the date and initials 17 D A M S 76 divided by a false keystone. The masonry is random rubble with dressed stones at quoins and voids; there is a moulded eaves-course, and the gables show plain tabling with a large roll skewput at each corner.

8573 NS 87 SE 20 March 1953

272. Larbert Village. Apart from the parish church and the old manse, which are described individually (Nos. 146 and 273), Larbert contains virtually nothing of architectural interest. The double dwelling of two storeys numbered 12 and 14 Denny Road shows the backset margins, returned eaves-courses and decorated roll skewputs that were fashionable about the turn of the 18th and 19th centuries; and two single-storey houses which adjoin the N. end of the Red Lion Hotel, Stirling Road, may likewise date from the 18th century. Otherwise the majority of the houses are Victorian, with a few remnants of small buildings of the early 19th century.

856822 (centre) NS 88 SE 17 August 1954

273. The Old Manse, Larbert. This building (Pl. 150 A) stands about 100 yds. W. of the cross-roads in the centre of Larbert, with its back to the Denny road. Its position was thus convenient for access to the old church, which stood in the graveyard just S. of the end of the garden (p. 156). It was built in 1635 (*infra*), and when visited by the Commission's officers in 1955 largely preserved its original arrangements apart from the construction of a new stair by the then owner, the breaking out of an entrance at the stairfoot, and the blocking of some of the windows. Since 1955 a new owner has reconditioned and re-roofed the house for preservation, modifying the internal arrangements to suit 20th-century conditions, and in so doing has uncovered some original features which had previously been obscured by harling. The present description and plan represent the building as it was in 1955.

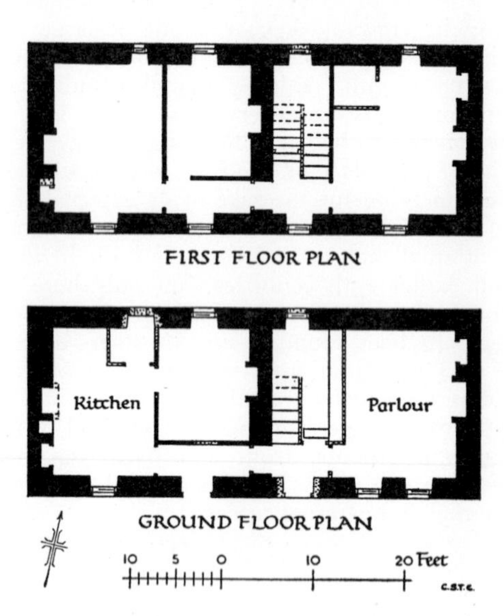

Fig. 124. The Old Manse, Larbert (No. 273)

The house is oblong on plan (Fig. 124), its major axis lying approximately E. and W. It is 49 ft. 6 in. long by 20 ft. over all, the gables being 2 ft. 10 in. and the lateral walls 2 ft. 2 in. thick. It contains two storeys and a garret. The masonry is rubble, the wall-heads finish in a cavetto-moulded eaves-course, and the gables are crow-stepped and end in ogival-faced skewputs. With the exception of a small inserted window, now blocked up, in the N. wall of the kitchen and the new door at the stairfoot, which was converted from a window, all the voids are original. The windows have plain-dressed margins with chamfered arrises, and the original entrance is wrought with a bead moulding. This entrance opens upon a passage which gives access to the rooms and also to the stair; the latter, though renewed (*supra*), is in the position of the original stair and the original flagged floor remains in the cellar behind it. The ground-floor rooms comprise a kitchen at the W. end and a parlour at the E. end, with the staircase and a smaller room between them, the last now entered from the kitchen. This arrangement is repeated in the bedroom accommodation on the first floor. All the rooms on these floors were originally lit by windows in the lateral walls; they are also provided with fireplaces, the one in the kitchen having plain jambs corbelled at the top to carry the lintel while the others are wrought with roll-and-hollow mouldings. There is a press in the end apartments on both floors. The garret has a window in each gable and a fireplace in the E. one. The lintel of the second window from the NW. corner on the first floor bears an inscription which records the date of construction. The lettering is clumsily spaced, the initials M / A N, for Mr. Alexander Norie, appearing on the sinister part of the stone and the date 1635 in the lower dexter corner; in addition the word BUILT, in smaller letters, appears in the upper line before the M. The Rev. Alexander Norie was presented in 1619.[1] Another inscribed stone, shown by its chamfering to have been the lintel of a small window, has been inserted in the S. front below the sill of the second window from the SE. corner on the first floor. The inscription reads 1684 / REPAIRED A M, the initials being those of the Rev. Archibald Muschet, who came to Larbert in 1662.[2]

WELL. The proprietor stated that there was a stone-lined well, 22 ft. in depth, about 15 ft. S. of the house at a point midway between the original entrance and the window of the kitchen.

855822 NS 88 SE 19 August 1955

274. Denny Town. Of the houses in Denny that are neither frankly Victorian nor disguised by reconstruction in the Victorian era, a few may be attributed to the later 18th century and the rest to the beginning of the 19th. A sample of the latter class is provided by the block comprising Numbers 3 and 5 Broad Street. The street façade of this shows, on the ground floor, two doors and three windows symmetrically arranged with eight pilasters; on the first floor three windows; and in the attic two large dormers, probably insertions. There is a moulded eaves-course and the gables finish in plain skews. A tablet above the central window on the first floor bears the date 1812 in Roman figures. Much of the SE. part of Stirling Street closely resembles this block, and may consequently be supposed to have been built at about the same time. Number 1 Broad Street, however, which adjoins it, is smaller and older, and probably dates from the end of the 18th century (Pl. 149 E); though now greatly altered, and provided with modern shop-windows, it preserves the roll skewputs and three first-floor windows of the original arrangement. With it may be classed an unnumbered block, also on the N. side of Broad Street but about 100 yds. to the W. This contains two houses, each with a door and two windows on the ground floor, while the W. one has two and the E. one three windows on the first floor. The margins of openings are backset, the walls are harled, and the gables finish in plain tabling with roll skewputs to the front and in crow-steps to the back. There is a cavetto eaves-course. A few other houses in the town likewise bear roll skewputs, and these are no doubt of approximately the same age as the buildings last mentioned above.

Another 18th-century house which deserves mention is Burnfoot, 14 West Boreland Road. This was originally a small dwelling of two storeys, with three rooms on each floor, but is now divided into two flats. The masonry is rubble, harl-pointed. The street façade has a central door with a moulded and lugged architrave, a window on either side and three others, symmetrically arranged, on the first floor, and a central gablet above topped by a chimney. Quoins and margins of voids are backset, and the three windows show narrow chamfers on their arrises. At the wall-head there is a moulded eaves-course with a band below it. The gables, which have chimneys at their heads, finish in plain tabling with moulded skewputs. The upper floor is reached by a stone newel-stair housed in a semicircular outshot at the back. There is a back entrance at the foot of the stair.

812827 (centre) NS 88 SW 1 July 1954

275. Dennyloanhead Village. Two buildings in Dennyloanhead deserve to be noted, the church, which is described separately under No. 151, and the Crown Hotel. Externally the latter, which stands at the junction of the roads from Falkirk and Denny, is an attractive example of a small house of the later 18th century, but internally it has been greatly altered. The façade (Pl. 149 D) shows a central entrance, reached by four stone steps with bent iron handrails, and a window on either side. Three windows are placed symmetrically on the first floor, with ornamental iron brackets in front of them. The slate roof shows no attic-windows, as the attics are lit from behind. The walls are of squared rubble brought to courses, with backset dressings and a moulded eaves-course returned at the gables; the gables finish in plain tabling, and each carries a substantial chimney-stack. The only interesting internal feature is the stair, which, instead of being of continuous newel-construction from bottom to top and housed in the usual rounded projection at the back of the building, rises in an internal staircase, counterclockwise, from the ground to the first floor, and continues thence, clockwise, in an upper staircase set somewhat to one side of the top of the lower one.

Mention may also be made of the remains, much altered and heavily damaged, of an old dwelling-house now incorporated in a range of sheds immediately W. of the church. One of the windows, which has evidently been converted from a door, shows wide chamfers and has a lintel bearing the date 1722 divided by the initials W D and I B.

809800 NS 88 SW 7 May 1954

[1] *Fasti*, iv, 310.
[2] *Ibid.*

276. Lennoxtown. Lennoxtown, or the Newtown of Campsie, was "new" in 1795,[1] and appears to have owed its origin mainly to the introduction into the district of the calico-printing industry—the Kincaid printfield having been started in 1785 and the Lennox-mill, or Westerfield, printfield in 1786.[2] Apart from the parish church, which is described separately under No. 156, the village contains little of architectural interest, and only the following buildings seem to deserve mention.

NUMBERS 1-4, WHITEFIELD. This block and its neighbour (*infra*) exemplify the industrial housing of 1795, the date of their building as recorded on panels set in their street fronts, and as such may be compared with similar structures at Fintry (No. 282); like these latter, however, they were reconstructed in the 20th century and much of their original character has consequently been lost. The block containing Numbers 1 to 4 measures 75 ft. by 20 ft. 4 in. The street-door opens on a small lobby, from which a straight stair rises to a landing lit by the central front window; at either end of this lobby a door leads into an apartment of two main rooms and a smaller bed-closet, all intercommunicating. Each of the main rooms occupies the whole width of the building. The two ground-floor apartments are entered at the back, each by its own door; these are similar to the first-floor apartments but are provided with larders. The panel over the street-entrance, though dating from the reconstruction, contains an original human head rudely carved in stone with the date 1795 on the neck.

NUMBERS 5-8, WHITEFIELD. The neighbouring block is somewhat smaller but is arranged on the same principle, though in this case the methods of access are reversed—ground-floor apartments, with their individual doors, opening on to the street and the entrance to the first-floor ones being at the back. In the panel on the front of this block there is set a small original iron plaque showing two men trying to pull a cow in opposite directions while a lawyer milks it; below is the legend "The Law Suit".

NUMBERS 48 AND 50, CROSSHILL STREET. This house may be mentioned for the sake of its Classical façade, unexpected, as here, in a small block of industrial apartments. The twin entrances are set under a simple dentilated pediment with triglyphs on the lintel, the frontage is flanked by flat pilasters, and there is a dentilated eaves-course. At the N. end of the ground floor filled-up doorways appear, opposed in the front and back walls. Internally there are now four apartments, two on each floor, the upper ones being approached by recent outside stairs at the back; they formerly contained box-beds, but these have been removed in the course of a reconstruction. The date 1821 on a panel on the opposite side of the street suggests that this house too may have been built at about the same time.

KALI NAIL WORKS. Apart from architectural remains, an interesting industrial relic is to be seen in the works of Messrs. J. and W. Somerville, Ltd. This is a so-called "oliver", a specialised type of work-bench formerly used in the making, by hand, of nails and other small objects formed from iron rods.[3] The oliver[4] (Pl. 155) is placed close to the forge, so that the smith, standing between them, can reach either simply by turning about. It comprises a massive cubical pedestal, with a pair of solid wooden uprights which support two transverse iron bars. To each bar there is fixed a hammer, which falls or rises as the bar is rotated through part of a circle. The hammers are depressed by a treadle, and raised by the upward pull of springy larch-poles fastened to the wall of the smithy. On the bench, below the hammers, there rests an iron block containing twelve sockets to receive the small specialised anvils ("jacks") that are required for different products.

6277, 6278 NS 67 NW 15 April 1958

277. Drymen Village. The village of Drymen is situated on the old road from Stirling to Dumbarton (No. 510) and was also a natural meeting-place for routes leading up the Endrick and Blane Waters, along the NE. side of Loch Lomond, and over the hill to Gartmore. At its centre there is a village green flanked on its W. side by a range of buildings none of which can be dated, in their present form, to before about 1800. "The Winnock", in a phase preceding the present, was evidently a row of cottages, but that these replaced earlier work is shown by the discovery, made during reconstruction, of a stone dated 1702 which had been used as building-material. It has now been reset in one of the downstairs rooms. The inn at the NE. corner of the green, though modernised, may very well have originated in the 18th century.

474886 NS 48 NE 3 October 1952

278. Killearn Village. In addition to the Old Manse and the converted cottage beside it, a few houses in the village of Killearn deserve a short notice.

The old cottages fronting on The Square, the street between the old church (No. 161) and the Black Bull Hotel, were recently modernised by the Killearn Trust. Mr. G. Innes, chairman of the Trust, informed the Commission's officer that three original but-and-ben houses had here been rebuilt as two, their original external appearance being preserved as far as possible, and also their fireplaces with aumbries alongside. He also explained that, in the original arrangement, each room had had two double box-beds set against the back

[1] *Stat. Acct.*, xv (1795), 355.

[2] *Ibid.*, 354. See also Cameron, J., *Calico Printing in Campsie*, 8, 12; this work was published as part of the same author's *Parish of Campsie*, but separately paged.

[3] The Commissioners are indebted to Mr. J. B. Webster, the Managing Director, for information and facilities given to their investigating staff, and particularly for the opportunity of interviewing Mr. J. Squair, the last of the "cottage" nail-makers, and of seeing him demonstrate the use of the oliver and forge.

[4] A fuller description is given in *Scottish Studies*, v (1961), 117 ff.

wall, and that it was, in fact, this arrangement of the beds that had governed the length of the houses.

Knowehead, which stands at the lower end of the row of cottages just described and is dated 1810, was likewise modernised and preserved by the Killearn Trust, additional dormer windows having been added.

The White Horse Inn, in the upper part of the village, still provides a fair example of a small inn of the late 18th or early 19th century. The Toll House opposite dates only from the middle of the 19th century, but is of interest as being a relic of a bygone system. It once had rising toll-bars, and a tariff of tolls which has suffered malicious obliteration.

The church of 1826,[1] now disused, is an uninteresting building which closely resembles the contemporary church at Fintry (No. 169).

523859 (centre) NS 58 NW 4 September 1952

279. The Buchanan Monument, Killearn. This monument (Pl. 51 A), which dominates the village from a position just N. of the Black Bull Hotel, was set up in 1788[2] in honour of the scholar and historian George Buchanan, who was born at Moss, near Killearn, in 1506. It was designed by James Craig, the Edinburgh architect, and was carried out by William Gray, mason in Camlachie.[3] The monument is an obelisk of grey sandstone ashlar, the material for which was quarried near the village, and stands to a total height of 103 ft. on a base 19 ft. square. As is shown by an inscription, it was repaired in 1850. The NE. face bears the name GEORGE BUCHANAN, with the dates of his lifetime 1506-1582; the inscription, which is on the NW. face, reads MEMORIAE AETERNAE / GEORGII BUCHANANI / VIRI / INTER FORTES FORTIS / INTER DOCTOS DOCTI / INTER SAPIENTES SAPIENTISSIMI / QUI TENAX PROPOSITI / IMPIORUM SACERDOTUM MINAS RIDENS / TYRANNORUM SAEVORUM MINAS SPERNENS / PURUM NUMINIS CULTUM / ATQUE / JURA HUMANI GENERIS / A PESSIMA SUPERSTITIONE ATQUE AB INFIMA SERVITUTE / IMPERTERRITUS VINDICAVIT / HOC MONUMENTUM / DOMUM PATERNAM ET NATALIA RURA PROSPECTANS / SUMPTIBUS ET PIETATE POPULARIUM / OLIM EXSTRUCTUM / AETAS POSTERA / REFICIENDUM CURAVIT / ANNO CHRISTI D. N. / MDCCCL. ("This monument, overlooking his father's house and his native countryside, was set up in past days at the charges and by the piety of the indwellers to the everlasting memory of George Buchanan, brave among the brave, learned among the learned, and most wise among the wise; who, holding fast to his purpose, deriding the threats of impious priests and despising those of savage tyrants, fearlessly defended pure spiritual worship and the laws of the human race against the vilest superstition and the basest servitude. A later age had the work repaired in the year of Christ, Our Lord, 1850.")

522859 NS 58 NW 1 September 1952

280. Balfron Village. The modern village of Balfron lies S. of the parish church and "Clachan" (Nos. 167, 281), stretching down the hill towards the Endrick Water. It grew up from 1790 onwards after the building of a cotton-spinning mill at Ballindalloch[4], and the institution of a printfield and bleachfield on the opposite side of the Endrick.[5] Many examples of the small houses belonging to this period can be seen in the village street, but they are too much altered internally to merit detailed description. A fully comparable example of contemporary industrial housing, in the Newtown of Fintry, is given under No. 282 (*q.v.*). A house of some individual character, named Rockbrae, is to be seen on the E. side of Buchanan Street, near the N. end of the village, and this seems to perpetuate the late 18th-century style better than the rest of the older houses. It measures 36 ft. 9 in. in length by 20 ft. 6 in. in breadth and, as seen from the street (Pl. 148 F), it appears to be three-storeyed, with a two-way forestair of stone rising to an entrance on the first floor, and four windows symmetrically placed; actually, however, the accommodation in the basement is merely cellarage, and only extends to about one-third of the length of the house, while the second floor is an attic. The walls are harled, but the windows, which are defined by marginal dressing, are not backset. The cellarage has had to be cut for the most part out of the living rock; it is entered by a door placed under the N. windows in the upper storeys, and is lit by a small window beside the door. The entrance, which has a moulded architrave, leads into a lobby which gives access to a room on either side, now modernised, and to a straight flight of wooden stairs which rises to the attic, also containing two rooms. The roof is modern, as is also a back door broken out at first-floor level on the steep slope behind.

5488 NS 58 NW 30 October 1952

281. The Clachan of Balfron. The original village of Balfron was in the vicinity of the parish church (No. 167), and the houses that now represent it are known as "The Clachan". None of these buildings is now in its original condition, but Orchardfield, which stands just S. of the approach to the church, deserves to be mentioned as a sample of good domestic building dating, presumably, from the late 18th century.

This house consists of an oblong, two-storeyed block with a single-storeyed addition, apparently of later date, built against its SW. gable (Fig. 125). The older portion measures 39 ft. 8 in. by 22 ft. 5 in., and the addition, which runs to the full width of the house, increases its length by 16 ft. 3 in. Originally the house contained two

---

[1] *N.S.A.*, viii (Stirlingshire), 66.
[2] *Stat. Acct.*, xvi (1795), 106 f.
[3] *Strathblane*, 161; see also Buchanan, G., *The History of Scotland*, tr. Aikman, J. (1827), i, xlviii f.
[4] *Stat. Acct.*, xvii (1796), 532; see also *N.S.A.*, viii (Stirlingshire), 298, and *Strathendrick*, 263.
[5] *Stat. Acct.*, *loc. cit.*

rooms on each floor, divided by a lobby on the lower floor and by a bed-closet on the upper; but a comparatively recent alteration has adapted it to accommodate four tenants, by the subdivision of the rooms and the insertion of extra fireplaces.[1] The walls have likewise been re-harled and the roof renewed, though the moulded eaves-courses have been retained. The gables now show no tabling. The entrance, which is in the middle of the SE. side, opens into the lobby from a garden. At the inner end of the lobby there is a geometric stone stair with

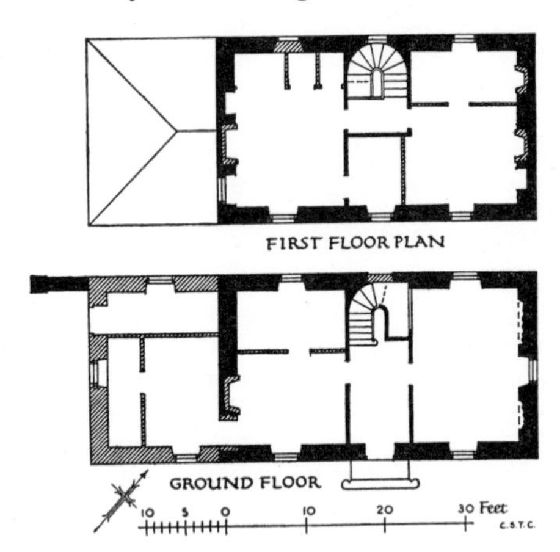

Fig. 125. Orchardfield, Clachan of Balfron (No. 281)

steps moulded at their edges, plain iron balusters and a mahogany handrail. The windows are symmetrically placed and have freestone dressings; below the staircase window a depression in the harling two inches deep may or may not mark the position of a closed-up back-door. The addition, originally separate from the house, has been put into connection with it by means of a doorway broken through the SW. gable. Like the house it has been partitioned off into apartments, three in number.

The original piers of the entrance through the garden wall, chamfered and with moulded cornices and coping, can be seen near the W. corner of the addition; a low divisional wall, with piers of similar type at its ends and on either side of a central opening, describes an arc across the garden in front of the SE. face of the house.

The only other house that calls for notice is the Old Manse, built in 1789,[2] which stands 500 yds. W. of the Clachan cross-roads. Its S. façade (Pl. 151 B), if dissociated from the extensive additions not shown in the illustration, can be regarded as a good example of the same type of building as has been described above at Orchardfield.

547892 (centre) NS 58 NW 14 May 1953

282. Fintry Village. Of the original village of Fintry, which was near the church (No. 169), there now remains only the old manse, the Clachan Inn, and what was once Gonachan schoolhouse. Of these, the two last are modernised out of recognition, while the first (Pl. 151 A), which was built in 1732 and must once have been a good example of its period, has suffered severely from more than a century's use as an outhouse and offices. The entrance, which carries the date of construction on its lintel, and the lower windows of the S. front have been built up, but the arrangement of the windows, the crow-steps, the skewputs and the eaves-course are all thoroughly characteristic. The wings, with their plain tabling, are later additions. The existing manse, which stands just W. of its predecessor, was "new" in 1841[3] and is an undistinguished structure measuring 40 ft. 6 in. by 34 ft. 2 in. The walls are harled, and on the W. there is a regular façade showing a central entrance and five windows symmetrically arranged; those that flank the entrance have moulded architraves, but the rest, and those in the other walls, have backset margins and the quoins are also backset. The staircase window in the E. wall has been partly covered by the roof of a single-storeyed addition.

The Newtown of Fintry, which lies a mile to the W., dates from the foundation of a cotton-spinning mill by Mr. Peter Spiers of Culcreuch at the end of the 18th century.[4] In 1794 sites were being feued for workers' houses along the S. side of the street, with garden ground opposite on the bank of the river[5]; a block of four dwellings, of the kind described in the *Statistical Account of Scotland*, is illustrated in Pl. 149 B. In each half of the block, which has a frontage of 21 ft. 3 in. on the street and is 28 ft. 3 in. deep, a ground-floor entrance opens from the street into a small lobby, and from this access is obtained to a single front room and, through this room, to two smaller rooms at the back. The dwellings on the upper floor are served by an outside stair at the back of the house; each of these contains a lobby and one room at the back and two rooms at the front. Above are garrets accessible by ladders from the first-floor dwellings. Mention may also be made of a pair of houses facing the bridge (Pl. 149 A); they show the normal arrangement of a central door and five windows, and the one to the W. has V-jointed quoins.

The cotton mill stood on the E. side of the road from Fintry to Kippen (B 822), some 500 yds. N. of the bridge. Not proving a commercial success, it fell into ruin before the end of the 19th century[6] and its remains are now of little architectural interest. The original plan has been obscured, and only one of the buildings still retains its roof; the N. and S. fronts of this structure are faced in ashlar, and its fenestration is simple and regular. The mill-lade, where it passes the site, is well constructed in masonry.

6186, 6187, 6286 NS 68 NW 9 December 1959

[1] The NE. room on the ground floor could not be inspected, but it is believed to be partitioned in the same way as the room above.
[2] *Stat. Acct.*, xvii (1796), 535.
[3] *N.S.A.*, viii (Stirlingshire), 46.
[4] *Strathendrick*, 261.
[5] *Stat. Acct.*, xi (1794), 377.
[6] *Strathendrick, loc. cit.*

283. Buchlyvie Village. There is little of architectural interest in the village of Buchlyvie, as the small houses in the main street seem to be undistinguished examples of work of the late 18th and early 19th centuries, all greatly modernised. On the strength of the rounded arrises of its door and the wide chamfers at its windows, the cottage immediately E. of the Red Lion Inn might perhaps be dated to the later 17th century.

5793 NS 59 SE 5 September 1952

284. Kippen Village. Apart from Taylor's Building, described separately under No. 285, there is little of real architectural interest in Kippen. Most of the earlier houses appear to date from the middle or later part of the 18th century, but they have been so much modernised that they no longer provide true samples of the work of their period. This applies in particular to the old manse, which, though a fine building, has been altered in appearance by improvements; and to some cottages at Cauldhame, on the SW. outskirts of the village, which have been very attractively restored. The houses most worthy of notice are all, like No. 285, in the narrow street W. of the church (No. 171), *e.g.* the former Black Bull Inn, now restored, with rolled skewputs; the smithy, with an outshot to the N. which bears the inscription 17 I K A H 63 on its door-lintel; and a crow-stepped house facing the war-memorial, together with the old bakehouse which adjoins it on the N. In the main street, SW. of the post-office, there can be seen a cottage with a doorway-lintel representing a flat arch with a large ornamental keystone; this lintel is so much too large for the cottage in question as to suggest that it is in secondary use, and a comparison with some of the lintels of neighbouring churches (Nos. 161, 168, 170) suggests further that it may have come from the old parish church (No. 171), having perhaps been placed there during the reconstruction of 1737[1]—a date which would suit its style. The old Free Church, probably built soon after 1843, is now unrecognisable as such, as it has been converted into dwellings and the original levels altered.

651948 (centre) NS 69 SE 21 October 1952

285. Taylor's Building, Kippen. This house stands on the SW. side of the lane known as the Old Glasgow Road, some 80 yds. below its junction with the main street of Kippen village. It is said locally to take its name from its builder and first owner, believed to have been a building contractor, and its style suggests a date for its construction before the middle of the 18th century. The house is oblong on plan (Fig. 126), measuring 37 ft. by 22 ft. 6 in. over walls just over 2 ft. thick, and contains three storeys and a garret. The façade (Pl. 148 C) has an entrance-doorway in the centre, with lugged architrave, convex frieze and moulded cornice, and a window on either side. The windows in the upper floors are uniformly placed above the ground-floor openings; all have backset margins. The walls are harled; the quoins, which are only present in front, are V-channelled; the wall-head has a moulded eaves-course; and the gables finish

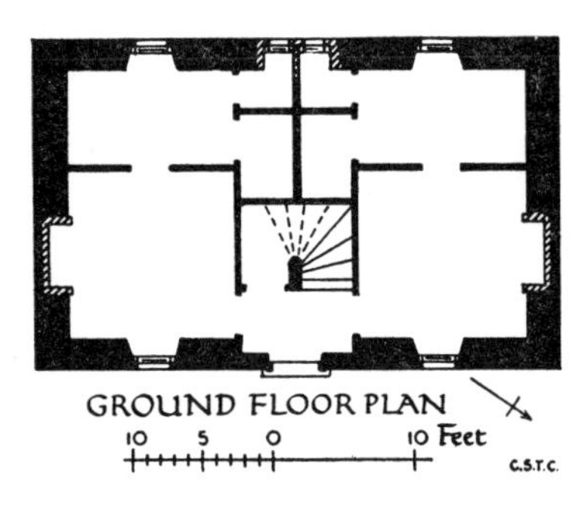

Fig. 126. Taylor's Building, Kippen (No. 285)

in tabling with wrought skewputs. The entrance opens into a small lobby, from which a stone stair rises in a rectangular stair-well and swings round a newel; above the first-floor landing the stair is wooden. From either side of the lobby and the landings a door opens into a small self-contained flat, each consisting of a living-room to the front and a smaller bedroom behind; each bedroom has a box-bed recess and a deep cupboard, formed in the mutual partition.[2] The third storey is coomb-ceiled. In the present condition of the house older and newer partitions cannot be distinguished, and it is consequently impossible to determine whether or how far the present internal arrangements are original.

651948 NS 69 SE 21 October 19[illegible]

286. Gargunnock Village. The village of Gargunnock extends for about a third of a mile along the old road from Stirling to Dumbarton (No. 510). It provides a fair sample of the rural housing described on p. 48 as none of the houses seems to date from before the later part of the 18th century, and one semi-ruinous example (Pl. 148 E), which has been built with clay mortar, shows a lintel dated 1722 (initials I F I A), perhaps in secondary use. An unaltered building, consisting of two blocks divided by a pend, was found to contain two houses in either division, the upper floor being reached by a forestair at the back. One of these upper houses, which was entered, proved to contain two rooms. The house next the hotel on the SSE., shown in Pl. 148 D, contained two rooms below and two above, with a straight stair immediately inside the entrance.

7094 NS 79 SW 24 October 1952

[1] *Stat. Acct.*, xviii (1796), 337.
[2] This description and the plan (Fig. 126) are based on an examination of a single unit on the first floor, the remainder not having been available for inspection.

COUNTRY

287. Airthrey Castle. Airthrey Castle was built by Robert Haldane in 1791,[1] to a design by Robert Adam,[2] but was extended on the N. in 1891 by the then proprietor, Donald M. Graham, with the result that nothing of Adam's design is now to be seen on that side. The building is now converted into a hospital.

The S. front (Pl. 201 B), however, is unaltered, and shows the adoption of Romantic elements in a scheme still predominantly Classical. Its central feature is a tower, with a convex front set between broad pilasters, which contains three storeys above a semi-basement. It is approached by a *perron* which contracts from a wide outer end and gives entry to the main floor by a French window. From this central tower lateral ranges swing backwards through a quarter of a circle to connect it with two terminal towers facing E. and W. respectively, both the connecting ranges and the terminal towers being one storey lower than the central tower. The connecting ranges are set back from the faces of the towers, thereby throwing the component blocks into relief; and the whole forms an agreeable symmetrical frontage of plain ashlar masonry, capped at the wall-heads by a battlemented parapet of slight projection borne on a row of miniature corbels. Small dummy bartizans rise from the parapet at the ends of the curved sections of the frontage, and these combine with the battlements, corbel-course and decoration based on mediaeval windows and archer-slits to create the Romantic atmosphere. The windows are regularly set in each floor, the main ones on the ground floor being round-headed and the rest lintelled; all have plain arrises. The wall-face is slightly intaken above the basement windows, a Classically moulded string-course divides the first and second floors, and the sills of the third-floor windows in the central tower are carried along in the form of a plain band. The balustrades of the *perron* are pierced with vesica-shaped openings, and end in circular pedestals each carrying a large shell-ornament.

Five original fireplaces of Adam type still remain in upper rooms.

812967 NS 89 NW 24 October 1952

288. Powis House. Powis House (Pl. 188 A) stands rather more than a mile E. of Causewayhead, between the main roads leading from Bridge of Allan to Dollar and Alloa respectively. It is said to have been built in 1746 or 1747 by Edward Mayne to replace an older house which had been acquired by his uncle, another Edward Mayne, from Stirling of Herbertshire.[3] Despite the addition of a large projecting bay on the S. front and some internal alterations, the building is an interesting example of a Georgian mansion-house.

The main block, which comprises the original house without the eastern additions, is almost square on plan, measuring externally 45 ft. 3 in. from E. to W. by 40 ft. from N. to S., and contains three storeys. The walls are harled, and the quoins and window-dressings, which are backset, are V-jointed in header-and-stretcher bond. A string-course, rebated to a convex section in the middle, returns all round the building and forms the sills of the first-floor windows. The wall-heads finish in a moulded cornice; the roof, which is slated, is low and of hipped type and has a flat top; and the bases of the chimney-stacks have ogival flanks. The entrance is in the middle of the N. front, and comprises a door with a narrow window on either side and a fanlight over all—the whole contained within a semicircular stepped portico consisting of two columns and two pilasters supporting an entablature. The windows above the entrance on both the upper floors are double, but those of the flights to E. and W. are single, as are also those on the other three sides. All have flat-arched lintels. The symmetrical arrangement of the windows is interrupted on the S. side by the addition of a projecting bay which rises to the full height of the building and contains three windows on each floor, the central one on the ground floor being a French window opening into the garden.

The entrance leads direct into a spacious hall from which the several ground-floor rooms open, and at the back of it a scale-and-platt stair, with bottle-nosed steps and an iron baluster, rises to the upper storeys. The stair-well is capped by a cupola, and over the first-floor landing there is a decorated segmental arch. The SW. room on the ground floor, the dining-room, incorporates the bay-window mentioned above; opposite to this it has a side-board recess flanked by two cupboards. On the first floor there is a drawing-room immediately over the dining-room, and in addition three bedrooms each of which has a mantelpiece in the Adam style (Pl. 166 A). The second floor contains four bedrooms and a boxroom.

The range of offices that adjoins the house on the E. appears to be of two different periods, both later than the mansion itself. The stable square (Pl. 189 A), which lies to the NW. of the house, is probably of late 18th- or early 19th-century date. It is a plain and dignified structure, but lacks any particular distinction.

SUNDIAL. A shafted stone sundial stands in the garden about 200 yds. S. of the house. The head bears the incised date 1745, together with a monogram which may represent Edward Mayne of Powis and his wife Janet Henderson.[4]

824955 NS 89 NW 30 April 1958

289. Craigforth House. Craigforth House stands on the NE. side of the hill of the same name, about two miles W. of Stirling, and commands an extensive prospect of the Carse and of the Ochil Hills. In its original form the building is no doubt of late 17th-century or early 18th-century date, but it has been altered from time to time

[1] Fergusson, R. Menzies, *Logie, A Parish History*, ii, 49.
[2] Bolton, A. T., *The Architecture of Robert and James Adam*, i, 132, n. 35.
[3] Fergusson, R. Menzies, *Logie, A Parish History*, ii, 94 ff.
[4] *Ibid.*

and was gutted by fire in 1930, since when it has been completely restored. The shell of the building survived the fire, and some care was taken in rebuilding to preserve the old external appearance of the house, the wall surfaces and window surrounds having been renewed where necessary in cement.

The main building is a rectangular block measuring 76 ft. in length by 42 ft. in breadth over walls which are 3 ft. 4 in. thick, while a later wing has been added on the NW. The main block rises to the height of three storeys and an attic and has a hipped and slated roof. The present treatment of the walls suggests that the house was built in ashlar. The principal façade (Pl. 195 C), which faces NE., is simple and symmetrical in treatment. The entrance-doorway is centrally placed on the ground floor and on either side of it there are three windows, but the addition of a heavy Doric porch has masked the regular spacing of the voids. The first- and second-floor windows are set over the openings below and all have moulded architraves. Those of the first floor are further emphasised by a moulded cornice supported on brackets, each alternate window having in addition a triangular pediment. There is a plain plinth and the walls finish in a moulded eaves-cornice above which there is a blocking-course, raised and corniced in the centre. The SW. façade is similar in treatment to the NE. one.

The interior has been entirely renewed in recent years and adapted for office accommodation, but the two original transverse partitions suggest that, before the rearrangement, the house contained three principal apartments on both ground and first floors.

The house was in the possession of the Callendars of Craigforth and their descendants until the present century, but is now occupied as business premises. An early view of the house is given in Fleming,[1] together with a sketch made about 1900.[2]

774948 NS 79 SE 6 September 1955

290. The Inclosure, Windsor Place, Stirling. This house, now surrounded by the substantial residences erected on the outskirts of Stirling in the latter half of the 19th century, originated, in the middle of the 18th century, as a country mansion standing in its own grounds. The building is two storeys and an attic in height, and was originally T-shaped on plan, having a central entrance-doorway in the NE. façade and a projecting staircase-tower at the rear. There are indications of a screen wall and a courtyard to the NW., but the original disposition has been masked by later additions. The masonry is of harled rubble; there is a cavetto-moulded eaves-course, and the gables finish in plain skewputs. The interior is of no special interest.

792931 NS 79 SE 3 June 1955

291. Laurelhill House, Stirling. Laurelhill House stands in its own grounds on the southern outskirts of Stirling, near the junction of King's Park Road and Park Place. On plan it is a rectangular block lying approximately W. and E.; the principal façade (Pl. 194 C) faces N. and the central portion of the S. façade projects as a semicircular bay. The house is a basement and two storeys in height, and the masonry is of harled rubble with dressed quoins and margins.

The central portion of the N. façade is slightly advanced, and contains on the ground floor the entrance-doorway, which is reached by a stone stair. On either side, a window is centrally placed in each of the flanking bays, the windows being square-headed but set within semicircular recesses which harmonise with the round-headed entrance-doorway. The three first-floor windows are symmetrically disposed over the voids below. A plain band runs across the façade between the basement and the ground floor, and at first-floor level a moulded string-course across the central portion only. The walls of the flanking bays finish in a plain parapet, but the advanced centre rises to a triangular pediment. The roof is hipped. The internal arrangements are conventional, the principal apartments being on the ground floor and the bedrooms above. The entrance-door opens into a hall within which a geometric stair rises to the first floor. Two other rooms face N. and there are three apartments to the S., the central one deriving additional light and warmth from the projecting semicircular bay in which it is set. Many of the rooms on both ground and first floors have fireplaces in the Adam manner, some of wood and others of marble.

The house, which was built about 1806 by James Duthie, a West India merchant, is[3] a typical representative of the late Georgian period. It may be compared, for example, with Parkhill (No. 313).

789924 NS 79 SE 10 June 1955

292. Borrowmeadow. The farmhouse of Borrowmeadow lies within the neck of a broad meander of the River Forth a mile E. of the town of Stirling. Although somewhat altered both within and without, it is a good example of a small, symmetrically planned laird's house of the first half of the 18th century, and has much in common with the substantial residences erected in the burgh of Airth during the same period (cf. No. 251 and Fig. 121).

The building is a simple rectangular block which rises to the height of two storeys and an attic and measures 39 ft. 6 in. by 22 ft. over walls which are 2 ft. in thickness. The masonry is harled rubble, but the quoins and window-margins, which are offset, are of dressed stone. The walls finish in a plain eaves-band, which is continuous with the lintels of the first-floor windows, and

[1] *Castles and Mansions*, 140.
[2] *Ibid.*, 143.
[3] *T.S.N.H.A.S.* (1937-8), 96.

above there is a moulded eaves-course. The gables are crow-stepped and have ogival-moulded skewputs, while the roof, which may originally have been pantiled, is of slate. The entrance-doorway is centrally placed in the S. façade (Pl. 175 B) at ground-floor level, but is masked by a later porch; it has a moulded and lugged architrave, a pulvinated frieze and a moulded cornice. There are two windows on each side of the doorway and a range of five on the first floor; all have chamfered arrises. The single-storey buildings that adjoin each gable, and the dairy that has been added at the NW. angle, are of later date than the house. The internal arrangements are typical of the period. A dog-legged stair occupies a central position within the building, having on either side of it a single large room on both the ground and first floors. The first floor also contains a small apartment in the NW. angle which is reached from the staircase landing, but this room may have been contrived at a later date. Some of the rooms have moulded plaster ceiling-cornices, and the W. room on the first floor retains a moulded stone fireplace of a usual 18th-century type. The stair is of wood and has a moulded newel-post; the treads measure 3 ft. 9 in. in width.

812938 NS 89 SW 23 April 1956

293. Steuarthall. This house (Pl. 163 B) is situated about two miles nearly due E. of Stirling, and stands at the base of a tongue of land enclosed by a narrow meander of the Bannock Burn. Though inhabited until recently, it has now fallen into disrepair and in 1957 was being used for poultry. It is L-shaped on plan (Fig. 127) and consists of a main block averaging 73 ft. 6 in. long by 22 ft. wide, the axis of which lies E. and W., and a kitchen wing of about the same width which projects 18 ft. 6 in. from the E. end of the N. side. To this wing a two-storeyed extension, containing a new kitchen, was added about 1824.[1] In the re-entrant angle there is a stair-tower housing a wheel-stair 4 ft. 6 in. in radius, the lower flight being of stone and the upper one of wood. Externally it has three flat faces, the W.-facing one of which no doubt contained the original main entrance; but this has been superseded by a new main entrance and a one-storeyed vestibule, with a dog-legged stair rising from its W. end, which was added along the N. face of the house probably in 1911.[2] The westernmost part of the main block consists of a tower, which rises to a height of four storeys, while the remainder contains two storeys and an attic and the wing two storeys only. It is clear that some further building once existed W. of the tower, as the S. wall of the main block runs on for 14 ft. in this direction and is broken and patched at its end, the W. wall of the tower is raggedly intaken at first-floor level, and at the base of this wall there is a doorway intended, as is shown by its checks, to open westwards into the vanished structure.

The walls are of rubble, are harled, and finish in an ovolo-moulded eaves-course. On S. and E. there are the remains of a plinth. All the gables are crow-stepped except that of the wing, on which the steps have been replaced by plain tabling. The roofs have been re-slated and the attic windows are insertions. Original windows have rounded arrises except those in the stair-tower, which show edge-roll mouldings. Some of them retain grooves and socket-holes which show that they were

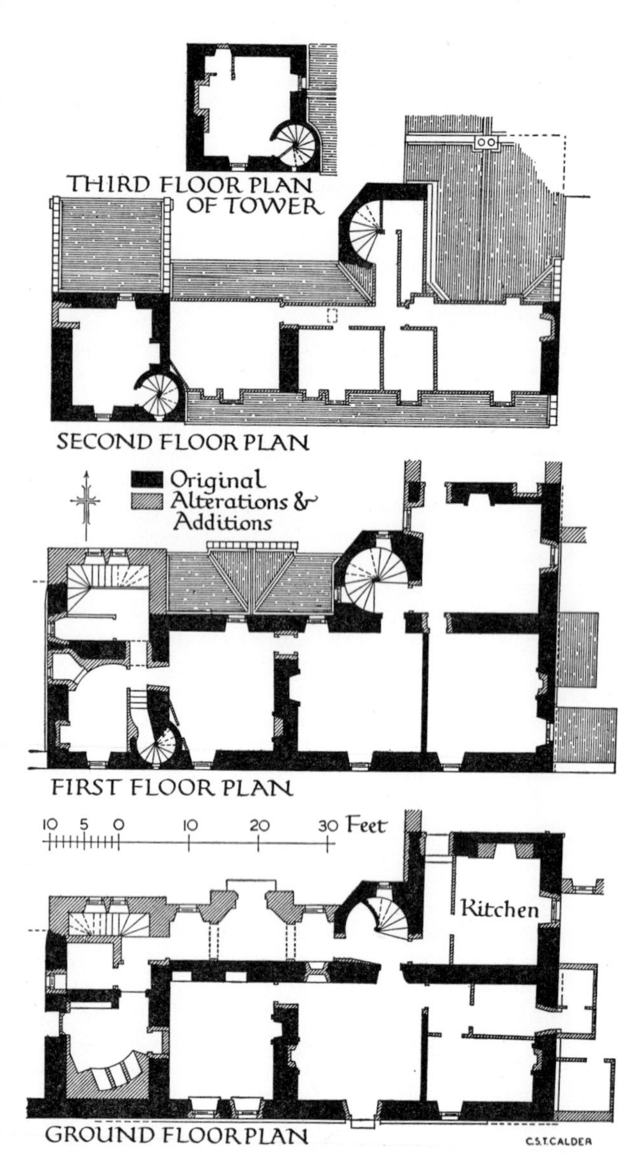

Fig. 127. Steuarthall (No. 293)

half-glazed, with shutters and bars. Windows which have been renewed, inserted or blocked up are indicated accordingly in Fig. 127; a French window in the S. wall

[1] Graham, H., *Parties and Pleasures*, 83.
[2] This date appeared on some internal panelling, removed since the date of visit.

and an entrance to a modern bathroom in the E. gable are both converted windows, and what may have been another window, just W. of the stair-tower, seems to have been turned into two small back-to-back cupboards. The doors have been treated similarly during alterations, some blocked up and others encased in plaster or woodwork, but apart from a few which have evidently been broken through walls, they are mostly in their original positions.

Internally the tower contains one room on each floor. The basement, which has been converted into a wine-cellar, has no fireplace and is windowless and dark; it is entered by an original doorway in its N. side and has, in addition, two blocked-up doorways, in its E. and W. sides respectively. The E. one has a heavy backset margin and is therefore most probably an insertion (*infra*); the W. one, which is original, has already been mentioned as communicating with the vanished building to the W. There is a recess in the N. wall. From the first-floor room there rises a small wheel-stair which provides the only access to the upper storeys. It is carried up to the wall-head in the SE. corner of the tower as a projecting turret supported on the E. by a continuous corbel-course of three members, but on the S. it is flush with the S. face of the tower. The corbelling is thus inside the adjoining room of the main block (*infra*). The room from which it is reached has been contracted by a partition so as to leave a narrow passageway leading to the stair, the doorway and steps at the bottom of which have been altered; this passageway contains four new steps rising to a platt which has evidently been adjusted so as to bring the foot of the stair to a new level. A doorway by the bottom of these steps, which communicates with the adjoining room to the E., seems to be slightly unsymmetrical and may or may not be an original feature (*infra*). The upper rooms of the tower are encroached on by the small wheel-stair; they possess no features of interest.

The internal arrangements in the main block and wing E. of the tower have been little affected by the later subdivision of the ground and attic floors. The rooms are reached through one another, all directly or indirectly from the stair in the re-entrant angle. Originally there were four good-sized rooms of similar arrangement on each of the two lower floors, all being provided with fireplaces. The attic floor is now sub-divided into four rooms opening off a passage, but the two central ones are little better than bed-closets formed within the original E. room. The fireplaces in the E. room on the ground floor and the central room on the first floor show roll-and-hollow mouldings on the jambs; the rest are plain, and all of them have been provided with wooden mantelpieces of late 18th- or early 19th-century date. The old kitchen-fireplace in the N. gable of the wing was originally 8 ft. wide, but has been contracted; its jambs and three-centred arch-head still survive. The fireplace on the first floor, just mentioned, formerly contained a cast-iron fireback now removed by the owner for preservation. This bears in low relief a representation of the Nativity with the initials I H K dividing the date 1533, and was presumably imported from abroad.[1]

In the masonry that blocks the doorway that opens W. out of the tower basement there is an heraldic panel (Pl. 204 D), of a kind which might once have been set above the main entrance. It bears a shield with helm and mantling and, for crest, a man's—presumably a Moor's—head looking towards the dexter. The shield is parted per pale and charged: Dexter, on a bend three buckles, for Stirling, with a crescent in chief for difference; sinister, the head of a fish couped, with an annulet in its mouth, between three cinquefoils, for Hamilton. A label above bears the motto GANG FORDWARD, and below there appear, on a panel, the relief initials A S and A H, for Archibald Stirling, 3rd of Garden, and his second wife Anna, daughter of Sir Alexander Hamilton of Haggs. What seem to be the same initials, dividing the date 1703, are carved in monogram in the tympanum of a round-headed pediment, presumably from an old dormer-window, now set in the W. wall of the later kitchen-extension between the first-floor windows.

Archibald Stirling having married Anna Hamilton in 1686,[2] it is natural to infer that the house was built by him in 1703. So much being granted, a question is bound to arise as to whether the whole of the building is to be attributed to Stirling, or only the portion that lies E. of the tower. This latter exemplifies a plan which was in use at the turn of the 17th and 18th centuries, but the tower might well have been built a century earlier, while some of its features further tend to suggest that it was part of a pre-existing structure. For example, neither the basement nor the first-floor doorway in the E. wall of the tower can be regarded with confidence as original, while the small stair-turret, which is now partly inside the building to the E. of it, would seem more naturally placed as an external feature. There is, however, no trace of structural evidence to support a theory of this kind. No race-bond can be found, at points where defects in the harling permit inspection, between the S. face of the tower and the adjoining work on the E.; the plinth is homogeneous along the whole of the S. face, and parallels to the internal corbelling of the turret are not unknown. It seems necessary therefore to regard the whole structure as a unit, and to attribute its pecularities to the persistence of obsolete fashions.

827929 NS 89 SW 18 June 1957

294. Torbrex Farm. This house, now a roofless shell, stands just outside the N. outskirts of Torbrex village (No. 259). It is rectangular on plan (Fig. 128), measuring 34 ft. 6 in. by 20 ft. over walls 2 ft. 6 in. and 2 ft. thick respectively in gables and sides. Its original height was two storeys and an attic, but it was later raised to three storeys and an attic. The masonry is rubble, containing many small water-worn boulders, and the floors were

[1] The British Museum, to which the owner supplied a description of the fireback, stated that nothing of the kind was produced in Scotland before 1700, and suggested a Flemish origin.

[2] Burke, *Landed Gentry*, ed. 1952.

joisted. Most of the old walling survives except on the S. side, where it has been entirely removed above the first-floor level. The quoins on this side are dressed with a backset margin, but on the N. this feature occurs only in the newer masonry above the old wall-head. On neither the old nor the new wall-head is there an eaves-course. The present W. gable is finished with tabling, as is also the S. rake of the E. gable, but the N. rake at this end is topped with crow-steps which end in an ogival skewput. Below this skewput a stone with the initials I W and B B (*infra*) has been inserted upside down. The walls

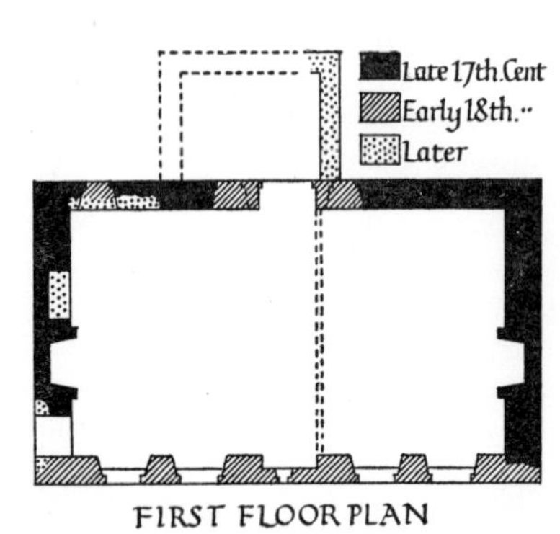

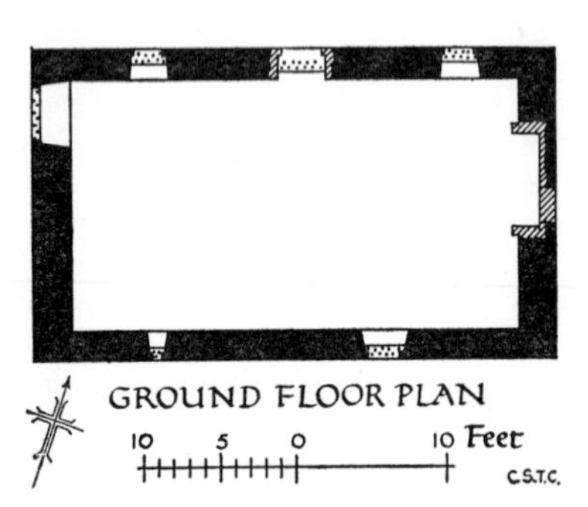

Fig. 128. Torbrex Farm (No. 294)

have been harled externally and plastered internally. Traces of wooden partitions showing in the plaster suggest that each floor was subdivided simply into two large rooms, one in each gable-end, presumably with a stair between them.

The original block appears to date from the 17th, the major alterations from the beginning of the 18th, and a few minor modifications from the 19th century. The ground floor was entered by a doorway, near the NW. end of the W. gable, which was subsequently formed into a window and, still later, blocked up. It may have been replaced by an inserted doorway in the middle of the N. wall, where an opening is now closed up with brickwork but shows a shallow recess. Two small windows in each of the side walls, which once lit this floor, have also been closed up, while one in the E. gable has been put out of use by the insertion of a kitchen fireplace. The openings of both the door and the original windows have chamfered arrises.

The present entrance, which gives access to the principal rooms on the first floor, is situated in the middle of the N. wall and was formerly covered by a later porch. Only the foundations of the E. wall of this porch now remain, and these seem to rest on made-up ground which rises to first-floor level and conceals the outside of the presumed doorway and the ground-floor window to the E. of it. The entrance-doorway, which has square arrises, is an insertion; in the process of its construction an original window on each side of it has been partly destroyed and filled up, as has also a similar window near the NW. corner. In the remodelled S. wall the windows are larger, and are dressed with backset margins and rounded arrises, as are those in the façade of the house at Dalquairn (No. 318) which is dateable to 1711. They are symmetrically arranged, two on each side of a small central window which may have lit the stair-landing. On the second floor, three windows are set symmetrically in the S. wall, and in the attic there is a single window, now blocked up, in each gable. The original attic was lit, at its W. end, by two windows, a single jamb of each of which was incorporated in the masonry of the gable when the house was heightened. No trace now remains of corresponding windows in the E. gable, but it is safe to assume that they existed. All the windows on the floors above the first have plain arrises. The fireplaces are all set in the gable-ends, but only the two on the first floor are original; these are wrought with a roll-and-hollow moulding. The others are inserted, the W. one on the floor above being finished with a finer roll-and-hollow moulding while the E. one is treated with a hollow moulding and has the soffit of its lintel sunk-wrought to a quarter-round at the corners. The attic fireplaces have plain jambs and lintels.

This house appears to have been a residence of the family of Wordie of Torbrex, and the initials quoted above are probably those of John Wordie, 4th of Torbrex, and his wife Barbara Bennet, whom he married in 1701.[1]

In the farm-steading, which adjoins the house on the W., a doorway and two windows are treated with backset margins and rounded arrises, in the same manner as the first-floor window described above. The walling in which they occur may therefore be assigned to the early 18th century, but the greater part of the steading is later and probably dates from some time in the century following.

789921 NS 79 SE 22 August 1955

295. Bannockburn House. Bannockburn House occupies a pleasant and secluded site about a mile S. of Bannockburn Town (No. 264) and a quarter of a mile E. of the main Glasgow-Stirling road (A 80). The building is of 17th-century date, and, although subsequently altered and enlarged, its unusual plan together with the fine plaster ceilings makes it one of the most interesting examples of its period in the county.

The lands of Bannockburn and Skeoch were granted

[1] *T.S.N.H.A.S.* (1937-8), 95 f.

by Charles I to John Rollo, second son of Sir Andrew Rollo of Duncrub, in 1636.[1] In 1666, Andrew, 3rd Lord Rollo, succeeded his uncle in the property, but financial difficulties forced him to sell the estate to Hugh Paterson after he had held it for less than ten years.[2] The new owner was created a baronet in 1686, and, although the Jacobite sympathies of the Patersons led to the forfeiture of the baronetcy after the rebellion of 1715, the family continued to live at Bannockburn until well on in the 18th century.[3] The house has since passed through a number of different hands. The exact date of its erection is not known, but two of the ceilings can be ascribed to about the year 1680 and this suggests that the house may have been built by Hugh Paterson soon after he acquired the property, although the strap-worked pediments of the dormer windows are a generation earlier in style. It was considerably enlarged at the end of the 19th century.

Bannockburn House is a symmetrically planned H-shaped building (Fig. 129), a basement and three storeys in height. It consists of a main block, which measures 44 ft. 3 in. by 24 ft. 6 in. over all and runs E. and W., together with two wings which run N. and S. and measure 42 ft. 11 in. by 22 ft. 6 in. over all. The plan differs widely from that of the typical Scottish house of the period and may derive from an English model, although the elevations and detail are characteristically Scottish. The building is of rubble, which may have been harled originally but is now covered with a cement rendering; the voids are of dressed sandstone, most of the original openings having chamfered arrises. The basement windows have been barred, while those on the ground and first floors seem to have been half-glazed and half-barred, the lower part of the window being protected by a shutter. The walls rise from a plinth to an ogival-moulded eaves-course; the gables are crow-stepped and finish in moulded skewputs. On the N. façade (Fig. 129) the main block contains three ranges of symmetrically placed windows which light the principal floors, those of the second floor being dormers. All the windows have moulded cornices, which in the case of the dormers support carved, strap-worked pediments. The entrance-doorway is centrally placed at ground-floor level and is now entered through an ill-proportioned porch which was erected about the year 1884.[4] A moulded panel-recess, now empty but designed to accommodate a coat of arms, is placed over the central window above first-floor level. The fenestration of the N. wing is symmetrical and corresponds with that of the main frontage, but there may originally have been two windows on each storey in the N. gable-ends. The ground level on this side of the house was probably raised a little when the new porch was erected. The S. façade corresponds closely with the N. one, but the wings have less projection. It has been altered through the conversion of the E. window on the ground floor into a garden door and the renewal of the dormer pediments. The S. projection of the W. wing is now concealed by the extensive additions carried out by Waller & Sons, architects, about the year 1884.[5] The bay window that projects at ground-floor level on the E. frontage of the E. wing is probably an addition of the same date. The offices to the W. of the house are of late 18th- or early 19th-century date, but were further extended in 1884.

INTERIOR. The plan is a symmetrical one, the main block being designed to accommodate two principal apartments, one on the ground floor and the other on the first floor; while the arms of the H contain the smaller rooms together with the twin stairs, which rise to the full height of the house. The stairs, which are of stone, are dog-legged; the treads are bottle-nosed and have a width of 4 ft. (Pl. 167 A). The front door gives access to a large room which occupies the greater part of the main block; this apartment may always have served as an entrance hall, but in the course of the alterations of 1884 it was carried up through the old first-floor drawing-room, and was provided with a gallery and otherwise remodelled. The floor of the drawing-room was removed and its fine plastered ceiling thus forms the principal feature of interest in the entrance hall. The ceiling (Pls. 168-171) is in the elaborate and highly ornamental style that was in vogue in the reign of Charles II. It comprises a number of panels of geometrical shapes symmetrically disposed around an oval compartment in the centre. The panels and the borders of the central oval are enriched with an abundance of detail in high relief, the ornament consisting for the most part of bunches of fruit, flowers and foliage. The frieze is decorated with a repeating pattern in the same style, and there is a rose-and-bracket cornice. Some of the background is painted in blue and brown and part of the ornament is picked out in gilt. The strong resemblance of this ceiling to those of the State Apartments at Holyrood Palace, Edinburgh,[6] and especially to that of the King's Bedroom, suggests that one or more of the Holyrood plasterers may also have worked at Bannockburn. East of the entrance hall, but also within the main block, there is a small room which retains an original plaster frieze and cornice. The frieze (Pl. 173 A) has a repeating pattern in low relief incorporating a vase, foliage, fruit and figures. The E. wing contains two rooms, one on each side of the staircase, but both have been very much altered. The arrangement of the W. wing is the same; the small room to the N. of the stair has some 18th-century panelling and a moulded plaster ceiling-cornice, while the cupboard in the N. wall may originally have been a window. The room to the S. of the stair was inaccessible at the date of visit.

The plan of the first floor repeats that of the ground

[1] *Th eScots Peerage*, vii, 196.

[2] H.M. General Register House, Inventory of Rollo Charters, Nos. 104 and 120.

[3] G.E.C., *Complete Baronetage*, iv, 342.

[4] A drawing of about 1820, reproduced by Fleming, *Castles and Mansions*, 282, shows the original porch, and this has been incorporated in the elevational drawing of the N. façade (Fig. 129).

[5] Plans of the house, dating from this time, are preserved by the owner, Miss Mitchell.

[6] *Inventory of the City of Edinburgh*, No. 87. Cf. also Turner, L., *Decorative Plasterwork in Great Britain*, 144 ff.

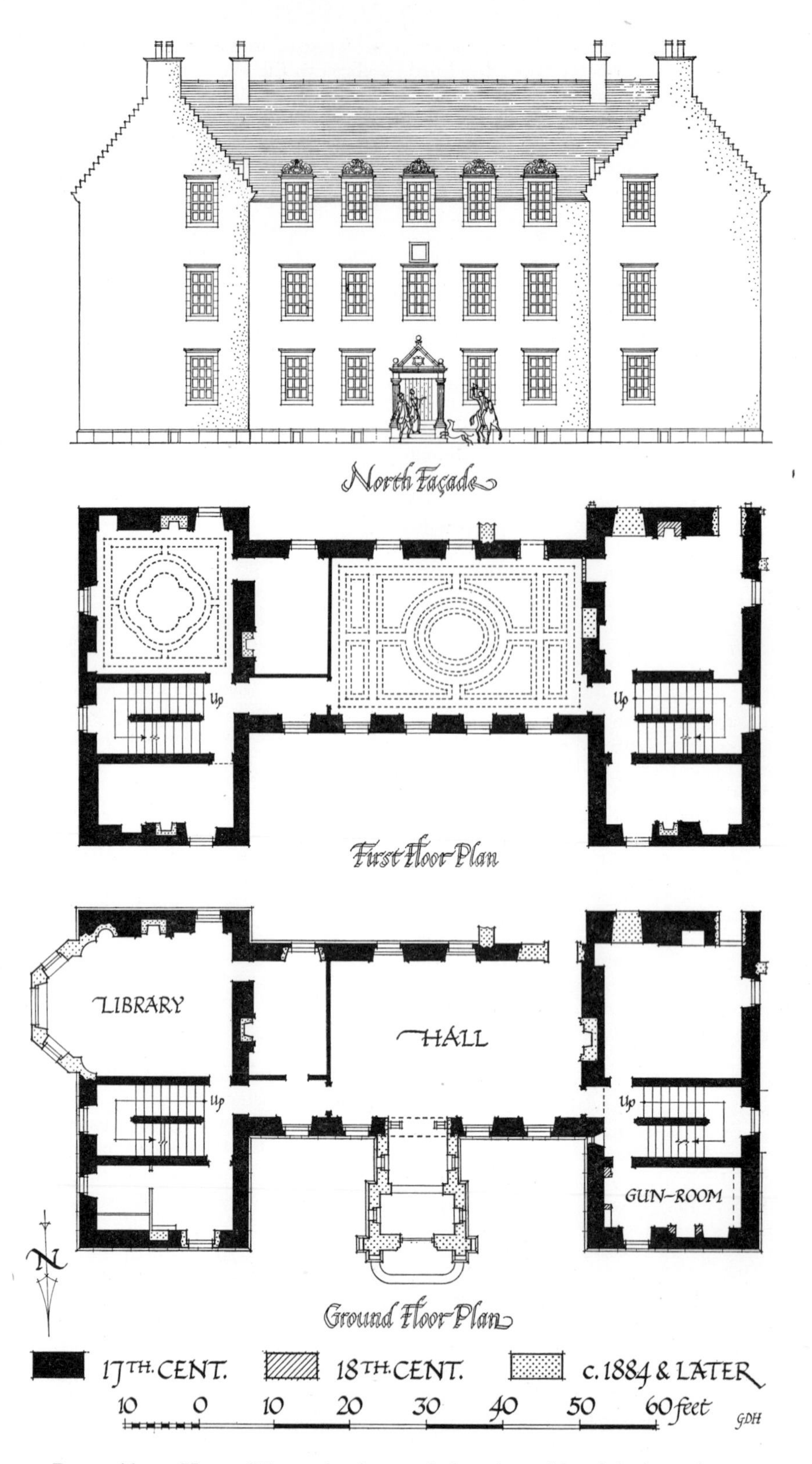

Fig. 129. Bannockburn House (No. 295); plans and elevation with original porch reconstructed

floor. Of the drawing-room, which occupied the greater part of the main block, nothing remains but the ceiling, and this has already been described. The original fireplace in the W. wall was blocked when the gallery was built, and at the same time the window at the W. end of the S. wall was converted into a door to give access from the gallery to the SW. addition. The room occupying the S. part of the E. wing has a plaster ceiling (Pl. 172), similar in style to that of the old drawing-room but more restrained in its ornamental detail; it comprises a central quatrefoil with an enriched border of fruit and flowers, together with corner panels, each of which is outlined with a rod-and-ribbon border and contains a vase of flowers. In the S. wall there is an original stone fireplace with a bolection moulding. To the W. of this room, to which it serves as a dressing-room, there is a smaller apartment which is contained within the main block; it has an ornamental plaster frieze (Pl. 173 B) similar to the one in the room that occupies a corresponding position on the ground floor. The small room to the N. of the stair has been remodelled but retains a moulded plaster ceiling-cornice. The larger of the two rooms in the W. wing (Pl. 167 B) has an 18th-century fireplace, some panelling of the same period and a low-relief plaster frieze of 17th-century date (Pl. 173 C) similar to the two already noted. The door in the S. wall is an insertion. The small room to the N. of the stair retains an original bolection-moulded fireplace and a moulded plaster cornice; the cupboard in the N. wall may originally have been a window recess. On the third floor the arrangement of the wings is like that on the two lower floors, but the main block contains a number of bedrooms which are entered from a corridor on the N. Some of the roof timbers are original and have incised positioning numerals; wooden slate-pegs are still in use. The basement has been much altered and is of little interest. The main block contains a range of cellars which are entered from a corridor on the N. and there are other rooms in the wings; the position of the original kitchen is uncertain. In the N. part of the W. wing, and at a lower level, there is an unlit barrel-vaulted cellar. Access is from above by a stair and a hatch, neither of which is original in its present form. None of the other basement rooms is vaulted and the only remaining features of interest are the chamfered stone surrounds of some of the doorways. Most of the windows have been enlarged.

DOVECOT. The dovecot that stands 250 yds. NE. of the house is described under No. 392.

808888 NS 88 NW 3 August 1956

296. Auchenbowie House. Auchenbowie House (Pl. 165 A) stands in its policies two and a half miles S. of the village of St. Ninians and rather less than half a mile W. of the main Glasgow-Stirling road (A 80). The oldest part of the building is an example of a laird's house of the 17th century, but extensive alterations and additions were made to the original structure both in 1768 and at the end of the 19th century. The original house is an L-shaped building, three storeys and an attic in height, and consists of a main block which measures 59 ft. 2 in. by 22 ft. 8 in. over all and runs roughly N. and S., together with an E. wing which measures 29 ft. 4 in. by 30 ft. 6 in. over all. An octagonal stair-tower rises in the re-entrant angle of the building and finishes in a pyramidal roof. The masonry is rubble, and has recently been re-harled; it is said that a number of blocked-up windows are concealed by the harling. There is a broad, tabled plinth, which is unlikely to be original, and the walls finish in a moulded eaves-course; the gables are crow-stepped and have ogival-moulded skewputs. The upper parts of the chimney-stacks have been renewed.

The old entrance-doorway is situated at the base of the stair-tower and has a bolection-moulded surround; above there is a stone panel on which there is carved in relief the Bruce arms together with the date 1506. This panel is said to have come to light in about 1952, during the re-harling of the house, and the coat of arms and date were cut on it then as the original inscription and carving could not be made out. The date 1506 is too early to suit the construction of the present house. Both the E. wall of the main block and the S. wall of the wing have two large windows symmetrically placed on the three main floors, but these, together with the windows in the gable-ends, have for the most part been renewed or enlarged during the 18th and 19th centuries. The attic storey of the wing is lit by two dormer windows which have plain triangular pediments; the wing may originally have had dormer windows also, but these would have been removed in the 18th century, when the attic storey was incorporated in a heightened third-floor room. The W. elevation of the old house is almost completely concealed by a later addition, which is for the most part in character with the 17th-century work. The addition incorporates an octagonal turret at the base of which is situated what is now the main entrance-doorway of the house. The pediment of a dormer window on the S. side of the addition bears the incised date 1768. The N. elevation of the original house is largely masked by a two-storeyed extension of late 19th-century date, above the roof of which there may be seen an attic window in the N. gable-end of the old main block.

Very few original features remain within the old house. The plan of the ground floor (Fig. 130) shows that the front door led into the stair-tower, from which a door to the N. gave access to a corridor, and this in turn gave access to the apartments on the ground floor. The main block originally contained two apartments of which the southernmost was a kitchen and the northernmost a cellar. When the W. addition with its new entrance-doorway was built in 1768, the N. part of the kitchen became a hall and a geometric stair was inserted at its N. end. The treads of the stair have moulded nosings and there is a simple iron balustrade. At the same time, the original stair in the re-entrant angle, which gave access to both main block and wing on the upper storeys, was removed, and the stair-tower was floored on each storey to form a closet. The old segmental-headed fireplace remains in the S. gable of the kitchen, but the stones of the jambs and voussoirs have been re-dressed or renewed. Within the fireplace there is now a cast-iron fireback which incorporates the figure of Europa in relief. The arched recess to the W., which is now a window, may originally have been an oven. The doorway in the W. wall was inserted in 1768 to give access to the addition; the splayed recess to the S. of it may have been either a window or a slop-sink, while the cupboard to the N. was

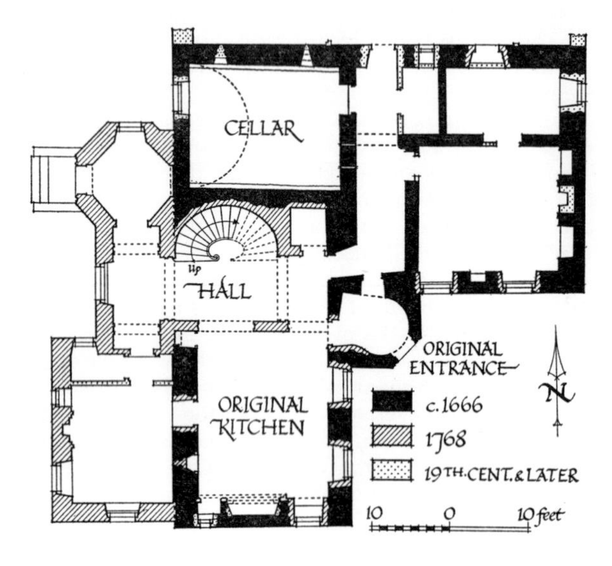

Fig. 130. Auchenbowie House (No. 296)

originally an external door of which the S. jamb still remains. Both these openings were blocked in 1768. The cupboard in the NE. angle of the kitchen was formed when the geometric stair was inserted against the N. wall. The cellar that occupies the N. part of the main block is barrel-vaulted; two wrought-iron meat-hooks hang from the ceiling. There are two original windows in the N. wall, both of which were blocked when the 19th-century additions were made to the N. side of the house. The cellar was originally reached by way of the small room in the NW. angle of the wing, but a blocked-up opening in the E. wall of the cellar suggests that a door was inserted at some time to give direct access to the corridor. The wing, which is considerably broader than the main block, seems originally to have contained a large apartment in the SE. angle and two smaller rooms to the N., as well as the corridor on the W. that communicated with the entrance-doorway. The corridor has been extended northwards, however, to communicate with the 19th-century addition by means of an inserted doorway, while the NW. room has been contracted and forms a wine-cellar. The other two rooms remain but contain no features of interest. In plan the first and second floors are similar to the ground floor and they have been modified in much the same way. The S. room of the main block on the first floor has a wooden fireplace in the Adam style and a plaster ceiling-cornice of the same period. The wing was remodelled in the 18th century to form an L-shaped dining-room with a smaller room in the NW. angle. The dining-room contains a wooden fireplace and other fittings of the period; the smaller room has been subdivided at a later date. On the second floor the N. room in the main block contains a pine fireplace in the Adam style. The E. wing was remodelled as a library in the latter part of the 18th century, and now forms a single large room which contains within its height part of the old attic-storey. The coved ceiling and the panelling (Pl. 164) are of 18th-century date.

During the 17th century Auchenbowie was in the hands of the Bruce family, which is said to have acquired the property at the beginning of the preceding century.[1] In September 1666 a contract for the erection of a house at Auchenbowie was drawn up between Robert Bruce, younger of Auchenbowie, and John Simson, a Glasgow mason, and his brother George Simson.[2] The building specified in the contract, however, a simple block with a turnpike stair, is considerably smaller in scale than the existing old house, and it would seem that the original plan was abandoned in favour of a more ambitious project. At the end of the 17th century the estate passed to the Monro family through the marriage of Margaret, a younger daughter of Robert Bruce of Auchenbowie, with Col. George Monro, son of Sir Alexander Monro of Bearcrofts, a descendant of whom possesses it today.[3]

SUNDIAL. A sundial (Pl. 214 B) stands on the lawn about 20 yds. E. of the house. The shaft, which is square in section, rises from a moulded base to support the head, which takes the form of a polyhedron; this has probably been truncated to incorporate the present copper dial. The shaft is divided into panels, most of which contain sunk dials; a panel on the W. side is carved in relief with a shield charged: Quarterly, 1st and 4th, an eagle's head erased, holding in the beak a laurel branch, for Monro of Bearcrofts; 2nd and 3rd, a saltire and chief, for Bruce of Auchenbowie. The panel below contains the initials G M and M B, for George Monro and Margaret Bruce (*supra*). The date 1702, which is incised below the initials, together with the initials and date on the lower portion of the E. side of the shaft, have been added within recent years.[4]

798874 NS 78 NE 26 July 1956

297. Braes. This house is situated about a mile NNW. of Dunipace, its position on a hillside, at the S. edge of Braes Wood, giving it an extensive view over the low ground of the Carron Valley. It is still inhabited, as a farmhouse, and the fabric, which probably dates from

[1] Inglis, J. A., *The Monros of Auchinbowie*, 45.
[2] H.M. General Register House, *Register of Deeds*, Mack., 19, 282.
[3] Inglis, *op. cit.*, 8 f., 45.
[4] *Castles and Mansions*, 216 ff.

the later 18th century, remains practically unaltered. The heraldic stone mentioned below suggests that there was an earlier house on or near the same site. Built with its main axis lying nearly E. and W., the house is oblong on plan (Fig. 131) and measures 56 ft. 3 in. by 23 ft. It contains two storeys and an attic, the disposition of the rooms in each being almost identical and comprising a large apartment at each end and two smaller ones, with a staircase and a passageway, in the middle.

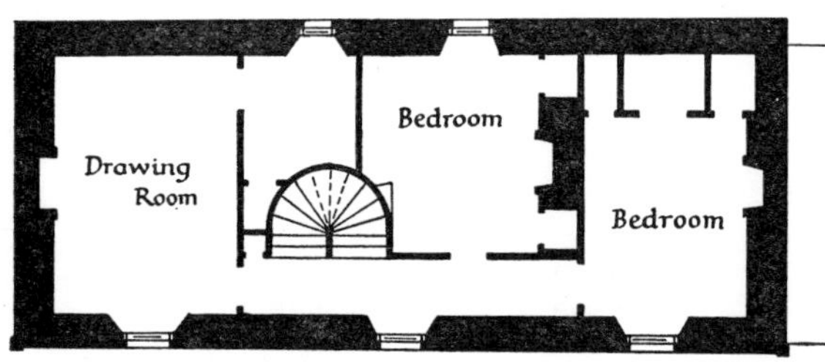

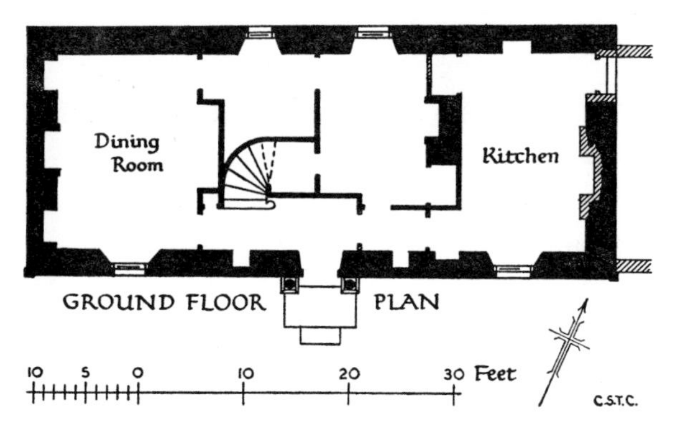

Fig. 131. Braes (No. 297)

The walls are founded on a rough projecting footing of large boulders; they are harled, and the frontal quoins and the margins of all the voids, which are of sandstone, are backset to receive the roughcast. An eaves-course along the S. façade is wrought with an ogee-and-cavetto moulding, but on the N. there is simply a cavetto. The gables are tabled, with scrolled and foliated skewputs in front and plain quarter-round ones at the back. The front faces of the quoins, which are 9 in. broad, have the effect of pilasters; they terminate at the eaves-course in moulded caps each with a mask and egg-and-dart ornament carved on the plain surface above the necking. The slated roof and two attic windows to the front have probably been renewed, but the rest of the windows are original; all of them are uniformly spaced, each room being lighted by one window.

The main entrance, which is wrought with an architrave, is set in the middle of the S. front within a shallow portico of the Roman Doric order; this consists of a pair of plain detached columns set on pedestals and supporting an entablature containing a frieze with triglyphs, a cornice and a blocking-course. The entrance leads into a lobby, alined with the main axis of the house, from which a wooden stair with winding treads rises to the attic. Within the lobby, on either side of the entrance, there is a very narrow recess. On each floor the principal rooms are entered directly from the lobby or a landing, only the smallest of them, which has no fireplace and lies behind the staircase, opening off a larger one. The kitchen occupies the E. end of the ground floor; its fireplace has been renewed and a back door has been broken through the gable to communicate with an outbuilding. The room W. of the kitchen is lined with plain panelling, framed and fielded, and there is a fireplace in the mutual wall. At the W. end of the house is the dining-room, which has a fireplace in the gable with a cupboard on either side of it and a sideboard recess in the partition opposite. This fireplace has a blue marble surround and a wooden mantelpiece of Adam type. The room above, the drawing-room, has a somewhat similar fireplace with a fluted mantelpiece; the fireplace in the room above the kitchen has moulded stone jambs. Each gable of the attic contains a fireplace and a press, and numerous other presses are provided throughout the house.

In the back wall of the house, 8 ft. 6 in. from the N. corner, an heraldic panel, now probably incomplete, has been set for preservation. It bears a shield parted per pale and charged: Dexter, three hunting horns below the initials I F; sinister, an unidentifiable charge, resembling a buckle between three mullets, below the initials A C. At the base of the shield is the date 1643. The shield and initials are evidently those of James Forrester (Forestar) "in Brayis of Mekill Denoven" and of his wife Agnes Crawford.[1]

GARDEN GATEWAY. From in front of the house steps lead down to the gateway of what was formerly a garden or orchard. The gate pillars finish in a moulded cornice and are of rusticated ashlar reconstructed without mortar.

798847 NS 78 SE 16 August 1955

298. Quarter. Quarter is a small Georgian mansion which stands a mile N. of the village of Dunipace and 300 yds. E. of the main Glasgow-Stirling road (A 80). The building consists of a rectangular block, which measures 59 ft. 9 in. by 29 ft. 9 in. and runs N. and S., with a wing measuring 10 ft. 10 in. by 20 ft. 2 in. projecting from the centre of its E. side. A courtyard adjoins the house on the E. and contains the kitchens and offices, some of which are of a later date than the main building. The house is of two storeys, and the masonry is of harled rubble with dressed margins and quoins; the walls finish in a moulded eaves-course and the roof is hipped. The principal façade (Pl. 194 A) faces W. and contains a Tuscan entrance-porch which is centrally placed on the

[1] Index to the General Register of Sasines, 1631-40, H.M. General Register House.

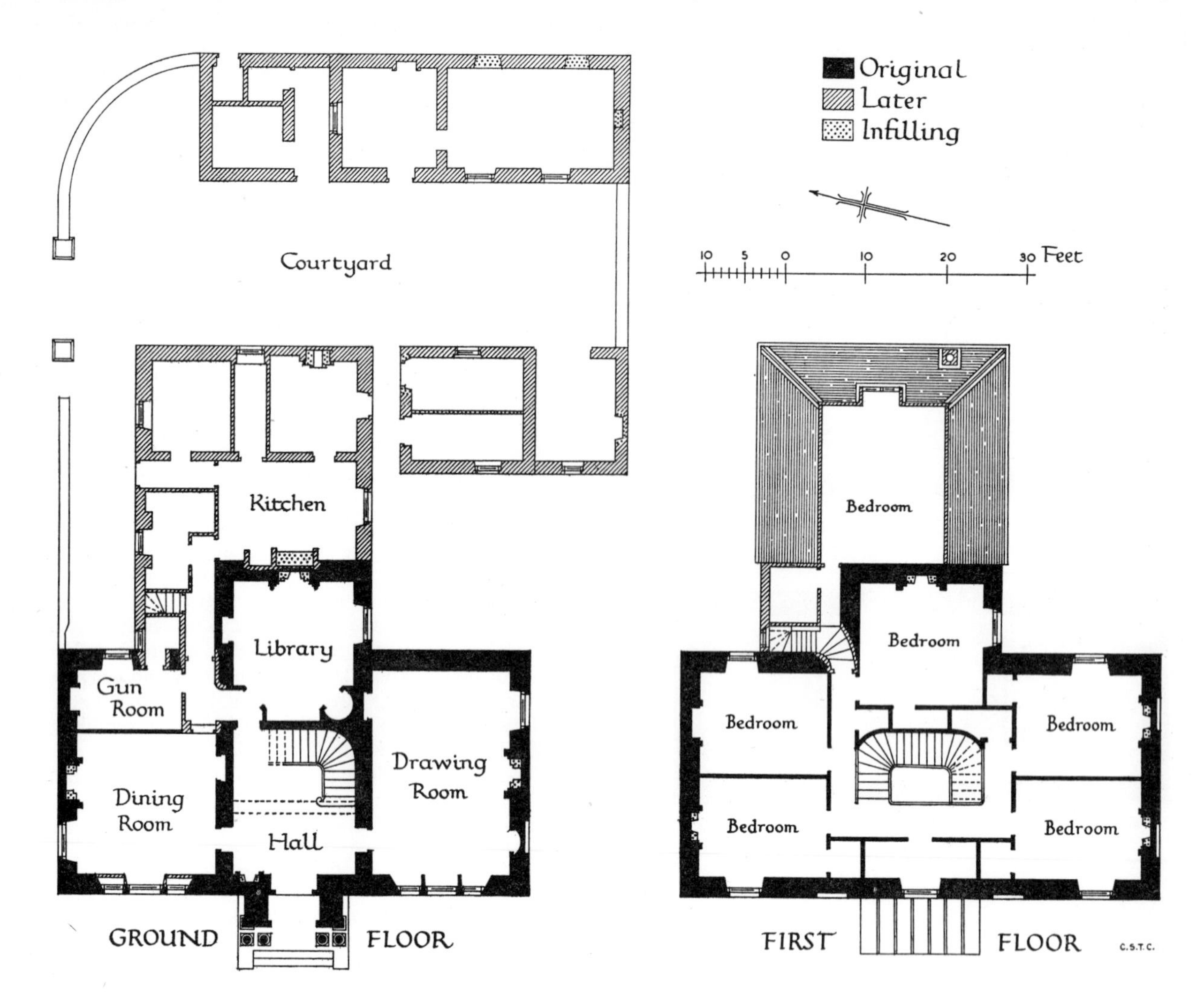

Fig. 132. Quarter (No. 298)

ground floor. On either side there is a single, large three-light window with a hood-mould, while on the first floor there is a range of five smaller windows, two of which are dummies. The central portion of the façade rises to form a plain triangular pediment in the centre of which there is a small circular light. At the back of the house the NE. re-entrant angle between main block and wing has been filled in to provide additional offices, while the wing itself has been extended eastwards to form kitchen premises.

The principal apartments are on the ground floor (Fig. 132). The front entrance gives access to a stone-flagged hall at the rear of which a geometric stair (Pl. 194B), lit by a cupola, rises to the first floor. To the S. and N. of the hall, doors lead to the drawing-room and dining-room respectively; the former occupies the full width of the main block, but to the E. of the dining-room there is a small gun-room which is reached from a corridor behind the hall. At the S. end of the corridor a door leads to the wing, which contains the library. This room has a plain marble fireplace with a decorated wooden surround in which Corinthian columns support an entablature, the frieze of which is carved with marine flora and fauna and other motifs. The other rooms are of no particular interest, although both drawing-room and dining-room have an ornamental plaster frieze and ceiling-cornice. There are five bedrooms on the first floor, four in the main block and one in the wing.

The lands of Quarter were held by the family of Brown of Quarter in the 17th century, and the present house is said to have been built by Alexander Brown, who succeeded to the property in 1776. The estate passed to another branch of the family during the 19th century.[1]

810849 NS 88 SW 6 September 1955

[1] Gibson, J. C., *Lands and Lairds of Larbert and Dunipace Parishes*, 189 ff.

299. Torwood Castle. In the Middle Ages the Tor Wood was an area of Royal forest, and the office of Forester was held, from the second half of the 15th century until about the middle of the 17th century, by the Forestars of Garden.[1] The castle appears to have been built in 1566—the date carved on a stone panel (Pl. 161 E) found, about 1918, in a stone dyke some 200 yds. NW. of the building[2] and now preserved in Falkirk Museum (cf. No. 428)—presumably by Sir Alexander Forestar of Garden, who was for a time Provost of Stirling and who died in 1598 (pp. 138 f.). On 31 October 1585 "the place of Woodhead, beside the Tor-wood" was taken and garrisoned by the "banished lords"—the Earls of Angus and Mar, the Master of Glamis and others—in preparation for their capture of Stirling.[3] Early in the 17th century the estate of Garden passed to the Stirling family,[4] but the Forestars retained their office of Royal Forester, together with their castle in the Tor Wood, until 1635, when the lands of Torheid and the forest of the Tor Wood were acquired by George, first Lord Forrester of Corstorphine.[5] The buildings enclosing the courtyard seem to date from the first half of the 17th century, and are therefore very probably the work of this new proprietor.

The castle stands on high-lying but fairly level ground at what is now the S. edge of the Tor Wood, and rather less than half a mile W. of the Stirling-Falkirk highway (A 9). It is L-shaped on plan (Fig. 133), consisting of a principal block alined approximately from E. to W. with a short wing extending N. from its W. end and a small square tower in the re-entrant angle. On the N. lies a large courtyard formerly enclosed by the later buildings just mentioned. The main building is roofless,[6] but is of particular interest in view of its evident transitional character between castle and mansion, the design tending towards the horizontal rather than the vertical (Pl. 160 A) and the plan being based on the hall in a way which decisively determines the lay-out and appearance of the whole. The gaunt appearance of the S. façade is more than counterbalanced by the attractive treatment of the re-entrant NE. angle, and by the finely moulded details seen in the interior.

The main block comprises a vaulted ground floor, a principal floor and an attic. Its length is 82 ft., including a projection 5 ft. 6 in. deep at the SW. corner, no doubt provided for defensive purposes to enfilade the wall to the N. of it; its breadth is 29 ft. 6 in. The thickness of the walls is, in general, 3 ft. 10 in., though that of the E. gable, which contains the kitchen fireplace and flue, is 9 ft. 3 in. while one of the walls of the SW. projection is only 1 ft. 6 in. thick. The gables are crow-stepped, and an intermediate gable interrupts the roof-line 30 ft. short of the E. gable, over a partition which separates the hall from the withdrawing-room; this gable serves to distinguish the symmetrical fenestration of the hall portion of the S. front, on the W., from the more casual arrangements in the E. end. The wing (Pls. 159 and 160 B), which contains the main stair, is a square tower with gables at N. and S., measuring 20 ft. each way over walls 2 ft. 6 in. thick; it rises two storeys higher than the main block, and has a string-course at first-floor level which stops abruptly on reaching the W. gable of the main block. The small tower in the angle, which also contains a stair, measures 8 ft. by 7 ft. over all. The walls of the whole building are of yellow sandstone rubble, weathering to grey, and were originally harled; they show masoncraft of a high order.

The S. façade (Pl. 160 A), W. of the intermediate gable, shows at first-floor level the four windows that light the hall; their margins are moulded and they originally had grilles. The larger ones were half-glazed, with shutters in their lower portions. The sills of the central pair are raised so high as to make these windows almost square. West of them two small diamond-shaped apertures pierce the wall of the projection, to light the stair within (Pl. 161 C). Symmetrically disposed below the hall windows are three small ground-floor windows with rebated chamfers, which originally had vertical bars (Pl. 161 D); and at eaves-level there are traces of three dormers with mouldings like those below and not quite symmetrically placed. East of the intermediate gable the fenestration is irregular, as there are two windows on the ground floor, two, at different levels, on the principal floor, the larger one being grilled and half-shuttered, and a single dormer in the attic. In the E. gable there is one small window with chamfered arrises lighting a small chamber N. of the kitchen fireplace, while on the principal floor there are two ranges of windows, at different levels, the lower one on the S. having been broken out or roughly enlarged. The function of these windows will be considered shortly. The N. façade, E. of the wing (Pl. 159), shows at ground-floor level two windows lighting the ground-floor passage (*infra*), a slit, and an aperture for the intake of water, giblet-checked externally, and the outlet of a shaft from a garderobe on the attic floor; above are two openings, the W. one a window and the E. one a doorway with chamfered arrises, now partly filled up, and evidently designed to give access to an E. curtain wall or an E. range of buildings such as was not actually built until the 17th century. In the W. end of the main block one large window with a gun-loop below it lights the end of the hall; the projection has a gun-loop, facing N., at ground-floor level, a small chamfered opening on the stair, a small window in each of the two small chambers that occupy the height of the first floor, and another in the attic. The walls of the wing and the tower in the re-entrant angle are based on a low splayed plinth, which stops where it reaches the main block. In the E. wall of the wing, and flanked by the tower in the re-entrant angle, is the entrance-doorway, the approach to which is covered by several gun-loops, as shown in Pl. 161 A. The

[1] *Castles and Mansions*, 165 ff.
[2] Information from Sir Ian Bolton, Bt., K.B.E., LL.D.
[3] Moyses, R., *Memoirs of the Affairs of Scotland, etc.*, 100.
[4] Fraser, W., *The Stirlings of Keir*, 83.
[5] *The Scots Peerage*, iv, 91. The later history of the property is given in *Castles and Mansions*, 171.
[6] Since the present survey was made, the proprietor, Mr. Gordon Millar, has begun restoration work and has also carried out excavations.

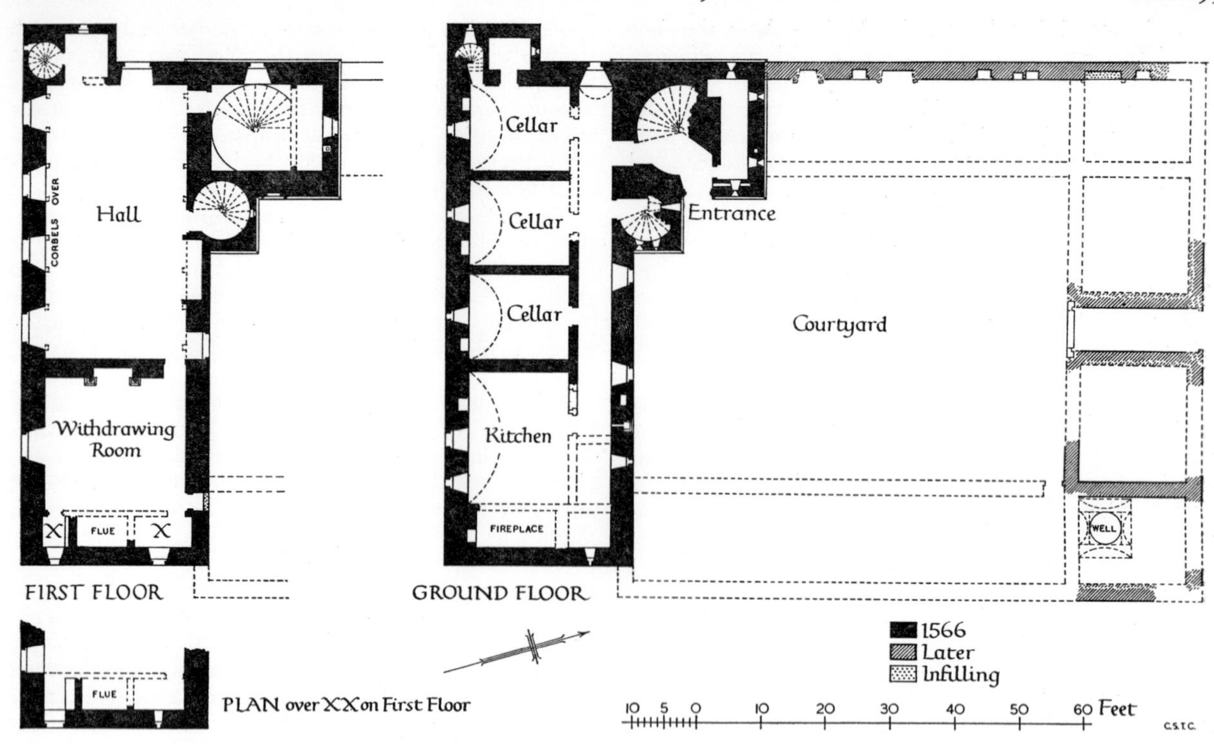

Fig. 133. Torwood Castle (No. 299)

entrance is square-headed, is checked for a door and a yett, and has stopped roll-and-hollow mouldings; in the N. jamb is a well-preserved bar-hole running through to a gun-loop in the guard-room, from which the bar was operated. Above the entrance, and incorporated in the first-floor string-course already mentioned, there is an assemblage presumably intended to hold an heraldic panel, though this has now disappeared. Enclosed within a moulded frame, with quatrefoils in its upper corners, there can now be seen a Classical niche with moulded sill and frieze, traces of pilaster-capitals topped by finials, and a semicircular pediment with a foliated shell in the tympanum. The main tower is lighted by square-headed windows with moulded arrises, of which there are five in the N. and two each in the E. and W. sides; and the tower in the re-entrant angle by three slits in the N. side. A moulded course is stepped down at the re-entrant angle, from the eaves of the main tower, to incorporate the roof of the small tower, which evidently did not rise as high as the main one.

The internal arrangements can readily be seen in Fig. 133. The entrance opens into a lobby, from which rises the main stair. A narrow door on the right opens into a guard-room, a narrow chamber which occupies the N. end of the wing and serves gun-loops facing E., N. and W. A doorway to the left of the main stair opens into a vaulted passage which runs E. and W. and gives access on the N. to the stair in the re-entrant angle, on the S. into a range of three vaulted cellars, and at its E. end into the kitchen. The stair, which is spiral and measures 8 ft. 6 in. in diameter, rises to the top floor but one of the tower (*infra*). Each of the cellars has an aumbry beside the window, and the W. one has two doorways into the projection—the N. one leading to a small room which serves a gun-loop and the S. one to the base of a spiral stair, 5 ft. 6 in. in diameter, which rises to the attic floor. The junction between the passage and the kitchen is now ruinous, but the lower part of the W. jamb of a door, with a serving-hatch beside it on the W., can be seen on the S. side of the passage. This doorway and hatch, like the rest of the ground-floor doorways, show rebated chamfers. The water-inlet already mentioned is opposite the kitchen door. The E. end of the passage is obscured by fallen debris. The kitchen fireplace (12 ft. 6 in. by 5 ft. 6 in.) has been almost entirely destroyed, but traces remain of a fine semicircular arch of ashlar with hollow-chamfered voussoirs; it has an aumbry in its S. end, and to N. of it was a small square chamber, independently lit, the method of access to which is uncertain. In the S. wall of the kitchen is another aumbry. The stair in the main tower is spiral and measures 13 ft. 9 in. in diameter. It rises no further than the principal floor, where it is roofed over by a fine barrel-vault. On the way it gives access, at an intermediate level, to a narrow room which corresponds with the guard-room below; it was probably a vestibule, as it is fitted with a laver and drainage shaft in the N. wall beside the window, and the partition separating it from the stair rises only to an intermediate level, indicated by joist-holes, so that the small square window gave light above it to the stair-well.

The hall, which measures internally 41 ft. by 22 ft., is entered from the main stair at its NW. corner and from the one in the re-entrant angle half-way along its N. side. At its NE. corner it communicates with the withdrawing-room, which occupies the E. portion of the principal floor, and near its SW. corner with a small ante-room and, through this, with the small turnpike in the SW. angle. The fireplace is in the N. wall, immediately E. of the entry from the stair in the re-entrant angle; it is 9 ft. wide, and has square pilasters with Classical mouldings on bases and capitals. Traces of plaster remain here and there on the walls. Moulded stone corbels, with joist-holes immediately above, can be seen on both side-walls and indicate the level of the timbering of the ceiling and of the floor above. The withdrawing-room is 20 ft. long by 21 ft. 6 in. wide, its length being reduced by the thickness of the E. gable which houses the kitchen flue. A curious arrangement seems to have been made at the E. end of the room, where two small rooms, each with a window—the S. one enlarged or broken out—have been contrived at floor level, one on either side of the flue, and above these, but still within the height of the withdrawing-room, a pair of corresponding spaces which acted as a kind of clearstorey, their windows giving light to the withdrawing-room over the rooms below (Fig. 133). It is this arrangement that explains the fenestration of the E. gable, as noted earlier. The S. room at the lower level is only 4 ft. wide, but its counterpart at the higher level is wider by a foot, as the flue has contracted correspondingly, and is provided with a serviceable window-seat; it is therefore to be supposed that the "clearstorey" spaces were put to some practical use. The fireplace of the withdrawing-room, which is in its W. wall, is comparable with that of the hall but has half-round jambs. The high-level doorway to an E. range of courtyard buildings, mentioned above, is in the NE. corner of the room. It is evidently an original feature, and shows that the construction of an E. courtyard-range was already anticipated in 1566. This room was joisted, like the hall, but no corbels are present.

Little survives of the attic floor, but traces of a fireplace remain at either end of the section W. of the intermediate gable. The E. one retains a square pilaster-jamb with Classical mouldings on its capital and base. These fireplaces suggest that the space over the hall was divided by a wooden partition, as do also the L-shaped garderobe recesses that alternate with the windows on the S. The garderobe of which the shaft was mentioned earlier is situated in the NW. corner of the space over the withdrawing-room, and is corbelled inwards by one course. The turnpike in the projection appears to have ended at this level, but the one in the re-entrant angle, after opening into the attic, continues upwards to give access to the upper floor of the tower and to another small turnpike which in turn leads to an uppermost floor in the main tower. This part of the building is now inaccessible and the precise arrangements are consequently somewhat uncertain. The small turnpike is contained in a half-round turret corbelled out into the attic just below its ceiling (Pl. 161 B). The room in the W. projection is entered direct from the main attic, the turnpike in the projection having ended after giving access to a chamber at intermediate level within the height of the hall.

COURTYARD BUILDINGS. The courtyard, which is cobbled, was evidently enclosed by three ranges of building, but much of the structure has now vanished, as shown in Fig. 133. The outer wall of the N. range is 88 ft. N. of the N. wall of the main block, and the W. range, which continues the line of the W. side of the wing, is thus 68 ft. long. The overall breadth is 82 ft., or 4 ft. 6 in. longer than the N. side of the castle, and the remains of tusking on the E. gable of the main block show that the outer wall of the E. range returned upon it here. The entrance-passage, no doubt originally a pend, pierces the N. range 37 ft. 9 in. (centre) E. of the outer wall of the W. range; it is cobbled, measures 6 ft. 6 in. in width, and has at its inner end a sill-piece showing checks for the frame of a door approximately 5 ft. 9 in. wide. The N. range is 21 ft. 2 in. in width as measured along the pend. The outer wall of the W. range, which is 2 ft. 9 in. thick, stands to a height of two storeys, but there is evidence that the range was reorganised at some time and re-roofed at a lower level. Fireplaces and presses alternate in a manner which suggests that it was subdivided into three compartments. The N. and E. ranges converge on a square well-house at the NE. angle. The well-chamber is curiously vaulted, having segmental main arches set N. and S. and supporting subsidiary arches set transversely to form a square aperture. Over this is superimposed a circular opening.

GARDEN. South of the castle there are traces of what was probably a large kitchen-garden, with some remains of stone foundations, as of a small enclosure, within its W. side.

835843 NS 88 SW 14 September 1955

300. Kersie Mains. This house stands close to the River Forth and about 250 yds. NW. of the junction of the Grangemouth-Stirling highway (A 905) with the secondary road that leads to South Alloa (B 966). It is an interesting example of a small laird's house of about the middle of the 17th century, the plan and general scale of the building being typical of the period. The exact date of its erection is unknown, but the house was the seat of John Wright of "Carsy" in 1707[1]; it subsequently passed into the possession of the Earls of Dunmore and later became a farmhouse.[2]

Kersie Mains (Fig. 134) is an L-shaped building, the main block of which runs E. and W. and measures 43 ft. 3 in. by 18 ft. 6 in.; there is a N. wing measuring

[1] Sibbald, *History*, 48.
[2] *Castles and Mansions*, 330.

29 ft. by 21 ft. 9 in., and a rectangular staircase-tower rises in the re-entrant angle. The house is three storeys and an attic in height, but the ground level has been raised on the W. and S. and this has partially hidden the basement floor, which is now disused. The walls, which have an average thickness of 2 ft. 4 in., are of harled rubble and finish in an ogival eaves-course. The roof is slated and the gables have a projecting table-course. The front door, which is centrally placed in the S. façade (Pl. 165 B) at the present ground-floor level, probably replaces an earlier window, the original entrance being at the foot of the staircase-tower. Two rows of symmetrically disposed windows light the principal floors, but the westernmost window of the lower range is now blinded; their jambs are wrought with an edge-roll moulding. A square sundial with two faces projects from the SW. angle at the present first-floor level. The W. façade of the N. wing also incorporates two rows of windows, but here too the original arrangement has been altered to suit the rise in ground level. The central window on the ground floor has been turned into a doorway which is entered from a porch; the ground-floor window to the S. of the porch has straight arrises and has probably been renewed, as the other windows have roll mouldings like those on the S. front. Below the window can be seen the upper portion of a doorway which gave access to the basement before the change of levels was effected. The porch, the shed that adjoins it to the N., and the single-storey extension of the N. wing have all been added. The original entrance-doorway, which has rounded arrises, is situated at the foot of the staircase-tower; there is said to be an inscription set over the lintel, but if so it is now completely hidden by harling.

The door enters into a lobby from which a spacious scale-and-platt stair rises to the full height of the house to give access to the principal apartments on each floor. The first flight of stairs, however, has been blocked by a partition since the making of the new entrance in the S. front, and there is now no internal access to the basement. Within the lobby, doors lead both to the main block and to the wing, each of which contains a single unvaulted apartment. The one in the main block contains a large kitchen-fireplace in the wall of the W. gable, but this has been altered and contracted and its roll-moulded lintel has been removed and re-used in a fireplace in the N. wing. To the S. of the fireplace is a mural recess, once shelved, in the W. wall of which there is a small oval window which is now blinded externally but retains its crown glass. The communicating door in the N. wall, and a cupboard to the E. of it which is now blocked up, are insertions, but to the W. of the door an original slit-window looks into the N. wing. Of the three windows that originally lit the apartment from the S., the two easternmost have been blocked up, as has the similar window at the E. end of the N. wall; the one in the wall of the E. gable is an insertion. The N. wing has a stone sink in the E. wall, and in the N. gable there is a fireplace which is now closed up. This incorporates the lintel already referred to, and in its present form seems to be of 18th- or 19th-century date. To the N. of the blocked-up doorway in the W. wall there is an original window and also a mural recess, but both have been filled in. The ground floor seems originally to have contained only three rooms, two in the main block and one in the wing, but this arrangement has been modified to include another small apartment in the wing and the central corridor that serves the new entrance-doorway of the S. front. The rooms have been much altered, and now contain little that is of interest apart from the unusual type of roll-moulded fireplace that remains in the W. gable-wall of the main block. The first-floor plan was originally similar to that of the ground floor and has been modified

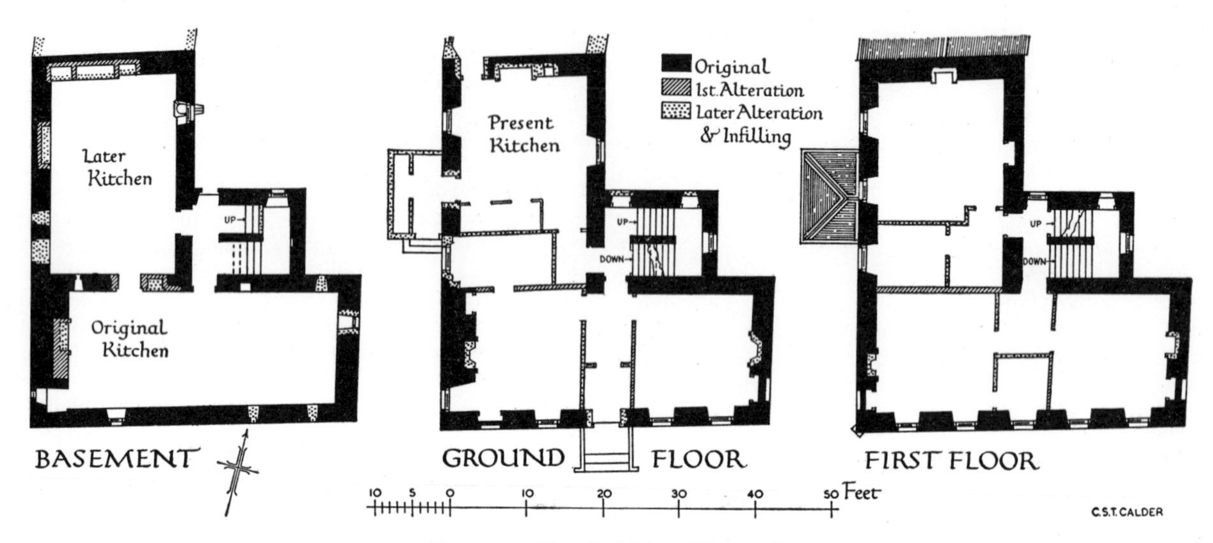

Fig. 134. Kersie Mains (No. 300)

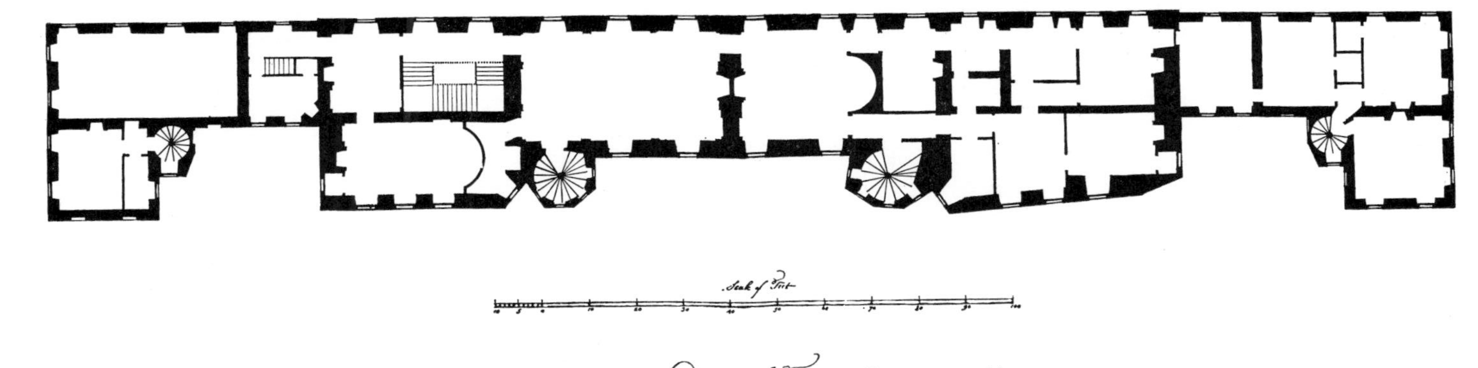

IMPROVED PLAN of the *Principal Floor* of CALLANDER HOUSE

Fig. 141. Callendar House (No. 311); principal floor, adapted from plan of 1785 by James Craig

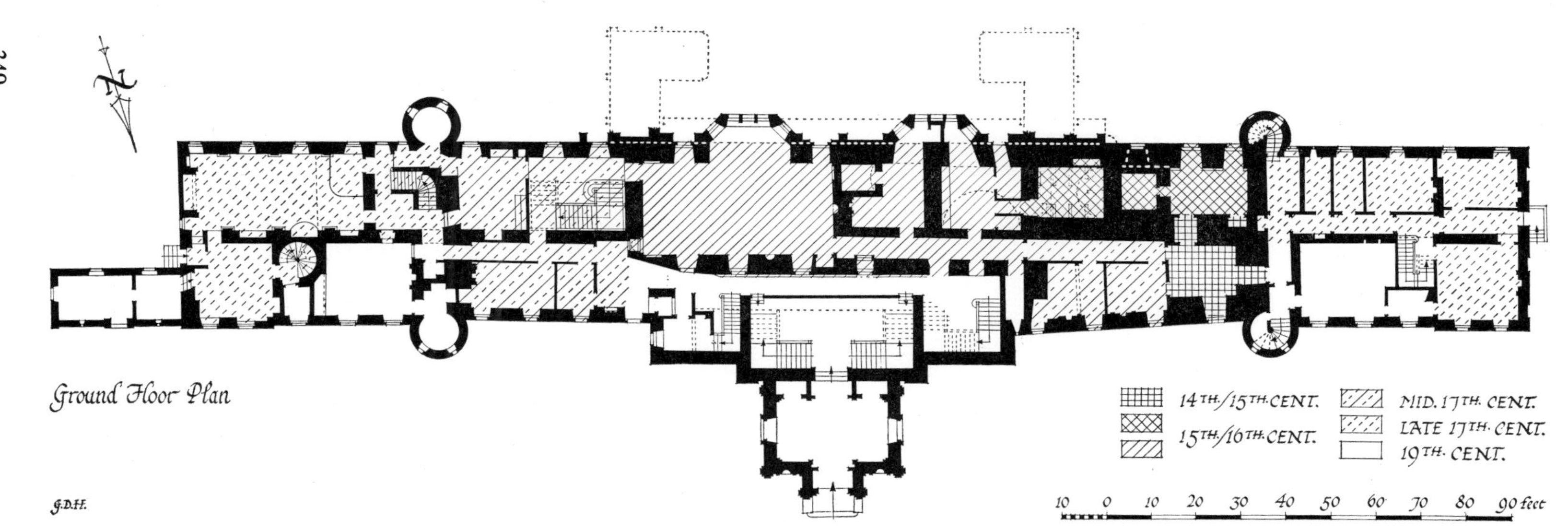

Fig. 142. Callendar House (No. 311); plan of ground floor

Callendar took up residence in the middle of the 17th century, however, they began a programme of additions and alterations which changed the whole character of the building, transforming it from a castle into a more or less symmetrically planned mansion, which must have been larger than any in the county. The house was once more extended eastwards, this time by about 40 ft., so as to bring what had now become the main block to a total length of about 182 ft. The new addition, however, was of greater width than those of the 15th and 16th centuries, and in order to make the building symmetrical the original tower at the NW. angle was itself extended eastwards to a length approximately equal to that of the new E. addition. The central portion of the façade was thus recessed, and octagonal stair-towers were erected in each of its re-entrant angles. At the same time an attempt was made to regularise the fenestration, particularly on the S. façade, where a number of roll-moulded windows were inserted.

Two further alterations seem to have taken place during the 17th century. In the first place the fenestration of the N. façade was modified, a number of windows with roll-and-fillet mouldings being inserted. Secondly, there was added to each end of the main block an L-shaped wing two main storeys in height, the E. wing also incorporating a sunk basement. An octagonal stair-turret stood in the re-entrant angle of each wing. These additions brought the building to its present length of 300 ft. The appearance of the house at this period may best be judged from a plan of 1785[1] (Fig. 141), which was drawn to illustrate some modifications proposed by James Craig. It is uncertain whether or not these alterations, which seem to have concerned only the interior of the house, were ever carried out. In 1830 plans for extensive alterations, and for the addition of a kitchen wing, were drawn up by David Hamilton but were not executed. Later in the 19th century, however, an ambitious scheme of alterations was carried out to give the house the appearance that it bears today. The central portion of the N. front was remodelled and a new porch and entrance-hall built. The octagonal stair-turrets, which had formed a conspicuous feature of the façade, were replaced by two scale-and-platt staircases while, in addition, a circular stair-turret was added to each angle of the main block. On the S. front two flights of stone stairs were built to give access to balconies on the first floor. The re-entrant angles of the L-shaped wings were filled in and an attic storey was added at each extremity. Finally, the upper part of the building was remodelled to give the house something of the appearance of a French château of the Renaissance, special attention being paid to the profile of the roof and to the ornamental detail. Most of this work was executed by Wardrop and Reid of Edinburgh between 1869 and 1877.

Of the small tower that seems to form the oldest part of the house, the N., W. and S. walls remain at ground-floor level where they average 7 ft. in thickness. The N. and W. walls probably extend upwards to second-floor level, but the E. wall of the tower has been removed, probably in the 17th century, so that its original dimensions are uncertain. The E. wing that was added to the S. wall of the tower probably comprised a range of three vaulted apartments on the ground floor, of which the easternmost, now a wine-cellar, was a kitchen. This room has a segmental-headed fireplace, now blocked, in the S. wall. At the E. end of the apartment the vault is reinforced by an arch, which, at its N. end, is pierced by a small rectangular aperture, now blocked. This may have been a communication shaft as it is too small to have served as a hatch; a similar aperture exists in the kitchen at Gargunnock House (No. 215). The purpose of the arch itself is uncertain; it may have been introduced to reinforce the vault during alterations to the wall above. The vaults of the two westernmost apartments, which were probably cellars, have been removed. The upper floors contain no features of particular interest and the diminished wall-thicknesses suggest that there has been considerable alteration and rebuilding.

The addition by which this E. wing was itself extended eastwards apparently comprised a range of four vaulted cellars entered from a corridor on the N. Two large bay-windows were incorporated in the S. wall of the addition during the 19th century, while in the same period the N. wall was masked by the new entrance-hall and staircases. The N. wall retains its plinth, however, together with a number of late 17th-century windows with roll-and-double-fillet mouldings. The two westernmost cellars remain, together with part of the N. corridor, but only one of the cellars retains its vault. The two easternmost cellars and the E. part of the N. corridor have been remodelled to form a single large apartment, now a dining-room. In the 19th century a range of spacious apartments arranged *en suite* was formed on the first floor; the rich *décor* of these rooms exemplifies the taste of the period.

The extensive alterations made in the 17th century have already been described. The most interesting internal feature of the period that survives is the scale-and-platt stair near the SE. corner of the main block (Pl. 197 B). The stair has a balustrade with heavy square newels and the stair-well is panelled; some of the wood-work has been restored. Above, there is a painted plaster ceiling in the Baroque manner, which incorporates a perspective vista framed within a large oval (Pl. 197 A). A room in the NE. angle of the main block at first-floor level (Pl. 198) has an elaborate carved wooden fireplace-surround and overmantel in the style of Grinling Gibbons, but this is understood to have been acquired within the present century. The sunk cellarage beneath the L-shaped wing at the E. end of the house contains a number of barrel-vaulted apartments, some of which have meat-hooks hanging from the crown of the vault. A doorway in the E. gable, now blocked, formerly gave external access to these cellars. In the 18th century a large kitchen, rising through two storeys, was formed by the

[1] The originals of this plan, and also of the others to be mentioned below, are preserved at Callendar; copies are in the possession of the Scottish National Buildings Record.

removal of a first floor; it is divided into bays by heavy pilasters which rise to support a moulded cornice above which there is a coved ceiling. In the E. wall of the kitchen there is a large elliptical-headed fireplace which retains a roasting-spit, while in the N. wall there is an oven (Pl. 199 A) and a hot-plate (Pl. 199 B), both apparently of 18th-century date and remarkable for the decoration of the cast-iron fittings. This wing retains the octagonal stair in the former re-entrant angle (*supra*), although it is now masked by 19th-century additions. The wing at the W. end of the house does not retain its octagonal stair; it has been much altered internally and is now used as an estate office.

POLICIES. Writing in 1707, Sibbald says, "The *Calander* has a large Wood adjacent to it, with Walks cut through it, and Fish Ponds near the House."[1] The policies, though still well wooded, have been remodelled to conform with later ideas of landscape gardening, a notable feature of the scheme having been the removal of a section of the Antonine Wall (No. 111) in front of the mansion to provide a vista to the north. The fish-ponds of Sibbald's day may perhaps be represented by the lake that lies SE. of the mansion, from which a small canal appears, at some time, to have run westwards through the policies. About half a mile SW. of the mansion the canal-bed is spanned by a stone bridge (Pl. 227 C), the parapet of which is borne on cast-iron baluster-shafts.

MAUSOLEUM. About half a mile SE. of the mansion, and forming a feature of the scheme of landscape gardening mentioned above, there stands a mausoleum built in the form of a circular Classical temple (Pl. 50 A). This was completed about 1816.[2] The heavily rusticated podium supports a cella and a peristyle of twelve columns of the Greek Doric order. The entrance is on the NW., and bears on its lintel Lucian's couplet[3]:

ΘΝΗΤΑ ΤΑ ΤΩΝ ΘΝΗΤΩΝ ΚΑΙ ΠΑΝΤΑ ΠΑΡΕΡΧΕΤΑΙ ΗΜΑΣ
ΗΝ ΔΕ ΜΗ ΑΛΛ ΗΜΕΙΣ ΑΤΤΑ ΠΑΡΕΡΧΟΜΕΘΑ

("Mortals' possessions are mortal, and all things pass us by; if not, at any rate we pass them by").

SUNDIALS. There are two sundials in the policies. One stands close to the summer-house, about 200 yds. S. of the mansion. An obelisk shaft rises from a square base to support a cubical dial-head. The angles of the dial are carved with masks, and one face bears the date 1677 and another the initials A N and E C, all incised. The significance of these initials is uncertain. The total height of the sundial is 3 ft., but there are indications that in its present form it is incomplete or has been remodelled. The other sundial stands about 80 yds. S. of the mansion. The shaft, which is square in section, rises from a moulded base to support a dial-head in the form of a bulged capital. Both shaft and head contain a number of geometrically shaped sunk dials. The structure is 4 ft. 1 in. high, but the shaft is shorter than in most sundials of this type and may have been truncated. One face of the shaft is carved in relief with a shield charged: Quarterly, 1st and 4th, three gillyflowers within a double tressure, for Livingstone; 2nd and 3rd, a bend between six billets, for Callendar; en surtout an escutcheon, now blank.[4] Above the shield there is an earl's coronet together with the incised initials E / I L, presumably for James, 5th and last Earl of Linlithgow, who succeeded to the title in 1695. A copper dial by Adie of Edinburgh has at some time been inset on the top of the dial-head.

ICE-HOUSE. An ice-house, which is now inaccessible, is set into an earthen bank rather more than 100 yds. to the N. of the house.

898793 NS 87 NE 30 June 1957

312. Polmont Park. This "genteel house", which was advertised for sale in 1793[5], was added to twice in the course of the 19th century and has also been considerably altered inside.[6]

The N. face of the original house is 45 ft. in length and shows squared rubble masonry brought to courses, V-jointed quoins, a central entrance flanked by Venetian windows, three square-headed windows on the first floor, a moulded eaves-course, plain tabling and decorated skewputs. All the windows have backset margins. The door has a moulded architrave, and is flanked by columns with moulded bases and capitals supporting an ornamented frieze and a curving broken pediment. On the S. elevation some of the windows have been altered, and the large dormers are no doubt an addition. Internally, the front door seems to have opened into a lobby containing a stair, though the existing stair is a replacement. The large rooms lit by the Venetian windows, to E. and W. of the entrance, are evidently in their original condition, and the one to the E. has an arch-headed alcove in its back wall and an Adam-type fireplace. On the first floor a landing gives access, to E. and W. through plaster arches supported on fluted pilasters with floreated capitals, to passages, each of which admits to a room on N. and S. Opening directly from the landing is a smaller room, now a bathroom. On the floor above there is one large room to E. and another to W., now lighted by the south-facing dormers; at the head of the stair is a small room lit by a skylight, also adapted as a bathroom.

932792 NS 97 NW 10 March 1953

313. Parkhill. The house of Parkhill stands in its policies 600 yds. SE. of the cross-roads (A 9 and A 905)

---

[1] Sibbald, *History*, 54.
[2] Information from Lt.-Col. W. Forbes of Callendar.
[3] *Anthologia Palatina*, x, 31.
[4] This escutcheon, which should bear an oak tree within a bordure charged with eight gillyflowers, is the augmentation for the title of Linlithgow.
[5] *Edinburgh Evening Courant*, 16th May 1793. The Commissioners are indebted for this reference to Lt.-Col. R. L. Hunter, T.D., F.S.A.
[6] This house has been gutted since the date of visit.

midway between Polmont and Laurieston. The earliest part of the existing complex, which alone is of interest, was built about 1790 by James Cheape of Sauchie,[1] who in 1788 had acquired the estate which was then known as "Parkend". This name seems to be first mentioned in 1602, in the will of the then proprietor Robert Bellenden; in 1788 it was changed to "Park Place", and this in turn was changed to "Parkhill" in 1794. The portion of the property W. of Polmont Burn originally formed part of the Forestlands of Redding and Abbotspark, while the remainder belonged to Over Polmont.

The house of 1790, together with what seems to be a later extension at either end, now constitutes the NE. range of the greatly extended mansion. Its interior has been considerably altered, but its exterior, as seen from NE. and SW., provides a good example of contemporary taste in small country houses. Its resemblance to Laurelhill House (No. 291) is marked. It consists of an oblong block three storeys in height, with a partly-sunk basement and a hipped and slated roof above a moulded eaves-course; the masonry is random rubble and the voids have squared rybats and dressed margins. The quoins are also dressed. The central portion of the NE. front forms a shallow, squared projection, finished with a gable, and contains, on the first or principal floor, a central three-light window with a fanlight, evidently the original entrance. This is flanked on either side by a Venetian window. The windows in the basement and the second floor are single and square-headed. In the centre of the SW. front there is a semicircular projection finished with a low conical roof; this contains a three-light window on the first and second floors but a single light in the basement. All the other windows on this side are likewise square-headed, except for two on the first floor NW. of the central projection.

CARVED DETAILS. Among the architectural fragments outside the lodge at the SE. entrance to the policies there may be mentioned: (i) A stone slab, inscribed in relief, the sides of which have been trimmed off as parts of the inscription are missing. It may be restored conjecturally as follows [CHRIST] IS MY ADVANTAG[E OVER / SIN A]ND DEATH 1610 / [BLISSIT BE] GOD FOR ALL H[IS GIFTIS] / R B I A. The first pair of initials would fit Robert Bellenden, but the laird of Parkend in 1610 was called David, not Robert, and his wife was Annas Livingstoun[2]; while neither his grandfather, from whom he inherited, nor his father, though both of them were named Robert, appears to have had a wife with the initials I A. The stone is thus probably not a relic of the earlier mansion-house of Parkend, and is more likely to have been brought from elsewhere—even, possibly, from Edinburgh (cf. No. 420). (ii) A dressed stone 5 ft. long, 1 ft. 3 in. deep and 7 in. thick, inscribed in large relief lettering of 17th-century appearance ANGVSTA ADVERSVM AVGVSTA / W F B G. The motto may perhaps be translated "Poverty is the adversary of renown". On the upper edge of the stone there are five sockets, as if for iron bars or dowels. (iii) A large slab worked on its face with an ogival arch-head moulded and crocketed and ending in a heavy finial. A small shield, now blank, appears above either haunch of the arch-head, and within the arch there are some traces of Gothic decoration. The style suggests a date in the 15th century.

928787 NS 97 NW 3 March 1953

314. Polmont House. Polmont House stands some 300 yds. NE. of Polmont Junction, on an eminence from which it overlooks the Polmont Burn and the village and lower-lying ground to the N. Its oldest portion seems to have been built about 1785,[3] probably by Gilbert Laurie, formerly Lord Provost of Edinburgh, who owned the estate in 1787.[4] However, like its contemporaries Polmont Park (No. 312) and Parkhill (No. 313), it has been considerably altered and enlarged, with the result that its original appearance, as a plain three-storeyed block, has been very largely obscured. As first built it comprised an oblong block measuring 47 ft. 4 in. from E. to W. by 30 ft. 4 in. transversely over walls 3 ft. 3 in. thick; the S. façade of this can be seen in Pl. 195 A, flanked by later wings and having its central portion covered and its entrance hidden by a tower, 14 ft. 2 in. wide by 8 ft. 7 in. deep, which has also been added to it.

The original block rises to a height of three storeys and finishes in a hipped roof above a moulded eaves-course. There is a sunk cellarage containing two apartments under the W. half, reached by a downward continuation of the main stair, and, on the ground floor, a large single room on each side of the hall which contains in its inner end a stone wheel-stair ascending anti-clockwise. On the upper floors the space appears to have been formerly divided into four apartments, opening two on each side of the landings; but the interior has been so much altered that no early details are now recognisable. As was usual in the latter half of the 18th century, single square-headed windows were regularly spaced in the front and back walls, and at least two are known to be closed up on the first floor of the W. gable where it is crossed by the roof of the wing. The first additions, probably made about the turn of the 18th and 19th centuries, are the single-storeyed wings seen in Pl. 195 A, which both measure approximately 32 ft. in length by 29 ft. 8 in. transversely. They are set back 6 in. from the face of the S. front; their double-pitched roofs end in gables which carry tabling with ornamental urn-finials on the skewputs, while pinnacles of obelisk form rise above the eaves in the centre of each side-wall. The W. wing contains a single room and is lit by a Venetian window

[1] The Commissioners are indebted to Miss Gray-Buchanan of Parkhill for the loan of unpublished notes by her father, the late Mr. A. W. Gray-Buchanan of Parkhill, from which the historical facts here given have been derived.

[2] Falkirk Proclamations of Marriage, 11th December 1611 (A. W. G.-B.).

[3] *The Edinburgh Evening Courant* of 10th March 1788 described it as "an excellent house . . . built within these few years with suitable offices".

[4] *Scots Magazine*, xlix, 467.

in each side-wall; the E. one has been partitioned into kitchen apartments and has a similar window, now partly blocked up, in the N. wall and two single-light windows on the S. A comparatively recent addition to the wing itself extends the kitchen premises still further E. The second addition increased the width of the original house by 11 ft. along the whole length of its N. side. It comprises a building of two storeys, each containing a long, narrow gallery-like apartment. The upper room was lit by single windows, but those on the ground floor were lit by a three-light window on each side of a central portico; this portico, which contains the front door, is built of ashlar and appears to be of still later construction. At the same time, a single-storeyed outshot lit by a double window and measuring 12 ft. 8 in. by 8 ft. 6 in., was built in extension of each end of the addition against the respective wings, and the tower was also added to the middle of the S. façade. The tower contains an entrance in its E. side, and provides space for bathrooms on its upper floors. The whole of this range of additions, as well as the tower, is flat-roofed and battlemented, and may be ascribed to about the middle of the 19th century.

933782 NS 97 NW 9 April 1953

315. Folly, Avondale House. This folly stands on a knoll a quarter of a mile S. of Avondale House and about 1 mile E. of the village of Polmont. It is a small square pavilion in the castellated style, with a circular tower at each angle and an embattled parapet. It contains a single apartment, which has a fireplace, but the building is now roofless and is falling into decay.

953788 NS 97 NE (unnoted) 3 May 1956

316. Muiravonside House. Muiravonside House stands on the left bank of the Avon, overlooking the deep glen through which this stretch of the river flows. The building has acquired its present somewhat U-shaped plan (Fig. 143) as a result of extensions, and of the addition of two parallel wings to what was originally a simple rectangular house. Few distinctive features of the original building have survived these and the other alterations that have taken place, but it can be identified as a two-storeyed block, probably dating from the early 17th century, which is alined from ENE. to WSW. and measures 46 ft. 7 in. in length by 20 ft. 8 in. in width over walls 2 ft. 7 in. thick. An attic is also present, but this may not be the original one but a replacement made when the roof was renewed. The exterior is rendered in a thin coating of cement, but the walls appear to be well built of random rubble; the quoins are dressed and a quirked edge-roll moulding is wrought on the voids. Towards the W. end of the S. front there is an outer door on the ground floor, while another on the first floor, which was presumably reached by a forestair, has been made into a window. To the E. of the entrance there are two original windows with a later one, which repeats the edge-roll moulding, inserted between them. This arrangement is repeated on the floor above. In the N. wall a window has been built up, its aperture appearing as a recess on the inner face. Most of the W. gable has been removed to allow the addition of a bowed W. end, and an extension with a similar rounded end has been made for symmetry outside the E. gable. On the ground floor, the interior is now divided into two rooms, both entered by doors broken through the N. wall, and the corresponding doors on the first floor have likewise been broken through—all these rooms being in communication with the additions. These rooms show no features of interest and their fireplaces are modern. Of the wings, the E. one is probably

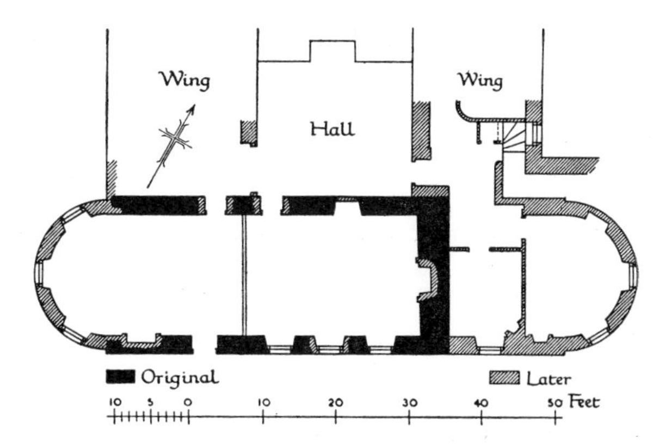

Fig. 143. Muiravonside House (No. 316)

the earlier as it seems to incorporate some older masonry in its lower part, whereas the upper part resembles the squared rubble-work of the W. wing; it may thus have been reconstructed at the time when the W. wing was built—*i.e.* probably in the late 18th or early 19th century. The inner part of the court, between the wings, has been cut off at a later date to form a hall with a porch; above the hall is a large room. A door leading into the W. wing from the court has a moulding of the same character as is seen on the S. front; it may well have been taken from the original house and reset in the wing when this was built. The same may be said of a panel set above the door and inscribed 1604 / I R M Q, and in this case the date would presumably refer to the construction of the original house. In the E. face of the E. wing there is set another panel, which bears the date 1630; this may be the date of the first construction of this wing, as evidenced by the older masonry mentioned above.

In the early 17th century the lands of Muiravonside belonged to the Lords Ross,[1] and the initials I R may possibly represent a member of this family. Since the beginning of the 19th century the property has been in the hands of the Stirlings of Muiravonside, a branch of the family of Stirling of Cadder.[2]

964753 NS 97 NE 18 March 1953

[1] *The Scots Peerage*, vii, 255.
[2] Burke, *Landed Gentry* (1952 ed.).

317. Compston. The farm of Compston stands on the N. side of the road from Linlithgow Bridge to Avonbridge, a third of a mile W. of its crossing over the Union Canal. The farmhouse seems to have been altered and enlarged early in the 19th or late in the 18th century, but its main portion, a two-storeyed block measuring 40 ft. by 25 ft. externally, evidently dates from a considerably earlier period. This is shown by the design of the front door, which has a bolection-moulded and lugged surround, a pulvinated frieze and a moulded cornice, as well as by the chamfered margins of the three first-floor windows. The two ground-floor windows, which are much larger and unchamfered, were no doubt inserted during the reconstruction. The stair-projection at the back, which contains a tall window, may or may not be an original feature, while the outshots at the two ends are likely to be additions. The Commission's officer was refused access to the interior.

Other survivals of the earlier phase are to be seen in the chamfered arrises of a yard-entrance, by which access is now obtained to the back door, and in two chamfered lintels re-used over windows in the N. wall of the range of farm-buildings that extends W. from the yard.

The house of "Compstone" is on record in 1723.[1]

957759 NS 97 NE 10 April 1955

318. Dalquhairn. This house stands nearly half a mile SW. of Avonbridge, on ground sloping gently to the left bank of a small burn which joins the Avon just above the village. On this slope, in front of the house, there has been a walled garden about 180 ft. square. Access is obtained by a track from the Avonbridge-Slamannan highway, which passes at about a hundred yards' distance on the right bank of the burn. The remains comprise a dwelling-house and two ranges of outbuildings projecting from it at right angles and enclosing, with it, a courtyard measuring 65 ft. by 44 ft. 9 in. (Fig. 144). The outer end of the courtyard seems to have been closed by a wall, which presumably had a gateway in the centre. Everything is now in a more or less advanced state of ruin, but the house is said locally to have been inhabited until the end of the 19th century. This is the earliest portion of the surviving complex; it bears the date 171[?1] above the front entrance but seems to incorporate parts of an earlier structure (*infra*). The two ranges flanking the courtyard were evidently added to the dwelling, either as stabling or as farm-buildings.

The house measures 49 ft. 9 in. by 20 ft. 3 in. over rubble-built walls 2 ft. 1 in. thick; the partitions, in which all the fireplaces and vents are conveniently gathered, are 2 ft. 8 in. thick. It stands to a height of two storeys and an attic; the slated roof, which has no dormer windows, still survives over the eastern half but only in a dilapidated condition. Evidence for the existence of an older house is provided by the re-use, here and there, of its dressed stonework—*e.g.* a 17th-century pediment (*infra*), bead mouldings more suggestive of the 16th or 17th than of the 18th century on the back door and on one jamb of a salt-box in the kitchen, and socket-holes for bars in the soffit of a window which shows no corresponding sockets in the sill. Again, the appearance of the masonry changes at a ragged race-bond between the back door and the window to the W. of it; all four windows E. of the back door have rounded arrises, while those to the W. of it have backset margins and sharp arrises; the same distinction applies to the voids in the W. and E. gables, with the exception of the E. attic window. The door to the outshot in the E. gable may, however, have been reconstructed, perhaps from a window. All these facts suggest that parts of an earlier building may survive in the E. end of the back wall and in the E. gable. The front, however, is of one build and is uniform in design. It shows, on the ground floor, a central doorway, now partly ruined, flanked on each side by two windows and a small oval light, and on the first floor five windows symmetrically placed. The architrave of the doorway is lugged and has a roll-and-hollow moulding; it is surmounted by a convex frieze, moulded cornice and broken segmental pediment, the latter bearing on the tympanum the initials J S and I M flanked by the date 171[?1]. The initials are those of James Shaw and his wife Issobel Mill.[2] The windows have backset marginal surrounds but the arrises of the rybats are rounded. The rear lintels of all windows and outer doors, as well as those of internal doors and presses, are of wood. Above the lintel of the back door there has been inserted what seems to be the broken-off top of a curved and moulded pediment, surmounted by a device resembling a fleur-de-lys finial with the date 166[?5]. Wall-heads both front and back finish in a heavy ogival-moulded eaves-course, and the plain tabling of the gables rests on a rebated cavetto skewput. At the apex of each gable there has been a finial, but the E. one is now missing.

Internally the space is divided into three portions, the narrowest being in the middle; the two end rooms are thus of much the same size and of almost square shape on all three storeys. On the ground floor the central hall, the kitchen to the W. and the parlour to the E. measure respectively 9 ft., 15 ft. 2 in., and 15 ft. 7 in., and each occupies the full internal width of the house (16 ft. 3 in.). The upper floors contain bedroom accommodation similarly arranged (see Fig. 144). The kitchen contains a fireplace which is plain except for ogival-moulded, corbelled caps on its jambs. Beside the S. jamb there is a small recess, and N. of the fireplace and in the N. wall there are cupboard-recesses, both originally shelved. In the SW. corner there is an external door covered by a later porch; this has been butt-jointed against the main wall, which has been raggled for a penthouse roof. The corresponding door in the parlour opens into a narrow outshot, also an addition, which has similarly been covered by a penthouse roof, as is shown by two channelled corbels projecting from the wall-face above the door—presumably supports for a runner-beam. In the N. wall of the parlour there is a cupboard recess and another,

[1] *Geogr. Collections*, i, 316.
[2] *Index to General Register of Sasines*, 1701-20, 755.

South-east Elevation

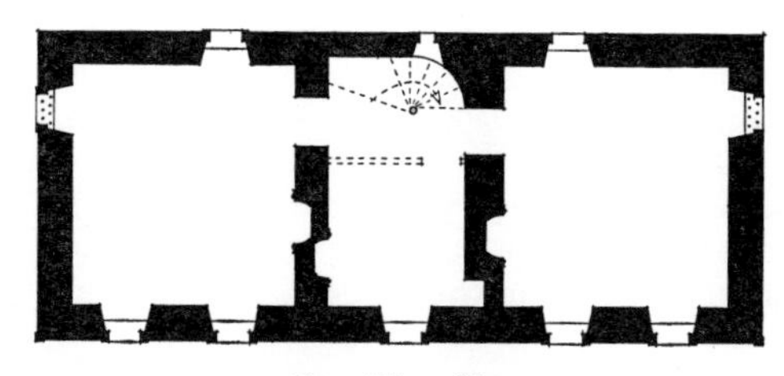

First Floor Plan

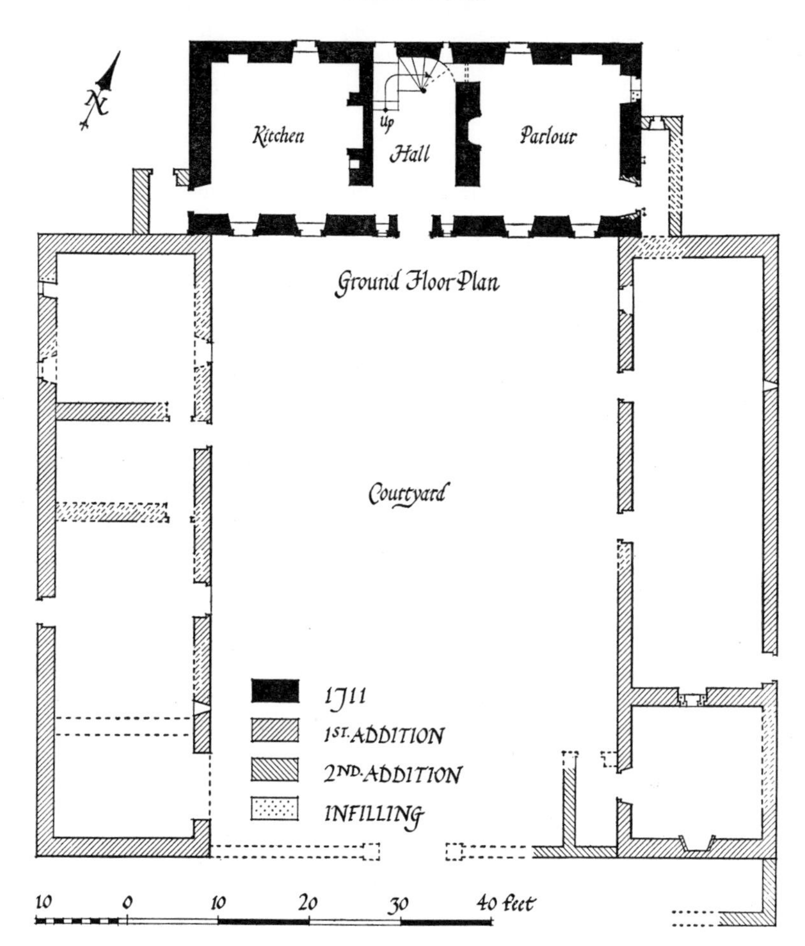

Fig. 144. Dalquhairn (No. 318); plan and reconstructed elevation

which was once shelved, appears in the NW. corner. The jambs and lintel of the fireplace are worked with a roll-and-hollow moulding. A stone wheel-stair, which has had a press underneath it, rises from beside the back door, at the back of the hall; this serves the first floor, but the upper flight, leading to the attic, was of wood and the winders are now missing. The small mid-room on the first floor is provided with a fireplace with plain upstart jambs and lintel, and in the SE. corner there is a locker with a rounded arris on its N. jamb. In each of the end rooms a window in the gable has been blocked up and converted into a shelved press; the fireplaces are similar to the one in the living-room. The mid-room on the attic floor is simply a closet, but each end-room is dimly lit by a small window in the gable and is furnished with a plain fireplace from which the jambs and the lintel have now fallen out. All the internal wall-faces have been finished in plaster.

The outbuildings flanking the courtyard are heavily ruined, and are in general reduced to or below the height of the window-sills. Where their walls make contact with the front of the house the masonry is butt-jointed. Both ranges measure 66 ft. 6 in. in length, and the W. one 18 ft. 10 in. and the E. one 17 ft. 9 in. in width, in each case over walls varying from 1 ft. 9 in. to 2 ft. in thickness. The W. range appears to have been divided into four apartments by three transverse partitions; remains of two of these survive, and the third, shown on the plan by unhatched dotted lines, has been added conjecturally to divide what was certainly a coach-house or cart-shed, on the S., from what was probably a stable on the N. The existence of the former is proved by the wide entrance (7 ft.) in its E. wall, by the surviving springer of an original arched head, and by the crooks for a hinged door; while the splayed, 3 in. slit to the N. of it, probably provided for ventilation rather than for lighting, combines with the arrangement of the doors in the E. and W. walls to suggest a stable. About 12 ft. W. of this range, and 21 ft. from its northern end, there is a well, lined with masonry.

The E. range is subdivided unequally into two apartments, the N. one of which may have contained a byre and barn and the S. one a bothy for a groom or farm-hands. The latter, which is 14 ft. 2 in. square, opens off a porch in the SE. corner of the courtyard and is provided with a fireplace in its S. gable. In the N. wall opposite there has been a communicating door now converted into a small window. In the gable above this converted door three ledged pigeon-holes have been formed, and there are slight traces of nesting boxes on the inside. The window and pigeon-holes, being external features, must have been inserted after the room at the end of the range had lost its roof and passed out of use. In the larger division there are two doors opening W. into the courtyard, while a third, in the SE. corner, opens E. In the E. wall there is also a single splayed slit. The fact that some of the door-margins in both ranges are backset with square arrises, while others show chamfered or rounded arrises, suggests that alterations and insertions have been made from time to time.

During the 17th and 18th centuries Dalquhairn was in the possession of the Shaw family,[1] the present house having evidently been built by James Shaw (*supra*) in the second decade of the 18th century.

The track leading to the buildings crosses the burn, mentioned above, by a bridge which seems to be at least as old as the house. This is described separately under No. 464.

905724 NS 97 SW 26 April 1954

319. Pirnie Lodge. This house was built by the Rev. William Hastie, sometime minister of Slamannan, whose initials, with those of his wife, Isabella Shaw, and the date 1735, appear on the lintel of the front door (Pl. 174 C). The house measures 29 ft. by 19 ft. externally, and the façade shows one window on either side of the central doorway, with two others on the first floor placed symmetrically above them. The jambs of the doorway bear roll-and-hollow mouldings returned at the top; the inscription on the lintel is in bold raised letters on sunk panels and reads M R / W H I S 1735. The front windows have all been enlarged, but a small original window, with rounded arrises, which lights the stair can be seen in the centre of the back wall together with a smaller one, of irregular shape, at ground-floor level. In the NE. gable a window on the first floor has been built up, but a small one remains to light the roof-space above. The gables are crow-stepped, and the existing slate roof replaces an original roof of thatch. Internally there is a room to the right of the entrance, a stair in the centre of the house, and a hall and pantry to the left. On the first floor there are two rooms.

870728 NS 87 SE 10 April 1954

320. Glorat. The house of Glorat, which stands about a mile due E. of Lennoxtown, was largely rebuilt in 1869, the tower being added in 1879, but some older structure, the date of which is not certain, is incorporated in the W. gable, and in the lower part of the wall on the N. side. The quoins of the NW. corner, and the heavy, backset margins of three windows in this part of the building, certainly antedate any Victorian reconstruction. Reset at lintel level beside the easternmost of the two windows in the N. side there is likewise to be seen a stone bearing the initials M S and the date 1625, probably re-cut; the initials are those of Mungo Stirling, at that time heir to his father, Sir John Stirling, 4th of Glorat, whom he succeeded in 1642.

In the E. face of the wing just N. of the present entrance there has been inserted a small triangular pediment, with a narrow moulded margin, bearing an arm issuing out of a cloud from the sinister side and grasping a sword in pale, all within a roundel. This is the honorable augmentation,

[1] *The Commissariot Record of Stirling, Register of Testaments*, 1607-1800, S.R.S., 145 f.

here separately represented, that was conferred on Sir George Stirling, 6th of Glorat, by Charles II in 1666 (*infra*).

The Stirlings of Glorat[1] are one of the oldest families in the county, tracing their descent through the Stirlings of Craigbarnet from the Stirlings of Cadder. William, 1st of Glorat, was the second son of Sir John Stirling of Craigbarnet; he received a charter for the lands of Glorat in 1508, and the family has continued in possession since that date. The Stirlings of Glorat were strong Royalists, and the patent creating Sir George Stirling's Baronetcy of Nova Scotia in 1666 refers especially to services rendered by him and his father Sir Mungo "in His Majestie's service". The coat was registered at the Lyon Office (1672-8) as "*Argent* a bend engrailed *azur* [properly Sable] charged with three buckles *or*, on a chief *gules* a naked arme issuing out of a cloud from ye sinister side, grasping a sword in pale, and therewith guarding ane Imperiall crowne placed in ye dexter canton proper, All within a double Tressur, counter flowered of thistles *vert*".[2]

641778 NS 67 NW 1 October 1953

321. Kincaid House. The main interest of this building, which is now a hotel, resides in its eastern block, which provides a good example of early 19th-century taste (Pl. 202 A). It was designed by David Hamilton, the architect of Lennox Castle (No. 324) and of the High Church of Campsie (No. 156), and was built about 1812.[3] It is said to have been inspired by Inveraray Castle.

The block in question is an oblong two-storeyed building of droved ashlar measuring 70 ft. by 43 ft., and having at each corner a round tower which rises higher than the wall-heads. The central portion of the E. face is slightly advanced. The frontal towers and the walls between them finish in corbelled and crenellated parapets, that of the projection, which rises above the wall-head, being pierced. The roof is hipped and slated, and above the centre of it rises a low square tower with a large pointed window in its E. and W. faces. The E. façade shows, in the centre, the front door, with fanlight and narrow flanking lights, covered by a semicircular, parapeted portico resting on four columns, reeded and rather slim in their proportions. Above the portico, on the upper floor, there is a window with three pointed lights, and to right and left other three-light windows, those on the first floor being square-headed and those on the ground floor having segmental heads in the centre and round heads at the sides. Each tower shows two single lights on each floor, round-headed below and square-headed above, one being blind in each case. All the lower windows have label mouldings. The sides have two-light windows on each floor, the easternmost ones being blind. A plain splayed plinth is present on all three sides, and a string-course at the level of the window-sills on each floor. The front door leads into a vestibule, and this communicates, through a glazed partition in which there are two thin fluted columns, with a spacious hall. A stone stair with bottle-nosed treads rises in its NW. corner.

The older portions of the house adjoin the N. part of the W. side of the 1812 block. They comprise, on the S., the remains of the original house, believed to date from about 1690,[4] and to the N. of this an addition of the mid-18th century. The original house seems to have been an oblong structure, of two storeys and an attic, measuring about 33 ft. by 19 ft. 9 in. Its masonry has been cemented over, but its crow-stepped W. gable still survives. The 18th-century addition is of droved ashlar and has a moulded eaves-course, a hipped roof and an outside stair on the west for access to the first floor. The windows, which have segmental arches on the ground floor and are square-headed on the first floor, show no signs of alteration, but a plan shown to the Commission's officers suggested that there had once been three storeys in the E. part of this building. The outbuildings and the basement cellarage are no doubt contemporary with the E. block.

Kincaid House was the residence of the family of Kincaid of that Ilk,[5] who formerly occupied an older house on the same site.

649760 NS 67 NW 28 September 1953

322. Birdston Farm.[6] The former house of Birdston is now incorporated in the steading of the farm, which stands about half-way between the Milton of Campsie and Kirkintilloch at the junction of a lane with the high-road. The Lennox Estate plan shows the farm-buildings as they existed in 1843, and their construction, and the conversion of the residence into a farmhouse, may well date from about that time, while the style and appearance of the house itself suggest a date about the middle of the 18th century. The house is an oblong block of two storeys and an attic, measuring approximately 45 ft. by 25 ft. and having its façade towards the S.; this shows, on the ground floor, a central entrance with two windows on either side of it and, on the first floor, five windows correspondingly arranged (Pl. 175 A). Quoins, windows and door have dressed and backset margins; the straight lintels of the lower windows and door have projecting false keystones. The wall-head finishes in a plain broad band in line with the upper lintels, and on top of this there is a moulded eaves-course; on the back wall, however, the eaves-course is a simple narrow band. Towards the E. end of the back wall there is a window on each floor, and the cement that now covers the masonry may hide built-up windows towards the W. end. About

[1] Bain, J., *The Stirlings of Craigbernard and Glorat*, 15 ff.
[2] *Ibid.*, 39.
[3] Cameron, J., *The Parish of Campsie*, 185.
[4] *Ibid.*
[5] On the connection of this family with that of Lennox of Woodhead see No. 205.
[6] The Commission's officers were not allowed access to this building by its proprietor, Mr. T. Reid; the following account has consequently had to be based on purely superficial observations reinforced by a plan dated 1843 (Fig. 145), which was kindly lent by Mr. W. R. Patterson, of the Lennox Estate Office.

the middle of this wall there is a staircase window with the suggestion of a built-up window below it. The back windows and quoins are not backset. The gables are topped with tabling which finishes in decorated roll-skewputs (Pl. 204 A); and in the middle of each a small window with a backset margin gives light to the garret. The plan of 1843 (Fig. 145) indicates that the entrance

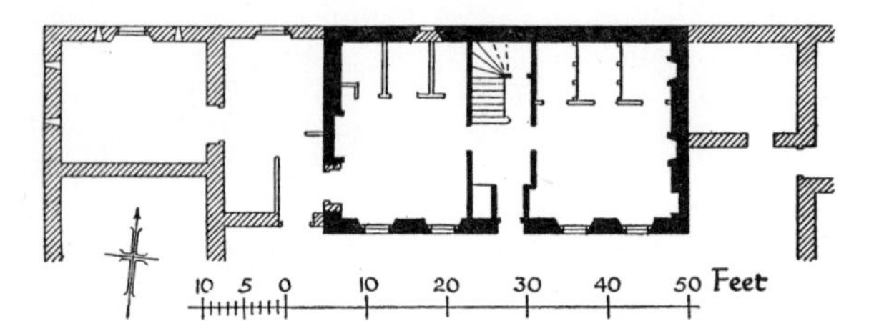

Fig. 145. Birdston Farm (No. 322); redrawn from an estate plan

then led into a hall containing the stair at its inner end and giving access to a single room on either side, the W. room being the kitchen and the E. one a parlour. The bed-closets shown on the plan are presumably not original. Bedrooms would no doubt have been similarly disposed on the floor above, probably with the addition of a small bed-closet, entered from the lobby, over the entrance hall.

654754 NS 67 NE 28 September 1953

323. Tower. Notwithstanding its name, the house of Tower, which stands some 700 yds. W. of Torrance, is simply a one-storeyed structure with an attic. Whatever its original status may have been, it now serves as a farm-house, the other farm-buildings flanking an open space in front of it. A late addition has been built against the SW. gable and communicates with the house through a broken-out doorway; but originally the house was, on plan, a simple oblong measuring 44 ft. 2 in. by 25 ft. The walls, 2 ft. 4 in. in thickness, are built of squared rubble brought to courses, with the gables finishing in a tabling stopped, on the front wall, on scrolled skewputs. On the front there is a moulded eaves-course, but on the back this is represented by a plain band. The roof has been re-slated.

The entrance is in the middle of the SE. face and is flanked on either side by two windows; all have backset margins, with keystones wrought on the lintels. The quoins also are backset, but the four windows in the back wall are plain and the south-westernmost one may be an insertion, its neighbour having been built up. On the upper floor there is a window in each gable, and two dormer windows to the front which are probably renewals. The entrance opens into a small lobby and passage leading to the back of the house, where a wooden dog-legged stair ascends to two attic bedrooms, one in each end of the building. On the ground floor there are similarly two rooms opening off the lobby, the south-western one being the original kitchen. In the kitchen the old lintelled fireplace has been contracted to take a modern range, and a bed-closet has been later partitioned off in the N. corner; in the other room the original fireplace is hidden by a subsequent contraction, and a partition has been inserted which cuts off space for a fireless bed-chamber on the NW. This north-eastern room, which has a sideboard recess on the SW., has been panelled, but the gable-end has been refaced with plain lining.

The lowermost part of the stair and its northern partition have been altered, and a bathroom above now occupies part of the space of the NE. attic. This is ceiled with boarding, but the ceiling of the SW. attic is plastered. The old fireplace in each gable on the attic floor has been renewed. The house may date from the end of the 18th century but more probably from the beginning of the 19th.

613741 NS 67 SW 28 September 1953

324. Lennox Castle. Lennox Castle stands in a conspicuous position above the high and steep S. bank of the Glazert Water, a mile and a half WNW. of Lennoxtown, and now serves as nurses' quarters in the Lennox Castle Institution (Glasgow Corporation). It was built between 1837 and 1841 by John Kincaid-Lennox, who succeeded to the estate of Woodhead in 1833, in preference to rebuilding the tower-house of Woodhead (No. 205). The architect was David Hamilton, who also designed Kincaid House (No. 321) and the High Church of Campsie (No. 156), and the structure deserves mention as a sample of contemporary taste. It is on record that the supposed style of a Norman castle was chosen for this house in the belief that it would be in keeping with the dignity of the earldom of Lennox, a claim which Mr. Kincaid-Lennox was pursuing at the time. In the upshot, however, the expense of the building was one of the main obstacles to the effective prosecution of this claim.[1]

The Castle is quadrangular on plan and consists of a massive U-shaped main block, measuring 154 ft. from N. to S. by 95 ft. from E. to W., with low ranges of offices and outbuildings, one or two storeys in height, enclosing a small courtyard on the west. The E. façade comprises a central portion, of three storeys with an attic in the roof, and wings which rise one storey higher and have their E. ends advanced from the plane of the central portion. Their W. ends extend backwards to flank part of the courtyard, and above the N. wing a large tower is carried up to a height of five storeys with its corner pilasters terminating in square turrets. This arrangement emphasises the importance of this tower as the chief feature of the N. front, and in it is set, on the first floor, the principal entrance, reached by an enclosed flight of wide stone steps which rise from an arched, vaulted and

[1] Cameron, J., *The Parish of Campsie*, 163 ff.

turreted *porte cochère*. Another tower of five storeys projects 22 ft. into the courtyard between the wings, and houses the main stair which is of stone with wooden balusters. All these features, except the stair-tower, will be recognised in Pl. 201 A, which also illustrates the use made by the architect of mediaeval models.

The masonry is red sandstone ashlar throughout, brought to courses, each of the upper storeys being defined by a continuous moulded string-course at window-sill level. The central portion of the E. face is topped by a plain parapet of slight projection, borne on continuous corbelling enriched at intervals by floriated ornament, while elsewhere on the higher wall-heads of the main block, and on the low buildings of the courtyard, the parapets are crenellated and supported on corbel-courses. Most of the corners of the main components are pilastered or shafted, and some of the pilasters themselves have shafts in the outer angles. Windows on the ground floor are heavily chamfered and lintelled, but above that level, with a few exceptions, the openings have moulded jambs and semicircular heads with label mouldings finishing on stops, some of which are carved with human heads. The majority are single lights, but some are grouped in twos or threes and, in some cases, they are set in a slight projection with a dentilated frieze, cornice and angle shafts.

Internally the apartments are roomy and high, especially on the principal floor. Striking of its kind, however unattractive to present-day taste, is the ceiling decoration in the dining-room, drawing-room and hall. The dining-room ceiling is divided into coffers by means of heavy ribs, moulded and carved, with carved bosses at the intersections, combined with lighter ribbing within in the form of the Greek cross. The drawing-room ceiling is of plaster and is subdivided in a generally similar manner; it is elaborately enriched and has pendants at the rib-intersections. The ceiling of the long hall, in the centre of the E. block, is subdivided by flat arches of wood, carved and moulded and resting on shafted pilasters; the main subdivisions are again broken up into coffers, and heavily enriched.

605783 NS 67 NW 1 October 1953

325. Ballencleroch. The house of Ballencleroch (Pl. 195 D) stands within its policies just outside the Clachan of Campsie and on the opposite (right) bank of the Kirk Burn. Originally a modest laird's house of the 17th century, it has grown to its present size as a result of extensive additions made in 1852-3 to the S. and W. of the original block, the walls of which, barring minor alterations introduced to suit the later work, are more or less entire. The original building comprised two storeys and an attic and was T-shaped on plan (Fig. 146), a small wing, now gutted of its staircase, projecting from about the middle of the S. side. The main block measures 49 ft. by 21 ft. and the wing 12 ft. by 10 ft. 5 in., the wall-head of the latter rising higher than that of the former. The walls are harled but show the dressed and backset margins of quoins and voids, and they finish in a moulded eaves-course carrying a slate roof which has been renewed. The gables are crow-stepped and end in moulded skewputs, the windows are chamfered on the arrises, and the original door, which is set in the middle of the N. side and has been converted into a window, is framed in a roll-and-hollow moulding. Above the entrance there is a panel enclosed by a moulded border

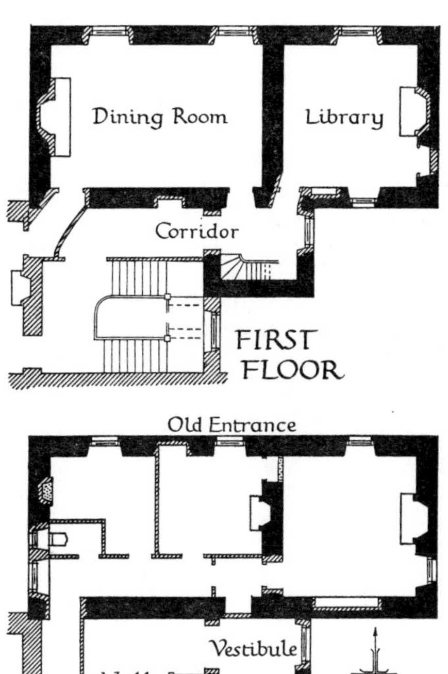

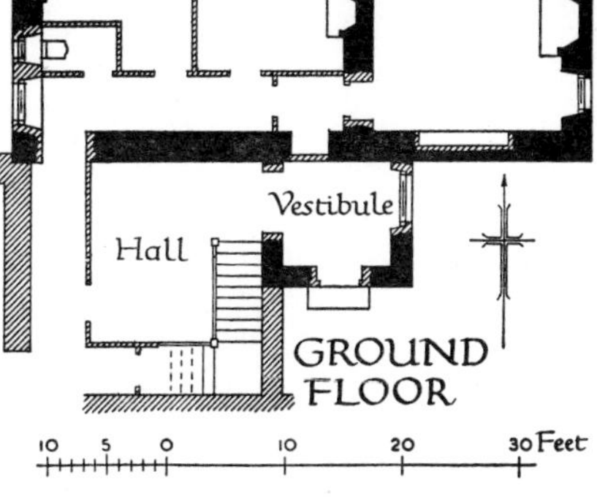

Fig. 146. Ballencleroch (No. 325)

and bearing a shield; this is parted per pale and charged: Dexter, a saltire between four roses, for MacFarlan; sinister, three pallets on a chief, for Keith. Respectively above and below the shield are the initials I M and M K, and the date 1665; the initials are those of James MacFarlan of Ballencleroch and his wife Mary Keith of Invermay, whom he married in 1652,[1] and the date is presumably that of the construction of the house. The two lower windows, one on each side of the doorway, are original, but the three above on the first floor have been enlarged. By the SE. angle of the house there are also three original windows, one on the ground floor and two on the first, but of the latter the one in the gable is harled over and its presence is indicated only by a later

[1] *Parish of Holyroodhouse or Canongate, Register of Marriages*, 1564-1800, S.R.S., 320.

cupboard formed on the inside. In the W. gable two windows have been broken through on the ground floor. The two smaller windows in the upper part of the wing are old, but the two larger ones on the E. side are insertions, as is also the entrance-doorway on the S. On the dismantling of the old staircase the ground floor of the wing became a vestibule, the original doorway from the main block being closed to form a press in the N. face of the wall. The vestibule communicated with the hall and staircase in the additions through a wide opening broken through the W. wall, while a similar opening on the floor above admitted an extension of a corridor off the new stair to replace the original first-floor landing. The attic of the wing, which is coomb-ceiled and lined with wood, and its narrow wooden stair were left intact.

The interior of the main block is divided by a heavy stone partition into two apartments on each floor, the original entrance having opened, on the level, into the larger one, which is to the west. The whole of the interior has been altered and modernised, but two fireplaces with roll-and-hollow mouldings remain *in situ* on the ground floor, one in the E. gable and the other in the partition. The E. room on the first floor, now the library, has been panelled—probably in the late 18th or early 19th century. The panelling is plain and fielded, and the fireplace, which is of similar type to those mentioned above but may only be a replica, is flanked by fluted pilasters. Around the room there is an elaborate frieze with a dentilated cornice, and the plaster ceiling has been grained to suit the woodwork.

SUNDIALS, ETC. In the garden, on the N. side of the house, there stands a fine sundial of obelisk type (Pl. 215 E), generally reminiscent of the one described under No. 444. It is said to have come from Lennox Castle (No. 324)[1] and, if so, may well have originated at Woodhead (No. 205). Its total height, including its base of three steps, is 6 ft.; its shaft is 9 in. square and its capital, which is octagonal, is 1 ft. 5½ in. high by 1 ft. 3 in. wide. The shaft is divided into three cubical sections by incised lines, which frame sunk dials of various designs; the capital bears hemispherical hollows on its central band, above and below which are four blank facets separated by triangular depressions. The obelisk-shaped uppermost portion is plain except for incised horizontal lines representing courses of masonry. It is topped by a small finial. This type of dial was in vogue during most of the 17th century and continued into the 18th. The capital of another obelisk-sundial, also octagonal and of approximately similar size, lies beside the entrance to the house; while a sundial of the cubical type is set on top of an arched gateway which opens into the back court. This latter is obviously not in its proper position, as the face bearing the dial is now turned towards the north; the reverse face is carved with a crescent-increscent and the dexter one with an eight-pointed star, while the sinister face is blank. The arch itself is said to have been taken from the kitchen of a house older than the one of 1665, which was demolished in 1852-3[2], and if so was presumably a fireplace-arch.

Another interesting fragment preserved in the garden is part of an heraldic panel which, when complete, measured 2 ft. 3 in. in height by 1 ft. 9 in. in width. It bears four shields, arranged quarterly and charged: 1st and 4th, a saltire wavy between four roses, for MacFarlan; 2nd and 3rd, two chevrons bendwise between six roundlets in two groups, two and one, and in dexter chief a canton. These appear to be the arms of Patrick MacFarlan of Keithton (*infra*) and his wife Christian Blair.[3] Yet another object which may be connected with the older house is a leaden water-tank, 2 ft. 6 in. long, 1 ft. 6 in. wide and 1 ft. 5 in. deep, which lies by the front door. It bears the date 1753 and is decorated with figures in relief. The fossil tree-trunk that has been set up in the garden in a socketed base is matched at the Old Manse of Kilsyth.

The lands of Ballencleroch belonged to the Brisbane family from the early years of the 15th century. In 1642 John Brisbane of Bishopton sold the estate to Patrick MacFarlan of Keithton, who was one of the MacFarlans of Arrochar, and it was his son James who built the house of 1665. John MacFarlan of Ballencleroch was responsible for the extensive additions of 1852-3, and the estate passed from the family in 1921.[4]

609794 NS 67 NW 29 September 1953

326. Middle Ballewan. Middle Ballewan stands about three-quarters of a mile NNW. of the village of Blanefield; it is a small laird's house of early 18th-century date which is now incorporated in a group of later buildings. The old house runs roughly E. and W. and measures 46 ft. 6 in. by 20 ft. 9 in. over walls 2 ft. 6 in. thick; it is a plain rectangular block, two storeys and an attic in height, and is built in rubble masonry with dressed quoins and margins. The walls finish in a plain eaves-band above which there may originally have been an eaves-course; the gables are crow-stepped and have ogee-moulded skewputs. The windows have chamfered arrises. The S. façade (Fig. 147), which is symmetrically disposed, incorporates two ranges of windows together with an entrance-doorway which is centrally placed on the ground floor. The surround of the doorway is wrought with a roll-moulding; above there is a stone panel which contains a monogram and the date 1702 carved in relief. The monogram appears to comprise the letters M I C I S and no doubt commemorates Master John Craig, second of Ballewan, and his wife whose name is unknown.[5] The three-light window to the E. of the entrance-doorway is an insertion, but the other openings are original; the windows were originally half-glazed, those on the ground floor being also barred. Internally the house has been much altered, but originally there seems to have been a central stair, with a single

[1] *T.G.A.S.*, new series, ix, pt. iv (1940), 277, 285.
[2] Cameron, J., *The Parish of Campsie*, 194 ff.
[3] *Ibid.*
[4] *Ibid.*; Burke, *Landed Gentry* (1952 ed.).
[5] *Strathblane*, 160.

large room on either side of it on both ground and first floors. A stone fireplace in the E. gable at first-floor level has an elaborate bead-moulding and seems to be an original feature; in the same room there is some plaster panelling.

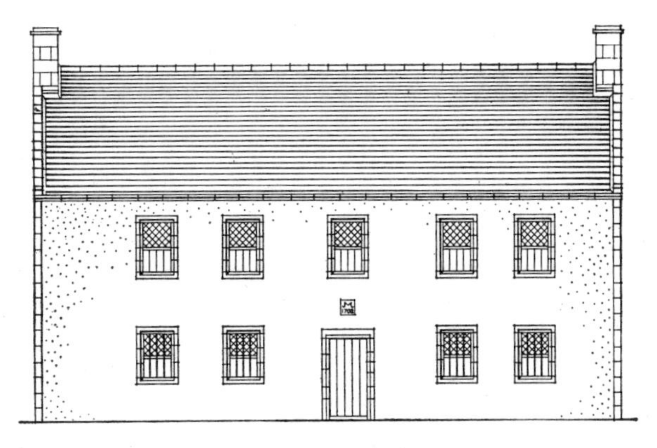

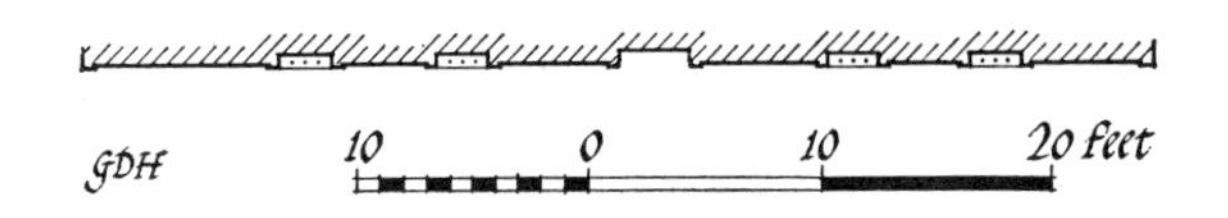

Fig. 147. Middle Ballewan (No. 326); S. elevation, reconstructed

The N. front of the old house is now masked by an extensive addition of 1890, while a single-storeyed outshot of 1773 adjoins it to the E. Another single-storeyed outshot, erected in 1766, adjoins the house to the W., and from it a single-storeyed range of offices returns to the S. Above a blocked doorway in the S. gable of this range there is incised the date 1774, while a re-used lintel over one of the doors in the E. wall bears the incised date 1684 and the initials I C and A K, for John Craig, first of Ballewan and his wife Agnes Kincaid, whom he married after 1648.[1]

Ballewan came into the hands of the Craig family in about 1628 and remained in its possession until 1835, when it was sold to James Graham.[2]

546807 NS 58 SW 12 August 1957

327. Carbeth Guthrie House. This house stands about 700 yds. E. of the point where a side-road to Blanefield branches from the Glasgow-Drymen highway; it was built soon after 1817 by John Guthrie of Carbeth.[3] The house, a plain Georgian building, comprises a block of three storeys and an attic with its front facing W. It measures on plan 61 ft. from E. to W. by 51 ft. from N. to S., the former dimension including an E. wing, in alinement with the N. side, which projects 4 ft. 9 in. beyond the main block. The basement is sunk, and the principal floor is reached by a short flight of steps in the middle of the W. front, spanning the sunk area. The revetting wall of the sunk area, which extends round the W. and S. sides only, is finished as a battlemented cope with square pedestals at intervals carrying urn-finials. The masonry of the house is squared rubble brought to courses, the windows having upstart jambs with moulded architraves and the lower ones cornices supported on scroll brackets. The original windows were regularly placed, but on N. and S. others have been inserted including a bay-window on the S. The quoins are back-set, and the wall-heads terminate in a cornice-course above which there is a slated hipped roof.

On the platt of the stair fronting the main entrance there is a portico of the Doric order, consisting of two plain pilasters and two fluted columns carrying a semi-circular entablature. The doorway itself is simple and is flanked by two narrow windows. The original internal arrangements have been altered.

528794 NS 57 NW 16 October 1953

328. Dalnair. Dalnair (Fig. 148) stands on the N. bank of the Endrick Water, two miles SE. of the village of Drymen and about five furlongs SSW. of Gartness. Although the building has been much altered and added to, it remains an interesting example of a late 17th-century manse (*infra*). The old house is T-shaped on plan and comprises a main block which runs roughly E. and W. and measures 47 ft. 3 in. by 20 ft. 9 in. over all, together with a staircase wing which projects to the N. and measures 11 ft. 5 in. by 10 ft. 2 in. over all. The building rises to a height of three storeys, the upper storey being lit by dormers. The masonry is harled rubble with dressed quoins and margins, and the original windows have rounded arrises and were formerly half-glazed; those on the ground floor seem to have been barred. The walls finish in a cavetto-moulded eaves-course and the gables were originally crow-stepped and had cavetto-moulded skewputs; this treatment may still be seen on the N. wing.

The old entrance-doorway, which has a rusticated surround, remains in the N. wall of the wing but is now converted for use as a window. The lintel bears the incised date 1682, which was recut in 1957, together with initials of which all but the letters M C and E are now illegible. Presumably the full inscription comprised the initials M I C and E G for Master James Craig and his wife Elizabeth Govane (*infra*). Above the doorway there is a moulded frame, evidently designed to contain an heraldic panel but now empty. There was originally a single window on each floor of the main block on either side of the wing, but only the first-floor window to the E. remains unaltered, the others having been either enlarged or else masked by the single-storeyed outshot that now fills the NW. re-entrant angle of main block and

[1] *Ibid.*, 158. [2] *Ibid.*, 157 ff. [3] *Ibid.*, 41 ff.

wing. The pediments of the dormer windows have been renewed.

The S. front has also been altered. Originally there seems to have been a range of three windows, more or less symmetrically disposed, on all three floors; but a central entrance-doorway has replaced a window on the ground floor, the westernmost window on the ground floor has been enlarged, and the pediments of the dormer windows have been renewed.

Inside the house the main features of the original plan may still be traced (Fig. 148). The old entrance-doorway in the N. wing opens directly on to a turnpike stair which gives access to the upper floors. Most of the stair treads seem to have been renewed, but those at the top have moulded nosings and are probably original. To the S. of the stair there is a hall, from which access is obtained to a single room at each end of the main block. A similar arrangement probably existed on the upper floors, a small bedroom perhaps taking the place of the hall. The thickness of the E. gable suggests that the ground-floor room at the E. end of the main block may originally have been a kitchen.

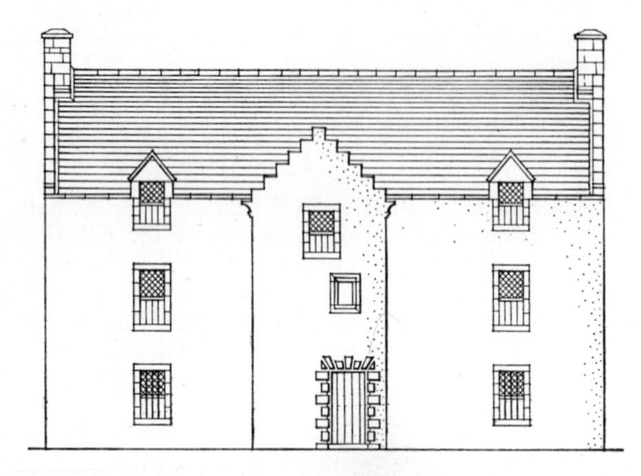

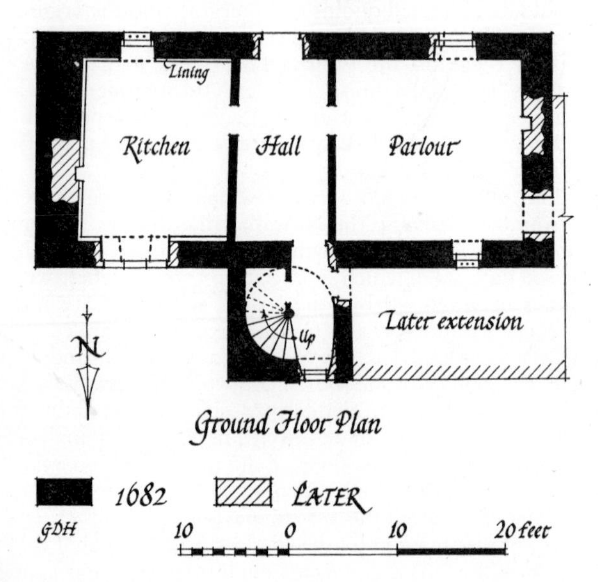

Fig. 148. Dalnair (No. 328); plan and reconstructed elevation

The lands of Dalnair were purchased by Mr. James Craig, Minister of Killearn, from Archibald, Lord Napier, in 1679,[1] and three years later Craig erected the present building to serve as a manse. His long tenure of the benefice of Killearn was not without incident, for in 1689, following the Revolution Settlement, he was brought before the Privy Council and charged with a number of offences such as not reading the Proclamation of the Estates and not praying for King William and Queen Mary. He was further accused of having said that he wished King William "were drowned in the mickle pot of Great Nesse, which is the deepest place in the Murray water".[2] These charges were found not proven and Craig was acquitted, only to be deposed in the following year after a ministry of thirty-two years. His descendants continued to live at Dalnair until 1775, when Captain William Craig sold the estate to Nicol Graham of Gartmore. At the end of the 19th century, Dalnair, together with some neighbouring properties, came into the hands of Thomas Brown, of Glasgow, who built the large mansion known as Dalnair House about three-quarters of a mile W. of old Dalnair.[3]

494860 NS 48 NE 15 August 1957

329. Buchanan Old House. This complex of remains stands about three-quarters of a mile NW. of Drymen and some 550 yds. WNW. of Buchanan Castle, its 19th-century successor. The site is regarded as being that of the ancient seat of the Buchanans of that Ilk,[4] but the surviving structures are the remains of a large house built by the first Duke of Montrose in place of an earlier building which was pulled down in about 1724.[5] This new house was in turn destroyed by fire in 1850, and the existing buildings are no more than the surviving remains of service wings which were situated behind the main block. A painting of the house as it was before the fire, which is preserved in the adjacent golf club-house, shows a great façade comprising a central block of three storeys, and flanking wings. Its position in relation to the Endrick Water, which also appears in the picture, shows that it faced SE., and the existing remains must thus represent two wings which originally extended NW. from the NE. end of the main building. This interpretation of the remains is confirmed by a set of plans by Charles Barry,[6] dated 1837, which present a projected scheme for alterations to the house which was probably

[1] *Strathendrick*, 56.
[2] *Fasti*, iii, 349.
[3] *Strathendrick*, 220 f.
[4] *Stat. Acct.*, ix (1793), 24.
[5] *Geogr. Collections*, i, 344.
[6] In the possession of His Grace the Duke of Montrose.

never carried out. The NE. wing, part of which was utilised as servants' quarters, is still more or less complete; it is a long building which contains three storeys in its SE. part but only a single storey towards the NW. Near the NW. end of the three-storeyed portion a small wing projects from its SW. side with a square stair-tower in the S. re-entrant angle; this transverse wing originally communicated with the SW. kitchen-wing, which is now a roofless shell reduced to the height of the first-floor window-sills. At its NW. end the SW. wall of this wing joins up with that of the club-house of the local golf-club, which preserves its line and stands on the site of vanished offices. At the W. corner of the club-house another fragment of the earlier work appears in the form of a small rectangular building with three tall, round-headed windows in its W. side. The NW. wall of this is in alinement with the back wall of the court-yard, which still retains its original entrance-gateway.

The outline of the main block of the house, as it appears on the plans of 1837, is now marked out in the turf by a setting of stones. The length of the house appears to have been about 230 ft. over all.

457888 NS 48 NE 24 April 1959

330. Craigivairn. The house of Craigivairn stands on high ground just less than two miles NE. of Drymen, and commands an extensive prospect of the valleys of the Blane and Endrick Waters. It is a laird's residence of about the second half of the 18th century, and was no doubt erected by one of the Buchanans of Craigivairn to replace an earlier building of the same name[1] (cf. No. 210).

The house, which is substantially built, is T-shaped on plan. It comprises a rectangular main block measuring 44 ft. 9 in. by 20 ft. 1 in. over all and alined from SW. to NE., together with a NW. wing measuring 18 ft. 10 in. by 8 ft. 7 in. over all. Both main block and wing rise to a height of three storeys and an attic; the walls finish in a cavetto-moulded eaves-course and the gables have a plain coping. The masonry, which is of random rubble, was formerly harled; the quoins and margins are roughly dressed and the windows have slightly rounded arrises. The SE. façade contains three ranges of windows, all symmetrically disposed, those on the first floor being larger than the others. The main entrance-doorway is on the ground floor and has a simply moulded, lugged architrave which is now for the most part concealed by a wooden porch. The re-entrant angle between the wing and the NE. part of the main block has been filled in on the ground floor by a later outshot, which conceals another original entrance-doorway in the NW. wall of the main block.

On plan (Fig. 149) the house contains three main

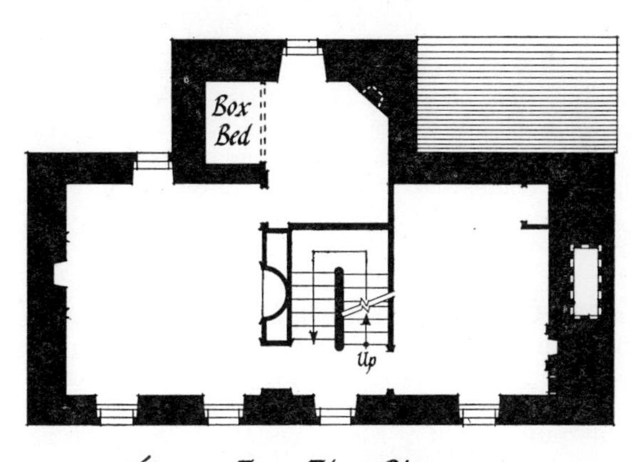

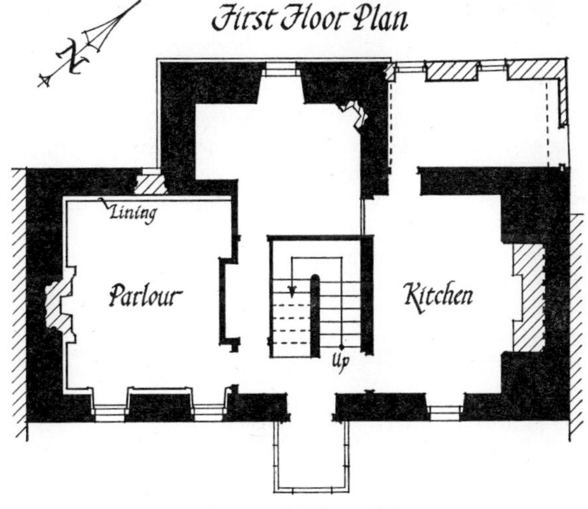

Fig. 149. Craigivairn (No. 330); plans and reconstructed elevation

[1] *Strathendrick*, 317 ff.

rooms on each floor, two in the main block and a small apartment in the wing. A dog-legged stair, which is centrally placed within the main block, gives access to the upper floors. The stair is of stone between the ground and first floors, but in the upper flights the treads are of wood; the wooden balusters are alternately plain and twisted. The NE. room in the main block at ground-floor level is a kitchen and contains a large segmental-headed fireplace, now contracted, in the gable wall. The original entrance-doorway in the NW. wall now gives access to a second kitchen, which is contained in the outshot. In the SW. room there is a blocked-up window, now visible only on the outside, in the NW. wall. On the first floor the SW. room in the main block contains some original panelling and a moulded plaster ceiling-cornice. A door to the NE. gives access to the room in the wing; this contains a recess for a box-bed. The NE. room in the main block and the apartments on the two upper floors are now of no special interest. Many of the roof timbers are old and bear incised carpenters' marks.

A single-storeyed range of offices projects to the SE. on either side of the house, with which they appear to be more or less contemporary. Part of a stone lintel, which is said to have come from one of these buildings, is built into the brick buttress of an outbuilding to the E. of the house. It bears an incised date, now incomplete, which originally read either 1732 or, more probably, 1752.

493910 N XIV S.W. 19 July 1956

331. The Old Manse, Killearn. The old manse, which stands on the W. margin of the village behind the Buchanan Monument (No. 279), was built in 1825[1]; it has been enlarged and modernised, but its main block is still quite typical of such houses as built in the early 19th century. It is a plain building of two storeys and an attic, having a central doorway on the E. with a window on either side on the ground floor and three above. The back has two windows on the ground and two on the first floor, with a long window in the centre lighting the stair and a small one below it. The attics are lighted from the gables. The front door opens into a central hall containing a stair at the back with iron balusters and a mahogany handrail. Below the stair is cellarage. There were originally four rooms on the ground floor, the right-hand one in front and the left-hand one behind having been larger than the others. On the first floor there are five rooms, one small one being over the entrance. The attic, which is reached by a small stair from the first-floor landing, contains two large rooms.

What was formerly a separate cottage has now been joined up with the S. side of the manse to form a wing. This building is one-storeyed, and its original part has on its W. side a central door with the date 1815 on the lintel and a window on either side.

Reset in the stables there is a block of red sandstone, evidently the keystone of a large round arch, bearing the date 1671.

522860 NS 58 NW ("Manse") 2 September 1952

332. Old Ballikinrain. The house of Old Ballikinrain stands two and a half miles NE. of Killearn and one mile SE. of Balfron. The structure is not all of the same date, but comprises an early 18th-century house to which an extensive NW. addition was made at the end of the 18th century. Further alterations and additions have been made at still later dates, and the most interesting features of the building today are the SE. façade of the original house and the NW. façade of the late 18th-century addition, each of which is a good example of its period.

The original house, which may be ascribed to about the second quarter of the 18th century, is T-shaped on plan and comprises a rectangular block, which runs NE. and SW. and measures 49 ft. 10 in. by 23 ft. 9 in. over all, together with a small wing, which projects from the centre of the NW. front. The building rises to a height of two storeys and an attic and is constructed in rubble, with dressed margins, except for the SE. front, which is of droved ashlar. The central feature of this façade (Fig. 150, Pl. 176 A) is the entrance-doorway on the ground

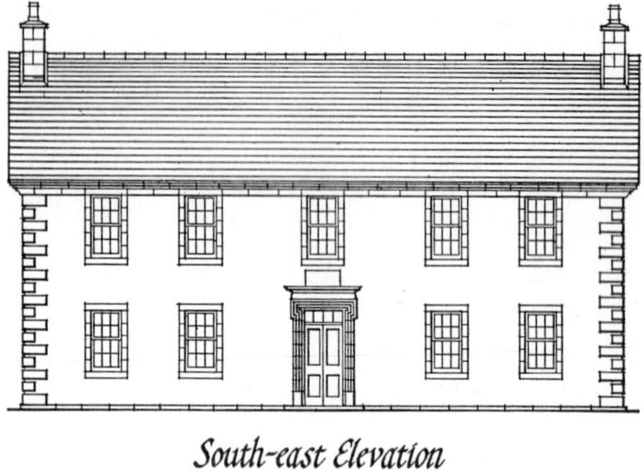

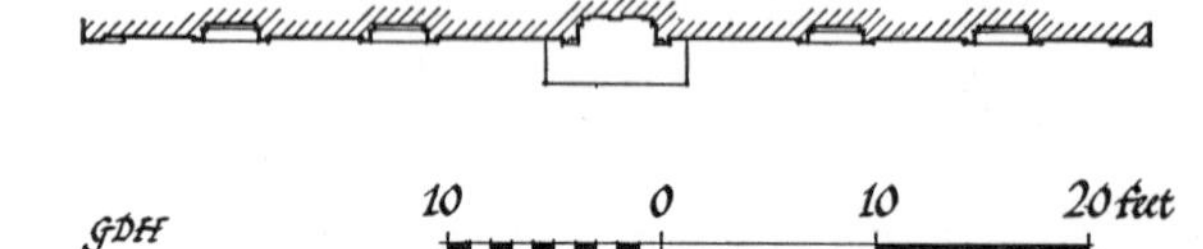

Fig. 150. Old Ballikinrain (No. 332); SE. elevation, reconstructed

floor; this has a lugged, bolection-moulded surround surmounted by a pulvinated frieze and moulded cornice. Above the doorway there is a plain stone panel which may have been intended to bear a coat of arms or a date. There is a range of windows on both the ground and the first floors, but the dormers that light the attic are insertions. The wall rises from a plinth and finishes in a plain eaves-band, which coincides with the lintels of the first-floor windows; above, there is an ogival-moulded eaves-cornice. The angles are defined by rusticated quoins and the roof has an overhanging verge at the gables. The NW. façade is concealed by the late 18th-

[1] *N.S.A.*, viii (Stirlingshire), 66.

century addition; a single-storeyed range of offices projects to the SE. on each side of the house.[1]

The interior of the house has been very much altered and now presents few features of interest, but the original arrangements may be deduced from the old plan (Pl. 176 B). This plan, which bears neither signature nor date, was certainly drawn out before the erection of the NW. addition at the end of the 18th century, and may perhaps be an original working-drawing for the house. The entrance-doorway formerly led into a hall within which a scale-and-platt stair rose to the first floor. From the hall access could be obtained to the kitchen on the SW. and to another apartment on the NE., apparently a bedroom with an adjacent dressing-room, which occupied the N. angle of the main block. The projecting wing on the NW. contained a cellar, which was reached by a doorway under the stairs. The disposition of rooms on the first floor was no doubt similar; the parlour must have occupied one end of the main block, the remaining space being taken up by bedrooms. The only features of interest that remain today are the old draw-bar, situated within the entrance-doorway, and a stone fireplace in the SW. gable at first-floor level. This has a sunk-moulded lintel and is wrought with a bead moulding on the arris.

The most notable feature of the late 18th-century addition is the NW. façade (Pl. 188 D), which rises to a height of two storeys and is built in ashlar. The wall rises from a plinth and finishes in a plain eaves-band, above which there is a moulded eaves-cornice and a blocking course. The central portion of the façade is framed within applied Ionic pilasters, and rises to a triangular pediment, in the tympanum of which there is a plain oval panel surrounded by a laurel wreath. The two ranges of windows are disposed symmetrically, but the mullions and transoms appear to be insertions. From each of the gable walls there projects a semi-octagonal bay, which rises to the full height of the façade. Within, a feature of some interest is the hall fireplace, which is of marble; the stone is said to have been quarried at Creag Dhubh, a little to the E. of Aberfoyle and 9 miles N. of Ballikinrain.[2] In the drawing-room there is a wooden fireplace-surround in the Adam manner, which is said to have come from Rosneath Castle, Dunbartonshire.

The lands of Ballikinrain were in the possession of the family of Napier of Ballikinrain as early as the 15th century.[3] The house that forms the oldest part of the present building may have been erected by James Napier, a prosperous Glasgow merchant, who succeeded to the estate in 1722.[4] The NW. addition was probably built by Robert Dunmore, another Glasgow merchant and husband of Janet Napier, who inherited the property in 1784.[5] An estate plan dated 1785[6] does not show the new building which, however, is likely to have been completed before the family suffered severe financial losses in 1793. Plans of about this period for proposed alterations also survive,[6] but there is nothing to suggest that they were ever carried out. The estate remained in the Napier family until 1862.

559879 NS 58 NE 13 June 1957

333. Old Place of Balgair. This house, now a roofless and dilapidated shell, stands 250 yds. N. of the right bank of the Endrick Water and a quarter of a mile nearly due W. of Over Glins. It is in the Classical style and was built in 1721,[7] presumably by James Galbraith, the second of the Galbraith lairds, who died in 1728.[8] It is shown as a laird's seat both on Roy's map of 1747-55 and on Grassom's map of 1817, and the statement that it was never finished, and was not much lived in by the lairds' families owing to an early subsidence of the foundations,[9] seems to be at variance with the fact that structural alterations were carried out at some time (*infra*).

The house is oblong on plan (Fig. 151) and measures 51 ft. in length by 34 ft. in width, the central portion on front and back being advanced 12 in. from the main planes for a length of 24 ft. Its longer axis is oriented approximately E. and W. There are three principal storeys, but the central block rises higher than the ends and thus has space to accommodate an attic floor. The walls are built of rubble, with backset margins at quoins and voids, perhaps for harling; the windows, which are all single lights and are lintelled, are provided with relieving arches, as are also the fireplaces. The ends and central projections of the house have pedimented gables finishing in moulded tabling, while a moulded eaves-course runs along the wall-heads and a moulded intake-course extends all round between the basement and first-floor levels. The openings are uniformly set in rows, one above the other—in threes on each floor in the frontal projecting feature, but in single order in the centres of all the other face-planes. On the S. façade there are two blank panels within moulded frames between the central windows of the second floor, and a similar moulding surrounds the attic window above. Internally the house is divided to its full height into three main divisions by two transverse partitions of stone, the central portion housing the staircase against the back wall and the gable-ends containing the living accommodation. Separate entrances in the middle of the front lead respectively into the basement and the main floor. The basement entrance, which has a segmental arch, gives ingress to the mid division, off which a door in the middle of the W. partition opens into a large room occupying the full width of the house, with what was probably a fireplace towards the S. end of the gable wall. In the E. partition, two adjacent doors open into separate compartments, each with an arch-headed fireplace in the gable; the fire-

[1] These buildings differ in some respects from the ones shown on an 18th-century plan of the house in the possession of the owner, Mr. A. R. Cross, M.C. This plan (Pl. 176 B), in so far as it concerns the offices, may therefore represent a project which was never carried out or, alternatively, the buildings may have been remodelled at some later date.

[2] *N.S.A.*, x, 1096.

[3] Cf. *Strathendrick*, 191.

[4] *Ibid.*, 202.

[5] *Ibid.*, 204.

[6] In the possession of Mr. A. R. Cross, M.C.

[7] *Strathendrick*, 261.

[8] *Ibid.*, 234.

[9] *Ibid.*, 261.

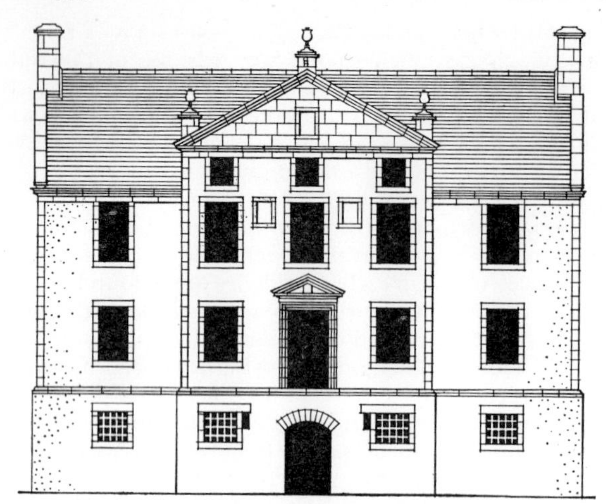

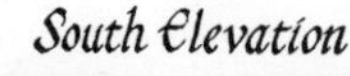

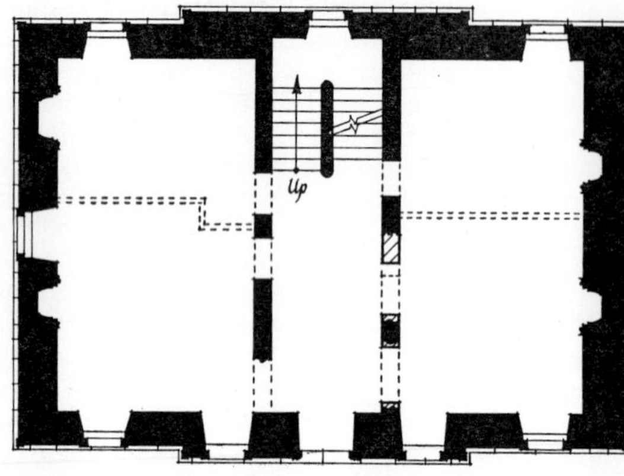

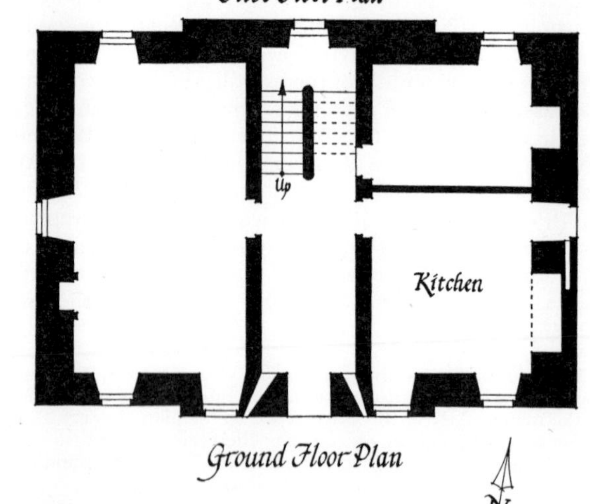

Fig. 151. Old Place of Balgair (No. 333); plans and reconstructed elevation

place in the front room, which was evidently the kitchen, being the larger of the two and having backset margins. The main-floor entrance must have been reached by a forestair or *perron* which no longer exists. It is ornamented with a moulded architrave and a triangular pediment and gives access to what was once a spacious hall, from the back of which a staircase ascended to the upper floors and presumably descended to the basement; but the staircase has been almost entirely destroyed, only the tusks of one or two steps, with bottle-nosed mouldings on the treads, remaining to suggest that the stair was of the scale-and-platt type. Two adjacent doors, centred on each side of the hall, originally gave entrance to four separate chambers, each provided, in the gable, with a fireplace wrought with roll-and-hollow mouldings on the jambs; but the original door to the SE. room has been replaced by two inserted doors although it is still traceable. This arrangement is repeated on the floor above and, in addition, there is a small bedroom S. of the landing in which a fireplace, moulded like the others, has been constructed in the angle formed by the front wall and the W. partition.

Part of a panel is built into the front of the house, near the SW. corner and at about eye-level. It bears the incised initials I G together with the numeral I, no doubt the first figure of a date, the remaining part of which was inscribed upon the missing portion of the panel. The stone seems to have been broken before its incorporation in the fabric of the present structure and may have formed part of an older building; the initials probably represent an earlier Galbraith laird.

603886 NS 68 NW 3 October 1952

334. Mains of Glins. The building known as the Mains of Glins stands by the old Kippen-Fintry road, two and a half miles SW. of Kippen and three miles NE. of Fintry. Once a small but attractive laird's house, and dating from the middle of the 18th century, it is now roofless and falling into total ruin. The remains comprise a dwelling-house, which runs NE. and SW. and measures 47 ft. 3 in. by 23 ft. 4 in. over all, together with later outbuildings which formed two sides of a courtyard to the NW. of the house. These latter are now completely ruinous.

The house is a plain rectangular block, two storeys and an attic in height. The masonry is harled rubble with dressed quoins and margins, the latter being wrought with a narrow chamfer. The walls rise to a moulded eaves-course; the gables have plain copings which finish in moulded skewputs, while the chimneys have ogival-moulded copings. The NW. façade (Fig. 152) is symmetrical and incorporates two ranges of windows together with the main entrance-doorway, which is centrally placed on the ground floor. The doorway has a Gibbs surround and a moulded cornice; the lintel bears the incised inscription M B M C 1743. In the 18th century the lands of Glins were held by the Buchanan family, and the initials M B are presumably those of Moses

Buchanan, second son of John Buchanan of Carbeth[1]; his wife's name, which is no doubt represented by the initials M C, is unknown. The ground-floor opening at the SW. end of the façade, now a window, was originally a doorway giving access to the kitchen. The other elevations are of no particular interest. An original window at ground-floor level on the SE. front has been converted into a doorway.

The plan (Fig. 152), which is rather more complex than in other houses of this type, is a symmetrical one. The staircase is central, and on either side of it there was originally both a large and a small room at each end of the house, while a fifth apartment was situated behind the stair. This arrangement obtained on both the ground and first floors. The main entrance-doorway opens into a lobby within which rises the stair; this is of geometric type, the lower flight being of stone with bottle-nosed treads and the upper one, which gave access to the attic, being of wood. From the lobby a door to the SW. opens into the larger of the two rooms that formerly occupied this end of the house. This room was probably the kitchen, though the fireplace in the gable is not original, and it seems to have been provided with two external doorways in the initial arrangement. The one opening to the NW., later turned into a window, has already been mentioned. A second doorway, in the W. corner of the kitchen, pierced the gable wall, but was turned into a cupboard when the kitchen was combined with the smaller room that lay to the SE. of it to make a single large apartment. At this time, too, a third doorway was struck through the gable to give access to the outshot to the SW. of the house. The small room that originally lay to the SE. of the kitchen, but was later combined with it, has two blocked-up windows in the SE. wall and a fireplace, also blocked, in the S. angle. The large room to the NE. of the entrance lobby, perhaps the parlour, has a stone fireplace, the jambs and lintel of which are wrought with a double concave and quirk moulding. The small room to the SE. of the parlour has an angle fireplace.

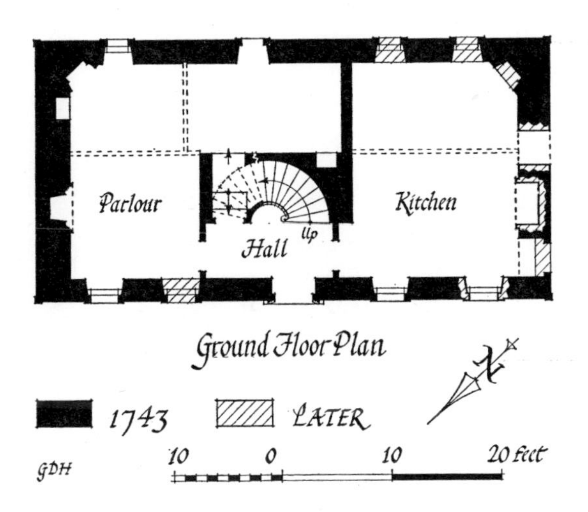

Fig. 152. Mains of Glins (No. 334); plan and reconstructed elevation

On the first floor, the two rooms at the SW. end of the house seem latterly to have been thrown into one, as on the floor below. The larger of the two rooms at the NE. end of the house has a fireplace, the arris of which shows a continuous bead-moulding; the lintel is sunk-wrought with rounded angles. Fireplaces of a similar type but lacking the bead moulding are found in some of the other rooms. The attic floor is ruinous and its arrangement is uncertain.

633910 NS 69 SW 9 October 1957

335. Wrightpark. This house stands within policies about a mile and a half SSW. of Kippen, facing approximately E. from high ground W. of the valley of the Boquhan Burn. It was built in 1750[2] and, apart from an addition made to the N. side, the provision of access to this addition, and some minor alterations such as the modernisation of fireplaces, it is still virtually complete in its original form—a Georgian mansion three storeys in height with a Classical front of ashlar, harled sides and back, and a hipped, slate-covered roof. The original portion measures 51 ft. 9 in. by 37 ft. 8 in. over walls which average 3 ft. 9 in. in thickness; the addition increases the length by 18 ft. and is 33 ft. 6 in. wide (Fig. 153). The façade (Pl. 188 B) embodies a central portion emphasised by a slight projection and finished with a moulded pediment; this is ornamented with three urn-finials and there is a circular opening in the centre of the otherwise plain tympanum. On the ground floor the frontage is treated in V-jointed masonry; the entrance, which is in the centre, is round-headed and has a fanlight over the door, and on either side of it there are two round-headed recesses, 1 ft. deep, in which the windows are

[1] *Strathendrick*, 348.
[2] Information from the proprietor, Mr. P. J. Laidlaw.

set. Above this level six plain pilasters, with moulded bases but plain unwrought capitals, are carried up through the two upper storeys to support an entablature with a convex frieze; the upper member of the cornice returns round the house as an eaves-course. There are five windows on each of the upper storeys, uniformly spaced to correspond with those below and finished with architraves; the windows in the back and side walls have backset margins, but all alike are square-headed. The quoins at the NW. and SW. corners are in header-and-stretcher bond and are V-jointed.

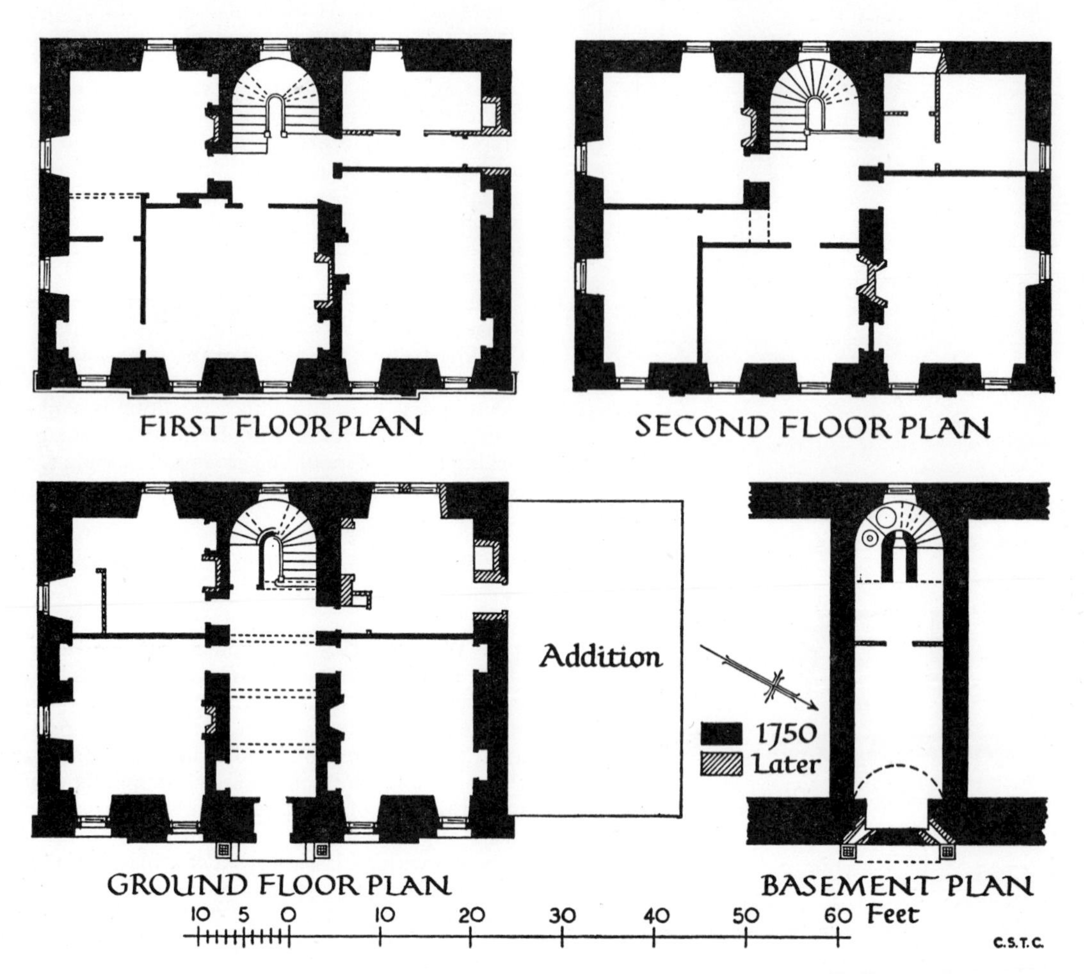

Fig. 153. Wrightpark (No. 335)

The entrance leads into a large hall, 22 ft. long by 9 ft. 6 in. wide; the walls are plastered and have dado rails, and the ceiling is divided into four panels by segmentally-arched ribs. On either side are two doors, giving separate access through partitions 2 ft. 6 in. thick to the four ground-floor rooms; of these, the two facing the front are larger than the others, the S. one having a simple dado-rail but the N. one a panelled dado. The NW. room has been turned into a kitchen, with access to the addition. At the back of the hall the main stair rises to the upper floors and, in continuation of it, a narrower flight of stone steps descends to a vaulted basement equal in area to the hall and now—though perhaps not originally—fitted out as a wine-cellar; this is ventilated by two narrow, grated flues broken out from an original recess at its E. end to open by the front-door step. The small lobby that gives access to the basement is lit by borrowed light from the newel, and where it extends under the stair a well has been constructed for the domestic water-supply with a small and shallow stone sink in front of it, no doubt to carry off water spilled from the buckets. The main stair in its lowest flight is of stone, with moulded treads, but above the first-floor landing is continued in wood. It turns round carved newels and the balusters are of turned wood. A dado-rail runs round each landing. Both the upper floors were originally partitioned into five rooms, but the NW. room on the first floor has been converted into a servery with access to the addition. The room above it is now a bathroom.

Most of the fireplaces have been renewed, but three

still show marble surrounds and in some of the rooms the original mantelpieces have survived. In the NE. room on the ground floor the mantelpiece, which is of wood, is carved on the frieze with grapes and scrollwork and there is foliaceous ornamentation on the shelf and jambs. What are believed to be the remains of one of the original fireplaces are preserved outside—the lintel, showing a human head and scrollwork (Pl. 204 C), being built into the inner range of the stable courtyard and two jambs into the garden wall behind, one on either side of the gate. Ample cupboard-space is provided in all the rooms; doors are six-panelled, with architraves; the window-recesses are panelled, and are fitted with internal shutters.

643926 NS 69 SW 29 September 1952

336. Old Auchentroig. The old house of Auchentroig (Pl. 174 A), which stands 70 yds. W. of the modern mansion, provides an interesting example of a small laird's residence dated by an inscription to 1702. Apart from a few minor alterations and repairs it can be regarded as virtually intact. An oblong rubble building of two storeys, with a garret above, it measures 37 ft. 6 in. by 18 ft. 9 in. externally; the side walls are 2 ft. thick, the NE. gable 2 ft. 7 in. and the SW. gable, which contains the kitchen fireplace, 5 ft. 6 in. The SE. front shows a central entrance framed by roll-and-hollow mouldings and four windows with chamfered arrises, symmetrically placed. The NE. gable has one original window on each floor and a built-up window in the garret, and another window has been built up in the NW. wall at first-floor level. The gables are finished in crow-steps with cavetto-moulded skewputs, and the roof is slated. The accommodation consists of four rooms, arranged two on each floor and with a straight flight of wooden stairs rising in the centre between wooden partitions. The house is now in use for handloom weaving.

The entrance (Pl. 174 B), which has an inscribed lintel and an heraldic panel above it (*infra*), still retains its original door, constructed of two thicknesses of wood lining, the boards being set vertically outside and horizontally inside. It is studded with wrought-iron nail-heads, and the original iron fittings—latch, lock-mounting, knocker and crook-and-band hinges—are all present. There is a bar-hole in the SW. jamb. The doorway leads into a small lobby which gives access to the stair and to the two ground-floor rooms (Fig. 154). This floor has been renewed in concrete. The room to the SW., which measures 15 ft. by 10 ft. 9 in., was the kitchen, and its fireplace, which has a segmental arch, is 10 ft. wide by 3 ft. 9 in. deep. The original window is on the SE. side and another has been inserted on the NW. The space below the upper part of the staircase has been left open as a recess. The NE. room, which is approximately 15 ft. square, is lit by two original windows, one in the SE. wall and the other in the gable. The fireplace is late, and probably replaces an original one. The door of this room has been renewed, but all the other doors, which are six-panelled, seem to be original.

The upper floor is carried on joists averaging 5 in. by 6 in. At the head of the stair a small landing ends against the NW. wall in a fixed door, which seems to be a dummy, and gives access on either side to the upper rooms. These

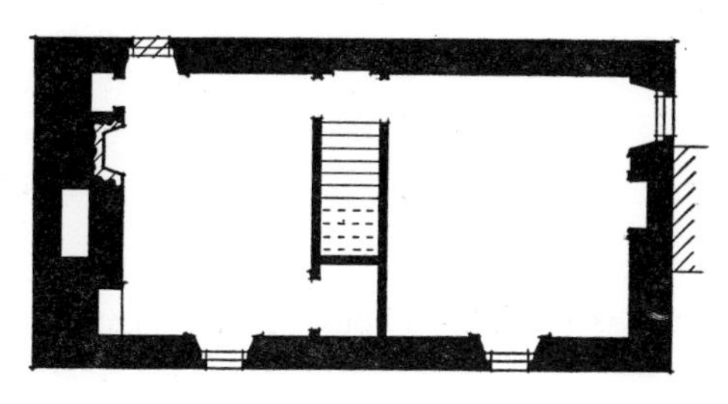

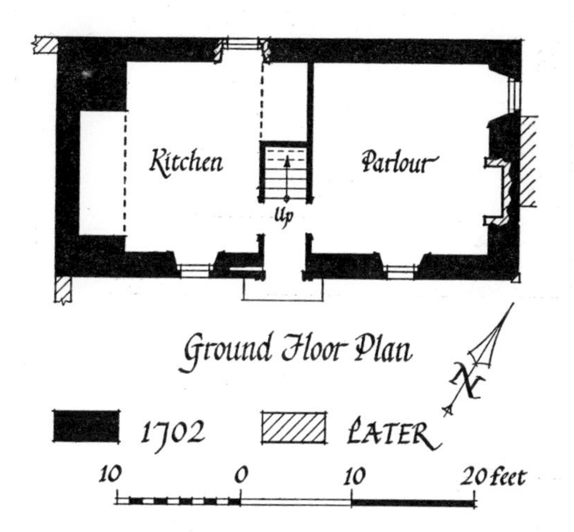

Fig. 154. Old Auchentroig (No. 336); plans and reconstructed elevation

correspond with the ground-floor rooms in size and in the arrangement of their windows and fireplaces. The fireplace in the NE. room is original, and has roll-and-hollow mouldings on jambs and lintel which are, however, framed in a later wooden mantelpiece. The fireplace in the SW. room has been either partially or wholly renewed and the window in the NW. wall is blocked. A press occupies the space above the ground-floor lobby, and there are in addition another press and an aumbry in the gable, one on either side of the fireplace. This room has a dado-rail, and a small, moulded wooden cornice finishing its plaster ceiling. In all the rooms the walls have been plastered, all the openings have architraves, and the windows have panelled shutters.

The entrance lintel bears the inscription 17 MS IM BG 02, evidently the initials of the contemporary laird, John MacLachlan,[1] and of his wives, whose names are not known. Set in the wall above the entrance there is an heraldic panel carved in relief. The dexter portion of the lower half is charged, for MacLachlan: Quarterly, 1st, a lion rampant; 2nd, a cross pattée palewise, on an indeterminate charge; 3rd, a galley; 4th, a salmon naiant; while the sinister portion is blank. Above is the crest, a castle resting on a cap of estate.

Auchentroig was in the possession of a family of MacLachlans for 600 years before its alienation in the 19th century. The house is said to have been attacked by Rob Roy in 1710, who is credited with having taken it by setting fire to the lower part of the door.[2]

544935 NS 59 SW 29 September 1952

337. Gartinstarry. This house (Fig. 155) stands by the road from Buchlyvie to Gartmore, three-quarters of a

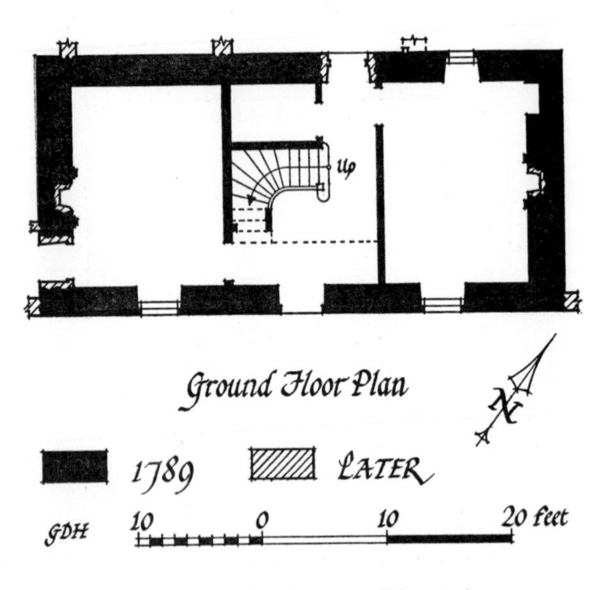

Fig. 155. Gartinstarry (No. 337)

mile W. of Buchlyvie Station. Though now thoroughly modernised as a dwelling, and modified by later outbuildings and connecting screen-walls, it yet deserves notice as the SE. front of its oblong central block (Pl. 175 C) is substantially unchanged, and gives a good example of the farmhouse of the late 18th century. It can, moreover, be dated with some confidence, as the figures 1789 have been scratched in plaster on the S. skewput —probably replacing something cut in the stone underneath. The central block measures 41 ft. 9 in. by 20 ft. externally; it is two storeys high and the front shows a central entrance, five windows, and eaves finished in a moulded cornice. In front the quoins and the margins of the openings are backset for harling. The gables are finished with plain tabling. The front door opens into a hall with a room on either side; from it a stair with a wooden baluster rises counter-clockwise to a landing from which access is had to two corresponding first-floor rooms.

Some facts about the Buchanans of Brachern, who owned Gartinstarry from the beginning of the 17th century, have been assembled by Guthrie Smith.[3]

553938 NS 59 SE 29 September 1952

338. Garden. This house stands on the N. side of the Stirling-Dumbarton highway (A 811) midway between Arnprior and Buchlyvie. It comprises work of two periods, an older W. portion dating from 1749 or immediately thereafter, and the E. portion, with the main façade, dating from 1830. Both dates are given by building contracts, the earlier one[4] entered into by John Stirling of Garden and David Tod, a mason in Gartmore. Additions were projected in 1824, but were only carried out, and then in a different form, in 1830,[5] the architect being William Stirling, who may or may not have been a relative of the Garden family.

The resulting structure is T-shaped on plan, the earlier and later buildings being juxtaposed, with their longitudinal axes running N. and S., and so designed that the addition of 1830 forms an impressive frontal block behind which is concealed the smaller 18th-century house. The masonry of both parts is rubble with red sandstone dressings, and the walls are covered with harling of a yellowish tint.

The original house, which retains its moulded eaves-course, has been much altered, but to judge from its surviving features, and the plan as incorporated in the 19th-century drawings of the alterations, it may be classed as a small mansion-house, having three main storeys, a basement and an attic. The W. façade is still in its original condition, and its symmetrical fenestration, which shows three windows on each storey, with plain backset margins, hints at the general external treatment of the house. A single-storey extension on the N. is 19th-century work. Internally, the house is divided trans-

[1] *Index to General Register of Sasines*, 1701-20, 555.
[2] *Strathendrick*, 267.
[3] *Ibid.*, 366 f.
[4] In the possession of Mrs. Stirling of Garden.
[5] Plans for the proposals of both 1824 and 1830 are preserved at Garden, and Stirling's E. elevation is reproduced in Pl. 200 B.

versely into three main divisions, the central one being occupied by a geometric stair with adjoining paved area, while originally the flanking ones were each subdivided into two living apartments. The N. pair is shown by the 19th-century plan to have been divided by a narrow passageway which linked the vestibule with an external doorway, situated as a solitary feature in the N. gable. In view of the awkwardness of this arrangement, it is interesting to note that the 19th-century plan shows no evidence of any other entrance having existed. The stair, which is a pleasing feature, has its lowermost flight constructed of stone, and the steps have moulded nosings; the two upper flights are of wood, the steps of the middle one again being moulded while those of the uppermost are plain, as if the attics had been intended for servants only. The wrought-iron balustrade and wooden handrail date from the alterations, but the brass door-handles in the attic are original. The NE. room on the ground floor retains its original fireplace-surround. The basement has been partially destroyed, but it presumably contained the kitchen and offices, and was approached by a small service-stair, now removed. When the new block was added, the ground floor of the old one was lowered by one foot; provision was made for this in the building-contract and evidence for the change is to be seen in the basement, where the ground-floor joists have been lowered, and at the foot of the stair, where a tread has been inserted.

The 19th-century block contains three floors and an attic, the lowermost floor being a semi-basement. Its E. front (Pl. 200) is now the best architectural feature of the house. The central portico-entrance, situated on the principal floor, is approached by a *perron* which bridges the sunken area in front of the basement. The side walls, which have a single central window on each floor, are uniformly treated with the façade, the broad, horizontal band at principal-floor level being continued and the windows on the principal floor being surmounted by triangular pediments.

The internal accommodation on the principal floor consists of a central vestibule with a large room on either side of it. The vestibule, which has a coved and coffered ceiling, communicates through a smaller inner division with a broad corridor which runs the full width of the building (N. to S.) on all floors. This corridor was evidently introduced to provide a junction between the older and newer blocks, and it communicates at its N. end with a scale-and-platt stair which leads to the upper floors.

597944 NS 59 SE 17 May 1955

339. Arnprior Farm. The dwelling-house attached to Arnprior Farm, originally a small mansion, stands in a garden on the S. side of the Stirling-Dumbarton road just W. of the bridge over Arnprior Burn. It is an excellent example of the minor domestic architecture of the later 18th century, as it is in perfect condition and has suffered a minimum of modernisation—the insertion of some fireplaces and the construction of a bathroom in the room at the corner of the first floor being the only material alterations. The garden being nearly on a level with the first floor, the house is divided from it on the NW. side by a narrow sunk area, spanned by a short flight of steps leading to the front door; but at the back the ground is on a level with the basement, which is entered by a back door in the middle of the SE. side.

The house is oblong on plan (Fig. 156) and measures 43 ft. 10 in. by 33 ft. 2 in. over walls which vary in thickness from 2 ft. 6 in. to 2 ft. 9 in. It comprises three storeys and an attic. The walls are rubble-built with backset quoins and window-dressings, and except at the back they rest on an ashlar base-course; the whole face of the basement in the sunk area is channelled rusticated work. The wall-heads finish in a moulded eaves-course, and the roof, which has been renewed, is slated. The front door is framed by plain pilasters supporting a plain frieze with a moulded cornice; there is a single window to right and left, and three windows symmetrically disposed in the floor above (Pl. 175 D). The dormer windows that light the attic open towards the SE.

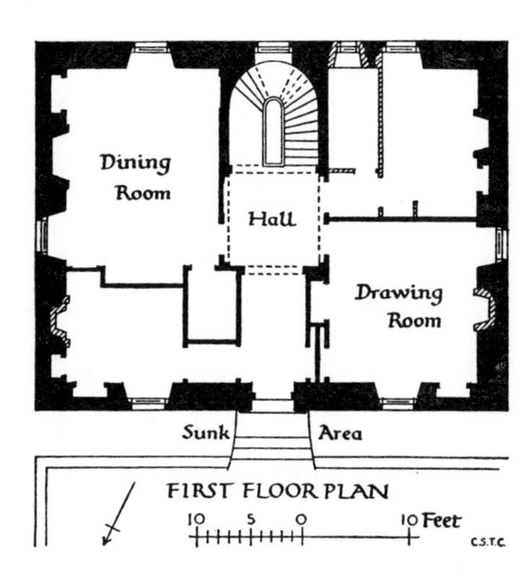

Fig. 156. Arnprior Farm (No. 339)

The entrance opens into a roomy vestibule and this into a square hall, the N. room being entered from the former and the other three from the latter. From pilasters in the angles of the hall, arches with panelled soffits are carried over the voids; at the back is the staircase, which has a rounded end. The woodwork and plaster cornices are enriched and delicately moulded. The E. corner of this floor is occupied by the dining-room which has a panelled dado, as has the W. room also, but the other two have dado-rails only. The stair, which is of stone and has cantilevered steps, descends to the basement and rises to the first floor. The basement contains the kitchen, store-rooms and offices, and on the first floor five bedrooms open off an ample landing. From the landing a small wooden wheel-stair mounts to two large attic-bedrooms each containing a fireplace.

613949 NS 69 SW 22 October 1952

340. Arnmore House. This is the ruin of a small, symmetrically planned, laird's house dating from the turn of the 17th and 18th centuries, which stands on high ground nearly two miles SW. of Kippen. The building is a simple rectangular block lying approximately E. and W. and measuring 46 ft. by 20 ft. 6 in. over walls 2 ft. 1 in. thick. The house originally comprised two main storeys, but at a later period was reduced to its present height of a single storey and an attic. The masonry is of rubble and has been harled. The entrance-doorway, centrally placed in the N. façade at ground-floor level, is wrought with an ogival moulding; above, there is a bolection-moulded surround, evidently intended to contain an armorial panel but now empty. The eaves-course, which has an ogival moulding, is probably original although it must have been rebuilt when the upper storey of the house was removed. The fenestration of both the N. and S. façades has been very much altered and the lintel of an inserted window in the S. front bears the incised inscription A L 1722 I S. The initials are probably those of Archibald Leckie, who seems to have possessed the property at this period,[1] and of his wife, while the date no doubt commemorates the completion of some of the structural alterations already described.

The interior is now gutted, but it would seem that in the original arrangement the front door opened on to a stair on either side of which there was a single apartment on each principal floor. The entrance-door was secured by a bar, the socket of which still remains. The W. room on the ground floor was the kitchen, and part of the fireplace, which had a corbelled lintel, still survives. Parts of three other stone fireplaces remain; two on the first floor have been wrought with an ogival moulding while the third, which is on the ground floor, has had a bead moulding.

Outbuildings have been added to each gable of the building, but these are now more ruinous than the original house.

626935 NS 69 SW 5 September 1957

341. Boquhan. The house of Boquhan, once evidently a fine Georgian mansion, has been unroofed and gutted, and is now fast becoming a ruin. In 1825, it was described as "a neat modern house".[2] The stables, which stand 470 yds. N. of the house and form part of the modern farm-buildings, are described under No. 342.

668950 NS 69 NE 21 October 1952

342. Stables, Boquhan. The stables belonging to the former mansion-house of Boquhan (No. 341) now form part of the modern steading, but they still provide a good example of this type of building as constructed early in the 19th century. The precise date of their construction has not been discovered, but they must presumably date from after 1817 as they are not marked on Grassom's map of Stirlingshire. They consist of four ranges laid out symmetrically about a quadrangular courtyard, the S. range (Pl. 189 B) being dominated by a domed clock-tower and the blocks at the corners being slightly higher than, and projecting 2 ft. from, the intervening wall-faces. The clock-tower and the block from which it rises are faced in ashlar, the other walls being harled; voids and corners have dressed margins, some of which are backset. The whole complex measures 115 ft. from E. to W. by 94 ft. 6 in. from N. to S., and the courtyard similarly 70 ft. 6 in. by 51 ft.

Entrance to the courtyard is gained on the S. by a pend set in the central block, which projects 7 in. from the face of the range and rises above the eaves level; the pend, which was closed by a double iron gate, has an arched head and is 11 ft. wide. The projecting block finishes in a pediment with a plain tympanum, and above this the clock-tower rises in two stages, the lower one being square and the upper one octagonal on plan, and is surmounted by a semi-elliptical cupola with a copper-covered roof. The octagonal stage has openings for clock-dials towards the cardinal points, with round-headed windows in the other faces. On either side of the pend, and entered from it, there is a four-stalled stable having round-headed windows to S. and ventilation openings to N.; above the stables are lofts, lit by low, lintelled windows, and entered from the courtyard by a stone forestair and a later spiral iron stair. The terminal blocks of the front range, which have hipped roofs, contain coach-houses, entered through round-headed doorways, with lofts above. The lateral ranges have been altered, but the rooms in the W. one, which have fireplaces, were probably designed as bothies for stable attendants, while those in the E. one may have been loose-boxes or harness-rooms. The N. range, like the S. one, has a projecting central block pierced by a round-headed pend and finishing in a pediment. The W. portion of this range contains a one-storeyed dwelling-house, with attic bedrooms reached by a straight internal stair; the E. portion contains one storey and a loft, now adapted to the purposes of the farm.

670951 NS 69 NE ("Boquhan Home Farm") 21 October 1952

343. Old Leckie House. Old Leckie House (Pl. 163 A) stands in well-wooded grounds at the foot of the Gargunnock Hills, two and a half miles E. of the village of Kippen. It is an attractive example of a laird's house of about the end of the 16th century, and comprises an original T-shaped building to which there has been

[1] Decennial Indexes to the Services of Heirs in Scotland, etc., i (1730-9), 20, H.M. General Register House.

[2] Graham, H., *Parties and Pleasures*, 167.

added an E. wing (Fig. 157). The 16th-century house consists of a main block of three storeys and an attic, which measures 62 ft. by 25 ft. 2 in. and lies E. and W., together with a S. wing of four storeys which measures 22 ft. 2 in. by 13 ft. 11 in. This wing contains a circular stair-tower in each of its re-entrant angles, the one to the W. rising from the ground floor to the second floor and the one to the E. beginning at first-floor level and rising to the full height of the S. wing. The E. wing is of two storeys and measures 29 ft. by 25 ft. 2 in.; it is of 18th-century date. The roofs are slated, those of the original building finishing in crow-stepped gables and ogival skewputs; the gables of the E. wing are tabled and have roll-moulded skewputs. The house is built of harled rubble, the masonry being a red sandstone similar to that which outcrops on the banks of the Leckie Burn 50 yds. SE. of the building. The window margins, of dressed stone, are now painted.

The original entrance-doorway, which is in the SE. re-entrant angle of the main block and S. wing (Pl. 162), is recessed beneath a broad segmental arch, in the soffit of which there are two square machicolations, now blocked. To the S. of the doorway is a window, in the sill of which there is a splayed gun-loop, but this too, like the spy-hole which overlooks the entrance recess from the N., is now blocked up. Within the doorway there is a stout wrought-iron yett which must have been rehung, as in its present position it would impede the working of a draw-bar for an original outer door. The elaborately guarded entrance is almost the only defensive feature of the house, and although in an authentic mediaeval tradition, it was probably designed more for appearance than for utility. Above the doorway the stair-tower is corbelled out on a continuous corbel-course of seven members; the uppermost member continues as a string-course on the E. and S. sides of the S. wing, returning round a stone panel which is centrally placed over the segmental arch of the entrance-recess. The panel is set within a moulded border but is quite plain and does not appear ever to have been inscribed. The stair-tower finishes in an ogival-moulded eaves-course above which there is a conical roof. The present entrance-doorway has been inserted in the S. gable wall of the S. wing at first-floor level, and is approached by an external stair at the top of which there is an entrance-porch. The small window to the E. of the porch has been inserted, but the two windows above, one at second-floor level and the other at third-floor level, are original. The stair-tower in the SW. re-entrant angle of main block and wing has a cat-slide roof; the door immediately to the W. of the tower at ground-floor level has been inserted. The E. gable of the main block is largely masked by the 18th-century wing, while a small single-storey outshot has been added to the W. gable; above there can be seen the outline of an original second-storey window, now blocked up. The N. front of the main block incorporates a small gablet which lights the central room on the attic floor. The door at ground-floor level, near the W. gable wall, is an insertion. The original windows of the 16th-century building are round-arrised, and many of the ground- and first-floor windows have been barred while some of the larger ones have been half-glazed. Some windows have been enlarged and others inserted, and these alterations are noted on the plans. The walls of both main block and wing finish in a moulded eaves-course, that of the former having a double roll-and-fillet moulding and that of the latter an ogee-and-fillet moulding.

The building has undergone many alterations within, but the main features of the original plan are still apparent. The old entrance-doorway on the ground floor leads into the S. wing, which probably at one time contained a flight of stairs rising to the first floor. The stair was removed when the new first-floor entrance-doorway was constructed, and, as many of the steps that rise to the new doorway are old and have moulded nosings, they may come from the original internal stair. The partitions in the old stair-lobby are late, as is the window in the W. wall; the window in the E. wall must have been enlarged or renewed as there is no internal access to the gun-loop in its sill. From this lobby a door leads into a corridor from which access was formerly obtained to the three main apartments that occupied the ground floor. The easternmost room was a cellar and the central one a kitchen, both vaulted, and each was originally entered by a separate door from the corridor. Now, however, the partition between the two rooms has been removed[1] and the doors from the corridor closed, so that access to what is today a single apartment has to be obtained from the 18th-century wing by means of a doorway inserted in the E. gable wall of the older building. To the N. of this doorway is an original window which was blinded when the E. wing was added, and beyond it there is a locker. There are two more lockers in the N. wall and two wrought-iron meat-hooks hang from the vault. At the W. end of the apartment the central voussoirs of a round-arched fireplace can be seen behind a later partition. The kitchen flue is thus placed centrally within the house and not, as is more usual, in a gable. A door has been broken through the N. wall of the corridor to give access to the fireplace, which is now used as a storage compartment; it is lit by an inserted window in the N. wall. The flue has been blocked and ceiled and a similar compartment contrived within it on the first floor. To the E. of the fireplace there has probably been a service-hatch in the S. wall; it is now blocked within but appears as a shallow recess in the N. wall of the corridor. At the W. end of the corridor a door to the S. leads to the stair in the W. re-entrant angle of main block and S. wing; this is a service stair and gives access to the main block only, at first- and second-floor levels. To the W. another door leads into the third of the original ground-floor apartments. This room is unvaulted and has been subdivided by later partitions; the fireplace in the W. gable wall has been inserted and subsequently contracted, but the window to the S. of it, now blocked, is original, as is the one at the W. end of the N. wall. The other two windows have been inserted or enlarged.

---

[1] It is shown on MacGibbon and Ross's plan of about 1892 (*Cast. and Dom. Arch.*, iv, 84).

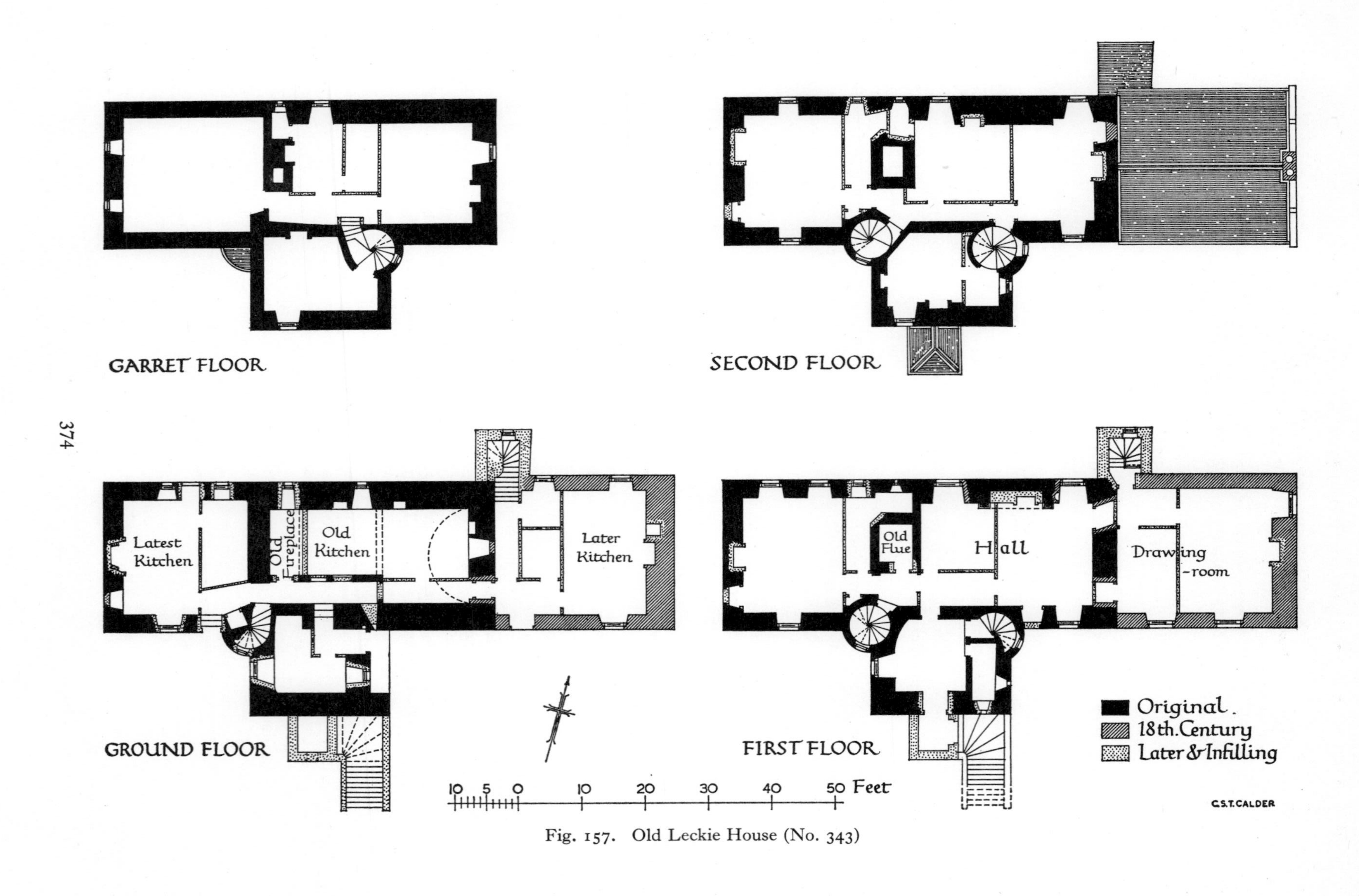

Fig. 157. Old Leckie House (No. 343)

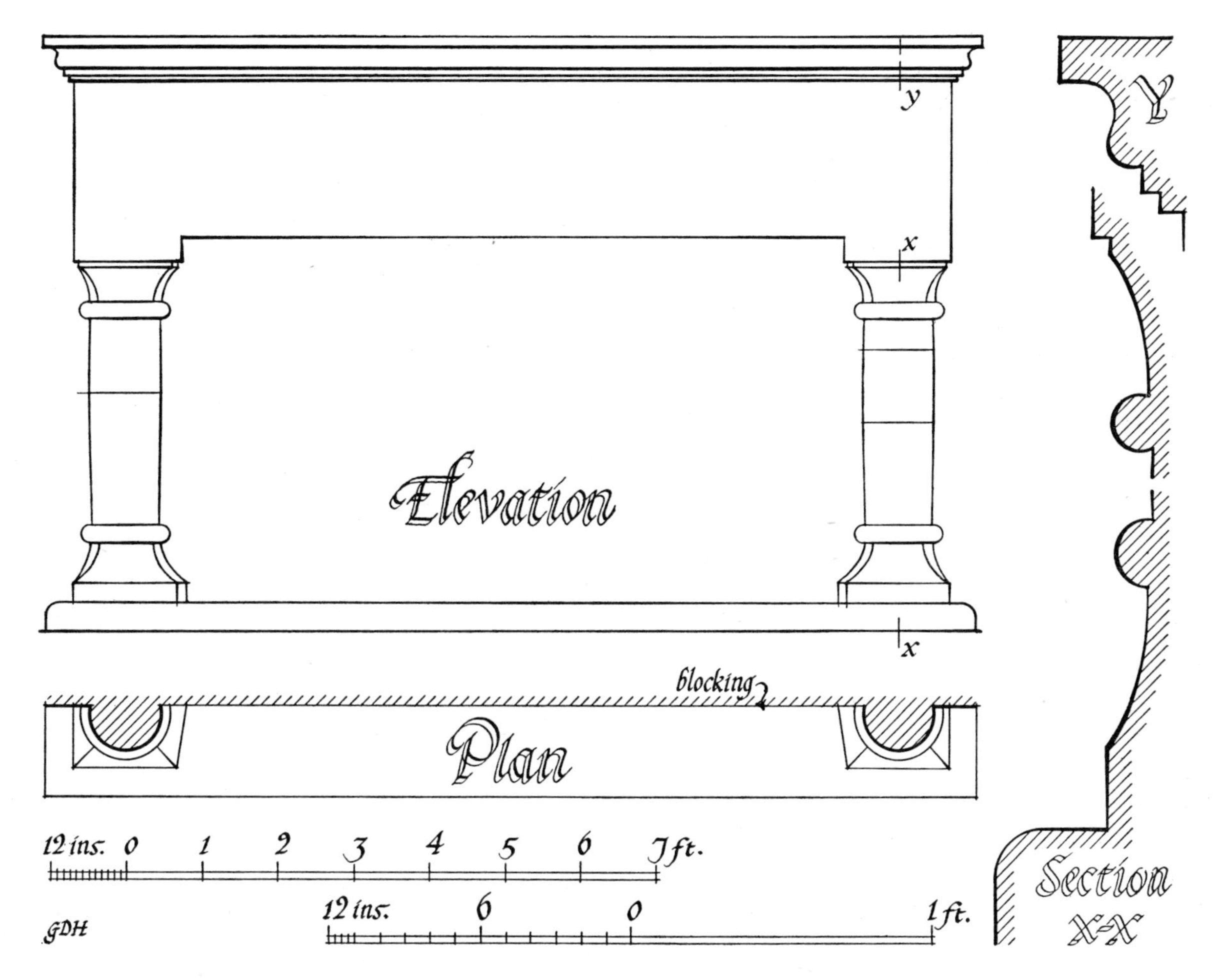

Fig. 158. Old Leckie House (No. 343); detail of fireplace

On the first floor the S. wing, which formerly contained the main stair, now serves as an entrance-hall to the new front door in its S. wall. The room is barrel-vaulted, and in the E. wall a doorway leads to a mural chamber from the NE. angle of which access could be obtained to one of the machicolations over the old entrance-doorway below. Another door in the E. wall leads to a turnpike-stair which rises in the E. re-entrant angle to give access to both main block and wing on the two upper floors. The main block originally contained two rooms at first-floor level, of which the larger, no doubt the hall, was entered directly from the S. wing. This room was altered in the 18th century, and has since been subdivided to form two smaller apartments and a corridor. The principal remaining feature of interest is the fine stone fireplace in the N. wall (Fig. 158), in which boldly carved half-columns rise from high bases to support a plain lintel and moulded cornice. The hall also retains a dado, some panelled doors and a moulded plaster ceiling-cornice of 18th-century date. To the W. of the hall is a small lobby which is accessible from the service-stair, and beyond it there is another large room which was subdivided in the 18th century. It retains an original garderobe-recess in the NE. angle and some 18th-century woodwork like that of the hall. The upper floors are of less interest, as most of the rooms have been divided up into smaller apartments and few original features remain. On the second floor there was formerly a single room in the S. wing and two or perhaps three in the main block. The arrangement of the third floor was similar, but at this level the rooms are accessible only from the turnpike in the NE. re-entrant angle as the service-stair rises no higher than the second floor. The central attic-room in the main block has a garderobe-recess in the NW. angle and there is another garderobe in a similar position on the floor below.

The E. wing now forms a separate dwelling. An outshot has been added to the N. front to house a staircase and the internal arrangements have been much altered. A large drawing-room originally occupied the first floor, and this, though now subdivided, still retains a panelled dado and moulded plaster ceiling-cornice.

The lands of Leckie were held by the family of Leckie of that Ilk from the middle of the 14th century until the year 1668, when they were conveyed to David Moir of Craigarnhall. Leckie remained in the hands of a branch of the Moir family until the beginning of the 20th century.[1]

SUNDIAL. Part of an obelisk-shaped sundial of 17th-century date (Pl. 215 D) stands in a rockery a few yards SE. of the old bridge (No. 453). The shaft, which has been broken at the top, is 9½ in. square and now rises to the height of 3 ft. 1 in. When complete it showed five stages, separated by incised lines, each of which contained four sunken geometrical dials, one on each face. The head, which is detached and lies about 20 yds. S. of the shaft, takes the form of a bulged capital the faces of which contain a number of dials; one face, however, bears two sunk shields charged, respectively, in low relief: Dexter, three unidentifiable charges; sinister, a fess checky. The significance of the dexter coat is uncertain, but the fess checky may be associated with the family of Moir of Leckie.

689946 NS 69 SE ("Leckie")
Various dates in September 1955

344. The Manse, Gargunnock. Gargunnock Manse, which stands in a garden adjoining the churchyard, was built about 1750 and had been twice repaired before 1833, when the relative article in the *New Statistical Account* was written.[2] A further addition has been made in recent times, and the interior completely remodelled. An original oblong block, however, still exists as a nucleus to the additions on E., W. and S.; this measures 40 ft. 9 in. by 21 ft. 3 in., is rubble-built and harled, and contains two storeys and an attic. Its N. façade, which seems to be virtually unaltered, shows general proportions and a regularity in the setting of the voids which accords very well with a date in the middle of the 18th century. The entrance, now covered by a porch of later construction, is central and is flanked on either side by a window; three windows are uniformly placed on the floor above, and the attics are lit from the gables. Quoins and windows have backset margins, there is a cavetto-moulded eaves-course at the wall-head, and the roof, which is slated, is finished against plain tabling on the gables. In the interior an old stair has been preserved, though whether original or dating from one of the early reconstructions cannot be decided with certainty; it carries slim wrought-iron balusters with a simple wooden handrail.

The old bell of the parish church (No. 172) is preserved in the manse garden. It is 14¾ in. in diameter and is inscribed FOR THE CHWRCH OF GARGWNNOCK BOWGHT / BY THE MINISTER AND SESION IOHN MEIKLE FECIT / ED^R 1702. This bell was made by the recasting and enlargement of an earlier bell, which was too small to be heard at a distance.[3]

707942 NS 79 SW 24 October 1952

345. Touch House. This house is pleasantly situated at the foot of the Touch Hills, just under three miles W. of Stirling and about half a mile S. of the main Stirling-Dumbarton road (A 811). The building (Fig. 159, Pls. 177 and 178) is a composite structure incorporating work of more than one period, but its most outstanding feature is the S. front which is perhaps the most distinguished example of Georgian architecture in the county. The name of the architect is not recorded, but there seems to be no reason to doubt the tradition that ascribes the 18th-century work to William Adam. The architectural development of the house is not entirely clear, but it seems likely that the original building, which is probably of 16th-century date, consisted of a main block alined from E. to W., from which there projected a rectangular tower at the NW. and SE. angles. Of this there remains today only the SE. tower, which is virtually complete, together with the lower portion of the NW. tower which is now incorporated in later work. During the 17th century, the NW. tower was largely rebuilt and at the same time extended eastwards in a range of buildings which now forms the N. side of the house. In the middle of the 18th century the main block of the original building was removed and replaced by the much larger Georgian block that has already been mentioned. The range of offices at the NE. angle is of 19th-century date.[4]

The SE. tower of the original building rises to the height of four storeys and an attic, and is built in whinstone rubble with dressed quoins and margins. Above third-floor level a double course of individual stone corbels bears a crenellated parapet within which rise the crow-stepped gables of the attic roof. At the NE. corner of the tower an original re-entrant angle was filled in during the 19th century to accommodate a chimney which serves a fireplace in the range of offices. The W. wall of the tower is concealed by later work; in the S. wall there is a single window on each of the four main storeys, the lowest one being an insertion. There is an inserted window in the E. wall at first-floor level and a small garderobe-window, perhaps original, on both the second and third floors. At second-floor level there is also an original window which lights a small mural chamber, and to the N. of the window a projecting drain-spout indicates that there was originally a sink or laver within. The lower portion of the N. wall is concealed by the range of offices, but above there are two original stair-

[1] *Stirling Antiquary*, iv, 289 ff.
[2] *N.S.A.*, viii (Stirlingshire), 57.
[3] *P.S.A.S.*, lxxxiv (1949-50), 79, with illustration; *ibid.*, pl. vi, 4, facing p. 96.
[4] A model of Touch House, now preserved in the Smith Institute, Stirling, is said to depict the building as it was before the erection of the Georgian block. The model, however, is unlikely to have been made before the 18th-century alterations to the house were carried out, and it does not altogether accord with what remains of the older buildings.

windows. The tower contains a large turnpike-stair which rises to the full height of the structure to give access to a small apartment on each floor; on the ground and first floors the treads have moulded nosings, but the upper part of the stair may have been renewed. The stair also communicated with the original main block, and when this was removed the openings in the W. wall of the tower were used to give access to the new 18th-century building. The ground floor of the tower is barrel-vaulted but otherwise retains no original features; the partition to the E. and the doorway in the E. wall are insertions.

Of the NW. tower, which is thought to have formed part of the original building, only the two lower floors remain, and these have been so much altered that almost no original features survive. The only external evidence for the existence of the tower is the change in the alinement of the N. wall of the present N. range. Within, however, the thickness of the outer walls on the ground floor is seen to average 4 ft. 6 in. at the W. end of the range as compared with about 2 ft. 3 in. at the E. end. At the W. end of the corridor that runs along the S. side of the range on the ground floor, a semicircular corbel-course

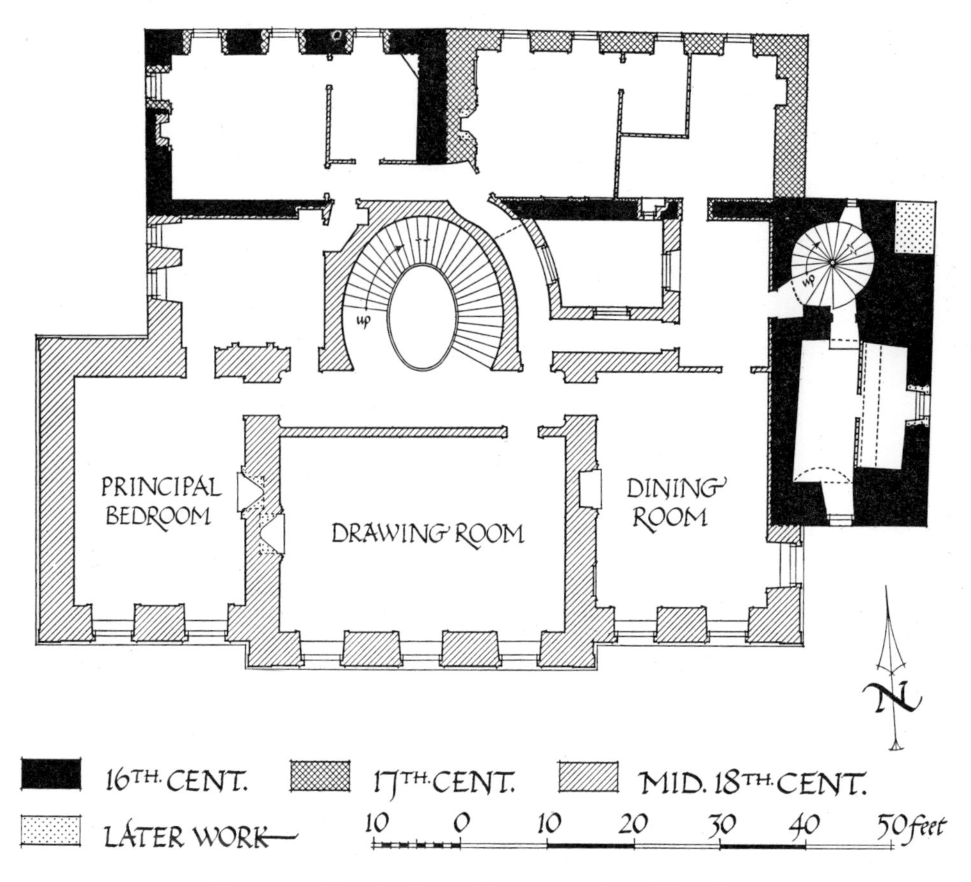

Fig. 159. Touch House (No. 345); plan of first floor

The room on the first floor is also barrel-vaulted, and has served as a kitchen although it is inconveniently small for this purpose. A large segmental-headed fireplace occupies the E. wall, but the recess is now partitioned off and used as a cupboard. The apartment on the second floor has a bolection-moulded fireplace of 17th-century date in the W. wall, and a garderobe and a cupboard in the E. wall. The room on the third floor also has a garderobe in the E. wall, and at the S. end of the same wall there is a mural recess which contains a shelved cupboard. The sink or laver, the outlet for which has already been noted, was probably situated within this recess. The attic floor has no features of interest.

projects from the S. wall; this may originally have supported some feature on the floor above, perhaps a small stair, all other trace of which has now disappeared. The E. portion of the N. range and the remodelled NW. tower, which adjoins it to the W., are not otherwise of much interest. The block that they form (Pl. 178 B) rises to the height of three storeys and is built in harled rubble with dressed margins; the gables are crow-stepped. The top storey is lit by dormers, the pediments of which were renewed in 1928, and some of the other windows may have been altered or renewed at the same time. The interior has been altered, both in the 18th century and in more recent times, and few original features remain. A

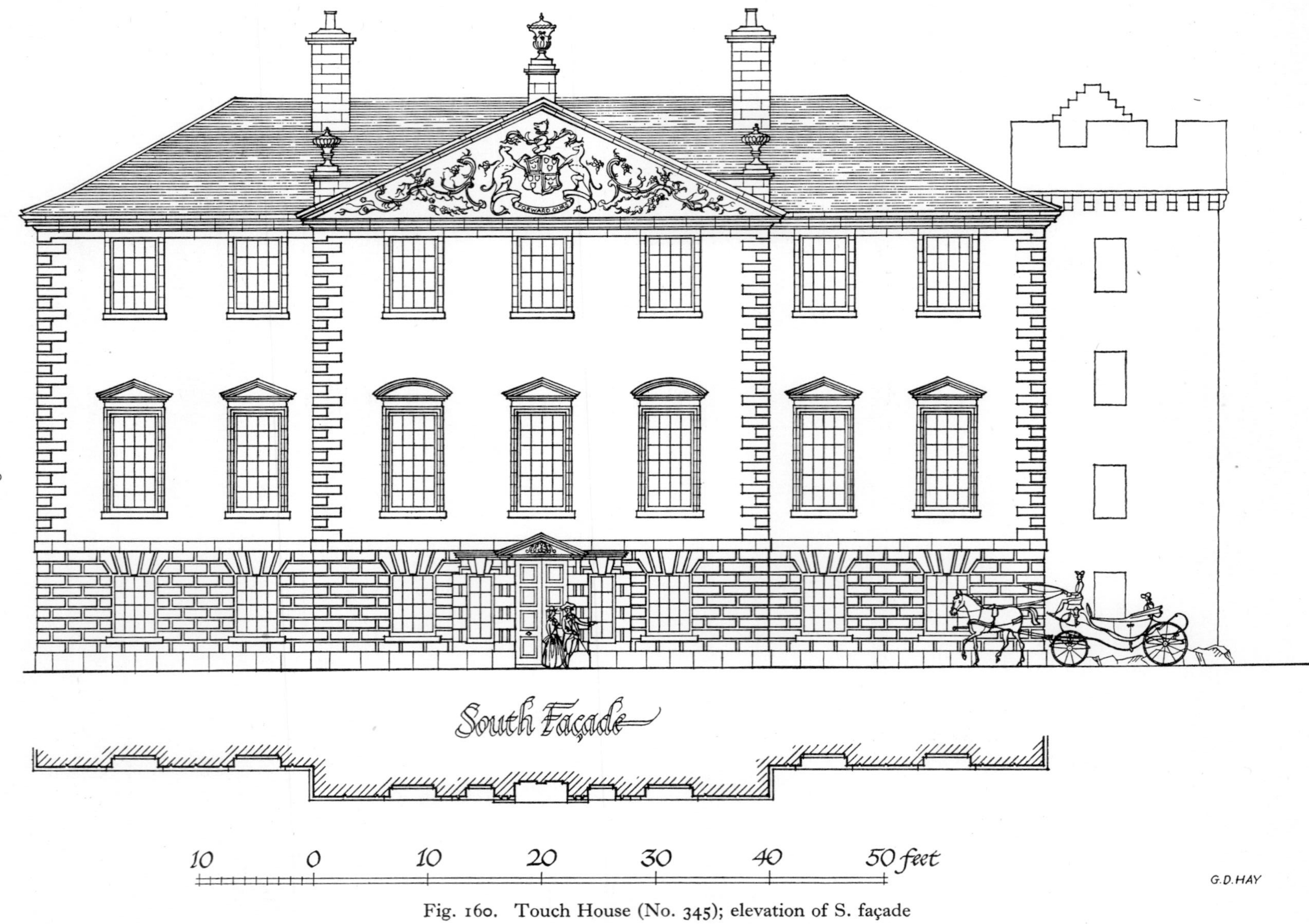

Fig. 160. Touch House (No. 345); elevation of S. façade

room on the first floor contains some 18th-century panelling and a plain marble fireplace. On the second floor the easternmost room has an original bolection-moulded fireplace in the E. wall, while the westernmost room, which was formerly a library, has a coved ceiling of 18th-century date, with plaster busts in the angles (Pls. 185 D, 186 and 187).

The S. block is three storeys in height; the S. façade is built in ashlar and the remainder in whinstone rubble with dressed quoins and margins. The walls finish in a moulded eaves-cornice and the roof is hipped with sprocketed eaves. The S. façade (Fig. 160, Pl. 177), although of conventional Classical design, is a well-ordered composition of considerable architectural merit. The fine mason-work and the careful execution of the ornamental detail are both worthy of note. The central portion of the façade breaks forward and is carried up to finish in a triangular pediment, the tympanum of which contains ornamental scroll-work incorporating the full heraldic achievement of the Setons of Touch. The shield is charged: Quarterly 1st and 4th, three crescents within a double tressure flory-counter-flory, for Seton; 2nd and 3rd, three escutcheons, for Hay. The supporters are greyhounds and the crest is a bear's head couped. Below is a label on which there is incised the motto FORWARD OURS. The masonry of the ground floor is rusticated; there is a basal plinth, and a plain horizontal band defines the junction of the ground and first floors. The main entrance-doorway, which is the least successful feature of the design, is centrally placed at ground-floor level. Above it there is a moulded triangular pediment, which is borne on carved brackets and has in its tympanum a reversing monogram of the initials H E S, for Hugh and Elizabeth Seton, who were married in 1745.[1] The erection of the S. front was probably begun soon after their marriage. The main ground-floor windows are symmetrically placed on either side of the entrance, and the first- and second-floor windows are ranged over those below. The windows on the first floor have moulded architraves, and are emphasised by entablatures which incorporate either triangular or segmental pediments. The second-floor windows have plain surrounds.

The new construction was designed primarily to provide a set of principal rooms on each of its two main floors, together with a staircase which could serve both the old and the new portions of the house; and its plan has of necessity been adapted to that of the buildings already standing at the time of its erection. The entrance-doorway gives access to the hall, at the N. end of which a spacious geometric stair (Pl. 183) rises to give access to the upper floors. The stair is lit from above by an elliptical cupola; the iron balustrade has probably been renewed. The ground-floor rooms are of little interest, though the one to the W. has a wooden fireplace-surround in the Adam manner, while the larger of the two rooms to the E. of the hall retains some original panelling. The first floor contains three large rooms, each reached from the stair-landing which also communicates with the N. range by means of a corridor on the E. side of the stair; on the S. wall of the landing there hangs the tapestry illustrated in Pl. 185 C. The E. apartment, which was the dining-room, retains its original pine panelling; there is a dado, and each door has a moulded surround and a carved frieze and cornice, the former incorporating an acorn-and-oakleaf design. The ceiling (Pl. 179) is divided into compartments which contain conventional designs in relief. The drawing-room (Pl. 180) immediately to the W. contains panelling like that in the dining-room and there is an ornamental plaster ceiling in the Rococo manner (Pl. 181). The W. room is said to have been the principal bedroom; it is not panelled, but the doors have moulded architraves. The ceiling is less elaborately treated than that in the drawing-room. The arrangement of the second floor is broadly similar to that of the first. The two easternmost rooms are partly panelled and each has its own dressing-room. The W. room has a fine ornamental ceiling (Pls. 184, 185 A-B) similar in style to that of the drawing-room, and the E. one portions of early fabric wall-covering. The three large rooms on the first floor and the W. room on the second floor are said to contain marble fireplaces, but these are now boxed in and could not be seen at the date of visit.[2]

A lead rain-water head from Touch House, apparently of 18th-century date, is preserved in the National Museum of Antiquities of Scotland.

The lands of Touch were acquired by the Setons at about the end of the 15th century, and continued in the direct line of that family until the middle of the 18th century. The property then descended through the female line and passed to the Seton-Steuarts of Allanton and Touch, who held it until about 1930.[3]

752927 NS 79 SE 9 June 1956

346. Seton Lodge. Seton Lodge stands about two and a half miles W. of Stirling and a quarter of a mile N. of Touch House (No. 345). Its original portion comprises a T-shaped house of two storeys and an attic, the main block running E. and W. and the wing projecting from the centre of the N. front. To this house, which may be ascribed to about the turn of the 18th and 19th centuries, a W. wing was added in 1947, while minor additions were made on the N. at about the same time. These extensions have been designed to harmonise as far as

[1] *T.S.N.H.A.S.* (1928-9), 37.

[2] These fireplaces were uncovered in 1960 when the main apartments were restored to their original functions after war-time adaptations. The dining-room and drawing-room chimney-pieces (Pl. 182) appear to be of mid-18th century date, the latter, with its bracketed cornice and carved frieze, being a particularly distinguished example of its period. The chimney-piece of the W. room on the second floor has a fine plaster overmantel, but the wooden fireplace-surround appears to be a renewal. These fireplaces have been indicated on the plan (Fig. 159), which has also been amended to conform with other minor alterations carried out in 1960.

[3] Seton, G., *The Family of Seton*, 335 ff.; Burke, *Landed Gentry* (1952 ed.), 1612.

possible with the older building, the original appearance of which is suggested in Fig. 161.

The house is built in rubble with dressed margins, and the masonry is harled; the roof is hipped, but the over-

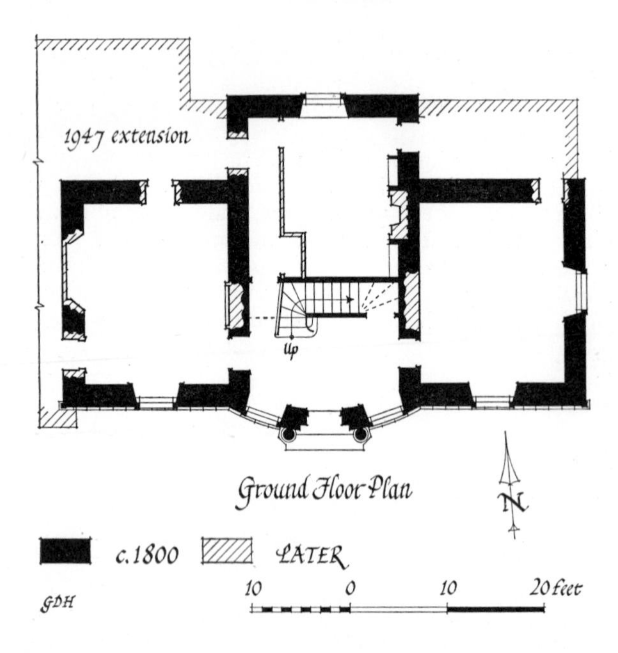

Fig. 161. Seton Lodge (No. 346); plan and reconstructed elevation

hanging eaves may not be original. The most interesting feature of the exterior is the S. façade, the central portion of which is bow-fronted and contains the entrance-doorway set within a Tuscan porch; over the door there is a radial fanlight. All the windows are symmetrically placed, but some are dummies. The plan (Fig. 161) is a symmetrical one. The entrance-doorway leads into a hall, at the rear of which there is a stone stair with a plain cast-iron handrail. There is a single room on either side of the stair and a smaller room in the N. wing; a similar arrangement originally existed on the first floor. The interior has, however, been very much altered, and the only remaining feature of interest is a simple wooden fireplace-surround, in the Adam manner, in the W. room on the ground floor. A more elaborate fireplace in the same style, which is incorporated in the 1947 wing, is said to have come from a house in Edinburgh.

Seton Lodge is on the estate of Touch, formerly the property of the Seton family (cf. No. 345); it may have been built as a dower-house, but on an estate plan of 1810[1] it is shown as the residence of the factor.

753931 NS 79 SE 12 June 1957

347. Carnock House (Site). Carnock House formerly stood in its policies two miles west of Airth and about the same distance south of the River Forth. The house was the work of two main building periods, the first in the middle of the 16th century and the second nearly a century later. It was demolished in 1941, and the brief account that follows has been compiled from photographs now in the possession of the Ministry of Works and from the more complete description of MacGibbon and Ross[2] to which reference should be made.

The lands of Carnock were gradually accumulated by the Drummond family during the 16th century,[3] and the original house was built by Robert Drummond of Carnock in 1548. Robert Drummond was knighted, and in 1579 became Master of Works to the Crown of Scotland,[4] so it may be that the design of the building, which is an unusual one, owed something to his own interest in the subject. The house was three storeys and an attic in height, and on plan was a simple parallelogram running E. and W. with two square projecting stair-towers to the N., one of which contained the main entrance. Both stairs rose the full height of the building and were so placed as to give access to each floor at opposite ends of the house. The ground floor contained vaulted cellars and a kitchen at the E. end. On the first floor, the hall occupied the central position, having at either end a smaller room, each of which connected both with the hall and with one of the staircases. A parapet-walk, borne on a continuous corbel-course and having open rounds at the angles, ran round the building.

In 1634, the estate of Carnock passed from the Drummonds to Thomas Nicolson,[5] an Edinburgh lawyer, who was shortly afterwards created a baronet of Nova Scotia. The alterations and additions to the house must have been begun almost at once, for the date 1634 was inscribed on a dormer pediment on the S. front of the house. Minor additions were made on the N. front, while a separate range of buildings, containing stables and a new kitchen, was constructed N. of the house and

[1] In the possession of the present owner, Col. E. P. Buchanan, M.C.
[2] *Cast. and Dom. Arch.*, ii, 490 ff.
[3] *R.M.S.*, iii, 1513-46 and iv, 1546-88, *passim*.
[4] Mylne, R. S., *Master Masons to the Crown of Scotland*, 54, 60.
[5] *R.M.S.*, ix, 1634-51, No. 26.

roughly parallel to it. A wall linked the new building to the old and formed the third side of a courtyard. At the same time, the old kitchen was turned into a cellar and the fireplace was built up.

An attempt was also made to give a more symmetrical appearance to the S. façade. The fenestration at first- and second-floor levels was regularised and the voids were enlarged and provided with simply moulded lugged architraves. On the ground floor, a central doorway, Classical in form, was somewhat awkwardly contrived to give access to the garden terrace from one of the cellars. This doorway was flanked by pilasters which supported an entablature and raking pediment.[1] The attic floor was enlarged and provided with dormers having triangular pediments, the tympana of which contained the initials of Sir Thomas Nicolson and his wife Isobel Henderson, together with their armorial achievements. The parapet was reduced in height to admit more light to this upper floor, and the round at the SE. angle, if such was part of the original structure, was removed.

The internal decoration of the house seems to have taken place a little later, when some fine ornamental plaster ceilings were inserted. A few fragments of one of these ceilings, together with some tempera-painted boards, were removed during the demolition and are now preserved at Kinneil House, West Lothian. The plaster fragments are part of the panelled ceiling of the hall or drawing-room, which was the principal first-floor apartment. They include a plain circular plaque from the circumference of which spring alternate roses, thistles and fleurs-de-lys; and also two identical heraldic shields. These are parted per pale and charged: Dexter, a lion's head between three falcons' heads, cantoned with the badge of Nova Scotia, for Sir Thomas Nicolson; sinister, second, three gillyflowers, fourth, a bend between six billets, for Margaret Livingstone. These are the coats of Sir Thomas Nicolson, 2nd Baronet of Carnock, and his wife, and the ceiling can therefore be ascribed to the period between the year 1646, when Sir Thomas succeeded his father, and his death which took place in 1664.[2]

The great oaken entrance-door of the house (Pl. 216 B) is preserved in the Smith Institute, Stirling, and is described under No. 405. A finial said to have come from Carnock is preserved in the garden at Bloemfontein, Airth, and is noted under No. 415.

Sir Thomas Nicolson, fourth of Carnock, became the fourth Lord Napier of Merchiston, but the house and lands of Carnock passed by marriage to the Shaws of Greenock about the beginning of the 18th century.

865882 NS 88 NE 14 October 1954

348. Tamrawer (Site). The house of Tamrawer, which is marked ("Tomrawyr") on Pont's map of the early 17th century,[3] stood about 320 yds. E. of Meadowside, on the W. lip of a small, steep gully. The site is now occupied by the ruins of a small farm, stated by the Ordnance Survey Name Book[4] to have been "originally the dwelling house of the proprietor of the estate of Tomrawer", but now too much dilapidated for dating.[5] A stone dated 1769, which is said to have been removed from it, is described under No. 408. The main interest of the place resides in the fact that it was a laird of Tamrawer, John Graham, who in 1739 first introduced the cultivation of potatoes as a field crop.[6] According to local report, the experimental planting was carried out in the field immediately S. of the house.

758796 NS 77 NE (unnoted; "Tomrawer, ruin" on sheet xxix of 1864-5 edition) 14 October 1953

SMALL HOUSES, FARMS, DOVECOTS, ETC.

349. Old Cottages, Dumyat. These remains are situated on the N. flank of Dumyat, at a height of about 900 ft. O.D. and at a distance of about one-third of a mile S. of Lossburn Reservoir. They consist of five rectangular foundations, measuring from 22 ft. to 30 ft. in length by from 11 ft. to 15 ft. in width within low, grass-grown, stony mounds. Four lie in a group and one stands by itself 120 yds. NW. of the others. A spring issues from the hillside at a point about equidistant between the group and the single foundation. The foundations forming the group are disposed about a comparatively level area of the hillside which measures some 120 ft. both from SW. to NE. and transversely; adjoining this on the NW. is a rounded enclosure defined by a ruinous stone wall and measuring about 50 ft. in diameter. The isolated foundation, which lies on a shelf facing NW., is associated with a small enclosure measuring 12 ft. by 9 ft. within a ruined and grass-grown stone wall. The foundations and enclosures are probably the remains of a small farmstead, possibly of the 17th or 18th century.

830983 NS 89 NW (unnoted) 28 September 1956

350. Old Mill, Milton. This building, which may at one time have formed part of a mill, stands a quarter of a mile SE. of the village of Whins of Milton and 100 yds. SE. of Milton farm, which it now serves as a storehouse. It measures 36 ft. in length by 25 ft. 9 in. in breadth over walls which average 2 ft. 2 in. in thickness; it originally

---

[1] *Cast. and Dom. Arch.*, ii, fig. 921.
[2] *Retours* (Stirlingshire), Nos. 184 and 235.
[3] Published in Blaeu's *Theatrum Orbis Terrarum*, v, *Sterlinensis praefectura*.
[4] Parish of Kilsyth, 93.
[5] William Graham of Tamrawer is on record in 1602 (Graham, J. E., *The Grahams of Tamrawer*, Edinburgh, 1895, printed for private circulation, 28). The subsequent history of this property is dealt with fully by Graham, J. St. J., *The Grahams of Auchencloich and Tamrawer*, Lisbon, 1952, printed for private circulation, *passim*.
[6] *Stat. Acct.*, xviii (1796), 282 f.; Symon, J. A., *Scottish Farming Past and Present* (1959), 115.

rose to a height of three storeys throughout, though the E. portion of the basement is now filled in. The gables are finished with plain tabling and have moulded skewputs. The building has evidently been altered from time to time and the present structure represents the work of more than a single period. The lowermost four or five courses of the central portion of the W. gable are built in coursed ashlar, and are probably of earlier date than the remainder, which is of rubble with dressed quoins and margins. The greater part of the building is no doubt of 18th-century date, the round-arrised windows in the S. and E. walls being of this period; but some of the walling has been renewed at a later time, and other windows have been inserted together with cart-shed openings in the N. wall. Three carved stones are incorporated in the building. A door-lintel which bears the initials S H P above the date 16[??] has been reset in the E. gable; the letters probably stand for Sir Hugh Paterson, 1st or 2nd of Bannockburn (cf. No. 392). A quoin set low down on the SW. angle bears the incised initials D Y and K E, with the date 1754; while another quoin, immediately below the skewput on the NE. angle, shows 1803, also incised. This last date no doubt refers to some work of reconstruction.

802899 NS 88 NW 31 August 1955

351. "Beaton's Mill", Milton. The house in which tradition says that James III was murdered[1] formerly stood about 70 yds. SE. of No. 350, beside a lane which leads up towards Milton from a ford over the Bannock Burn. When first visited, in 1954, it was ruinous, having been damaged by fire in 1952, and possessed no architectural features apart from a small window with widely chamfered arrises in the surviving gable. Its general appearance, however, was that of a cottage of the 17th or early 18th century, and this is borne out by an early photograph[2] which depicts a simple, one-storeyed building with a thatched roof. It is quite unlikely to have been in existence as early as 1488. The house has now been almost wholly demolished, but its foundations, which remain, show rubble construction with lime mortar. There is no evidence to support the idea that it was ever used as a mill, for which function its position would in fact have been quite unsuitable.

802899 NS 88 NW 31 August 1955

352. Round House, Dalgrain. The house that stands in the angle formed by the Forth and Clyde Canal and the W. side of the Edinburgh-Stirling highway (A 905), at the S. approach to the swing-bridge at Dalgrain, is remarkable for being circular on plan. It is stone-built and harled, measuring 83 ft. 6 in. in circumference (corresponding diameter 26 ft. 7 in.) outside a wall 2 ft. thick. The roof is slated, but the original roof is said to have been of thatch and at a lower level, the wall-head having been raised. The door, which is towards the Canal (approximately N.), opens into a very small lobby, with doors on all three sides; those to right and left open into the two semicircular rooms into which the interior is divided, and the third gives access to a steep, ladderlike stair, which rises in the line of the partition between the rooms to a circular attic. Each of the ground-floor rooms has a fireplace in the partition, the flues from which are carried up through the centre of the attic, and a two-light window in the centre of its arc. The attic has a skylight.

This building is understood to have been the toll-house for the highway-bridge, and its construction is therefore to be associated with that of the Canal.

912818 NS 98 SW 27 March 1953

353. Old Building, Bowhouse. The farm of Bowhouse is situated some five-eighths of a mile NNE. of Beancross, on the by-road leading thence to Grangemouth by Abbotsgrange. The range of barns, etc., that stands immediately NE. of the farmhouse is now, as a result of various reconstructions and alterations, substantially a 19th-century structure, but it evidently incorporates, in its NW. wall, some remains of a building which may go back to the 17th century. Thus the NE. jamb of the blocked doorway near the NE. end of this wall has a widely chamfered arris up to a height of 5 ft. above the ground, while the masonry immediately adjoining it seems to be of the same build. Again, the rebuilt doorway near the SW. end of the wall contains some rybats showing a similar chamfer, and others on which the arrises are rounded.

Bowhouse was formerly a property of Holyrood Abbey. A tack of the lands to one Andrew Callendar is recorded in 1552.[3]

930804 NS 98 SW 2 April 1958

354. Old Building, Upper Candie. The cottage of Upper Candie, with its gardens and outbuildings, is situated on the E. outskirts of Grangemouth, overshadowed by the oil refineries of British Petroleum Chemicals Limited. The cottage itself has evidently been reconstructed, and though recent harling disguises structural details there is no reason to date it earlier than the end of the 18th century. The front garden, however, is flanked on its NE. side by a length of walling which incorporates two doorways, the arrises of which show wide chamfers; all other details are hidden by dense ivy, but it seems likely that this wall once belonged to a byre or outhouse, perhaps dating from the 17th century.

The title-deeds of this property indicate that it once formed part of the estate of Saltcoats.[4] This was formerly a property of Holyrood Abbey, the grant of Easter and

---

[1] *Stat. Acct.*, xviii (1796), 410.

[2] Drysdale, W., *Auld Biggins of Stirling*, unnumbered illustration.

[3] *Holyrood*, No. 131.

[4] The Commissioners are indebted for this information to Mr. R. Porteous, Grangemouth.

Wester Saltcoats, with some cotlands and other neighbouring property, by the Commendator to the Duke of Châtelhérault being on record in 1552.[1]

941814 NS 98 SW 2 April 1958

355. Windmill, Myrehead. Near the NW. corner of the farm-buildings at Myrehead, some 650 yds. NW. of Manuel Station, and partly encroached on by them, there stands the empty shell of a windmill.[2] It is roughly built of rubble, with large freestone quoins at the doors, and is circular on plan, measuring about 19 ft. in diameter at ground level over a wall 3 ft. thick, but contracts markedly above the second floor (Pl. 205 A). The height is estimated to be about 40 ft. The top is open and the interior has been gutted, but the arrangement of doors and joist-holes shows that there were originally three floors in all in the lower part of the tower. At ground level, in the W. arc, there is a door, now blocked to half its height, with a massive lintel and a relieving arch; on the N. and the SE. respectively a small window and a door have been broken out. On the first floor the inside of a blocked door, clearly original, can be seen on the S., the exterior of which is obscured by the abutting farm-buildings. On the second floor, in the W. arc, there is a door with a relieving arch but no lintel; the lower edge of this opening, from which the threshold seems likewise to have been removed, is some 8 ft. directly above the lintel of the ground-floor entrance. A ring of putlog holes runs round the exterior at this level. The appearance of the quoins would agree with a date in the late 18th or early 19th century.

965775 NS 97 NE 20 March 1953

356. Summerhouse. This farmhouse, which stands a mile and a quarter W. of the village of Avonbridge, although much altered externally and modernised within, incorporates the remains of a building which may date from the 17th century. The only remaining features of interest are some old window-openings, now blocked up, in the N. wall and the W. gable; these have rounded arrises.

890725 NS 87 SE 8 October 1957

357. Old Building, Stoneridge. The doorway that gives entry to what is now the scullery of Stoneridge farmhouse has widely chamfered jambs and an inscribed lintel, all heavily weathered. The lintel appears to have borne initials and a date, but today the initials are illegible and the date has nearly disappeared. It is probably to be read as 1694, the last two digits being fairly clear. The doorway is no doubt *in situ*, but the building as a whole must have been greatly altered. The barn at the E. end of the steading bears the date 1720 on the lintel of its outer door, and both this door and its counterpart in the opposite wall have chamfers of the period and also internal lintels of wood shaped to a slightly arched form.

879700 NS 87 SE 1 April 1956

358. Binniegreen, Balquhatstone. The house of Binniegreen, now converted into a forester's cottage, stands within the Balquhatstone policies 70 yds. SSE. of the mansion. Though the building is greatly altered, enough of the original features remain on the NW. face to show that it originally possessed a central entrance with two windows on either side and five others set symmetrically at first-floor level. The masonry is rubble and there is a cavetto eaves-course. The doorway, now changed into a window, shows a lugged roll-and-hollow moulding interrupted by blocks, and is surmounted by a moulded pediment containing the date 1734. Apart, perhaps, from a small window with an unusual moulding, the SE. face is probably of somewhat later construction.

858725 NS 87 SE 16 April 1954

359. Hallhouse. This house, which is still inhabited, stands about three-quarters of a mile WSW. of the centre of Denny, on ground which slopes to the left bank of the Castlerankine Burn. On plan (Fig. 162) it is oblong, measuring 63 ft. 9 in. in length over an extension 18 ft. 6 in. long at its NE. end, by 18 ft. 6 in. in width. It is built of rubble faced partly with cement and partly with harling, and is subdivided into three main parts by mutual gables; the SW. part containing two storeys, the central part one storey and a garret, and the NE. extension a single storey only. The two-storeyed portion has crow-stepped gables and an ogival eaves-course while the lower gables finish in tabling. The slated roofs are probably renewals.

The first construction is probably to be dated to the late 17th or early 18th century, but many alterations are known to have taken place, and the fact that all details are obscured by harling and cement makes a proper analysis impossible. That the SW. and central portions are contemporary seems very probable, as both are based on a continuous foundation of large boulders and the floors of both are also known to have once been paved with flagstones. On the other hand, no original means of communication between the two parts can now be identified, as the doorway in the E. corner of the SW. room is shown by its skew-wise position to have resulted from some alteration, while its counterpart on the upper floor only gives access to the stair, which was inserted by the present owner. Before the insertion of the stair the first-floor room was reached by a hatchway in the floor and a ladder in the room below. The owner further stated that a covered-up press existed near the N. corner of the

[1] *Holyrood*, App. II, No. 37.

[2] Notes in *P.S.A.S.*, lxxix (1944-5), 12. This same article explains the mechanism of these mills.

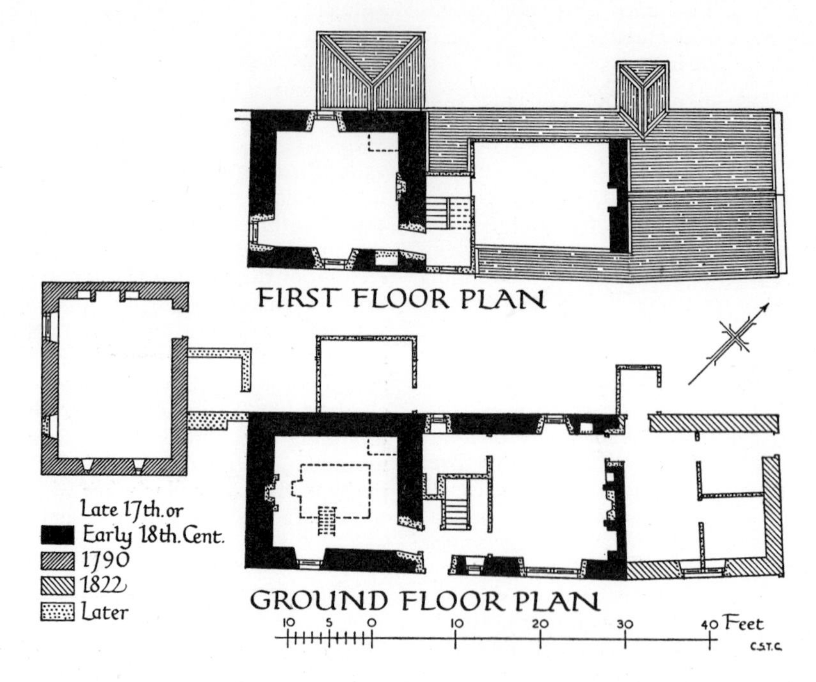

Fig. 162. Hallhouse (No. 359)

upper room, and this might conceivably represent an original door reached by a forestair. The NE. subdivision is evidently an addition, probably of 1822 (*infra*); this was originally a byre, and communicated with the central room, the kitchen, by a door in the NE. gable of the latter NW. of the fireplace and small oven.

In the absence of a complete analysis of the structure, mention may be made of some original or early details. For example, chamfered arrises are seen in the window of the SW. room on the ground floor, in its counterpart in the room above, and in the back door in the NW. wall of the extension. The window beside the front door has rounded arrises and was once barred. The NW. window of the kitchen may represent a restoration of an original one. The kitchen fireplace is original but has been contracted; its lintel is supported by an ogival corbel on either jamb. A small recess in the NW. wall of the kitchen, now plastered over, served to hold a bucket of water before a supply was piped in. Witness to alterations and additions is borne by five inscriptions—the front-door lintel bears the date 18[?3 or 6]8 flanked by the initials T J, for Thomas Johnstone, and those of his wife, which are illegible; the entrance in the NE. gable of the extension similarly shows T J with the wife's initials J N, flanking the date 1822; the sill of the chamfered window in the first-floor room at the SW. end of the house is inscribed REP(AIRE)D 1834, while the blocked-up window in the NW. wall was likewise repaired in 1934; and the doorway lintel of a one-storeyed, single-chambered outbuilding, which stands just clear of the SW. end of the house, is inscribed with T J and E A, flanking the date 1790. This outbuilding presumably served some domestic purpose, as it is provided with a fireplace and two ordinary windows in addition to the two 4-inch slits in the SE. gable. The shallow cellar in the SW. room of the main building is not a feature of any interest, as the proprietor states that it was constructed as a heating-chamber for a greenhouse, the ruins of which can be seen on the outside of the gable.

SUNDIAL. On one of the crow-steps of the SE. gable of the outbuilding referred to above there has been placed a single-faced sundial bearing the date 1670. The proprietor believes that it was brought from the old church of Denny (cf. No. 149).

From records in the possession of the proprietor, Mr. Bryson, it would appear that Hallhouse had been in the possession of the Johnstone family or of their descendants from the late 16th century to the present day.

801824 NS 88 SW 18 July 1957

360. Leys. The remains of the farm of Leys are situated on the SE. outskirts of Denny Muir, some three miles WSW. of Denny. The farmhouse was demolished at the beginning of the 20th century, and only a fragment of it (Fig. 163) now survives; formerly, however, it constituted the SW. end of a long range of buildings, the other end, which is still used as a byre, having been separated from it by a through lobby 7 ft. in width. As will appear shortly, the farmhouse probably dates from 1702, while the original NE. portion of the block is older and may go back at least to the 1660s. The total length of the block is judged from doubtful surface indications of foundations to have been a little over 90 ft.; the width is 19 ft. The greater part of the walling, which is of rubble averaging 2 ft. in thickness and bound with lime mortar, has been rebuilt on older foundations in which clay mortar was used; but on the SE. side of the byre the original walling, 2 ft. 5 in. in thickness, still rises to a height of 4 ft. or so. In the inner facing of this wall the sawn-off stumps of three crucks are embedded; a fourth was lately removed during the formation of the door in the SE. wall, and is now utilised as a lintel. These crucks were originally arranged in pairs, so as to form the principal trusses supporting a purlined roof; according to Mr. Erskine, Leysbent, who lived in the house before its demolition, the feet of the crucks did not reach down to the floor but were housed in the wall about 2 ft. above it. A doorway with rounded arrises, which once entered from the lobby but is now built up, appears to have been the original means of access; all other openings in the side walls and gables have either been inserted or belong to the part of the walling that was renewed when the building was converted into a byre. The roof is also a replacement. On the lobby side of the partition between byre and house there is a small locker at each end and, at a lower level on each side of the blocked-up entrance, a recessed slit, 6 in. wide and 12 in. or so in depth, containing the rounded stump of a horizontally placed timber. The purpose of these slits and timbers is unknown. In the gable of the partition a flat slab projects as a pigeon-rest, and above it there have been several rows of holes by which pigeons could enter, but these are now built up. In the wall at the SE. end of the lobby a press has been hollowed out, and beside this a door has been opened; this last was probably done in the 19th century, though the door carries a re-used chamfered lintel incised with the date 166[?] flanked by the initials W L and A S. At the opposite end of the lobby there is another small locker. The older entrance to the lobby is in its NW. end; this has chamfered arrises and still retains its lintel, which is inscribed W L C D 1702. The initials are said to be those of William Laing and Christina Dunsmuir. Immediately beside it, in the partition between the lobby and the farmhouse, there is another door, also with chamfered arrises but now lacking its lintel. The partition, which now stands barely 3 ft. high, has been thinned on its SW. face as if to accommodate a press, corresponding with the doorway from the lobby, and perhaps a fireplace in the centre. The rest of this building has been demolished, but Mr. Erskine stated that it comprised, on the ground floor, two rooms with a cellarage between them under an internal stair, and on the first floor two rooms and a closet. In his time the lobby was a scullery, communicating with the byre, while the adjoining room of the house was a kitchen which also contained box beds. The plan is plainly of the "long house" variety (cf. p. 49).

767817 NS 78 SE 5 August 1954

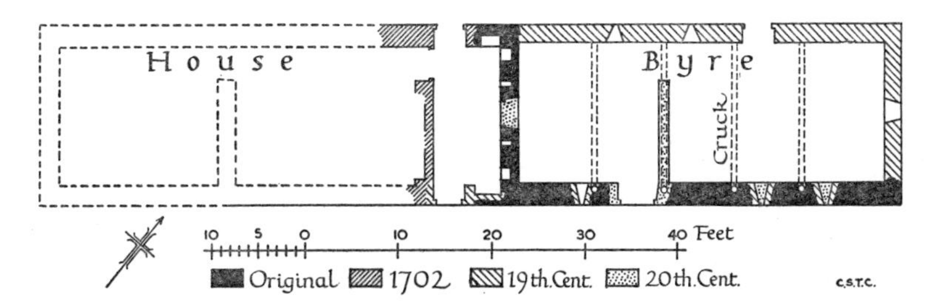

Fig. 163. Leys (No. 360)

361. Old Farm, Wester Barnego. The farm of Wester Barnego, which is now ruinous, stands two and a half miles NW. of the village of Dunipace. The structure is for the most part of 19th-century date, but a building on the S. side of the enclosure is probably as old as the 17th century. It consists of a rectangular block, a single storey in height, which runs N. and S.; the S. part has been removed to make way for a later building and the surviving portion now measures 31 ft. by 18 ft. 6 in. over walls which have a thickness of 2 ft. 3 in. The masonry, which is of rubble, has been laid in mud mortar and the voids have chamfered arrises. Apart from one or two blocked-up doors and windows in the E. and W. walls, the building now contains no features of interest.

BEE-BOLES. About 100 yds. N. of the farm, four square recesses (Pl. 205 C), formed of stone slabs, are built against the S. wall of a dyke. A fifth recess, which adjoins to the W., is now blocked; the remainder measure about 1 ft. 9 in. in width and 2 ft. 3 in. in height and have a depth of 2 ft. They were originally fitted with doors or shutters, and no doubt contained beehives.

783840 NS 78 SE 3 May 1956

362. Cruck-framed Byre, Hallquarter. This structure, an outbuilding of Hallquarter Farm, although latterly in use as a byre, may originally have been a dwelling-house. It measures 26 ft. 8 in. by 14 ft. 5 in. internally, and the walls, which are of rubble masonry laid in mud mortar, have a thickness of 2 ft. and rise to a height of 6 ft. The roof, which was originally thatched, was supported by two pairs of crucks; the roof has been renewed, however, and the crucks sawn off at wall-head level so that only the stumps survive (Fig. 164). Enough remains to indicate that each cruck blade was formed of two separate members, scarf-jointed a little below wall-head level.

782860 NS 78 NE 18 June 1955

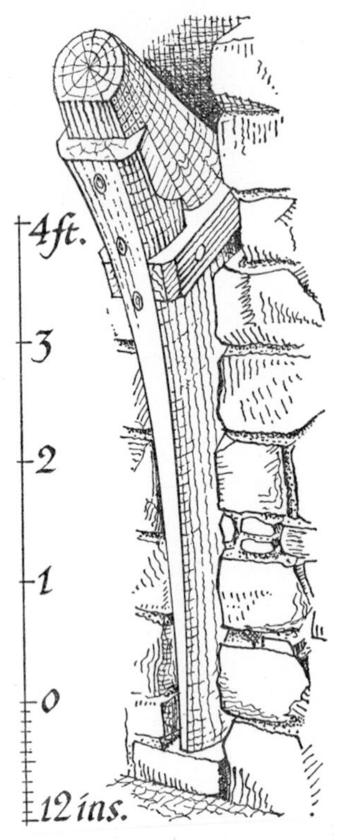

Fig. 164. Cruck-framed byre, Hallquarter (No. 362); detail of cruck

363. Garrel Mill-house. Garrel Mill and its mill-house stand on opposite sides of the Kilsyth-Stirling road (No. 511) 200 yds. N. of its junction, in Kilsyth, with the Falkirk highway. The mill-house, which is on the NW. side of the road, has been renovated, harled in cement and re-roofed, but its walling and internal arrangements are substantially original and the structure probably dates from the end of the 17th century. The house is oblong on plan, 37 ft. 3 in. long by 19 ft. 9 in. wide, with a semicircular projection housing a geometrical stair in the centre of the back wall, and is two storeys high. The SE. façade, which is unaltered, has an entrance in the centre with two windows on either side of it and five others on the floor above, symmetrically spaced. The entrance has a lugged and bowtell-moulded architrave, and above it a moulded corbel carries a plain shield. Another corbel on the S. corner carries a cubical sundial. The arrises of the windows are chamfered, and the wall-head finishes in a plain eaves-band. The entrance opens into a lobby, with a room on either side of it; on the first floor there is similarly a room on either side of a landing and modern bathroom. The stair and the baluster rail are of wood, and the balusters of iron. To the original house there have been added a one-storeyed outshot on the S., used as a bedroom, and a two-storeyed extension abutting the NE. gable; doors to these have been broken out, as well as a back entrance from the stair.

720783 NS 77 NW 2 October 1953

364. Old House, Campsie Manse. In the back yard of the manse at the Clachan of Campsie, a low range of buildings, now used as outhouses, embodies details which seem to suggest a 17th-century date. The range is a single-storeyed, oblong block, measuring 49 ft. by 20 ft. 10 in., and is divided into three compartments by transverse stone partitions. The stonework of the S. front is large squared rubble brought to courses, but the ends seem to have been broken and rebuilt with random rubble. Each division is entered from the S., and each is lit by a window on that side, the central division having also a small window, probably inserted, in the N. wall. The original doorway to the central division is edged with a roll-and-hollow moulding, but the other doors have sharp arrises and appear to be later. The reverse is the case with the windows, the end ones appearing to be old and the middle one an insertion. There are no fireplaces on the ground floor, but high up in the E. partition what looks like a built-up fireplace suggests the former existence of an upper storey or an attic; in that case the present eaves-course, which is wrought with an ogival moulding, may have been lowered when the building was converted to a single storey.

611794 NS 67 NW 8 September 1953

365. Old Inn, Barraston. The easternmost of the farm-buildings at Barraston is said locally to have once been an inn, though this need not necessarily have been its original role. The structure has, however, been gutted and converted into a piggery, with the result that no original features now survive except a doorway in the W. wall, which has itself been partly built up to act as a window. Internally this doorway shows rounded arrises, and externally its lintel is inscribed, in relief, 1609 / A B A H, the pairs of initials being separated by a cross. A local historian relates[1] how one Abraham Hannay obtained these lands in 1609, and gives his wife's name as Ann Blyth, transcribing the initials incorrectly as A H A B. If this had been their true order, the identification would have seemed most natural, as the husband's initials would then have been, as was usual, on the dexter side; and in any case the reversal many be simply due to a mistake on the part of the stone-cutter.

A built-up doorway of 18th-century character in the E. wall has a lintel inscribed W H 1789 L C. No doubt this also refers to a Hannay.

606754 NS 67 NW 13 August 1953

[1] Cameron, J., *The Parish of Campsie*, 203 f.

366. Old Cottages, Edinkill. Two examples of what are no doubt country cottages of 18th-century date were noted in Edinkill. The first, Number 6 Dumbrock Road, originally consisted of a one-storeyed building with an attic, measuring 34 ft. by 20 ft. over walls 2 ft. 6 in. thick, though later additions have been made at the back. The masonry is rubble with dressed quoins, the wall finishes in a cavetto eaves-course and the gables are crow-stepped with cavetto skewputs. The door, which is central in the front, and a small window in the back wall both have rounded arrises and appear to be original, the back window being also provided with crooks for external shutters; but the windows flanking the door have been altered and the large attic-window is a recent insertion. The raggle of a lower building, with a built-up fireplace, may be seen on the outer face of the W. gable. The whole of the interior is now a single room, though this may not have been the original arrangement as there is, or has been, a fireplace at either end.

The other cottage stands opposite, at the corner of Dumbrock Road and Old Mugdock Road. It is of the same general type as the one described, but shows no characteristic features apart from three windows with rounded arrises.

562791 NS 57 NE 11 August 1953

367. Huts, Auchineden Burn. Two huts, represented only by foundation mounds, can be seen on a small bluff overlooking the streamlets and ditches at the head of the Auchineden Burn. Their position is about a quarter of a mile WSW. of Catythirsty Well. Both measure about 18 ft. in diameter over all, one being approximately circular and the other having slightly flattened sides. They are not thought to be prehistoric.

506811 NS 58 SW (unnoted) 3 July 1958

368. Old Farm, Braefoot. About a quarter of a mile W. of the farm of Braefoot, and about half a mile E. of the main Glasgow-Drymen highway (A 809), there are the ruins of a small farmstead, which is of some interest as an example of a cruck-framed building of comparatively late date. The remains are of more than one period, but the oldest portion comprises a small house which measures 36 ft. 5 in. by 20 ft. 10 in. over walls 2 ft. thick. The building is of rubble masonry laid in lime mortar and the voids have pink-sandstone dressings; the appearance of the house suggests a date not earlier than the late 18th or early 19th century. The building seems to have been single-storeyed and probably contained two main rooms, which were entered from the central entrance-doorway. There were two pairs of crucks, which sprang from a height of about 1 ft. 6 in. above ground level; the crucks have now disappeared, but the slots in which they stood remain as cavities in the inner faces of the walls. At a later date a byre or barn, which measures 52 ft. 9 in. by 19 ft. over all and appears to have contained four pairs of crucks, was added to the E. gable of the original house. Subsequently a third structure, perhaps another byre, was added to the W. gable of the original house, but this latest addition was not cruck-framed.

514828 NS 58 SW 13 August 1957

369. Old Cottage, Cameron Muir. Fifty yards N. of the road across Cameron Muir, at spot-level 378, a low, rush-covered mound bears the foundations of a small house measuring about 30 ft. by 25 ft. over all. It is no doubt to be associated with the remains of enclosures and traces of former cultivation that are visible further N., at the head of the valley of the Green Burn.

472832 NS 48 SE (unnoted) 9 September 1956

370. Old Mill, Gartness. The old mill, now ruinous and overgrown, stands on the right bank of the Endrick Water, 300 yds. SSE. of Gartness Bridge. Though a mill has functioned here since 1739,[1] the existing ruin almost certainly belongs to the late 18th or early 19th century. A re-used window-lintel with a wide chamfer, and the stone bearing the date 1574 that appears in the S. gable of the adjoining store-house, probably came from Gartness Castle (No. 220).[2]

502866 NS 58 NW ("Mill, Dis.") 1 September 1952

371. Old Farms, Crockeild. About a quarter of a mile NE. of Rudha Curraichd, on the E. shore of Loch Lomond, and just above the present tree-line, the slope of the hillside becomes slightly easier after rising very steeply for some 500 ft. from the water's edge. Here stand the remains of a small farming settlement, comprising four or five units, each of which consists of a house with some smaller outhouses, and an oval enclosure, presumably for animals. The largest house measures 46 ft. by 15 ft. over all, the walls standing only to a height of some 3 ft. to 4 ft. There is little evidence as to the age of the remains, but there is no reason to suppose that they are older than the 18th century. The footpath from Ptarmigan Lodge to Inversnaid (cf. No. 521) passes through the settlement.

NN 344022 N iv S.E. 12 May 1954

372. Old House, Corheichan.[3] This house stands on a knoll overlooking the left bank of Allt Phadruic, just above what is now the S. shore of Loch Arklet; before the level of the surface was raised, by the damming of the Arklet Water, fields and marsh lay below it at the

---

[1] *Stat. Acct.*, xvi (1795), 108.
[2] Ordnance Survey Name Book, Drymen parish, 95.
[3] The authority for this spelling is unknown. Locally the name is pronounced as if spelt Corrieechan, and it is so spelt on Grassom's map of 1817.

original W. end of the loch. It is now no more than a ruin, but some at least of its original features still appear.

The long axis of the house runs from E. to W. and the structure, which is of random rubble laid in mud mortar, measures 57 ft. 3 in. by 19 ft. 6 in. (average) over walls 2 ft. 6 in. thick. The W. gable, which shows massive quoins, is nearly complete and stands to a height of about 13 ft.; in the centre of the interior there is a small fireplace, strongly built in lime mortar, and a small window, set high up, may suggest the former presence of a loft. There are traces of two doors in the N. wall and of one in the S. wall, but it is not clear whether all are original. Much of the N. wall is completely ruined, but it stands 8 ft. high at the NE. corner and, in addition to the doors, it shows the remains of a splayed window at either end. The roof was supported on two pairs of jointed crucks, recessed in the walls, which appear to have been irregularly spaced; the lower portion of one of these remains in the S. wall. Externally several projecting stones have evidently served as thatch-pegs, and abutting on the E. gable are the remains of a small outbuilding.

About 35 yds. E. of the dwelling-house there stands a smaller building, 41 ft. long by 20 ft. 6 in. wide over walls 2 ft. 3 in. thick; though now much altered and partially reconstructed in lime mortar, it was originally dry-built, in random rubble, and was roofed with two pairs of crucks. These were jointed and pegged, and were recessed in the walls; their lower portions still remain *in situ* on the N. side (Pl. 207 A). The two doorways in the N. wall, the two slit-windows in the S. wall and the drainage channel that crosses the floor near the E. end are none of them original features; taken in conjunction with the absence of a fireplace they suggest that, latterly at least, the building served as a byre.

Corheichan is on record as the home of Rob Roy's uncle, Alastair McGregor, at the time of the former's marriage in 1693,[1] but it is by no means certain that the existing house was standing at that time.

NN 377086 N iii 15 May 1959

373. Huts, etc., Glen Gyle. The following remains were noted in Glen Gyle. (i) On a rocky outcrop about 100 yds. up a small burn which joins the Glengyle Water 270 yds. below the forks at the head of the glen, part of a ring of large boulders once forming the foundations of a hut about 10 ft. in diameter. (ii) At spot-level 568 on the right bank of the Glengyle Water, three small occupation-scoops, with boulders, on a knoll. (iii) A flattish site scooped out of another knoll a short distance to the W., between two tributary burns. (iv) On a low, dry knoll in a swamp, close to the Glengyle Water at spot-level 443, a hut measuring 24 ft. by 16 ft. over foundation mounds up to 2 ft. high, with a doorway on the S. and a flat area outside it. In spite of their primitive appearance, these structures are not considered to be prehistoric.

NN 360146, NN 365143, NN 373138 N ii, N iii (unnoted)
9 September 1952

374. Old Houses and Site of Graveyard, Lag a' Chuirn. The head of Glen Gyle is formed by the union of two glens between which the county boundary continues the line of the main valley up the flank of Beinn Ducteach. At the foot of Lag a' Chuirn, the glen on the Stirlingshire side, and just above the junction of the burns, there may be seen the ruins of an old drystone house measuring 32 ft. by 14 ft. over all, but too much altered by conversion to the purposes of the sheep-farm for any original features to be distinguished with certainty. Other remains of the group of structures that once stood here, on both banks of the burn, include the foundations of a house measuring about 27 ft. by 15 ft., and of a stone hut originally measuring 12 ft. by 8 ft. but now rebuilt as a sheep-shelter. Somewhere close to these houses is said to have been the site of a graveyard, now vanished, which was formerly known as Kilmacallach[2]; in this connection the name "Bealach nan Corp", given on the O.S. map to a pass (365157) leading into Glen Gyle from Balquhidder, is worth noting for its suggestion of the former existence of a coffin-road. This dedication is probably to Abbot Cellach of Iona (802-815).[3]

About 750 yds. further up Lag a' Chuirn a small tributary comes down from the slopes of Beinn Ducteach. On this there are the ruins of some further small houses, one of which is said to bear the name of Tigh na Cuirte and to have been the "court-house" in which cattle-thieves were tried.[4] Lag a' Chuirn was on the line of an important drove-road from Argyll,[5] of which, however, no physical traces were seen; and this glimpse of raiding over what was later an ordinary drove-road lends force to Dr. Haldane's suggestion[6] as to the illicit origin of the trade.

NN 359147, NN 352147 N ii (unnoted)
14 September 1952

375. Old Farms, Comer. Though now too much dilapidated for detailed record, the remains of some old houses near Comer, about two and a half miles up Glen Dubh from Stronmacnair (No. 377), are of interest both for comparison with the older houses at Big Bruach-caoruinn (No. 379) and also because some evidence exists as to their age. Comer was the home of Gregor McGregor, the father of Rob Roy's wife,[7] and consequently some, if not necessarily all, of these buildings are likely to be at least as old as the end of the 17th century. The one that is situated about 600 yds. N. of Comer farmhouse measures 70 ft. in length by 15 ft. in width over all, and seems to have contained three

---

[1] Howlett, H., *Highland Constable*, 34 f., quoting Buchanan parish register.
[2] Information from Mr. Duncan Sinclair, Stronaclachar.
[3] Mackinlay, J. M., *Ancient Church Dedications in Scotland, Non-Scriptural Dedications*, 144.
[4] Information from Mr. Donald McLaren, Dow of Glengyle.
[5] Haldane, A. R. B., *The Drove Roads of Scotland*, 99.
[6] *Ibid.*, 2.
[7] Howlett, *op. cit.*, 34.

compartments with a lean-to building attached to its S. gable. The central compartment is the largest, and has an external entrance; the N. one is also entered from the outside, and was probably the byre. This was the largest of the houses, and if, as is locally believed, it was McGregor's residence, it points to the singularly modest material standards that might have sufficed a gentleman of the period (cf. No. 372).

NN 387045 N V (unnoted) 5 May 1955

376. Old Farms, Loch Dubh. The remains of a settlement of small houses, similar to those noted at Comer (No. 375), and lower down Glen Dubh (No. 378), are to be seen close to the head of Loch Dubh, on either side of the road leading to Comer. One of the houses measures 40 ft. 6 in. by 19 ft. 6 in. over drystone walls averaging 3 ft. in thickness. Three pairs of cruck recesses are present. A byre 42 ft. 6 in. long extends westwards from the W. gable. The ground to the N. of the settlement is enclosed by a turf dyke.

NN 403035 N V 5 May 1955

377. Cruck-framed Byre, Stronmacnair. The croft of Stronmacnair, which is marked on Grassom's map of 1817, occupies an isolated position in Glen Dubh, about 100 yds. W. of the county boundary of Stirlingshire and Perthshire. About 30 yds. SW. of the house there is a small rectangular building (Fig. 165, Pl. 206 B),

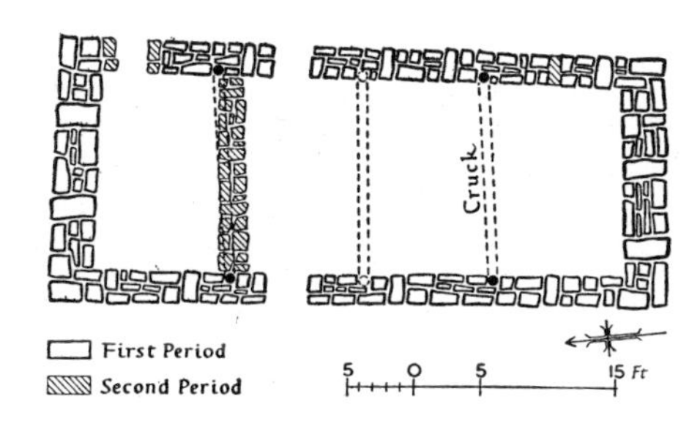

Fig. 165. Cruck-framed byre, Stronmacnair (No. 377)

a single storey in height, which measures 45 ft. 4 in. by 18 ft. 5 in. over all. The masonry, which is of rubble, is built without mortar although some of the external wall-surfaces have been patched with mortar at a later date; there is a corrugated iron roof, but the original covering was no doubt of thatch. The building runs roughly N. and S.; an original doorway is set a little to the N. of centre in both the E. and W. walls, but the doorway at the N. end of the E. wall is an insertion. There is a single window high up in the N. gable and a small slit, now blocked, at the S. end of the E. wall.

The building originally contained a single compartment only, and the partition wall to the N. is an insertion. The original roof was supported by three pairs of crucks, set at intervals of approximately 10 ft. The centre pair of crucks has been removed and the wall cavities filled up; the other two pairs remain *in situ* but have been truncated at wall-head level to accommodate the new roof. The feet of the southernmost pair of crucks rest on stone slabs about 1 ft. 8 in. above ground level. Each cruck has been of two members, the lower and the upper portions having been joined with wooden pegs at about wall-head level; only the lower members (Pl. 207 B) now remain. The feet of the northernmost pair are set about 3 ft. 3 in. above ground level and each cruck appears to have consisted of a single member only. The southernmost pair are of coniferous timber and the crucks have a diameter of about 8 in.; the northernmost pair are of oak and the crucks have a diameter of about 6 in. There is no trace of a fire-place and the provision of windows is inadequate for a dwelling-house; the disposition of the two original doorways suggests that the structure was erected for use as a byre.

NN 424025 N V 2 May 1956

378. Old Farms, Glen Dubh. At many places on the steep hillside falling to the right bank of the Duchray Water, from N. of Allt na Seilcheig to Little Bruach-caoruinn (No. 380), there may be seen larger or smaller patches of ground from which boulders have been cleared and which have evidently been under cultivation at some time. Scattered about the same area are the remains of several small houses which were not noted in detail; one of them measured 20 ft. by 7 ft. 6 in. internally and had slightly rounded corners and a door in the middle of one side. Cf. Nos. 379 and 380.

NN 4201 N vii N.E. (unnoted) 14 May 1959

379. Old Farms, Big Bruach-caoruinn. This large and somewhat scattered settlement (Fig. 166), which is marked on Grassom's map of 1817, lies on the left (W.) bank of the Bruach Caoruinn Burn 600 yds. WSW. of its confluence with the Duchray Water. Its lowermost end, in the angle between the Bruach Caoruinn Burn and a small unnamed tributary, is at 450 ft. O.D., and above it the cultivable ground slopes gently upwards with an aspect slightly E. of S. Below the settlement the ground flattens out to the main valley of the Duchray Water. The nucleus of the settlement consists of two long buildings set at rather less than a right angle to one another, with a gap 23 ft. wide between their ends; while a few feet beyond the NW. gable of the longer one there are the remains of an earlier building, and another some 120 yds. distant on the opposite side of the small burn. In addition, there is a kiln for drying corn, together with extensive remains both of subsidiary enclosures and of larger field-boundaries; it is probable that a comparatively large area was cultivated (cf. No. 378).

HOUSE A. The larger house (A on Fig. 166), the axis of which runs approximately from NW. to SE. and across the contours, is 103 ft. long by about 20 ft. broad over walls generally about 2 ft. 6 in. thick; the NW. compartment, however, is only 13 ft. 3 in. broad. The masonry is rougher than that at Little Bruach-caoruinn (No. 380) and the construction less good; the cruck-recesses are also less well preserved, though enough evidence remains to show that this method of roofing was used. The house contains four compartments, of which the SE. one was probably the dwelling-house, or at any rate the main portion of the habitable quarters, while the other three may have served as barns and byres. The SE. compartment is 40 ft. 6 in. long internally; its gable, which stands 14 ft. high internally and higher externally owing to the fall of the ground, contains a well-preserved fireplace and flue built in lime mortar, while mud mortar is used in the rest of the house. There is a central door in the SW. wall, with a splayed window on either side of it, and traces of another window in the NE. wall. The adjoining room is about 19 ft. long and lies 18 in. higher than the SE. one. It is entered by a doorway through the partition, which stands 13 ft. high and reaches to what was the level of the roof-ridge; it also has an external entrance in its SW. wall, and is shut off from the third compartment by a partition standing 10 ft. high through which there is no communicating doorway. This third compartment averages 13 ft. 6 in. in length and has a well-preserved doorway on the SW. with its lintel still in position; it has no internal communication with the NW. compartment, and the partition between them seems to have once been a gable-end as it has a high-level window in its centre. The NW. compartment, on this showing, must presumably have been an addition. There is also evidence, particularly in the substantial foundation-stones that survive at the W. corner, to show that its original SW. wall was at some time taken down and replaced by the existing one, which represents a contraction of about 3 ft. 6 in. in the breadth of the compartment. The existing SW. wall shows traces of a central doorway.

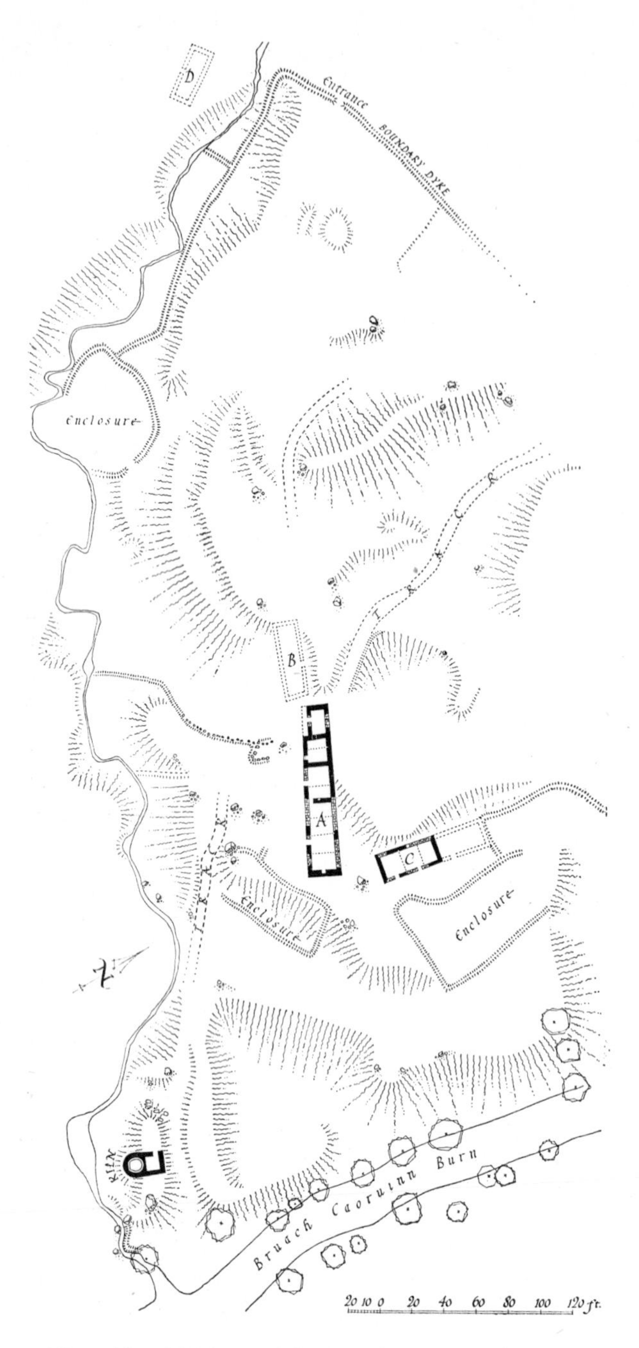

Fig. 166. Old farms, Big Bruach-caoruinn (No. 379)

HOUSE B. This house, which is reduced to its foundations, lies immediately NW. of House A. It measures only 46 ft. by 16 ft. over all, and thus corresponds with the house on the other side of the small burn and with others noted at Comer (No. 375). It may have been the predecessor of House A.

HOUSE C. This house (C on Fig. 166) is set with its axis approximately N. and S. It measures 38 ft. 6 in. by 16 ft. 4 in. over walls about 2 ft. 2 in. thick; but remains of further construction at its N. end suggest that it was originally about 32 ft. longer. The walls are built with mud mortar, and a pair of cruck-recesses and some projecting stones for thatch-ropes are preserved. There are two doorways in the E. side and at least one window, with splayed jambs, on the W. The presence of a drain outlet issuing from under the W. wall near its S. end indicates that this end of the building was a byre. This drain gives into a ditch which flanks the W. wall of the house and no doubt served to cut off water seeping downwards from the ground in the re-entrant angle between Houses C and A.

HOUSE D. This building, mentioned above as lying on the other side of the small burn, is featureless, but its dimensions (34 ft. 6 in. by 14 ft. 6 in.) suggest a comparison with House B. They may both be remains of an earlier settlement.

THE KILN. The corn-drying kiln[1] is situated close to the junction of the burns, some 60 yds. SE. of House A; the track serving it can still be made out. It is built on sloping ground and comprises a circular funnel, in which the corn was placed on a wooden rack, together with a rectangular storage-chamber or barn. The funnel, which takes the form of an inverted and truncated cone, measures about 8 ft. in diameter at its mouth; its entry flue, which lies 8 ft. 3 in. below the level of the mouth of the funnel, measures 1 ft. 9 in. by 1 ft. 4 in. at its outer end. The barn measures about 7 ft. 6 in. by 5 ft.

ENCLOSURES, ETC. Only vague and disjointed traces could be recovered of the dykes and enclosures adjoining the houses, and the general character of these can be seen in Fig. 166. Attention may be drawn, in particular, to a partially preserved, dyked enclosure, having a well-marked entrance and measuring about 20 yds. in diameter, which lies beside the small burn some 60 yds. W. of House A; and to a stretch of boundary-dyke which runs up the side of the burn from it for 70 yds., and then returns at right angles for 47 yds. to die out in boggy ground. The returned stretch is pierced by an entrance. Traces of enclosures are also seen SE. of House A, and E. and N. of House C; and there is some dyking near the N. corner of House A, by the side of a roadway which approaches from the N. Further field-boundaries can be seen on the hillside for a quarter of a mile or more to the N. of the settlement.

NN 418007 N vii N.E. 19 May 1955

380. Old Farms, Little Bruach-caoruinn. This settlement, which is marked on Grassom's map of 1817, stands rather less than a quarter of a mile SW. of the Duchray Water, on the left (NW.) bank of a small unnamed burn which joins the Duchray Water 270 yds. downstream from the confluence of the Bruach Caoruinn Burn. Its site is a shelf which slopes SE. towards the small burn and an intervening strip of wet ground, while further away, to E. and NE., there is the flatter valley-bottom of the Duchray Water, which here lies at about 420 ft. O.D. Behind the settlement, to the NW., the ground rises to a low ridge, beyond which, about a quarter of a mile distant, lies the comparable settlement of Big Bruach-caoruinn (No. 379).

The Little Bruach-caoruinn settlement consists of three houses, with their outbuildings and enclosures, disposed as shown in Fig. 167. The houses are alined roughly crescentwise, along the contour, the lower side of the site being levelled up as a platform (*infra*). The following structural details were recorded about them in order from NE. to SW.

HOUSE A (Fig. 167, Pl. 206 A). This is the best preserved house in the group, and may be the most recent; its walls, at any rate, are thinner than those of the others. It measures externally about 73 ft. by 16 ft. 10 in., and is constructed of random rubble with mud mortar. The side walls are slightly battered, the height of the wall-head being about 7 ft.; both gables stand intact and are 11 ft. high. The S. wall shows a splayed window and doorway, together with traces of what may have been a second doorway and a gap which may represent a third. Stones project from the wall-faces at certain points, no doubt for the attachment of ropes to retain the thatch; the E. gable has also two flat, projecting members, at a

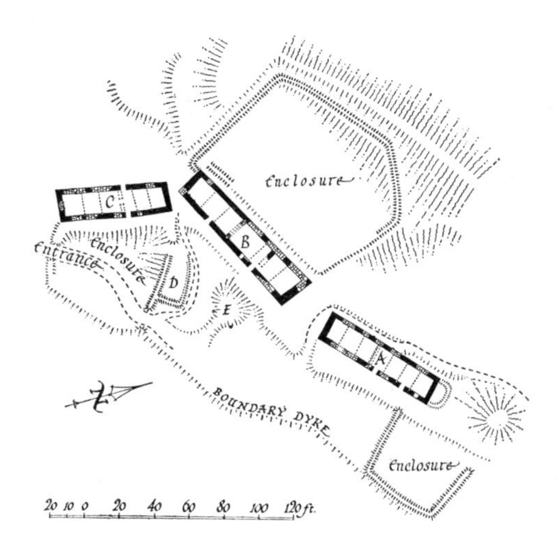

Fig. 167. Old farms, Little Bruach-caoruinn (No. 380)

higher level than these stones, which probably served to ride the ropes clear of the wall-face. The internal arrangements are uncertain, but the building probably comprised a dwelling-house at the E. end and a byre, of smaller size, at the W. end. The presence of two doors in the E. portion suggests that this may itself have been subdivided. A pair of cruck-recesses in the E. portion are well preserved. Abutting on the outside of the E. gable are earthfast stones which suggest the foundations of a small outhouse.

HOUSE B (Fig. 167). This house, the central one of the group, is larger than its neighbours and somewhat irregular in shape, its external length averaging 88 ft. and its width varying from 17 ft. 8 in. to 21 ft. 6 in. The walls are built with mud mortar, the lateral ones being battered; the E. gable is 4 ft. thick and the other walls 3 ft. thick. The building is divided into three compartments, of which the two easternmost appear to have comprised a dwelling-house, with a central entrance flanked by splayed windows, while the W. one, which has a separate entrance, was presumably the byre. The E. partition, which subdivides the dwelling-house, probably had a doorway near its S. end for internal

[1] A plan and section of a kiln of this type appear in *P.S.A.S.*, xc (1956-7), 47.

communication; the W. partition is built on the line of a cruck-frame and probably never rose to the full height of the roof.

HOUSE C (Fig. 167). This is the smallest of the three houses, measuring externally 63 ft. 6 in. in length and from 16 ft. 4 in. to 18 ft. 6 in. in breadth. It differs in plan from the others in the possession of two doors set opposite to one another in its long sides. The position of the internal partitions that may once have existed cannot now be determined, but the opposed doors could have served a feeding-walk,[1] which could also have been used for winnowing, in a through current of air. The N. gable is intact, and stands to a height of 10 ft., the wall-head being at 5 ft. 6 in. The masonry both of the gable and of the surviving parts of the side walls is of high quality, and is clearly the work of a skilled craftsman; the gable, in particular, is excellently bonded and pinned, and has a perfectly uniform surface. High up on the outer face of the gable two stone thatch-pegs are symmetrically placed, and above them, 1 ft. below the apex, there are two projecting members similar to those noted on House A. There have evidently been four pairs of crucks, and the cruck-recesses that remain are very well preserved.

No evidence as to the position of the fire was found in any of these houses. This suggests that use was made either of a central hearth, with a smoke-hole in the roof, or, more probably, of a chimney-hood of wood and clay fixed against the interior of a gable.[2]

OUTBUILDINGS AND ENCLOSURES. The platform flanking the SE. fronts of the houses (*supra*) is about 12 ft. wide and has been carefully built up in places with dry-stone masonry. Below it the ground slopes gently towards the burn; the upper part of this slope is bounded at either end by a turf dyke, the one at the SW. end originating at the SE. corner of House C and standing to a height of 3 ft. with a thickness of 4 ft. A roadway enters the enclosed space through a well-defined entrance in this dyke, but it fades out after passing a second dyke which comes down from the NE. corner of the same house; this second dyke is itself interrupted by an entrance into the smaller enclosure that the two dykes form in front of the house, and has on its N. side a small platform (D on Fig. 167). North of this again a hollow path leads up to the platform, and still further N. there is a small scooped-out enclosure (E on Fig. 167) which probably had a roof borne on posts, as two circular stones, suggestive of post-bases, flank its entrance. Another path leads up to the SW. end of House A and round its back, and at the NE. end of the enclosed strip, SE. of House A, there is a plot enclosed on three sides by turf dykes and on the fourth by the face of the platform. North of House B there lies a large enclosure of which the house itself forms the S. side; the other sides are formed by dykes of mixed stone and turf about 3 ft. high, with ditches 4 ft. wide outside them. A good deal of ground higher up the slope behind the houses has evidently been more or less improved and partially cleared of boulders.

About 200 yds. SE. of the settlement there is a corn-drying kiln similar to the one at Big Bruach-caoruinn (cf. No. 379).

NN 421006 N vii N.E. 18 May 1955

381. Old Farms, Balgair. These remains are situated, at a height of 320 ft. O.D., on gently sloping ground 570 yds. NE. of Hill of Balgair farmhouse and a quarter of a mile E. of Croftalpine farmhouse. They occupy a field of rough pasture, and consist of a group of rectangular foundations and irregular courts and enclosures (Fig. 168). The remains are bounded on the NW. by a

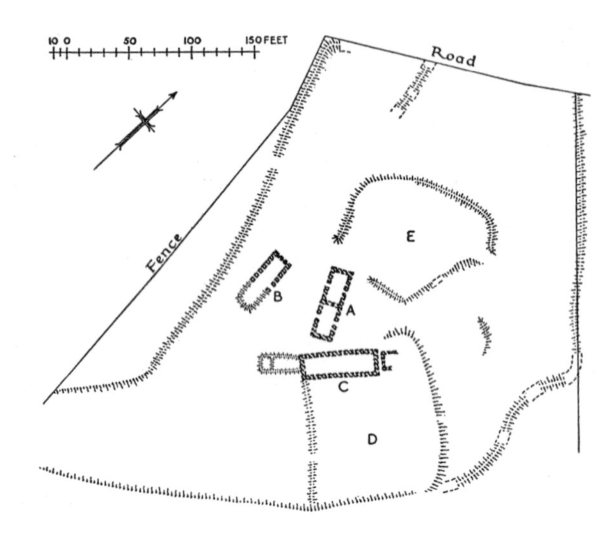

Fig. 168. Old farms, Balgair (No. 381)

stretch of the bank that borders the modern road; this measures 200 ft. in length and probably incorporates a sector of the original boundary of the farms. A low bank, which measures about 8 ft. in width, springs from the SW. end of the NW. boundary and runs SSE. for a distance of 300 ft. before turning SW. and running for a further distance of 70 ft., beyond which it is lost in a cultivated field. A similar low bank runs SE. from the NE. end of the NW. boundary on a somewhat sinuous course for a distance of 200 ft. After a break 25 ft. in breadth it continues generally southwards for a further 125 ft., and then gives way to a scarp which runs thence SW. for 330 ft. before dying out at a point only 60 ft. SSW. of the end of the W. boundary-bank.

Within the irregular area thus outlined are the remains of houses and farm-buildings. The most conspicuous of these is the one marked A on the plan; it consists of the ruins of a stone wall, measuring 3 ft. 6 in. in width and now standing to a maximum height of 2 ft., which forms

[1] Peate, I., *The Welsh House*, 56.

[2] An example of this type of chimney is illustrated in the *Inventory of Roxburghshire*, fig. 46.

two contiguous rectangles. Each measures 24 ft. in length by 12 ft. in breadth and each has a narrow gap in both its long sides. The long axis of this structure runs from NNW. to SSE. At a distance of some 13 yds. to the W. of A there is another rectangular structure (B); part of this is defined by the ruins of a wall measuring 3 ft. 6 in. in width and part by a low grass-grown bank. This structure measures internally about 45 ft. in length by 12 ft. in breadth, and its long axis runs from N. to S. A narrow gap pierces the E. side at about its middle point.

A third rectangular foundation (C) lies close to the SSE. end of A; it measures internally 56 ft. in length from NE. to SW. by 15 ft. transversely within a ruined stone wall 3 ft. 6 in. in thickness. This structure is not so well preserved as are A and B, and it is impossible to distinguish the position of an entrance. A rectangular structure defined by a low, narrow grassy bank adjoins the SW. end of C; it contains two compartments, the larger of which measures 20 ft. in length by 10 ft. in breadth and the smaller 10 ft. in breadth by 8 ft. in length. Close to the SE. end of C, but not quite contiguous with it, are the scanty remains of another small straight-sided structure the walls of which measure 2 ft. in thickness.

The rectangular foundation C may represent a barn, as it forms a substantial part of the NW. side of a square court or yard (D) which measures about 100 ft. along each axis. This court is bounded on the SW. by a low grass-grown bank about 7 ft. in width, and on the SE. by a stretch of the scarp that forms the SE. border of the site. On the NE. there is a scarp about 3 ft. in depth which falls to boggy ground outside the court. The remaining major feature is an irregular enclosure (E) which lies N. of the principal rectangular foundation A. This enclosure is bounded by a grass-grown stony bank which stands to a maximum height of 2 ft. and is spread to a maximum width of 9 ft. It measures 110 ft. in length from NE. to SW. by a maximum of 90 ft. transversely. There is an entrance 12 ft. in width in the E., and a gap 33 ft. in width in the S. which lies close to ruin A.

Numerous slight and amorphous remains of banks lie in the E. sector of the enclosed area; a shallow depression 45 ft. in length and 10 ft. in width which lies in the N. part of the enclosure may represent the remains of a road.

It is probable that these structures were part of the vanished hamlet of the Hill of Balgair, which was once a larger place than Balfron and was occupied by cottars and weavers and possessed a public house and shops.[1] Some of the carved stones now seen in the neighbourhood (Nos. 447 and 448) may well have come from this hamlet.

601892 NS 68 NW (unnoted) 9 October 1952

382. Old Cottage, Drove Hill. This structure lies on a slight eminence on the NE. slope of Drove Hill, at a height of about 1100 ft. O.D. and at a distance of 100 yds. SE. of the natural boulder marked "Gray Stone" on the O.S. map. It consists of a ruined wall, about 2 ft. 6 in. thick, which encloses an area measuring 24 ft. by 10 ft.

653826 NS 68 SE (unnoted) 21 April 1954

383. Old Toll-house, Campsiemuir. This cottage, a former toll-house, stands by the Craw Road (p. 426) close to its highest point. Architecturally it is of no special interest, as it does not differ from the generality of the cottages built at the turn of the 18th and 19th centuries, and it has also been altered and added to. A feature worth noting, however, is the large slab that is built into its S. side, near the E. end; this, though now covered with whitewash, is reported by the occupier to have been formerly covered with writing, and it was no doubt a tariff of tolls similar to the one recorded in the village of Killearn (No. 278).

634821 NS 68 SW ("Muir Toll") 10 September 1956

384. Old Farm, Broomhole. The ruins of this old farmhouse (Fig. 169) stand 70 yds. S. of the Fintry-Denny highway at a point 260 yds. E. of Broomhole Bridge, overlooking the Endrick Water from an elevation

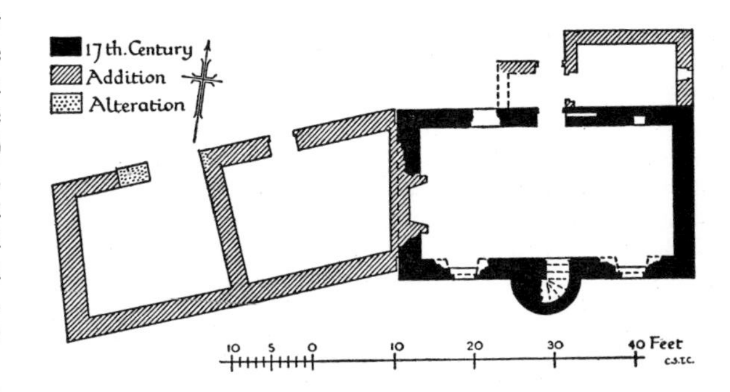

Fig. 169. Old farm, Broomhole (No. 384)

of about 100 ft. above it. Apart from the W. gable, which still retains some of its crow-steps, the walls are now reduced for the most part to the level of the ground-floor window-sills, while the interior is full of debris. In its earliest phase the house was an oblong two-storeyed building, of which the upper floor was probably an attic, and measured 36 ft. 8 in. from E. to W. by about 20 ft. 6 in. transversely over walls about 2 ft. 6 in. thick; while its ground floor may probably have contained two rooms there are now no traces of a partition. In the centre of the S. side there is a semicircular projection with an overall radius of 4 ft. 4 in.; this housed a wheel-stair 5 ft. in diameter and was entered from the interior by a giblet-

[1] *Strathendrick*, 262.

checked doorway. To E. and W. of the projection can be seen the weathered sill and lower rybats of a window. The front door is placed near the centre of the N. side; a bar-hole in its E. jamb still retains the wooden casing for the bar, which measures 2½ in. square internally. A break in the wall to the W. of the door may indicate the position of a window; to the E. of the door there is a small recess in the inner face of the wall. No openings can be seen under the debris of the E. gable, but in the W. gable there is a fireplace on either floor—both probably renewals, or insertions made when the gable was rebuilt and thickened (*infra*). The one on the ground floor has chamfered jambs, and once carried a segmental arch which is now missing. The masonry is rubble throughout, and the three-inch chamfers worked on the arrises of door and window openings suggest a date of construction in the 17th century.

A later phase is represented by additions made respectively at the W. end and on the N. side; but the recurrence, in both of these, of the three-inch chamfers, together with a general similarity in the work, suggests that they were built not long after the original block. The western addition consists of two single-storeyed outhouses extending lengthwise slightly S. of W. from the W. gable, their axis having been deflected 10° from that of the original block; this extension measures 42 ft. 7 in. by 19 ft. in average length and breadth, the side walls being 2 ft. 4 in. and the gable 3 ft. 2 in. thick. The W. gable of the original house was evidently rebuilt and thickened by 1 ft. when this addition was made; it can be seen that the inner faces of the walls of the extension are bonded with the gable although their outer faces abut against it without any bonding. A sherd of green-glazed pottery was found embedded in the mortar on the W. face of the gable. The two outhouses are divided by a thick masonry partition, the inner one being slightly longer than the outer; the entrance to the former survives, with its lowermost rybats in position, near the centre of its N. wall, but that of the latter has been replaced by an opening which extends 6 ft. 6 in. from the line of the W. face of the partition.

The other addition is a small lean-to outshot, alined with the E. gable of the original block and extending along two-thirds of its N. side. It comprises a single room, and a lobby covering the entrance to the original house. The room measures 12 ft. 2 in. by 8 ft. 3 in. internally, the walls averaging about 1 ft. 10 in. in thickness. It is entered off the lobby by a door adjacent to that of the house, and has a small window in its E. wall. The lobby is entered by a door in a re-entrant angle, 5 ft. 4 in. in front of the house-door; its W. side was once extended as a press or recess, but how far is now uncertain.

The house was described in 1861 as "a small farm-steading, slated and in bad repair".[1]

KILN. Associated with the house is a system of old fields enclosed by dykes of stone and turf, and in the line of one of these dykes, about 60 yds. SE. of the house, there is a circular stone construction identifiable as a lime-kiln.[2] This structure, which is ruinous, measures about 21 ft. in diameter over all and is battered on the inner as well as on the outer face, with the result that the hollow interior has the shape of an inverted and truncated cone. This cavity is 13 ft. in diameter at the level of the broken wall-head, *i.e.* up to 5 ft. above the ground on the side away from the dyke, but it narrows to 9 ft. at a depth of 2 ft. 6 in., to which level the floor is silted up with debris.

644860 NS 68 NW 15 May 1953

385. New Mill, Broich Burn. The ruins of the New Mill stand on the Broich Burn half a mile downstream (NNE.) from Loch Laggan. The site is just below a low cliff over which the water falls in two channels, both artificial, the original course of the burn turning the end of the cliff a little further W. Notwithstanding the fact that a "new" mill is said to have been built here in the reign of James V,[3] the date 1774 appears on a lintel of the mill-house and the whole of the structure evidently belongs to this period. However, the existence of two mill-lades and two mill-ponds above the cliff, and the fact that the westernmost of these systems, which is alined with the vanished wheel-house at the W. end of the ruin, appears to have encroached on the other, which must consequently be the older of the two, suggest that an earlier mill may have stood just E. of the existing ruin, with its wheel under the superseded eastern lade. The tradition of a 16th-century foundation should therefore, perhaps, be taken as referring to a demolished building in this more easterly position.

630933 NS 69 SW ("New Mill, in ruins") 22 October 1952

386. Auldhall. Notwithstanding the resemblance of this name to the "field of Old Hall" mentioned under No. 224 as the site of the old tower of Boquhan, the house, though probably somewhat older than most of the comparable farmhouses in the neighbourhood, pretty certainly dates only from the later 18th century. Nor were signs of any ancient structure seen in the vicinity.

661935 NS 69 SE 29 September 1952

387. Kildean Mill, Old Mills Farm. Above a door in the SW. wall of the mill-house at Old Mills Farm there is set a stone panel bearing the date 1697 and the initials I C and A N, all in raised letters. The incised date 1783 has been added at a later period. Part of the present structure may be as old as the earlier of the two dates, but the mill has been much altered from time to time and, apart from the seatings for its two wheels and the double sluice, it possesses no features of interest.

778957 NS 79 NE 9 August 1955

[1] Ordnance Survey Name Book, Fintry parish, 39.
[2] *P.S.A.S.*, xc (1956-7), 50.
[3] *Stat. Acct.*, xviii (1796), 331.

388. Dovecot, Manorneuk. The dovecot that once stood just SE. of the farm-buildings of Manorneuk has now been reduced to a pile of debris. The foundations of a square structure with dressed quoins, measuring 15 ft. 4 in. a side, can be made out, but no other features survive. Doubtless, however, it belonged to Manor Castle (No. 194), which stood about 110 yds. away to the E.

826949 NS 89 SW 5 May 1953

389. Dovecot, Touch. A dovecot (Fig. 170) stands in a wood about 250 yds. NNE. of the mansion at Touch (No. 345); it measures 17 ft. 9 in. by 14 ft. 10 in. over all and is built in rubble with dressed margins. There is a penthouse roof and the gables are crow-stepped. Above the door is incised the date 1736 and the initials I [S], probably for James Seton of Touch who died in 1742.[1]

752929 NS 79 SE 9 June 1956

390. Dovecot, Old Sauchie. An early 18th-century dovecot (Fig. 170), now in a ruinous condition, stands in a field 500 yds. NE. of the castle (No. 195). The structure is rectangular and measures 24 ft. 11 in. by 15 ft. 3 in. over all; it is built in rubble with dressed quoins and margins, and has had a penthouse roof. There are two compartments within, each of which has its own entrance-doorway in the S. wall; both chambers are lined with nesting-boxes and a double perch is set above each doorway. Originally a carved stone panel was centrally placed at the same level, but this has now fallen and lies among debris at the foot of the S. wall; it measures 2 ft. 4 in. by 1 ft. 8 in. and contains, within a moulded border, a coat of arms, two sets of initials and the date 1700, all in relief. The initials are now much worn, but have been read as I G and M F for John Glas of Sauchie and his wife Margaret Foulis, whom he married in 1695.[2] The coat is largely illegible, but what remains of it corresponds with Nisbet's description[3] of the arms of Glas of Sauchie: A fleur-de-lys between three mullets, within a bordure.

781886 NS 78 NE 25 May 1956

391. Dovecot and Carved Stones, Lower Polmaise. This dovecot (Pl. 209 A) stands about 200 yds. NW. of the site of Old Polmaise House, now demolished, and close to the courtyard that contains the ruins of offices and stables once pertaining to the mansion. It is circular on plan, having an internal diameter of 11 ft. 1 in. and walls 1 ft. 10 in. thick. The masonry is rubble, patched with brick, and the walls rise to a plain string-course set a little below the wall-head. Below the string-course there is a large pigeon-port facing S., while immediately above the string-course there is a series of small ports. The conical slated roof is surmounted by a ball-finial. The entrance-doorway is contained within a straight screen-wall set tangentially to the main structure on the NE. side. The interior (Pl. 209 B) is lined with brick nesting-boxes and there is a well-preserved potence which appears to be of comparatively recent construction. The dovecot is probably of late 18th- or early 19th-century date.

On the NW. side of the courtyard there is a 19th-century cottage, the entrance-porch of which incorporates a roll-moulded doorway of 16th-century date.

834925 NS 89 SW 26 April 1959

392. Dovecot, Bannockburn House. An old dovecot, now in a ruinous condition, stands 250 yds. NE. of Bannockburn House (No. 295). It measures 18 ft. by 18 ft. over all and is built in rubble masonry with pronounced V-jointed quoins. The roof has been of the penthouse type, and has finished in an ogival-moulded eaves-cornice of which part still remains. A square string-course returns round the building below eaves-level, and lower again there are two circular openings, each cut from a single stone, one in the S. wall and the other in the E. wall. The entrance-doorway is centrally placed in the S. wall and has a rusticated surround and an external door-check. On the lintel is the incised date 1698 divided by the initials S H P for Sir Hugh Paterson, 2nd of Bannockburn (cf. No. 350). Above the lintel there is a stone panel with the incised date 1768 divided by the initials M P, and above are the initials D P R. The initials M P probably represent Mary, daughter of Sir Hugh Paterson, 3rd of Bannockburn,[4] while the date may be that of some alteration or repairs. The upper set of initials seems to have been added at a later date; it may represent Mary Paterson's husband, David Paterson Rollo.[5] There are indications that the dovecot has been reconstructed in part, perhaps in 1768, and it also incorporates a number of carved stones of 17th-century date which are in secondary use. The most interesting of these is a crudely formed Ionic capital, set half-way down the rake of the W. gable; this suggests that, latterly at least, the roof was stepped at this point, perhaps to provide a ledge or perch.

810889 NS 88 NW 3 August 1956

393. Dovecot, Carron House. Some 300 yds. S. of Carron House (No. 310) there stands a dovecot, an octagonal Georgian structure of red brick with freestone dressings (Fig. 170, Pl. 208 C), which measures 18 ft. in diameter over walls 2 ft. thick. The door has an ogival pediment, and an oval window above it. At half-height there is a string-course, with a range of oval windows

[1] Seton, G., *The Family of Seton*, 345.
[2] *T.S.N.H.A.S.* (1933-4), 85; *Miscellany of the Scottish History Society*, i, 309; *Castles and Mansions*, 393.
[3] *A System of Heraldry* (1722 ed.), i, 387.
[4] *T.S.N.H.A.S.* (1933-4), 128.
[5] *Ibid.*

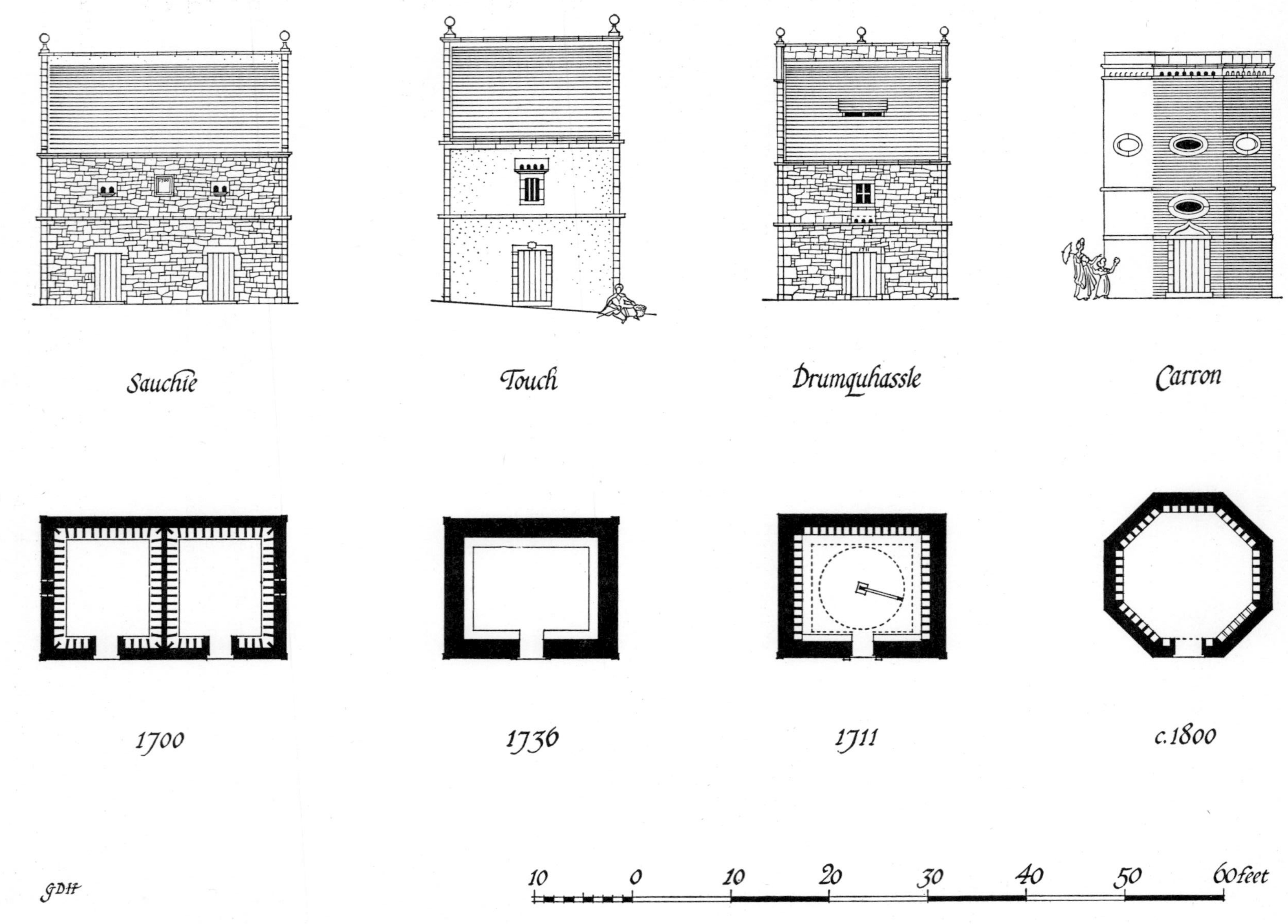

Fig. 170. Dovecots: Old Sauchie (No. 390), Touch (No. 389), Drumquhassle (No. 398), Carron House (No. 393)

above it, blind except in the side containing the door. The wall finishes in a moulded cornice, with a perching-course and entries for the birds, some of them blind, below it. There is evidence to suggest that it was surmounted by a plain parapet-course, and the roof, behind this, may have been pyramidal or virtually flat. The nests are brick-built.

897826 NS 88 SE 5 April 1960

394. Dovecot, Muiravonside House. Projecting from the E. end of the wall that divides the garden from the offices of Muiravonside House (No. 316), there is a large dovecot now adapted as a garden store-house. It measures 19 ft. 3 in. in breadth by 15 ft. 5 in. in depth externally, is built of rubble with backset dressings, and has a lean-to roof sloping up between flights of crow-steps to a high back-wall, entries for the birds arranged in the form of dormers, and a string-course for perching at eaves level. Although it thus exemplifies a type which was in use from the 17th century onwards, it shows no features suggestive of a date before the earlier 19th century. The building has been considerably altered; in particular the original entrance has been built up and a larger one substituted beside it.

965753 NS 97 NE 18 March 1953

395. Dovecot, Compston. The dovecot that formerly stood just W. of the farmhouse of Compston (No. 317) is now reduced to a featureless pile of rubble.

957759 NS 97 NE (unnoted) 10 April 1955

396. Dovecot, Westquarter, Redding. This dovecot stands near the W. end of Dovecot Road, Redding, where new houses have spread over what were once the lands of Westquarter House. It is in excellent preservation, and apart from a renewed roof is virtually in its original state (Pl. 208 B). Slightly oblong on plan, it measures 18 ft. 3 in. from E. to W. by 16 ft. 3 in. transversely over walls 2 ft. 10 in. thick, and is built of random rubble with dressed quoins and door-rybats. The door is in the centre of the S. side, and above this a heavy, rounded perching-course runs all round the building. Resting on this, above the door, is an heraldic panel which will be described below; it is topped by a small moulded cornice above which there is a row of three openings for the birds. From the wall-head of the S. wall the roof slopes upwards to the N. wall, which is considerably higher, the slope being interrupted to provide space for a further row of six openings for pigeons. The side walls are crow-stepped to a point about half-way up the upper portion of the roof, where they meet the returns of the tabled parapet that tops the N. wall; this parapet is finished with scrolls and pilasters, and bears ball-finials at the corners. The inner faces of the walls consist wholly of stone-built nests, which must number several hundreds; they are built in regular rows, each about 9 in. high, and the openings, which are separated by spacing stones of uniform thickness, average 8 in. in width and 1 ft. 6 in. in depth. The floor is laid with bricks, in which a circular setting marks the socket-hole of the vanished potence.

The panel above the door (Pl. 210 C) bears, on a slightly sunk field, a shield enclosed by a line which probably represents a bordure and charged: Quarterly, 1st and 4th, three cinquefoils, two and one, within a tressure; 2nd and 3rd, a bend between six billets.[1] Above the shield appear the letters S / D, and separated by it are the initials W L / H L; taken together these stand for Sir William Livingstone of Westquarter and his wife Dame Helenore Livingstone, whom he married in 1626.[2] The arms are those registered as of Livingstone of Westquarter, and may either have been evolved from Livingstone's paternal arms, with a bordure for difference, or have been those of Dame Helenore, the heiress of Westquarter, and borne by Livingstone *jure uxoris*. Below the shield is the date 1647. While the heraldic panel undoubtedly dates from the year 1647, the general appearance of the dovecot suggests that it is not older than the 18th century. In particular, the sharp arrises of the entrance-doorway and the droved dressings of its jamb stones are unlikely to be of 17th-century date. It seems probable, therefore, that the heraldic panel originally formed part of some other building, perhaps an earlier dovecot, and was incorporated in the present structure during the course of its erection.

The Livingstones of Westquarter, a branch of the family of Livingstone of Callendar, were in possession of the estate of Westquarter by the beginning of the 17th century. In the middle of the 17th century Sir William Livingstone built the old house of Westquarter, which stood until about the end of the 19th century; it was then replaced by a "magnificent mansion",[3] now in its turn demolished to make way for a housing estate.

913787 NS 97 NW (indicated but not named) 26 March 1953

397. Dovecot and Old House, Dunipace. This structure stands just N. of the former avenue of Dunipace House, 140 yds. NNE. of the graveyard (No. 147). It consists of a tower which, though it is now converted into a dovecot, evidently once contained the external stair of a mansion, together with two short lengths of walling set at right angles to one another and evidently representing the last remains of an L-shaped house of a type commonly dateable to the turn of the 16th and 17th centuries. Too little of this structure survives, and what survives has been too much altered

[1] In the second quarter only five billets are carved, no doubt for lack of space.
[2] *Castles and Mansions*, 304.
[3] *Ibid.* A sketch of the old house of Westquarter is given on p. 306.

and patched, for any idea to be formed of its original size or appearance; but it was clearly older than the tower, which has been fitted into its re-entrant angle as an addition, presumably as a more dignified substitute for an original forestair. The tower may date from about the middle of the 17th century.

The fragment of wall standing S. of the tower shows at ground level on its S., or inner, face an arched opening with a segmental head and above this a doorway. Both are now blocked, but they are assumed to have been, respectively, an access to cellarage and the main entrance of the house. The latter would have been approached in the original arrangement by the forestair, and later by the stair inside the tower; the former, which presumably opened under the forestair, could have been reached through the base of the tower after this had been constructed. East of the position of the threshold of the first-floor entrance are two moulded corbels, which suggest the supports of a floor. East of these corbels the wall has been removed, but from about 12 in. above their level the vertical edge of the wall is not ragged, as it is below, but is formed by the jamb of a door chamfered on its S. face. Four of the rybats, placed about the middle of the jamb, show socket-holes for the bars of an iron grille, and are no doubt in secondary use. The fragment of walling that stands E. of the tower shows, at ground level, a small window with a segmental head and, at its broken N. end, the chamfered jamb of a door. At first-floor level in this wall, where it abuts on the other fragment, a tall recess has been formed 3 ft. 6 in. wide by 6 in. deep.

The tower appears externally as part of an octagon, though only three of its sides are completely free. Each of the free sides measures 5 ft. 11 in. except the W. one, which is enlarged to 7 ft. 3 in. at its base to accommodate the entrance-door. The masonry is rubble with neatly squared dressings, and there are two moulded string-courses, at first-floor and second-floor levels respectively. Octagonal construction ends about 1 ft. 6 in. above the upper string-course; the uppermost portion of the tower is circular, finishing in a moulded eaves-course, and was no doubt added when the tower was turned into a dovecot. The roof is slated, and carries an ornamental lantern adapted for the entry of pigeons; another large opening for pigeons has been made on the S., just below the level of the upper string-course which, however, terminates before reaching this point. The entrance, which is now only 5 ft. 4 in. high owing to a rise in the level of the ground, and 3 ft. 3 in. wide, seems originally to have had a roll-and-hollow moulding, but the roll has been cut away to allow an external door with giblet checks to be fitted to the dovecot. The checks of the original house-door are still present inside. In the NW. face of the tower there is a built-up window at ground-floor and another at first-floor level; the former measures 3 ft. 6 in. by 2 ft. 3 in. and the arrises of both are chamfered. Internally the tower has been lined with stone nests, which have covered up any traces of the stair; in the E. arc, however, there can be seen the jambs of the ground-floor window mentioned above in the description of the older building, and above it some rybats, with sockets for bars, belonging to a first-floor window not now visible from the other side. A single jamb of the first-floor entrance to the S. block can also be seen.

The old house of Dunipace is probably to be associated with the family of Livingstone of Dunipace, which possessed the property from the end of the 15th until the middle of the 17th century.[1] A later house, built by the Spottiswoodes at the end of the 18th century and restored, after a fire, in 1897-8,[2] has since been demolished.

838819 NS 88 SW 18 May 1955

398. Dovecot, Drumquhassle. This fine dovecot (Fig. 170, Pl. 208 A), dated 1711 on the door-lintel, stands in the policies of the Park of Drumquhassle, 250 yds. NNE. of the house. It is built of red sandstone and is nearly square on plan, measuring 17 ft. 3 in. across the front by 15 ft. transversely over walls 1 ft. 9 in. thick. The front wall rises to a height of 14 ft. 3 in., having a wide ledge at 7 ft. 6 in. above the ground and a cornice at the wall-head which becomes a ledge on the other three walls. From the cornice, the roof, which is slated, slopes upwards to a line considerably below the top of the back wall, which is about 26 ft. 6 in. in height. The side walls rise with the slope of the roof, at first with crow-steps and then vertically, with a rounded pilaster facing the vertical edge, to the full height of the back wall, the wall-head at sides and back being ornamented with a cornice and five stone balls. The door, which is in the centre of the front, is square-headed; above the ledge, also in the centre, are three small arched openings for the birds, and above these a small square window. Internally the base of the front wall is thickened to 2 ft. 5 in., and some kind of wooden shelf appears to have rested on the intake and to have continued, cantilevered or strutted, round the other three sides. In the centre there is a restored potence turning on a stone pedestal. The nests are of brick.

483871 NS 48 NE 4 April 1960

399. Dovecot, Laraben. This dovecot (Pl. 208 D) stands just N. of the Stirling-Glasgow road 120 yds. E. of Laraben farmhouse. It is of brick on a foundation of red sandstone, and probably dates from the later 18th century. On plan it is square, measuring 18 ft. 6 in. a side over walls 2 ft. 6 in. thick, and the height to the wall-head is about 17 ft. 6 in. The roof has disappeared, and the upper part of the W. side is partly broken down. In the S. side, under a relieving-arch, there is a square-headed doorway, the lintel of which may have been re-used; it is giblet-checked for an outer as well as an inner door and measures 5 ft. by 2 ft. 10 in. At 7 ft. 6 in.

[1] Gibson, J. C., *Lands and Lairds of Larbert and Dunipace Parishes*, 84 ff.
[2] *Ibid.*, 118 ff.

above the ground, a decorative string-course 18 in. deep runs all round the building; and there is another ornamental belt, with a blocking-course, at the wall-head. Internally there is a scarcement 1 ft. 6 in. above the ground; the walls, except the damaged W. wall, are lined with brick nests, and above these there is another scarcement, evidently to support the roof. In the centre of the floor there stands an upright stone with a pivot-hole in the top, in which the potence rotated (cf. No. 398).

626954 NS 69 NW 29 August 1952

400. Old Cottage, Beancross (Site).[1] On the NW. side of the by-road from Beancross to Lauriston, and next door to the house that stands at the junction of the by-road with A 905, there is a small cottage, roofless and ruinous, which appears to have been reconstructed in the late 18th or early 19th century. Some work of an earlier period remains, however, in the E. jamb of a door showing a wide chamfer, and in the lower part of a window, just E. of the door, which, although its lintel has been renewed, shows similarly chamfered rybats and a sloping sill.

923796 NS 97 NW 7 November 1954

ARCHITECTURAL DETAILS AND CARVED STONES

401. The Mercat Cross, Broad Street, Stirling. The Mercat Cross (Pl. 142) was restored and re-erected in its original position in front of the Town House (No. 232), in 1891,[2] but only the unicorn finial formed part of the original monument. The animal is posed in a sitting position and wears a collar from which a chain is carried round the body. In front of the breast there is a crowned shield bearing the Royal Arms of Scotland, and this is surrounded by the collar of the Order of the Thistle. The figure of St. Andrew with the Cross can be seen on the badge.

792937 NS 79 SE 29 September 1954

402. Inscribed Lintel, 85 Lower Bridge Street, Stirling. A lintel over the passageway of this house is incised with the initials R S I W between the date figures 1706.

794944 NS 79 SE 30 September 1954

403. Inscribed Rock, Gowan Hill, Stirling. This rock is difficult to find, as it lies inconspicuously just below the lip of the steep, broken NW. slope of the Gowan Hill among a number of small, rounded outcrops. By 1933 its position had been forgotten, but in that year it was again located and was cleared of turf.[3] It is situated about 120 yds. due N. of the N. corner of Ballengeich Cemetery and 30 yds. NE. of a small but noticeable flattened shelf at the NW. margin of the summit-area of the hill; a narrow foot-track, made by people scrambling up the slope, passes beside and partly over the inscribed surface, which is flat and serves as a step, with the result that the inscription is suffering a certain amount of wear. The flat surface seems to have been exposed by the splitting-off of a piece of the rock, which has a naturally rounded profile at this point; this rock, a dolerite, is everywhere heavily fissured, and the missing piece need not necessarily have been removed by human agency.

Fig. 171. Inscribed rock, Gowan Hill, Stirling (No. 403)

The inscription in its present form is reproduced in Fig. 171.[4] It was first recorded in Gibson's edition of Camden's *Britannia*,[5] with a faulty transcription. A slightly different transcription is given, on the authority of an informant, by Sibbald,[6] who, like Gibson, regarded the inscription as Roman, and yet another one by Horsley.[7] The latter writes "[it] does not appear to be Roman. Some suppose it to be in the *Highland* tongue. It was thus taken by a careful and impartial hand." It is to be noted

[1] This cottage has been demolished since the date of visit.
[2] Ronald, J., *Landmarks of Old Stirling*, 319 ff.
[3] *T.S.N.H.A.S.* (1934-5), 71.
[4] The Commissioners are indebted to Mr. R. P. Wright, F.S.A., for making this drawing and for collaborating with their staff in the study of the inscription.
[5] First edn. (1695), 958.
[6] *Auctarium Musei Balfouriani* (1697), 206; *Historical Inquiries* (1707), 35.
[7] *Britannia Romana* (1732), 206.

that Horsley's transcription, though faulty, includes the D F, as D E, and the R C, as R E, both of which had been omitted by Sibbald and Gibson and which may consequently have been fairly recent additions when Horsley's correspondent copied them. These letters, and likewise the two ES, can be discounted as idle scribings, and need not be supposed to bear on the meaning of the main inscription.

The primary text, though far from clear, can best be transcribed as Ɨ[?]EXCOIIEALIS / LETΛLΛ. If it is supposed that the Ɨ, the second E, and the T are superfluous and that the [?] represents a V with some other letter, perhaps a K, cut on top of it,[1] the whole could be regarded as purporting to be a list of Roman army units—⟨*Ɨ*⟩*vex*(*illatio*), *co*(*hors*) *II*, ⟨*E*⟩*alis*, *le*(*gio*), ⟨*T*⟩, *ala*.[2] If the [?] is read as N rather than as V,[3] the opening words might be taken as *in ex*(*ercitu*), the general character of the whole inscription remaining unchanged. In either case the whole would be, in Roman eyes, fantastic, though not beyond the imagination of a falsifier who had a slight acquaintance with Roman inscriptions. It will be recalled that, as early as the beginning of the 17th century, a number of major inscriptions had been found, which could have created an interest and a fashion, and have formed a background for this falsified text. These inscriptions, moreover, contain the A with a V-shaped cross-bar, which is a rare form and one which a falsifier might well have used to give an air of verisimilitude to his work. A further pointer to the date of the inscription is given by the first letter; unlike the As, this Ɨ is un-Roman but represents a form seen on local post-Reformation tombstones. There is no reason to suppose that it is a later addition to the rest of the main inscription.

A cast of the stone, made in 1891,[4] is preserved in the Smith Institute, Stirling.

79099435 NS 79 SE (unnoted) 11 March 1956

404. Carved Stones, 14 Abercromby Place, Stirling. (i) The heraldic panel (Pl. 212 C) that was once set over the entrance to Manor Castle (No. 194) is now preserved at 14 Abercromby Place, Stirling. It is bordered by baluster-posts with finials, with cherub heads above and below, and bears in the centre, enclosed within a garland, a shield parted per pale and charged: Dexter, a bend between six billets, for Callendar of Manor; sinister, a stag's head erased, for Reid. Above the shield there appears a scroll with the date 1572, and below it the initials R C and M R, for Robert Callendar and Margaret Reid. The estate of Manor was held by the family of Callendar during the 15th and 16th centuries, the laird of 1572 being Robert Callendar, who appears to have succeeded in 1567.[5] It is to be inferred that he built the castle in that year. (ii) At the same place there is also preserved an inscribed panel (Pl. 210 D) from the small farmhouse of Long Kerse, which formerly stood near Manor Farm in Logie parish. Its upper portion bears two ducks naiant, facing inwards towards the initials I A / M H; below an ornamental band is incised the date 1762.

793932 NS 79 SE 5 May 1953

405. Carved Woodwork, Carved Stones, etc., Smith Institute, Dumbarton Road, Stirling. Apart from the Stirling Heads, which are described elsewhere,[6] the Institute contains the following pieces of carved woodwork, all of which are supposed to have come from Stirling Castle (No. 192). (i) A set of fifteen medallion panels (Pls. 217-220) which, according to local tradition,[7] once formed part of the wainscotting of the Palace of Stirling (p. 203); they were purchased at the sale of the effects of Miss Lucas, a Stirling resident, in 1876. It is known that when the panels came into the possession of Miss Lucas they were set within a frame.[8] The panels,[9] which measure 14 in. by 10½ in., may be ascribed to the first half of the 16th century, and contain busts set within strapped and carved garlands surmounted by scroll-work, masks and other devices. The subject-matter is similar to that of other contemporary medallion-heads, some of the figures wearing fanciful costumes and others a stylised version of the dress of the period. Although smaller in scale than the Stirling Heads, the carvings exhibit a high standard of craftsmanship; the name of the sculptor is not known, but a set of eight panels of unknown provenance now preserved in the Victoria and Albert Museum, London,[10] appears to be the work of the same hand. (ii) A panel (Pl. 220 D) measuring 10½ in. by 9¼ in., and crudely carved in relief with a medallion head. This panel was acquired with the set of fifteen described above and is said to have come from Stirling Castle.[11] (iii) A fragment[12] of a pierced panel measuring 1 ft. 5 in. in length; the carving is Gothic in character and the fragment is said to have come from the Douglas Room, Stirling Castle (cf. p. 218). If so it most probably formed part of some article of furniture, for the apartment in question was built only in 1594.

Of the other objects in the Institute's collection only the following call for mention in this Inventory. (i) A stone panel, from the upper part of the gable of a demolished house which was formerly numbered 13

---

[1] The author of the article in *T.S.N.H.A.S.*, read the first letter as KI

[2] Superfluous letters are indicated by pointed brackets.

[3] A drawing made by Miss Maclagan, which is preserved in the Library of the National Museum of Antiquities of Scotland (II. D. 4), shows a nondescript letter apparently combining K and reversed N.

[4] *T.S.N.H.A.S.*, *loc. cit.*

[5] Fergusson, R. Menzies, *Logie, A Parish History*, ii, 103-6.

[6] Royal Commission on Ancient Monuments (Scotland), *The Stirling Heads*, H.M.S.O., 1960.

[7] *T.S.N.H.A.S.* (1924-5), 168 f.

[8] *Ibid.*

[9] Illustrated in *P.S.A.S.*, lx (1925-6), 402.

[10] Museum nos. 217-'98 to 224-'98.

[11] *T.S.N.H.A.S.* (1924-5), 168 f.

[12] Illustrated in *P.S.A.S.*, lx (1925-6), 391.

Baker Street. It bears, after a damaged date which may be read as 16[?7 ?], the incised couplet:

HEIR I FORBEARE / MY NAME OR ARMES / TO FIX
LEAST I OR MYNE / SHOWLD SELL THOSE / STONES AND STICKS.

(ii) The jambs, lintel and pediment of a dormer window of early 17th-century date from Number 18 Broad Street[1] (pp. 296 f.). The arrises of the jambs are rounded, the lintel is moulded, and the pediment is curved, with a break at the apex. The tympanum contains three raised panels. Originally three pointed finials stood on the pediment, but one of these is now missing. (iii) The massive oaken entrance-door from Carnock House (No. 347). The door is constructed in three thicknesses of boarding, but the lower part has been restored. It is 6 ft. 3 in. high, 3 ft. 9 in. broad and 2½ in. thick. The exterior (Pl. 216 B) is studded with large round-headed nails, and has a latch and knocker. Inside, two hinge-bands stretch right across the door, and there are also a hook for a chain, an iron handle and a bolt; the last two look newer than the other fittings, and may have been added at some time when the original heavy bolt had become obsolete. At a height of 1 ft. 7 in. above the bottom there is a hinged opening, measuring 1 ft. 2 in. by 1 ft. 1 in., which is secured by a massive lock in a wooden case; it may possibly have been designed as a loop-hole for a small cannon. An old photograph, exhibited beside it, shows the door *in situ* in a doorway with a heavy angle-roll perhaps about 7 in. in diameter. (iv) A model of Touch House, which is mentioned under No. 345.

790935 NS 79 SE 15 October 1954

406. Painted Ceiling, Westerlands, Stirling. The late Dr. Thomas Ross, in his paper on the tempera panels discovered in 1866 in the house of Wester Livilands, Stirling,[2] and now preserved in the National Museum of Antiquities of Scotland, notes that the joists in the oratory and the bedroom that were divided by the screen bearing the panels were "painted with conventional patterns, but these were very much destroyed, the ceilings having at a later period been lathed and plastered".[3] A fragment of one of these ceilings has been reset above a small landing on the principal stair at Westerlands, a modern house which has replaced Wester Livilands; it may be dated, like the panels, to about 1629. It measures 11 ft. by 9 ft. 2 in., and both joists and ceiling-boards are painted in red, green, blue, black and white. The strips of boarding that appear between the joists are divided into oblong panels, bearing alternately formal floral designs and bunches of figs and grapes, very stiffly composed. The joists themselves are decorated with arabesques and stars.

798923 NS 79 SE 8 October 1954

407. Carved Stone, Craigforth Dairy, Raploch Road, Stirling. Reset for preservation in the S. façade of the farmhouse, a little below the coping of the W. gable, there is a cavetto-moulded skewput bearing the date 1699 in raised letters. Another skewput, with the incised date 1817, occupies a similar position below the E. gable.

786942 NS 79 SE 2 June 1955

408. Carved Panel, Logie Cottage. The carved panel, mentioned under No. 348 (*q.v.*) as having been removed from Tamrawer, is now preserved at Logie Cottage, near the old parish church. The panel has a cabled border and originally bore,[4] at the top, the date 1769, but superficial splitting in the dexter corner has removed the first two figures. Below the date there appears a six-pointed star, and below this, flanked by the initials I G and A C, a very large merchant's mark in the form of a 4 with decorated terminals. At the bottom, on the dexter side, there are two escallops and a plant, with a six-pointed star above them, and on the sinister side two roses. The initials are those of James Graham, who succeeded his brother William as laird of Tamrawer in 1772, and of his wife Agnes, daughter of Thomas Campbell; he disposed of the property immediately after acquiring it.[5]

815970 NS 89 NW 23 August 1952

409. Carved Stone, Kerse Mills. A stone panel set in the W. gable of one of the buildings at Kerse Mills bears the incised initials D M S, flanked by the date 1672; above are the initials I M flanked by the date 1754. The earlier set may possibly represent Dame Mause Stirling, *née* Murray, second wife of Sir Archibald Stirling of Garden, who died in 1668. The lands and barony of Polmaise had been settled on Dame Mause in terms of a marriage contract of 1646.[6]

812924 NS 89 SW 10 August 1955

410. Sundials and Carved Stones, Sauchieburn House. Two sundials and a number of carved stones, all apparently of 17th-century date, are preserved in the grounds of Sauchieburn House, two miles SW. of the village of St. Ninians. All are said to have been brought from Barnton House, Midlothian. (i) An obelisk-shaped sundial of a type not uncommon in the late 17th and early 18th century stands about 50 yds. W. of the house (Pl. 215 B). The shaft rises to support a polyhedron on

[1] Illustrated in *Castles and Mansions*, 181.
[2] *P.S.A.S.*, xxxiii (1898-9), 387 ff., with illustrations.
[3] *Ibid.*, 395.
[4] As shown by the illustration in Graham, J. **St. J.**, *The Grahams of Auchencloich and Tamrawer*, Lisbon (1952), 52.
[5] *Ibid.*, 35.
[6] Fraser, W., *The Stirlings of Keir*, 456.

which there is set a tapering finial. The total height of the sundial above the base is 9 ft. 3 in. The shaft is divided into panels most of which contain sunk dials of various geometric shapes. The date 1692 is carved on one of the bottom panels in incised numerals. (ii) On the E. side of the sundial there stands a stone panel which measures 1 ft. 6 in. by 1 ft. 11 in.; it bears the date 1630, carved in relief. (iii) Two lions couchant, carved in stone, are set close to the sundial; they measure about 3 ft. in length. (iv) A stone door-lintel, which measures 6 ft. by 9 in. over all, lies on the ground about 10 yds. SE. of the house. It is inscribed in relief with the initials R S and A [?], the date 1612 and the motto BLEST BE GOD FOR ALL HIS GIFTS. (v) A second obelisk-shaped sundial, which is illustrated by MacGibbon and Ross,[1] stands about 50 yds. N. of the house. The lower part of the structure, however, which is square in section and has a mask carved on each face, has been removed and now stands at the foot of the first sundial about 50 yds. W. of the house. The bore-holes visible in this stone confirm the suggestion[2] that the structure originally incorporated a fountain. An heraldic achievement is carved in relief on the N. side of the sundial (Pl. 215 C). The shield is charged: Three buckles on a chevron between three boars' heads erased. The supporters are griffins and the crest a dove, crowned, with a snake twined about its legs. The arms are those of the Elphinstones, Lords Balmerino, and the sundial was probably erected at Barnton shortly before the sale of the property by the Master of Balmerino, son of the 3rd Lord Balmerino, in 1680.[3]

774892 NS 78 NE 3 April 1957

411. Carved Panels, St. Andrew's Church, Dunmore. In the chancel of St. Andrew's Church, which was built about the year 1850, there is a wooden seat[4] in the back of which there have been set five carved panels of late 16th- or early 17th-century date. The panels (Pl. 221) are of oak and have an average measurement of 1 ft. 3 in. by 9 in.; they are carved in relief with religious scenes and allegorical figures, all set within decorative architectural frames. One contains a representation of the Annunciation, and another of the Circumcision, while a third depicts the figure of Hope; the remaining two contain unnamed allegorical figures which are somewhat different in feeling from the other three subjects. The work is of a style which spread to England and Scotland from the Low Countries in the 16th and 17th centuries, but whether the Dunmore panels were at one time incorporated in some other building in the neighbourhood, or were acquired as antiques in the middle of the 19th century, cannot now be ascertained.

889889 NS 88 NE 17 August 1955

412. The Mercat Cross, Airth. The Mercat Cross (Pl. 143)[5] stands at the NW. end of the High Street, and consists of a stepped octagonal pedestal, an octagonal shaft with a splayed base, and a square head with a finial apparently representing an acorn. Its total height is 17 ft. 2 in. The pedestal proper, without the base of the shaft, is 3 ft. high, and rises in five steps which contract progressively from a basal diameter of 13 ft., the SE. side of the octagon measuring 5 ft. 9 in. at ground level. The shaft, including its base and footing, is 10 ft. 5 in. high and shows considerable entasis, being 1 ft. 2 in. thick at 3 ft. 6 in. above the top of the pedestal. The splayed portion was originally octagonal, like the pedestal, but has been worn almost to a circular section. The shaft finishes in a square moulded capital; above this the head, which is also square in section and has sides 1 ft. 8 in. long, rises a further 3 ft. 9 in. to the top of the finial. Each face is carved, and has a curvilinear pediment above it. On the NW. face is a shield, with helm and mantling and a griffon for crest, charged: A chevron between three boars' heads erased. The initials C E appear on the pediment, and signify Charles, 9th Lord Elphinstone, who evidently set up the cross in 1697 (*infra*). The NE. face bears a similar heraldic assemblage, but the shield in this case is charged: Quarterly, 1st and 4th, a chevron between three boars' heads erased; 2nd and 3rd, a saltire and chief with a mullet in the dexter corner. These are the arms of Charles Elphinstone's parents, Sir Richard Elphinstone and Jane Bruce of Airth, whose initials appear on the pediment above. Beneath both shields runs the motto DOE WELL LET THEM SAY. The SW. and SE. faces bear shield-shaped sundials, the metal gnomons of which are still in place; they have scrolled cresting above them and swags below. On the SW. pediment there are crossed sprays of foliage and on the SE. one the date 1697.

899875 NS 88 NE 4 April 1955

413. Old Market Cross, Airth. A square stone pillar, which is locally believed to have been the market cross of the "Old Town of Airth" (p. 306), stands just E. of the north drive of Airth Castle, about midway between the Castle and the site of the old settlement. The pillar, which has no pedestal, is 7 ft. 2 in. high and 9¾ in. square in section, while its head, which comprises the uppermost 10½ in., is slightly larger, being 11 in. square. This head was evidently once a sundial, as its SE. face bears the remains of a gnomon together with some traces of dialling which suggest a 17th-century date. The shaft has been fractured and shows traces of two phases of repair—the first with iron cramps, now removed, and the second with cement.

899870 NS 88 NE ("Cross") 23 June 1955

[1] *Cast. and Dom. Arch.*, v, 480-1.
[2] *Ibid.*
[3] *T.G.A.S.*, new series, ix, 252 f.
[4] This seat has been removed to St. Mary's Episcopal Cathedral, Edinburgh, since the date of visit.
[5] The Cross is also illustrated by Small, J. W., *Scottish Market Crosses*, pls. 1 and 2.

414. Carved Stone, Overseer's House, Airth. A carved panel from the vanished Ship Inn, Airth, is preserved at the Overseer's House in the policies of Airth Castle (No. 199). It measures 2 ft. by 1 ft. 10 in., and bears in relief a representation of a barque under sail (Pl. 210 F). The paint has been applied within the last few years.

896867 NS 88 NE 14 October 1954

415. Carved Stones, Bloemfontein, Airth. In the garden at Bloemfontein, in High Street, Airth, there is preserved a collection of carved details formed by Mrs. Hall. Besides a number of Victorian corbels—lion and human heads—from the demolished house of Westquarter, near Redding, the following items were noted. (i) A panel (Pl. 210 E) from a demolished house in Main Street, Airth, measuring 2 ft. by 1 ft. 9 in. and bearing in the centre an anchor dividing the initials and date J G / M C 1732. The anchor and inscription are flanked by a pair of sea-serpents, with forked tails ending in fins, while above there is a grotesque human head flanked by leafy tendrils. The initials are said to be those of John Graham and Mary Callander. (ii) A cubical block of stone formerly built into the side of the fireplace in the demolished Tolbooth of Airth. One face shows a round hollow 10 in. in diameter and 9 in. deep, and it is thought to have been a salt-fatt. (iii) A stone pillar which formerly supported the forestair of a cottage standing on the site of the garden. Being in use as a sundial, its present height is only 3 ft. 1 in.; its upper portion is oblong in section (12 in. by 9 in.), but from 13 in. below the top its corners are widely chamfered (3¼ in.). (iv) Numerous sills and lintels, largely from houses in Airth. Most of these show sockets for bars, and some have bead-ornamentation. (v) A small palmate finial, said to have come from Carnock House (No. 347).

899875 NS 88 NE 25 June 1955

416. Architectural Fragment, Eastfield. In the E. face of the W. range of the farm-steading at Eastfield, at its S. end, there can be seen part of a blocked-up doorway, the rest of which is covered by a lean-to structure occupying the SW. corner of the farmyard. The architrave of this doorway has a roll-and-hollow moulding, presumably of 17th-century date, but no further remains of the house to which it must have belonged can now be identified.

908872 NS 98 NW 10 September 1954

417. Carved Stone, Greendyke. In the W. gable of a barn at Greendyke farm there has been reset a dormer pediment inscribed with the initials D / M S / [? R or B] E. It closely resembles the one noted close by at Powfoulis (p. 343), the letters being of the same character and similarly cut in relief on sunk fields, but the initials have not been identified.

912859 NS 98 NW 29 June 1955

418. Architectural Details and Sundial, Kinnaird House. Neither Kinnaird House, a 19th-century mansion, nor its stables and offices, which may date from the turn of the 18th and 19th centuries, is of any particular interest. Some richly carved Classical details, evidently from an 18th-century house, are preserved outside the N. wall of the kitchen garden (No. 307), and the stair of the same house has been re-used in the existing mansion. As now arranged, this stair, which is of grey freestone, rises to a small landing and then, dividing into two, turns back on itself to right and left to continue its ascent to first-floor level.

The sundial stands on a modern pedestal in the re-entrant angle of the eastern block of offices. It is of the cubical type, with a decorative finial, but now lacks its vanes; it measures 2 ft. 4 in. in height by 1 ft. 8 in. across each face. One face bears the date 1690 and the opposite one a shield charged, for Bruce of Kinnaird[1]: A saltire; on a chief, in the dexter corner, a mullet. Above the shield appears the motto SIC TRANSIT GLORIA MUNDI ("Thus passes the glory of this world"). The sundial was presumably erected by Alexander Bruce of Kinnaird, who owned the estate in the second half of the 17th century.

885848 NS 88 SE 13 April 1954

419. Sundial, Howkerse. A sundial (Pl. 215 A) stands within the garden of the house of Howkerse, which is situated beside the Grangemouth-Stirling highway (A 977) about a mile N. of Skinflats. It has a columnar shaft set within the socket of an old mill-stone, which now serves as a base. The shaft supports a cubical dial-head surmounted by a ball finial; one face of the dial bears the incised date 1699 and another a shield charged: A lion rampant. Below the shield are the incised initials I C and I A. Neither the achievement nor the initials suggest any of the local families, and it is consequently possible that the sundial may have been brought from some other part of the country.

907838 NS 98 SW 5 September 1957

420. Carved Stones, Millfield. A small collection of architectural details, evidently brought from elsewhere for preservation, have been set up as ornaments in the Millfield policies, about 150 yds. NNW. of the mansion. Those numbered (i) to (iii) below have been formed into a doorway spanning a path beside the right bank of the

[1] Bruce, M. E. Cumming, *Family Records of the Bruces and the Cumyns*, 348 ff.

Polmont Burn, while the rest are on the left bank a little further downstream.

(i) A dormer-pediment (Pl. 212 B) bearing, on a sunk panel in the centre, a triple-towered castle. To right and left of this appears a rose above a thistle, and above it a large thistle. The finial is formed by a crown. This assemblage forms the S. face of the doorway superstructure. (ii) Back to back with the foregoing, a similar tympanum inscribed in large raised letters GOD BLISS THIS WARK, with the date 1619 above. This inscription, and the emblems of the Crown and of the City of Edinburgh, suggest that both these tympana probably came from the King's Wark at Leith, which was under construction by Bernard Lindsay at about the date recorded.[1] The lowermost stone in each assemblage has been defaced with socket-holes for iron bars. (iii) Stones with rounded arrises and, in some cases, glazing grooves which show that they were originally in use as window-jambs. These now form the rybats and sconcheons of the doorway. (iv) An heraldic panel measuring 3 ft. by 2 ft. 6 in. which seems originally to have been set in a moulded framework on the outside of a building. It is carved in low relief with the arms of the City of Edinburgh, and above appears the motto NISI DOMINUS FRUSTRA with the date 2 IVNII 1623. Arms and motto point to an Edinburgh origin for this panel. (v) A stone lion, sitting upright on a square base, the whole being 3 ft. 9½ in. high. It holds in its forepaws a cartouche charged: Quarterly, 1st and 4th, a stag's head cabossed; 2nd and 3rd, a flame; at fess point the badge of Nova Scotia. Above the charges are the letters S / G MCK, indicating that the arms are those of Sir George Mackenzie of Tarbat, later 1st Earl of Cromartie; the figure is thus likely to have come from Caroline Park, Granton, which he built in 1685.[2] The remains of a metal dowel on top of the lion's head suggest that the figure was intended to support a sundial; a lion sundial of the late 16th century has been recorded at Pitfirrane, Fife,[3] and others, of the same or of the following century, at Lee Castle and Waygateshaw, Lanarkshire.[4]

In the canalised bed of the Polmont Burn, just upstream from the doorway mentioned above, there may be seen some of the square stone blocks that originally took the place of sleepers on the Edinburgh and Glasgow Railway (cf. No. 559).

931788 NS 97 NW 18 March 1953

421. Heraldic Panel, Gilmeadowland. An heraldic panel (Pl. 210 A) measuring 2 ft. by 1 ft. 5 in., which is said to have come from Almond Castle (No. 202), has been reset for preservation in the front wall of the porch at Gilmeadowland farmhouse. The shield is charged, for Livingstone: Quarterly, 1st and 4th, three cinquefoils; 2nd and 3rd, a bend between six billets. The initials T L and E N, which flank the shield, are those of Thomas Livingstone of Almond, 3rd son of Alexander, 5th Lord Livingstone, and his wife Elizabeth Nicholl; and, as these two were married before 1582,[5] the date 1586 which also appears on the panel is likely to record the completion of some building work at the Castle, presumably the second set of alterations described under No. 202 (*q.v.*).

954766 NS 97 NE 6 March 1953

422. Doorway, Babbithill. The farmhouse of Babbithill, just over a mile WSW. of Avonbridge, is of little interest in itself as it was originally formed out of two small weavers' houses and has since undergone extensive reconstruction. Its doorway, however, is an interesting sample of contemporary taste with its massive columns, plain capitals and lintel, and pyramidal finials with a moulded cornice above. The panel above the cornice is inscribed W B 1845 J B, and commemorates William Boyd and his wife Janet Bryce; the date no doubt records the year in which the house assumed its present form.

892722 NS 87 SE 19 April 1953

423. Carved Stones, North Arnloss. The dwelling-house at North Arnloss, which forms part of the range of buildings running E. and W., has gone out of use, but may be identified by the lintel over the doorway inscribed 17 J W J P 91. The initials are for James Waugh and Janet Paton. In the same wall there is set a small dormer-pediment bearing the date 1691 in large incised figures, with traces of paint. The gable at the W. end of this range has decorated roll-skewputs. In the wall of the small boiler-house opposite the dwelling-house door there is a stone bearing a thistle, in relief, which measures 10 in. in height by 12 in. across the leaves. Like the dormer-pediment it shows traces of paint.

877720 NS 87 SE 10 April 1954

424. Carved Stones, Balquhatstone House. Balquhatstone House has been rebuilt and enlarged, though in fact some masonry of an earlier building is known to be embedded in its NE. end and N. corner. At the time of the alterations, the entrance-lintel of the earlier house was reset for preservation in the SE. wall, over the kitchen window; its inscription, which is in relief on a sunk panel and has been recut, reads 1632 G W E A, the initials being those of George Waddell and his wife whose name is unknown. Another inscription, on a stone reset over a window opening on the yard, is illegible but probably begins G P. The date may be 18[?]3.

857726 NS 87 SE 16 April 1954

[1] Cf. *Inventory of Edinburgh*, p. 267. The Commissioners are indebted for this identification to the late Dr. C. A. Malcolm, C.B.E.

[2] *Inventory of Midlothian*, No. 41, *q.v.*

[3] *Inventory of Fife, Kinross and Clackmannan*, p. 126.

[4] *Cast. and Dom. Arch.*, v, 453, 456.

[5] *The Scots Peerage*, v, 437.

425. Carved Stones, Loanhead. Loanhead Cottage, as it now stands, represents a recent reconstruction of part of a row of cottages, the other end of which stands roofless; the date 1829 appearing on a chimney is presumably that of their construction. In the N. side there is an outshot with a window in its centre; the lintel of this window, evidently in secondary use, has borne an inscription, no doubt initials and a date, but only the final figures 70 are now legible. Inside the outshot, in its W. wall, there is a recess 1 ft. 8 in. wide across the front, 1 ft. 2½ in. deep, and rhomboidal on plan. Its floor is formed by a stone hollowed out to form a circular basin 2 in. deep, the rounded front of which projects 2 in. from the face of the wall. Running back into the inner side of the stone from the bottom of the basin, with which it is flush in the centre, there is a slot three-quarters of an inch wide; this ends in a small hole which gives into the wall behind in the manner of a drain. Nothing is known as to the origin or purpose of the stone but, like the lintel, it has probably been reset here for preservation.

844721 NS 87 SW 10 April 1954

426. Carved Stones, 36 Silver Row, Falkirk. The Masonic Arms, which stands at the corner of Silver Row and Manor Street, is a two-storeyed house built in 1762[1] by the Falkirk Lodge of Free and Accepted Masons. It retains its rolled skewputs but has been greatly altered from its original condition; in particular the original arched entrance in the street frontage has been built up, only the projecting keystone having been left *in situ*. Above this stone there is a panel carved in relief and painted; it bears a shield charged: On a chevron between three castles, a pair of compasses. On a ribbon below the shield appear the words LODGE FALKIRK. The sill of the window immediately above the panel (Pl. 212 E) bears the inscription L IↄↄIↄCCII to which a Roman origin is wrongly ascribed in a notice painted on the wall below the keystone. It seems probable that this is a lintel from an older Lodge, and that it has been cut down to fit the breadth of this rather small window with the result that an F, balancing the L and standing, with it, for LODGE FALKIRK, has disappeared from the sinister end. On this showing the inscription would have corresponded with the normal initial-and-date inscriptions of the 17th and 18th centuries, and might be supposed to have commemorated the foundation of the Lodge or the building of its first meeting-place.

The meaning of the Roman numerals is uncertain. The first group signifies 5000,[2] but the resulting date 5702 would be absurd unless, as has been suggested,[3] it is intended to reckon from the supposed creation of the world in 4004 B.C., in which case it would correspond with A.D. 1698. It is also possible that Iↄↄ has been used in place of CIↄ to signify 1000, and that the date should accordingly be read as 1702.

889799 NS 87 NE 1 April 1956

427. Carved Stone, 9 Pleasance, Falkirk. A moulded corbel-head of late mediaeval date, which is said to have come from the old Parish Church (No. 140), is built into the external gable-wall on the SW. side of this building.

887798 NS 87 NE 3 August 1957

428. Carved Stones, Falkirk Museum. The following stones preserved in Falkirk Museum, Dollar Park, deserve to be noted. (i) A scrolled, ansate panel (Pl. 161 E), bearing the date 1566, believed to have come from Torwood Castle (No. 299, *q.v.*). (ii) A greatly wasted demi-lion from the Cross Well, Falkirk, as mentioned under No. 540. (iii) A panel inscribed in relief 1626 / S W L / D H L. These are probably the initials of Sir William Livingstone of Westquarter and his wife Dame Helenore Livingstone; the same initials occur on the heraldic panel on Westquarter dovecot (No. 396). (iv) A rectangular panel measuring 2 ft. 9 in. in height and 2 ft. 5 in. in width (Pl. 211 B). On a sunk field it bears, in relief, a shield, parted per pale and charged: Dexter, a mullet between three gillyflowers within a double tressure flory-counter-flory; sinister, three roundels on a fess between six mullets. The shield is flanked by the initials S W L and D A B and above it there is a label bearing the motto SPE EXPECTO ("I wait in hope"). The margin of the slab bears the following inscription in relief DOM(INVS) WILEM LEVINGSTON DE KILSAY BARO AEQVES AVRAT(VS)[4] ET DOM(IN)A ANTONIA DE BORD. The arms are those of Sir William Livingstone of Kilsyth, who died in 1626 or 1627 and of his first wife Antoinette de Bord, the daughter and heiress of Pierre de Bord.[5] The stone is understood to have come from Kilsyth, but whether from the Old Place of Kilsyth (No. 218), from Colzium Castle (No. 204) or from some other site, is uncertain. (v) A segmental-headed panel, 3 ft. 1 in. high by 1 ft. 11 in. wide, bearing a shield charged: Quarterly, 1st and 4th, three gillyflowers within a double tressure flory-counter-flory; 2nd and 3rd, a bend between six billets (Pl. 211 A). The supporters are lions and the crest a dexter hand, holding a sword; above the crest there is a label with the incised inscription ET DOMI ET FORIS ("Both at home and abroad"). Notwithstanding the reversal of the quarterings, the arms are evidently those of one of the earls of Callendar,[6] and the stone, which is understood to have come from Callendar House (No. 311), may be ascribed to the second half of the 17th century. (vi) A stone corbel measuring 1 ft. 9 in. by 11 in. by 1 ft. 5 in. and carved with a human

---

[1] The historical matter here quoted is taken from an article by the late Mr. T. McGrouther in *P.F.A.N.H.S.*, i (1935-6), 11 ff., where an illustration of the carved stones is given.

[2] Capelli, *Dizionario di Abbreviature Latine ed Italiane*, 2nd edn., 415.

[3] *P.F.A.N.H.S.*, i (1935-6), 18 f.

[4] "*Baro, aeques auratus*" may be translated "Knight banneret".

[5] *The Scots Peerage*, v, 190.

[6] Cf. *ibid.*, ii, 364, and v, 450.

face (Pl. 212 A); it is of late mediaeval date and is understood to have come from Falkirk Parish Church (No. 140; cf. also No. 427). (vii) A stone fragment measuring 1 ft. 6 in. by 1 ft. 5 in. by 1 ft. One face is wrought with a hollow moulding, which contains a stop in the form of a shield bearing the Five Wounds of Christ. The stone, which is of late mediaeval date, is understood to have come from the Castlecary district, but its exact provenance is unknown.

880802 NS 88 SE ("Arnotdale") 23 March 1959

429. Carved Stone, Herbertshire Castle. This stone rests in a leaning position on the crest of the bluff on which Herbertshire Castle (No. 216) once stood. It is about 100 yds. NW. of Denny Bridge over the River Carron, and can be seen from the highway just N. of the bridge. In its present position the exposed part of its upper face measures 2 ft. 2 in. by 2 ft., and it is 7 in. thick. The stone is heavily weathered and, though it shows some indefinite signs of carving near the top, the irregular raised strip that runs down the centre might well be a natural feature. The carving was described in 1892 as a band, bounded by two horizontal lines, running across the top, with some incised marks below it. An[1] earlier note on what was evidently the same stone calls these marks "unintelligible characters", and records that the stone itself bore the name of "Hornbean".[2]

807831 NS 88 SW 24 June 1954

430. Carved Stone, Orchard. A triangular panel 2 ft. 5 in. wide by 1 ft. 10 in. high, evidently from a dormer pediment, has been set for preservation in the wall of one of the outbuildings at Orchard farm, between Auchencloch Mill and Kelvinhead. It is now covered with a heavy coat of whitewash, which obscures its details, but these were recorded and photographed many years ago, when they appeared more clearly.[3] The centre of the panel is occupied by a shield charged: Quarterly, 1st and 4th, three escallops; 2nd and 3rd, three roses. The lower part of the shield is flanked by the initials R G, and above it is a date read in 1910 as 1585. Robert Graham of Auchencloich is mentioned in a document of this same year,[4] and the panel may be presumed to have come from the mansion-house of Auchencloich, which probably stood, in the later 16th century, on or near the present site of Orchard. A sundial, which no doubt originally belonged to the house of Auchencloich, was formerly preserved at Orchard, but it[5] was sold about 1930 and efforts to trace it have failed. It had a shaft of rectangular section, divided into panels which contained sunk dials.

762790 NS 77 NE 7 May 1954

431. Heraldic Panel, Kelvinhead. The implement shed in the steading at Kelvinhead farm, at the junction of the Banton by-road with the highway from Falkirk to Kilsyth, seems to comprise the shell, gutted and much altered, of an 18th-century dwelling-house. The entrance, now built up, is in the centre of the S. wall, and above this is set an heraldic panel (Pl. 210 B); but it is impossible to be sure that this is its original position as the building has suffered so much disturbance. The panel bears a shield charged: Quarterly, 1st and 4th, three roses; 2nd and 3rd, three escallops. The shield is flanked by the initials R G and below these [?M] P, while above it, on a label, appears the date 1765. Although this date is incised, while the heraldic achievements, the initials, and the associated palmettes are in relief, the whole assemblage is unquestionably of one and the same date,[6] the more so as the upper part of the stone, above the moulded border, shows droving of 18th-century character. The initials would suit Robert Graham of Kelvinhead, mentioned in a sasine of 1771[7]; his wife's name has not been traced but she may well have been a Patrick seeing that David Patrick, portioner of Wester Auchencloich, is associated with this Robert Graham and with John Graham of Auchencloich in the transaction.[8] The transposition of the dexter and sinister achievements is probably due to the design having been copied from the matrix of a seal.

757786 NS 77 NE 7 May 1954

432. Carved Stones, Garrel Mill. Garrel Mill, which faces No. 363 across the Takmadoon Road (No. 511), has been converted into a garage and is now of no particular interest. It was probably built in 1774, the date appearing on the keystone of the wide, arched entrance at the roadside. Immediately above this keystone there has been inserted an older carving—a shield bearing in relief the date 1700 and, below it, a reversing monogram of what appear to be the letters W, M, B and L.

720783 NS 77 NW ("Mill") 2 October 1953

433. Heraldic Panel, Craigengoyne, Kilsyth. In the hall at Craigengoyne House there hangs a carved wooden panel which, though it is not connected with any Stirlingshire monument, is of some intrinsic interest.

---

[1] *T.S.N.H.A.S.* (1892-3), 134 f.
[2] *Stirling Journal*, 12th June 1828.
[3] Graham, J. St. J., *The Grahams of Auchencloich and Tamrawer*, Lisbon (1952), 38 f., 48.
[4] *R.P.C.*, iv (1585-92), p. 22. See also Graham, J. St. J., *op. cit.*, 22 ff., and Graham, J. E., *The Grahams of Tamrawer* (Edinburgh Press, 1895, for private circulation), 8 ff., correcting what seems to be an erroneous account of this family given in *T.G.A.S.*, new series, i (1881-90), 383 ff.
[5] Graham, J. St. J., *op. cit.*, 43, with illustration.
[6] Additional disproof of the contrary suggestion, made by Graham, J. St. J., *op. cit.*, 49, is given by the fact that the surface of the label bearing the incised date is level with the highest parts of the relief design.
[7] *Ibid.*, 35.
[8] *Ibid.*

The panel bears a shield, with helm and mantling and, for crest, a battleaxe held in two hands. It is charged: Three piles issuing from a chief. Above the shield appear the initials S W A, for Sir William Anstruther of that Ilk, with the date 1645, and over all the motto PERIISSEM NISI PERIISSEM ("I should have perished had I not perished"). Sir William Anstruther was retoured heir to his father in the barony of Anstruther in 1606, married Euphemia, daughter of Sir Andrew Wemyss of Myrecairnie, in 1601, and died in 1649.[1]

721783 NS 77 NW 29 October 1953

434. Carved Stones, Gospel Hall, Kilsyth. In the Gospel Hall, which stands in the High Street next door to the first of the houses described under No. 254 and on the site of a house which is known to have resembled its neighbour closely,[2] there have been re-set some carved stones belonging to the earlier building. Above the entrance there is a panel with a moulded border (Pl. 212 D), bearing a man's figure in a skirted coat and knee-breeches; this figure divides the inscription J H H [?K] 1764, and the motto RENOVATE AN[IMAS] ("Renew your spirits") appears above on a ribbon.[3] In the back wall of the Hall there is a fragment of stone bearing the initials I H H [?K]: the final letter is again damaged, but in both cases K seems more probable than R, a possible alternative.

Behind the Gospel Hall there stands a small outhouse, in the S. gable of which two other carved stones have been reset. Nothing is known about their provenance. One of them shows a human face crudely executed in 18th-century style, and the other a cabled roundel with other decoration inside it.

718777 NS 77 NW 5 May 1954

435. Sundial and Carved Stone, Torrance. A cubical sundial, of a type in use in the 17th and 18th centuries, has been mounted on the SE. corner of Number 84, Main Street, Torrance. One gnomon is still present. On top of the sundial is set a crudely carved female head. The provenance of neither monument is known.

618739 NS 67 SW 8 September 1956

436. Carved Stone, Balgrochan Mill. Balgrochan Mill stands about a third of a mile NE. of the level crossing in Torrance, by the E. side of the road to Lennoxtown. The building itself is of no interest and was badly damaged by fire in 1958, but a small inscribed stone set in its W. face, about 10 ft. above the ground, bears witness to the existence of an earlier structure on the site. The inscription now legible, which is in relief on a sub-oval sunk panel, reads A F / 1653, and some marks in the top dexter region of the panel may be the remains of further initials.

624743 NS 67 SW 23 June 1958

437. Carved Stone, West Balgrochan. The farmyard at West Balgrochan occupies the former site of Balgrochan House, and the wall that bounds it on the SSE., dividing it from the garden of the adjoining property, embodies the lower part of that building's façade. The remains of window-margins can be seen in it, apparently of 18th-century character. West of the remains of this façade, part of a 17th-century lintel has been built into the face of the boundary wall; its dexter end has evidently been cut off, and the surviving inscription reads M M M 1642. It may be inferred that there were originally two pairs of initials, and that the first one of the first pair was on the missing end of the stone; if so they may well have represented John Marshall, portioner of Balgrochan, and his wife Margaret Marshall, who are on record at this period.[4]

617745 NS 67 SW 12 August 1953

438. Carved Stone, Campsie Manse. A lintel bearing the date 1621 in raised figures on a sunk panel has been set above the entrance to the walled garden of Campsie Manse, immediately W. of the house.

611794 NS 67 NW 8 September 1953

439. Carved Stones, Craigbarnet Mains. The steading of Craigbarnet Mains has been made out of the stable buildings of Craigbarnet House,[5] and these are shown by a date cut on a lintel in their E. range to have been built in 1785. The barn, on the W. side of the yard, incorporates the following architectural details, said to have come from the older house of Craigbarnet, which stood S. of the present course of the Kilsyth-Glasgow highway. (i) A lintel, with a moulded edge, bearing the date 1698. (ii) Two egg-shaped finials, mounted on the E. skewputs of the gables and bearing initials and figures in relief. The S., or dexter, one has near the top a single S, and beside it the bend and three buckles of the Stirling arms. Below appears I S / 16. The N., or sinister, finial bears M [S] / 62, the intention being that the two, taken together, should give I S M [S] / 1662, for John Stirling, 9th of Craigbarnet, and his wife Mary Stirling, youngest daughter of Sir Mungo Stirling of Glorat, whom he married in 1656.[6] (iii) On the gable-heads, two fluted balls each with a raised horizontal rib round its middle.

The Stirlings of Craigbernard were descended from

---

[1] Burke, *Peerage* (1925 ed.), 119.

[2] Information from Mr. Bell, Kilsyth.

[3] This motto seems to be founded on Eph., iv, 23, which reads in the Vulgate "*Renovamini autem spiritu mentis vestrae*".

[4] *The Commissariot Record of Stirling, Register of Testaments*, 1607-1800, S.R.S., 108.

[5] This important house, built in 1786, was under demolition at the date of visit, and was too far gone for any useful record of it to be prepared.

[6] Cameron, J., *The Parish of Campsie*, 178.

the Stirlings of Cadder and had acquired Craigbarnet by the middle of the 15th century. The old house of Craigbarnet was built by John Stirling, probably in 1662, and the later one, of 1786, by his grandson. The direct male line of the family ended with the death of the latter in 1805.[1]

594790 NS 57 NE ("Craigbarnet") 15 September 1953

440. Carved Stone, Leddriegreen House. A carved stone panel, which is built into the wall of the stables at Leddriegreen House, bears the incised inscription: G C O I C V / I 6 M 7 2 Y. The V and the Y seem to be additions, but the rest of the inscription is probably original in its present form in spite of some traces of re-cutting. The O and the M are difficult to account for, but, whatever interpretation is put on them, it seems clear that the stone commemorates Gilbert Craig, 2nd of Leddriegreen, who died before 1719,[2] and his wife, whose name is not known. The date may be that of their marriage or of the erection of the old house of Leddriegreen.

565797 NS 57 NE 15 July 1957

441. Carved Stones, Dumgoyach. In 1924 a slab bearing two Latin crosses was recorded at Dumgoyach Farm,[3] about half a mile W. of Duntreath Castle (No. 209). It was believed to have once been in use as the cover of a well. Of late years, however, and since this record was made, the farm has been converted into a residence, and in the altered surroundings no trace could be found either of this stone or of certain others, bearing cup-like markings, which had been noted at the same time. Another slab, however, of large size and slightly tapered outline, evidently a grave-cover, was seen lying at the threshold of an outbuilding on the S. side of the courtyard; and it is not impossible that a number of gravestones may at some time have been obtained from a churchyard—perhaps that of Strathblane (No. 158), which is only three miles distant—for use in the farm-buildings.

528812 NS 58 SW 30 September 1953

442. Sundials and Carved Stones, Park of Drumquhassle. In the garden at the Park of Drumquhassle there are preserved: (i) The central block, 15 in. high, of a columnar sundial similar to the one at Ballindalloch (No. 444). It shows twelve facets, of which four are cupped. (ii) A bronze dial, bearing a Latin inscription which records that it was made by William Govane of Drumquhassle in 1710. The dial has been fully described elsewhere.[4] (iii) A pair of red sandstone pine-cones, 1 ft. 8 in. high.

The carved stones probably came from Gartness Castle (No. 220).[5]

482869 NS 48 NE 30 August 1952

443. Carved Stone and Sundial, Boquhan House. Incorporated at eaves-level into the N. front of Boquhan House, which was erected in 1784, there is an old door-lintel bearing the incised inscription 17 T B M B 04. The initials are those of Thomas Buchanan, fourth of Boquhan, and of his first wife, Margaret, daughter of John Buchanan of Carbeth,[6] and the date no doubt commemorates the erection of the house that preceded the present one. In front of the house there is a copper sundial, dated 1689, which is mounted upon a later stone shaft.

544874 NS 58 NW 11 October 1957

444. Sundial, Ballindalloch. A fine columnar sundial stands on the lawn at Ballindalloch, its original position having been on the upper lawn a short distance to the north. Its general appearance is shown in Pl. 214 A, and it has been fully described elsewhere.[7] The height of the shaft, the tip of which has been broken off, with the drum-shaped pedestal, is 8 ft.

540884 NS 58 NW 30 August 1952

445. Sundial and Carved Stones, Camoquhill Douglas. The small mansion-house of Camoquhill Douglas stands about half a mile W. of the village of Balfron. The building is of no great antiquity, but the fragments of carved stone now preserved there suggest that the present structure occupies the site of an older house. These fragments comprise: (i) An angle sundial of 17th- or 18th-century date, which stands a little to the W. of the house. (ii) A stone baluster-shaft, probably of 17th-century date, which is built into the wall of a garage to the NE. of the house. (iii) A lintel, which is built into a wall a little to the W. of the house. This bears the incised inscription P N M N 1717. The initials are probably those of Patrick Neilson,[8] who possessed the property at that time, and of his wife.

The lintel of the entrance-doorway of the present house bears the date 1778 and the initials W N, as well as some later dates and initials, all apparently commemorating members of the Neilson family.

539893 NS 58 NW 16 August 1957

[1] Bain, G., *The Stirlings of Craigbernard and Glorat*, 6 ff.
[2] *Strathblane*, 65.
[3] *P.S.A.S.*, lix (1924-5), 147.
[4] *T.G.A.S.*, new series, ix (1940), 235.
[5] Ordnance Survey Name Book, Drymen parish, 95.
[6] *Strathendrick*, 358.
[7] *T.G.A.S.*, new series, ix (1940), 271, 285.
[8] *Strathendrick*, 353.

446. Heraldic Panel, Easter Ballochairn. A carved stone panel is built into the W. wall of a barn on the farm of Easter Ballochairn, two miles E. of the village of Balfron. It bears a shield charged: A saltire engrailed between four roses, within a bordure. The crest is a dexter hand holding an eagle's leg erased. Above is the motto [V]INCIT [VERI]TAS, with the initials M T N. Although the coat does not correspond in all respects with the one described by Nisbet,[1] the achievement and the initials no doubt represent Mr. Thomas Napier of Ballochairn, who possessed the property at the end of the 17th century.[2]

587889 NS 58 NE 15 July 1957

447. Carved Stones, Hill of Balgair. Over the front door of the farmhouse, inside the porch, there is a lintel with a rounded arris, bearing the date 1695; and into the SE. wall of the house there have been inserted a stone dated 1721 and a small oval light, perhaps of a similar date. Another lintel dated 1695 is to be seen over the SW. window in the NW. face of a small building which is now used as a boiler-house and store. The stone dated 1721 has been brought from the Old Place of Balgair (No. 333),[3] and the others may well have come from buildings in the vanished hamlet of the Hill of Balgair (cf. No. 381).

597890 NS 58 NE 29 August 1952

448. Sundial and Carved Stones, Harvieston. Over one of the windows on the NW. side of the farmhouse of Harvieston, locally known as Croftalpine, there has been re-set a lintel dated 1694. In the S. end of the byre of the same farm there have also been re-set (i) a sundial, dated 165[?], having two tabular faces and surmounted by a female head with flowing hair at the sides; (ii) two corbels showing grotesque human masks. These pieces may well have come from buildings in the vanished hamlet of Hill of Balgair (cf. No. 381).

598893 NS 58 NE 31 August 1952

449. Milestone, Craw Road. By the E. side of the Craw Road (p. 426), half a mile N. of the point where it crosses the Clachie Burn, there stands a partly mutilated milestone (Pl. 230 C) which presumably dates from the reconstruction of the road in 1792. The stone has been dressed to a rectangular section of 1 ft. 3 in. by 8 in.; its present height is 2 ft. 1 in., the upper part having been broken away. Near the top of the undamaged surface there has been carved an index hand pointing S., and above this there has been a word of which only a damaged O can now be made out. Below this hand there have been two lines of inscription, the lower one of which can be read as FINTRY; and near the base there is a second hand, this one pointing N.

646843 NS 68 SW ("MS., Def.") 12 July 1955

450. Carved Stone, Arngomery. What appears to have originally been a lintel, inscribed I E 1686 A L, has been built into the S. side of the transe that gives access to the stable yard at Arngomery. It is believed to have come from an old building which formerly occupied the site, and may originally have been set in the old house of Broich, which stood hereabouts.[4] The initials no doubt represent one of the lairds of Broich and his wife, perhaps James Edmonstone of Broich who received a grant of the property in 1662, or his son, another James, who succeeded him[5]; but as the former is said to have married Margaret Graham and the latter Jean Wordie,[6] the initials A L do not seem to correspond with any member of the family mentioned by Guthrie Smith.

640949 NS 69 SW 16 September 1952

451. Milestone, Fordhead. Beside the hollow track that rises from the Fords of Frew (No. 524) there stands a small block of red sandstone inscribed with the Roman numerals VI. Of this the Ordnance Survey Name Book[7] says, "An old road crossed the Ford of Frew leading to Glasgow, an old mile stone still standing adjacent to and on the south side of the Ford states it to be 6 miles to Burnfoot at a place at the south west end of the Parish." This note is correct, as the distance from the ford to Burnfoot (675884) is actually six miles if measured along the line of the road described under No. 525.

670960 NS 69 NE (unnoted) 24 August 1952

BRIDGES AND VIADUCTS

452. Cardross Bridge. This bridge (Pl. 226 B) carries the road from Arnprior to Port of Menteith (B 803) over the Forth at the SW. corner of the Cardross policies. It is a well-proportioned, triple-arched structure measuring 200 ft. in total length over splayed approaches and providing a roadway 13 ft. 9 in. wide between parapets 3 ft. 7 in. high by 1 ft. 5 in. thick. The roadway rises about 5 ft. to the centre of the bridge. The piers and abutments are built of coursed, rusticated masonry, the former having boldly projecting cut-waters which die out on the walls at springing level. The arches have rough-dressed voussoirs and rubble infilling; the spandrels and superstructure are of random rubble. Drain-holes are provided at the base of the parapet, which is plain. The arches are all of approximately the

[1] *A System of Heraldry* (1722 ed.), i, 141.
[2] *Strathendrick*, 184 f.
[3] *Ibid.*, 262.
[4] *Geogr. Collections*, i, 351.
[5] *Strathblane*, 98.
[6] *Ibid.*
[7] Gargunnock Parish, 12.

same size; the crown of the central one is 23 ft. 3 in. above the water, its span is 41 ft. and its height above the springing level 11 ft. 1 in.

In the S. face of the E. abutment there is set a panel bearing the following inscription beautifully executed in incised capitals: THIS BVILDING ERECTED A.D. 1774./ HIS MAIESTY / GAVE IN AID TO IT OUT OF THE ANNEXED / ESTATES £250 STR. / VIATOR / TUTO TRANSEAS / SIS / MEMOR / REGII BENEFICII ("Traveller, may you cross safely. Be mindful of the Royal benefaction").

An 18th-century plan for a proposed bridge at Cardross is preserved in H.M. General Register House,[1] but it does not correspond with the existing structure.

598972 NS 59 NE 13 May 1959

453. Old Bridge, Leckie. The old bridge lies about 200 yds. S. of Old Leckie House (No. 343) and 25 yds. upstream from the new bridge, which is of 18th-century date. It is built of rubble, and has a single semicircular arch with a span of 11 ft. which rises to a height of 9 ft. above the level of the Leckie Burn. The width of the roadway between the parapets is 6 ft. 9 in. and the overall length of the bridge excluding the approaches, which are staggered, is 15 ft. A stone set into the parapet on the S. side of the bridge bears the incised inscription 1673 / EX BENEVOLENTIA / OB SALUTEM ("[Built] out of benevolence, for safety's sake").

690945 NS 69 SE ("Bridge") 6 September 1955

454. Old Bridge, Drip. The old bridge of Drip (Pl. 225) spans the Forth about 600 yds. upstream from the inflow of the Teith. It was built by public subscription,[2] perhaps before 1745,[3] and formerly carried the traffic from Stirling to Aberfoyle and Callander; but the modern highway A 84 now passes over a new bridge which stands immediately to the N. of it. It is a dignified and well-proportioned structure containing five arches, and is built of red and grey sandstone rubble brought to courses; the voussoirs and the blocks used in the piers and cut-waters are large and carefully squared though the under-surfaces of the arches have been left rough. Its total length, exclusive of the splayed approaches, is 206 ft. and its width 16 ft. 2 in. over parapets each 1 ft. 1 in. thick; but the effective width of the roadway is reduced to 11 ft. 6 in. by strips of raised pavement. The roadway rises about 6 ft. from the right-bank level to the top of the central arch. The cut-waters of the two central piers are carried up and intaken to form small semi-hexagonal refuges on the roadway. The arches are graduated in size, the central one being 45 ft. wide and 13 ft. 3 in. high above the springing-line; the two that flank it are both 37 ft. 3 in. wide and respectively 11 ft. 3 in. and 11 ft. high above the springing-line; while the outermost two are respectively 24 ft. (left bank) and 24 ft. 6 in. (right bank) wide and rise 7 ft. 6 in. above the springing-line. They all spring at slightly over 7 ft. above the water. The top of the parapet over the central arch is 27 ft. 10 in. above the water.

770956 NS 79 NE ("Old Bridge") 8 June 1954

455. Old Bridge, Stirling. The paramount importance of the Forth crossing at Stirling has already been mentioned on p. 4, and records of bridges on this site go back to early times. If Boece's fables are ignored, we can still point to the word *pons* on three maps of the mid-13th century[4] and to the representation of a bridge on the burgh seal of Stirling in 1296,[5] a date which is only earlier by one year than Wallace's battle in which the breaking down of the bridge was traditionally an episode. This tradition implies that the bridge of that time was wooden, and the representation of a stone bridge on the seal need not be taken as evidence to the contrary as the design was most probably a conventional one. In 1304 an allusion to boats suggests that no bridge was available; in 1305 a bridge, presumably of timber, was repaired; in 1336 a bridge was in existence, and between 1361 and 1391 a ferry replaced the bridge. In 1407 the bridge was said to be very ruinous on account of its great age, and a Papal indulgence was offered to those willing to assist in its rebuilding.[6] The work carried out at this time was evidently of some importance, and payments to the fabric are recorded in 1408 and 1415. This structure may again have been of wood, as the possibility of its being broken is mentioned by an English spy between 1424 and 1437. "Bridgend" is alluded to in 1501 and 1502, the bridge is mentioned incidentally in 1525, and in 1527 James V crossed it after his escape from Falkland.[7] By this time we are certainly dealing with the existing bridge, the appearance of which suggests a date in the 15th or early 16th century. References to the repair of the structure in the 17th century are to be found in the Burgh Council records, while in 1745 one of the arches of the bridge was cut by General Blakeney, the commander of the troops in the Castle, to prevent the Highland army entering the town.[8] The bridge was closed to wheeled traffic when the new bridge was built (1831) about 100 yds. downstream; it is now in good preservation and is maintained under the guardianship of the Ministry of Works.

The bridge (Pls. 222 A and 223) stands at the end of the old route through the town (pp. 275 ff.), and spans the river on an axis running from WSW. to ENE. It is built

[1] Forfeited Estates Papers, No. 22.
[2] *Stat. Acct.*, vi (1793), 488.
[3] A bridge is marked here on Edgar's map of that date, which was, however, only published in 1777.
[4] *The Early Maps of Scotland*, Royal Scottish Geographical Society, facing pp. 18, 19.
[5] Stevenson J. H., and Wood, M. *Scottish Heraldic Seals*, i, Burghs, 80.
[6] *T.S.N.H.A.S.* (1928-9), 83 ff.
[7] All the foregoing historical references except the one otherwise noted are taken from *P.S.A.S.*, xlvii (1912-3), 320 ff.
[8] *Stirling Burgh Records*, 1667-1752, 272 ff.

of squared rubble brought to courses, on which masons' marks are visible here and there, and contains four semicircular arches supported on piers which, like the abutments, stand on massive oval foundations, mortar-built of coarse rubble. The basal courses of the cut-waters are protected by rubble jackets set 2 ft. to 3 ft. out. The main structure, between the abutments, is 268 ft. long by 17 ft. wide over parapets 1 ft. thick; these are 4 ft. 4 in. high at the crown of the bridge and finish in weathered copes slightly stepped on the haunches. The piers are provided, on either face, with triangular cut-waters, which finish in splayed tops about half-way up to the parapets; from the two central ones, however, the masonry has been developed into square projections and carried up to form refuges for pedestrians, the mouth of the SE. one being slightly askew. The walls of these recesses were originally much higher and finished in crow-stepped gables; they can be seen roofed in this manner in the early 18th-century painting formerly preserved in the Council Chambers,[1] and, less clearly, in one of Slezer's drawings[2] (Pl. 222 B). The arches, which spring from or slightly above the rubble foundations, are similar in construction, as each is formed of two ring-members, the lower one being recessed from the upper and the voussoirs of both being heavily chamfered while the intrados is plain. Their spans, from SW. to NE., are respectively 39 ft., 54 ft., 56 ft. and 48 ft. The crown of the road is about 38 ft. above the low-water level and about 30 ft. above the pier-foundations. A good deal of restoration has evidently been done, and in particular the NW. face of the SW. arch has evidently been rebuilt, no doubt after the demolition of 1745 (*supra*). The parapets have also been renewed. There were originally archways at each end of the bridge (Pl. 222 B), the one to the NE. having an iron gate; but both were removed during the 18th century and were replaced by the small square pillars with pyramidal finials that remain today.[3]

The bridge is extended at both ends in substantial abutments, which run well back from the bank and carry the approaches. The SW. approach is in alinement with the bridge, but the other swings through an angle of thirty degrees in the outermost two-thirds of its length. The walling of the approaches shows two splayed intakes, and the NE. one has been strengthened by the addition on each side of three rubble buttresses with splayed tops. The parapet walls of the approaches have been renewed with random rubble and plain coping-stones.

The roadway, which is cobbled and measures 15 ft. in width on the bridge, widens on entering the NE. approach to 17 ft. 6 in. and increases further to 36 ft. in the 170 ft. of its length to Bridgehaugh Road. In the SW. approach the roadway is 23 ft. 9 in. wide, but contracts to 15 ft. 2 in. in the 87 ft. to its junction with Lower Bridge Street. An excavation made in 1912 at the NE. end of the bridge revealed three earlier causeways underlying the existing road;[4] these no doubt represent periodic attempts to ease the gradient of the access. Two or three of the gargoyles that discharged surface water from one of these earlier roadways still survive.

The foundations of two piers of an earlier bridge, which presumably had a wooden superstructure, were discovered in 1905 in the bed of the river some 65 yds. upstream. The piers were about 28 ft. long by 14 ft. broad; they were 25 ft. apart, the centre of the NE. one being about 25 yds. from the left bank and that of the SW. one between 25 yds. and 30 yds. from the right bank.[5]

797945 NS 79 SE ("Bridge") 21 November 1955

456. Bridge, Chartershall. This bridge (Pl. 227 A) spans the Bannock Burn at the hamlet of Chartershall (No. 263). A panel in its W. face reads THIS BRIDGE WAS RE/BUILT BY THE JUSTICES / OF THE PACE 1747, and the evidence of reconstruction is clear in the contrast between the foundations of the N. abutment on the W. side and most of the rest of the structure. The 18th-century work is rubble, with dressed voussoirs and intrados, the arrises being rectangular; the parapet is plain, and was formerly secured by iron cramps. The lower W. part of the N. abutment, however, is built of larger blocks, its arris is widely chamfered, and it is deeply intaken by means of a sloping scarcement. Some masonry of the same character can be seen on the W. face of the S. abutment, but it is impossible to say how much of the interior of the archway is original as some of the old stonework seems to have been re-dressed and re-used in the reconstruction. The bridge is 119 ft. long over the mill-lade that runs under its N. end. The arch spans 26 ft. 8 in., springs at 7 ft. 7 in. above the water and rises 5 ft. 7 in. above the springing. The total height to the parapet is 17 ft. 4 in. The roadway is 12 ft. wide between parapets each 1 ft. 4 in. thick.

About the year 1900 a carved panel was found, incorporated in an old building in Chartershall, which bore the inscription THIS BRIDG WAS BU/ILT BY THE IUSTIC OF / PEACE OF STERLING / SHYER AN(N)O 1696.[6] The oldest portions of the existing bridge are no doubt of this date.

792902 NS 79 SE 18 May 1955

457. Old Bridge, Bannockburn. This bridge (Pl. 224 A) stands at the foot of The Brae, which, with Main Street, Old Town and The Path, formed the principal thoroughfare through the town of Bannockburn (No. 264) until

[1] Ronald, J., *Landmarks of Old Stirling*, 165.
[2] P.R.O., M.P.F. 246.
[3] Ronald, *op. cit.*, 167. The corbels set over the springing of the S. arch on both faces of the bridge may have been associated with one of these gateways.
[4] Contemporary record by Ministry of Works. Inglis' statement (*P.S.A.S., loc. cit.*) that there were five causeways in all is evidently an error.
[5] *T.S.N.H.A.S.* (1905-6), 33 ff.; *S.H.R.*, ii (1905), 487. The foregoing details were confirmed by Mr. R. Swift, Bridge of Allan, during the drought of 1955.
[6] *Stirling Antiquary*, ii, 278 f.

the construction of the present main road and bridge about 200 yds. to the E. The bridge spans the Bannock Burn from S. to N. and has an overall length of 158 ft. including the approaches. It consists of a single segmental arch which has a span of 33 ft. 10 in. and rises to the height of 14 ft. 7 in. above the level of the water. The width of the roadway between the parapets, which have an average height of 3 ft. 6 in., is 22 ft. 9 in. A straight joint visible in the soffit of the arch clearly indicates that the bridge has been widened, the width of the original structure, which lies to the E., being 11 ft. 10 in. and the present overall width 24 ft. 6 in. The older part is well built in coursed ashlar and many of the stones have masons' marks. The E. voussoirs are wrought with a broad chamfer, but those to the W. have been cut back during the widening of the bridge. The later portion is also in ashlar, but the voussoirs are distinguishable by their sharp arrises. The upper courses of masonry on each side of the bridge are of rubble, and this suggests that the parapet was renewed or heightened after the widening of the bridge.

A panel, set within a moulded border, is placed over the crown of the arch on the W. side of the bridge and bears the following inscription: THIS BRIDGE WAS / BUILT BY ROBERT / SPITALL TAYLOR / TO KING JAMES / THE FOURTH 1516 / PRO PATRIA / ET POSTERIS / REPAIRED BY THE JU/STICES OF PEACE 1710/12 FEET ADDED TO/THE BREADTH BY THE/ TRUSTEES 1781. The inscription is incised and incorporates a pair of scissors carved in relief. Although the panel itself can hardly be earlier in date than the late 18th century, its inscription may embody an authentic tradition.[1] If this is so, the older part of the present structure would date from the early 16th century, repairs having been effected in 1631[2] and 1710 and a more general remodelling of the bridge having been undertaken in 1781.

807904 NS 89 SW 27 April 1956

458. Old Bridge, West Westfield. Though hardly more than a culvert, its span being only about 10 ft. 6 in., this bridge, which carries the by-road B 9124 over the Little Pow Burn just SW. of West Westfield farm, is of interest as being probably older than most of the other local bridges except the Abbeytown Bridge (No. 460). This may be inferred from the less careful dressing of its masonry, and from the analogy between the projecting keystone seen on its SE. face and the ones on the bridge of 1750 at Gonachan (No. 467). It is also clear that its superstructure has had to be widened to carry the modern by-road.

880874 NS 88 NE (unnoted) 20 October 1954

459. Old Bridge, Airth. This bridge spans the Pow Burn 350 yds. WNW. of Abbeytown Bridge (No. 460). Its narrow breadth—only 11 ft. over parapets which were probably about 1 ft. 8 in. thick—combined with the absence of any associated road suggests that it was merely intended to provide communication between fields. Little of the structure now remains except the actual arch, and the appearance of the voussoirs suggests a date in the late 18th or early 19th century. The arch spans 25 ft. and rises 4 ft. 9 in. above the springing-line.

893866 NS 88 NE 14 October 1954

460. Abbeytown Bridge, Airth. This bridge (Pl. 227 B) spans the Pow Burn in the SW. corner of the policies of Airth Castle (No. 199), and gives access to the Castle from a secondary road (B 9036) coming from Carronshore. In 1723 it carried the highway from Falkirk to Airth.[3] A panel with a moulded border, set in the E. face of the bridge just below the parapet, records that the structure was FOUNDED UPON / WOOD AND / REBUILT BY THE / SHIRE 1726. Evidence of rebuilding, either at this date or later, is no doubt to be seen in the large, uncoursed rubble used in the abutments and parapets, which contrast with the courses of smaller, squared rubble in the spandrels. The bridge was repointed within the last few years.

The bridge is 110 ft. long including the approaches, 13 ft. broad over parapets 1 ft. 2 in. thick, and rises to a greatest height of 13 ft. above the water. The arch is rebated so as to form a narrower inner member, and both members are chamfered on their arrises; it has a span of 25 ft., springs at 3 ft. 6 in. above the water and rises 5 ft. 6 in. above the springing-line. The corners of the abutments are splayed.

The name Abbeytown Bridge no doubt arises from the former possession of rights and property in Airth by Holyrood Abbey.[4]

896865 NS 88 NE 14 October 1954

461. Bridge, New Mills. This bridge spans the Pow Burn, near its mouth, at a point about 700 yds. E. of Eastfield, and carries a minor road which runs from Airth to Higgins Neuck. A bridge stood here in 1723,[5] but it is impossible to be certain that the existing bridge is the same one as was then recorded as, apart from its comparatively narrow roadway (10 ft.) and some general resemblance to Abbeytown Bridge (No. 460), there is nothing to differentiate it from a 19th-century structure. The masonry is rubble, and seems to have been pointed fairly recently. The single arch has a span of 51 ft. 3 in. and rises 8 ft. above the springing-line, thus raising the roadway about 3 ft. above its level at the E. end of the bridge. The whole structure, including the slightly

[1] A further example of Robert Spittal's munificence is noted under No. 246.
[2] *Stirling Burgh Records*, 1519-1666, 167.
[3] *Geogr. Collections*, i, 329. Cf. also No. 514.
[4] Lawrie, *Charters*, No. XCIII.
[5] *Geogr. Collections*, i, 329.

splayed approaches, is 83 ft. in length. The W. abutment shows signs of subsidence towards the N.

915872 NS 98 NW 9 May 1958

462. Old Bridge, Larbert. This bridge spans the River Carron some 500 yds. SE. of Larbert cross-roads, on the general line of the Roman and post-Roman route to Stirling (cf. p. 115). A bridge certainly existed here in 1651,[1] and it is natural to suppose that the one mentioned by Pitscottie, which he evidently believed to have existed in 1488,[2] was likewise in the immediate vicinity. In 1723 the bridge of that time was recorded as having two arches.[3] The bridge now in question is shown by an inscribed roundel, inserted in the NW. parapet towards its SW. end, to have been built in 1782. Including the approaches, it is 56 yds. in length and is 27 ft. wide over its parapets. It is carried by two arches, the larger one, to the SW., spanning the main channel of the river (*c.* 44 ft.) and the smaller one, to the NE., providing a passage for flood-water. A single pier stands on the NE. margin of the main channel and has a splayed and pointed cut-water both upstream and downstream; the arches are defined by drip-moulds similar to those noted on the Low Bridge, Gonachan (No. 467), built some thirty years earlier.

Part of the abutment of an older bridge, the masonry of which does not, however, suggest a date earlier than the 18th century, can be seen flanking the lower part of the NE. abutment on its upstream side. This older bridge, and the roadway corresponding with it, were evidently at a lower level than the existing highway and bridge, and the road turned on to the bridge at a considerably sharper angle.

859818 NS 88 SE ("Larbert Bridges") 21 March 1956

463. Bridge, Almond Castle. This bridge is situated 30 yds. S. of Almond Castle (No. 202), and originally carried the approach-road over the ditch, now filled up, that surrounded the building. It consists of a single segmental arch with a span of 10 ft. 10 in., the space below which is filled up with debris and soil to above the springing-line. The superstructure has been demolished, but the width of the roadway was about 8 ft.

956772 NS 97 NE (unnoted) 24 March 1959

464. Bridge, Dalquhairn. The track leading to Dalquhairn from the Avonbridge-Slamannan highway is carried over a small burn by a bridge which may well be as old as the house (No. 318, *q.v.*). It is built of rough rubble, but much of the masonry has fallen out of the approaches and there is no parapet. Of the actual span little more survives than the voussoirs of the arch, which was originally segmental but has now been distorted by stress. The span is 12 ft. and the springing, soffit and crown of the roadway rise, respectively, about 1 ft., 4 ft. 6 in. and 6 ft. 6 in. above the water level. The total length is approximately 48 ft. and the breadth in the centre is 13 ft. over all.

904724 NS 97 SW (unnoted) 26 April 1954

465. Bridge, Faughlin Burn. This bridge carries the old road from Fintry to Denny (No. 528) over the Faughlin Burn, 175 yards. above its discharge into the Carron Water, near Carron Bridge (No. 466). The site has evidently been chosen for the comparative narrowness of the stream-bed, and its rocky sides. Though the superstructure and most of the facing on the upstream side have vanished, the remainder shows that the overall breadth was 12 ft. 6 in.; the span of the arch, which is segmental, is 19 ft., and its height above the water is 9 ft., the face being corbelled out from the voussoirs. The voussoirs and the facings of the abutments are neatly dressed, but the rest is roughly constructed of large stones and boulders.

742833 NS 78 SW 1 July 1954

466. Carron Bridge. This bridge carries the road from Stirling to Kilsyth and Glasgow (No. 511) over the River Carron, just S. of the point where it crosses the road from Denny to the west by Fintry. It was known as the New Bridge of Carron in 1707[4]; an inscribed stone set in the structure seems to indicate that it was built in 1695, while others record reconstructions carried out in 1715 and 1907 respectively. The evidence of these works is also very plain to see; for example, the S. arch has been completely rebuilt in brick, a concrete buttress has been added on the E. face of the N. end, and there are signs of disturbance at many points in the fabric. Nevertheless, the main features of the structure remain as they were in 1796, when the *Statistical Account of Scotland* described it as possessing one large and one small arch[5]; and it is also possible that the N. arch may either be intact or have been rebuilt very much on its original lines. What seems to be the oldest masonry is large squared rubble brought to courses. The structure comprises a straight central section, the bridge proper, measuring 126 ft. in length by 13 ft. 3 in. in width over parapets 1 ft. 3 in. thick and 4 ft. high. Curving approaches at either end bring up the total length to 182 ft. The roadway on the bridge proper falls about 5 ft. 6 in. from S. to N., the right bank being higher than the left, and the S. arch is much larger than the N. one to provide for the road's descent. The S. and N. arches spring respectively 3 ft. 6 in. and 15 ft. from the ends of the bridge and at a

---

[1] *Geogr. Collections*, i, 331.
[2] *Historie and Cronicles of Scotland*, S.T.S. edn., i, 206.
[3] *Geogr. Collections*, i, 326, 329.
[4] Sibbald, *History*, 28.
[5] Vol. xviii (1796), 225.

height of 5 ft. 6 in. above the water; they are supported by a pier 12 ft. 9 in. wide with a cut-water on its upstream face. The span of the S. arch is 47 ft. 6 in. and its height above the springing-line 10 ft. 2 in.; corresponding figures for the N. arch, which is inset 7 in. from either face and is heavily chamfered, are 22 ft. 6 in. and 5 ft. The top of the parapet over the S. arch is 21 ft. 6 in. above the water and over the N. arch 17 ft.

Set in the W. face of the bridge, over the S. arch, there is a stone bearing the date 1695 incised in large figures of the period; they strongly resemble those on the stone at St. Mirren's Well (No. 542). To the N. of this is another inscribed stone, perhaps once recording a mortification but now seriously damaged; of its upper three lines no more can be read than . . . . ON / . . . . N / . . . . . [?S] . . . . . D, after which it continues THIS BRIG THE / SOVME OF THRE H/VNDRED MARKS. North of this again is a stone inscribed REBUILT 1715, the 7 having a crossbar; and above the stone first mentioned is another with the inscription REBUILT 1907.

741835 NS 78 SW 16 September 1953

467. Low Bridge, Gonachan. This bridge, which was built in 1750,[1] carries the highway across the Endrick Water 750 yds. E. of Fintry Church (No. 169). It consists of a main arch with a smaller one at its S. end, both defined by drip-moulds (Pl. 224 B). The span of the main arch is 51 ft. 6 in. in breadth and rises 14 ft. above the springing, which in turn is 3 ft. 6 in. above low-water level. The height from the tabling of the parapet in the centre of the arch to the water is 23 ft. The keystone on the downstream side is decorated with a palmette surmounted by a panel dated [1]75[0], and above there is a defaced human mask; the upstream keystone shows the palmette only. Very similar keystones are to be seen at Edinbellie Church (No. 168), Killearn Church (No. 161) and elsewhere in the district. The smaller arch springs, on the cut-water of the pier, 5 ft. above the water; its rise above the springing is 3 ft. 3 in. and its span 18 ft. Numerous masons' marks are to be seen on the voussoirs of both arches. The breadth of the roadway between the parapets is 11 ft., splaying out to 17 ft. 6 in. at the ends. The total length of the bridge, including the splays, is 98 ft.

This bridge is on the line of the old road from Glasgow by Campsie[2]; its newer counterpart, in Fintry village, is mentioned under No. 468.

633863 NS 68 NW 3 October 1952

468. Bridge, Fintry. The bridge that carries the Fintry-Kippen highway over the Endrick Water in Fintry village is a somewhat undistinguished structure of three arches (Pl. 226 A), built in 1804.[3] It must thus have quickly superseded the first bridge built at this site, a four-arched structure which dated from about 1792 and was one of a number of local improvements undertaken at that time.[4] With the pilasters on the piers, the projecting course marking out the voussoirs, and the string-courses at the springing-line and above the arches, it exemplifies a type of bridge which was evidently in local favour at the turn of the 18th and 19th centuries.

615868 NS 68 NW ("Fintry Bridge") 28 August 1952

469. Moss Bridge. A document of 1732[5] mentions a stone bridge over the Blane Water, then newly built, which was evidently situated at Moss, and there is no reason to doubt that the existing bridge, though patched and partly reconstructed, is the one in question. It is of very plain construction, of large rubble with cut voussoirs and coping-stones; much of the coping has been renewed, but the joints in both the old and new portions are joggled. The total length of the bridge, over its splayed approaches, is 70 ft., and its breadth over the parapets is 11 ft. 6 in.; the roadway is thus only 9 ft. 2 in. wide. The arch, which has sagged from its original height and is now strengthened with iron straps, has a span of 26 ft. and springs at a height of 2 ft. above the flood level of the stream.

515839 NS 58 SW 26 June 1958

470. Bridges on the Rowardennan Road. With the improvement of the Rowardennan road (No. 520) as a highway, the bridges originally built on its line[6] have naturally had to be widened and strengthened. A nucleus of original construction, however, can be seen from place to place, and details of two bridges were recorded as exemplifying the local work of the later 18th century. One of these, at Blairvockie Cottage (377964), seems to have been rather sharply humped, its arch having a span of 11 ft. with a height of 3 ft. above the springing-line, which is itself 2 ft. 6 in. above the water. The other, over the Cashell Burn (395941), is flatter; its span is 17 ft. 6 in., but its arch, which springs at 3 ft. 6 in. above the water, is only 3 ft. 6 in. high. Both were approximately 14 ft. wide over all before they were widened, and would thus have provided a carriage-way of 11 ft. or less.

377964, 395941 N vii S.W., N xiii 4 May 1954

471. Railway Viaduct, Avonbank. The viaduct that carries the branch line from Manuel Junction to Bo'ness over the ravine of the River Avon, 300 yds. E. of Avonbank, deserves to be mentioned among the early railway constructions, as this branch was originally built as part

1 *Strathendrick*, 259.
2 *Stat. Acct.*, xi (1794), 380. On this road see pp. 425 ff.
3 *Strathendrick*, 261.
4 *Stat. Acct.*, xi (1794), 379 f.
5 H.M. General Register House, Duntreath Writs, No. 678 (1732).
6 Mentioned in *Stat. Acct.*, ix (1793), 24.

of the Slamannan and Borrowstounness Joint Railway, authorised in 1846. The viaduct is about 135 yds. in length by 25 ft. in breadth, and consists (Pl. 229 B) of six segmental arches with a span of 51 ft. and rising 20 ft. above the springing-line. The arches are borne on tapering piers of rock-faced, block-in-course masonry with string-courses at the springing-line, the voussoirs being of droved ashlar with V-channelled joints. Below the wall-head there runs a cornice, and the wall-head course supports an iron handrail. The river runs between the second and third piers from the N., 80 ft. below the level of the road-bed; these piers are intaken at 6 ft., and again at 11 ft., above the water, and have shallow rounded cut-waters both upstream and downstream. The other piers, which are founded on the steeply-sloping sides of the valley, show no intakes. The terminal arches abut on the ramps of the railway embankment.

The left bank of the river, on the downstream side of the viaduct, is revetted with stone blocks showing seatings for the chairs that evidently held the rails of the earliest line (cf. No. 559).

967785 NS 97 NE 21 April 1956

472. Avon Viaduct. The Avon Viaduct (Pl. 229 A), which spans the valley of the Avon between Linlithgow and Manuel stations, is an original feature of the Edinburgh and Glasgow Railway (cf. No. 558) opened in 1842. It is 442 yds. long and consists of a main arcade of twenty segmental arches each with a span of 50 ft., with a subsidiary one containing three arches of 20-ft. span which rise from the sloping end of the E. abutment. The river runs under the fourth and fifth arches from the E. end of the main arcade, the springing-line being 66 ft., the underside of the arches 82 ft., and the top of the masonry 92 ft. above the water level.[1] The masonry of the piers is block-in-course, and they measure 28 ft. by 7 ft. above the intake that occurs just above the ground at the W. end and is repeated throughout the arcade at the same level; the ends of the main arcade are emphasised by shallow buttresses applied to the westernmost pier and to the junction between the easternmost pier and the adjoining 20-ft. arch. The piers have plain capitals, and a string-course runs from end to end at the wall-head; above this rises the brickwork that retains the road-bed, and a heavy iron railing.

979769-983769 NS 97 NE ("Viaduct") 6 March 1953

473. Railway Viaduct, Manuel. An area of low ground lying about a quarter of a mile N. of Manuel House is crossed by the viaduct, now disused, that once carried the Slamannan and Borrowstounness Joint Railway (cf. No. 558). The Manuel Burn passes under the viaduct at its NE. end and the Crownerland Burn near its centre. As the railway was authorised in 1846, the viaduct must have been built very soon after that date.

The structure is approximately 250 yds. long,[2] and contains twenty-three arches. The masonry of both piers and superstructure is rock-faced block-in-course, the piers have dressed V-channelled quoins, and the parapet finishes in a flat coping; but the archivolts are of brick, the general appearance is undistinguished, and the whole work compares poorly with either the Avon Viaduct (No. 472), of 1842, or with the aqueduct of the Union Canal (No. 474), of about 1820. The piers, which taper slightly, are spaced with their centres 35 ft. apart; their basal thickness varies, on account of their taper, with changes in the level of the ground, but may be taken as averaging just under 6 ft. The transverse breadth of the work is 15 ft. 9 in. The highest arch—the one that spans the Crownerland Burn—springs at a height above the water of 32 ft., and rises 9 ft. 6 in. above the springing-line; its total height, to the parapet, is 48 ft. Where the ground is higher, however, these figures are naturally smaller; for example, the arch that spans the road from Linlithgow Bridge to Maddiston springs only 25 ft. above the surface of the road. The two terminal arches abut, to NE. and NW. respectively, on the ends of earthwork embankments.

966765-967767 NS 97 NE ("Viaduct") 12 April 1955

474. Avon Aqueduct. The Avon Aqueduct carries the Union Canal (No. 553) across the valley of the Avon some 600 yds. NNE. of Muiravonside House. It is a dignified and interesting structure (Pl. 228), built between 1818 and 1822, but a view of it is difficult to obtain as the valley is here steep-sided, sinuous and partly wooded. Including the splayed-out ends, where the narrower waterway of the aqueduct expands to the normal breadth of the canal, the structure measures just over 270 yds. in length by 23 ft. 8 in. in breadth and stands 86 ft. above the observed water-level of the river. The aqueduct proper, within the splayed ends, is supported by twelve segmental arches of 50-ft. span, which spring 50 ft. above the water level and rise 25 ft. above their springing-line. The piers, which are hollow, taper slightly on all faces; basal measurements taken on the fifth pier from the W. end at ground level—*i.e.* about 10 ft. above the water at the foot of the fourth pier—gave a breadth of 37 ft. 8 in. and a thickness of 12 ft. 7 in. Flat, tapering buttresses carry on the lines of the piers upwards across the face of the superstructure, which shows one string-course above the arches and another at the wall-head. The tops of the buttresses rise 5 ft. 6 in. above the wall-head, and the spaces between them are filled by heavy iron balustrades having uprights of X section. The masonry is block-in-course, rock-faced at quoins, voussoirs and string-courses. The upper surface carries, along its outer edges, stone bases 12 in. thick for the balustrades and, inside these, stone-paved tow-paths 4 ft. wide. The waterway consists of an iron trough, such as was first used by

[1] The Commissioners are indebted for these figures to the District Engineer, British Railways, Edinburgh.

[2] This figure was taken from the 6-inch O.S. map.

Telford for the Pont Cysyllte aqueduct on the Ellesmere Canal[1]; this trough measures 13 ft. in width, exclusive of the wooden fenders with which it is provided, and 6 ft. in depth in so far as its silted bottom permitted accurate measurement. Access to the interior of the superstructure, under the trough, is obtained through a small doorway 3 ft. high by 2 ft. 6 in. wide, which is situated in the N. face just W. of the westernmost pier.

965758-968757 NS 97 NE ("Aqueduct") 12 June 1953

475. Railway Viaduct, Camelon. This viaduct carries the line of what was originally the Edinburgh and Glasgow Railway (cf. No. 558) over the hollow up which the Union Canal (No. 553) once mounted, by a ladder of locks, from its junction with the Forth and Clyde Canal (No. 552) at Camelon. It consists of an arcade of six arches, finishing at either end on an earthwork embankment; the masonry is block-in-course with V-channelled quoins, and the piers are intaken at the base and have shallow tapering buttresses. A moulded cornice runs along the base of the parapet. The work is 384 ft. long between the faces of the abutments and 26 ft. wide between the parapets. The spans of the arches, in order from E. to W., are 130 ft., 20 ft., 64 ft., 20 ft., 15 ft. 8 in. and 15 ft. 8 in.; the height of the highest, the easternmost, is 44 ft. to the soffit.[2] The Union Canal passed under the easternmost arch, and this necessitated the construction of so wide a span.

866795 NS 87 NE ("Viaduct") 15 May 1955

476. Railway Viaduct, Castlecary. This viaduct carries the line of what was originally the Edinburgh and Glasgow Railway (cf. No. 558) over the valley of the Red Burn, near Castle Cary. It consists of an arcade 583 ft. long between the faces of the abutments and 26 ft. 9 in. wide between the parapets. There are eight arches each spanning 50 ft., the height of the highest one to the soffit being 88 ft. 3 in. above the water.[2] In style this viaduct closely resembles the one over the River Avon, described under No. 472.

788782 NS 77 NE ("Viaduct") 18 May 1955

477. Bridge of Offers (Site). No structure remains at the site of this bridge, a quarter of a mile NW. of Gargunnock Station; but boulders and large stones, some set and some tumbled, extend in a broad belt across the river-bed, some of the tumbled stones having apparently been squared, as if for use in regular masonry. It is on record[3] that the bridge "was never anything more than a heap of stones in the centre of the river; between which and each bank were laid logs of wood, thus forming a rude bridge, but which was inevitably washed away by the first flood. It was used by the natives in this neighbourhood up to the time of building the suspension bridge, for the purpose of carting the peats from Kincardine Moss, and after the peat season was past the bridge was removed until the following season with the exception of one plank which was left for foot passengers. . . . All that now remains of this once celebrated bridge are the stones in the centre which can almost be seen when the water is very low. . . ." The appearance of some dressed stones suggests that the original structure, "part of the ruins" of which were visible in 1841,[4] may have been more elaborate than the foregoing description suggests, and a comparison may be made with the bridge at Bridgend, in Melrose parish.[5]

712954 NS 79 NW 24 August 1952

478. Bridge, Kildean (Site). In the earlier editions of the 6-inch O.S. map the site of a bridge over the Forth is marked in Gothic character at Kildean farm, but in the current edition this item has been omitted. There is no good reason to believe in the former existence of a bridge at this point,[6] as the stonework that was being removed from the river-bed in the middle of the 19th century[7] seems to have been the bottoming of a ford; while the question has no doubt also been obscured by confused statements made at various times about the Roman crossing (cf. No. 124) as well as about the earlier position of Stirling Bridge (No. 455). No trace of construction can be seen at Kildean today, and the river can still be forded at times just upstream from the farm.

783951 NS 79 NE (unnoted) 17 August 1952

479. Denny Bridge (Site). Slight traces of an earlier bridge over the River Carron, linking Denny with Dunipace, are to be seen in some fragments of masonry just upstream from the left-bank abutment of the existing structure. This older bridge is presumably the one that was taken down in 1828, "being considered unfit, from its height and narrowness, for the wheel-carriages of the present day".[8] A bridge is on record at Denny in 1707[9] and again in 1723,[10] the second of these references stating that it had two arches.

807830 NS 88 SW (unnoted) 24 June 1954

---

[1] Rolt, L. T. C., *Thomas Telford* (1958), 44. The Pont Cysyllte aqueduct was opened in 1805 (*ibid.*), 56.
[2] The Commissioners are indebted to the British Transport Commissioners for these dimensions.
[3] Ordnance Survey Name Book, Gargunnock parish, 23 f.
[4] *N.S.A.*, viii (Stirlingshire), 52.
[5] *Inventory of Roxburghshire*, No. 593.
[6] See *S.H.R.*, ii (1905), 486 f.
[7] *T.S.N.H.A.S.* (1904-5), 49.
[8] *N.S.A.*, viii (Stirlingshire), 386.
[9] Sibbald, *History*, 28.
[10] *Geogr. Collections*, i, 332.

MISCELLANEOUS EARTHWORKS AND ENCLOSURES

480. Earthwork, Peel of Claggans. The slight remains of this structure lie on the right bank of the Claggans Burn, a quarter of a mile SE. of the bridge that carries the road from Gartmore to Dalmary over the burn, and at a height of a little under 100 ft. O.D. All that can now be seen is a shallow ditch in the form of an arc 300 ft. in length. The NE. end of the arc rests on the bank of the burn, and originally the ditch no doubt continued to rejoin the bank at a point about 300 ft. lower down, thus forming a D-shaped enclosure measuring about 300 ft. along the chord by about 200 ft. transversely.

The account of this monument in the Ordnance Survey Name Book[1] states that the tenant of the ground said that "he took up part of the foundation of what appeared to have been a strong building", and that the stones were "roughly hewn and squared".

521965 NS 59 NW 8 October 1952

481. Earthwork, Ballochneck. Scarcely anything is now visible of the earthwork, formerly known as the "Keir of Cashley", which is situated on the left bank of the Ballochneck Burn, 200 yds. ESE. of Allen farmhouse. It occupies a natural, steep-sided mound some 40 ft. in height, the top of which consists of an uneven but generally level area measuring about 65 ft. in diameter. Round the margin of the top there are very slight remains of a bank, while on the SW. flank, 6 ft. below the crest, there is a broad terrace 35 ft. in length which may or may not be artificial. Old farm-tracks traverse the lower slopes of the mound on the NW., N. and NE.

The superficial resemblance between this earthwork and the Keir Knowe of Drum (No. 187) suggests that it may have been a motte (cf. Introduction, p. 41).

556929 NS 59 SE ("Keir") 15 October 1952

482. Earthwork, Arngibbon. This earthwork, 550 yds. E. of Wester Blairgorts farmhouse, is situated at a height of about 170 ft. O.D. on a promontory which is formed by the confluence of a nameless right-bank tributary with the Arngibbon Burn. The site is strongly protected by nature on three sides, where the flanks of the promontory fall steeply for some 35 ft. to stream level, and the only easy access is across level ground from the E. Subrectangular on plan (Fig. 172), the earthwork measures internally 135 ft. in length by about 70 ft. in width, and has been defended by a single rampart with the addition of an external ditch at the E. end. In its original state the rampart was no doubt continuous along the N. and S. margins of the promontory, but it has been almost completely obliterated on these sides. At the W. end it is clearly visible in the form of a scarp, 8 ft. in height, but the best preserved sector is on the E., where it measures no less than 40 ft. in thickness at the base and stands to a height of 8 ft. internally and 12 ft. above the bottom of the ditch. The ditch is 18 ft. in width but is not more than 2 ft. in depth at the present time. A modern track which crosses the site is clearly responsible for the gap in the rampart on the W. side, and the original entrance is indicated by interruptions in both the bank and ditch on the opposite (E.) side, close to the N. margin of the promontory. The work, which is probably of mediaeval date (cf. Introduction, p. 51), is covered with trees and shrubs, and shows no superficial remains of internal buildings.

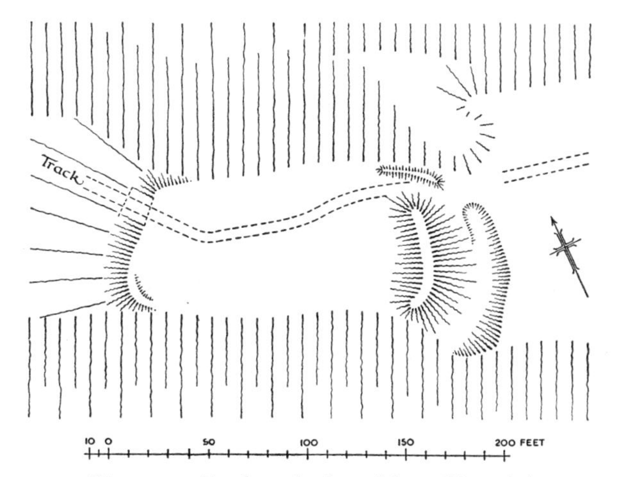

Fig. 172. Earthwork, Arngibbon (No. 482)

599939 NS 59 SE (unnoted) 28 March 1956

483. Earthwork, Keir Knowe of Arnmore. This earthwork is situated 400 yds. SE. of the Mains of Arnprior at a height of 320 ft. O.D. To N. and E. the adjacent ground is level, but it falls gently away to S. and W. The remains of the earthwork (Fig. 173), which

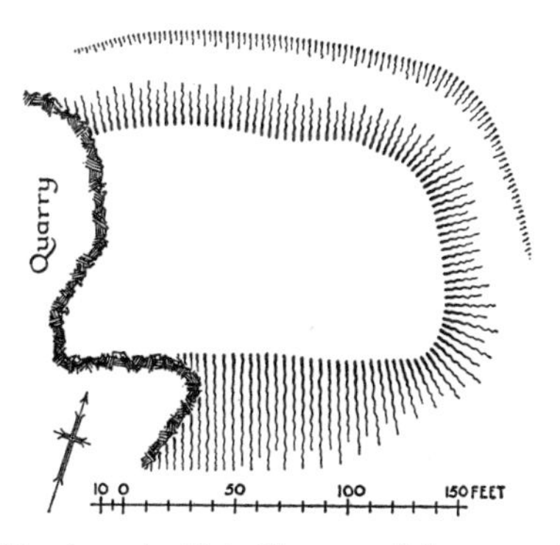

Fig. 173. Earthwork, Keir Knowe of Arnmore (No. 483)

[1] Drymen parish, 29.

have been under the plough, consist of a subrectangular level area, measuring 170 ft. in length by 100 ft. in breadth, bounded to the N. and E. by a ditch about 45 ft. in width and to the S. by the natural slope. The western end has been destroyed by a quarry. No traces of a bank can now be seen along the inner lip of the ditch or on the crest of the slope to the S. On the N. side, where it is best preserved, the ditch has a maximum depth of 2 ft. 9 in. below the inner lip and 1 ft. below the outer lip. The appearance of the work suggests that it is of mediaeval, rather than prehistoric, date.

621942 NS 69 SW 14 October 1952

484. Earthwork, Dasher. This earthwork, 700 yds. ENE. of Dasher farmhouse, stands at a height of about 150 ft. O.D., on the brink of the defile, some 80 ft. in depth, in which the Boquhan Burn flows N. towards its confluence with the River Forth. The earthwork is sub-oval on plan (Fig. 174) and measures 125 ft. from E. to

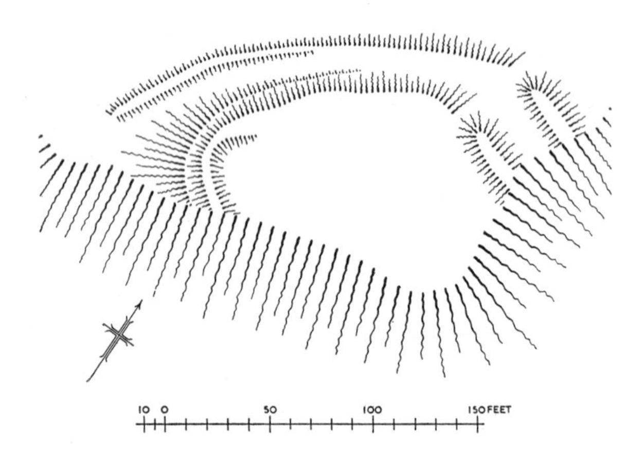

Fig. 174. Earthwork, Dasher (No. 484)

W. by a maximum of 80 ft. transversely. The NW. half is defended by two rubble ramparts, but any similar fortifications which may have existed in the SE. half have been destroyed by erosion of the face of the defile. Both ramparts are in a dilapidated condition, appearing either as low banks or simply as scarps; narrow gaps in each one, on the NNE., probably represent the original entrance. The interior is covered with bracken and shows no sign of buildings.

It is possible that, to S. and E., the defile itself was considered by the builders of the earthwork as sufficient for defensive purposes, and that the structure was thus a form of promontory fortification, possibly of mediaeval date.

668942 NS 69 SE (unnoted) 22 November 1956

485. Earthwork, Keir Hill of Dasher. This earthwork (Fig. 175) is situated about a quarter of a mile NE. of Kippen and 100 yds. NE. of Cuthbertston Cottage. It stands on a rocky promontory on the left bank of the Cuthbertston Burn at a height of 110 ft. O.D. It measures internally 135 ft. from E. to W. by 100 ft. transversely, and is defined partly by a stony bank measuring up to 33 ft. in thickness and 4 ft. in height, and partly by the crest of the steep rocky bank of the burn. At the E.

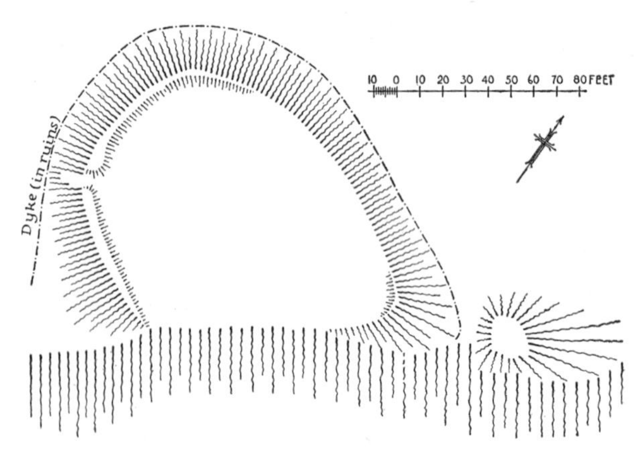

Fig. 175. Earthwork, Keir Hill of Dasher (No. 485)

apex the bank is accompanied by an external ditch which cuts off the tip of the promontory; the height from the bottom of the ditch to the crest of the bank is 14 ft. 6 in., while that to the outer lip is 2 ft. 6 in. A gap in the W. side of the earthwork, 5 ft. in width, presumably represents the original entrance. The interior has been under cultivation and is featureless.

The date and purpose of the work are unknown, but it is reported in the Ordnance Survey Name Book[1] that "on this hill it is supposed that the old church stood, which was dedicated to St. Mauvais, who is the tutelary Saint of this Parish, and the hill is frequently called the Kirk Hill on this account; but there are no records of this being the case, it is merely traditional".[2] An alternative possibility is that it was a motte (cf. Introduction, p. 40).

653951 23 June 1952
NS 69 NE ("Keir Hill of Dasher" in ordinary type)

486. Enclosure, Spout of Ballochleam. This enclosure is situated at a height of about 950 ft. O.D. one mile S. of the farmhouse of Easter Glinns, and 200 yds. W. of the Spout of Ballochleam. D-shaped on plan, it lies on a shelf at the foot of a sheer rock-face 80 ft. in height, and is formed by an arc of ruinous wall which springs from the base of the rock. The wall is about 3 ft. in thickness, constructed loosely of boulders, and encloses an uneven, grass-covered area measuring 80 ft. from WNW. to

[1] Kippen parish, 22.
[2] Cf. Nos. 171 and 545.

ESE. by 45 ft. transversely. There is a gap 3 ft. in width in the W. arc which probably represents an entrance. The date and purpose of this structure, which may be compared with No. 488, are unknown.

Immediately to the WNW. a subrectangular area measuring 140 ft. by 60 ft. has been cleared of boulders, but it has never, apparently, been surrounded by a wall.

651900 NS 69 SE (unnoted) 29 January 1958

487. Enclosure, Touch Muir. This enclosure is situated on open moorland 100 yds. WNW. of the dun (No. 85). A few large boulders appearing among scattered rubble indicate the course of a ruinous stone wall which appears originally to have measured about 4 ft. in thickness. The area enclosed measures 57 ft. in length from NW. to SE. by 47 ft. transversely. Two fallen boulders in the SE. arc may mark the position of the entrance. The enclosure is featureless, and may have been a fold, possibly belonging to the dun.

723919 NS 79 SW (unnoted) 4 July 1955

488. Enclosure, Dumyat. This structure is situated at a height of 800 ft. O.D. close to the right bank of a nameless burn which runs down the NW. flank of Dumyat into the W. end of the Lossburn Reservoir. D-shaped on plan, it lies on a sloping shelf between the burn and a sheer rock-face 20 ft. in height, and is formed by an arc of ruinous wall which springs from the base of the rock. The opposite ends of the wall join the rock at points 55 ft. apart, and the greatest width of the enclosure, measured from E. to W., is 60 ft. The remains of the wall consist of a few large, earthfast boulders protruding from a grass-grown, stony mound, with a gap in the W. arc which probably represents the entrance. The interior is uneven and featureless except for a line of rubble about 30 ft. in length which runs W. from a point on the rock-face 27 ft. S. of the N. end of the wall. The date and purpose of this structure are unknown.

827984 NS 89 NW (unnoted) 28 September 1956

489. Enclosure, Cowie. This enclosure, first discovered on an air-photograph, is situated at a height of about 170 ft. O.D., on the end of a low ridge which runs W. from the fort (No. 72) on the summit of the Berry Hills. It is formed by an earthen bank, now incomplete, and measures internally about 60 ft. from E. to W. by about 50 ft. transversely. The bank is best preserved where it crosses the ridge, being here about 2 ft. in height and spread to a thickness of about 12 ft. The remaining stretches are of insignificant proportions. No entrance is apparent, and there are no internal features.

834892 NS 88 NW (unnoted) 12 March 1952

490. Earthwork, Wester Barnego. This earthwork (Fig. 176), 200 yds. S. of the ruined farmhouse at Wester Barnego, is situated at a height of a little over 500 ft. O.D. on the NW. end of a rocky promontory which projects from the NE. side of the valley of the River Carron. It

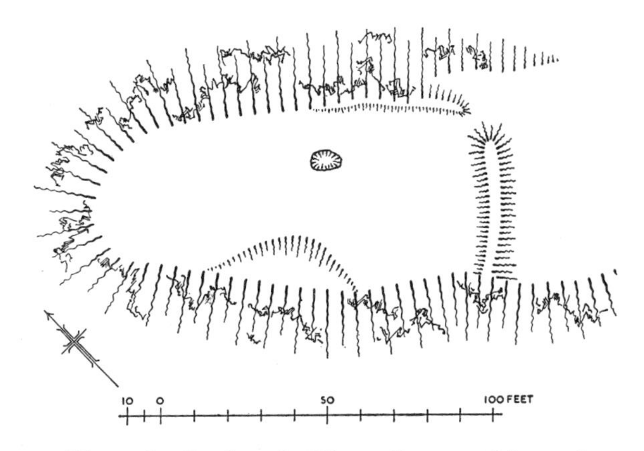

Fig. 176. Earthwork, Wester Barnego (No. 490)

has been made by drawing a bank of earth and stones across the promontory, thereby isolating a subrectangular area which measures 110 ft. from NW. to SE. by 50 ft. transversely. Traces of the bank can be seen returning north-westwards along the NE. margin of the promontory, and no doubt it was originally continuous round all four sides of the enclosure; where best preserved it measures 3 ft. in height and 14 ft. in thickness at the base. The entrance is situated on the E. and is 5 ft. in width.

The interior of the earthwork is uneven and contains only a steep-sided depression measuring 9 ft. in length, 5 ft. in width and about 1 ft. in depth. A strong growth of rushes in the bottom suggests that this may have been a water-hole.

783839 NS 78 SE (unnoted) 15 April 1954

491. Earthwork, Easter Glinns. Some slight remains of an earthwork can be seen on the natural knoll, known as Keir Knowe, that lies 500 yds. due W. of Easter Glinns farmhouse. The knoll is some 14 ft. in height, is oval on plan, and has a flat top measuring about 90 ft. in length from E. to W. by 60 ft. transversely; the sides are steep except to the E., where there is a gentle slope down from the crest to a small unnamed burn. At intervals round the margin of the summit area there are traces of a turf-covered bank measuring about 10 ft. in width but not more than 2 ft. in height, while three terraces of varying sizes, which occupy the greater part of the E. flank of the knoll, may represent the remains of additional ramparts. The work may have been a motte, comparable with the one at Drum (No. 187).

645915 NS 69 SW ("Keir Knowe" in ordinary type) 15 October 1952

492. Earthwork, Keir Brae of Garden (Site). It is recorded[1] that "the marks of some ancient military work", in the form of an oval rampart, once stood at a height of a little over 100 ft. O.D. on the highest point of the ridge 300 yds. ENE. of Keirbrae farmhouse. All traces of the work had however vanished by 1860,[2] and at the date of visit the site was occupied by a felled plantation.

588946 NS 59 SE (unnoted) 7 December 1953

493. Earthwork, Lower Greenyards (Site). This earthwork formerly stood 600 yds. SW. of Lower Greenyards farmhouse at a height of 100 ft. O.D. Its position was on a low promontory, the flat surface of which measures about 200 ft. in width from E. to W. by a similar distance from N. to S. It is bounded to E., W. and N. by gentle, grassy slopes, that to the W. falling to the right bank of an unnamed burn and the others to marshy land. A level field adjoins the site to the S. No remains are visible on the surface today, but crop-markings on National Survey air-photographs[3] indicate that the promontory was cut off from the adjacent ground by two ditches, about 70 ft. apart, which ran in an arc across the neck of the promontory for a distance of about 200 ft. Each ditch is accompanied externally by a very narrow, dark line which may represent a palisade. The entrance may have been towards the E. end of the defences.

816904 NS 89 SW (unnoted) 30 August 1955

494. Earthwork, Hill of Dunmore (Site). A nearly circular earthwork, with an external diameter of about 450 ft., can be seen on National Survey air-photographs[4] on the top of the Hill of Dunmore, 400 yds. SE. of the mansion of Dunmore Park and at a height of a little under 100 ft. O.D. The earthwork has been wrecked by ploughing, the planting of trees, and quarrying; and at the date of visit the only visible remains were a stretch of bank and outer ditch on the NW. arc, about 40 yds. in length, both so dilapidated as to be barely perceptible. The remains start on the N. side of a farm-track which crosses the site from E. to W., and run NW. from that point.

886889 NS 88 NE (unnoted) 6 October 1952

495. Earthwork, Gallamuir (Site). Crop-markings on National Survey air-photographs[5] reveal the double ditches of an oval earthwork on cultivated land, 250 yds. ESE. of Gallamuir farmhouse and at a height of about 150 ft. O.D. No traces of this structure can normally be seen on the surface, but at the date of visit, when the site was covered with wheat stubble, stretches of both ditches were clearly visible, as shown on the plan (Fig. 177), by reason of the stronger growth of the stubble overlying them. The ditches are from 20 ft. to 30 ft. apart, and the enclosed area measures 300 ft. from ESE.

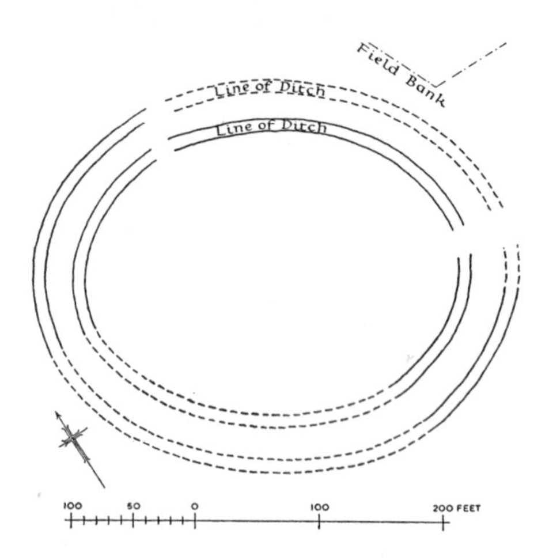

Fig. 177. Earthwork, Gallamuir (No. 495)

to WNW. by about 240 ft. transversely. Two narrow gaps in the inner ditch, on the N. and E. arcs respectively, may represent original entrances.

845877 NS 88 NW (unnoted) 15 October 1951

496. Enclosure, Bonnywood (Site). The farm of Bonnywood is situated on a rounded knoll which rises to a height of a little over 100 ft. O.D. When the top of the knoll was being levelled in 1888, in preparation for the building of the steading, a large hollow was observed "showing a circular formation about 50 to 60 feet in diameter, the surrounding margin being at least 9 inches higher than the interior".[6] No further details are recorded, but it is possible that the enclosure may have been an early homestead or settlement since a complete rotary quern was found in 1911 in the bed of a stream 60 yds. SE. of the site.[7] The quern is at present on loan to Falkirk Burgh Museum.

828809 NS 88 SW (unnoted) 24 November 1956

497. Earthwork, Middle Bankhead (Site). This earthwork, 300 yds. NNE. of Middle Bankhead farmhouse, was situated at a height of 350 ft. O.D. on a narrow ridge running from ENE. to WNW. No remains are now

1 *Stat. Acct.*, xviii (1796), 329.
2 Ordnance Survey Name Book, Kippen parish, 46.
3 540/RAF/1645, F 22, 0274-5.
4 106 G/SCOT/UK 85, 3390-1.
5 CPE/SCOT/UK 251, 5083-4.
6 *P.S.A.S.*, xlvi (1911-12), 367-9.
7 *Ibid.*; *Smith Institute Catalogue*, No. KA 40, 41.

visible on the ground, but double ditches are clearly revealed by crop-markings on National Survey air-photographs.[1] The inner ditch encloses an oval area measuring about 210 ft. in length from ENE. to WSW. by about 180 ft. transversely, and the outer ditch lies about 25 ft. outside it. At the narrow gap in the SSE. arc, which probably represents the original entrance, the ditches appear to turn towards one another and unite. The ENE. arc of the outer ditch is covered by the road that approaches Middle Bankhead farm from the NW., but otherwise the whole structure lies in the open field SW. of the road.

807807 NS 88 SW (unnoted) 11 September 1952

498. Earthwork, Bankier (Site). This structure, stated by Gordon to have occupied the top of a hill "opposite to Castlecarey",[2] was considered by the parish minister of Kilsyth in 1796 to have been the most important monument of its kind in the vicinity, on account both of its position and of its strength.[3] Gordon's description and illustration[4] indicate that the main defence was a rampart of earth and stone and not a stone wall; and this is further substantiated by the report that trees were then planted upon it. The rampart measured about 20 ft. in height and about 120 ft. in diameter, and was surrounded by a ditch about 24 ft. in width. The interior was paved with flat stones, and the entrance was on the E. Cottages built in the interior had increased the damage done to the remains by the trees on the rampart, but Gordon's account describes a structure which corresponds very closely to a type of mediaeval earthwork exemplified, for instance, by that at Scraesburgh, in Roxburghshire.[5]

Gordon does not locate the earthwork precisely, but Roy[6] marks "Bankier Castle" a few hundred yards S. of "Hollin Buss" (Hollandbush). This corresponds with the place marked on the O.S. map as Hillhead, 280 yds. SE. of Bankier House, where there is an isolated round-topped hill upon which, until recently, there was a group of cottages and a circular enclosure-wall. These have now given way to part of a housing estate, and it has been reported that some sherds of 16th-century pottery were found when excavations for this were proceeding. It is almost certain that this was the site of the earthwork.

The unknown author whose note is preserved by Macfarlane[7] concludes his list with a structure "over against Castle Carry at Dunglass". No place bearing this name has been noted in the lands N. of Castle Cary, and it might have been thought that the name Dunglass was applied to the structure at Bankier; but Pont includes in his inventory[8] two names, "Bankyr" and "Dunbass", and despite the difference in spelling between "Dunglass" and "Dunbass", it may be supposed that both referred to one and the same structure and that therefore Bankier was distinct from this. Sibbald shows "Banker" at this place.[9]

784790 NS 77 NE (unnoted) 19 June 1954

499. Earthwork, East Carlestoun (Site). This earthwork was situated 300 yds. SSW. of East Carlestoun farmhouse, on a low hill the summit of which attains a height of nearly 200 ft. O.D. The flanks of the hill slope gently down to level ground in all directions except to the NNW., where a steep scarp falls to the Red Burn. While no signs of the earthwork appear on the ground, National Survey air-photographs[10] show traces of three ditches in the form of crop-markings. The outer pair, which lie about 30 ft. apart, run round the gentler slopes of the hill and rest at either end on the left bank of the Red Burn. They enclose a D-shaped area which measures about 300 ft. in length from ENE. to WSW. by about 170 ft. transversely. Slight indications suggest entrances in the ENE. arcs of both these ditches. The third ditch lies higher up the hill and is not strictly concentric with the other two. It rests at either end on the scarp, which here forms the left bank of the burn, and encloses an area measuring about 160 ft. in length from ENE. to WSW. by about 90 ft. transversely. There may have been an entrance in the SE. arc.

629745 NS 67 SW (unnoted) 6 July 1955

OLD CULTIVATIONS

500. Cultivation Terraces, Sauchieburn House. The slight remains of what appears to be a group of cultivation terraces are situated on the N. slope of the valley of an unnamed stream which rises near Middlethird and joins the Sauchie Burn in Stockbridge Plantation. The terraces are distant a quarter of a mile NNE. of Sauchieburn House at an elevation of 300 ft. O.D. Observations on the ground and on air-photographs[11] suggest that four terraces ran from W. to E., parallel to the stream, for a distance of about 500 ft. on the S. flank of a knoll; and that three or four other terraces ran from NW. to SE. on the N. flank of the same knoll, the two groups merging at their E. extremities. In this they recall the groups of terraces that occur at the junction of the Buckie Burn with the River Carron (No. 501).

776896 NS 78 NE (unnoted) 22 April 1954

501. Cultivation Terraces, Buckie Burn. This group of terraces is situated on the left bank of Buckie Burn at its confluence with the River Carron, and continues for a

1 CPE/SCOT/UK 256 Part III, 5236-7.
2 *Itin. Septent.*, 22.
3 *Stat. Acct.*, xviii (1796), 295 n.
4 *Loc. cit.*, and pl. iii, 2.
5 *Inventory of Roxburghshire*, No. 466.
6 *Military Antiquities*, pl. xxxv.
7 *Geogr. Collections*, iii, 125.
8 *Ibid.*, ii, 369.
9 Sibbald, *Historical Inquiries*, map facing p. 3.
10 CPE/SCOT/UK 265A, 5121-2.
11 106G/SCOT/UK 93, 4056-7.

short distance on the left bank of the latter. The lowest terrace is close to the burn at an elevation of 500 ft. O.D. and the uppermost lies about 40 ft. above it. The main portion of the group, which is about 430 yds. in length from NW. to SE., contains at least seven terraces which measure up to 30 ft. in breadth by 7 ft. in height. Parts of the terraces have fallen away in land-slips, but the group can be traced round the angle formed by the junction of burn and river and thence eastwards for a distance of 130 yds. At this point a small unnamed stream which runs parallel to Buckie Burn joins the river, and while some of the terraces die out at its mouth two or three turn back to run NW. up its right bank for a distance of 170 yds.

763848 NS 78 SE (unnoted) 24 June 1952

502. Cultivation Terraces, Stenhouse. There are two cultivation terraces, varying in breadth with the steepness of the slope, in the corner of the Stenhouse policies, WSW. of the house (No. 200). Cf. also No. 513.

878829 NS 88 SE (unnoted) 3 December 1957

503. Cultivation Terraces, Avonbank. These terraces lie on the N. and E. slopes of a sandy knoll which is situated 400 yds. W. of Avonbank farmhouse and attains an elevation of a little over 200 ft. O.D. The slight remains of four terraces can be traced; two are close together near the bottom of the slope and the other two, more widely spaced, lie above them. These terraces, described as being at Sighthill, and two adjacent groups (Nos. 504 and 505), are referred to as remains of fortifications in *The New Statistical Account.*[1]

It is possible that this hill was once the site of some sort of defensive structure. In the Ordnance Survey Name Book,[2] after a statement that no fort could be seen at the site, the observations continue: "The Works of the Fort would appear to have been constructed of stone; the present tenant of Avonbank having destroyed it about 15 years since for the purpose of obtaining material, in the shape of stone, to erect outhouses; and from which he obtained an ample supply."

961786 NS 97 NE (unnoted) 8 December 1953

504. Cultivation Terraces, Castle Hill, Avonbank. This group of four terraces lies on the N. and E. slopes of a sandy hill which is situated rather more than half a mile ESE. of Avonbank farmhouse and attains an elevation of a little over 200 ft. O.D. The hill is separated from the pasture immediately to the S. by a hedge which lies on the crest of a scarp, and the three upper terraces terminate at or close to the N. side of the hedge. The uppermost one starts at a point 40 ft. above the bottom of the hill and 46 ft. below the summit. It is inclined across the E. slope of the hill, rising and turning through NW. to run W. horizontally across the N. slope; it thus reaches and runs along the level which at this point marks the angle between the gentle slope of the summit area and the steeper slope that forms the N. face of the hill. On the E., before the positive lynchet merges with the summit area, it measures about 5 ft. in width; the negative lynchet rises to a height of 19 ft.

The second terrace runs right round the N. face of the hill from near the hedge on the E. to a point close to the W. end of the hedge. On the NNE. the positive lynchet measures 9 ft. in width and the negative 14 ft. in height. The third terrace starts near the hedge on the E. but ends on the N. slope of the hill; on the NNE. the positive lynchet measures 10 ft. in width and the negative 9 ft. 6 in. in height. The fourth terrace is merged, on the E., with the fence that separates the hill from the adjacent field. It leaves this boundary in the NE. sector and runs thence right round the N. face of the hill, ascending the NW. and W. slopes and eventually joining the W. end of the scarp which, with the hedge, forms the S. boundary of the hill. On the NNE. the positive lynchet measures 18 ft. in width and the negative 6 ft. 6 in. in height.

The top of the hill and the positive lynchets have been planted, but only decaying stumps now remain. It is probable that the remains of a stony bank which border the positive lynchet of the lowest terrace represent a plantation bank.

This group of terraces and the two adjacent groups (Nos. 503 and 505) are mentioned in the *New Statistical Account*,[3] where they are described as the remains of fortifications.

973782 NS 97 NE (unnoted) 8 December 1953

505. Cultivation Terraces, Easter Manuel. This group of four terraces lies, at an elevation of from 170 ft. to 200 ft. O.D., on the N. face of a rough knoll, forming the summit of a low ridge in cultivated ground, about 160 yds. NNW. of Easter Manuel. It is easily visible from the Linlithgow-Falkirk highway. The terraces are now about 190 yds. long, but have been longer; they are comparatively steep and narrow, the positive lynchets being from 5 ft. to 18 ft. wide and the negative ones from 6 ft. to 9 ft. high.

A reference to this group of terraces, in which they are described as lying on "Harlelaw near Easter Manuel", appears in the *New Statistical Account*.[4] The author associates them with two adjacent groups (Nos. 503 and 504), but classes all three as the remains of fortifications.

975774 NS 97 NE (unnoted) 16 August 1952

506. Cultivation Terraces, Clachan of Campsie. The lower and less steep part of the hillside that slopes down

[1] Vol. viii (Stirlingshire), 210.
[2] Muiravonside parish, 53.
[3] Vol. viii (Stirlingshire), 210.
[4] *Ibid.*

from the Lennoxtown-Fintry highway immediately E. of the Clachan of Campsie bears at least nine cultivation terraces on an area measuring some 450 yds. from WNW. to ESE. by 200 yds. transversely. The strips are of irregular length and breadth as they are arranged to suit the lie of the ground, and they curve obliquely across the contours so that in their lower portions the low banks that divide them become negative lynchets. Their surfaces are marked with rigs alined along the axes of the terraces, and above them, on the steeper ground, an air-photograph shows traces of some paddocks or other small enclosures of irregular shape within a head-dyke. The westernmost of the terraces is overrun at its edge by some hollow tracks, but, as the origin of these is uncertain (cf. p. 426), the fact throws no light on the date of the terraces. It is interesting, however, to note a suggestion quoted by the parish historian,[1] that the vanished tower of Balcorrach stood somewhere at the base of this terraced area.

6179 NS 67 NW (unnoted) 11 August 1953

507. Cultivation Terraces, Troughstone. From a point just E. of Troughstone Cottages as far as the E. boundary of the policies of Ballagan House, the lowermost slopes of the hillside, just above the highway, are marked with numerous lengths of terracing, irregularly placed. Though less distinct than those at Campsie (No. 506), they are evidently cultivation terraces which have survived on an area which was unsuitable for other agricultural methods. The negative lynchets are generally up to 2 ft. or 3 ft. high, but one close to Troughstone reaches a height of about 7 ft.

576794 NS 57 NE (unnoted) 11 August 1953

OLD ROADS AND TRYSTS

508. Sheriffmuir Road. Although this is part of the old road from Stirling to Perth,[2] the portion of it that lies within Stirlingshire shows little evidence of antiquity. Traces of an earlier track are, however, to be seen on the NW. side of the cutting through which the road finally comes down to the lower ground at the former site of Pathfoot (805970)[3], where a hollow track appears to have made a precarious descent through a natural cleft in the rocks. The base of this cleft has been cut out, at one point, to a minimum breadth of 5 ft. The drystone walls that flank the upper parts of the road speak clearly of its use for droving[4] after the enclosure of the adjoining lands[5]; they are laid out with singular irregularity, as they enclose a strip of ground which varies in breadth from 20 ft. to as much as 100 ft. (Cf. also No. 546.)

826016-805969 NN 80 SW, NS 89 SW 16 August 1952

509. Old Road, Bridge of Allan to Blairlogie. An old road formerly ran from the crossing of the Allan Water at Bridge of Allan to Blairlogie, Menstrie and eastwards. Parts of its line are still indicated by the lane that diverges from the W. end of Henderson Street and passes behind the houses described under No. 255; by the footpath and lane that pass East Lodge (No. 256) and cross the Sheriffmuir Road (No. 508) at the former site of the village of Pathfoot[6]; and by the track from the old churchyard (No. 127), past Logie Cottage and through Blairlogie Village (No. 257), to the modern highway at Cotkerse.

791975-833968
NS 79 NE, NS 89 NW (indicated but not named)
16 August 1952

510. Military Road from Stirling to Dumbarton. The existing highway B 811 originated in a military road built after the Forty-five to give direct connection between the castles of Stirling and Dumbarton.[7] Roy's map of 1747-55 marks it as "Road from Stirling to Dumbarton". West of Kippen its line, from Drymen Bridge by Drymen, Kepculloch and Buchlyvie, corresponded closely with that of B 811; but between Kippen and a point 230 yds. S. of West Carse it ran at a rather higher level, and is now represented by lengths of by-road and farm tracks passing Boquhan and Leckie and forming the main street of Gargunnock. The E. end seems also to have diverged from the modern line; Taylor and Skinner show it[8] as keeping above the low-lying carse lands and approaching the South Port of Stirling by Cambusbarron. These alterations are noted in the *New Statistical Account.*[9] The existence at Leckie of a 17th-century bridge (No. 453) suggests that in this section, at least, an earlier local road was taken over and adapted by the military engineers.

473874-796931
NS 48 NE, NS 58 NW, NS 59 SW, NS 59 SE, NS 69 SW, NS 69 NW, NS 69 SE, NS 79 SW, NS 79 SE (variously indicated)
Various dates to 1955

511. Old Road from Stirling to Kilsyth and Glasgow. The road that runs from Stirling to Kilsyth by Carron

[1] Cameron, J., *The Parish of Campsie*, 187 f.
[2] Ordnance Survey Name Book, Logie parish, 37.
[3] Taylor and Skinner, in their *Survey and Maps of the Roads of North Britain* (1776), indicate that the Sheriffmuir Road debouched from the hills at Logie Church (816970) and not at this point, but the place-name Pathfoot is suggestive and a cattle-tryst was formerly held at the village (cf. No. 533).
[4] On which see Haldane, A. R. B., *The Drove Roads of Scotland*, 113.
[5] The common land at Sheriffmuir was divided in 1772 (*ibid.*, 52).
[6] Fergusson, R. Menzies, *Logie, A Parish History*, ii, 239.
[7] Chalmers, G., *Caledonia*, vi, 895.
[8] *Survey and Maps of the Roads of North Britain*, pl. 48.
[9] Vol. viii (Stirlingshire), 59.

Bridge must certainly have existed as early as 1695, as this date is inscribed on the bridge (No. 466); and it was probably in use considerably before that time as, for example, Montrose's movement from the Fords of Frew (No. 524) to the battlefield of Kilsyth suggests that it was available in 1645, while the name Carronfoorde on Pont's Map, of the early 17th century[1] is likewise significant. It is marked on Roy's map of 1747-55 with the legend "Road from Glasgow to Stirling", and at Kilsyth it appears to have joined an Edinburgh-Glasgow road probably corresponding with the modern A 803; this route, which is marked on Edgar's map of 1777, was at any rate the principal one between Glasgow and Edinburgh before the opening of the road by Cumbernauld in 1794,[2] and it would likewise have been natural for the Covenanters' gallows described under No. 176 to have been placed beside a much-frequented road.

In Roy's day this route evidently branched off the Stirling-Falkirk line at or near St. Ninians; but its original course at this end has been masked by the complex of modern side-roads and by the construction of an approach to Sauchieburn House and Old Sauchie. This private road, however, no doubt perpetuates its line, and SW. of Old Sauchie it appears in the characteristic form of a flat-bottomed, dug-out roadway, while as it rises from the right bank of the Sauchie Burn (775882) it is flanked by three deep hollow tracks. After passing along the W. end of a strip of plantation, it falls into the line of the access-road from the E. to Sauchie Home Farm, and continues past the steading for three-quarters of a mile until it reaches and crosses a modern by-road near the head of the Auchenbowie Burn (763876). The whole of this stretch has been improved for farm or estate purposes. From the hollow up which the modern by-road runs, it rises south-westwards in a rock-cutting 9 ft. to 12 ft. wide, made without provision for roadside drainage, and further on a much broader and shallower excavation is accompanied by three well-marked hollow tracks as it mounts a steepish pitch. Where the main track passes under a drystone dyke to the moorland it is about 24 ft. wide.

On reaching this area of moorland between Muirpark and Burnside, which is wet and mossy, the road becomes much less definite, but traces of the main hollow can be seen in the moss as it approaches the modern highway from Stirling to Kilsyth. With this it seems to coalesce just W. of Burnside (759868). From this point onwards no further signs of the older roadway appear for nearly five miles, and it must presumably have been obliterated by the modern highway itself or, perhaps, in places by the cultivation of the adjoining ground; but on a very steep pitch between the Banton Burn and Berryhill (729803) a short length of it can be seen cutting a corner and taking an even steeper course than the highway. The line of both roads has evidently been determined here by the necessity of turning the rocky chasm near the head of the Banton Burn. A more considerable divergence takes place about half a mile on, below Brockieside, where the old road can be seen to have crossed the Colzium Burn at 725796, the point where the gully is shallowest and its sides least abrupt, and to have continued thence across Belt Moss and over some rising ground beyond. It reaches the boundary dyke of the cultivated land at a point 150 yds. W. of the Colzium Burn (726790), this course having enabled it to avoid some of the wet, low-lying ground through which the modern highway runs. In the cultivated land it has been ploughed out, but it may well have resumed the existing course of the modern road at the bridge over the Colzium Burn at the head of Colzium Glen.

No further traces can be seen from that point onwards to the town of Kilsyth, but the topography hardly seems to admit of any other course than that now followed by the modern road.

c. 788898-*c.* 720781
NS 78 NE, NS 78 SE, NS 78 SW ("Takmadoon Road"), NS 77 NW ("Takmadoon Road")
14 September 1953

512. "Cadgers' Loan", Plean. The name "Cadgers' Loan" is applied, on the O.S. map, to the by-road that flanks the NW. side of the Plean House policies and extends NE. to East Plean and SW. to a minor cross-roads 370 yds. WSW. of Muirmailing. The Ordnance Survey Name Book[3] describes this road, which it states was formerly used for pack-horse traffic, as running "from the Stirling and Falkirk T.P. road, near East Touch-hill, to the Roman road near Muirmailing", and further records that "formerly this was the only road between Airth and Glasgow. This is the only part of it now in existence." No traces of the old roadway can now be seen.

Similar use of an ancient route by "cadgers" (hawkers) has been noted in Roxburghshire and Dumfriesshire.[4]

817859-829872 NS 88 NW 15 September 1956

513. Old Road, Stenhouse. Within the wall of the Stenhouse policies, immediately across the highway from Carron Company's works, the ground rises in a moderate slope, on which Arthur's O'on (No. 126) formerly stood. Immediately W. of the site of the O'on, a ditch-like hollow runs almost straight up the slope for a distance of 115 yds., from a point just inside the policy wall, until it is obliterated on the flatter ground above, which has evidently been under cultivation. Its course is approximately from SSE. to NNW., but its upper end swerves slightly westwards shortly before fading out. At its widest point it measures 10 ft. across the bottom, which is approximately flat, and 40 ft. over all; its greatest depth is from 7 ft. to 8 ft.

---

[1] Blaeu, *Theatrum Orbis Terrarum* (1654), v, *Stirlinensis praefectura.*
[2] *Stat. Acct.*, xviii (1796), 312.
[3] St. Ninians parish, 35.
[4] *Inventory of Roxburghshire*, p. 403, n. 4.

This hollow has every appearance of a disused roadway, and in fact the Crosshillmuirhead road from Carron to Airth evidently passed close by and on approximately this line in the later 18th century.[1] The scale of the map is too small for the course of the road to be determined with greater exactitude. It is no doubt a record of this same road that is preserved by a local writer of 1870, who states that "In olden times a road to Alloa and Airth went . . . through the estate of Stenhouse. Arthur's O'on was situated on the east side of that old road."[2] On the other hand, Sibbald, in 1707, described the hollow simply as "a broad Ditch",[3] which proves that it was not in use as a roadway in his time. This difficulty may be resolved by supposing that a road, which had previously run up the hollow, had been moved a short distance south-westwards, to permit the enclosure of policies, when Stenhouse Tower (No. 200) was built in the 17th century, and that Sibbald was unaware of the fact; or alternatively that this road, like so many old roads, possessed multiple tracks, and that Sibbald saw, but failed to recognise, one that had perhaps been out of use for some time.

879827 NS 88 SE (unnoted) 3 December 1957

514. Old Roads from Falkirk to Airth and Alloa. Some very explicit evidence, dating from 1723, is preserved in Macfarlane's *Geographical Collections*[4] about routes from Falkirk to Airth at the beginning of the 18th century, and it points, in the first place, to a road running approximately on the line of the modern highway B 9036. The Carron was crossed by a ford and a ferry, the latter known as the "west boat" or "Blacks boat", a little below Stenhouse, and by another ferry at "the coal-shore", *i.e.* Carronshore, the roads from these two river-crossings joining up "at the foot of Quarrell yeards", no doubt somewhere near the existing road-fork just S. of Carron Hall, formerly Quarrel (892836). From this junction there was "a fine road to Airth either by horse or foot called the Long Dyke", and this, with the "coal road" from Carronshore, formed the E. boundary of Larbert parish, just as B 9036 still does as far as the Muirdyke Burn, the "Muir dyke" of 1723. The road crossed this stream, which divided Airth and Bothkennar parishes, on a one-arched bridge which was no doubt situated at or near 894846, and the Pow Burn at Abbeytown Bridge (No. 460). The name "Long Dyke" suggests that this road, or part of it, may have had to be raised on an embankment to escape the floods of the carse-lands (cf. p. 440).

Further routes running northwards to Bothkennar and Airth are described as crossing the Carron by the "Newtons" and "Burns" ferries, neither of which can be located with confidence. The former, however, may well have been on a route approximating to the modern highway A 905, as it evidently came from the direction of Linlithgow or Bo'ness and is said to have passed "the Mains", which name may be compared with North Mains and South Mains, both about a mile N. of Skinflats. An undated map preserved in the Register House,[5] which appears to have been made in the later 18th century, marks "Bell's Dyke" along this line, though without indicating that a road followed its course.

Mention is also made of a "horse road to Airth from Fallkirk by the road called the Mossband", which is said to have passed W. of Kinnaird House (No. 307); and this is presumably to be identified with the "Crosshill-muirhead road", as marked on the same late 18th-century map. This road ran NNW. from the Carron Works, apparently through what are now the Stenhouse policies, turned N. and NE. along a line much resembling that of the existing by-roads past Gutterhead and Letham, and ultimately joined the Long Dyke road, which is also marked on this map at or near the existing junction (895863). (Cf. also No. 513.)

c. 883824-*c.* 895863
NS 88 SE, NS 88 NE (indicated but not named)
21 February 1958

515. Old Glasgow Road. It is on record[6] that, in 1723, a "Muir road" from Linlithgow to Glasgow crossed the Avon at Dalquhairn, *i.e.* at or near Avonbridge, and passed S. of Black Loch; and it is tempting to suppose that its line is perpetuated by the modern by-road that runs along the ridge separating the Drumtassie Burn from the valley E. of Little Black Loch. This ridgeway course is a natural one in view of the nature of much of the adjoining country, and the 17th-century building that evidently existed at Stoneridge (cf. No. 357) is likely to have been on or near a track; but no traces of an old road are identifiable today as the ground has either been improved for cultivation or is thickly covered with peat. The North Calder Water could have been forded conveniently at the apex of the loop that it forms 200 yds. ESE. of Lochstank, and from here a road might well have led past Hillhead towards Caldercruix; this area however is in Lanarkshire, and the search was not carried beyond the county boundary.

870694-*c.* 900713
NS 86 NE, NS 87 SE, NS 97 SW (indicated but not named)
1 April 1956

516. Old Roads from Campsie to Kippen. Roy's map of 1747-55 marks a road running up the W. side of Campsie Glen, entitled "Road from Glasgow to Fintray",

[1] H.M. General Register House, Map No. 701. Cf. also No. 514.

[2] M'Luckie, J. R., *Accounts of Arthur's O'on by Dr Stukely, Mr Alex. Gordon, and subsequent writers*, reprinted from the *Falkirk Herald and Linlithgow Journal*, 1870, 7.

[3] *Historical Inquiries*, 45.

[4] Vol. i, 324-7, 329 f. The data have been conflated to form the statement here given without further references to individual points.

[5] H.M. General Register House, Map. No. 701.

[6] *Geogr. Collections*, i, 317 f.

and also another the "Craw Road of Campsie",[1] rising from the valley somewhat E. of what is now Lennoxtown, passing obliquely up the hillside below Crichton's Cairn, and ultimately joining the other on the Nineteentimes Burn, some distance above Alnwick Bridge. The joint road thence follows a line to the Endrick Water at Gonachan, and further on from beyond the Newtown of Fintry to Kippen, which corresponds in a general way with highway B 822. By the end of the 18th century it seems to have been the Craw Road proper, rather than the road on the W. of Campsie Glen, that served the villages on the Endrick Water for communication with Glasgow and with the coal-mines in the neighbourhood of Lennoxtown; at this time the route as a whole was "extremely bad, and often impassable in winter",[2] while up the steep ascent from Lennoxtown "horses could scarcely crawl with half of a load".[3] In 1792 it was made a turnpike and regraded to make it suitable for wheeled traffic[4]; the reform being due to the proprietors of Culcreuch and Ballindalloch,[5] who were interested in the improvement of access to their cotton-mills (cf. Nos. 280 and 282).

The remains of the old Craw Road can be seen diverging from the highway just W. of some abandoned mineral workings, one-third of a mile NNW. of Balgrochan, which mask its lower end (624792). After rising across the hill-face above the highway it turns the shoulder overlooking Campsie Glen at a height of some 1050 ft. O.D., its average gradient over this length of three-quarters of a mile having been about 1 in 6. From the elevation so gained, however, its next stretch is able to keep well above the gorge of the Kirk Burn, which is very steep-sided and is interspersed with crags, and to pursue a slightly descending course towards Alnwick Bridge. In this section it consists of a terrace some 10 ft. to 15 ft. wide, heavily overgrown and showing no sign of metalling; and at Alnwick Bridge, where it dips down sharply to the junction of the Alnwick and Nineteentimes Burns, it becomes a hollow track. It is worth while noting here that the conspicuous hollow tracks just E. of Campsie Glen do not appear to have connected with the road above the gorge; the topography, indeed, would seem to make this impossible, and on the ground they simply fade out. They may, however, represent an attempt to realise an improvement suggested in 1795; it was then pointed out[6] that to cut a line of road from Campsie Kirk to the Craw Road, a horizontal distance of only 500 yds. though with a rise of some 400 ft., would shorten the distance to Stirling by as much as three miles.

Above Alnwick Bridge the gorge gives place to moorland, and here the old Craw Road seems to have been obliterated by the modern highway while Roy's other road approaches from the W. side of the Kirk Burn. The lower end of the latter can be identified by the W. end of the bridge that crosses the Kirk Burn in the Clachan of Campsie (609795); and from here it mounts the W. side of the valley, as a steep and twisty green track, on the right bank of the Heron Burn. After crossing this it holds a northward course past Maggie Lapslie's Knowe and along the lip of the chasm of Campsie Glen; and again appears quite clearly near Allanhead (610803), and running on thence up the glen on a parallel course to that of the old Craw Road (*supra*). From the neighbourhood of the Priest Burn (625813) a grass-grown terraced track, representing Roy's two roads after their junction, can be seen running close to the W. side of the highway and on a generally similar line. Small quarries, which seem to be contemporary, occur from place to place.

On reaching the watershed at the source of the River Carron the old road diverges uphill, traversing Campsie Muir on a course much higher than the modern line. Its greatest elevation must be about 1200 ft. O.D. After passing the parish boundary 108 yds. NW. of the highway, it rises gradually clear of the wettest ground and continues along the lower edge of rather steeper and better-drained slopes. This part of the roadway is often deeply hollowed, and duplicate stretches occur NW. of Campsiemuir Toll-house and again near the top of the descent to Clachie Burn. At difficult places, such as the crossing of the burn above the Toll-house, several subsidiary tracks have been worn by traffic. North of the Clachie Burn, which it crosses 360 yds. W. of the highway, it passes a ridge at some 970 ft. O.D. and thereafter keeps to the better-drained ground lying W. of the fan-shaped hollow at the head of the Tochan Burn. A hundred yards N. of the ridge-top the remains of a direction cairn can be seen by the E. side of the road.[7] This part of the road takes the form of a flat-bottomed hollow 8 ft. to 12 ft. wide, apparently dug out but not provided with side-drains, or of a terrace up to 12 ft. wide where it crosses lateral slopes. At difficult places, such as the crossings of tributary burns, the main track is accompanied or replaced by narrower hollows evidently worn by traffic. After the road has begun to dip into the main valley of the Endrick Water the descent becomes fairly steep, and the track is interrupted in places by old cultivation; it is here approaching the highway, and can be easily seen as a well-defined grassy terrace just W. of a march dyke at 641847. Thence it continues, to coalesce with the highway 110 yds. above the junction of the farm-road leading to Lurg. In the succeeding quarter of a mile below this point the old road makes two minor diversions from the SW. side of the highway, but apart from these appears to have followed the same course as the highway down into the valley-bottom.

The next section of the road Roy marks as crossing the Endrick Water by the Low Bridge at Gonachan (No. 467), after having been joined by one entitled "Road

---

[1] The name "Craw Road", though used specifically of this section in 1794 (*Stat. Acct.*, xi (1794), 380), and though still applied to it on the 6-inch O.S. map, seems now to be commonly used of the whole length between Lennoxtown and Gonachan.

[2] *Ibid.*, xviii (1796), 351.

[3] *Ibid.*, xi (1794), 379.

[4] *Ibid.*, xviii (1796), 351; Cameron, J., *The Parish of Campsie*, 247.

[5] Cameron, J., *loc. cit.*

[6] *Stat Acct.*, xv (1795), 352.

[7] Similar direction-cairns were noted in the *Inventory of Selkirkshire*, No. 112.

from Fintry to Falkirk" (No. 528). The Low Bridge was built just at the time of Roy's Survey, and was described in 1794[1] as "the bridge on the old line of road" in contradistinction to a new one at the Newtown of Fintry, then recently constructed (cf. No. 468). After reaching the right bank of the river, the road evidently turned downstream through what are now the policies of Craigton, and ran on NW. towards Culreuch Castle (No. 213); traces of a grassed-over road were noted approaching the Castle policies on this line below the shepherd's house (622874), and it was further learned from Mr. Archibald Kennedy, Fintry, that a row of large trees which runs approximately from E. to W. through the field immediately S. of the western avenue represents its westward continuation. At the W. margin of this field the old road again connects with highway B 822, which is here running N. towards Kippen after having crossed the Endrick Water at the Newtown of Fintry; the remainder of the road to Kippen from this point, as marked by Roy, appears to have approximated to the modern line although, on the steep rise from the right bank of the Lernock Burn, a hollowed roadway with one subsidiary track has been preserved in some rough grassland and, further N., the section that traverses square 6191 can be seen to the W. of B 822. Guthrie Smith believed that this road over Balgair Muir had been in use "from time immemorial".[2]

It may be remarked here that, in the stretch just N. of Fintry, Roy marks two side-roads branching off to the W. One of these leaves the Kippen road near the West Lodge at Culcreuch, crosses the Endrick Water S. of Nether Glins, and runs on to Killearn along a line approximating to that of highway B 878, though perhaps coming nearer to the river in parts of its course. Grassom's map of Stirlingshire shows that it was still in use in 1817. The other diverged less than a mile further N., probably between the modern farms of Over Glins and Provanston, and ran past the back of the policies of the Old Place of Balgair (No. 333) to the Clachan of Balfron (No. 281) and, ultimately, to Drymen. This line seems to be quite distinct from that of the modern by-road from Lernock Toll to Balfron, by Dalfoil, but the latter is associated in places with hollow tracks which might well be as old as Roy's time. The best example of these, flanking the suburban road named "Roman Road" from the fork near No. 184 towards the Clachan of Balfron, was being obliterated by a mechanical plough when visited in 1954 and is unlikely to be visible in future.

609795, 624792-652948; 6088-5588
NS 67 NW, NS 68 SW ("Crow Road"), NS 68 NW, NS 69 SW, NS 69 SE (indicated but not named)
Various dates to 4 May 1954

517. Old Roads, Stockie Muir. The route from Glasgow to Drymen, now represented by highway A 809, is evidently one of old standing; in 1796 it was a turnpike, and had recently been much improved,[3] while Roy had previously marked it on his map of 1747-55. It was evidently by this route that Scott thought of Jarvie and Frank Osbaldistone as travelling to Rob Roy's country.[4] The older roadways along the route have been largely obliterated by modern improvements and the cultivation of the adjoining ground, but some significant traces were noted in the stretch of a mile and a half between Stockiemuir (501827) and Young's Wood (511807), near Auchineden Lodge.

At the NW. end of this stretch, an old road can be seen emerging from the improved land at Stockiemuir, where the cart-track to Ledlewan leaves A 809; it runs parallel with the highway and about 70 yds. NE. of it until a swerve in the highway brings them together just SE. of the milestone. This old road is flanked by low turf-dykes, up to 25 ft. apart; its centre is hollowed, to a depth of 5 ft. at its lower end, and no metalling now appears. Parallel to it on the NE. there is a belt of hollow tracks up to 50 yds. in width, evidently representing an earlier, unorganised road; the tracks are of varying breadth and depth, run into one another from place to place, and shortly disappear where they are cut across by the walled stretch of drove road that leads NNE. towards Ledlewan (cf. No. 518), beyond which the ground has been improved.

In the course of the next half-mile, two stretches of hollow track can be seen in places running parallel with A 809 on its SW. side; and beyond the felled plantation at Catythirsty Well a flat-bottomed hollow, from 8 ft. to 10 ft. wide, strikes off SE. from the highway, but disappears in mossy ground about a third of a mile further on. Close to the highway it overlies a much narrower hollow track. At the point just short of spot-level 613, where A 809 swerves S. to skirt Young's Wood, another length of hollow track runs straight on, crossing the top of the steep rocky feature on which the wood is planted. At one point it is cut deeply into the rock, being here about 7 ft. wide at the bottom. Another track leaves A 809 at the NW. corner of Young's Wood, and is similarly cut into the rock though on a lower and less difficult course. No further investigations were made SE. of Young's Wood.

The evidence thus points to roads of two types as having preceded A 809, and possibly also the turnpike of the seventeen-nineties. The first was a system of unorganised hollow tracks, certainly earlier than the agricultural improvements of the 18th century and probably of mediaeval date. The second was a crudely constructed roadway, hollowed and narrow but provided with a flat bottom; the existence of stretches of more than one of these suggests experiments made from time to time with alternative courses.

501827-511807 NS 58 SW (unnoted) 25 June 1958

[1] *Stat. Acct.*, xi (1794), 380.
[2] *Strathendrick*, 261.
[3] *Stat. Acct.*, xviii (1796), 576.
[4] *Rob Roy*, ch. xxvii.

518. Drove Road, Cameron Muir to Strath Blane. Local information was obtained[1] that some, at any rate, of the West Highland droves heading to Falkirk (cf. pp. 53 f.) used to make their way by Cameron Muir, a ford on the Carnock Burn, Stockie Muir, and the farm of Ledlewan, thereafter crossing the Blane Water at a point near Lettremill. This tradition accords with a document of 1732[2], which states that these droves crossed the Blane Water by two fords, respectively near Croy and Ledlewan. Traces of a drove road were accordingly searched for on this line and the following observations were made. (1) *Finnich Glen.* The Carnock Water is difficult to cross owing to the depth and generally precipitous character of the Finnich Glen, through which it runs. There is, however, a practicable crossing-place for droves at a point about 500 yds. (direct measurement) downstream from the county boundary (472822), and the left bank here shows several hollow tracks descending towards the ford. The right bank, which was bracken-covered, could not be reached on the date of visit owing to the flooded condition of the stream. With these hollow tracks should perhaps be associated a belt of comb-like marks in the herbage which were observed some 400 yds. away to the NW. (*c.* 470825), and which suggest the passage of animals from some ford on the Cameron Burn, probably at Wester Cameron.[3] (2) *Stockie Muir.* Of the several small headwater streamlets of the Dualt Burn, which join up near and above the point where the parish boundary-wall strikes off from the burn's course, only two are marked on the 6-inch map—one running N. from the flank of Auchineden Hill and the other ESE. from the point marked "Rises" on Stockie Muir. These two coalesce at 495816, and it is clear that the latter, a mere ditch, has adopted the line of a hollow roadway up to 20 ft. wide, scarped along its uphill side and having a flattish bottom. The scarping is very plain, and is up to 3 ft. high in places. Higher up on the moor the line of the road is marked out by distinctive light-coloured herbage, and at the skyline it seems to be alined more or less on the ford on the Carnock Burn (*supra*), about a mile away to the W. Traces of the road are lost where the glen of the Dualt Burn begins to deepen and steepen, slightly above its junction with the boundary wall. (3) *Dualt and Auchineden Burns.* A further section of the drove road is probably to be seen in the line of light-coloured herbage, similar to the one just mentioned, that cuts across the arc of the Dualt Burn in the NW. corner of square 5081. No corresponding mark was found on the strip of moorland separating the Dualt and Auchineden Burns, nor any obvious signs of approaches to a ford on either side of the latter; in particular, the wide, shallow hollow that rises from its right bank towards the Glasgow-Drymen highway just E. of the thirteenth milestone may well be a natural feature.[4] It is to be noted, however, that this is the lowest point at which the Auchineden Burn could be crossed easily by droves, and also that it is just opposite the end of the well-defined stretch of the drove road that is described in the following section. (4) *Ledlewan.* The ground NE. of the Glasgow-Drymen highway has been improved, and the stretch of the drove road that traverses it has consequently been enclosed. It leaves the highway 100 yds. SE. of the thirteenth milestone, being here up to 17 ft. wide between its low and rather dilapidated lateral dykes; it shows a little metalling in places, and a ditch on its lower side. It runs practically straight NE. for over 700 yds., first over a low ridge and then downhill through the enclosures of Ledlewan farm; thereafter, debouching from the E. corner of a small open space, it descends steeply to the N. end of the farmyard. That this stretch must have been out of use for something like a century is suggested by the presence of a mature Scots pine, growing in the middle of the roadway. Below the farm the steepness of the gradient has been eased by quite extensive rock-cutting, but this may well have been done as a farm-improvement as this part of the drove road, which is up to 25 ft. wide, is also the way of access to the farm. (5) *Strath Blane.* On reaching the bottom of the slope below Ledlewan, the drove road, now marked by a double row of hedge-timber, pursues a less direct but generally easterly course across the haugh to the Blane Water at 518832. The footpath leading from the river to Lettremill, the by-road thence to Dumgoyne level-crossing, and the double hedges running from the railway to the Glasgow-Aberfoyle highway (A 81) just S. of Baptiston evidently mark a further extension of the drove road, bringing it to the edge of the moors above Killearn and Ballikinrain; and a road is in fact shown along this line on Grassom's map of 1817.

472822-526836
NS 48 SE (indicated in part), NS 58 SW (unnoted)
3 July 1958

519. Old Road, Cameron Muir. Some scanty traces of an old road can be seen here and there beside the by-road that crosses Cameron Muir, from the county boundary at Wester Cameron towards Finnich Toll. They are most easily recognisable just N. of the modern road at spot-level 399, a quarter of a mile E. of the Wester Cameron enclosures, where hollow tracks can be seen on either side of a small burn; stretches of a roadway, once hollowed but now grown up with moss and rank grass, also appear just N. of the modern road in the last 500 yds. short of the woods that flank the Carnock Burn. Elsewhere the track has been obliterated by cultivation, mossy growth, and the modern road where this has adopted its line.

This route was being used by drovers in the later 19th century.[5]

458830-477834 NS 48 SE (dotted lines)
9 September 1956

[1] From Mr. Dickie, Auchineden Farm.

[2] H.M. General Register House, Duntreath Writs, No. 678.

[3] It is to be noted that such a route would have been quite distinct from the road described under No. 519, except in so far as it may have followed the walled-off roadway through the enclosed ground of Wester Cameron.

[4] Similar indeterminate indications can be seen on the right bank of the Dualt Burn about a quarter of a mile downstream (501826).

[5] Cregeen, "Recollections", 152, 155.

520. Road to Rowardennan. The road from Drymen to Rowardennan was finished in 1792 after thirty years' work.[1] It was provided with bridges over the burns, and with a "quay" at Rowardennan (cf. No. 574) from which a ferry plied across Loch Lomond to Inverbeg on the Dumbarton-Inveraray road. The modern highway presumably perpetuates the 18th-century route, though in a widened and improved form, as no traces of an earlier abandoned road were observed anywhere beside it and the two bridges that were examined (No. 470) contained a nucleus of original structure.

The main engineering difficulties were evidently created by the knolls and ridges extending across the route from the mountain sides on the NE., as well as by burns and areas of swampy ground. The road adapts itself to these features, and for the most part keeps back from the actual shore of the loch. A good deal of cutting evidently had to be done in the Pass of Balmaha (417909), in part of which the highway now runs between rock-faces allowing it a space no more than 20 ft. wide. The rock on the E. side here shows a cut face up to 15 ft. in height, and it would seem that whatever track this route took before the road was made must have been as breakneck as the S. end of the original Sheriffmuir road (cf. No. 508).

Vestiges of what may have been the predecessor of the 18th-century road are perhaps to be seen, just E. of the highway, above Lochan Maoil Dhuinne (364974). The track here crosses a rocky knoll and runs northwards into a moss; it is quite unimproved, but the outcrops of rock round the summit of the knoll have been quarried as if, perhaps, to provide filling for the boggy stretch.

Beyond Rowardennan a rough road skirts the shore as far as Ptarmigan Lodge, and from there a footpath leads to Inversnaid, a distance of five miles. As this track provides the only overland communication with the settlement at Crockeild (No. 371), it must date at least from the 18th century, and no doubt some traffic has followed this route since very much earlier times. A military road from Inversnaid to Dumbarton was evidently projected as early as 1718, but no actual construction was done (cf. No. 521).

In the early years of the 19th century the route from Rowardennan was used by drovers bringing cattle from Argyllshire to Falkirk. The beasts were ferried or swum across Loch Lomond from Inverbeg.[2]

474886-359985
NS 48 NE, N xiii, N vii S.W. (indicated but not named)
4 May 1954

521. Old Road from the Garrison of Inversnaid to Rowardennan. The military survey made by Lieutenants Dumaresque and Bastide in 1718 marks a "Road to Dumbarton" from the Garrison of Inversnaid to Rowardennan, but indicates only the first half-mile or so of its length.[3] This corresponds with the first part of the track noted on the 6-inch O.S. map as running from the junction of the Snaid Burn and the Arklet Water to Loch Lomond by way of the lower slopes of Cruachan. It is likely, therefore, that this track represents the 18th-century route which, after reaching Loch Lomond, presumably continued southwards towards Balloch and Dumbarton.

After leaving the Garrison, the road ran SW. to the junction of the Snaid Burn and the Arklet Water, crossing the latter a little to the E. of the present wooden bridge. Today it first becomes visible as a track climbing steeply up the lower slopes of Cruachan from the Arklet Water, and forming a well-defined hollow way at the first crest. As the road continues to climb it becomes little more than a footpath and at times disappears almost completely. It reaches a height of about 600 ft. at Maol Reamhar, from whence it begins to descend towards Loch Lomond. Below the tree-line the track again becomes well defined, alternating between a banked road 8 ft. in width and a hollow track 6 ft. broad and 4 ft. 6 in. deep. Three hundred yards N. of the abandoned settlement of Stuickinruagh it joins the Rowardennan-Inversnaid track, along which the old route no doubt continued towards Dumbarton (cf. No. 520). It seems unlikely that this road can ever have been suitable for wheeled traffic.

NN 348096-NN 341071 N ii, N iv N.E. (dotted lines)
4 May 1955

522. Old Road from the Garrison of Inversnaid to Inversnaid Harbour. This road is marked on the military survey made in 1718[4] and also on a contemporary site-plan[5] (Pl. 117), where it is referred to as "Road to Loch Lomen Harbour". Today it survives as a well-defined track, the course of which is shown on the 6-inch O.S. map. The road crossed the Snaid Burn 100 yds. W. of the Garrison, where a drystone bridge-abutment can be seen and also traces of a ford. Beyond the Snaid Burn, a straight section of roadway, 10 ft. in width, climbs to a crest which overlooks Loch Lomond, and from this point the road descends, in the form of a hollow track 6 ft. to 9 ft. in width, until it is crossed by a small burn. Twenty yards further on the stream re-crosses the road, passing through a well-preserved culvert 14 ft. in length; quarry-pits can be seen in this area. After passing a boundary fence the track continues its descent towards the loch, becoming less well defined at first, but developing into a banked roadway just above the tree-line. As the descent steepens the banked roadway gives place to a hollow track, the sides of which rise to an average height of 10 ft.; the causeway, however, maintains a width of 12 ft. From this point a series of sharp turns brings it to the line of the modern highway about 200 yds. NE. of the Inversnaid Hotel. The course of the

[1] *Stat. Acct.*, ix (1793), 24.
[2] Cregeen, "Recollections", 154.
[3] National Library of Scotland MS. 1648, Z 3/15. See also *Ibid.*, Z 3/16 (Pl. 117).
[4] *Ibid.*, Z 3/15.
[5] *Ibid.*, Z 3/16.

old road becomes difficult to follow here, but it seems to cut across the hairpin bend of the modern road and to descend directly to the old harbour, which lay just N. of the present jetty.

NN 348096-NN 336088 N ii (dotted lines) 4 May 1955

523. Old Road from the Garrison of Inversnaid to Stronachlachar. This road is shown on the military survey made by Lieutenants Dumaresque and Bastide in 1718.[1] It ran from Inversnaid to Glengyle via Loch Katrine and then, after leaving Stirlingshire, continued via Balquhidder, Lochearnhead and Loch Tay to join the military road from Dunkeld to Ruthven at Blair Atholl. The principal reason given for the siting of a Barracks at Inversnaid was the preservation of communications along this route.[2]

In Stirlingshire the road is best represented by the three-mile stretch between the Garrison (No. 225) and Stronachlachar, most of its length being marked on the 6-inch O.S. map. It first appears in the field immediately to the S. of the Barracks, and from this point it can be seen quite plainly, running in an easterly direction about 100 yds. N. of the present road. The old and new roads gradually converge to meet near the Loch Arklet Dam, but 100 yds. E. of the small fir-wood that borders the northern shore of the loch the old road can again be seen taking a more northerly course towards Corrarklet, while the modern road continues to skirt the loch shores. After passing through Corrarklet, which appears on a contemporary survey as a settlement of about a dozen houses,[3] the old road continues towards Bruach, running parallel with the present road and about 150 yds. N. of it. About half-way between Corrarklet and Bruach a well-preserved culvert carries a small burn beneath the road (Pl. 230 D). On the S. side the culvert measures 1 ft. 9 in. in width and 2 ft. 5 in. in height from below the lintel to the surface of the water. Above Bruach a small reservoir has obliterated all traces of the road, which can be seen, however, on either side of it. A well-preserved section immediately to the E. of this reservoir has been formed by cutting back into the hillside and banking up the roadway with the material thus obtained. It is noticeable that in the absence of efficient drainage the causeway has become very boggy at this point. The road then continues towards Stronachlachar, but its later course becomes obscured by houses and gardens.

NN 348096-*c.* NN 400091 N ii, N iii (dotted lines) 6 May 1955

524. Fords of Frew, Fordhead. The Fords of Frew, which were used both by Montrose in 1645[4] and by the Highland army in 1745,[5] when Stirling Bridge (No. 455) had been broken by the Government forces in the town, today show much less conspicuous features than might have been expected in view of their earlier strategic importance[6] and of their extensive use by the drovers.[7] All that can now be seen is a wide but shallow hollow track leading towards the Stirlingshire bank just W. of the stackyard behind Fordhead farm, the bank itself being steep. Access on the Perthshire bank appears to have been some 80 yds. downstream. Roy shows no route across the Forth here on his map of 1747-55, and marks in place of it a road running northwards from Gargunnock and crossing the river a mile and a half to the E., in the neighbourhood of Nether Kerse. Nothing seems to be recorded about a road following this latter line, and no traces of a ford were found on it; but it would correspond more or less with a route from Gargunnock to Thornhill, by way of Fleuchams and Kepdarroch, which is locally said to have been used by tinkers within recent years.

On the road running southwards from the Fords of Frew see Nos. 525 and 526.

670960 NS 69 NE (unnoted) 24 August 1952

525. Old Road, Boquhan Burn to the Endrick Water. As was mentioned under No. 451, the milestone at Fordhead is said to mark the distance from the Fords of Frew to Burnfoot. The six miles indicated by the stone represent the distance fairly enough, by way of the Boquhan Burn and the Spout of Ballochleam. Grassom's map of 1817 marks a road from Ballochleam to Burnfoot, though not beyond, and remains of it can be seen running up the valley of the Boquhan Burn southwards from Ballochleam farm; it surmounts the lip of the escarpment just E. of the Spout of Ballochleam, at an elevation of about 980 ft. O.D., and thence, after crossing the watershed, descends the left bank of the Backside Burn to Burnfoot. This section, which is evidently still in use for farm purposes, was followed as far as the former site of Backside ("Sheepfold" 666894), beyond which it is no longer passable for wheels; its line was found to have been laid out with care, and the road itself has been fairly well constructed, though some of the gradients on the rise to the top of the escarpment are extremely steep. On easy ground the track is roughly metalled and is up to 12 ft. in breadth, though less where side-cutting and terracing have been required, and it has been carried through the barrier created by the cliff that forms the lip of the escarpment on a steep, rock-cut terrace. Improvement seems to have ended at Burnfoot, but traces of rough tracks were found leading in two directions beyond that point (cf. Nos. 526 and 527). The comparatively

[1] "The Roads between Innersnait, Ruthven of Badenock, Kiliwhiman and Fort William in ye highlands of North Britain". National Library of Scotland MS. 1648, Z 3/13. See also MSS. 1648, Z 3/15 and Z 3/16 (Pl. 117) ("Road to Monteth").
[2] P.R.O., W.O. 47/30, 229.
[3] National Library of Scotland MS. 1648, Z 3/15.
[4] *History*, 392.
[5] *Stat. Acct.*, xviii (1796), 332.
[6] Crawford, O.G.S., *Topography of Roman Scotland*, 18 ff.
[7] Haldane, A. R. B., *The Drove Roads of Scotland*, 83.

large amount of constructional work would accord with the idea of a regular traffic-route, perhaps leading to Glasgow as suggested by the Ordnance Survey Name Book (cf. No. 451) or perhaps planned to that end but never completed beyond the parish boundary. A short length of hollow track was observed near Backside, suggesting that the route had been in use before the improved roadway was built. The Commission's officer was informed locally that the Burnfoot route was a drove road (cf. No. 527).

657924-675884 NS 69 SE, NS 68 NE (dotted lines)
29 June 1955

526. Old Road, Burnfoot to Walton Reservoir. The road described under No. 525 appears, as there stated, to end at Burnfoot, in the sense that no traces of construction were observed beyond the Burnfoot Burn, just SE. of the house, to which a narrow track descends as a steeply-cut terrace. Unmade traffic-tracks do, however, continue its line in two directions, in addition to a shepherd's footpath which descends to the farmhouse of Cringate. One of these,[1] which descends to the ground now occupied by the Walton Reservoir, is marked for a short distance on the first edition of the 6-inch O.S. map; today it can be seen turning downwards towards the Endrick Water on the left bank of the Burnfoot Burn and, after crossing the former, dying out above its right bank some 400 yds. downstream from the confluence. Further traces of this road can be seen just E. of the fank above Todholes, swinging W. from the bottom of a V-shaped notch in the hillside below the fank, and thence pursuing a course somewhat S. of W. towards the ruined house on the N. shore of the Reservoir (667868). It is hollowed or terraced according to the lie of the ground, and in places disappears altogether, but it consistently keeps to the drier ridges and knolls, avoiding a series of small mosses. After passing the ruined house the track probably crossed ground now covered by the E. section of the Reservoir, on a line which would have brought it to the modern highway (B 818) at about 663864, but its traces are now very dim; the track across the dam that divides the two sections of the Reservoir is naturally later than the waterworks, which were undertaken for the benefit of Culcreuch Mill.[2]

On the facts stated, the route would seem to have led down the valley towards Fintry.

c. 676832-667868 NS 68 NE (unnoted) 6 July 1955

527. Old Road from Fintry to Stirling. Roy's map of 1747-55 marks a "Road from Fintray to Stirling" as running north-eastwards from a point E. of the Endrick Water, about half a mile N. of Sir John de Graham's Castle (No. 186), along the general line of the existing moor road by Cairnoch Lodge and Easter Cringate. Its SW. end is not shown as connecting with the contemporary road in the Endrick Water valley (No. 528), though this is probably no more than a draughtsman's oversight; while its NE. portion, after passing near King's Yett and Berryhill, runs straight to the present position of Touchadam Quarry in the valley of the Bannock Burn, then turns sharply NNW. towards Castlehill, and swings round W. of Murray's Wood to connect with the Stirling-Kippen road a short distance W. of Cambusbarron. Traces of this old road have evidently been obliterated, over much of its length, by the moor road just mentioned; but they can be found here and there beside the latter, for example near Cairnoch Lodge and E. of Easter Cringate, and appear quite clearly at and E. of the King's Yett cairn (No. 8), where the modern road has diverged from the older line. They take the usual form of hollowed or terraced tracks, and number at least six between the cairn and the head-dyke of the enclosed ground. North-east of this dyke cultivation has obliterated everything, but it is noticeable that here the alinement of the tracks agrees exactly with Roy's map while footpaths and farm-tracks again correspond with Roy's line past Castlehill, Woodside and Gartur. In its day this road was no doubt a regular highway, not merely a drove road, and, in so far as it was used for droving, the beasts that followed it must have been destined for Stirling market, and not for Falkirk Tryst (No. 534). Beasts are still driven to Stirling along the modern moor-road, and some remains of old tracks can be seen where it crosses the King's Yett Burn (740891).

This route appears further to have been connected with the region NE. of the Gargunnock Hills, by way of Burnfoot (cf. Nos. 525 and 526). As stated under No. 526, the road from Ballochleam (No. 525) is continued S. of Burnfoot by two tracks, of which one goes down the Endrick Water to Walton Reservoir (No. 526). The other rises obliquely towards the shoulder of Cringate Law, where it is soon lost, but what is probably a continuation of it joins the moor road at 691868, just west of a gravel-pit.

c. 684865-767926
NS 68 NE, NS 78 NW, NS 78 NE, NS 79 SE (dotted lines, unnoted)
13 July 1955

528. Old Road from Fintry to Denny. Roy, on his map of 1747-55, marks a road running up the upper valley of the Endrick Water and down that of the River Carron, with the legend "Road from Fintray to Falkirk and Edinbr" beside it just E. of Carron Bridge. Near Low Bridge, Gonachan (634863), it must have crossed the line of what is now called the Craw Road (p. 426). Here and upstream it is shown as keeping to the left bank of the Endrick, but no trace of this stretch can now be seen as the ground has either been cultivated, afforested or flooded by the Carron Reservoir. Edgar's map of 1777[3]

[1] For the other, see No. 527.

[2] Ordnance Survey Name Book, Fintry parish, 37.

[3] This map was based on a survey made in 1745, but as it was brought up to date for publication in 1777 it cannot safely be used as evidence for conditions existing before the latter date.

also shows a road running E. from near Walton, N. of the NW. end of the Reservoir as this now exists, along the left bank of the Carron to a point somewhat W. of Muirmill (*c.* 724838),[1] and there crossing to the right bank and coalescing with Roy's line. The eastward continuation of the route seems to be perpetuated by a farm-road which joins the Kilsyth-Stirling highway (No. 511) at 741833, crosses the Faughlin Burn by a bridge (No. 465), and continues straight up and over Tarduff Hill; it is flanked by drystone walls, and may be followed as far as the waterworks near the head of the Overton Burn (768834), but beyond that point its line is continued by an improved by-road which joins the highway B 818 at Crummocksteps (781831). West of the summit of Tarduff Hill the road throws off a branch which connects with B 818 near Tops (758841); this latter appears to have superseded the older high-level route by 1801.[2]

634863-811827
NS 68 NW, NS 68 NE, NS 68 SE, NS 78 SW, NS 78 SE, NS 88 SW (indicated but not named)

8 October 1954

529. Drove Roads in Denny Parish. Two drove roads can be identified in the parish of Denny, and as both seem to be variants of the main route leading from the west by the Endrick and Carron valleys they can best be discussed in conjunction.

Droves reached the Endrick Water principally from two directions, Balloch and Gartmore[3]; the drovers are said to have used both banks of the Endrick[4], and Dr. Haldane records that one, at least, of their routes crossed the S. shoulder of the Fintry Hills.[5] Spittalhill and Kirk o' Muir are mentioned as points in this section.[6] These routes appear to have entered Denny parish at two points —over the Faughlin Burn, by the road described under No. 528, and on or near the watershed W. of Doups. In the 18th century the former route, which runs between drystone dykes over Tarduff Hill, was evidently a regular highway; but it has also been used for droving as the rectangular enclosures on the right bank of the Carron, downstream from the Faughlin Burn, are locally known to have been intended to hold droves on passage.[7] Local information was further obtained to the effect that the droves did not continue eastwards to Denny, but turned S. at the Overton cross-roads and went on to Bonnybridge by way of the present site of Drumbowie Reservoir. The roads in this area have now all been improved, and no traces remain by which this report can be checked, but it is likely to be correct as a road following this course would have joined up conveniently with the one next to be described.

The second of the main drove roads that traverse this parish shows its first remains, again in the form of double walls, at the edge of the enclosed ground about a third of a mile SSE. of Linns (761809); after an easterly course of rather more than a mile the walls fade out in the swampy ground W. of Drumbowie Reservoir. The roadway is here 45 ft. wide. It is said to have come down past Doups from the higher ground to the W.,[8] though it was not walled outside the enclosed area; and thus it was probably a prolongation of a variant of the Carron valley route which crossed the upper slopes of Tomtain (7281) and passed the highway from Stirling to Kilsyth at or about the watershed.[9] That a drove road did cross the highway here is made likely by the presence of openings for stock on opposite sides of it at two points—one on the parish boundary (735815) and the other a quarter of a mile further to the south. Eastwards from its present point of disappearance this drove road no doubt coalesced with the one previously described, and is therefore probably perpetuated by a by-road, now flooded by the Drumbowie Reservoir but marked on the 2nd edition of the 6-inch O.S. map, the continuation of which runs from near the E. corner of the Reservoir to the Glasgow-Stirling highway (A 80) one mile N. of Dennyloanhead. A road which diverges eastwards from a point on A 80 close to the junction of this by-road is called "Drove Loan", and is said[10] to have formed the next section of the drove road, though it is also recalled locally that droves used to come into Dennyloanhead itself by a "loan" which passes immediately W. of the Crown Hotel.[11] Probably alternate routes were in use in this final stage to Stenhousemuir, as Denny, Dunipace (presumably the old site, as in Nos. 147 and 397) and Dennyloanhead are all recorded by one of the last of the drovers.[12]

742833-768834, 761809-783810
NS 78 SW, NS 78 SE, NS 88 SW (unnoted, double line)

2 July 1954

530. Corduroy Road, Parks of Garden (Site). The Rev. W. Wilson records[13] that "a causeway composed of the trunks of trees, with marks of bolts in the longitudinal sleepers", was found near the farm of Parks of Garden; and the earlier editions of the 6-inch O.S. map mark "Remains of Roman Road discovered" at a point some 300 yds. ESE. of the steading. No remains can be seen today, but Wilson's description suggests a corduroy road of the kind that has been found elsewhere in Neolithic

---

[1] A drove road ran here in the 19th century (Cregeen, "Recollections", 152).
[2] This is to be inferred from what is said about access to Auchenlillylin Spout in *N.S.A.*, viii (Stirlingshire), 118 f.
[3] Haldane, A. R. B., *The Drove Roads of Scotland*, 99 f. Cf. also pp. 53 f.
[4] Information from Mr. Archibald Kennedy, Fintry.
[5] *Op. cit.*, 101.
[6] Cregeen, "Recollections", 152.
[7] For confirmation see Cregeen, *op. cit.*, 155.
[8] Information from Mr. Erskine, Leysbent.
[9] Information from Mr. Adam, Muirmill. See also *P.F.A.N.H.S.*, i, 44.
[10] *P.F.A.N.H.S.*, *loc. cit.*
[11] Information from Mr. Baxter, Crown Hotel, Dennyloanhead.
[12] Cregeen, *op. cit.*, 152.
[13] "Kippen", 10.

and Bronze Age contexts.[1] What was probably another example occurred in Kincardine Moss, which lies just outside Stirlingshire and some six miles distant to the east.[2]

A road-like mound which runs NE. for 200 yds. from a point 180 yds. E. of the farm need not be considered in this connection. It is composed of peat, with which the whole of this ground must have been covered before its reclamation, and the stones appearing in it were placed there by the present farm-tenant.

604970 NS 69 NW (unnoted) 5 September 1952

531. Old Road, Bearside (Site). Some remains of an ancient road were found on the farm of Bearside in the late 1830s,[3] though the statement that they represented a west-going branch of the Roman road from Camelon to the north (No. 124) need not be taken as valid. It is interesting to note that a road evidently existed in this same vicinity in the late 12th or early 13th century, as a charter of William the Lion[4] mentions a *magna strata* as running somewhere close to Cambusbarron, which is less than a mile NNW. of Bearside. The place to which this road is described in the charter as leading, Cuiltedovenald, cannot now be identified.

?7891 NS 79 SE (unnoted)

532. Tryst Ground, Hill of Balgair (Site). The tract of land lying SW. of the junction of the road from Fintry to Arnprior with that from Kippen, called the Hill of Balgair, is an expanse of comparatively level open moorland which stands at a height of a little under 600 ft. O.D. Dispersed over an area of it about half a mile in extent there are about twenty mounds and enclosures, among which two principal types can be distinguished. One of these comprises featureless mounds, approximately circular on plan, measuring about 12 ft. in diameter and standing to about 3 ft. in height, and the other subrectangular banked enclosures with rounded corners. The enclosures measure, over all, about 24 ft. in length by about 16 ft. in breadth, while their banks are 5 ft. wide and 1 ft. 6 in. high from the level of the ground outside. In addition, two more complicated structures occur, each consisting of a subrectangular banked enclosure of similar dimensions to those described above, within which is a circular bank some 5 ft. in thickness enclosing a small area only about 5 ft. in diameter. The small circular enclosure is raised upon the larger rectangular one, as if it was of later build. The remains are blurred by tussocks and coarse heather and show no details. The unmade road marked on the O.S. map by dotted lines passes through the group and appears to cut into two of the structures. Some generally similar structures occur on the Touch Hills, seven miles to the E.

Although the nature of these structures cannot be determined, it is natural to connect them with the former Balgair cattle-market, the site of which is marked in this position on the 1899 edition of the O.S. map. At some date before 1812 a fair was established "at Balgair near Fintry", and in that year it was "fast rising into consequence".[5] Balgair Market ceased to be held about the end of the 19th century,[6] but was still remembered by old residents in Fintry in 1954.

6191 NS 69 SW (unnoted) 1 July 1954

533. Tryst Ground, Pathfoot (Site). A cattle-tryst was formerly held at the village, now vanished, of Pathfoot, but was later moved to Falkirk.[7] The site, which was near the westernmost of the standing stones in the Airthrey policies (No. 47), must have been a convenient one for droves moving down the Sheriffmuir Road (No. 508).

8096 NS 89 NW (unnoted) 23 August 1952

534. Tryst Ground, Stenhousemuir (Site). The ground on which Falkirk Tryst[8] was held after 1785 lies immediately NW. of Stenhousemuir, and is traversed by Tryst Road. It is now occupied by a golf-course and playing-fields, and shows no features recalling its former use. On the trysts see Introduction, p. 53.

8683 NS 88 SE 26 September 1954

535. Tryst Ground (Site) and Drove Road, Reddingrig Muir. As has been said on p. 53, Falkirk Tryst was originally held on Reddingrig Muir and Whitesiderig Muir, until the subdivision of these commonties necessitated a removal to Rough Castle. Nothing connected with the Tryst now remains on the site, but a map[9] prepared in 1772, to accompany a surveyor's deposition made before the Commissioner appointed for dividing the commonties,[10] marks "Place of the Tents" in the angle between what is now the main street of Shieldhill and the E. side of the lane (*infra*) that leaves it opposite the end of the road from Falkirk (897767), together with "Herdshillock" at what is now Herdshill, about 700 yds. away to the ENE. These indications

[1] *P.P.S.*, xxvi (1960), 1 ff.
[2] *T.R.S.E.*, iii, pt. ii, 276 f.
[3] *N.S.A.*, viii (Stirlingshire), 322.
[4] *Dunfermline*, 39.
[5] *General View*, 334.
[6] *P.F.A.N.H.S.*, iii (1938-9), 51.
[7] Fergusson, R. Menzies, *Logie, A Parish History*, ii, 244.
[8] Haldane, A. R. B., *The Drove Roads of Scotland*, 138 ff.
[9] The Commissioners are indebted to Mr. R. S. Taylor, F.S.A.Scot., for showing to their officer a copy of this map, made in 1869, which is in the possession of his firm, Messrs. Gair and Gibson, Writers, Falkirk. The original was by John Scott, Surveyor.
[10] An account of the proceedings is given in *P.F.A.N.H.S.*, i (1935-6), 25 ff., and the map is reproduced at the end of the volume.

suggest that the main focus of the tryst was probably on the site of the existing village of Shieldhill.

The same map marks the drove road approaching from Falkirk along the line of the modern road that leaves the town by Cow Wynd and Glenbrae and crosses the Westquarter Burn by Pirleyhill Bridge. From the "Place of the Tents" it is shown as running for some 780 yds. to the edge of the Gardrum Moss; here it turned E. along the edge of the moss, crossed the head of the Gardrum Burn at "Greenshiel Ford", where the highway to Avonbridge now leaves the SW. corner of California village, and then continued rather E. of S., evidently along much the same line as the modern highway (B 8028). A section of this drove road still survives between Shieldhill and Gardrum Moss, though no doubt a good deal altered in appearance since 1772 as it presumably served for the southward passage of droves throughout the history of the Falkirk trysts. Its N. end is the lane, already mentioned, at 896767; its S. end, near Gardrum Moss, where it seems to have been left without recent upkeep, is a grassy, slightly hollowed, way some 22 ft. wide and showing some traces of coarse metalling. It is flanked by low turf dykes, which still bear a few remains of old thorn hedges.

8976, 9076, 9077
NS 87 NE, NS 97 NW (indicated but not named)
6 June 1957

WELLS

536. St. Ninian's Well, Stirling. In 1777, Nimmo wrote: "Near the south-port is a very copious and pure spring, called *St Ninian's well*, on account of its having been dedicated to that saint. . . . The remains of a chapel are also to be seen, which, having been repaired, are much used by the inhabitants as a washing-house. This well . . . furnished the inhabitants of Stirling with the greatest part of their water till 1774, when, to the great benefit of the place, water was brought in pipes from Gilles-hill, about a mile distant, which now supplies every quarter of the town."[1] The well stands in what is now the NW. corner of the children's playground in Wellgreen. The existing structure is a rectangular, single-storey building of rubble measuring about 21 ft. by 16 ft. over all. It is roofed with a barrel vault and contains washing-troughs within.[2] Although Nimmo and later writers[3] state that part of an earlier chapel is contained within the present building, there is nothing to suggest that the structure visible today is other than the "common washing house . . . at St. Ninians well" erected by the Burgh Council in 1737 to the designs of Robert Henderson, mason.[4]

796930 NS 79 SE (unnoted) 8 October 1954

537. St. Thomas's Well, Cambusbarron. The original well, a spring, has been submerged in the artificial pond at St. Thomas' Well farm,[5] about 600 yds. NNE. of the centre of Cambusbarron village. The name is now attached to a dipping-well just in front of the embankment of the pond.

779930 NS 79 SE (unnoted) 28 October 1954

538. Old Well, Milton. About 50 yds. SE. of No. 350, and on the W. side of the lane that leads down to a ford on the Bannock Burn, a drystone well-head has been constructed in the face of a bank. The well itself, which presumably once served "Beaton's Mill" (No. 351), which stood close by, is now dry and filled up with debris, but the rounded back of the well-head and its lintelled cover still remain. Its internal height is 3 ft. 2 in., its breadth is 2 ft. 2 in., and its depth from front to back is 1 ft. 10 in.

802899 NS 88 NW ("W") 28 October 1954

539. Well, Airth Castle. This well is situated 130 yds. NW. of the Castle (No. 199). It could not be examined as it was covered up with massive stone slabs.

899869 NS 88 NE (unnoted) 23 June 1955

540. Cross Well, Falkirk. This fine stone fountain (Pl. 216 A) stands in the High Street immediately W. of the Town Steeple (No. 253). It is a circular structure about 12 ft. 6 in. high, constructed of grey-sandstone ashlar rendered in reddish plaster to match the red-sandstone finial. The column forming the lower part of the structure contracts from a plinth-course to a diameter of 4 ft. 6 in., and finishes in a cornice, above a string-course and plain frieze, at a height of 7 ft. 6 in.; the water issues from a tap in the S. arc of the column below an iron plaque showing two Classical figures and the date 1817. In the E. arc there is an iron door secured by a bar; both are curved to conform with the shape of the masonry column. Above the cornice a fluted and flattened dome supports a fluted drum, and on this is set the finial, a crowned demi-lion with a heavily curled mane holding a shield of which the sinister portion has been damaged. Below the shield the date 1817 appears on a fluted band which encircles the S. arc of the finial. The shield is parted per pale and was originally charged[6]: Dexter, quarterly, 1st and

---

[1] *History*, 313.
[2] Plans and elevations can be found in *P.S.A.S.*, xvii (1882-1883), 170 ff. There is now no trace of the upper floor that existed in 1882.
[3] *E.g.* Fleming, J. S., *Old Nooks of Stirling*, 111 ff.
[4] *Stirling Council Records*, ii, 239. The idea of substituting horizontal beams for the barrel vault was evidently rejected.
[5] Ordnance Survey Name Book, St. Ninians parish, 61.
[6] The charges on the vanished portion have been supplied from a sketch preserved in the Dollar Park Museum, for the use of which, as well as for other information about this monument, the Commissioners are indebted to Miss D. M. Hunter, the Curator.

4th, three gillyflowers slipped within a double tressure flory-counter-flory; 2nd and 3rd, a bend between six billets: sinister, quarterly, 1st and 4th, three cinquefoils; 2nd and 3rd, a galley. These are the arms of Alexander, 2nd Earl of Callendar, who succeeded in 1674 and died in 1685, and his wife Mary, third daughter of the 2nd Duke of Hamilton,[1] and it is known that the structure was erected at the Earl's expense.[2]

The well was originally built in 1681,[3] an imperfectly documented record[4] stating that its original position was on the S. side of the High Street and that it was subsequently moved to the N. side before being finally rebuilt on its present site. The existing structure was no doubt copied from its predecessor, as the demi-lion resembles in a general way the greatly wasted remains of the demi-lion from the original well, which are preserved in the Dollar Park Museum (No. 428).

888799 NS 87 NE (unnoted) 1 April 1956

541. Well, Denny Paper Works. On a steep bank immediately N. of the buildings of the Denny Paper Works (Vale Board Mills, Ltd.), 300 yds. S. of Kirkland farm, there can be seen the bricked-up top of a well. This is perhaps to be identified with St. Alchenter's, or St. Alexander's, Well, described in 1723[5] as "a spaw well, famous in old times for severall cures, then much frequented". At that time there were vestiges of a chapel and churchyard, called St. Alchenter's Chapel, thirty or forty yards W. of the well.[6] St. Alexander is said to have been the son of a Scottish king, and to have become a Cistercian monk in France.[7]

827826 NS 88 SW (unnoted) 24 June 1954

542. St. Mirren's Well and Carved Stone, Brockieside. St. Mirren's Well is situated on the hillside above Belt Moss, about a quarter of a mile SW. of Brockieside and 250 yds. W. of the Stirling-Kilsyth highway (No. 511) at B.M. 536.3. The spring is now enclosed in a considerable masonry structure of no great age, and its waters, which must originally have drained into the moss, are now piped away to Colzium. Beside the building that covers the well there lies an unshaped stone measuring 3 ft. by 2 ft. 4 in. by about 10 in. in greatest length, breadth and thickness, and bearing near the top the date 1687 incised in large contemporary figures. The stone could not be raised for its other face to be examined.

Dedications to, or other traces of, St. Merinus (Meadhran) in Scotland are recorded at Paisley and in the parishes of Kelton, Kilmaronock, Coylton and Edzell.[8]

723795 NS 77 NW ("St. Mirren's Well", "Stone") 14 September 1953

543. Old Well, Tower. A covered well of drystone masonry has been built in the bank on the S. side of the old road 100 yds. NW. of Tower (No. 323). The aperture in the face of the bank, which now contains a wooden door, is well constructed of squared blocks, with a lintel, and measures 3 ft. 6 in. by 2 ft. 3 in. The well-chamber, which has a lintelled roof, measures 3 ft. 10 in. each way and the water, when examined, was about 2 ft. deep above a stone floor on which there were the remains of lead piping. The sill-stone within the opening is much worn.

612742 NS 67 SW ("W") 28 September 1953

544. St. Maha's Well, Muirpark. This name is attached to a spring, enclosed in a small well-head of drystone masonry, which forms the source of the easternmost of the three small burns that join together and descend to Milton of Buchanan. It is situated in a swampy hollow some 350 yds. SSW. of Muirpark. The well-head is of horseshoe shape, measures 2 ft. by 3 ft. internally and stands about 1 ft. above the surface of the water. A few yards to the NE. there can be seen some vestiges of a similar structure, now turfed over, which may represent the remains of an earlier and more substantial well-head.

Watson states that the saint's name now anglicised as Maha was the Irish Tua, in Scottish Gaelic Tatha.[9] Guthrie Smith records that the well had been resorted to for healing within the memory of persons then living (1896).[10]

458917 N xiv S.W. ("Saintmaha Well") 13 May 1953

545. St. Mauvais' Well, Kippen. At the site of the well as marked on the O.S. map, about 250 yds. NNE. of the centre of Kippen village, there appears to be some stonework now covered up with turf. From here water is carried some ten feet by an iron pipe, and this discharges into a large round stone basin; the overflow from the basin is in turn carried away underground by a stone-built drain. It is to be noted that the site is only about 100 yds. distant from that on which a pre-Reformation church has been alleged to have stood (cf. No. 171).

The saint to whom this well is sacred is Mobhi, abbot of Glas Naoidhen,[11] who died in 544.[12] "St. Mauvie's Fair" was formerly held in this parish on 26th October.

---

[1] *The Scots Peerage*, ii, 363.
[2] Sibbald, *History*, 51.
[3] Livingston, E. B., *The Livingstons of Callendar*, ed. 1887, 122 and n. 12.
[4] *P.F.A.N.H.S.*, iv (1946-9), 26.
[5] *Geogr. Collections*, i, 332.
[6] *Ibid.*
[7] Forbes, A. P., *Kalendars of Scottish Saints*, 270.
[8] *Ibid.*, 397 f.
[9] *Place-Names*, 297 f. He compares *Cill Mo-Thatha* on Loch Awe and *Loch Mo-Thatháig* in the Braes of Doune. See also *ibid.*, p. 152.
[10] *Strathendrick*, 98, n. 1.
[11] Mackinlay, J. M., *Ancient Church Dedications in Scotland: Non-Scriptural Dedications*, 79.
[12] *Annals of Ulster*, Rolls edn., i, 49.

Other Scottish dedications to this saint are given[1] as in Perthshire, Mull and Kintyre, the name in all these cases appearing in the form Dabhi (Davie). Forbes draws attention[2] to the insertion of St. Mobhi and St. Bean, in a late hand, in the Bute Portiforium as evidence of the restoration to favour of Celtic saints in the later Middle Ages.

652950 NS 69 NE 21 October 1952

546. "Highlandman's Well", Sheriffmuir Road (Site). Where it passes the head of the swamp that drains NW. into Bridge of Allan Reservoir, the Sheriffmuir Road (No. 508) makes a sharp turn, and the so-called "Highlandman's Well" is by the E. side of the road here. The well itself has been filled up, but the stream of water issuing from it can still be seen. *The Statistical Account of Scotland*[3] records that it was called the "Holy Well", and was said "to have formerly been much resorted to by the Roman Catholics".

813980 NS 89 NW ("Spring") 12 September 1952

547. Chapel Well, Cambusbarron (Site). This well cannot now be seen as it has lately become covered up with debris and forced soil. Its position is pointed out as close to the marked site of the chapel (No. 174), and just E. of the bottom of a flight of steps descending to a small burn. There is a tradition in the village that its water was used medicinally.

778925 NS 79 SE 28 October 1954

548. Lady Well, Airth (Site). There are no structural remains on the site of the Lady Well, on the right bank of the Pow Burn 180 yds. E. of Abbeytown Bridge (No. 460). The well was supposed to have obtained its name "from the holy water, in the time of Popery, being taken from it, to supply the abbacy, or Catholic chapel, then at Airth", and the water was still used medicinally at the end of the 18th century.[4]

898865 NS 88 NE 14 October 1954

549. St. Laurence's Well, Slamannan (Site). This well, which is marked on the O.S. map by the right bank of the Culloch Burn some 275 yds. SSE. of the church (No. 145), no longer exists as such, as it has been covered with a concrete and iron manhole and has been made part of the sewerage system of the village. The "High St. Laurence Well", marked on the map about 60 yds. SSE. of it, has been filled up.

Scottish dedications to St. Laurence, who was martyred in 258, are fairly numerous.[5]

857732 NS 87 SE 20 March 1953

550. St. Machan's Well (Site). No structural remains survive at the site marked on the O.S. map, just W. of the lane leading up Campsie Glen and 140 yds. N. of the Clachan of Campsie; but there is still a spring at this point, reinforced by surface drainage from across the lane. A runnel of water leads from it through the wood N. of the old church (No. 157), and this seems once to have been covered over, in parts at least, as stone slabs may be seen lying beside it from place to place. For St. Machan see No. 157.

610797 NS 67 NW 29 September 1953

551. St. Vildrin's Well (Site). Though a spring still runs strongly a short distance below the site of this well as shown on the O.S. map, *i.e.* a quarter of a mile NW. of the farm of Finnich, no remains of any structure now survive. As late as 1851 the well still appears to have been "ornamented with an image, said to be of its patron saint", and was resorted to on the strength of supposed healing virtues[6]; but by 1883 the "image" had been broken up and used as building material in the farmhouse.[7] It was stated at that time that the image "was shaped like a cross, stood about 2 feet 6 inches high, and had a figure incised on the centre".[8] This is the only dedication to St. Vildrin recorded by Bishop Forbes.[9]

491856 NS 48 NE 30 August 1952

CANALS, WATERWAYS, ETC.

552. The Forth and Clyde Canal. The project of a Forth-Clyde waterway was first ventilated in the reign of Charles II,[10] and surveys on which no action was taken were made in 1723 and 1761. A few years later the well-known engineer John Smeaton was called in, and he estimated a cost of £80,000 for a canal 5 ft. deep; but the work that was ultimately authorised by Parliament in 1767[11] was a canal 7 ft. deep, the cost of which was estimated at £150,000. The preamble of the Act sets forth that the making of a "navigable Cut or Canal" will "open an easy Communication between the Firths of *Forth* and *Clyde*, as also between the interior Parts of the Country, which will not only be a great *Advantage* to

1 Mackinlay, *loc. cit.*
2 *Kalendars of Scottish Saints*, xxv.
3 Vol. iii (1792), 288.
4 *Stat. Acct.*, iii (1792), 495.
5 Mackinlay, J. M., *op. cit.*, 388 ff.
6 *Origines*, i, 38.
7 *P.S.A.S.*, xvii (1882-3), 201.
8 *Ibid.*, 202.
9 *Kalendars of Scottish Saints*, 458.
10 *History*, 468. Most of the historical facts cited below have been taken from the 1777 edition of Nimmo's work, pp. 468 ff., from the 1880 edition of the same, vol. i, pp. 288 ff., or from *Stat. Acct.*, xix (1797), pp. 88 ff. Some dimensions, etc., have been taken from Pratt, E. A., *Scottish Canals and Waterways* (1922), 108, 161.
11 8 Geo. III, cap. 63.

the Trade carried on between the said two Firths, but will also tend to the Improvement of the adjacent Lands, the Relief of the Poor, and the Preservation of the public Roads, and moreover be of general Utility". Construction began at the E. end, under Smeaton's direction, in 1768, and by 1775 the Canal had reached Stockingfield, near Glasgow. Progress was then held up by financial difficulties, but in 1784 the Government made a loan from the forfeited Jacobite estates, work was resumed in 1786 under the superintendence of Robert Whitworth, and navigation from sea to sea was opened in 1790.

The total length of the Canal is 38¾ miles, of which approximately nine miles are in Stirlingshire. Its normal breadth at the surface of the water is 63 ft., and at the bottom 30 ft.; the raising of the banks has increased its depth from the 7 ft. of the Act to 9 ft. 6 in. The locks (Pl. 230 A) measure 68 ft. 6 in. by 19 ft. 10 in., with a rise of 8 ft., and admit vessels drawing 8 ft. 9 in. Nimmo states[1] that they are "founded upon piles and platforms of wood, and lined with strong walls of hewn stone upon each side". The Canal's greatest elevation above sea level is 156 ft.; this it reaches from the E., after passing Lock 20, just W. of the boundary of Stirling and Dunbarton counties, the remaining nineteen locks of the eastern series all being in Stirlingshire.[2] The waterway is contained by massive earthen embankments, the tow-path following the N. one; where the canal runs along the face of a slope, as it does for most of the way from Camelon to the county boundary, it forms a great channelled shelf, supported by a massive embankment along its northern or downhill side. Lateral hollows, valleys and watercourses are crossed on solid earthworks, through the bases of which the streams are led by arched conduits. Roads pass the canal on swing-bridges, though the Falkirk-Glasgow highway was originally led under an aqueduct-bridge between Locks 11 and 12.[3] Water is supplied to the eastern portion of the canal from Townhead Reservoir, near Kilsyth, which was constructed for the purpose in 1778[4] and is fed principally by the Banton and Craigdouffie Burns, the Boiling Glen, and a lade from the Garrel Burn at Garrel Mill (*infra*).

The canal is entered at Grangemouth through the Old Harbour (Pl. 230 B), a cut about 500 ft. long by up to 200 ft. wide which dries out to mud at low water. The upper portion, which is in line with the adjoining stretch of the canal, is faced with ashlar, and the margins of the wharves that flank it are formed of very large stone slabs with iron clamps. The lower portion, which turns slightly northwards to enter the Carron estuary, has sloping sides faced with drystone masonry. The Basin, to which access is obtained through a lock at the inner end of the harbour, is sub-oval in shape and measures approximately 230 ft. by 150 ft.; the Harbour and the Basin together, with their wharfage, form the core of the small block of streets described under No. 266. At the inner end of the Basin there is a second lock, and this leads into a stretch which runs more or less straight for approximately two miles and a quarter to Bainsford Bridge, in Grahamston. As this ground is largely "carse", the rise in level from the Basin is provided for by only three locks (3 to 5). In Grahamston the canal turns SSW., passes another lock (6), and then turns more westerly again to make the ascent to Camelon; on this no less than ten locks (7 to 16) are required in a distance of some 1600 yds. Immediately W. of Bainsford Bridge the tow-path is flanked for 50 yds. by a rubble wall 10 ft. 6 in. high to the bottom of the coping, which once enclosed Carron Company's basin. It has been pierced by an entry for a branch-canal, 20 ft. 6 in. wide, and by two wide archways and a square-headed doorway, all of which are now blocked up. The basin has itself been filled in, but the side walls of the enclosure still survive in a damaged condition. In 1810 a waggon railway was built to connect this basin with the Company's works,[5] but no remains of this now survive. The basin of Carron Company's coal-wharf between Locks 8 and 9 has also been filled in, as has another basin between Locks 11 and 12. It was just W. of Lock 16 that the Union Canal branched off; its terminal basin has been filled up (*infra*, p. 438), but the position of its entrance is still visible in the S. bank, which here forms a shallow bay.

Westwards from Camelon the canal maintains the same level for just over 4 miles, the stretch immediately W. of Camelon being terraced on a gentle northward-facing slope while the ground E. of Bonnybridge is flatter. At Bonnybridge the canal has to pass a considerable side-valley, in which stands Messrs. Smith & Wellstood's foundry; this it does by means of a long and high earthwork, pierced by a tunnel which is shared by a burn and a by-road; from the W. end of the earthwork the canal passes on to the face of a slope overlooking the Bonny Water. Between Bonnybridge and the county boundary, at the Red Burn, it goes through three locks (17, 18, 19), and, as the transverse slope steepens, the bank that sustains the waterway becomes very high and massive, measuring up to 15 ft. in width at the top. The side-valley at Castle Cary is traversed by a solid earthwork about 130 yds. in length, under which the Red Burn is carried by an arched masonry tunnel.

Westwards from the Red Burn the canal is outside the county, but the boundary runs parallel with it for several miles at only a few yards' distance, and consequently the feeder by which water is supplied to it from Townhead Reservoir (*supra*) runs almost wholly through Stirlingshire. The aqueduct channel branches off from the outlet of the reservoir about 140 yds. SW. of the point where this is crossed by the Falkirk-Kilsyth highway, and is thence led along the flank of some rising ground, over the headwaters of the Kelvin—here no more than a ditch—by a short length of earthwork, and into the canal just E. of the Craigmarloch swing-bridge (737773). At Craigmarloch there can be seen the stabling, now ruinous, that

---

[1] *History*, 473.
[2] The structural details that follow refer to the Stirlingshire section.
[3] *History*, 476.
[4] Ordnance Survey Name Book, Kilsyth parish, 86.
[5] Dott, G., *Early Scottish Colliery Wagonways*, St. Margaret's Technical Press, 1947, 30 f.

housed the horses employed in towing boats on this part of the canal.[1]

The feeder-canal that leads water from the Garrel Burn to Townhead Reservoir also deserves mention as a work of considerable proportions. From the mill-pond of Garrel Mill the water is led under the Kilsyth-Stirling highway (No. 511) by a masonry conduit 4 ft. wide, which is replaced E. of the highway by a channel, 10 ft. or more in width and formed, like the canal itself, by an earthwork embankment. This follows a course along the contours for about a mile, and then discharges into the NW. corner of the reservoir. Alongside this feeder-canal are to be seen a number of squared stone blocks inscribed F C N, for Forth and Clyde Navigation, together, in most cases, with the date 1823; these must not, however, be taken as indicating that the feeder was not built until that year, as the water of the Garrel Burn "was carried off by the canal company, by a small canal . . . into a large reservoir about a mile to the east" at or about the same time as the main work was carried out.[2]

785784-923824

NS 77 NE, NS 87 NW, NS 88 SW, NS 88 SE, NS 98 SW
Various dates in 1955

553. The Union Canal. The Union Canal was projected in 1818 and finished in 1822, its designer being Hugh Baird, of Kelvinhead. Its purpose was to carry passengers and goods between Edinburgh (Port Hopetoun) and the Forth and Clyde Canal at Camelon (Port Downie), but its results were disappointing from the outset and in 1848 it was acquired by the Edinburgh and Glasgow Railway. By 1880 it was carrying only coal and manure.[3] It is now no longer usable for transport, as the locks that connected it with the Forth and Clyde Canal have been demolished, and its terminal in Edinburgh has also been filled in and built over; but it still holds water throughout the rest of its length, and is an interesting survival of a past industrial epoch. Its original length was 31½ miles; it is 40 ft. wide at the top of the banks, 37 ft. at the surface of the water, and 20 ft. at the bottom; the depth is 5 ft.; and the locks measured 69 ft. by 12 ft. 6 in.[4] The canal is fed from Cobbinshaw Reservoir, the water running down the Bog Burn into the Almond and being deflected, near Midcalder, into a feeder which discharges into the canal where it crosses the Almond.

The W. terminal of the Canal consisted of a basin which opened into the Forth and Clyde Canal just W. of Lock 16 (p. 437). This basin has now been filled in, but the position of the gate can be seen on the S. bank of the Forth and Clyde Canal. From the terminal basin the demolished series of eleven locks rose 110 ft. in just over half a mile to an elevation of 242 ft. above sea level, and this elevation the Canal maintained all the rest of the way to Edinburgh, without any further locks. The former course taken by the series of locks can still be traced on the ground, curving up the hillside under the railway viaduct (No. 475) and ending at the remains of a gate where the topmost lock joined the Canal proper. The locks are marked on the 6-inch O.S. map, which shows further that they were provided with side-ponds.

The Canal extends 570 yds. westwards from the top of the series of locks, its W. end being closed by a masonry embankment. The westernmost section of the work runs along a north-facing slope, and in consequence has had to be excavated along the contour and embanked on its N. side. The tow-path tops the embankment. About a mile E. of the locks, however, the Canal is confronted by a ridge which links up with the high ground overlooking Callendar Park, and it passes under this obstacle by a tunnel 700 yds. long—its course being deflected south-eastwards so that the tunnel debouches into a convenient natural feature, the valley of the Glen Burn. Deep cuttings lead the Canal into and out of the tunnel, which is itself rock-cut but is patched with masonry and brick-work, and at either end there is a round arch set in a concave masonry facing. The tow-path inside the tunnel has been renovated and provided with a handrail for the use of pedestrians. This tunnel is of some interest in that it is earlier than the railway-tunnels and therefore, presumably, the oldest tunnel in Scotland.[5]

The valley of the Glen Burn runs eastwards, and has been ingeniously adapted to carry the Canal on its way by the displacement of the burn itself into an artificial channel. This is led along the S. side of the glen, and at a distance of 700 yds. from the tunnel is carried below the Canal by a large masonry conduit to follow its natural course, which here turns away from the Canal north-eastwards. The Canal, meanwhile, continues in an easterly direction, either terraced on the hillside as before or passing transverse features by means of cuttings. None of these cuttings is deep, as the terrain is comparatively even; their sides are revetted with stonework, either squared or rough, and generally dry-built, but just W. of Polmont Station a stretch of well-cut, droved masonry can be seen alongside the tow-path. Transverse streams, of which the Westquarter Burn is the only one of any size, are led under the Canal through well-built masonry conduits; roads are carried over it by bridges (*infra*), with the exception of the by-road from A 9 to Rumford by Nicolton, which goes through a tunnel with headroom of only 7 ft. 6 in. The ends of this tunnel are concave and faced with squared masonry in much the same way as the mouths of the Canal tunnel (*supra*). Individual sections of the Canal can be cut off from the remainder, for drainage, by the insertion of temporary barriers of boards puddled with clay; the slots for one of these barriers can be seen at the W. end of the Avon aqueduct (*infra*). Just W. of this same point there is a small repairing dock, and bays and the remains of jetties can be seen at various places.

Mention should be made here of the terminal dock of

[1] Ordnance Survey Name Book, Kilsyth parish, 101.
[2] *Stat. Acct.*, xviii (1796), 225.
[3] *History* (1880 ed.), ii, 34.
[4] Pratt, E. A., *Scottish Canals and Waterways* (1922), 160.
[5] A contemporary "pamphlet" which gives details about the dimensions of the tunnel, the method of its construction, and so on, is reproduced by Love, *Local Antiquarian Notes and Queries*, iii, 88 ff.

the Slamannan Railway (cf. No. 559), though, as this line was not opened until 1840, it is presumably not an original part of the Canal. It lies on the SW. bank of the Canal 170 yds. NW. of the road from Linlithgow to Slamannan (961761), and consists of a basin 150 ft. square which communicates with the Canal through an opening 15 ft. wide at its narrowest point. The SW. side of the basin is formed by a quay of massive stonework, its coping bearing some remains of loading machinery. The grooves in its edge are understood to have been made by pigs of iron being slid down into barges. The NE. side and the entrance are also faced with, if not wholly built of, masonry, part of the coping here being made of blocks to which railway-lines had once been bolted. As far as could be seen under a heavy covering of herbage, the NW. and SE. sides are of earth.

The tow-path varies in width according to the space available, but does not seem to be less than 5 ft. wide even under the bridges. The large bay by the tow-path, and the roughly paved pathway leading down to it, that can be seen just E. of the highway bridge at Glen Village were provided to facilitate the changing of the horses that belonged to the local colliery. Distances are marked not only at every mile but often at half-mile intervals; a typical milestone being a dressed stone pillar up to 2 ft. 9 in. high above an undressed base, square in section and measuring 10 in. a side. The stones are set with one arris towards the Canal, the distances to Camelon and Edinburgh being incised on the adjacent faces. The one by the W. end of the Avon Aqueduct is thus marked 7½ and 24. Beside this milestone stands a larger pillar, marking the division between two stages; this stands 3 ft. 6 in. high above its base, measures 13 in. by 10½ in. in section, and is inscribed DIVISION / BETWIXT / THIRD AND / FOURTH STAGES. The bridges are well built of dressed stone, and have segmental arches with serial numbers, which run from E. to W., incised on the keystone on each face. Bridge 54, which carries a highway southwards from near Polmont Station, will serve as a sample of the series as a whole; it is of squared rubble brought to courses, with voussoirs neatly droved, and shows a string-course of square section along the base of the parapet. Its overall breadth is 25 ft. measured along the tow-path but somewhat less in the centre, as both faces are slightly concave. The arch springs 6 ft. 4 in. above the tow-path and spans 33 ft.; the arrises of the abutment are rounded, and are deeply scored by the tow-ropes. The highway bridge at Glen Village shows no serial number, but the projecting keystones bear human masks —laughing on the E. side and weeping on the W.—and above each of them appears the date 1821 on a panel defined by a cable moulding.

The most interesting feature of the Stirlingshire section of the Canal is the aqueduct by which it is carried across the valley of the Avon, and so into West Lothian. This structure is described separately under No. 474.

869800-966758
NS 88 SE (unnoted), NS 87 NE, NS 97 NW, NS 97 NE
Various dates in 1954

554. River Improvements on the River Kelvin. In the upper part of its course the Kelvin runs through flat haughlands, in or on the boundaries of Kilsyth, Campsie and Baldernock parishes. In its natural state this ground was waterlogged and liable to flood, but improvements were begun about 1780 when the riparian proprietors of the section in Baldernock united in forming embankments on either side.[1] Work in Kilsyth parish, upstream from Baldernock, began about 1793, when Sir Archibald Edmonstone of Duntreath organised and largely financed a scheme for the straightening and deepening of the channel.[2] This scheme was planned and controlled by Robert Whitworth, who had been responsible for the completion of the Forth and Clyde Canal (No. 552). The length of the New Cut, as given by the contemporary minister of Kilsyth,[3] was something over four miles, but in 1795 work was evidently in progress in Campsie parish as well,[4] presumably through the co-operation of Mr. Lennox of Antermony.[5] The artificial straightness of much of the waterway is obvious, and the manner in which the embankments are set back from the water's edge corresponds with the descriptions given in both *The Statistical Account of Scotland* and the *General View*; but original improvements cannot now be identified with certainty as they are likely to have been more or less completely masked by the effects of more recent work.

5673-7176
NS 57 SE, NS 67 SW, NS 67 SE, NS 67 NE, NS 77 NW
(hachures in part)
8 September 1956

555. River Improvements, etc., between Larbert and Grangemouth. The operations of Carron Company, which was founded in 1759, have produced some interesting examples of early industrial engineering. At Carron itself there is a large mill-reservoir, and this is supplied by a lade which leaves the river at a dam just S. of Larbert Church (No. 146); these works were built by John Smeaton,[6] and can be dated to 1772 by an inscribed stone found during repairs to the lock-gate at the dam. The lade, which may be compared with the canal feeder at Colzium (p. 438), is some 2700 yds. long by 25 ft. to 30 ft. wide, and is formed by a stout earthen embankment founded, in places, on masonry. On issuing from the Works the water supplied a canal, which passed through a lock, about half a mile downstream, into the Carron, itself straightened and shortened about 1765, for the convenience of shipping,[7] by Lord Dundas.[8] This canal, which originated in a loading bay within the

[1] *General View*, 280 f.
[2] *Stat. Acct.*, xviii (1796), 220 ff.
[3] *Ibid.*
[4] *Ibid.*, xv (1795), 317.
[5] *General View*, 279.
[6] *N.S.A.*, viii (Stirlingshire), 354.
[7] *History*, 454.
[8] *General View*, 277.

Works,[1] was used for the transport of produce to Carronshore, the village lower down the Carron that served as the Company's seaport.[2] The canal is now disused and the lock dismantled, but the earthen embankment remains. Carronshore, or what was described as "the Coalshore upon the north side of Carron", was regarded, at least as early as 1723, as "a good harbour for small boats and barks yea sometimes at spring tides there comes ships here of 60 tun burden".[3]

The improvement of the river for navigation has entailed the straightening of much of its course, by means of embankments, right down to and including its mouth. The extent of the earlier meanders can still be judged from the serpentine curves of the parish boundary-lines, which evidently perpetuate their courses. A good example of the riverside embankments can be seen W. of the Edinburgh-Stirling highway at Kerse Bridge; the work here, on the left bank, consists of an earthen mound, faced in part with a triple revetment of stout wooden posts with heavy sheeting, and measuring up to 20 ft. in height on the N., or landward, side.

These works had a further important effect in controlling floods, to which this ground had previously been liable. Sibbald wrote, in 1707, "the Inhabitants are obliged to make large Dykes, which in a few years must be altered and placed elsewhere"[4]; and at some time before 1723 the course of the river had had to be altered "by cutting throw some necks of land" to prevent the undermining of Kerse House.[5] The original Ordnance surveyors further recorded that, before the improvements, the navigable part of the river "was very crooked, overflowed its banks and left waste a considerable area of valuable land".[6] They add, however, that "since it was straightened and strong embankments erected on both sides to improve its navigation, the land which it once flooded and left almost useless is now the most valuable land in the locality".[7]

855820-936822
NS 88 SE ("Mill Lade", "Old Canal"), NS 98 SW (unnoted)
11 December 1955

556. River Dyke, Airth. In the twenty-five years preceding 1792, three hundred acres of land were reclaimed from the foreshore of the Forth, in Airth parish, by means of a "strong dike of sods".[8] A survey of 1823[9] suggests that this was accomplished in stages, as it marks various lengths of protective dyke between the village and the Forth, dating them 1720, 1780 and 1795, while the main dyke along the foreshore is dated 1802 and 1814. This system has now been modified, as some of the internal dykes have been removed and those at the foreshore have probably been raised and improved. The section of foreshore dyke lying NE. of the village consists of a massive earthwork about 24 ft. thick at the base, 5 ft. high above the general level of the tidal mud outside, though apparently only just topping the level of the highest tides, and falling internally to a drainage ditch at a lower level, which discharges through a sluice at low tide.

At and near the mouth of the Pow Burn, a mile distant to the SE., the foreshore dyke is slighter, being about 9 ft. thick and standing about 3 ft. above the tidal mud. Part of it is faced with three or four courses of large and roughly squared stone blocks. No remains were seen suggestive of the harbour established by James IV.[10]

9088, 9087, 9187 NS 98 NW (hachures)
20 October 1954

557. Old Harbour, Airth. A free port was created at Airth in 1597,[11] and up till about 1760 this was the county's principal outlet to the sea; but its trade was then transferred to the "newly built" village of Carronshore,[12] and this in turn was superseded by Grangemouth, the terminal of the Forth and Clyde Canal (No. 552). Vessels plying out of Airth obtained access to the Forth by the tidal channel of a small stream, which now runs, as a marshy hollow almost dried by land-drainage, along the NW. side of the track that leads to the shore from the end of Shore Road. Of the harbour works almost nothing survives today, though the site of a "quay", which existed in 1823,[13] can be identified in a very low grassy hummock on the SE. side of the channel about 200 yds. NE. of the last house in Shore Road. The Register House plan also shows that the dyked enclosure that extends from above the site of the quay to the village was a "Bason or Reservoir" which evidently served, with a system of sluices, to regulate the drainge and tidal waters in the channel.

Airth Harbour is mentioned in the following note written in 1723[14]: "Here is a dock for the building of ships, a saw miln, which goes by wind of a figure never before seen in Scotland invented by the ship builder himself, and a harbour called the Pow for ships of very considerable burden, which are built here very ingeniously and frequently as in any dock in the firth." It should not be confused[15] with James IV's harbour at

[1] Plan dated 1873 in the Company's archives.
[2] Ordnance Survey Name Book, Larbert parish, 18. Carronshore was "newly built" about 1760 (*History*, 453).
[3] *Geogr. Collections*, i, 330.
[4] Sibbald, *History*, 56.
[5] *Geogr. Collections*, i, 334.
[6] Ordnance Survey Name Book, Larbert parish, 42.
[7] *Ibid.*
[8] *Stat. Acct.*, iii (1792), 488. More details about the construction of foreshore embankments are given by Graham, *General View*, 276.
[9] H.M. General Register House, Plan No. 49.
[10] *Accts. L.H.T.* (1507-13), 280 f.; *Exch. Rolls* (1508-13), 403, 565. Cf. also No. 557.
[11] *R.M.S.* (1593-1608), No. 634.
[12] *History*, 453. In 1745 the Government troops burned the vessels belonging to the village to prevent their use as transports by the rebels, and this caused further loss to the traders of the place (*Stat. Acct.*, iii (1792), 492).
[13] H.M. General Register House, Plan No. 49.
[14] *Geogr. Collections*, i, 327.
[15] As by Balfour Paul in *Accts. L.H.T.* (1507-13), xlviii, notwithstanding the evidence that he had himself assembled on this and the previous page.

"Polerth", which was evidently situated at or near Higginsneuk.

In 1792, Airth still had about 140 "tradesmen and seamen" in a total population of about twelve hundred.[1] A certain James Younger, described as "shipmaster in Airth", is commemorated on a headstone, probably of 1737, in the parish graveyard of Dunbar.

899878-900879 NS 88 NE, NS 98 NW 18 March 1960

RAILWAYS

558. Railways, general. Apart from Nos. 471-473, 475, 476, 559 and 560, no railway works in Stirlingshire call for mention as monuments, but a note on the origins of the system may be of some historical interest. The Slamannan Railway is the oldest of the component lines, having been authorised by Parliament in 1835[2]; it ran from Stanrig and Arbuckle, near Airdrie, to the Union Canal at Causewayend (cf. No. 559), providing "easy and cheap Means for the Conveyance of Coal, Lime and Manure . . . and of Coal and Ironstone and other Minerals to the said Canal". In 1844 a link was formed with the Edinburgh and Glasgow Railway (*infra*), by means of a short length of line from near Causewayend Basin to near Myrehead,[3] and an extension to Bo'ness followed in 1846.[4] Meanwhile, in 1838, the Edinburgh and Glasgow Railway had been authorised, connecting those cities and having a branch to Falkirk[5]; while in 1845 the Caledonian Railway and the Scottish Central Railway followed—the former to run from Carlisle to Edinburgh, Glasgow and the North of Scotland,[6] and the latter from Perth to the Edinburgh and Glasgow Railway by Stirling,[7] the junction being at Greenhill. In the following year the Stirlingshire Midland Junction Railway, running between Larbert and Polmont,[8] gave Edinburgh a direct connection with the north by way of Stirling. The main network in the eastern part of the county was completed by the construction of two branches of the Scottish Central Railway—one from near Plean to Alloa (1846)[9] and the other from Larbert Junction to Denny (1856)[10]; while industrial areas in the southern and southwestern parishes were further opened up by the Blane Valley Railway (1861),[11] the Kelvin Valley Railway (1873)[12] and the Kilsyth and Bonnybridge Railway (1882).[13] Access to the Forth Valley and the area E. of Loch Lomond was provided by the Forth and Clyde Junction Railway of 1853, running from Alexandria to Stirling,[14] and by the Strathendrick and Aberfoyle Railway of 1880[15]; this latter connected the Forth and Clyde Junction line with Aberfoyle, by a branch from Buchlyvie, and with the Blane Valley line by one from Gartness.

It may be of interest to record here that, in Stirlingshire, as elsewhere, horse-drawn waggons were being run on rails before the advent of railways proper. At the beginning of the 19th century two such private railways existed,[16] one running from Lord Dundas's Carron Hall coalfield to the harbour at Carronshore, and the other, which has been identified (No. 560, *q.v.*), from Banton, near Kilsyth, to the Forth and Clyde Canal.

559. Slamannan Railway, Terminal Yard. The Slamannan Railway was one of the earliest public railways in Scotland,[17] having been authorised by Parliament in 1835. Though extended to Bo'ness by the Slamannan and Bo'ness Railway Act of 1846, its original terminus was the dock on the Union Canal (No. 553). Some interesting relics of the railway's earlier phases can be seen in the area immediately W. of the dock, where the line debouched into a large triangular yard. Some 260 yds. W. of the dock, and on the S. side of the existing line, there stands a partly ruinous brick water-tank into the N. face of which has been inserted a large stone panel bearing an inscription beginning THE SLAMANNAN RAILWAY / AND WORKS THEREWITH CONNECTED WAS / COMMENCED 1836 / OPENED 1840. After the word DIRECTORS, the following names are given: Kirkman Finlay of Castle Toward; Andrew Mitchell of Maulside; Robert Downie of Appin; Robert Grahame of Whitehill; William Brown of Kilmardinny; John Young, merchant, of Glasgow; James Donaldson of Thornwood; John E. Ralston of Glenellrigg; John Freeland, writer, Glasgow; together with John Mitchell, London, and Thomas T. Mitchell, the principal and resident engineers respectively. The sidings in the yard are still marked by their empty sleeper-trenches, but that these sleeper-borne sidings do not represent the oldest construction on the site is shown by some massive stone blocks, bored with holes for the bolting-down of the chairs, which still remain—some of them earthfast—near the NW. corner of the dock. A typical specimen of these blocks (Pl. 230 E) is roughly squared to a length, breadth and thickness of 1 ft. 10 in., 1 ft. 7 in. and 11 in., and shows a neatly prepared bed for the chair outlined with a groove; the holes are $1\frac{3}{8}$ in. in diameter and 6 in. apart (centres). Other similar stones have been re-used in the coping of the dock near its SE. corner. They were quarried at Bowdenhill in West Lothian.[18]

960761 NS 97 NE (unnoted) 12 June 1954

1 *Stat. Acct., loc. cit.*
2 5 and 6 William IV, cap. lv.
3 7 and 8 Victoria, cap. lxx.
4 9 and 10 Victoria, cap. cvii.
5 1 and 2 Victoria, cap. lviii.
6 8 and 9 Victoria, cap. clxii.
7 8 and 9 Victoria, cap. clxi.
8 9 and 10 Victoria, cap. clxv.
9 9 and 10 Victoria, cap. cl.
10 19 and 20 Victoria, cap. cxxxix.
11 24 and 25 Victoria, cap. ccxlviii.
12 36 and 37 Victoria, cap. clxxv.
13 45 and 46 Victoria, cap. clxxxvi.
14 16 and 17 Victoria, cap. cxxv.
15 43 and 44 Victoria, cap. clvi.
16 *General View*, 326.
17 For a private railway serving a colliery, see No. 560.
18 Information from Mr. J. MacLachlan, Maddiston.

560. Old Railway, Banton to Kelvinhead. The Rev. Patrick Graham records[1] that a private railway was running in 1813 from a colliery at Banton to the Forth and Clyde Canal. The waggons, which were horse-drawn, had unflanged wheels, and the rails on which they ran had consequently to be provided with iron bars to retain them. The rails were of iron, but were mounted on wooden rails which were, in turn, supported by wooden sleepers. The railway, on the line of which a "tramway" was evidently still in use at least as recently as 1895-6,[2] ran SSW. and S. from workings situated SE. of Banton, past the cross-roads in Low Banton, along the by-road to Kelvinhead, and thence SSE. to a wharf ("Kelvinhead Jetty") on the Canal, just outside the county. Remains of the earthen embankment of the railway, revetted or finished as necessary in good squared masonry, can be seen NNE. of Low Banton, where a stretch of it runs through fields on either side of the Craigdouffie Burn, and again between the Falkirk-Kilsyth highway at Kelvinhead and the bank of the Canal. At the bridge over the Craigdouffie Burn the embankment is faced with masonry and is 17 ft. in breadth; but it is reduced to 7 ft. at the actual opening, which must have been spanned by timbers or iron girders. Between Kelvinhead and the Canal the embankment is about 10 ft. broad at the top and 30 ft. over all.

750796-758782 NS 77 NE 14 April 1956

MINES AND QUARRIES

561. Old Copper-mine, Bridge of Allan. The entrance to this mine is situated in Mine Wood, about 100 yds. N. of the junction of Sunnylaw Road and Mine Road. An adit, about 15 ft. high by 4 ft. wide at the mouth, here enters the steep S. slope of the Hill of Airthrey, while directly above it there are traces of surface workings in the form of a deep, rock-cut channel which follows approximately the same line as the adit. The underground workings have been investigated and described by the Geological Survey of Great Britain.[3] It is reported locally that there was formerly a large pile of debris in front of the mine-entrance, but that this was used to level up part of the grounds of the Allan Water Hotel.

This mine, described as being at "Aithree", seems to have been in operation early in the 17th century,[4] when it is said to have produced "50 of ane 100 of the ore; besides that, of silver to the value of an £100 ster., and to the value of £200 ster. it affords of gold". It is again on record in 1661,[5] and from that time it and other mines in the district were worked intermittently until about 1815, when all work ceased. The latest operations were those of the Caledonian Mining Company, which re-opened the Airthrey mine about 1805.[6]

The medicinal properties of the water coming from a spring in these rocks were discovered during the working of the mine, and led to the development of Bridge of Allan as a spa.

795978 NS 79 NE ("Mine, disused") 30 April 1958

562. Old Copper-mine, Logie Burn. Two hundred yards N. of the old church of Logie (No. 127) the Sheriffmuir Road (No. 508) turns away from the Logie Burn in a hairpin bend, and 10 yds. upstream from this point, on the E. bank of the burn, an adit can be seen running horizontally into the hillside. This adit, which measures 4 ft. 6 in. in height and 3 ft. 6 in. in width, no doubt marks the site of an old copper-mine. A few yards further upstream traces of a trial adit are also visible in the E. bank of the burn.

815972 NS 89 NW (unnoted) 31 May 1955

563. Old Copper-mines, Ewe Lairs. The entrances to two old copper-mines are to be seen about 60 yds. apart on the steep SW. face of Ewe Lairs, rather more than 200 yds. NNE. of the centre of Blairlogie village. They are approximately on the line of the 500 ft. contour, which here coincides more or less with the junction between the exposed rocky scarps and the scree slopes below. The upper adit is 3 ft. high by 4 ft. 6 in. wide at the entrance, and can be seen to end after running almost horizontally into the hillside for about 20 ft. The ground outside it has been embanked to form a rough platform. The entrance of the lower adit is largely choked up, but seems to have been about the same size as the upper one; the adit seems to rise slightly, and there is again a platform outside.

828971, 829970 NS 89 NW (unnoted) 5 May 1953

564. Old Quarry and Coal Workings, Hill of Airth. The small plantation about 400 yds. E. of Douglashole covers a large group of sandstone quarries driven into the SW. slope of the Hill of Airth. Most of the quarry-faces are now covered up with debris and are overgrown, but at and near the inner end some, though not the majority, of the exposures show oblique or criss-cross lines suggesting that, in some cases at least, the surface was first worked smooth with a pick and the blocks then broken out along natural lines of fracture. The quarry is known, from a record in the possession of the Geological

[1] *General View*, 326.

[2] So marked on the 2nd edition of the 6-inch O.S. map, revised at that date.

[3] Wilson, G. V., *The Lead, Zinc, Copper and Nickel Ores of Scotland* (Memoir of the Geological Survey of Scotland; Special Reports on the Mineral Resources of Great Britain), xvii, 140 f.

[4] Cochran-Patrick, R. W., *Early Records relating to Mining in Scotland*, xxv.

[5] Wilson, *loc. cit.*

[6] *Ibid.*

Survey of Great Britain, to have been in existence before 1764, but it is probably not the one mentioned in 1723[1] as this is stated to have been "at the house of Airth", a description which agrees better with No. 565.

At the bottom of the exposed rock-face at the innermost end of the quarry, about 30 ft. below the original surface, the entrance to an old coal-mine has lately been re-opened; the workings were not accessible at the date of visit, but it is understood[2] that they are of the "stoop-and-roume" type and are of considerable extent. As the coal-seam, known as the "Crow-Coal", was here comparatively thick (over 3 ft.), and could be reached easily from the surface, these workings may well be of considerable age, though there is nothing to show whether the mine or the quarry is the older. "Stoop-and-roume" working was still practisd at Campsie at the end of the 18th century.[3]

A licence to export coal out of Scotland, granted to Sir Alexander Bruce of Airth in 1596,[4] shows that coal was already being mined on the estate by that time. It mentions, among other operational difficulties, "the continuall drawing of water to keip yair saidis coil-heuchis dry", and the same trouble is recorded at Campsie in 1795.[5] The coal on the Elphinstone estate is likewise on record in 1707,[6] and a "fire engine to work the coall", probably a Newcomen pumping-engine, was in use at Elphinstone as early as 1723.[7]

893876 NS 88 NE (unnoted) 13 July 1955

565. Old Quarry, Airth Church. The S. and E. faces of the bluff on which the old parish church (No. 137) stands have been quarried right back to the confines of the graveyard, the lip of the quarry being at one point only 9 ft. from the NE. corner of the church itself. Work was in progress here in 1723,[8] and as part of the retaining wall of the E. side of the graveyard is founded on quarried rock, and interment is shown by one of the gravestones E. of the church to have begun hereabouts at least as early as 1735, this portion, at any rate, of the quarry can hardly have been used since the latter date. In the upper part of the quarry the sandstone is a golden yellow and in the lower a pale grey; similar yellow and grey stone is used in the older and newer parts respectively of the church, and it is natural to suppose that the material was obtained from here.

900868 NS 98 NW (unnoted) 11 April 1956

566. Old Quarries, Tor Wood. The escarpment that forms the site of Tor Wood broch (No. 100) runs through part of the centre of Tor Wood on an alinement from NNW. to SSE. It faces across the hollow through which runs the Roman road (No. 124). It is everywhere steep, and is broken up in places by steps of outcropping rock, many of which have evidently been quarried in the past—quite probably at many different periods. It is impossible to estimate the age of any of the workings from the degree of weathering of their faces, as the rock, a sandstone in the Millstone Grit, varies much in this respect from place to place[9]; but it is easy to imagine that quarries in this position could conveniently have supplied material for the broch, the Roman road, or Torwood Castle (No. 299), which last is less than half a mile distant, besides serving farmers and dyke-builders all through the centuries. The quarries extend for at least 200 yds. southwards from the broch, and now appear as rock-faces from which larger or smaller blocks have been split off or levered out; in many places cavities are left under widely overhanging ledges, and though, here and there, a block remains lying in front of a corresponding cavity, it is clear that the present condition of the outcrops is due to human activity and not to natural causes. None of the faces seems to have been dressed back with oblique strokes of a pick, but marks which seem to have been made by wedges or levers are not uncommon.

CARVING. At a point about 100 yds. S. of the broch, a quarried outcrop descends the face of the escarpment obliquely from N. to S.; it is up to 10 ft. in height and parts of it have been deeply undercut. The back wall of the resulting series of cavities shows, on an arris which projects slightly between two planes, a human face executed in pocked technique. The head narrows to the chin from a broad forehead, the eyes and nose are clearly indicated by pocking, there is a faint suggestion of a mouth, and projections at the sides are presumably intended for ears. The carving is 4 in. high by 4½ in. wide over the pocked outlines; it is heavily weathered in spite of its comparatively sheltered situation at the back of a cavity, though a sharp fracture immediately to its left suggests that a small block has fallen out or been removed at some more recent time. The lip of the overhang above the cavity shows some of the marks attributed above to wedges.

833849-833848 NS 88 SW (unnoted) 7 August 1959

567. Millstone Quarries, Craigmaddie Muir. Craigmaddie Muir lies in the N. part of Baldernock parish. Its surface is relieved by numerous lava outcrops, and the quarries are located on two of these. It is possible that others may exist in the vicinity (cf. also No. 568).

One quarry is situated on the extensive outcrop of

[1] *Geogr. Collections*, i, 329.
[2] The Commissioners are indebted for information about these workings to Mr. W. A. Read, of the Geological Survey of Great Britain.
[3] *Stat. Acct.*, xv (1795), 331.
[4] *P.S.A.S.*, xxiv (1889-90), 474.
[5] *Stat. Acct.*, *loc. cit.*
[6] Sibbald, *History*, 48.
[7] *Geogr. Collections*, i, 329.
[8] *Ibid.*
[9] Similar variation was observed in the recent (19th- and 20th-century) workings of the same sandstone in Blackcraig Quarry and the adjacent cutting of the Plean Colliery railway (8286). Local cover, afforded by vegetation or overhanging ledges, appears to influence the process.

which the S. face forms a ragged cliff, about 400 yds. in length, lying parallel to and about 120 yds. N. of the public road immediately W. of North Blochairn farm-house. Millstones in different stages of completion (Pl. 158 A-B) and of various dimensions can be seen here and there on the exposed surface of the rock. The earliest stage in the process of manufacture is exemplified by rings pecked out on the flat surfaces of suitable expanses of rock. Measuring about 2 in. in width and half an inch in depth, they vary in diameter from 6 ft. 6 in. to 5 ft. A later stage in the process, also to be seen here, is the cutting of a channel some 6 in. to 9 in. wide, along and on the outer side of the pecked ring; this provided the space in which the quarryman could define and roughly dress the outer edge of the millstone, deepening the channel to give it the desired thickness. At this stage, which is also represented, the millstone was complete except for being freed from the living rock beneath, but it seems that the central hole was made before this final operation was carried out. No complete and free millstones are to be found in the vicinity of the quarry, but bowl-shaped depressions in the rock indicate places from which such stones have been removed.

The other quarry is situated on a bold outcrop which rises from the moor at a point about 130 yds. NE. of the cottage, now demolished, named Craigmaddie Muir on the 1923 edition of the O.S. map. At this site the millstones measure 4 ft. in diameter, but otherwise the traces of their manufacture are similar to those just described at North Blochairn. The millstones at both quarries may have measured about 1 ft. in thickness.

A windmill of about 1700, in which the stones are of the same size as those found on Craigmaddie Muir, has been recorded at Dunbarney, in Strathearn.[1]

578763-581762, 587765 NS 57 NE (unnoted)
23 November 1956

568. Millstone Quarry, Spittal. This quarry is situated 70 yds. NE. of a disused croft named Spittal, just over a mile NNW. of Dalmary. It consists of two contiguous saucer-shaped hollows (Pl. 158 C) which have been cut out of a ridge of conglomerate. Each hollow measures 6 ft. in diameter across the top and about 1 ft. in depth, and represents the cavity from which a millstone has been removed.

507973 NS 59 NW (unnoted) 17 March 1958

BLOOMERIES

569. Bloomeries, etc., Loch Lomond. The woods bordering the eastern shores of Loch Lomond, both N. and S. of Rowardennan, contain many traces of old iron-workings from place to place. The majority of them probably date from the 17th or 18th centuries (pp. 56 f.); and as no mention of the industry in this parish is made in either *The Statistical Account of Scotland* or *The New Statistical Account* it is likely to have lost its importance by the closing years of the 18th century. To locate and describe all these remains would be otiose, but some typical examples may be quoted to illustrate their general characteristics (cf. also No. 570).

(i) Immediately NE. of a sheep-fank, which stands about 200 yds. E. of the Snaid Burn a quarter of a mile N. of Inversnaid Garrison (No. 225), there can be seen several mounds, about 4 ft. high by 6 ft. in diameter, in which appear typical fragments of iron-slag. (ii) Remains of another bloomery can be seen on the S. side of the unnamed burn that runs down past Tigh an Eas, between the road leading from Rowardennan to Ptarmigan Lodge and the loch-side. A mound containing iron-slag lies immediately to the W. of the road where it crosses the burn,[2] and a second mound, measuring 15 ft. by 10 ft. and covered with bright green vegetation, lies a hundred yards downstream. (iii) Two more can be seen on the S. bank of the Allt a'Mhuilinn Burn in Sallochy Wood, two miles SE. of Rowardennan. The first lies a few yards E. of the bridge that carries the Balmaha-Rowardennan road over the burn; much of this mound has been washed away by the burn, but the exposed cross-section shows its height to be 2 ft. Lumps of slag can be seen lying in the stream-bed. Two hundred yards upstream a second mound, grass-grown but composed of slag, lies in a bend of the burn. From this site a well-defined track, now disused, runs south-westwards, crosses a track now used by the Forestry Commission and continues towards the Balmaha-Rowardennan road. (iv) A bloomery comprising a larger and a smaller heap of slag is to be found 180 yds. NE. of Blairvockie Cottage, close to the right bank of an unnamed burn which flows down through a rocky gorge to Dubh Lochan. The larger mound is conspicuous, being 24 ft. in diameter by 5 ft. in height and covered with bright green moss through which the slag appears plentifully. Its upper side has been dug into. The smaller mound, which lies close beside it to the NW., measures 12 ft. by 10 ft. and is 2 ft. 6 in. high. (v) Another site lies in what is now open country and at a height of about 100 ft. O.D., on the lower slopes of Coille Mhor Hill, some 240 yds. NNW. of Cluan. It consists of a conspicuous grass-covered knoll, some 15 ft. in diameter and 4 ft. in height, which contrasts sharply with the surrounding bracken-covered ground. A solitary hawthorn-tree grows out of the westernmost part of the mound, which appears to be composed entirely of slag. To the E. of this mound a rough platform measuring about 6 ft. by 8 ft., on which lie several large stones, may represent the site of the furnace, the construction of the mound showing that the material has been thrown from this side and the soil of the platform being studded with small lumps of slag. There is no burn in the immediate neighbourhood, but the site is well placed to take advantage of the wind.

[1] *P.S.A.S.*, lxxix (1944-5), 9.

[2] This is probably the example mentioned in *P.S.A.S.*, xxi (1886-7), 101.

All these sites, with the exception of the last, lie close to burns, but no traces of dams or lades were seen such as would indicate that water-power was harnessed for bellows to blow the furnaces. Charcoal was essential to the process, and three or four platforms, which lie close to the track leading from Rowardennan to Inversnaid, about half a mile NW. of Ptarmigan Lodge, may perhaps be "pitsteads" used in its preparation.[1] They measure 19 ft. by 19 ft. and have been formed by cutting into the face of the steeply sloping hillside and levelling out the platform with the excavated material. It is reported locally that other similar platforms occur elsewhere in the same area.

NN 347105, NS 360994, NS 380959, NS 382959, NS 378965, NS 366977, *c.* NN 348015
N ii, N vi N.E., N vii N.W., N vii S.W. (all unnoted)
14 May 1954, 6 May 1955

570. Bloomeries, Stronmacnair. Information was obtained at Stronmacnair that large numbers of bloomeries existed in this neighbourhood, up and down Glen Dubh, and two which were readily accessible were examined and noted. Both of these are close to the right bank of the small burn that here forms the county march, one about 60 yds. downhill from the burial-ground (No. 165) and the other at the confluence of the burn with the Duchray Water. The first is about 24 ft. in diameter and up to 4 ft. high, and has been dug into on the W. side; very vague traces of an oblong hut, measuring internally about 30 ft. by 8 ft., appear just to the S. of it. The second is rather smaller. Both are now turfed over, but show plentiful traces of slag and charcoal if the surface is disturbed.

NN 423022, NN 424023 N V (unnoted) 2 May 1956

MISCELLANEOUS

571. Bore Stone, Brock's Brae. The Bore Stone is situated at the top of Brock's Brae, on a minor public highway, and is within the western roadside fence. The fields surrounding this place were bought after a public appeal in 1930, and were handed over to the National Trust for Scotland to prevent housing development and thus to protect a site which had become associated with the Battle of Bannockburn.

According to the most recent conclusions regarding that battle,[2] fought on 24th June 1314, the main engagement would have taken place in the Carse, about a mile and a half away to the NE.; but the first contact of the opposing armies on the previous day would have been in the neighbourhood of the Bore Stone, as the English advanced up the mediaeval road to Stirling (cf. No. 124), and the single combat between Bruce and de Bohun would also have taken place hereabouts.

The Bore Stone itself is recorded by the Ordnance surveyors in 1859, who state that it "was nearly circular and measured 3 feet in diameter and two in thickness. In the centre was a hole 3 inches wide".[3] Nimmo's account made the width and depth of the hole about 4 in.[4] Nothing is known as to the origin of the stone or the purpose of the hole, but the tradition that Bruce's standard was set up in it does not appear on record before 1723[5] and seems improbable.

The stone, which had become broken into three larger pieces and a number of smaller ones, was in 1960 built into the top of a pedestal of granite setts about three feet high, and protected above by a heavy iron grill.

795906 NS 79 SE 16 February 1961

572. Pottery Kilns, Stenhouse (Sites). In December 1953 and July 1959 the remains of some mediaeval pottery-kilns were exposed by sand-pit and other workings in a field about 300 yds. N. of Stenhouse (No. 200). Sites of at least four kilns were located, the chambers of the best-preserved examples having an average internal length of 6 ft. 6 in. The study of the associated pottery is not yet complete, but a preliminary examination suggests that it may be of 14th- or early 15th-century date.[6]

8783 NS 88 SE (unnoted) 12 July 1959

573. Cave, Garrel Glen. *The New Statistical Account of Scotland* records[7] a cave in Garrel Glen, associating it with the Covenanters and stating that the date 1669 was carved over the entrance. In 1859 the Ordnance surveyors found that the cave had been damaged by quarrying, though the date was clearly legible; they stated that it "was never wholly covered over the top, but the rocks slightly overhang it".[8] What may or may not be the same cave, situated on the left bank of the Garrel Burn 50 yds. above the mill-house (No. 363), is now blocked by a wall bearing the inscription BUILT 1819.

719783 NS 77 NW (unnoted) 15 July 1954

574. Jetty, Rowardennan. The remains of a stone jetty are to be seen on the shore of Loch Lomond 120 yds. SSE. of Rowardennan pier. Its landward portion has been washed away, but it is partially preserved for about 100 ft. inwards from its outer end, which is virtually

[1] For parallels in Kintyre, see *P.S.A.S.*, liii (1918-9), 109 ff.; liv (1919-20), 197.
[2] *P.S.A.S.*, xc (1956-7), 170 ff.; Christison, Gen. Sir P., *Bannockburn* (National Trust for Scotland), 10 ff.
[3] Ordnance Survey Name Book, St. Ninian's parish, 113.
[4] *History*, 189 f.
[5] Macky, J., *A Journey through Scotland*, 199. The story is repeated by Nimmo, *loc. cit.*
[6] The Commissioners are indebted for this report to Miss D. M. Hunter, Curator, Falkirk Museum.
[7] Vol. viii (Stirlingshire), 152.
[8] Ordnance Survey Name Book, Kilsyth parish.

intact. It is 12 ft. 6 in. wide, and is constructed without mortar, of large boulders filled in with smaller material; the sides and end are finished with a kerb of large squared blocks held together by iron cramps. Some iron rings are provided for the attachment of boats' painters. The stumps of a few wooden posts can be seen below water level close to the E. side. This jetty is no doubt the "quay" provided for the ferry that ran across the loch from Inverbeg to the end of Rowardennan road (No. 520, *q.v.*),[1] and as such may be supposed to have been built towards the end of the 18th century.

359985 N vii S.W. 5 May 1954

575. "Hills of Dunipace". The numerous natural mounds that occur in the valley of the River Carron have been identified by geologists as the remains of the 100 ft. raised beach. The "Hills of Dunipace", though marked in Gothic characters on earlier editions of the O.S. map, are examples of this class of mound and are not monuments of human construction. They have, however, long been associated with tradition and legends.[2] Cf. also No. 20.

836818, 837816 NS 88 SW 13 March 1954

576. "Auld Wife's Lift", Craigmaddie Muir. The rock formation named "Auld Wife's Lift" on the O.S. map[3] is situated on Craigmaddie Muir at an elevation of a little under 600 ft. O.D. and at a distance of a quarter of a mile slightly E. of N. of North Blochairn farmhouse (Fig. 5). Two large boulderss tand close together and a third lies on top of them. All three are of the local carboniferous sandstone and, although at first sight they might be thought to be a cromlech, their arrangement is unquestionably natural.[4] A shallow incised groove, in the form of a circle 3 ft. in diameter, has been cut on the upper surface of the uppermost boulder,[5] but it does not appear to have any archaeological significance, and may well have been made by a quarryman engaged on cutting out millstones near by (see No. 567).

581764 NS 57 NE 19 June 1954

577. Mound, Ballinjour Wood. The mound beside the Burn of Achlais, marked "Camp" on the 6-inch O.S. map, is a natural feature and not an ancient monument.

458910 N xiv S.W. ("Camp") 18 May 1953

INDETERMINATE REMAINS

578. Indeterminate Remains, Kippen Muir. These remains are situated, on open moorland, 60 yds. E. of the road from Arnprior to Fintry and 670 yds. SE. of Lintmiln farmhouse. They consist of a mound about 42 ft. in diameter, the irregular, grass-grown surface of which rises to a maximum height of 3 ft. above the adjacent ground. The mound is certainly artificial, but may be nothing more than a lime-kiln and of no great age. A well-preserved example of a lime-kiln may be seen in the same neighbourhood, near Garrique farmhouse, Gargunnock.[6]

616921 NS 69 SW (unnoted) 29 March 1956

579. Indeterminate Remains, Touch. These remains are situated, at a height of about 150 ft. O.D., on the uneven, open ground E. of Millburn Wood and at a distance of 400 yds. S. of Touch West Lodge. They consist of two rectangular enclosures, each measuring about 40 ft. by 14 ft. and formed by grass-grown, stony banks. One structure lies, with its axis running N. and S., on the W. part of a low, rocky bluff which projects from the hillside; while the other, the axis of which runs E. and W., is situated a short distance away to the SW. The remains are probably those of an old farm.

749930 NS 79 SW (unnoted) 21 November 1956

580. Indeterminate Remains, Househill. In the open woodland close to the S. side of the old road from Denny that joins highway A 9 at North Broomage, at a point 640 yds. NW. of Househill farmhouse, there is an earthen bank in the form of an arc which measures 210 ft. in length. It is spread to a width of about 18 ft. and stands to a height of 3 ft. above ground level. It is broken by two gaps, one about 4 ft. in width in the W. sector and one about 17 ft. in width in the N. sector. There is nothing at either extremity of the bank to show that it ever continued beyond its present length, and its origin and purpose are uncertain. The narrow ditch that runs SW. from the N. arc appears to have been made for land drainage.

838828 NS 88 SW (unnoted) 22 April 1954

581. Indeterminate Remains, King's Hill, Antermony. Antermony House, now demolished, stood half a mile E. of the Milton of Campsie. A quarter of a mile E. of its former position there is a knoll called the King's Hill, which has been almost entirely removed by quarrying. Pont refers[7] to a structure at "Achterminnie" and an

---

[1] *Stat. Acct.*, ix (1793), 24.
[2] *N.S.A.*, viii (Stirlingshire), 379; *History*, 59 ff.; *Geogr. Collections*, i, 331.
[3] So also in *Stat. Acct.*, xv (1795), 280; but it is often referred to as the "Auld Wives' Lift" or "Lifts".
[4] Gregory, J. W., in *The Scottish Geographical Magazine*, xxxii (June 1916), 279.
[5] *P.S.A.S.*, xl (1905-6), 299.
[6] *P.S.A.S.*, xc (1956-7), 50.
[7] *Geogr. Collections*, ii, 369.

unknown author to "Auchterminume",[1] while Sibbald marks "Achtermmy"[2] and Gordon illustrates an "artificial Mount" at "Anterminny".[3] It is possible that this is the feature referred to, and that it may have been a motte.

665765 NS 67 NE ("King's Hill") 19 June 1954

582. Indeterminate Remains, Kettlehill. These remains (Fig. 178) are situated on a low rocky knoll

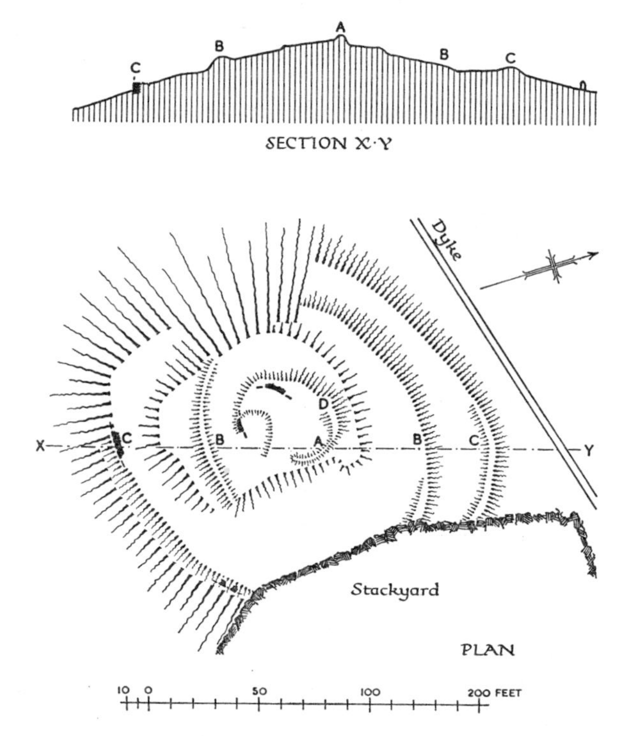

Fig. 178. Indeterminate remains, Kettlehill (No. 582)

immediately N. of Kettlehill farmhouse, at a height o 246 ft. O.D. The lower part of the E. flank of the kno has been quarried, the resulting space being used as a stackyard, while smaller quarries and emplacements for farm buildings have impinged upon the S. flank. While most of the knoll is covered with whins and brambles, the part E. and SE. of the summit is flat and open, and may have been cultivated in the past. The summit, which measures about 70 ft. in diameter, is partly enclosed by a heavily ruined stone wall (A); a few inner facing-stones are still visible protruding through the turf, but otherwise the wall is reduced to a low stony bank of irregular width. Excavations carried out on the N. sector of the wall,[4] at the point marked D on the plan, revealed a passage alined from N. to S. and measuring 8 ft. in length, 2 ft. in width and 3 ft. in height, the walls being built of large upright stones, interspersed with drystone masonry, and the roof of undressed slabs. The passage was surrounded and covered by rubble and earth, and excavation showed that, while the N. end had been roughly but effectively blocked, the S. end adjoined at right angles the foundation of another passage of similar build but with no surviving lintels. The latter passage, which measured 11 ft. in length and 3 ft. 6 in. in width, terminated to the W. in a bay with a clay floor, and to the E. in a paved floor from which a paved extension 3 ft. square protruded to the S. Food-refuse and a stone spindle-whorl were found in the W. bay.

Slight remains of two other banks occur lower down the knoll. The first of these, a grass-grown stony bank (B) from which a few large blocks protrude, starts at the brink of the quarry forming the stackyard at a distance of 50 ft. NE. of the NE. arc of wall A. It runs thence across the N. flank of the knoll, and, after a gap of 80 ft. on the steep W. flank, is traceable for a further 65 ft. before finally dying out on the margin of the former cultivated area. The other bank (C) lies about 25 ft. outside B, lower down the flanks of the knoll. The entrances to both B and C were probably in the sectors destroyed by the stackyard quarry. Like the innermost bank, banks B and C evidently represent the remains of walls, since, in addition to the few large blocks that protrude through the turf at various points along the courses of both, a stretch of wall-face three courses in height and 12 ft. in length is exposed in the S. arc of C.

The purpose and the date of these remains are alike obscure and can only be determined by further excavation.

576748 NS 57 SE (unnoted) 9 April 1959

583. Indeterminate Remains, Ceardach. Ceardach is a small islet in Loch Lomond, lying about 300 yds. from the E. side of the much larger island of Bucinch. It consists of a low, rocky reef capped with boulders and pebbles, and the whole is heavily overgrown with rank herbage, bushes and small trees. The name means "smithy", and evidence of what may have been a smith's or a smelter's activity is probably to be seen in the stones showing the effects of heat which were picked up near the landing-place. Specimens of these stones were submitted to Mr. R. Eckford, of the Geological Survey of Great Britain, who reported that their condition was due to artificial, and not to volcanic, heating.

391917 N xiii (unnoted) 13 May 1953

584. Indeterminate Remains, Clairinch. This island is so densely overgrown that no proper examination of the remains that exist on it is possible, and the Com-

[1] *Ibid.*, iii, 125.
[2] Sibbald, *Historical Inquiries* (1707), map opp. p. 3.
[3] *Itin. Septent.*, 21 and pl. ii, 1.
[4] The Commissioners are indebted to Mr. J. G. Scott for information concerning this excavation in advance of publication.

missioners are accordingly indebted to Mr. J. M. Davidson, O.B.E., F.S.A., for some information regarding them which he obtained, under great difficulties, in 1935. Near the NE. end of the island Mr. Davidson identified the foundations of an oblong drystone building some 37 ft. 6 in. long by 19 ft. wide, divided transversely into two compartments of equal size and having what may have been an oven or a small corn-drying kiln set like an apse in the centre of the N. side. This small structure had a circular paved bottom, about 4 ft. in diameter, which was extended inwards, to communicate with the interior of the building, by a single large flat slab—its level being 1 ft. 10 in. higher than that of the floor inside. Further but less definite remains included (i) foundations, perhaps representing a hut-circle about 20 ft. in diameter, with traces of some associated structures and a little paving; (ii) another set of foundations, with some paving, which yielded the head of an iron ring-headed pin; (iii) a building close to the shore at the NE. end of the island, which measured 46 ft. by 23 ft. 6 in.; it showed no traces of habitation and may be of no great antiquity.

The head of the pin to which reference has just been made is of a La Tène I (c) type, examples of which have been found in Scotland in contexts which were thought to suggest that they were lost in the 1st century B.C. or the 1st, or even the 2nd, century A.D.[1] The presence of this pin might indicate that some of the structural remains on the island were occupied in the Early Iron Age, a suggestion which might also apply to the adjacent crannog (No. 108).

4189 N xiii (unnoted) 29 July 1957

585. Indeterminate Remains and Cultivation Terrace, Cùil Mhuilinn. On the haugh beside the left bank of the Bruach Caoruinn Burn, about 300 yds. S. of the buildings at Big Bruach-caoruinn, there is an accumulation of boulders which does not resemble the remains of any structure except at its N. end, where earthfast boulders in alinement suggest rectangular foundations. From a point close to the bank of the burn about 80 yds. upstream a ditch, now considerably filled up, runs along the foot of the slope that bounds the haugh, fading out in marshy ground some 40 yds. SW. of the assemblage of boulders. Although this ditch does not now make junction with the burn, the occurrence of the name Cùil Mhuilinn on the O.S. map suggests that it may have been a mill-lade, with the implication that a mill existed somewhere here in association with the old farm mentioned under No. 379. In this case, however, no mill could well have stood at the point where the boulders are assembled as the level of this ground is appreciably higher than the ditch.

A small terrace at the foot of the slope flanking the haugh has evidently been improved for cultivation, as piles of stones from its surface have been formed along its outer margin.

NN 418007 N vii N.E. (unnoted) 14 May 1959

586. Indeterminate Remains, Dungoil. Some slight remains of four rectangular structures can be seen on successive natural shelves on the ESE. flank of Dungoil, about three-quarters of a mile W. of the Fintry-Lennoxtown highway. Three, which lie close together (Fig. 179), are situated about 260 yds. ESE. of the

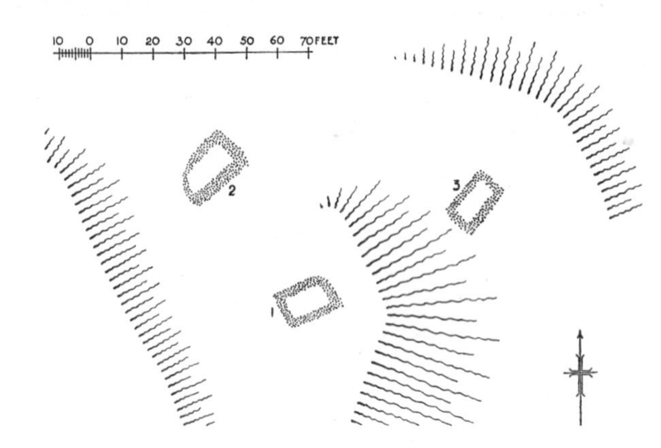

Fig. 179. Indeterminate remains, Dungoil (No. 586)

summit of the hill and at a height of about 1200 ft. O.D., while the fourth lies 70 yds. further to the ESE., lower down the hillside. The remains consist of ill-defined lines of stones and boulders which are for the most part covered with grass; no details are apparent. Measured externally they vary in length from 20 ft. to 24 ft. and in width from 12 ft. to 16 ft.

It seems probable that the structures are the temporary or permanent dwellings of pastoralists, but their date is unknown.

636844 NS 68 SW (unnoted) 7 October 1952

587. Indeterminate Remains, Dunbeg. These remains are situated on an isolated rocky knoll called Dunbeg, which stands out from the steep slope leading up from the valley of Endrick Water to Dunmore, the northernmost feature of the Campsie Fells. The site is half a mile W. of the road-junction in Newtown of Fintry and at a height of 650 ft. O.D. Except on the WSW., where there is a fall of only 20 ft. to the saddle that links the knoll to the main hillside, the flanks are steep and even precipitous in places. The top of the knoll is oval on plan and measures 150 ft. in length by 90 ft. in greatest breadth. It is largely covered with turf, but considerable quantities of stones appear here and there upon it, while the remains of a bank (possibly a ruined wall) can be traced all round the perimeter except on the WNW., where a gap probably represents an original entrance. No facing-stones can be seen, and the character and date of the work cannot be determined without excavation.

608866 NS 68 NW (unnoted) 20 May 1953

[1] *P.S.A.S.*, lxxxiv (1949-50), 129 f.

588. Indeterminate Remains, Hillhead. These remains (Fig. 180), 300 yds. ENE. of Hillhead farmhouse, are situated at a height of 180 ft. O.D. on the brink of a defile, some 50 ft. deep, in which a nameless burn flows N. to join the Gargunnock Burn half a mile away. They lie on a natural platform, sub-oval on plan and measuring

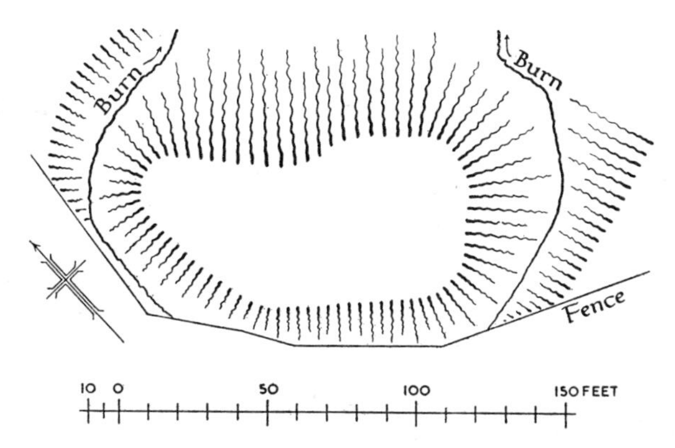

Fig. 180. Indeterminate remains, Hillhead (No. 588)

110 ft. in length from NW. to SE. by a maximum of 55 ft. transversely; the NE. part has collapsed into the defile. To NW. and SE. the platform is bordered by water-courses, the NW. one, which is at the foot of a very steep descent, being 17 ft. below it and the SE. one 14 ft. To the SW. the platform is bordered by a gentle slope, 3 ft. in depth, beyond which the land gradually rises again, but there is no sign that a ditch or other defensive work ever crossed SW. of the base of the platform between the two watercourses. The surface of the platform is level, and sparsely planted with conifers. Upon it there is a quantity of rubble suggesting the debris of a building, while a considerable number of large stones and boulders lying in the beds of the watercourses, and on the slope that falls NE. into the defile, appear rather to have fallen from above than to have occurred naturally. Although no actual foundations can be observed on the surface, the remains may be those of a dun or of some other drystone structure.

718940 NS 79 SW (unnoted) 22 November 1956

589. Indeterminate Site, Castlehill. A natural mound lies in open ground at a height of a little under 300 ft. O.D. and at a distance of a quarter of a mile ENE. of Castlehill farmhouse. It measures 200 ft. in length from WNW. to ESE. by 150 ft. transversely, and rises to a height of 15 ft. The top is cut by a broad and shallow trench, of no great age and measuring about 70 ft. in length; immediately beyond the SW. end of this there is a terrace which appears to have been formed as a spoil-heap from the cutting. No other recognisable traces of artificial work appear, but there exists a record[1] of "an old fortification . . . called Castlehill near to the house of Compstone, where are a great many vaults". Compston farmhouse (No. 317) is situated 230 yds. N. of the mound.

957756 NS 97 NE (unnoted) 8 December 1953

590. Indeterminate Site, Polmonthill. The rounded SW. corner and parts of the adjacent sides of an earth-work were observed as crop-markings by Dr. St. Joseph in the field immediately E. of the S. part of Millhall Reservoir, and were recorded on air-photographs.[2] No traces of the earthwork can be seen on the surface of the ground, and the subsoil is too soft to enable the ditches to be located by probing.

946789 NS 97 NW (unnoted) 31 January 1955

591. Indeterminate Site and Carved Stones, Zetland Park, Grangemouth. Beside the children's paddling-pool in Zetland Park, Grangemouth, there is a small area, surrounded by trees, which is locally known as "The Orchard". Its surface is now on a level with the rest of the Park, but until after the First World War it stood at least 4 ft. higher than the adjoining ground, which has now been levelled up on dumped rubbish.[3] Again, before these improvements, the Grange Burn touched its W. side, and it was also flanked, on S. and SE., by a wide ditch which held water when the burn was high. The earlier editions of the 6-inch O.S. map indicate this ditch, together with a traverse interrupting it to which is appended the legend "Site of Drawbridge". The words "Abbots Grange (site of)"[4] appear in the current edition. Whether these attributions are correct or not, such remains of a raised enclosure, on a spot which no doubt enjoyed slightly better natural drainage than the surrounding flats, suggest a former walled garden, if not an actual house-site. No traces of structure remain, and the mansion of Abbotsgrange, itself now vanished, stood some 300 yds. distant towards the SE.

Within The Orchard there is a pillar containing two carved stones. These are locally believed to have come from Abbotsgrange, along with the bronze sundial that surmounts the whole. The lower stone was evidently once set in masonry with only a single face exposed; this face measures 1 ft. 4 in. by 11 in. and bears, in raised letters, the initials B K / V B and, below, the date 1618. The initials are those of Elizabeth, daughter of Sir William Ker of Cessford and wife of Sir James Bellenden of Auchenoull, who owned the lands of Abbotsgrange from 1611 to 1630, and of her son William Bellenden.[5]

[1] *Geogr. Collections*, i, 317.

[2] Nos. L 32, Q 38 and Q 46 in the C.U.C.A.P.; cf. *J.R.S.*, xli (1951), 62.

[3] The Commissioners are indebted to Mr. R. Porteous, Grangemouth, for information about this site.

[4] Thomas Levingstone in Abbotsgrange is mentioned in 1543 (*R.M.S.*, iii (1513-46), No. 2935), and the lands are again on record in 1552 (*Holyrood*, 279) and in 1563 (*R.M.S.*, iv (1546-80), No. 1662).

[5] *R.M.S.*, as in previous note.

The upper stone is a decorated respond-capital, which is probably a 19th-century essay in 13th-century style. The sundial is of 18th-century design. A third stone, recorded in 1900[1] as being inscribed with a chevron and three mullets, for Ker, has now disappeared.

929814 NS 98 SW ("Abbots Grange, site of") 27 June 1958

592. Indeterminate Site, Larbert. It is recorded[2] that in the 18th century a "small tumulus" stood at the E. end of Larbert village, but that it was demolished during the construction of the main road to Stirling (A 9). This road runs NW. from Larbert Bridge through a cutting to Larbert cross-roads, passing E. of a district named Castlehill, and it is probable that the mound stood hereabouts. *The Statistical Account of Scotland*[3] mentions that there was a "fort" at Larbert, and an account of 1723[4] records that "At the north end of Larbert bridge is a little mount where was a batterie of cannon in defence of the bridge and ford, when King Charles the Second his army lay in the muirs of Dunipace and Larbert 1651".

c. 857821 NS 88 SE (unnoted) 7 December 1953

593. Indeterminate Site, Cowden Hill. At "a Place called *Wester Coudon*, a little above the Bridge of *Bonny* Southward" Gordon recorded[5] numerous ruins of buildings and walls, and rows of terraces on the northern slopes of the site. The terraces are described as being faced with stone to a height of about 10 ft., and to have measured from 15 ft. to 18 ft. in breadth; and it seems likely that they were cultivation terraces, although stone-faced cultivation terraces are rarely reported[6] and none have been found in Stirlingshire. There is no further information about the walls and buildings.

826802 NS 88 SW (unnoted) 19 June 1954

594. Indeterminate Site, Chapel Hill. Gordon noted a similar structure to that described under No. 595 at a place he called Chapel-Hill.[7] As this place was one mile E. of East Bankier and about half a mile W. of Wester Coudon (Cowden Hill, No. 593), it is likely to have been in the vicinity of the area marked on the O.S. map "Chapel Haugh", in the E. part of Dennyloanhead. The structure measured about 200 ft. "in Circumference"; if it was square (cf. No. 595), each side would thus have been 50 ft. in length. Within there were the foundations of stone buildings.

c. 8180 NS 88 SW (unnoted) 19 June 1954

595. Indeterminate Site, East Bankier. There is now no trace of the square, walled enclosure reported by Gordon[8] a quarter of a mile E. of "Bankier Castle" (No. 498), and its date and purpose are uncertain. It is said that the wall measured 18 ft. in thickness and 500 ft. in total length, and that the entrance to the enclosure was on the E.

c. 787790 NS 77 NE (unnoted) 19 June 1954

596. Indeterminate Site, Keir Hill of Glentirran. The Keir Hill of Glentirran is a natural mound which lies 300 yds. SW. of the ruins of Boquhan House and is occupied by a disused modern burial-ground. It is recorded[9] that "the marks of some ancient military work" in the form of an oval rampart existed on the hill, but all traces of this have now disappeared.

c. 667945 NS 69 SE (unnoted) 14 October 1952

ADDENDA

The Monuments described below were reported too late for inclusion in the appropriate sections of the Inventory.

597. Kilsyth Castle. All that now remains of this castle is a fragment of walling which lies in the corner of a field on the northern outskirts of Kilsyth, on the W. side of the road that leads from Kilsyth to Allanfauld. The plan of the building is not now discernible, but the walls appear to have had a thickness of about 6 ft. About 20 yds. to the SW., in the vicinity of a prominent outcrop of rock, some further fragments of masonry can be seen, but it is uncertain whether these are to be associated with the castle or not.

Kilsyth Castle appears to have been a residence of the Livingstones of Kilsyth (cf. pp. 12 f. and No. 204).

717786 NS 77 NW ("Kilsyth Castle, site of") 21 December 1960

598. Carved Stone, Shankhead. Built into the W. gable of the porch of the farmhouse of Shankhead there is a vaulting-boss bearing a shield, measuring 1 ft. 9 in. over all, on which there are carved in relief representations of the Five Wounds of Christ. The boss is evidently of late mediaeval date, but its origin is unknown.

751859 NS 78 NE 14 July 1960

1 *The Grangemouth Advertiser*, 29th December 1900.
2 *History*, 15.
3 Vol. iii (1792), 335-6.
4 *Geogr. Collections*, i, 331.
5 *Itin. Septent.*, 23.
6 *Inventory of Roxburghshire*, p. 49.
7 *Itin. Septent.*, 22.
8 *Ibid.*
9 *Stat. Acct.*, xviii (1796), 329.

599. Sundial, Inchyra Grange. Opposite the front door of Inchyra Grange, Polmont, there stands a sundial with a modern shaft and head and an 18th-century dial-plate of copper or bronze, heavily patinated. This plate is 1 ft. 7½ in. square and elaborately marked. The main dial, in the northern half, is numbered in the usual manner, the Roman figures having apparently been struck with a chisel-like tool; in its upper part are the words GEO: / JAMESON FECIT in cursive script, and on either side of it is a table of small Arabic figures, struck with punches. The gnomon bears on either side the Royal Arms of the United Kingdom, the shield being charged: Quarterly 1st, a lion rampant; 2nd, three leopards; 3rd, three fleurs-de-lys; 4th, a harp. The motto is HONI SOIT QUI MAL Y PENSE. Close to the southern edge of the plate, and on the same north-south line as the main dial, there is a smaller dial marked counter-clockwise with small punched Arabic numbers 1 to 29, evidently for the days of the month; the position of 30 is occupied by the north-south line, and the middle figures of the series are missing as the edge of the plate cuts off the southernmost segment of the dial. The gnomon has vanished. Flanking the dial is inscribed HAMILTON 1728 in Roman script. The remainder of the plate is ruled with lines associated with the names of months and of zodiacal figures; most of these are poorly preserved.

George Jameson is on record as the maker of a dial at Mount Charles, Alloway, dated 1735.[1]

934796 NS 97 NW 15 September 1960

[1] *T.G.A.S.*, new series, ix (1940), 286.

ARMORIAL

Anstruther of that Ilk. Three piles issuing from a chief (p. 407).
Balmerino, Lord. Three buckles on a chevron, between three boars' heads erased (p. 402).
Blair, see *MacFarlan of Keithton.*
Boyd of Trochrigg, see *Bruce of Stenhouse.*
Bruce of Airth. A saltire, on a chief two mullets (pp. 136, 145).
Bruce of Airth. A saltire, on a chief two mullets, within a bordure (p. 136).
Bruce of Airth. A saltire and chief (pp. 145, 147).
Bruce of Airth. A saltire bearing a mullet, in dexter chief a mullet (p. 147).
Bruce of Airth. A saltire and chief, with a mullet in dexter chief (p. 147).
Bruce of Airth. A saltire, in dexter chief a mullet (p. 148).
Bruce of Airth, see *Elphinstone of Calderhall.*
Bruce of Auchenbowie, see *Monro of Bearcrofts.*
Bruce of Kinnaird. A saltire, on a chief a mullet (p. 157).
Bruce of Kinnaird. A saltire, in dexter chief a mullet (p. 157).
Bruce of Kinnaird. A saltire, on a chief, in the dexter corner, a mullet (p. 403).
Bruce of Kinnaird impaling Douglas of Pittendreich. Dexter, a saltire, on a chief two mullets; sinister, a heart over the initials M D, on a chief two mullets (p. 345).
Bruce of Newtoun. A saltire and chief (p. 150).
Bruce of Powfoulis. A saltire and chief (p. 343).
Bruce of Stenhouse impaling Boyd of Trochrigg. Dexter, a saltire and chief, with a mullet at the dexter end of a blank space where the chief should properly be; sinister, a fess checky between three mullets (p. 238).
Bruce of Stenhouse impaling Boyd of Trochrigg. Dexter, a saltire and chief; sinister, a fess checky, a mullet in dexter chief (p. 239).
Bruce of Stenhouse impaling Douglas of Cavers. Dexter, a saltire and chief, with a mullet at the dexter end of a blank space where the chief should properly be; sinister, a heart below three mullets (p. 239).
Buchanan. A lion rampant (p. 313).
Buchanan impaling Graham. Dexter, a lion rampant; sinister, three escallops (p. 163).
Bully. A bull's head cabossed, in chief a cinquefoil (p. 136).
Callendar. A bend between three billets in sinister chief and a boar's head erased in dexter base (p. 153).
Callendar, Earl of. Quarterly, 1st and 4th, three gillyflowers within a double tressure flory-counter-flory; 2nd and 3rd, a bend between six billets[1] (p. 405).
Callendar of Manor impaling Reid of Ackinhead. Dexter, a bend between six billets; sinister, a stag's head erased (p. 400).
Callendar, see *Linlithgow* and *Livingstone.*
Campbell of Ardkinglass. A gyronny of eight cantoned with the badge of Nova Scotia, within a bordure (p. 268).
Carstairs of Kilconquhar. A chevron between three floral slips (p. 157).
Cochrane impaling McGregor. Dexter, a chevron between three boars' heads erased; sinister, a pine tree eradicated and surmounted of a sword (p. 163).
Colquhoun. A saltire engrailed (p. 255).
Cosour impaling Fotheringham. Dexter, three coursers' heads, bridled, couped; sinister, three bars (p. 135).

[1] Normal quarterings reversed.

Crawford, see *Forrester in Braes.*

Cunningham, see *Lennox of Woodhead*, and *McFarlan.*

de Bord, see *Livingstone of Kilsyth.*

Douglas. Three piles, in chief three mullets (p. 119).

Douglas of Cavers, see *Bruce of Stenhouse.*

Douglas of Pittendreich, see *Bruce of Kinnaird.*

Douglas of Whittingehame, see *Livingstone of Callendar.*

Drummond of Blair. A fess undy, in centre chief a mullet (p. 147).

Durham of Mollet impaling Murray. Dexter, on a fess three mullets, in base a crescent; sinister, a hunting horn, three mullets in chief (p. 138).

Edmonstone of Duntreath. Three crescents with an annulet at fess point, within a tressure flory-counter-flory (p. 259).

Elphinstone. A chevron between three boars' heads erased, each holding a shuttle in its mouth (p. 301).

Elphinstone, 3rd Lord. A chevron between three boars' heads erased (p. 147).

Elphinstone, 4th Lord. A chevron between three boars' heads erased (p. 148).

Elphinstone (4th Lord) impaling Livingstone. Dexter, a chevron between three boars' heads erased; sinister, quarterly, 1st and 4th, three gillyflowers, 2nd and 3rd, a bend between six billets (p. 145).

Elphinstone, 9th Lord. A chevron between three boars' heads erased (pp. 237, 402).

Elphinstone (Sir Michael). A chevron between three boars' heads erased, at honour point a small cross[1] (p. 148).

Elphinstone of Calderhall quartering Bruce of Airth. Quarterly, 1st and 4th, a chevron between three boars' heads erased; 2nd and 3rd a saltire and chief, a mullet in dexter chief (pp. 237, 402).

Elphinstone of Quarrel. A chevron with a crescent for difference between three boars' heads erased (pp. 156, 157).

Elphinstone [? *of Quarrel*]. A chevron between three boars' heads erased (p. 156).

Erskine. A pale (p. 282).

Erskine (differenced from Stirling or Leslie). On a pale, a buckle (p. 138).

Erskine (of the Shielfield branch). On a pale, a cross-crosslet fitchée (p. 139).

Erskine, see *Mar.*

Forestar [? *of Arngibbon*]. A hunting horn (p. 138).

Forestar [? *of Denovan*]. A hunting horn (p. 138).

Forestar of Garden. Three hunting horns (p. 139).

Forestar [? *of Garden*]. A saltire, in base a hunting horn (pp. 134, 139).

Forrester in Braes impaling Crawford. Dexter, three hunting horns below the initials I F; sinister, an unidentifiable charge between three mullets below the initials A C (p. 335).

Fotheringham, see *Cosour.*

Gibb. In chief a broken spear chevronwise, held by a hand issuing from the sinister; in base a spur (p. 139).

Glas of Sauchie. A fleur-de-lys between three mullets, within a bordure (p. 395).

Graham of Auchencloich. Quarterly, 1st and 4th, three escallops; 2nd and 3rd, three roses (p. 406).

Graham of Dundaff. Three escallops (p. 152).

Graham [? *of Kelvinhead*]. Quarterly, 1st and 4th, three roses; 2nd and 3rd, three escallops (p. 406).

Graham, see *Buchanan.*

[1] Presumably for the inescutcheon of a Baronet of Nova Scotia.

Hamilton, see *Livingstone.*

Hamilton (Dame Margaret), see *Kincaid of that Ilk.*

Hamilton of Bardowie. A chevron between three cinquefoils, within a bordure (p. 255).

Hamilton of Haggs, see *Stirling of Garden.*

Hay. Quarterly, 1st and 4th, three fancy inescutcheons; 2nd and 3rd, two bars;[1] over all an escutcheon charged: Three escutcheons (p. 160).

Hay, see *Seton of Touch.*

? *Innes of Blairton* (accompanying initials R I). A fess between six mullets (p. 152).

Jonson. A saltire (p. 134).

Keith of Invermay, see *MacFarlan of Ballencleroch.*

Ker of Cessford (from record). "A chevron and three mullets" (p. 450).

Kincaid of that Ilk. A triple-towered castle and in chief two mullets[2] (p. 162).

Kincaid of that Ilk impaling Hamilton. Dexter, a crenellated tower, in chief two mullets; sinister, three cinquefoils (p. 162).

Kincaid of that Ilk impaling Leslie of Rothes. Dexter, a crenellated tower, in chief two mullets; sinister, 1st and 4th, a lion rampant, 2nd and 3rd, three buckles on a bend (p. 162).

Lennox of Woodhead quartering Cunningham. Quarterly, 1st and 4th, a saltire between four roses; 2nd and 3rd, a shakefork (p. 248).

Leslie of Rothes. Quarterly, 1st and 4th, a lion passant; 2nd and 3rd, three buckles on a bend, the quarters being here reversed (p. 147).

Leslie of Rothes, see *Kincaid of that Ilk.*

Linlithgow, 5th Earl of, quartering Callendar. Quarterly, 1st and 4th, three gillyflowers within a double tressure [flory-counter-flory], for Livingstone; 2nd and 3rd, a bend between six billets, for Callendar; en surtout an escutcheon, now blank[3] (p. 351).

Little. A saltire within a bordure (p. 344).

Livingstone (Lady Jane). Quarterly, 1st and 4th, three gillyflowers; 2nd and 3rd, a barrulet between six billets; over all an inescutcheon (illegible) (p. 147).

Livingstone of Almond. Quarterly, 1st and 4th, three cinquefoils; 2nd and 3rd a bend between six billets (p. 404).

Livingstone of Callendar. Quarterly, 1st and 4th, three gillyflowers within a double tressure flory-counter-flory; 2nd and 3rd, a bend between six billets (p. 151).

Livingstone of Callendar impaling ? Douglas of Whittingehame or Pedefer. Dexter, dimidiated, 1st and 4th for Livingstone, 2nd and 3rd for Callendar, the 2nd and 4th quarters being elided by the dimidiation; sinister, a fess or chief charged with three stars accompanied by a rose or gillyflower in base, a three-point label in chief (p. 151).

Livingstone of Callendar impaling Hamilton. Dexter, quarterly, 1st and 4th, three gillyflowers slipped within a double tressure flory-counter-flory; 2nd and 3rd, a bend between six billets: sinister, quarterly, 1st and 4th, three cinquefoils; 2nd and 3rd, a galley (p. 435).

Livingstone of Kilsyth impaling de Bord. Dexter, a mullet between three gillyflowers within a double tressure flory-counter-flory; sinister, three roundels on a fess between six mullets (p. 405).

Livingstone of Westquarter. Quarterly, 1st and 4th, three cinquefoils within a tressure; 2nd and 3rd, a bend between six billets (p. 397).

[1] The intention may have been to represent three bars.

[2] The two circular marks seen in base may or may not be true heraldic charges.

[3] This escutcheon, which should bear an oak-tree within a bordure charged with eight gillyflowers, is the augmentation for the title of Linlithgow.

Livingstone, see *Elphinstone* and *Nicolson.*

Logan. A heart pierced by three Passion nails (p. 147).

Macalastair, see *Stirling, Viscount.*

McFarlan. A saltire between four roses (p. 163).

McFarlan impaling Cunningham. Dexter, a saltire between four roses; sinister, a shakefork (p. 163).

MacFarlan of Ballencleroch impaling Keith of Invermay. Dexter, a saltire between four roses; sinister, three pallets on a chief (p. 359).

MacFarlan of Keithton quartering Blair. Quarterly, 1st and 4th, a saltire wavy between four roses; 2nd and 3rd, two chevrons bendwise between six roundlets in two groups, two and one, and in dexter chief a canton (p. 360).

McGregor of that Ilk. A pine-tree debruised of a baton sinister (p. 167).

McGregor, see *Cochrane.*

Mackenzie of Tarbat. Quarterly, 1st and 4th, a stag's head cabossed; 2nd and 3rd, a flame; at fess point the badge of Nova Scotia (p. 404).

MacLachlan of Auchentroig. Quarterly, 1st, a lion rampant; 2nd a cross pattée palewise, on an indeterminate charge;[1] 3rd, a galley; 4th a salmon naiant. For crest, a castle resting on a cap of estate (p. 370).

Mar and Erskine impaling Murray of Tullibardine. Dexter, quarterly, 1st and 4th, a bend between six cross-crosslets fitchée; 2nd and 3rd, a pale; sinister, three mullets within a tressure flory-counter-flory (p. 288).

Mar quartering Erskine. Quarterly, 1st and 4th, a bend between six cross-crosslets fitchée; 2nd and 3rd, a pale (p. 288).

Masonic. On a chevron between three castles, a pair of compasses (p. 405).

Moir of Leckie. A fess checky (p. 376).

Monro of Bearcrofts quartering Bruce of Auchenbowie. Quarterly, 1st and 4th, an eagle's head erased, holding in the beak a laurel branch; 2nd and 3rd, a saltire and chief (p. 334).

Montrose, Marquess of. Quarterly, 1st and 4th, three escallops on a chief; 2nd and 3rd, three roses (p. 162).

Murray, see *Durham of Mollet.*

Murray of Tullibardine, see *Mar.*

Nairn. Parted per pale, Sable and Argent, on a chaplet four quatrefoils, all counter-changed (p. 136).

Napier of Ballochairn. A saltire engrailed between four roses, within a bordure (p. 409).

Nicolson impaling Livingstone. Dexter, a lion's head between three falcons' heads, cantoned with the badge of Nova Scotia; sinister, 2nd, three gillyflowers, 4th, a bend between six billets (p. 381).

Nova Scotia. A saltire, surtout an escutcheon, with a lion rampant within a double tressure flory-counter-flory, ensigned by a Royal Crown (p. 279).

Pedefer, see *Livingstone of Callendar.*

Rankine of Orchardhead. Three boars' heads erased, in dexter base a lance and in sinister base a Lochaber axe, all within a bordure (p. 344).

Reid of Ackinhead, see *Callendar of Manor.*

Schort. A tree, with a hunting horn at its base, between, dexter, a bow at full bend, stringed and arrowed, and, sinister, a hunting knife (p. 301).

Scotland. A lion rampant within a tressure flory-counter-flory (pp. 287, 399).

Seton of Touch quartering Hay. Quarterly, 1st and 4th, three crescents within a double tressure flory-counter-flory; 2nd and 3rd, three escutcheons (p. 379).

[1] Apparently not a dexter hand couped.

Smith of Craigend. Gules, a chevron between two crescents in chief and a garb in base (p. 163).

? *Somerville.* Two mullets and a cross-crosslet fitchée between three cross-crosslets fitchée in chief and another three in base (p. 160).

Stirling Burgh. A wolf on a crag (p. 292). A wolf couchant on a rock (p. 295).

Stirling (Viscount). A chevron, in base a crescent (p. 282).

Stirling (Viscount) quartering Macalastair. Quarterly, 1st and 4th, a chevron, in base a crescent; 2nd and 3rd, a galley, oars in action, sails furled, flagged, between three cross-crosslets; over all, on an escutcheon, the badge of Nova Scotia (p. 279).

Stirling of Craigbarnet. Three buckles on a bend (p. 407).

Stirling of Garden impaling Hamilton of Haggs. Dexter, three buckles on a bend, with a crescent in chief for difference; sinister, the head of a fish couped, with an annulet in its mouth, between three cinquefoils (p. 329).

Stirling of Glorat (from record). "*Argent* a bend engrailed *azur* [properly Sable] charged with three buckles *or*, on a chief *gules* a naked arme issuing out of a cloud from ye sinister side, grasping a sword in pale, and therewith guarding ane Imperiall crowne placed in ye dexter canton proper, All within a double Tressur, counter flowered of thistles *vert*" (p. 357).

Unidentified (A.D.). On a fess three mullets, in base a crescent (p. 138).

Unidentified (I.C.). A lion rampant (p. 403).

Unidentified (I.F.). In chief three rosettes between three piles; in base an annulet (p. 162).

Unidentified (W.M. and M.H.). A weaver's shuttle (p. 139).

Unidentified. On a bend between two mullets, two [? roses], within a bordure (p. 136).

Unidentified. A woman's head and neck, in chief three mullets (p. 147).

Unidentified. Quarterly, 1st and 4th, a chevron; 2nd [? and 3rd], a stag's head erased (p. 150).

United Kingdom (Scottish version). Quarterly, 1st, a lion rampant; 2nd, three leopards; 3rd, three fleurs-de-lys; 4th, a harp (p. 451).

GLOSSARY

Abacus. The uppermost member of a capital.
Affrontée. In heraldry, full-faced to the spectator.
Agger. Mound, used of the raised track of a Roman military road.
Aisle. (1) An internal subdivision of a church, formed by an arcade separating it from the main body of the nave or chancel. (2) A projecting wing or chapel, often for purposes of family burial (Scots).
Ala. A regiment of Roman Auxiliary cavalry, with a numerical strength of 500 (*quingenaria*) or 1000 (*milliaria*).
Annulet. (1) A small raised moulding encircling a shaft or column. (2) In heraldry, a ring.
Ansate. Having handle-like extensions.
Antefixes. In Classical architecture, small upright ornaments erected at regular intervals above an eaves cornice.
Apse. A projection, semicircular or polygonal on plan, from the wall of a church or other building.
Arch-braced. Of a roof in which the tie-beams or collars are supported on curved braces.
Architrave. (1) A moulded frame round a door, window or similar opening. (2) The lowest member of an entablature, resting directly upon the column or pier.
Archivolt. The underside of an arch, and so also applied to mouldings on the curve.
Argent. In heraldry, white or silver.
Arris. The external angle at the meeting of two surfaces.
Ashlar. Masonry wrought to an even or rusticated face and square edges, and bedded with a fine joint.
Aumbry. A small cupboard or closed recess in a wall.
Azure. In heraldry, blue.

Back-set. Of masonry in which part of the face of the stone is cut back, in such a way that rendering, if applied to it, is flush with the remainder (Scots).
Badge. An heraldic finial on a roof.
Bailey. An open space or court within a castle enclosure.
Ball-flower. A globular flower-ornament, composed of three petals enclosing a small ball.
Barbican. A tower or advanced work defending the entrance to a castle.
Barmkin. A defensive enclosure, usually attached to a tower.
Barrel-vault. A continuous vault, semicircular, segmental or pointed in section.
Barrulet. In heraldry, a small bar.
Bartizan. The open parapet of a tower.
Basque. A downward extension, slightly below the waist, of a doublet or bodice.
Baxter. Baker (Scots).
Bay. The unit of building between piers or buttresses.
Beaker. A type of pottery used in the early 2nd millennium B.C.
Benatura. A stoup or basin for holy water.
Bend. In heraldry, an oblique band across a shield.
Bezant. In heraldry, a gold roundel or disc.
Billet. In heraldry, a small oblong charge representing a billet of wood.
Block-in-course. Of masonry similar to regular coursed rubble except that the blocks are larger and of a better quality.

Blocking-course. A plain course of stones laid on the top of a cornice, crowning the wall.

Bolection moulding. A moulding raised above the general plane of the framework of a door or panel.

Bordure. In heraldry, a margin or border round a shield.

Bottle-nosed steps. Steps in which the tread-nosings are finished in a semi-round.

Bowtell moulding. A convex moulding or roll, usually three-quarters of a circle in section.

Bracteate. A coin or medal formed of gold or silver beaten very thin and impressed with a die, the design impressed on one side appearing in relief on the other.

Bretasche. A defensive gallery of wood.

Buckler. A small shield.

But-and-ben. A two-roomed cottage, strictly one with an outer and an inner room (Scots).

Butt-joint, see *Race-bond.*

Cabossed. In heraldry, of an animal's head cut off at the ears and shown full-faced.

Canton. In heraldry, the first quarter of a shield, or a similar but smaller subdivision in a corresponding position.

Cap-house. The small roofed superstructure of a stair leading to the parapet walk or garret of a building.

Caponier. In fortification, a covered passage giving flanking fire along a ditch.

Casemate. In fortification, a bomb-proof chamber in the thickness of a rampart, for artillery, etc.

Cat-slide roof. Any portion of a roof which is continued downwards below the general eaves-line.

Cavetto. A concave moulding of one-quarter of a circle.

Cella. In ancient architecture, the part of a temple within the walls.

Chalmer. Chamber (Scots).

Chamfer. The bevelled surface left by cutting away an angle or arris (*q.v.*).

Chaplet. In heraldry, a wreath.

Chase. Groove.

Checked. Recessed to receive a door-frame, etc., or to act as a stop (Scots).

Checky. In heraldry, divided into squares or chequers.

Chevron. In heraldry, a charge of pointed gable form.

Chief. In heraldry, the upper third of a shield.

Cinerary Urn. A type of pottery used for containing a cremated burial in the 2nd millennium B.C.

Cinquefoil, see *Foil.*

Clearstorey. A lighting storey or range of windows in the highest part of a building, especially the nave, chancel, etc., of a church.

Coffer. A sunk panel in a ceiling or soffit.

Cohort. A unit of Roman troops, constituting the tenth part of a legion.

Collar-beam. A tie-beam fixed above wall-plate level.

Composite. The fifth Classical order, Ionic grafted upon Corinthian.

Coomb-ceiling. The sloping ceiling of a room partially or wholly contained in the roof-space (Scots).

Corbel. A block of stone or timber projecting from a wall to support a superincumbent weight.

Cordiner. Shoemaker (Scots).

Cornice. (1) In Classical architecture, the uppermost member of an entablature. (2) A moulded projection which crowns or finishes the part to which it is attached.

Couchant. In heraldry, of an animal lying prone but with the head raised.

Coudes. Pieces of armour protecting the elbows.

Counterchanged. In heraldry, of a shield divided so that part of the field is of a metal and part of a colour, the charges in either part being of the opposite colour or metal.

Counterscarp. The outer slope of the ditch of a fortified place, facing the scarp.

Couped, see under *Erased.*

Coving. The concave profile sometimes formed between a ceiling and the wall of a room.

Credence. A side-table or shelf, often in a niche, for the Elements before consecration.

Crenelle. An opening in an embattled parapet, between two merlons (*q.v.*)

Crocketted. In Gothic architecture, having ornaments such as buds or curled leaves on the angles of pinnacles, etc.

Cross, Calvary. A cross set on a mound or steps.

Cross, Greek. A plain cross in which shaft and limbs are of equal length.

Cross, Latin. A cross of which the shaft is longer than the limbs.

Cross-crosslet. In heraldry, originally a cross with limbs ending as trefoils, but later one with limbs ending in squarely-cut plain crosses.

Cross-patty. In heraldry, a cross with expanding arms cut square at the ends.

Crossing. The part of a church where the transepts cross the main axis.

Crow-stepped. Of a gable having a stepped profile (Scots).

Cruck. A principal roof-member springing from a point below wall-plate level.

Cusping. The projecting points between the small arcs or "foils" (*q.v.*) in Gothic tracery, arches, etc.

Dado. A decorative covering or lining applied to the lower part of the walls of a room and representing a continuous pedestal.

Debruised. In heraldry, surmounted.

Demi-lion. In heraldry, half a lion.

Dentilated. Of cornices having small square blocks or projections in their bed-mouldings.

Dexter. In heraldry, the right-hand side, opposite to the spectator's left.

Dimidiation. In heraldry, the cutting through of two shields per pale and the joining up of the dexter half of one with the sinister half of the other.

Dog-legged stair. A stair so called because of its appearance in vertical section, the upper flight returning above the lower one without a well.

Dog-tooth. In Gothic architecture, an ornament consisting of a series of pyramidal flowers of four petals.

Droved. Of ashlar, finished with the hammer and boaster to show a series of more or less parallel tool-marks over the whole surface.

Easter Sepulchre. A recess for the reception until Easter Day of the Elements consecrated on Maundy Thursday.

Edge-roll. A rounded or circular moulding set on an external angle.

Egg-and-dart. In Classical architecture, a series of ornaments alternately oval and shaped like the head of a dart.

Einzelhof. A peasant establishment for a single family-unit.

Engrailed. In heraldry, edged with a series of concave curves.

Entablature. In Classical architecture, the whole of the horizontal members above the column (architrave, frieze, cornice).

Entasis. A slight convex deviation from a straight line in the profile of a column, employed to overcome an optical illusion of concavity.

Equilateral arch. A pointed arch of which the radii are equal to the width of the opening.

Erased. In heraldry, ragged, as if torn off, as distinct from *couped*, or cut evenly.

Escallop. In heraldry, a scallop shell.

Escutcheon. In heraldry, an heraldic shield.

Escutcheon of pretence. In heraldry, a wife's shield placed in the middle of that of her husband.

Fess. In heraldry, a horizontal band across the centre of a shield.

Fess-point. In heraldry, central point.

Feu or *feu-ferme.* A perpetual lease granted in return for an annual fixed money-rent.

Fibula. A safety-pin.

Fillet. A narrow, flat band running down a shaft or along a moulding, or separating two mouldings.

Fitchée. In heraldry, terminating in a point.

Flory. In heraldry, decorated with fleurs-de-lys.

Flory-counter-flory. In heraldry, of a tressure (*q.v.*) which bears fleurs-de-lys pointing alternately outwards and inwards.

Foil (*trefoil, quatrefoil, cinquefoil, multifoil*). The lobe, often leaf-shaped, of three, four, five or more arcs, formed by the cusping (*q.v.*) in an arch or other opening, or in panelling.

Food Vessel. A type of pottery used in the 2nd millennium B.C.

Forestair. An external stair, usually unenclosed.

Four-centred. Of an arch the curve of which has been struck from four centres.

Frieze. In Classical architecture, the member in the entablature of an order that occurs between the architrave and the cornice. Also applied to a band below a ceiling cornice.

Gablet. A small gable.

Galilee. A porch at the W. end of a church.

Garb. In heraldry, a sheaf of corn.

Garderobe. A mediaeval privy, known as a close garderobe when it has no shaft.

Geometric stair. A stair in which the flights run continuously round a well-hole, without newels.

Gibbs surround. The surround of a door or window containing either alternating larger and smaller blocks of stone, set quoinwise, or intermittent large blocks, often connected by a narrow raised band.

Giblet-checked. Of an opening rebated externally to receive a door-frame (Scots).

Gnomon. The vane or indicator of a sundial.

Gorget. Armour for the throat.

Groined. Of a vault without ribs, the groin being the sharp edge formed at the meeting of two vault-cells.

Gules. In heraldry, red.

Gyronny. In heraldry, applied to a field divided into eight triangular segments by two lines drawn quarterly and two drawn saltirewise.

Harled. Rough-cast (Scots).

Harl-pointing. Pointing of rough texture, partly spread over the surface of the masonry (Scots).

Henge. A circular embanked sanctuary of the 2nd millennium B.C.

Heritor. The proprietor of a heritable subject, and as such responsible, before the legislation of 1925, for the upkeep of the parish church and manse (Scots).

Herm. A pillar carved at the top with the head of Hermes, or, more loosely, with any male bust.

Hipped roof. A roof pitched back at the ends as well as at the sides, on a building constructed without gables.

Honour point. In heraldry, the point just above the centre of the shield.

Hood-moulding. A projecting moulding above an arch or lintel, also called a drip-stone or label.

Impaled. In heraldry, of two coats of arms side by side on one shield divided down the middle; usually that of the husband impaled with that of the wife.

Impost. The member from which the arch springs.

Increscent. In heraldry, of a crescent with its horns turned towards the dexter.

Inescutcheon. In heraldry, a shield borne as a charge.

Intake-member. A member carrying a wall-face back, e.g. from the top of a plinth.

Jamb. (1) The side of a door or window. (2) A wing of a building (Scots). (3) In heraldry, the leg of an animal.

King-post. In mediaeval roof-construction, an upright post connecting the ridge-piece with the centre of a tie-beam or collar-beam.

Label. (1) In Gothic architecture, a hood moulding (*q.v.*). (2) In heraldry, a narrow band on the chief of a shield from which hang "points" at right angles, usually borne as a "difference" or mark of junior membership of a family.

Laigh. Low (Scots).

Laird's loft. A private gallery in a church for a laird and his family (Scots).

Laver. A small stone wash-basin, usually recessed in a wall.

Lierne vault. A vault which incorporates short ribs or struts (liernes) connecting ribs with one another, and not springing from the impost or rising to the central boss.

Limes. A fortified frontier-line.

Loggia. A gallery open to the air.

Louvres. Inclined boards with spaces between them, set in windows or lanterns for ventilation.

Lucarne. An opening in a roof to admit light.

Machicolations. Slots or shafts, particularly openings between corbels, through which missiles could be directed downwards.

Merlon. The part of an embattled parapet that stands between two openings (cf. *Crenelle*).

Messuage. Land with residential buildings.

Microlith. A very small implement fashioned of flint, chert, etc.

Milliary, see *Ala*.

Mill-rind. The metal fitting at the centre of a mill-stone.

Mortsafe. An iron frame placed over a coffin as a protection against body-snatchers (Scots).

Motte. The mound of a Norman castle.

Mullet. In heraldry, a five-pointed spur-rowel, like a star, but with a hole in the centre.

Mullion. An upright member dividing a window into two or more lights.

Naiant. In heraldry, swimming.

Nail-head. Ornamentation resembling a series of square nail-heads.

Newel. (1) The central column of a spiral staircase, from which the steps radiate. (2) The principal posts at the angles of a dog-legged or well stair.

Nook-shaft. A shaft set in an angle or nook.

Ogival. Having a double curve, one concave and the other convex.

Oillet. A small window-opening.

O'on. Oven (Scots).

Oppidum. A hill-fort whose exceptional size and particularly commanding position suggests that it was a tribal centre.

Or. In heraldry, gold.

Oriel. A window projected on corbelling.

Orle. A border within a shield at some distance from the edge.

Outshot. An appendage to a main building.

Ovolo moulding. A convex moulding.

Pale. In heraldry, a vertical band down the middle of a shield.

Parterre. An area of garden laid out formally with flower-beds.

Passant. In heraldry, of an animal walking and looking straight forwards.

Patera. As used in Gothic architecture, a small ornament usually taking the form of a four-petalled flower, normally set at intervals in a moulding.

Peascod. A kind of breastplate, fashionable in the later 16th century, having an overhanging hump in the lower part of the front.

Pelta-shaped. Shaped like a crescent, and so resembling a *pelta* (a small shield) seen from the side.

Pend. A covered passage (Scots).

Peristalith. A member of the ring of upright stones on the edge of a cairn.

Peristyle. A colonnade surrounding a building.

Perron. A platform outside a building ascended by steps.

Pilaster. A rectangular column, of shallow projection, engaged in a wall.

Piles. In heraldry, a series of triangular wedge-shaped figures issuing from the top of the shield and pointing downwards.

Pinked. Of garments showing ornamental perforations.

Pinnings. Small stones used to fill irregularities in coursed masonry.

Piscina. A basin in which the sacred vessels were washed, set in a niche or recess usually S. of the altar, and provided with a drain discharging into the thickness of the wall.

Pit. A castle prison, usually in the form of a sunk chamber entered from above through a hatch.

Plinth. The projecting base of a wall or column.

Podium. A continuous pedestal.

Porte-cochère. An entrance provided with a porch under which a carriage could draw up.

Potence. A rotating ladder used in dovecots to give access to the nests.

Praesidium. A fortified post.

Praetentura. The part of the interior of a Roman fort that lies in front of the headquarters building.

Praetorium. The residence of the officer commanding a Roman fort.

Prebend. (1) The stipend of a cathedral canon, or member of a collegiate church. (2) Ecclesiastical property from which such a stipend is drawn.

Presbytery. The part of the church reserved for the officiating clergy, east of the choir.

Press. A wall-cupboard (Scots).

Principia. The headquarters building of a Roman fort.

Proper. In heraldry, denoting that a charge appears in its natural colour.

Pulvinated. Of a frieze, having a convex or bulging section.

Purlin. A horizontal timber lying on the principal rafters of a roof to distribute the weight borne by the common rafters.

Putlog holes. Openings left in the face of a wall for the insertion of scaffolding.
Putto. A small figure of a naked boy.

Quadripartite. Of a vaulting-bay divided into four compartments by ribs or groins.
Quaich. A small shallow drinking-cup with two lug-handles (Scots).
Quatrefoil, see *Foil.*
Quillons. The arms forming the cross-guard of a sword.
Quirk. A sharp-edged groove separating other members of a moulding.
Quoin. A corner stone of a building.

Race-bond. A vertical or otherwise unbonded joint in masonry (Scots).
Raggle. A groove cut in masonry to receive the material forming a joint, especially on the face of a wall to receive the edge of a roof.
Rake. Slope, as of a roof or gable.
Rampant. In heraldry, of an animal standing erect on the hind legs, with both forelegs elevated and the head in profile.
Rear-arch. A constructional arch used in place of a lintel to carry the inner side of a wall over the back of a door or window.
Rebated, see *Checked.*
Relieving arch. An arch built over a lintel, to relieve it of superincumbent weight.
Rendering. Plastering applied to the external face of a wall.
Rerebrace. A piece of armour protecting the upper arm.
Respond. A half-pier attached to a wall to support an arch.
Retentura. The part of the interior of a Roman fort that lies behind the headquarters building.
Reticulated. Of masonry in which the surfaces of the stones are worked to give a net-like pattern in raised veins.
Reveal. The part of a jamb that lies between the frame of a door or window and the outer face of the wall.
Rock-faced, see *Rusticated.*
Roll-and-hollow moulding. A roll-moulding combined with one or more concave ones.
Round. A turret projecting from the upper angle of a building.
Rubble. Masonry of rough unsquared stones.
Rusticated. Of masonry in which only the margins of the stones are worked, the faces being left rough, e.g. "rock-faced"; also of ashlar having the joints emphasised by channelling.
Rybat. A side-piece of dressed stone in a window or door (Scots).

Sacellum. The regimental chapel in the headquarters of a Roman fort.
Saltire. In heraldry, St. Andrew's Cross.
Sarking. Boarding laid on the rafters, as a base for the roofing material.
Sasine. (1) Symbolical delivery of possession of a feudal property by the superior to his vassal. (2) A notarial instrument narrating that the symbolical delivery has been made (Scots).
Scale-and-platt. Of a stair having straight flights of steps with landings.
Scarcement. A narrow ledge formed where a wall is set back.
Scarf-joint. A longitudinal joint between two timbers, bevelled or notched at their ends and pinned through the bevelled portion.
Scarp. The inner slope of the ditch of a fortified place.
Sconcheon. The side of an aperture, from the back of the jamb to the interior of the wall (Scots).

Screens. A partition separating the hall from the service space; also applied to the space so cut off from the hall.

Segmental arch. A rounded arch the arc of which is less than a semicircle.

Seisin, see *Sasine.*

Sejant. In heraldry, sitting.

Shakefork. In heraldry, a charge resembling a Y with the points upwards.

Shalloon. A closely-woven woollen material used chiefly for linings.

Shouldered arch. A lintel supported on a corbel at either end, the corbels usually being cut to a concave profile.

Sinister. In heraldry, the left-hand side, opposite to the spectator's right.

Skew. The slope of a gable-head.

Skewput. The lowest stone in the coping of a gable (Scots).

Slipped. In heraldry, torn off from the stalk.

Snecked. Of masonry in which some blocks are rebated to fit adjoining ones.

Soffit. The underside of a stair, lintel, cornice, arch, canopy, etc.

Sollerets. Shoes made of overlapping steel plates.

Spandrel. The triangular-shaped space above the haunch of an arch.

Sprocket. A short member nailed to the foot of a rafter to form tilted eaves or a bell-cast roof.

Squinch arch. An arch spanning the angle between two walls.

Stile. The vertical part of a piece of framing into which are fixed the ends of rails.

Stoop-and-roume. A method of mining coal by which pillars of coal are left uncut to support the roof of the gallery.

String-course. A projecting horizontal band or moulding carried along the face of a wall.

Study. A small room usually contained within a corner turret (Scots).

Stugged. Of masonry dressed with a punch so as to produce close pock-markings.

Sunk-wrought. Of work executed below the plane of the general surface.

Surcoat. An outer coat, often worn over armour and displaying armorial bearings.

Taces. Rows of overlapping steel bands below the breastplate, defending the hips and lower part of the body.

Tack. Lease (Scots).

Tas-de-charge. A form of construction in which two or more arches or vaulting-ribs, instead of beginning separately, have one or more courses of stones as springers in common, these being bedded horizontally and bonded into the wall.

Tierceron vault. A vault having, in addition to the main ribs, intermediate (tierceron) ribs which rise from the main springers but end at a point short of the central boss.

Transe. A through passage (Scots).

Transom. A beam or beams sub-dividing a window horizontally into two or more lights.

Tressure. In heraldry, a border within the shield narrower than the *orle* (*q.v.*), generally borne double.

Triforium. A gallery or arcade, usually without windows and so a "blind-storey", above the main arcade and below the "clearstorey" (*q.v.*).

Triglyph. A vertically grooved tablet occurring at regular intervals in the Doric frieze.

Turnpike stair. A spiral stair (Scots).

Tusking. Stones left projecting from the surface of a wall to allow the bonding in of another wall. Also used of the ragged end of a ruinous wall.

Tutulus. An external traverse protecting the entrance to a Roman fort or temporary camp.

Tympanum. An enclosed space in the head of an arch, doorway, etc., or in the triangle of a pediment.

Undercroft. A vaulted under-building.
Undy. In heraldry, wave-like.
Upstart. Part of the jamb of a void equivalent in height to several rybats (Scots).

Vallum. Rampart.
Vambrace. A piece of armour protecting the forearm.
Venetian window. A window having three apertures, of which the central one is arched and wider than the others, separated from one another by slender piers.
Vert. In heraldry, green.
Vesica. A sub-oval window with pointed ends.
Via praetoria. The roadway leading through the front gate of a Roman fort to the headquarters building.
Via principalis. The roadway leading through a Roman fort from side to side, in front of the headquarters building.
Vicus. A civil settlement attached to a Roman fort.
Voussoirs. The wedge-like stones that form an arch.

Warming-house. An apartment in a monastic building in which a fire was kept burning to provide warmth.
Water-guard. An attachment preventing the entry of water into a scabbard.
Water-holding. Of a hollow moulding, in the base of a plinth, or column, so deeply undercut that water would lie in it.
Wavy. In heraldry, wave-like.
Wheel stair, see *Turnpike stair.*
Woodhouse. In heraldry, a wild man.
Wyvern. In heraldry, an animal having a barbed tail and two feet like those of an eagle.

Yale. In heraldry, an animal with horns and tusks.
Yett. A grated iron door (Scots).

INDEX

References are to pages and not to article numbers. Where more than one reference is given for any item, the main entry is printed in bold type.

[1] Excluding those which form part of other monuments.

[1] *Italics* indicate significant remains of pre-Reformation construction.

[1] *Italics* indicate vitrifaction.

[1] For details see under locality headings.

[1] *Italics* indicate use for droving.

PLATES 117-230

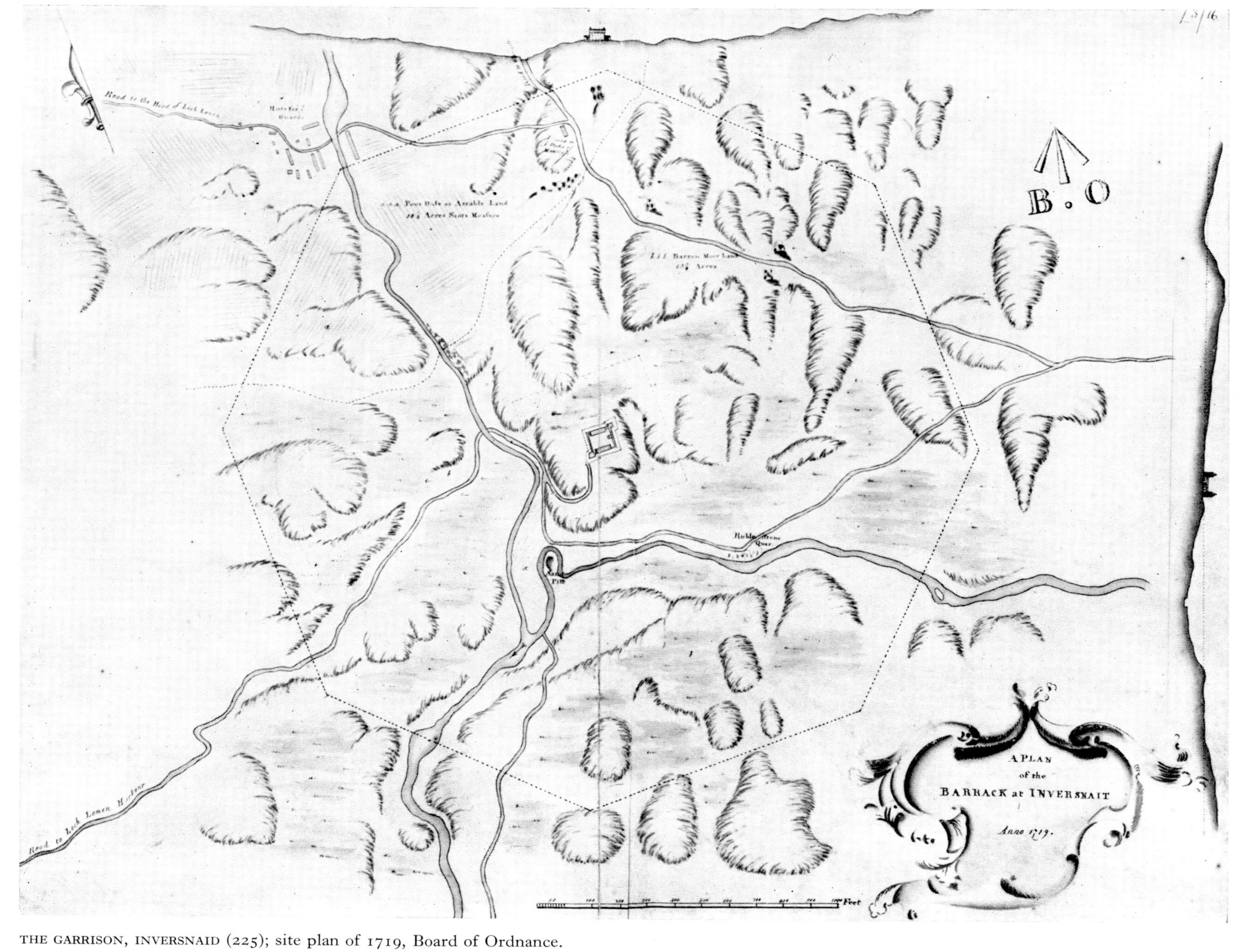

THE GARRISON, INVERSNAID (225); site plan of 1719, Board of Ordnance.

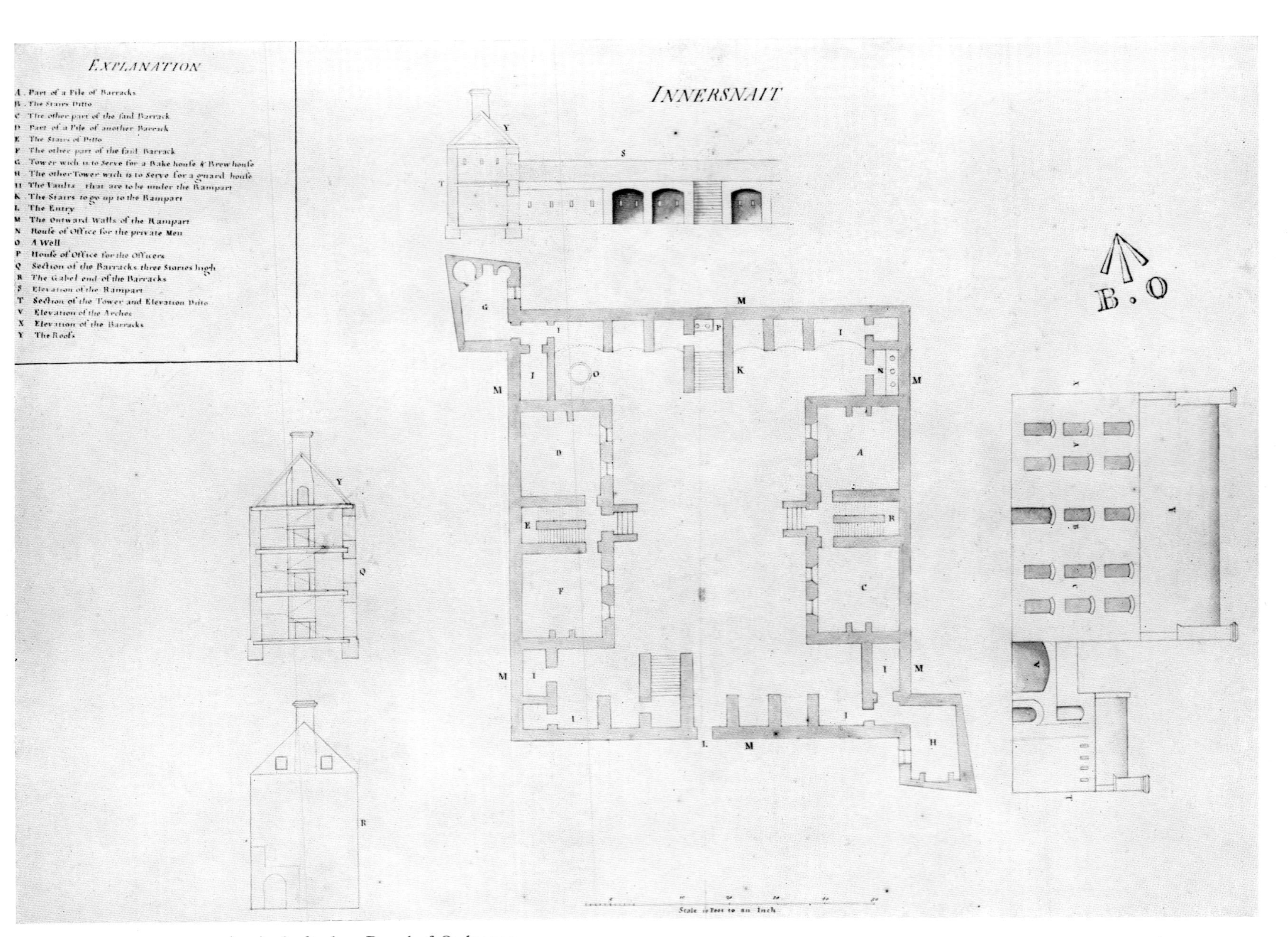

THE GARRISON, INVERSNAID (225); draft plan, Board of Ordnance.

A

B

C

THE GARRISON, INVERSNAID (225);

A. remains of N. barrack-block.

B. loopholes in N. barrack-block.

C. remains of well.

PLATE 119

PLATE 120

VIEW OF THE BURGH AND CASTLE OF STIRLING, 1673-4, by Vorsterman.

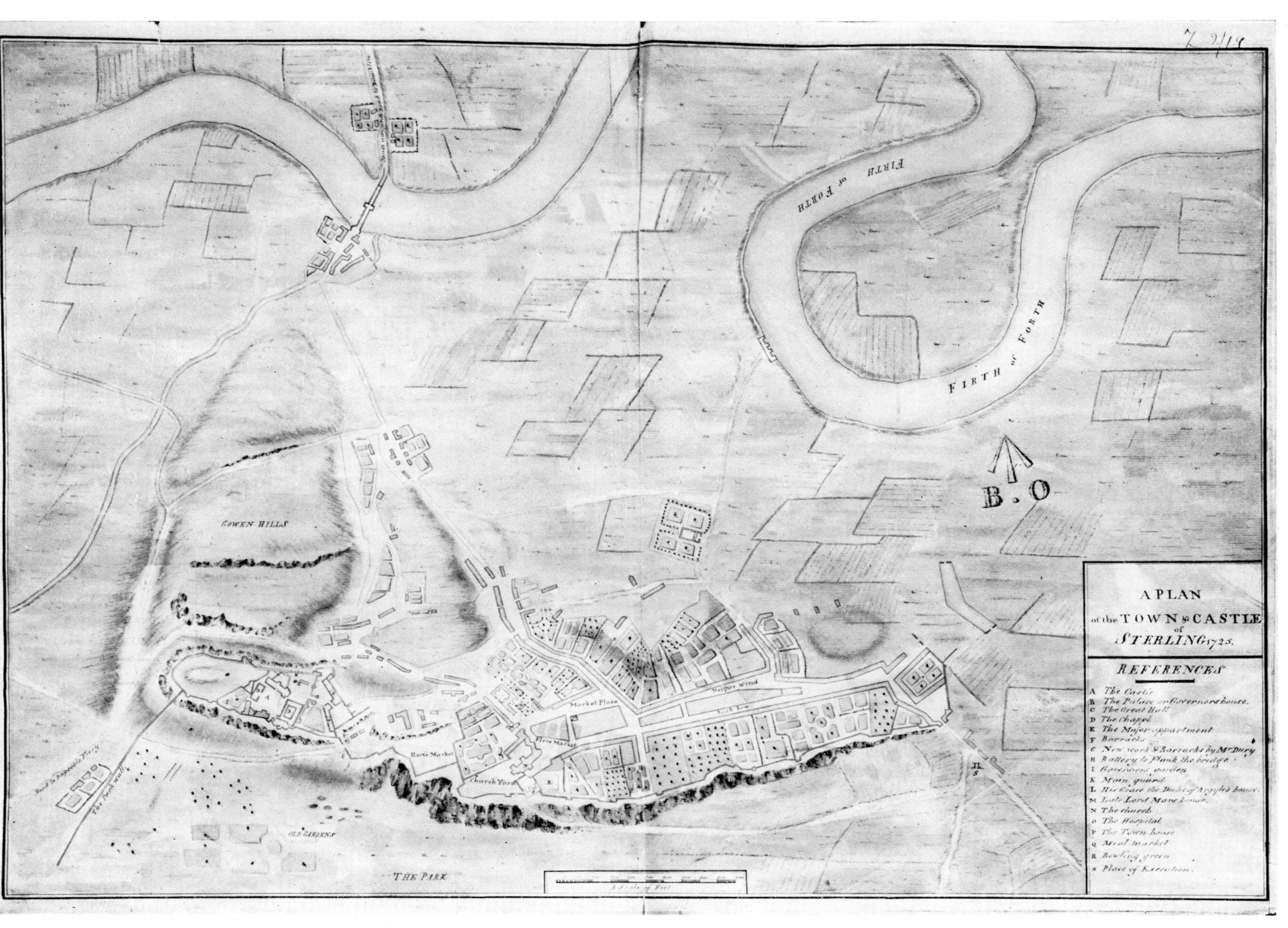

PLAN OF THE BURGH AND CASTLE OF STIRLING, 1725, by Laye.

A

B

ARGYLL'S LODGING, STIRLING (227); A. from NW. B. E. range from SE.

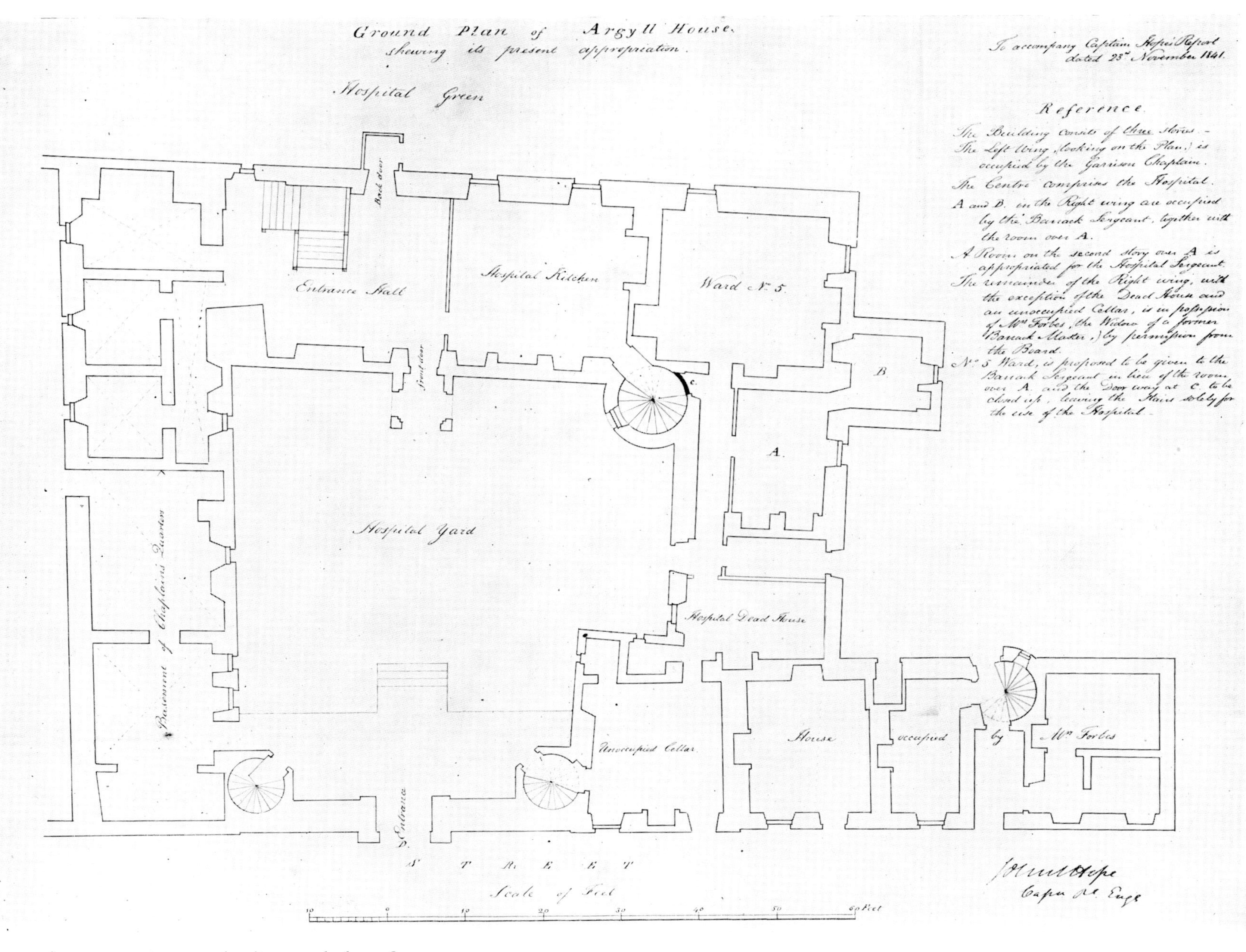

ARGYLL'S LODGING, STIRLING (227); ground plan, 1841.

A

B

C

ARGYLL'S LODGING, STIRLING (227); A. E. range from courtyard. B. heraldic panel, Viscount Stirling. C. entrance-porch, E. range.

A

B

C

D

E

ARGYLL'S LODGING, STIRLING (227);

A. entrance-gateway.

B. window architrave in SE. stair-tower.

C, D, E. window pediments in E. range.

A

D

B

C

ARGYLL'S LODGING, STIRLING (227); A, B, C. fireplace in the Upper Hall. D. fireplace on first floor of E. range.

A

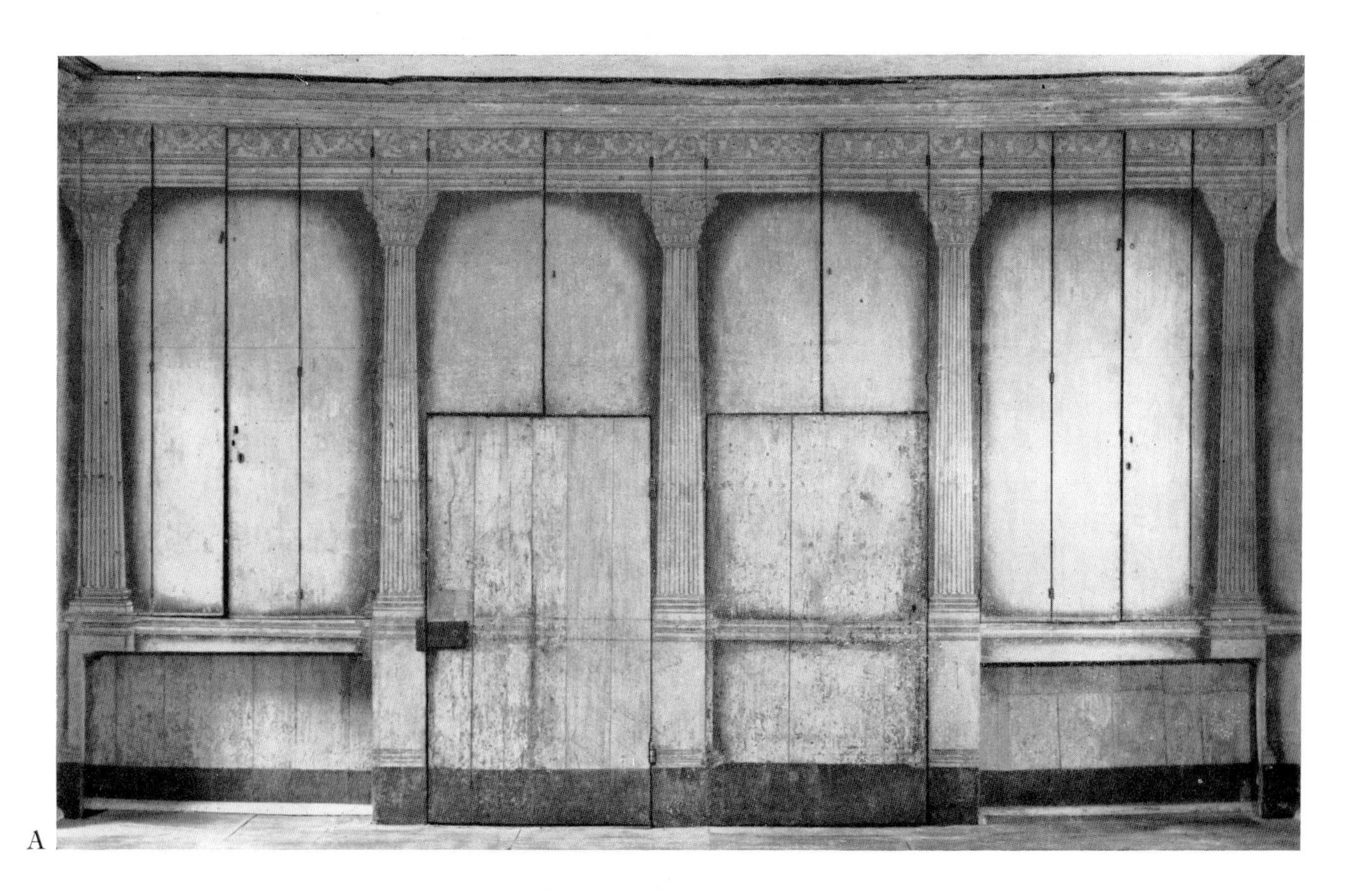

B

ARGYLL'S LODGING, STIRLING (227); painted decoration in the Upper Hall.

A

B

ARGYLL'S LODGING, STIRLING (227); A. doorway to the Upper Hall. B. staircase in E. range.

MAR'S WORK, STIRLING (230); E. façade.

A

B

MAR'S WORK, STIRLING (230); E. façade. A. heraldic panel (Mar quartering Erskine).
B. heraldic panel (Mar and Erskine impaling Murray of Tullibardine).

MAR'S WORK, STIRLING (230); E. façade. A. heraldic panel (Scotland). B. statuette (16). C. base-stop (31). D. base-stop (29).

PLATE 132

COWANE'S HOSPITAL, STIRLING (231), from NE.

A. COWANE'S HOSPITAL, STIRLING (231); Founder's statue.
B. COWANE'S HOSPITAL, STIRLING (231); oak chest.
C. COWANE'S HOUSE, STIRLING (237), from NE.

A

B

A. THE TOWN HOUSE, STIRLING (232), from NW. B. THE ATHENAEUM, KING STREET, STIRLING (247), from SE.

A

B

THE TOWN HOUSE, STIRLING (232); A. belfry.
B. fireplace and panelling on first floor.

GLENGARRY LODGE, SPITTAL STREET, STIRLING (248), from S.

BROAD STREET, STIRLING; right, 34, Norrie's House (233); left, 36-38 (234).

A

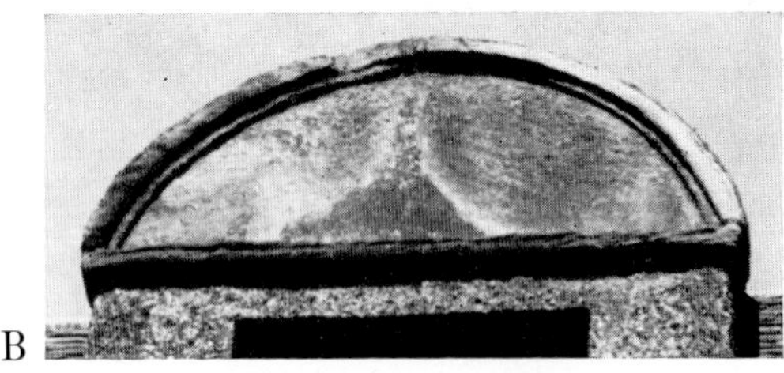

B

C

D

24-26 BROAD STREET, STIRLING (234);

A. general view.

B. dormer pediment.

C. view from close.

D. DORMER PEDIMENT, 38 ST. JOHN STREET, STIRLING (245).

A

B

C

D

BRUCE OF AUCHENBOWIE'S HOUSE, ST. JOHN STREET, STIRLING (244);
A. from NW. B. crow-stepped gable. C. moulded skewput.
D. DARNLEY HOUSE, BOW STREET, STIRLING (235), from W.

A

B

C

A. GATEWAY, THE HIGH SCHOOL, SPITTAL STREET, STIRLING (248). B. DOORWAY, 72-76 ST. MARY'S WYND, STIRLING (238).
C. DOORWAY, 42 UPPER BRIDGE STREET, STIRLING (241).

A

B

C

THE TOWN WALL, STIRLING (249); A. bastion, Back Walk. B. Port Street bastion. C. return at lower end of Back Walk.

THE MERCAT CROSS, STIRLING (401).

PLATE 142

THE MERCAT CROSS, AIRTH (412).

A

B

THE BURGH OF AIRTH (251);

A. house at corner of Shore Road.

B. doorway of "The Herring House".

C. door-head of house in High Street.

D. doorway pediment of "The Smithy".

C

D

THE TOWN STEEPLE, FALKIRK (253).

PLATE 146

A

B

THE BURGH OF KILSYTH (254); A. 11 High Street. B. house in High Street.

A

B

C

D

BANNOCKBURN TOWN (264); A. the Brae. B. 17 the Brae. C. 26 Newmarket. D. 54 and 56 Station Road.

A

B

C

D

E

F

A. CHARTERSHALL VILLAGE (263); cottages.

B. TORBREX VILLAGE (259); weavers' cottages.

C. TAYLOR'S BUILDING, KIPPEN (285).

D, E. GARGUNNOCK VILLAGE (286); houses in main street.

F. BALFRON VILLAGE (280); Rockbrae, Buchanan Street.

A

D

B

E

C

F

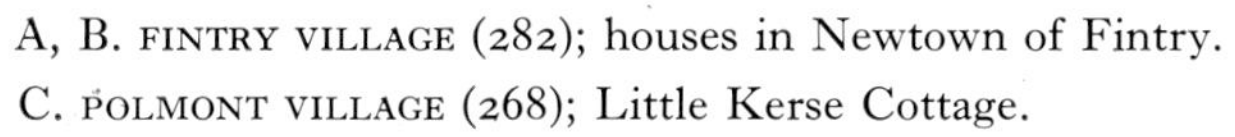

A, B. FINTRY VILLAGE (282); houses in Newtown of Fintry.

C. POLMONT VILLAGE (268); Little Kerse Cottage.

D. DENNYLOANHEAD VILLAGE (275); the Crown Hotel.

E. DENNY TOWN (274); 1 Broad Street.

F. SCHOOLHOUSE, POLMONT (269).

A

B

A. THE OLD MANSE, LARBERT (273). B. THE MANSE, POLMONT (270).

A

B

A. FINTRY VILLAGE (282); old manse.

B. THE CLACHAN OF BALFRON (281); the Old Manse.

ENGINEERING SHOP, CARRON IRONWORKS (265); roof structure in W. section.

A

B

ENGINEERING SHOP, CARRON IRONWORKS (265); A. tie-beam in W. section. B. S. elevation.

ENGINEERING SHOP, CARRON IRONWORKS (265); details of floor structure.

A

B

LENNOXTOWN (276); "Oliver" machine, Kali Nail Works.

A

B

C

BANNOCKBURN TOWN (264); Skeoch Mill.

A. general view from S.

B. inscribed stone.

C. roofs of dye-houses.

BANNOCKBURN TOWN (264); the Royal George Mill.

A, B. MILLSTONE QUARRIES, CRAIGMADDIE MUIR (567). C. MILLSTONE QUARRY, SPITTAL (568).

TORWOOD CASTLE (299) from N.

PLATE 159

A

B

TORWOOD CASTLE (299); A. from S. B. from W.

TORWOOD CASTLE (299); A. entrance-doorway. B. remains of stair-turret, attic floor. C. diamond-shaped lights in S. façade. D. ground-floor window in S. façade. E. stone panel with date 1566.

OLD LECKIE HOUSE (343); original entrance-doorway.

A

B

A. OLD LECKIE HOUSE (343) from SE. B. STEUARTHALL (293) from S.

AUCHENBOWIE HOUSE (296); the library.

A

B

A. AUCHENBOWIE HOUSE (296) from SE.

B. KERSIE MAINS (300) from SW.

A

B

A. POWIS HOUSE (288); fireplace on first floor.

B. KERSIE MAINS (300); fireplace on first floor.

A

B

BANNOCKBURN HOUSE (295); A. staircase.
B. first-floor room in W. wing.

BANNOCKBURN HOUSE (295); ceiling in old drawing-room.

A

B

BANNOCKBURN HOUSE (295); ceiling in old drawing-room. A. detail. B. centre-piece.

BANNOCKBURN HOUSE (295); detail of ceiling in old drawing-room.

A

B

BANNOCKBURN HOUSE (295); details of ceiling in old drawing-room.

A

B

BANNOCKBURN HOUSE (295);
ceiling of first-floor room in E. wing.

A

B

C

BANNOCKBURN HOUSE (295);

A. plaster frieze in room E. of entrance-hall.

B. plaster frieze in room E. of old drawing-room.

C. plaster frieze and cornice in first-floor room in W. wing.

A

B

C

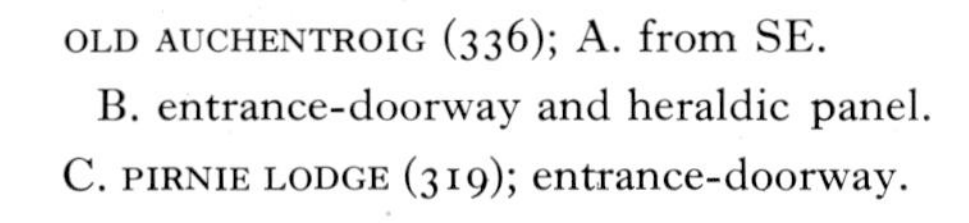

OLD AUCHENTROIG (336); A. from SE.
B. entrance-doorway and heraldic panel.
C. PIRNIE LODGE (319); entrance-doorway.

A

B

C

D

A. BIRDSTON FARM (322) from S.
B. BORROWMEADOW (292) from S.
C. GARTINSTARRY (377) from SE.
D. ARNPRIOR FARM (339) from NW.

A

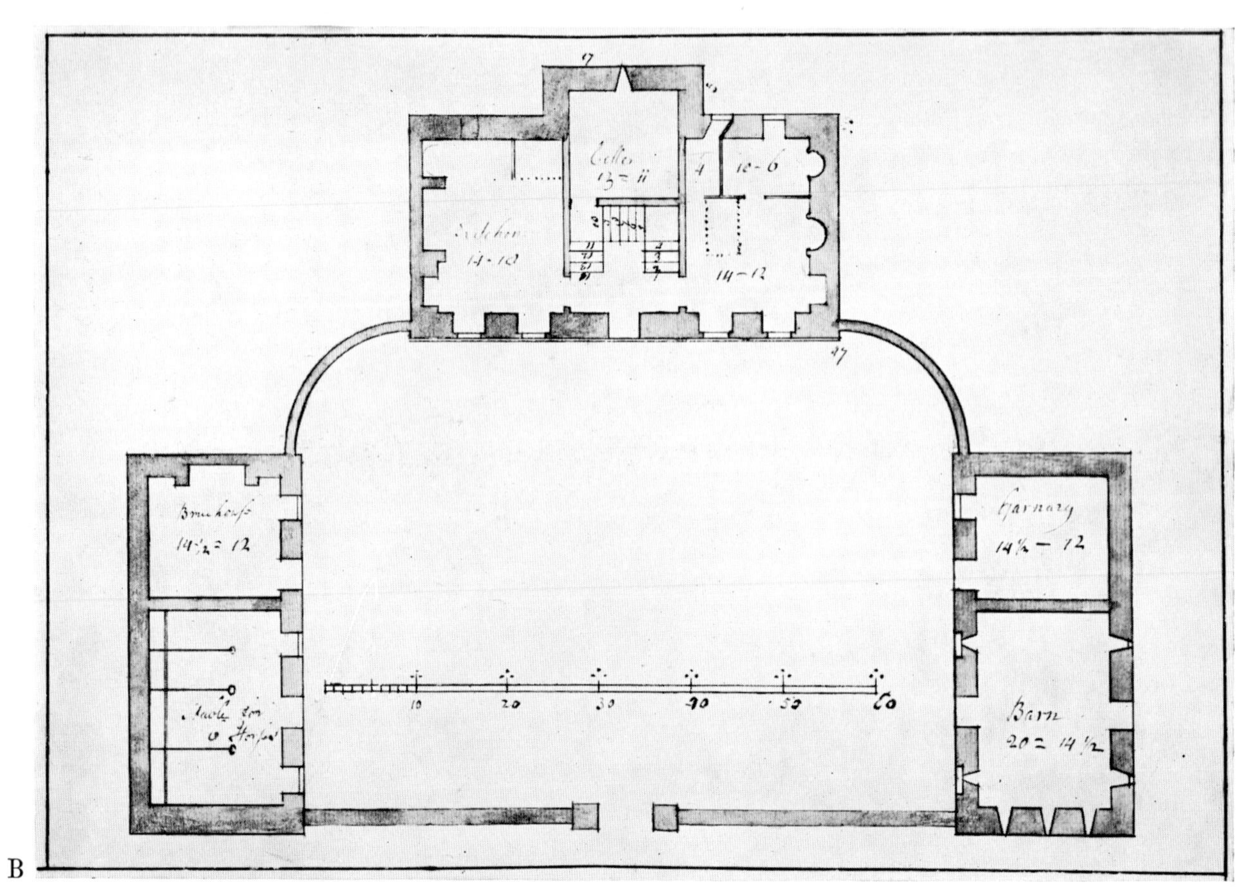

B

OLD BALLIKINRAIN (332); A. from SE. B. 18th-century plan.

TOUCH HOUSE (345) from SE.

A

B

TOUCH HOUSE (345); A. from SE., showing early tower. B. view from NE.

TOUCH HOUSE (345); ceiling in dining-room.

TOUCH HOUSE (345); the drawing-room.

A

B

TOUCH HOUSE (345); details of ceiling in drawing-room.

A

B

TOUCH HOUSE (345);
A. chimney-piece in drawing-room.
B. chimney-piece in dining-room.

TOUCH HOUSE (345); principal stair.

A

B

C

TOUCH HOUSE (345); ceiling, with details, in W. room on second floor of S. block.

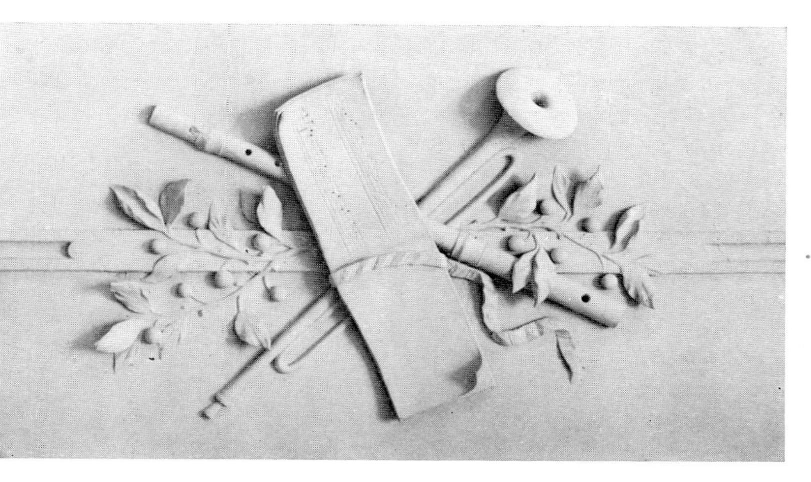

A

C

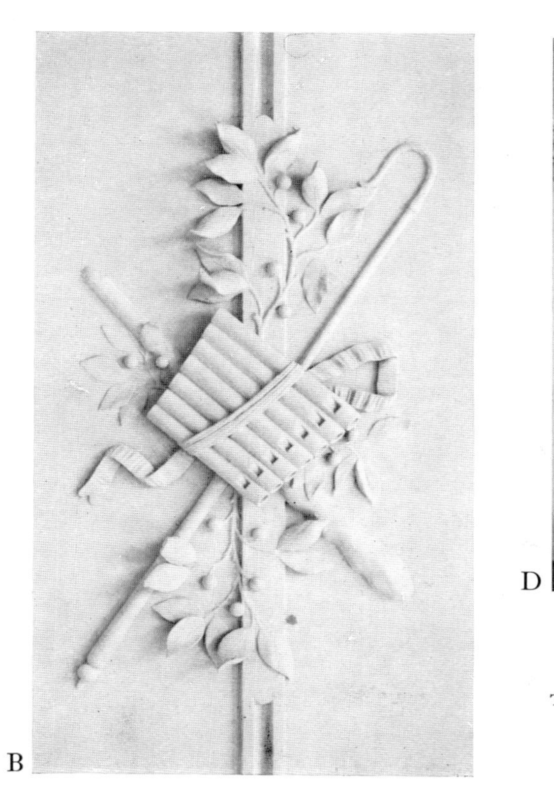

B

D

TOUCH HOUSE (345); A, B. details of ceiling in W. room on second floor of S. block.
C. tapestry on stair landing.
D. library in N. range.

A

B

TOUCH HOUSE (345); plaster busts, library in N. range.

A

B

TOUCH HOUSE (345); plaster busts, library in N. range.

A

B

C

D

A. POWIS HOUSE (288) from NW.
B. WRIGHTPARK (335) from SE.
C. CARRON HOUSE (310) from SE.
D. OLD BALLIKINRAIN (332) from NW.

A

B

A. POWIS HOUSE (288); the stables. B. BOQUHAN (342); the stables.

GARGUNNOCK HOUSE (215) from S.

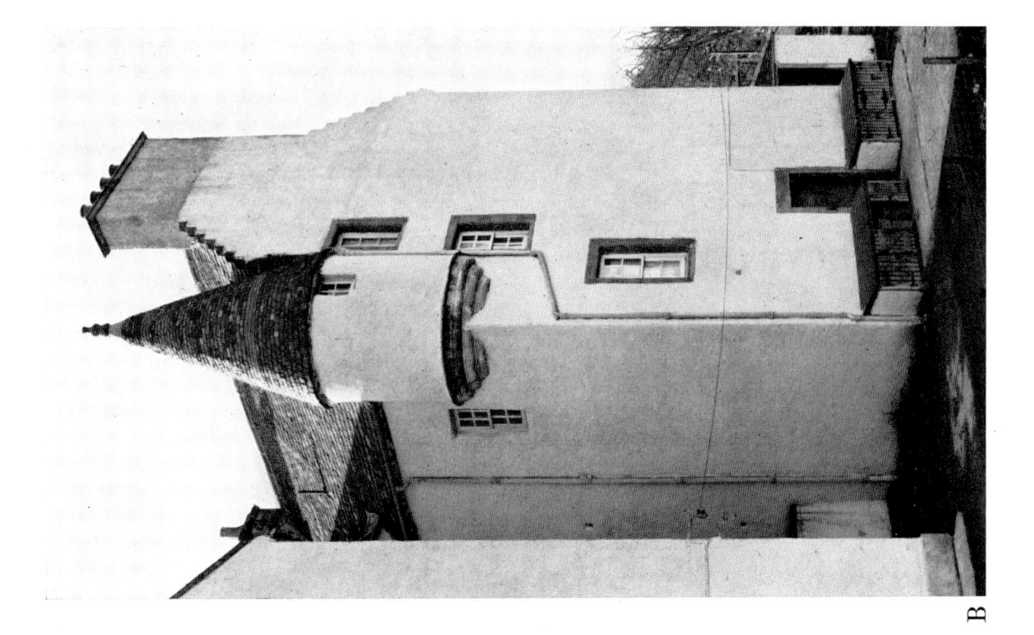

B

A

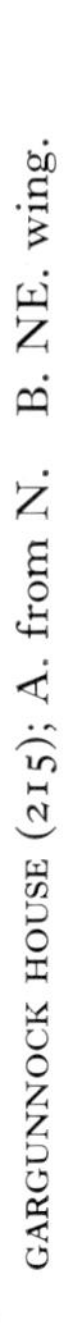

GARGUNNOCK HOUSE (215); A. from N. B. NE. wing.

A

B

GARGUNNOCK HOUSE (215);

A. ceiling in drawing-room.

B. S. end of dining-room.

PLATE 192

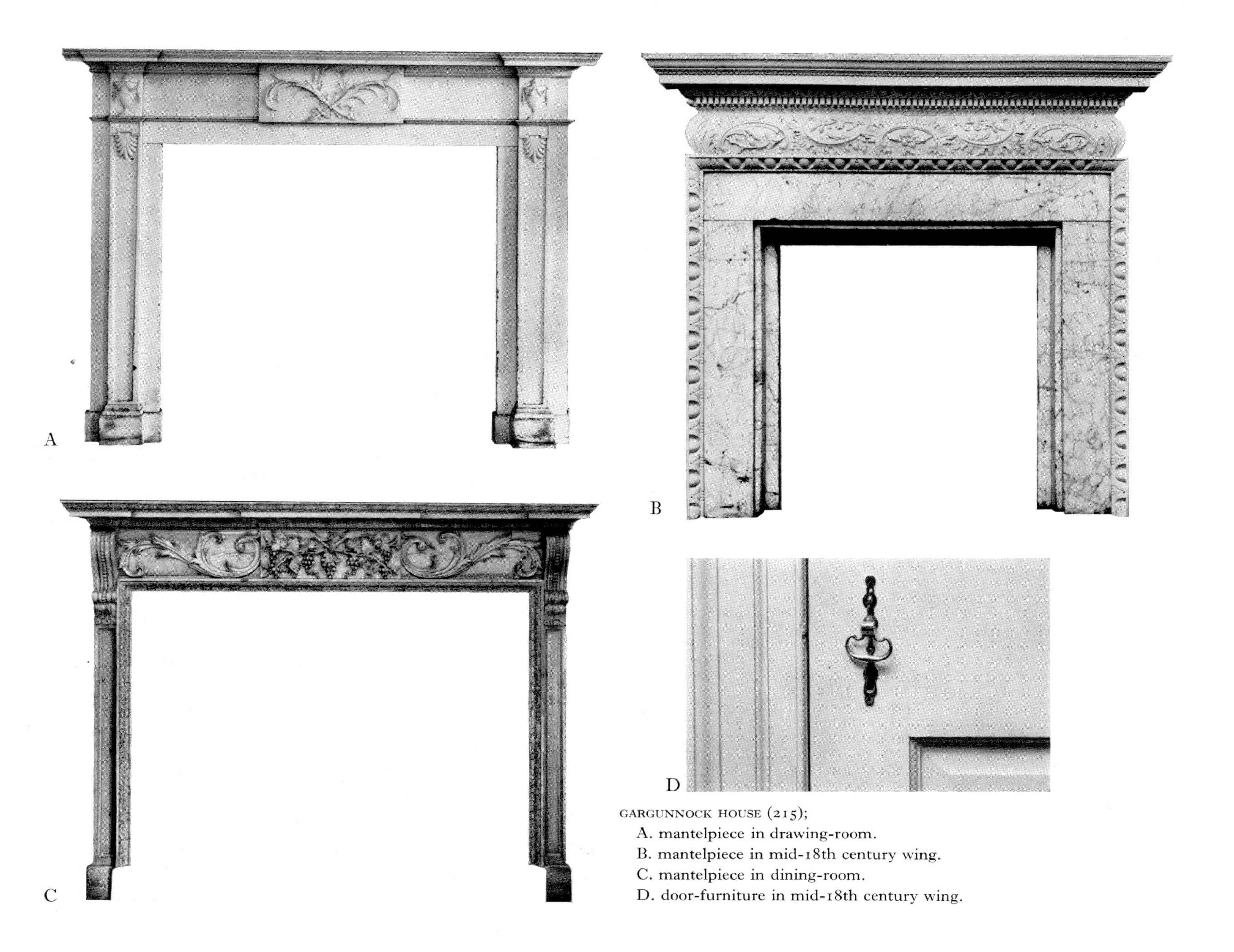

GARGUNNOCK HOUSE (215);

A. mantelpiece in drawing-room.
B. mantelpiece in mid-18th century wing.
C. mantelpiece in dining-room.
D. door-furniture in mid-18th century wing.

A

C

B

QUARTER (298); A. from W. B. stair.

C. LAURELHILL HOUSE, STIRLING (291), from N.

A

B

C

D

A. POLMONT HOUSE (314) from S.
B. NEUCK (303) from NW.
C. CRAIGFORTH HOUSE (289) from NE.
D. BALLENCLEROCH (325) from SE.

CALLENDAR HOUSE (311) from SW.

A

B

CALLENDAR HOUSE (311); A. ceiling over scale-and-platt stair. B. scale-and-platt stair.

A

B

CALLENDAR HOUSE (311);

A. interior of first-floor room in NE. angle of main block.

B. door-furniture.

A

B

CALLENDAR HOUSE (311); kitchen. A. oven. B. hot-plate.

A

B

GARDEN (338); A. view from E. B. architect's drawing of E. elevation.

A

B

A. LENNOX CASTLE (324) from NE. B. AIRTHREY CASTLE (287) from S.

A

B

A. KINCAID HOUSE (321) from E. B. POWFOULIS (304) from W.

A

B

DUNMORE PARK (301); A. SE. elevation, architect's drawing. B. view from SE.

A

B

C

D

A. BIRDSTON FARM (322); skewput.

B. "THE PINEAPPLE", DUNMORE PARK (302); keystone of portico.

C. WRIGHTPARK (335); fireplace lintel.

D. STEUARTHALL (293); heraldic panel, Stirling and Hamilton.

A

B

C

A. WINDMILL, MYREHEAD (355).

B. THRESHING-MILL, NORTH BELLSDYKE FARM (p. 47).

C. OLD FARM, WESTER BARNEGO (361); bee-boles.

A

B

A. OLD FARMS, LITTLE BRUACH-CAORUINN (380); House A from W.

B. CRUCK-FRAMED BYRE, STRONMACNAIR (377), from NW.

A

B

A. OLD HOUSE, CORHEICHAN (372); remains of cruck in byre.
B. CRUCK-FRAMED BYRE, STRONMACNAIR (377); remains of cruck.

A

B

C

D

A. DOVECOT, DRUMQUHASSLE (398).
B. DOVECOT, WESTQUARTER (396).
C. DOVECOT, CARRON HOUSE (393).
D. DOVECOT, LARABEN (399).

A

B

DOVECOT, LOWER POLMAISE (391); A. exterior.
B. interior showing potence.

A. HERALDIC PANEL, GILMEADOWLAND (421); Livingstone of Almond.

B. HERALDIC PANEL, KELVINHEAD (431); Graham (probably of Kelvinhead).

C. HERALDIC PANEL, WESTQUARTER DOVECOT (396); Livingstone of Westquarter.

D. CARVED PANEL, 14 ABERCROMBY PLACE, STIRLING (404).

E. CARVED STONE, BLOEMFONTEIN, AIRTH (415).

F. CARVED STONE, OVERSEER'S HOUSE, AIRTH (414).

A

B

HERALDIC PANELS, FALKIRK MUSEUM (428); A. Earl of Callendar.
B. Livingstone of Kilsyth impaling de Bord.

A. STONE CORBEL, FALKIRK MUSEUM (428).
B. CARVED STONE, MILLFIELD (420).
C. HERALDIC PANEL, 14 ABERCROMBY PLACE, STIRLING (404); Callendar impaling Reid.
D. CARVED STONE, GOSPEL HALL, KILSYTH (434).
E. CARVED STONE, 36 SILVER ROW, FALKIRK (426).

A

B

ST. NINIAN'S VILLAGE (260); carved panels on Randolph Buildings, Randolph Crescent.

A

B

A. SUNDIAL, BALLINDALLOCH (444). B. SUNDIAL, AUCHENBOWIE HOUSE (296).

A

B

E

D

C

A. SUNDIAL, HOWKERSE (419).

B. SUNDIAL, SAUCHIEBURN HOUSE (410).

C. SUNDIAL, SAUCHIEBURN HOUSE (410); detail.

D. SUNDIAL, OLD LECKIE HOUSE (343).

E. SUNDIAL, BALLENCLEROCH (325).

A

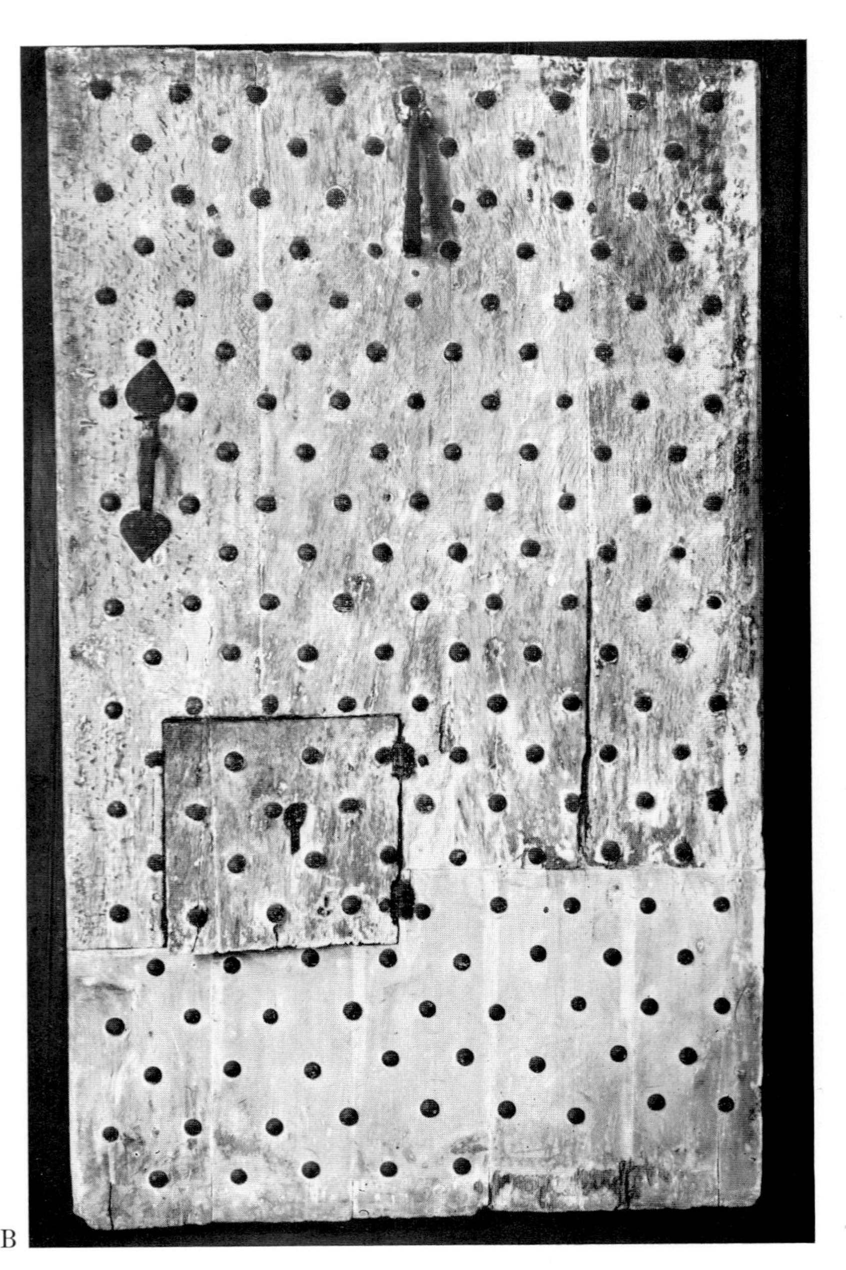

B

A. CROSS WELL, FALKIRK (540). B. SMITH INSTITUTE, STIRLING (405); door from Carnock House.

A

B

C

D

SMITH INSTITUTE, STIRLING (405); medallion panels.

A

B

C

D

SMITH INSTITUTE, STIRLING (405); medallion panels.

A

B

C

D

SMITH INSTITUTE, STIRLING (405); medallion panels.

A

B

C

D

SMITH INSTITUTE, STIRLING (405); medallion panels.

A

B

C

D

E

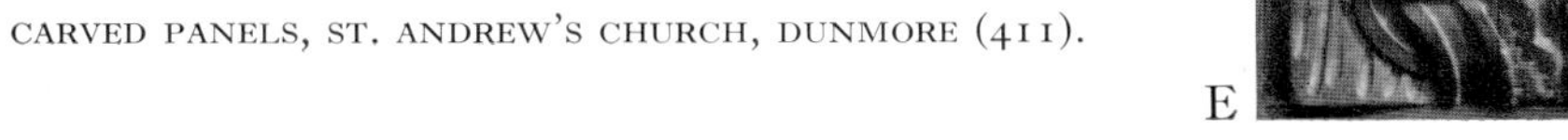

CARVED PANELS, ST. ANDREW'S CHURCH, DUNMORE (411).

A

B

OLD BRIDGE, STIRLING (455); A. from E. B. in relation to Stirling Castle, by Slezer.

OLD BRIDGE, STIRLING (455), from SE.

A

B

A. OLD BRIDGE, BANNOCKBURN (457), from W. B. LOW BRIDGE, GONACHAN (467), from E.

OLD BRIDGE, DRIP (454), from SE.

A

B

A. BRIDGE, FINTRY (468), from W. B. CARDROSS BRIDGE (452) from SW.

A

B

C

A. BRIDGE, CHARTERSHALL (456), from W. B. ABBEYTOWN BRIDGE, AIRTH (460), from W.
C. CALLENDAR HOUSE (311); bridge in policies.

A

B

AVON AQUEDUCT (474);
A. from SE.
B. detail of bay design.

A

B

A. AVON VIADUCT (472) from W. B. RAILWAY VIADUCT, AVONBANK (471), from SW.

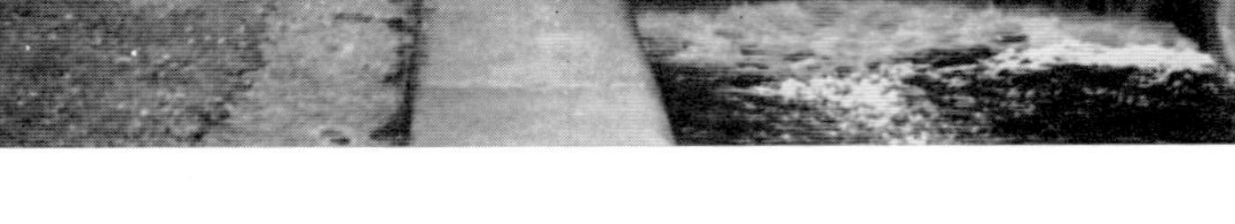

A

B

C

D

E

THE FORTH AND CLYDE CANAL (552); A. locks 15 and 16.
B. lock entry, the Old Harbour, Grangemouth.

C. MILESTONE, CRAW ROAD (449).

D. OLD ROAD FROM THE GARRISON OF INVERSNAID TO STRONACHLACHAR (523); culvert.

E. SLAMANNAN RAILWAY, TERMINAL YARD (559); stone used as base-plate.

S.O. Code No. 49-140-16-0*